The Ageless Chinese

A H I S T O R Y

The Ageless Chinese

A H I S T O R Y

D U N   J.   L I

Charles Scribner's Sons   New York

#410947

MAPS BY JEANYEE WONG

Facing the title page is the design of a lattice from a residence in Chengtu, Szechuan, 1825, as rendered in *A Grammar of Chinese Lattice* by Samuel Sheeps Dye.

Preface

In writing this book I hope to meet what I have considered as an important need in Chinese history: a one-volume book covering China's past from the very beginning to the present. Many books on modern China have been published in the United States in recent years, but there are few that relate modern China to its ancient past. It is my belief that modern China can be better understood by analyzing China's historical forces as well as forces that are mostly Western in origin. Aside from whatever merits it might have as a complete history, this book, I hope, will help students to understand contemporary China from a historical perspective and perhaps in a more profound manner. Since most of the basic forces that shape modern China have been accumulative and were in operation many centuries before the modern period, I have chosen to title the book *The Ageless Chinese*.

As the book covers the entire history of China, I have been forced to be extremely selective in the choice of topical materials. Generally speaking, I have tried to follow four criteria in the selection of topics to be discussed in each historical period. First, they must be the most significant events, whether they be political, cultural, or economic. Second, they must be generally known. Third, since the book will have an English-speaking public, the topics discussed must be meaningful to persons brought up in the Western culture. Political feuds and military battles, which occupy the attention of China's traditional historians, are generally omitted unless they are related to larger, more important issues. And fourth, these topics must have some bearing on contemporary affairs, however indirect that bearing might be. For instance, farm problems are given considerable attention in this book because by and large the same problems still exist today.

In writing this book I have followed a chronological arrangement so that students can follow the development of Chinese culture from one period to another, and so that the tendency towards over-simplification, which so often occurs in discussing Chinese culture, is reduced. What is true of one period may not be necessarily true of another. The chronological order is discarded only when there are compelling reasons for doing so. Printing was invented in the Sui-T'ang period; yet I discuss it under "The Two Sungs" because movable type was not invented until the Sung dynasty. To discuss printing under "Sui and T'ang" would have meant the splitting of one topic into two disconnected parts. The dynastic cycle is discussed in Chapter X instead of Chapter III because I believe that a student has to acquire some knowledge about dynasties before he begins to philosophize on the theory of dynastic change.

In allocating space for each historical period, my major criterion is cultural achievement. A complete chapter is devoted to the pre-Ch'in philosophers; Sung, one of the weakest regimes in Chinese history, is nevertheless discussed in two chapters because Sung was perhaps the most Confucian (and therefore most "Chinese") of all Chinese regimes. For the same reason, the space allocated to the Mongol regime is one of the shortest of all major regimes. This criterion of cultural achievement is no longer used when I come to the discussion of modern China. The reason for this deviation is twofold: the tremendous importance of the Western impact and the direct bearing of the recent past on contemporary China. It is too early to tell whether the modern period is also a period of great cultural achievement.

Having in mind readers to whom Chinese names all sound similar and often confusing, I have tried to introduce as few names as I could without sacrificing the content of the book. (See "Romanization of Chinese names," p. 553.) For each historical period I introduce a few key figures to whom a great deal of attention is given. They are chosen because they represent the spirit of their age. For the Ch'in period the

key man is Shih Huang-ti; for the Former Han it is Han Wu-ti. Wang
Mang also becomes a key man in this book because Han's social and
economic problems are reflected in his reforms. As the spirit of the
time changes, the nature of the key men also changes. They may not
even be political leaders. In the discussion of the Sung dynasty, for instance, a considerable space is provided for people like Li Ch'ing-chao
while barely mentioning three or four of the Sung emperors. Before he
died in 1925, Sun Yat-sen was the key man, even though his political
power was largely ineffective. Needless to say, the key man in China
today is Mao Tse-tung.

Though the main body of this book—the chronological history—begins with Chapter I, the "Introduction: The Geographical Setting" is
not unnecessarily or superficially imposed. It sets the tone for the entire
work. Though the theory of geographical or economic determinism has
been abandoned by most, if not all historians, it is nevertheless true that
geography imposes limitations as well as provides opportunities for a
nation's development, especially in a sedentary, agricultural society like
China. It helps to explain, for instance, the repeated occurrences of
famine, revolt, and dynastic change, the land problem which almost
every Chinese regime has to face, and even customs and mores generally associated with the Chinese. Above all, it gives us some insight
with regard to China's prospect, or the lack of it, of becoming a great
industrial power in the sense that we think of the Soviet Union or the
United States. The study of temperature and rainfall in different geographical regions of China seems to be very remote from the study of
Chinese history, but the development of Chinese history would have
been entirely different if, say, the northwestern half of China had the
same climatic conditions as those of the southeastern half.

However, to students who take a Chinese history course for the first
time, the numerous names of mountains, rivers, and cities that are
mentioned in the Introduction are nevertheless a great burden. As an
alternative, they might read the Introduction rather quickly before they
study Chapter I, and then return to the Introduction after they study
the rest of the book. Though closely related to the rest of the work, the
Introduction could also be studied as a separate unit.

I wish to express my thanks to Professor Derk Bodde of the University of Pennsylvania and to Professor Laurence G. Thompson of Po-
mona College who examined an early draft of the manuscript on behalf
of the publishers and provided a number of helpful suggestions. To my
colleagues at Paterson State College who have read one or more chapters
of the manuscript I wish also to express my thanks. They are Professors
Charlotte C. Brown, Albert Resis, Paul P. Vouras, Edward F. Willis, and
Alfred Young. Professor Stanley Hirshon of Queens College also read two
chapters. My wife June, who has been very patient with me during the

preparation of this work, read the entire manuscript and made many valuable suggestions. Lastly, I wish to mention my own son David whose frequent incursions into the study room each day has doubtless delayed the early completion of this work but without whose repeated presence the preparation of this work would have been much less pleasant.

DUN J. LI

Paterson State College
Wayne, New Jersey
December, 1964

Contents

List of Illustrations

List of Maps

The Ageless Chinese

A H I S T O R Y

Introduction:
The Geographical Setting

If history is a continuous and, let us hope, unending drama, geography is the stage on which such drama is performed. While on the one hand the kind of drama man plays modifies the environment in which he lives, the environment itself influences or sometimes dictates what kind of drama can be played. Man and nature modify each other in a reciprocal manner. Though man is the most intelligent of all creatures, he is by no means omnipotent. He can exploit nature to his advantage, but he cannot change nature's basic pattern. Often does he work in vain when nature is harsh and unrewarding, and especially did his ancestors who had less knowledge and who lacked the experience which has evolved and accumulated through thousands of years. Though geography does not deter-

mine history, history is very much influenced by it. To understand a nation's history, we have to familiarize ourselves with its geography. Thus
we begin our story of the Chinese with a description of the place where
they live.

The Chinese live in Chung-kuo ("Central Nation") or Chung-hua
("Central and Flowery Land"), better known in the English language as
China. The Chinese call their country "Central Nation" or "Flowery Land"
because until modern times they had believed that they lived in the
center of the civilized world, rich and beautiful beyond comparison. A
better knowledge of the world reveals something different, but the old
names have persisted. Americans and Europeans often refer to China as a
Far Eastern country, a term as misleading as the "central nation," because
such a term can only be justified if somehow we believe that the world
begins somewhere east of Japan. China is located in the southeastern end
of the Eurasian land mass, and since the eastern portion of this land mass
is called Asia, it is more correct to say that China is an East Asian country,
or a country in East Asia.

In terms of size China is the third largest country (after the Soviet
Union and Canada) in the world, with an area totalling 3,760,000
square miles. From Pamir to the Pacific it extends 2,300 miles, and it
measures 2,500 miles from northern Manchuria to the Himalayas. It lies
between 18° and 54°N, from the tropical to the subarctic, excluding four
groups of coral islands in the South China Sea which extend as far as 4°N.
If China were imposed on North America, it would cover an area from
the Atlantic to the Pacific, and from the southern Hudson Bay to the
island of Jamaica in the Caribbean Sea. This vast expanse gives China a
variety of climates and regional characteristics.

In the north China shares its longest boundary with the Soviet Union. At the eastern end of the boundary the Tumen and Yalu Rivers
separate it from Korea. The Himalayas form a natural boundary between
China in the north, and Pakistan, India, Nepal, and Bhutan in the south.
Across its southwestern border China faces Burma, Laos, and North Vietnam. China's coastline of 4,000 miles is washed by the extensions of the
Western Pacific: the Yellow Sea in the north, East China Sea in the middle,
and South China Sea in the south. At the end of World War II, it had
thirty-five provinces and two territories. One territory, Outer Mongolia,
has since then become independent.

LANDFORMS

The land of China may be compared to a gigantic watershed, with
Pamir and the Tibetan Plateau as the water divide and the Western
Pacific as the water's final resting place. The entire area slopes eastward,

MAP 1

CHINA: LANDFORMS

Boundaries as of 1962

National Boundaries
Disputed Boundaries

Scale of Miles
0   300   600

and the altitudes of mountains and rivers diminish with it. Travelling westward, one ascends higher and higher, and when one reaches the Tibetan Plateau, the altitude is so high and the air so thin that breathing might be difficult. The Tibetan Plateau, nicknamed "the roof of the world," rises as high as 12,000 feet above sea level and is surrounded by even more formidable mountains. In the north are the Karakorum Range, the Altyn Tagh, and the Kunlun Mountains; all of them have peaks of over 20,000 feet. In the south are the Himalayas whose insurmountable height had guaranteed the "eternal" friendship between India and China until recent years. Their highest peak (also the world's highest), Mt. Everest, is located between Tibet and Nepal and rises 29,141 feet above sea level. Its towering height and treacherous slopes have been a challenge to the world's best mountain climbers.

Stretching northward and then eastward from Pamir is Tien Shan ("Heavenly Mountains") whose 1,000-mile length divides the Chinese Sinkiang province into two arid basins, Dzungaria in the north and Tarim in the south. Dzungaria has a greater annual rainfall than Tarim and is partially desert and partially pastoral. Tarim, on the other hand, is extremely dry and contains one of the world's most desolate deserts, the Takla Makan. However, fertile oases are found along the Tarim River which receives its water from the melting snow on surrounding mountains. Through these oases ran the ancient Silk Road to the Near East, and at one time camel-driving merchants risked their lives so that the Roman world could enjoy the luxuries from the East.

East of Sinkiang is the Mongolian Plateau which rises 3,000 to 6,000 feet above sea level and trends eastward. The southern and Chinese portion of the plateau is generally referred to as Inner Mongolia, as contrary to the larger, northern portion which is known as Outer Mongolia. Inner Mongolia is covered by deserts: the Gobi, the Ordos, and the Ninghsia. On the southern and eastern margin of the deserts are the steppe lands where rainfall is sufficient for a sparse growth of drought-resistant short grass and capable of supporting small herds of sheep and cattle. Oases are found wherever there is sufficient surface or underground water. Over the possession of these oases the Chinese and the non-Chinese nomadic groups fought many ancient battles.

South of the steppe lands are a loess plateau in the west and the North China Plain in the east. The plateau is formed by aeolian dust and silt blown from the northern deserts. Rainfall is light, and steppe conditions prevail over most parts of this region. Rivers dissect loess hills into deep valleys, and only the valleys can be cultivated fruitfully. The plateau is bordered in the east by the T'aihang Mountains which slope down eastward to merge with the North China Plain. The plain is drained by the Yellow River and the Ku River, together with their tributaries. The soil is the mineral-rich loess, and the plain, unlike the plateau, is one of the largest cultivated regions in China. At the eastern end of the plain and south of the Yellow River delta rise the Shantung Hills which stretch northeastward to form the Shantung Peninsula. The highest peak of this hilly complex is the historically famous Tai Shan which was visited often by Confucius.

East of the Mongolian Plateau are the Manchurian mountains and hills. The mountains—Greater and Lesser Hsingan Mountains—are located in northern and western Manchuria, slope down southeastward to merge with the Manchurian Plain, and rise again to form the Manchurian Hills. The Manchurian Plain consists of the drainage basins of the Liao and the Sungari and is a rich agricultural area. The Ch'angpai ("Everlasting White") Range stands majestically above the Manchurian Hills, and from here the Manchus once swooped down to conquer the Manchurian Plain and eventually all of China as well.

From the point of view of climate, the most important mountains in China are Ch'inling (also Tsinling) and its eastern extensions. They separate the dry north from the humid south, the Yellow River drainage from that of the Yangtze. The Yangtze and its tributaries create many fertile alluvial plains along their paths, from the Szechuan basin in the west to the Lower Yangtze in the east. In the east the Lower Yangtze plain merges imperceptibly with the North China Plain; together they form a vast, flat expanse from Shantung to Chekiang. The easternmost extension of Ch'inling, trending eastward, disappears in the Kiang-Huai Plain, the middle section of this vast expanse.

South of the Yangtze River the terrain follows the same pattern of diminishing its altitude eastward. Southeast of the Tibetan Plateau lies another plateau of lesser but equally staggering height. It is called Yun-Kwei Plateau because it covers Yunnan and Kweichow provinces. It averages 7,000 feet in its western, or Yunnan, portion and drops down to an average of 4,000 feet in its eastern, or Kweichow, portion. In its southeastern section are the Parallel Ranges where high mountains and deep valleys run southward and form a sharp, unique contrast. Water rushes its way along these valleys to join the Salween and Mekong Rivers. In some areas valleys are so deep and mountains so high that people who live on opposite sides of the same valley could say good morning to each other, but would have to journey all day before they could shake hands.

East of the Yun-Kwei Plateau the terrain lowers to become less rugged, more prosaic hills. South of the Yangtze drainage hilly regions dominate the terrain from Kwangsi to the East China Sea. These hilly regions are often named after the provinces in which they are located. They are, from west to east: (1) the Liangkwang (Kwangsi and Kwangtung) Hills, (2) the Kiangnan Hills (Hunan and Kiangsi excluding the central lakes region), (3) the Che-Huan (South Anhwei and East Chekiang) Hills, and (4) the Fukien Hills. In the hilly regions rivers are short and drainages are small. The only exception is the Si ("West") River which will be discussed later.

Wherever the hilly regions are washed by the sea, the coastline tends to be more serrated and contains many bays and harbors. Thus, in the Manchurian hilly region we find two superb harbors, Dairen and Port Arthur, located on the southern tip of the Liaotung Peninsula. Across the Gulf of Pohai is the Shantung Peninsula where the Shantung Hills make possible the fine ports of Weihaiwei and Tsingtao. South of Shantung and north of the Hangchow Bay the coastline is round and flat, as its hinterland is a vast expanse of alluvial plains. The prominent position of Shanghai does not depend on its importance as a harbor but on the fact that it stands at the mouth of the richest drainage basin in China. South of the Hangchow Bay the coastal areas are again hilly, and there are such fine harbors as Ningpo, Wenchow, Amoy, Swatow, and the historically famous Ch'üanchou. The potentiality of these harbors has not been fully developed, largely because transportation is extremely difficult over the hinterlands, and the rivers leading to them are short and swift.

DRAINAGE

As mountains in China trend eastward, so do all major rivers. The Yellow River and the Yangtze, the two largest rivers in China, are not exceptions. At their origin on the eastern fringe of the Tibetan Plateau, the two rivers are less than a hundred miles apart, but they become further apart as they wind their way eastward. Leaving the Tibetan Plateau, the Yellow River flows northwestward and then eastward to form the Ordos Bend. Moving southward, it serves as the boundary line between Shensi and Shansi. After receiving water from its two largest tributaries, Fen and Wei, it is blocked in its southward path by the Ch'inling Mountains; it turns eastward to enter the North China Plain. It passes across the Grand Canal in western Shantung before it pours into the Gulf of Pohai.

Economically, the Yellow River is less beneficial than the Yangtze and is in fact sometimes called the "Sorrow of China." Through its upper valley it is swift and, as it cuts through the loess plateau, it carries with it tons of sediment. From its muddy appearance the river acquired its present name. In Lungmen (between Shensi and Shansi) the river current is so swift that, according to an ancient myth, "fish which jump upstream across the rapids will automatically become dragons." East of Lungmen the river enters the North China Plain; as its current slackens, it begins to deposit its content. As a result, the river bed continues to rise and dykes have to be built higher and higher to confine the river within its course. In some areas the river bed is higher than the adjacent land, and once a dyke

MAP 2
CHINA: DRAINAGE

Scale of Miles
0   300   600

is broken during a heavy downpour, no little Dutch boy can save the area from a devastating flood. The eastern section of the North China Plain is only a few feet above sea level for the most part, and the river meanders through its own creation like a dying reptile. Consequently it often changes its course, and several major changes, with great loss of men and animals, have been recorded since history began. The last of such changes occurred in 1938 when Chinese field commanders, unable to check the advance of Japanese invaders, decided to break the dykes and cause a man-made flood. The Japanese were stopped for the time being, but countless Chinese lives were also lost in this catastrophe.

As the river is shallow, navigation on a large scale is all but impossible. Only the smallest boats of junk size can take advantage of the water surface. Irrigation, however, is practiced on a vast scale. Numerous canals, large and small, have been built to irrigate the adjacent fields. The irrigation works in the North China Plain were historically famous. Here the ancient Chinese civilization was born, and for more than 2,500 years it was the center of the civilized world known to the Chinese. Beginning in the Sung dynasty (960–1279), however, the situation changed. The once magnificent works of flood control and irrigation began to deteriorate, and this deterioration has never been successfully arrested. The economic and cultural center of China began to shift southward and, economically at least, the Yangtze basin has been more important than North China for the past one thousand years.

In its upper valley the Yangtze is the Chinsha River ("River of the Golden Sand") which collects the water of numerous streams on the eastern fringe of the Tibetan Plateau and flows southward. Cutting through the northernmost portion of Yunnan province, it goes northeastward to Szechuan. From then on it is called the Yangtze. Szechuan is a basin formed by the Yangtze and three of its major tributaries, and Szechuan, in fact, means "Four Rivers." Leaving Szechuan, the river cuts through the Tapa Mountains and passes through the famous Three Gorges. Overlooking one of the gorges is Mount Wu where, according to an ancient myth, a king of Ch'u had once met intimately the beautiful river nymph. The mountains rise almost vertically on both sides of the gorges, and the river rushes eastward over hundreds of treacherous rapids.

After the Three Gorges the river current slackens and travels more leisurely over the central lakes region. There are hundreds of lakes in this area, among which Lake Tungting and Lake Poyang are by far the largest. Here the Yangtze receives its longest and largest tributaries. From the south come the four rivers—Hsiang, Tzu, Yüan, and Li—which jointly drain the Hunan province and pour into Lake Tungting. From the north comes the Han River which joins the Yangtze at the Wu-Han metropolis. Further east, the Kan River drains the Kiangsi province, winds its way northward, and discharges its content into Lake Poyang.

Leaving the central lakes region, the Yangtze turns northeastward, cuts across the Grand Canal near Yangchow, and receives more tributaries before it pours into the East China Sea near Shanghai.

The third river in importance is the Si River and its drainage is the largest south of the Yangtze Valley. Its source is a dozen or more streams originating at the foot of the Yun-Kwei Plateau. As it travels eastward, it receives water from joining tributaries. West of Canton it merges with the Pei ("North") River and is then called the Chu ("Pearl") River. It pours into the South China Sea.

Three more rivers need to be mentioned. One is the Heilung ("Black Dragon") or Amur River which originates on the western slope of the Greater Hsingan Mountains, travels northeastward and then southeastward to serve as a common boundary between the Soviet Union and China, and pours into the Sea of Okhotsk through Russia's Maritime Province. Its most important tributary is the Sungari River which, together with the Liao River, drains the Manchurian Plain. The second river is the Huai River which winds its way eastward from one of the Ch'inling extensions to pour into Lake Hungtze, between Anhwei and Kiangsu provinces. Climatically, it is the dividing line between the North and the South in this part of China. Lastly, the Chekiang River drains its namesake province. It cuts the province into two parts, West and East Chekiang, as it goes northward to pour into the Hangchow Bay. The Hangchow Bay is geographically famous for its tidal waves. The tide enters as a racing wave of water up to 15 feet high and speeds up to 15 miles per hour on top of the normal water surface. Each year people travel far to see this unusual spectacle.

CLIMATE

There are many factors that affect the climate of China. First, continental China has a latitudinal difference of 36 degrees, which means large variations in temperature throughout the country. Hainan Island, below 20°N, is tropical, and the northernmost part of Manchuria, near 54°N, is subarctic. Between these two extremes are most parts of China which enjoy a middle latitude or temperate climate. Cyclonic activities are most active in middle latitudes, and in China's case, are an important factor in determining the amount of annual rainfall. The four seasons are sharply divided, though the lengths of summer and winter vary with latitude. Second, China faces the Pacific in the east and has as its hinterland one of the largest land masses in the world. The seasonal changes of temperature and air pressure on the continent vis-à-vis those on the ocean create what is known in this part of the world as the monsoon. The monsoon is a seasonal wind reversal and is responsible for the bitter cold winter in the

Northwest and heavy, summer rainfall in the Southeast. In summer, the continent is heated up faster than the ocean, and wind blows from the ocean towards the continent. The moisture-laden air discharges its load on the continent and causes heavy rain, especially along the coastal areas. In winter, as the continent cools off faster than the ocean, wind direction is reversed. The northern and northwestern winds, originating in continental polar regions, are cold and dry. They become even drier as they blow southward, for relative humidity becomes less as the air is heated up. Winter, therefore, is the dry season in China. Third, as major mountain ranges in China run along a west-east direction, they are effective barriers to the moisture-bearing winds from the ocean. Reaching a mountain, the air rises along the southern slope, discharges its water content as it ascends, and becomes comparatively dry on the lee side of the mountain. It becomes drier and drier as it passes over succeeding mountain ranges. Annual rainfall, consequently, diminishes northwestward.

There are three factors that determine the temperature of various parts of China: latitude, distance from the sea, and altitude. Temperatures—annual averages—range from 68° to 77°F in the Si River valley, 59° to 68°F in the Yangtze basin, 50° to 59°F along the Yellow River, 41° to 50°F in South Manchuria, and below 41°F in the northernmost section of Manchuria. Average temperatures, however, do not tell the whole story. Compared with many other parts of the world located on the same latitudes (North America, for instance), China has a much wider range of temperature between the coldest and warmest months. In other words, summer tends to be hotter, and winter much colder. Most parts of China have recorded maximum temperature exceeding 95°F; in some areas it exceeds 104°F. Kirin, located at 44°N in "cold" Manchuria, has recorded a maximum temperature at 104°F. In winter the high pressure system originating from Siberia dominates all of China. Its cold wind blows southeastward and penetrates as deep as areas south of the Tropic of Cancer. Canton, at 23.1°N, has recorded temperature at 27°F. The temperature of northernmost Manchuria sometimes falls to 40°F below zero.

The further an area is away from the ocean, the more continental its climate will be. Shanghai, on the coast, has a January average of 38°F and a July average of 80°F, with an annual range of 42 degrees. On the other hand, Urumchi, located deep in the hinterland in Sinkiang, has a January average of −3°F and a July average of 75°F, with an annual range of 78 degrees!

As in other parts of the world, altitude is also an important factor in determining temperature. In the southwestern section of the country are located high plateaus and many of the world's highest mountains. Northwestern Tibet, for instance, is located in comparatively low latitude (32–35°N); yet its annual temperature averages only 23°F in many

MAP 3
CHINA:
ANNUAL AVERAGE
TEMPERATURE
—— National Boundaries

0   300   600
Scale of Miles

SOVIET UNION

SOVIET UNION

Lake Baikal

OUTER MONGOLIA

MANCHURIA

32-39°F

Below 32°F

32-39°F

Ürumchi

SINKIANG

46-54°F

39-46°F

32-39°F

TIBET

39-46°F

39-46°F

46-54°F

54-61°F

Kirin

MANCHURIAN PLAIN

39-46°F

46-54°F

46-54°F

YELLOW RIVER

54-61°F

Yellow Sea

Sea of Japan

Shanghai

54-61°F

61-68°F

YANGTZE RIVER

61-68°F

61-68°F

SI RIVER

68-75°F

Canton

KWANGTUNG

TROPIC OF CANCER

68-75°F

68-75°F

HAINAN ISLAND

TROPIC OF CANCER

Bay of Bengal

places. Because of its high altitude, a large portion of this region is permanently frozen.

The reasons described above cause the length of the growing season to decrease northward, and to a lesser extent, westward. Kwangtung, on the southeastern coast, has a growing season all year round, because rarely would temperature drop below 32°F. The middle and lower Yangtze valley, further north but close to the coast, has a growing season of eight to ten months. On the other hand, the Manchurian Plain has a growing season of only five to six months, and some of the mountainous regions in Tibet have practically no growing season at all.

Rainfall in China is mostly frontal or cyclonic in origin; only a small portion comes from convectional and orographic sources. The southern and southeastern monsoon brings precipitation to China from May to September and is responsible for much of the rainfall during the summer months. If in certain years the southern and southeastern winds are weak, they can only go as far as the Yangtze Valley, discharge all their water content, and leave little for North China. In such case, there are floods in the Yangtze and drought in the Yellow River region. If, on the other hand, the winds are unusually strong, they cause heavy rainfall in North China and little precipitation in the Yangtze Valley. Thus a flood or drought in North China is often accompanied by a drought or flood in the Yangtze region. Only when the winds are of the right strength will the rainfall be properly distributed and will all parts of China be benefited by its presence. In other words, when crops fail in the Yangtze, it is likely that they will also fail in North China, though for different reasons. If it is a good year, it would be a good year in both regions. Not surprisingly, the erratic behavior of the monsoon is a major concern to the Chinese people.

Superimposed on this monsoon pattern are the migrating cyclonic and anticyclonic disturbances which move along a west-east direction towards the coast and then northeastward towards Japan. Approximately eighty cyclonic depressions move across China each year. These storm centers are responsible for much of China's rainfall, expecially in the interior regions. Generally speaking, they are most widespread in the Yangtze and appear less often north of the Huai River. They occur every month of the year and are most numerous in the winter and spring. In late spring when they are blocked by the polar front in the north, they become stationary in the Lower Yangtze and cause continuous rain which the Chinese call *mai-yü,* or plum rain. It is most welcome to farmers because this is the time when rice seedlings, newly planted, need a great deal of moisture.

More intense and violent than the normal, mid-latitude cyclonic depressions are the typhoons. The typhoons originate in the ocean east of the Philippine Islands and cause strong winds and heavy storms on their destructive paths. In late summer and early autumn they repeatedly in-

MAP 4
CHINA:
ANNUAL RAINFALL
—— National Boundaries

0   300   600
Scale of Miles

Lake
Baikal

OUTER MONGOLIA

5-10"

0-5"

0-5"

Urumchi

TARIM RIVER

5-10"

5-10"

Hulun
(Hailar)

5-10"

10-20"

10-20"

Mukden

20-30"

Sea of
Japan

Peking

10-20"

20-30"

10-20"

Lanchow

5-10"

10-20"

Sian

YELLOW RIVER

20-30"

20-30"

Yellow
Sea

HUAI RIVER

30-40"

LOWER
YANGTZE

Shanghai

40-50"

East
China
Sea

20-30"

10-20"

30-40"

Chengtu

30-40"

YANGTZE RIVER

40-50"

40-50"

50-60"

60-70"

70-80"

60-70"

Taipei

70-80"

50-60"
60-70"

40-50"

50-60"

60-70"

50-60"

60-70"

SI RIVER

Canton

50-60"

60-70"

South China Sea

50-60" 60-70"

Bay of
Bengal

vade China's southeast coast and cause heavy damages. Fortunately they curve northeastward once they hit the coast areas, and rarely do they penetrate far into the interior.

Three conclusions can be reached with regard to China's rainfall. First, it is heavily concentrated in summer; second, it is most plentiful on the southeast coast and diminishes northwestward towards the continent; and third, it is unreliable and unpredictable. Since rainfall is essential to the growth of vegetation and since it diminishes towards the hinterland at an accelerated speed, a large portion of China is unfit for cultivation. If we say that an annual rainfall of twenty inches is the minimum for profitable agricultural engagement, then about half of China's land surface would be unfruitful as farm land, no matter how good other conditions are. Actually, total arable land is much smaller, because other conditions, such as those of terrain and soil, are not so good as they should be.

Though China is fortunate in the sense that rainfall is concentrated during the growing season—in Lower Yangtze, for instance, almost seventy percent of annual rainfall falls between March and August inclusive —the unreliability of precipitation in a given year works havoc among farmers. Annual averages are often misleading, because what looks good in average may be disastrous in reality. In China's case, a wet year may have three or four times as much rain as a dry year. The disparity is more pronounced in North China than in the Yangtze Valley and the Si River basin. Flood follows drought and vice versa, even though the average appears to be the right amount. In view of these facts, it is not surprising that crops fail often and that they fail more often in North China. Since history began, the unreliability of rainfall has caused the greatest distress to Chinese farmers. During summer when rain is needed most, often none comes. The cumulus clouds drift slowly across the sky, and nothing happens. An ancient Chinese poet was so angry with them that he asked them pointedly:

> While myriads of seedlings
> Are dying of thirst,
> How can you leisurely
> Make peaks of mountains
> As if nothing had happened?

Today nature is as unmerciful to the Chinese as it has always been.

GEOGRAPHICAL REGIONS

Customarily, the Chinese speak of their country as composed of the Northeast, the Northwest, North China, South China, the Southeast, the Southwest, and finally, Mongolia and Tibet. There are two disadvantages in this division. First, each region is loosely termed, and individuals might

MAP 5
CHINA:
GEOGRAPHICAL REGIONS *
——— National Boundaries
-■-■- Disputed Boundaries
* For Provincial Divisions,
see MAP 31

0   300   600
Scale of Miles

NORTHEAST

INNER MONGOLIA

MONGOLIA

SUNGARI RIVER
Harbin
Changchun
Mukden

YALU RIVER
LIAO RIVER

Dairen
Port Arthur
Tsingtao

Yellow
Sea

NORTH CHINA

Kalgan
Peking
Tientsin
Kailan
Tsinan

Soochow
Shanghai
Hangchow

Foochow
Taipei
TAIWAN
Amoy

SOUTHEAST

Nanking

TAIHANG MTS
Taiyuan
FEN RIVER
YELLOW RIVER
WEI RIVER
Sian

Kaifeng
YELLOW RIVER
HUAI RIVER
TAPIEH MTS

HANCHUNG

SOUTH CHINA

Han-
Hankow
yang Wuchang
Nanchang
Changsha

Canton
Hong Kong
Macao

HAINAN
ISLAND

NINGHSIA
SUIYUAN

Lanchow
YELLOW RIVER

Chengtu
Chungking

Kweiyang
Kweilin
Liuchow
SI RIVER

SOUTHWEST

NORTHWEST

Urumchi
(Tihwa)
Turfan

TARIM RIVER

CHINSHA RIVER

YANGTZE RIVER

Kunming

TIBET

Lhasa
Zhikatse
TSANGPO RIVER

BRAHMAPUTRA RIVER

Bay of
Bengal

differ as to exactly what areas or provinces it contains. Second, this is not a division based entirely on geographical factors. These disadvantages, however, are more than offset by the advantage of a customary usage commonly understood. Furthermore, based on geographical factors alone, no two geographers could agree as to how China should be divided, because each geographer emphasizes a different factor or factors.

The Northeast   The Northeast is often referred to as Manchuria, because this was the ancient home of the Manchus. Chinese migration to Manchuria began more than two thousand years ago and most of the immigrants settled in the rich farm land in South Manchuria. When the Manchus ruled China beginning in the seventeenth century, Chinese were barred from moving to Manchuria for permanent settlement; this bar, however, was revoked during the last century. Subsequently Chinese from nearby Shantung and Hopeh provinces moved in in large numbers, and today there are approximately fifty million Chinese in Manchuria as compared to less than one million Manchus. The Manchus have even begun to identify themselves as Chinese.

Of all the geographical regions Manchuria is by far the richest in China. It offers great opportunities for agriculture and industry. Though rainfall and temperature diminish northwestward, South Manchuria is humid and warm enough to sustain an intensive farming as practiced by the Chinese. Only in the northwestern parts of Manchuria does rainfall become too light and growing season too short to practice agriculture profitably. The Manchurian Plain—sometimes referred to as the Sung-Liao Plain—is one of the major agricultural areas in China, and produces a variety of food and industrial crops. Since its population density is small compared with other agricultural areas in China, it has a food surplus. Soy beans are its most important food export.

Manchuria also has China's largest forest reserves. Lumbering is an important industry in eastern Manchuria, timber being shipped out downstream to the market via the Yalu and the Sungari Rivers. Fur trapping is a major source of income in forest regions, and sable is the most famous among a variety of furs produced. Harbin, located in the center of Manchuria, is its largest fur market.

Manchuria is the only region in China that is highly industrialized. It contains more than half of China's known iron ore reserves, and its coal reserves are also very large. It produces a variable amount of copper, manganese, lead, and sodium. China's largest gold reserve is located along the Amur River in northern Manchuria, though production has not been large. Modern hydroelectric plants along the Yalu River provide much of the electric power for industrial uses. All major cities and industrial centers are linked by railroads; in fact, Manchuria has more miles of railroad track than any other region in China. Mukden, with a population of more than 1,500,000, is the largest city in this region.

The Northwest   The Northwest extends westward from the T'aihung Mountains to the eastern border of Russian Turkestan. It includes Sinkiang, Kansu, Chinghai, the Shensi province north of the Ch'inling Mountains, and Shansi. Rainfall diminishes westward and climate becomes more continental along the same direction. The annual rainfall of Shansi, the easternmost province in this region, is about twenty inches. It steadily diminishes westward until it is less than four inches in southern Sinkiang (Tarim).[1]

Agricultural activities are greatly hampered by climatic limitations. In the eastern portion of the region where rainfall is comparatively heavy, agriculture is practiced on riverine plains where irrigation water alone is available. Thus the Fen River basin, the Wei River plain, and the Lanchow area (Kansu) are the three major agricultural areas. The Wei River plain has one of the best soils and produces high-quality cotton besides the regular food crops. Sian (Ch'angan), an ancient capital, is still the largest city in the area.

Outside the riverine plains, the landscape is dominated by steppes and deserts. Here and there oases are found, and they please a man's eyes with their trees, shrubs, and cultivated fields. In addition to food crops, farmers in oases grow a variety of fruits, such as grapes, peaches, cherries, apples, apricots, and watermelons. Oases are by definition isolated areas, and most parts of the Northwest are agriculturally unproductive. As the land is unable to support a large population, the Northwest remains as one of China's least populated regions.

Unfit for agriculture, a large portion of the Northwest is devoted to the livestock industry. Cattle and sheep are raised simultaneously, though sheep are more important in most areas. The best kind of pastures is often found in areas adjacent to high mountains where the melting snow provides the much needed moisture. The raising of livestock is the major occupation of non-Chinese groups, such as the Uighurs in Sinkiang. The Chinese, on the other hand, are mostly farmers and are concentrated in riverine plains and oases.

Containing China's largest coal reserves, the Northwest possesses great potentials for industrial development. There are also unknown quantities of gold, nitrate, lead, bauxite, and manganese reserves. However, these reserves will remain in the ground until better means of transportation can be built to reach them. Recently the Communist regime has begun to carry out an ambitious railroad-building program in this region.

North China   North China is bordered by the Great Wall in the north, and its southern boundary is the Tapieh Mountains in the west and the Huai River in the east. From the T'aihang Mountains it extends eastward to the Yellow Sea. Except for Shantung which is mostly hilly, North China is a vast plain. It includes Hopeh, Honan, Shantung, and the

---

[1] To locate provinces and cities, see Map 31, page 472.

northern sections of Anhwei and Kiangsu. It is sometimes called Chung-yüan, or Central Plain.

Among the factors that hamper North China agriculturally the most important is the lack of adequate rainfall. On the average, the amount of annual rainfall is only half as much as that of South China and is only one-third as much as that in the Southeast. The shortage of rainfall and its unreliability make farming extremely hazardous. Whenever it does rain, the rain floods the denuded earth. Since farmers have no other source of income except what can be gained by cultivating the field, a crop failure means famine for them. Thousands of years of settlement have made North China one of the most densely populated areas in China, and the supply of food can barely meet the demand even in good years. Time and again famine raises its ugly head, and famine is followed by rebellion and war.

North China has two major coal fields, one along the T'aihang Mountains and the other in northern Hopeh. The Kailan coal mine is the largest of its kind in North China. The region is served by four major railroads: Ching-Han (from Peking to Hankow), Chin-P'u (from Tientsin to Nanking), Pei-Ning (from Peking to Mukden), and Lung-Hai which passes across North China along an east-west direction. (Map 6, page 27) All major cities are located along the railroads. Peking, the old imperial city, is now the capital of the Communist regime. It is famous for its libraries, museums, and scenic spots. Tientsin is the largest industrial and commercial center in this region. Industries include flour-milling, manufacturing of wool and cotton textiles, oil-pressing, leather-tanning, and paper-making. Its handwoven rugs, together with those from Peking, are internationally famous.

South China Since China's main wealth comes from agriculture, South China, by producing large quantities of agricultural products, is economically better off than its northern counterpart. For one thing, enjoying a warmer and more humid climate, the southerners are able to raise paddy rice which yields more calories per acre than wheat or any other northern crop. Besides, the Yangtze and its tributaries are far less troublous than the Yellow River.

South China consists of Hupeh, Hunan, Kiangsi, the Shensi province south of the Ch'inling Mountains (the Hanchung area), the sections of Anhwei and Kiangsu south of the Huai River, and the northern section of Chekiang (West Chekiang). Much of this region is hilly; only areas adjacent to lakes and rivers are intensively cultivated. Thus the central lakes region, Lower Yangtze, and the Hanchung area are three of the most productive areas in China, and their population density is also among the highest. The four major products are rice, cotton, tea, and silk, though considerable amounts of soy beans, sweet potatoes, and tobacco are also produced. Kiangsi and Hunan produce the finest hemp in China which, after being bleached, is woven into an airy cloth for summer wear. Besides timber, the most important forest products are tung oil and lacquer. The region is well supplied with fish, since it contains numerous lakes, rivers, and ponds and is close to the sea. Coal reserves have been found in every province, though production has not been large. In eastern Hupeh where coal and iron ore happen to be located together, there is an iron-steel center, the largest south of the Great Wall. South China also produces most of the nation's tungsten, antimony, lead, zinc, and silver.

Around the lakes and beside the rivers stand many of China's prosperous cities. Shanghai, with a population of seven millions, is by far the largest. It is the financial center of China as well as its largest port. Industries include the manufacturing of textiles, cement, tiles, glass, cigarettes and tobacco products, the milling of rice and flour, shipbuilding, printing and publishing, and a variety of others. West of Shanghai and on the southern bank of the Yangtze is Nanking, the former capital of Nationalist China. Nearby are Soochow and Hangchow which, rich and prosperous, are popularly referred to as the two "paradises on earth." Further up on the Yangtze is the Wu-Han metropolis. It consists of three cities: Hankow, Wuchang, and Hanyang. Hankow is the largest of the three and is the commercial center of the central lakes region.

The Southeast   The Southeast is mostly hilly, and level land can only be found in localized riverine plains and deltas. It includes the southern section of Chekiang (East Chekiang), Fukien, Kwangtung, Taiwan, and Hainan Island. It stretches from the subtropical to the tropical; south of Chekiang, there is little or no winter snow at all. Rainfall is plentiful and is concentrated in summer when the southeastern monsoon dominates the entire region.

As the growing season is long and rainfall is heavy, most areas in this region can grow two or even three crops a year. Whenever level land can be found or slopes are not too steep, rice is intensively cultivated. Thus, despite the limited areas available for cultivation, the Southeast is a major rice producing region in China. Taiwan serves as a good example to show the advantage of intensive farming. It is smaller than Denmark and less than twenty-five percent of the island is arable. Yet it produces enough rice to feed more than eleven million people and exports large quantities besides. In addition to rice, there are also other crops, notably sugar cane. Taiwan is a major producer of cane sugar in the world and exports most of its refined sugar overseas. Located in the low latitudes, the Southeast produces a variety of tropical and subtropical fruits, including bananas, pineapples, oranges, and lichis.

As this region is mostly hilly, forests can be found in every province, and lumbering is an important industry. Its irregular coastline contains many fine bays and harbors, and fishing is an important means of earning a livelihood. The catches are dried, salted, or peppered to be shipped to

ARCHITECTURE IN PEKING

Marble Screen with Nine Dragons
Marble Arch Bridge
Walking Corridor
Temple Lion
The Cornice of a Palace
Marble Boat in the Summer Palace
Marble Pagoda of the Yellow Temple

A NARROW, CROWDED STREET IN HONG KONG Notice the Chinese signs with, in some cases, their English equivalents. While most Chinese in this British colony are attired in the Western style, the woman in the foreground wears the traditional *ch'i-p'ao* which dates from the time of the Manchus.

many parts of the country. Mawei, ten miles east of Foochow (capital of Fukien province), has one of China's best shipyards.

Historically the Southeast is the seafaring section of the nation. Millions of its children have emigrated to other parts of the world, especially Southeast Asia. Macao and Hong Kong along the Kwangtung coast remind many Chinese of a colonial past. Hong Kong, once a rocky island with scattered fishing villages, has been prosperous ever since the British took it over in 1842 and is now one of the greatest commercial centers in East Asia. Canton is the capital of Kwangtung province and the largest city of this region within Chinese jurisdiction. Taipei, the major city of Nationalist China on Taiwan, is a commercial center as well as a political capital.

Because of its rugged terrain, the Southeast is poor in transportation. Poor transportation creates a unique situation: the diversity of dialects. There are so many dialects and subdialects in this region that sometimes people living less than a hundred miles apart cannot understand each other. In a less generous mood, ancient Chinese in the north often referred to these dialects as *niao-yü,* or birds' chatterings. Fortunately, all China uses the same written language, one of the oldest in the world. When a northern Chinese goes to a chop suey restaurant in the United States, he has to write his order because most Chinese-Americans came from China's Southeast.

The Southwest The Southwest has two distinct regions: the Yun-Kwei Plateau and its eastern slopes, and the Szechuan basin. It includes four provinces: Yunnan, Kweichow, Kwangsi, and Szechuan.

Because of its high altitude, the Yun-Kwei Plateau is generally cool in summer and mild in winter. Kunming, for instance, has an average January temperature of 46°F and an average July temperature of 62°F. However, as the plateau slopes down eastward, annual range of temperature increases. The average July temperature of Kwangsi rises as high as 82°F. Szechuan, surrounded by high mountains, is also hot in summer. Winter, on the other hand, is comparatively mild; the eastward trending mountains protect this region from the bitter cold winds which plague most parts of China during this time. These same mountains also block the northern movement of summer monsoon and cause a large amount of precipitation throughout the entire region.

Climatic conditions being generally favorable, agriculture is intensively engaged in, wherever level land can be found. Szechuan, which has extensive alluvial plains, becomes one of the most important agricultural areas in China. Its most important crop is rice, followed by soy beans, cotton, wheat, corn, and sweet potatoes. Cane sugar is produced in the southwestern section of the province, and total annual production is only second to that of Taiwan. Nearby are China's famous salt wells, some of which, dug centuries ago, reach a depth of more than four thousand feet. In addition, Szechuan is first in the production of tung oil, and third (after Chekiang and Kiangsu) in the production of raw silk. The richness of Szechuan earns it the enviable title "Heavenly State" (*t'ien-fu chih kuo*) and, during World War II, enabled China to hold out against the Japanese demand for surrender for more than eight years.

Compared with Szechuan, the other three provinces in the Southwest are less fortunate. For the most part the terrain is too rugged to be useful. In the Yun-Kwei Plateau where level land is hard to find, terracing is widely used to wrest arable land from mountains. In Kweichow some of the terraced farms climb for several hundred feet and are a remarkable sight to see.

Chengtu, located in western Szechuan, is the industrial and commercial center of the surrounding area. The recently completed Ch'eng-Yü Railroad (from Chengtu to Chungking) has enhanced its position as a commercial market. Chungking serves as an entrepot for a large drainage basin in central Szechuan and was the wartime capital of Nationalist China. Kunming is the capital of Yunnan and is noted for its "spring

RICE TERRACES IN CHINA   Notice the neat rows of rice plants in the field. The lower parts of the plants are covered by water during their growth. On the left side of the picture is a farmer's thatched hut. The clearing in front of the hut is used, among other things, for threshing harvested crops.

weather all year round." Kweilin is the largest city in Kwangsi and, located beside a lake, is famous for its scenery.

Mongolia and Tibet   Though geographically apart, Mongolia and Tibet are often grouped together because first, under the Nationalist regime they were both territories contrary to the rest of the nation which was divided into administrative provinces; second, each is inhabited by an ethnic minority; and third, there are geographical characteristics common to both of them. Since 1945 when Outer Mongolia became officially independent, the word Mongolia has come to mean Inner Mongolia only. Inner Mongolia is sandwiched between Outer Mongolia in the north and the Great Wall in the south. Under the Nationalist regime it was divided into four administrative provinces: Ninghsia, Suiyuan, Chahar, and Jehol. Since then the Communists have made a realignment of administrative units. Ninghsia was joined with Kansu, and an Inner Mongolian Autonomous Region was created to cover most of the other provinces.

The climate of Inner Mongolia is decidedly continental; summer is unusually hot and winter is extremely cold. Rainfall is small, and its annual amount diminishes westward. It averages between eight and twenty inches a year in the eastern section (Jehol) to less than two inches in the extreme western section. The region is a land of deserts and steppes.

Whenever rainfall is adequate to make grass grow, livestock is raised to take advantage of the natural environment. Sheep skin and wool are the two major items for export. Farming is conducted only in oases. That part of the Yellow River which separates Suiyuan from Ninghsia has a string of almost continuous oases which are cultivated by the Chinese. This is the only densely populated area in the entire region. The major mineral resources of Inner Mongolia are coal, iron ore, sodium, and sulphur.

Historically Tibet consisted of the Tibetan territory and the Sikang province. In 1954 Sikang was divided into two parts. The western part joined the Tibetan territory to form a newly created Tibetan Autonomous Region, and the eastern part was made a part of Szechuan province. That is the situation as it stands today.

The climate of Tibet varies a great deal, from a tundra type of climate in the northwestern section to a more humid, warmer climate in the southern section. Lhasa, located in the southern section, is cool in summer (average July temperature, 61°F) but cold in winter (average January temperature, 19°F). Rainfall for most parts of Tibet is very small, though the extreme southern section has a wide range of annual rainfall, from 10 to as much as 160 inches. The amount received each year varies with the strength of the Indian monsoon.

Agriculture is practiced along the river valleys of the southern section. The most important native crop is the hardy *ch'ing-k'o* (literally, green grain), though wheat, barley, and a variety of vegetables are also produced. Agricultural areas being extremely limited, the occupation of most Tibetans is the raising of livestock. The most important animal is the yak, an animal unique to the Tibetan region. The Tibetans drink its milk, eat its meat, and wear its fur and skin. Its fur is also woven into tents and rugs; its dung is burned as fuel; and its bones are made into utensils. The yak is also used as a means of transportation. The Tibetans drink a large amount of tea, which they do not grow, often mixed with butter. To obtain tea from outside sources, they ship out wool, animal hides, rugs, and such specialities as musk, deer antlers, and rhinoceros' and antelope's horns. These specialities, which are supposed to possess the power of rejuvenation, are highly priced, and they find their best customers among the well-to-do Chinese.

Tibet has a population variously estimated as between one and two millions. A sizable portion of it consists of Lamaist monks who until recently were the temporal as well as religious leaders in each community. Lhasa, with a population of sixty thousand, is by far the largest city. The thirteen-story Potala Palace, from which the Dalai Lama once ruled all of Tibet, towers above the entire city. Zhikatse, the second largest city, is the seat of the Panchen Lama, and most of its population are monks. Until recently there had been neither motor roads nor motorized vehicles in Tibet. When the Communists took it over in 1951, they began an intensive highway building program. Now there are more than three thousand miles of motor roads linking all major cities in Tibet with those in China proper. Following the highways came the Chinese whose number was insignificant before and is now estimated to be more than half a million.

ECONOMIC RESOURCES AND INDUSTRIAL PROSPECTS

Despite its emphasis on industrialization in recent years, China remains an agricultural country, and more than 75 percent of its people, directly or indirectly, depend upon farming for their livelihood. Yet, due to the presence of a number of unfavorable conditions—the lack of adequate rainfall, rugged terrain, poor soil, etc.—the amount of land which can be profitably used for agriculture is less than twenty percent of China's land surface. This percentage is further reduced by the amount of land allocated for other purposes, such as commercial and industrial establishments, houses, schools, roads, and cemeteries. Land under cultivation is roughly ten percent of total land surface, approximately 260 million acres. This would mean only 0.37 acres per capita in a land of 700 million people. Land shortage, combined with an accelerated rate of population increase in recent decades, has been one of China's most serious problems.

Agriculturally unpromising, China does not have large mineral resources either. Among major minerals coal is the only item of which China has plenty. Total reserve is estimated anywhere from 444 billion to 1,200 billion metric tons, a large portion of which seems to be of excellent quality. Even if the smaller figure is used, China still ranks fourth (after the United States, the Soviet Union, and Canada) in the world. The advantage of having large coal reserves is offset to a great extent by

MAP 6

CHINA: RAILROADS

++++++ Railroads

------ Railroads Under
Construction

Scale of Miles

0   300   600

SOVIET UNION

SEA OF JAPAN

Vladivostok

Aigun

Harbin

Changchun

Pyongyang

Chita

Hailar

Tsitsihar

Mukden

Antung

Dairen

Port Arthur

Chefoo

Tsingtao

YELLOW SEA

Shanghai

Ningpo

CHINA SEA

Foochow

Taipei

Amoy

Ulan Bator

OUTER MONGOLIA

Peking

Tientsin

Tsinan

Tunghai

Suchow

Nanking

Hangchow

Kalgan

Paotow

Tatung

Taiyuan

Chengchow

Hankow

Nanchang

Nanyang

Hengyang

Canton

Hong Kong

Hami

Sining

Lanchow

Sian

YELLOW RIVER

Chengtu

YANGTZE RIVER

Chungking

Changsha

Kweiyang

Liuchow

SI RIVER

Hanoi

Urumchi

SINKIANG

TIBET

Kunming

Bay of Bengal

insufficient iron-ore deposits. Known iron-ore deposits are estimated to be between four and eleven billion tons, and most of them are located in South Manchuria. Before World War II annual production of pig iron (including the production in Manchuria) never exceeded one million tons, and the figure has risen to something like fourteen million tons in recent years. Even the latter figure is a far cry from the approximately 100 million tons produced annually in the United States.

Among major minerals China is most in need of petroleum. Before World War II practically all petroleum products were imported. At present the most important oil field is the Yümen Field in northern Kansu which produced nearly half of Communist China's petroleum products in recent years. Total production in 1960 is estimated to be 26 million barrels. This figure, though impressive historically, is only a fraction of what China needs and is an insignificant amount compared with the 2,575 million barrels produced by the United States and 1,080 million barrels produced by the Soviet Union (both 1960 figures).

As for minor minerals, tungsten and antimony are the only two items of which China has a large amount of reserves. It is inadequately supplied with copper, zinc, lead, gold, and silver deposits. Bauxite, from which aluminum is extracted, is widely distributed in China. However, only those in Manchuria and Taiwan have been exploited commercially.

While insufficiently supplied with some of the key minerals, China is favorably endowed with water power potential. However, with the exception of Manchuria where hydroelectric developments were undertaken by the Japanese before the war, little of this vast potential has been fully developed. There are excellent sites along the upper and middle valleys of the Yangtze and the Yellow River where dams can be built to generate hydroelectric power. It is estimated that enough electricity can be produced to supply the need of all major cities from Hankow to Shanghai if the turbulent water along the Three Gorges can be somehow harnessed. In 1957 Communist China announced an ambitious program of building 46 dams along the Yellow River, scheduled to be completed in 1967. When completed, the dams would not only provide irrigation water and generate 100 billion K.W.H. of electricity each year but would also decrease the river flow and thus reduce the chance of floods in the North China Plain. Since most of China's water potential is located deep in the interior, its development would mean not only the establishment of new industrial centers away from the more developed, densely populated coastal areas but also a better, more balanced population distribution for the entire country.

Since the Communists took over the country in 1949, there have been concentrated efforts to industrialize on a massive scale. The success or failure of China to industrialize will not only affect the future of China but perhaps the world as well. A strong, industrialized China will inevitably make its influence felt. The question arises as to whether China can industrialize. If it can, the next question is, how successful will its industrialization be?

To industrialize, a country has to satisfy a number of primary conditions. Among them are: (1) favorable social and cultural environment, (2) the availability of trained personnel, managerial as well as technical, (3) easy access to fuel and raw materials, and (4) capital. In China's case, the problems posed by the first two conditions are transitional and will be eventually solved, if they have not been solved. The traditional Chinese society did not provide a favorable environment for industrial development. It looked down upon industry and commerce and dissuaded young men of promise from looking forward to them as a career. Because this society has been slowly undermined since the impact of the West and is virtually destroyed under the Communist rule, no longer does it pose any problems for industrial development, not in the traditional sense at least. As to the availability of trained personnel, it is ultimately determined by the educational level of the country as a whole. Until recently education has been the privilege of a few. As mass education is being emphasized today, inevitably there will be more industrial and research personnel.

As far as China is concerned, the problems posed by the second two conditions—insufficient supply of raw materials and the lack of capital savings—are much more basic. China's known mineral resources will not be adequate to meet its needs, even when they are fully developed. As previously stated, it is insufficiently supplied with iron ore and is totally lacking in petroleum, though it has a large coal reserve. The nonmineral resources are not very promising either. It has only a limited amount of forest reserve, and it does not produce natural rubber. Cotton production is not enough to meet domestic demand; the extension of its acreage can only be made at the expense of wheat and rice production which is in short supply at times. To be sure, there are a few items of which China produces a surplus, such as tungsten and antimony, tea, silk, tung oil, and soy beans. They can be exported to earn much needed foreign exchange, but they are insufficient to finance any sizable industrial program. Often they have to be used to purchase food, instead of industrial equipment. Coal is a potential item of export, but its resources have not been fully tapped; even when they are, transportation will be a great problem. The supply of tin, copper, lead, zinc, and other metals will not be enough to satisfy domestic needs, even when a minor industrialization program begins.

The basic problem with the Chinese economy is that it cannot and does not produce a surplus and consequently there are no capital savings. It has little to offer in the world market to obtain capital goods from more industrialized countries. Chinese agriculture is conducted on a subsistence level, producing enough to feed all in good years but not enough in bad years. The extraction of savings from the agricultural section of the economy would mean undernourishment, if not mass starvation. The improvement of sanitation and medical care has speeded up the growth of population, and the increased population reduces the amount of food available to each person. As population continues to increase, the prospect of savings becomes smaller and the hope of industrialization also diminishes.

In view of the difficulties involved, the prospects of large-scale industrialization do not seem encouraging at the moment. However, situations might arise which can change the prospects to a great extent, such as, for instance, the discovery of hitherto unknown mineral resources, a series of technological revolutions, a decreasing birth rate, and massive foreign aid, or better still, a combination of all of them. Moreover, there is China's determination to industrialize; it cannot see any other alternative if it wishes to become a modernized, prosperous nation. Such determination can make a great deal of difference. Of course, a long time will have to elapse before there can be any conclusion with regard to China's success or failure in becoming a highly industrialized society.

示 i

The Formative Period

The Chinese are a Mongoloid people who have lived in China for many thousand years. Despite theories to the contrary, there has been no proved evidence that they migrated to China from somewhere else. In 1927 skeletal remains were found in a small village near Peking of what is called the Peking Man, who is believed to have lived in this part of the world some 400,000 years ago. The Peking Man was a predecessor of *Homo sapiens* or modern man, and the fact that he possessed certain Mongoloid features has led many people to wonder whether he might have been the forerunner of the early inhabitants of North China. The question cannot be definitely answered because we know little about the transitional period during which subhuman beings were replaced by *Homo sapiens*. When the transitional period was over and when the first modern man appeared in this part of the world, he was a Mongoloid. Presumably, he was the ancestor of the modern Chinese. However, a long span of time had to elapse before his descendants could develop a semblance of culture. Throughout these long years progress was painful and extremely slow.

The question often arises as to why the Chinese civilization developed in the Yellow River basin instead of the Yangtze which, as we have said in the Introduction, is more beneficial economically. There have been many theories to explain this phenomenon, including the theory that a harsh environment stimulated better efforts on the part of the inhabitants and that they had to be inventive in order to survive. For instance, the frequency of floods necessitated creative work in irrigation and flood control. Furthermore, as both types of work required communal efforts, political organization was necessary to achieve the desired result. As floods in the Yellow River usually covered a large area, the political organization had to be strong and extensive enough to force cooperation among people of the area involved. There is even reason to believe that North China of ancient times was an easier place to live in than it is today. Centuries of deforestation have made flood-control more difficult and thousands of years of intensive farming have reduced the natural fertility of the soil. At one time North China was both challenging and rewarding enough to stimulate man to creative efforts but not rich enough to reduce him to lethargy and inactivity.

Unfortunately, we know little about his early activities. Archaeological findings, extensive as they are, are still inadequate in reconstructing a clear, reliable picture. Three major sites of Paleolithic culture have been located in North China, two near Peking and one in the Ordos Desert. Most common among the findings were stone choppers which, presumably, were all-purpose instruments used for cutting, boring, scraping, etc. Next numerous was a stone spade which might have been used for digging earth. The excavations at the Ordos Desert revealed a stone culture of a more advanced stage, as the findings included ground stone knives and bone needles. As the Paleolithic culture merged imperceptibly with that of the Neolithic period, the stone instruments became more refined and varied. What made the Neolithic culture remarkably distinct from its predecessor was the invention and the increasing use of potteries. Neolithic potteries have been found all over China, from Manchuria to Kwangtung, indicating wide diffusion of an advanced culture. However, most of the findings were made in North China, which might have been the source of the diffusion. Towards the end of the Neolithic period two pottery cultures stood as the most outstanding, the Yang-shao (Honan) and the Lung-shan (Shantung), named after the two sites where most of the typical potteries were unearthed. The Yang-shao culture spread from Manchuria westward to Kansu, but for reasons unknown it never extended eastward to the rest of China proper. Its typical product was a red pot painted with black, geometric designs and was perhaps used as a water container. The Lung-shan potteries were more advanced as they were more complex in pattern and design. They were found in the Yangtze Valley as well as North China. As they were typified by a shiny black hue, the culture they represented is sometimes called the black pottery culture.

We do not know whether the Chinese Neolithic culture was an independent development or had been influenced by the older cultures in West Asia. The similarity in geometric designs between the Yang-shao potteries and those unearthed in West Asia has led to the belief that borrowings did exist, but evidences have been too scanty to be conclusive.

How did the Neolithic people live? For one thing, we know that by the latter part of the Neolithic period they had entered the agricultural stage. Among the Yang-shao findings there were stone instruments which could only be interpreted as farm implements. Some kind of knitting and weaving must have also existed in view of the plaid patterns on the painted potteries and the discovery of spinning wheels in the Shansi and Honan excavations. For protection against wild animals as well as human enemies, many people lived together in villages. As villages existed, there must have been some kind of political organization among the villagers. Pig bones were numerous in these village ruins; the pig was perhaps the first domesticated animal. Towards the end of the Neolithic period potteries were not merely functional utensils; they were art pieces through which the potters gave vent to their sentiment and exercised their artistic skill. Sometimes animal images were engraved on these potteries such as those of cattle, horses, and sheep. These animals must have been domesticated by then. Since the potters were obviously experts devoted to their craft, it is safe to assume that a division of labor existed among the villagers and that the exchange of goods and services existed side by side with the division of labor. Among the Lung-shan findings not only were the tools, utensils, and ornaments skillfully fashioned from stone, shells, or bones but there were also animal bones that had been used for divination purposes. The belief in supernatural forces implied the existence of some kind of religion, albeit animistic.

While archaeological findings are too scanty to enable us to reconstruct the life of the Neolithic period, there are numerous written works which purport to describe it in detail. As these works were composed long after the alleged events they described had occurred, we cannot accept them as history in their entirety. Some of the described events are legendary, if not fictional; others are fairly reliable. The question as to where the line should be drawn has been a matter of debate ever since these works were written some twenty-two or twenty-three hundred years ago. Some of these works will be discussed in connection with Confucianism in the next chapter; the present concern will be the amount of information that can be derived from them with regard to the Neolithic culture. Generally speaking, the earlier the described events, the more legendary they tend to be, and the degree of reliability increases as the period during which the events had allegedly occurred comes closer to the time when these books were written. When reconstructing the history of this very ancient age, each writer has obviously to use his own judgment to differentiate facts from mere legends.

In a typically oversimplified way, the legends give a few culture heroes the major credit for bringing culture to the Chinese. Fu-hsi, one of these culture heroes, taught the domestication of animals, and thus the people were spared the daily necessity of hunting and fishing; he introduced the institution of marriage in order to remedy the rather awkward situation "when people knew only their mothers, with no knowledge of who their fathers were"; he invented the first musical instrument; and he was credited with the introduction of a calendar that numbered "360 days for each year." Another hero, Yu-ch'ao, persuaded people to come down from their "nests" in the trees or out from their dens in the caves to start building houses on the ground. Culture hero Shen-nung ("Divine Farmer") taught people the art of farming and the craft of trade; he even invented the art of prescribing herb cures, "after testing hundreds of herbs himself." Emperor Huang-ti ("Yellow Emperor") made the greatest contribution of all. He defeated the barbarian Miaos, thus clearing North China for Chinese settlement; introduced governmental institutions; and was even credited with the invention of coined money and the compass. His wife taught silk culture and domestic work. His minister Ts'ang Chieh invented the first written signs, thereupon "all spirits cried in agony, as the innermost secrets of nature were thus revealed."

When we come to the second half of the third millennium, the legend says that there was a golden age, when rulers were chosen from the best of men and ruled through their own examples and virtues. The best known of them were Yao and Shun whose virtues, it was said, were so great that by doing nothing in particular they brought peace and prosperity to all of their subjects. One thing, however, marred the history of the good emperors, namely, an unprecedented flood which occurred during their reigns. According to the legend, the Great Flood lasted for several decades, causing heavy damage to men and animals, for none was able to devise a means to stop it. First the incompetent Kun was appointed to supervise flood control. After nine years of building more dykes, the situation remained serious. Yü, the son of Kun, succeeded as supervisor of flood control after his father's death. He dug canals following the natural routes of the Yellow River and planted trees alongs its banks and those of its tributaries. After thirteen years of diligent work during which he was said not to have visited his home even once, the turbulent current was tamed and was led calmly towards the sea. Yü became a popular hero, and the reigning monarch Shun decided to designate him as his successor.

Many historians wonder whether the good emperors had ever existed, let alone their good deeds. That these emperors sought "the most virtuous men," instead of their sons, to be designated as their successors seems to have been a legend too idealized to be true. If they did exist at all, these so-called emperors were perhaps the tribal chieftains best known among the numerous tribes then in existence in North China and might have governed better than other chieftains. Conceivably the various Chinese tribes had formed a confederation as a defense measure against non-Chinese tribes who lived around them and posed a constant threat. The "good emperors" could have been the heads of the confederation to whom all Chinese tribes owed some kind of allegiance. The designation of virtuous men as successors might have been an election process whereby the heads of the confederation were chosen. The incumbent chief of the confederation nominated "the most virtuous man" (which probably means "the ablest and the wisest") as his successor, and the nomination was subject to approval by all Chinese tribes other than his own. Once approval was secured, the nominee became officially the successor. When Yü was installed as the confederation chief, "ten thousand nations" (which means "numerous tribes"), we are told, came to him to pay their homage and tribute. It seems that once a tribal chief was proclaimed as the common suzerain of all Chinese tribes he was free to use whatever means at his command, including military force, to compel allegiance from the recalcitrant tribes. In any case, he could count on the support of those tribes which had already pledged allegiance to him.

If the above description is close to reality, the question arises as to why the "good emperors" are idealized beyond credibility in some of the earliest written records. To ancient historians, history was not merely an objective record of past events; it was also the means of providing moral lessons. The necessity of serving a moral purpose was such an overwhelming concern to these early historians that it often led them to a distortion of facts. The most unscrupulous among them even forged documents in order to drive home a point which to them was extremely important. In writing political history, most of these traditional historians subscribed to two basic principles, the principle of legitimacy and the principle of using the past to teach the present. These two principles were of course closely related. Legitimacy was not legitimacy in its biological sense; it was a legitimacy of "virtue" (tao-t'ung) which came to mean that only the most virtuous men were entitled to rule. This concept antedated Confucianism, though it was Confucianism which later strengthened it. It is not surprising that the most detailed description of Yao and Shun appears in the book of Mencius (372–289 B.C.), an architect of Confucian philosophy. As the theory of legitimacy was popularized, the tendency was to extend the line of legitimacy to the remotest years. One historian even composed an "imperial chronology" which extended the line beyond 4,000 B.C. Many of these "emperors" were said to have reigned more than one hundred years, which of course was a physical impossibility. Since traditional historians believed that history should serve as a moral guide to teach the present, they tended to glorify the past as the present became more unpleasant. Those who wrote about the "good emperors" lived between the eighth and the third century B.C., an age of chaos and war, and they were longing for a reappearance of the golden age which had allegedly existed in the past. To men like Mencius, history was always more important as a book of ethics than as history, and they read into it their own beliefs.

Unreliable as these early writings are as historical materials, it is totally unwarranted to dismiss everything in them as fictional or legendary. Each individual event has to be evaluated and judged according to its own merit. Skepticism, when carried to great extremes, could be as harmful as credulity. The Great Flood might serve as an example. While we cannot take as historical fact every detail about the Great Flood, it is nevertheless true that the flood could have occurred, because of the condition of the Yellow River and its tributaries, as we have described these in the Introduction, and because of the frequency of floods in North China during the historical period. It might have been a series of floods which occurred intermittently for a number of years. The fact that there was a legendary flood in West Asia does not necessarily mean that the Chinese had borrowed such a legend.

The accession of Yü as the common suzerain of all Chinese tribes was traditionally placed at 2205 B.C. Towards the end of Yü's reign, his tribe had become so strong and prosperous that the other tribes proclaimed his son Ch'i as his successor. The fact that Ch'i was an able and wise man might also have had something to do with this decision. A precedent was established and from then on the position of the common suzerain became hereditary. The dynasty which Yü established was called Hsia, the first dynasty in Chinese history. Though nominally suzerain, the Hsia was but one of the hundreds of tribes in the North China Plain. Inter-tribal warfare was frequent. Outside of forming a common front against the non-Chinese tribes ("barbarians") whenever it was necessary, they were free to conquer and annex one another. Even the Hsia tribe itself was eager to join the game. Originally located in western Honan, it expanded eastward until it covered parts of the modern Shantung and Hopeh provinces. As time went on, however, the Hsia rulers gradually lost the vitality which had characterized earlier leaders. Secluded in their palaces and sunk in sensual pleasures, they became puppets of their own ministers. In the twenty-second century B.C. one of the ministers actually ousted the king and usurped the throne. A dynastic revival ensued shortly afterwards, but it proved to be only temporary. In the eighteenth century B.C. one of the eastern tribes, called Shang, eventually replaced the Hsia as the common suzerain of all Chinese tribes.

SHANG

Shang originally was the name of a nomadic tribe, moving from place to place until it finally settled in Shangch'iu of modern Honan province. Through contacts with the more advanced Chinese tribes, it gradually adopted agriculture and acquired the sophisticated culture of a sedentary society. Meanwhile, it lost none of the vigor and vitality of a nomadic horde. In the eighteenth century B.C. a great leader emerged who, through diplomacy and warfare, annexed most of his neighboring states. This leader, T'ang, was not only noted for his military exploits, but even more so for his enlightened domestic policy. He ran an efficient government, worked hard for the welfare of his people, and was held in great esteem by them. In his struggle for supremacy, he promoted agricultural production to sustain his military campaigns, made alliances with those tribes that submitted to his will, and conquered those that resisted. As a showdown drew near with the Hsia, he successfully convinced most Chinese tribes as well as his own people how oppressive and corrupt the Hsia regime had become and why he had no choice except revolt. As a result, an increasing number of Chinese tribes switched their loyalty to him. Instead of rising up to meet the challenge, the last Hsia ruler, Chieh, became depraved and cruel. He reportedly killed his best ministers simply because they had offended him and he wasted manpower needlessly by building elaborate palaces for his concubines. As the military campaign progressed, more and more tribes joined T'ang's revolt. In the final battle Chieh was captured. After he had been exiled, the new dynasty, Shang, was formally established. The establishment of the dynasty was traditionally placed at 1766 B.C.

As the Shangs are closer to us than the Hsias in terms of time, we know a great deal more about them. Recent archaeological findings have further enriched our knowledge. For one thing, we know that they moved their capital often. This could have meant that they were not yet completely out of the pastoral stage or that they had repeatedly exhausted land fertility by constant cultivation. Both theories have perhaps an element of truth. Anyhow, agriculture was their main occupation. Crops included millet, wheat, and rice; millet seems to have been the main staple crop and was also used to make wine. Sericulture had been discovered before, and the silk produced was used to make clothes, kerchiefs, curtains, etc. For meat there were cattle, sheep, chicken, and hogs. Dogs had been domesticated. Other animals like oxen, horses, and elephants were used

YELLOW RIVER

T'U-FANG
(barbarian)

CH'IANG
(barbarian)

Yen

☐ Yin

Yi
Yüfang
Wei
ch'i

Chou
Shang
ch'i
Shangch'iu
Huo

Yellow
Sea

HUAI YI
(barbarian)

YANGTZE RIVER

SI RIVER

MAP 7
CHINA of the SHANG DYNASTY
(c. 1766 – c. 1122 B.C.)
● Tribal Sites
☐ Shang's Capital after 1401 B.C.

0   300   600
Scale of Miles

for transportation; we know that the nobility and the wealthy had car-
riages drawn by animals. On the battlefield, while common soldiers
fought on foot, the nobles attacked each other in horse chariots. Elephants
were sometimes used for charging the enemy's defense lines. As forests
could still be found in most parts of North China, game was abundant,
and hunting was the most popular sport among the nobles. Even around
the capital city Yin (after 1401 B.C.) there were large undeveloped areas
to which agriculture had not been extended. We know that in one hunting
trip a Shang ruler bagged 348 deer, and in another, 113 boars.

As for shelter, a peasant's house was no more than a thatched hut;
the whole family lived in one large, rectangular room, divided by wooden
boards or thatched curtains to make kitchen and living quarters. The
houses of the wealthy were more elaborate. Stone and bronze foundations
have been found on the Yin ruins; columns must have been extensively
used for supporting the main beams. Since no tiles or bricks have been
found on these sites, it is presumed that even among the wealthy, thatched
roofing was common. Walls were generally made of hardened earth; doors
usually faced south to admit more sunlight.

During the Shang dynasty two of the most epochal events occurred,
namely, the discovery of bronze metallurgy and the development of a
written language. Though we cannot place the date when bronze metallurgy was discovered in China, it must have undergone a long process of
development before it reached the perfection evidenced by the bronzes
unearthed in the Yin ruins. Experts have opined that the technique of
casting bronze in the Shang dynasty was even superior to the famed
craftsmanship of the European Renaissance. The unearthed bronzes were
of many kinds, mostly household utensils and religious implements. There
were wine pots, cups, plates and dishes, drinking vessels, and food containers of various shapes and designs. There were also religious vessels
covered with elaborate designs in incised lines or in high relief. One
bronze piece, perhaps serving the same purpose as our lazy Susan, had a
beautifully designed central column around which four sculptured dragons rotated. Bronze was also cast into military weapons. The points of
spears, javelins, and arrows, together with swords and knives, were made
of bronze, as were warriors' helmets. However, bronze did not replace
stone completely, as some weapons were still made of stone or animal
bones.

Though overshadowed by bronzes, other handicraft products of the
Shangs were scarcely less impressive. Some of the glazed potteries were
made of clay of the finest quality, with paintings or relief drawings of
animals and geometrical patterns. Jade was carved into many shapes
representing men, wild animals, birds, fishes, and frogs; stone was sculptured into statues of men, tigers, rabbits, and birds. There was also a
variety of ornaments made of jade and precious stones used for women's

hairdressing. Since none of these materials were produced in the areas in which they were found, trade must have been very extensive. Cowrie shells were used as a medium of exchange; coined money was not yet invented.

The Shangs were said to be a religious people. They believed in spirits who, they thought, existed everywhere: in the forests, mountains, rivers, fields, and even in one's own house. However, most of the spirits were those of harmless, deceased ancestors. After a man died, his spirit presumably left the body and was wafted into the air, but it would extend protection to the family if properly humored and worshipped. By means of sacrifices and by magic incantations the spirits could be summoned before a priest and could be persuaded to reveal what the future held for the family. The Shangs would not do anything important without consulting the spirits, whether it be making a trip or fighting a war. For the kings who had to make important decisions affecting the entire nation, religious rituals became exceedingly elaborate affairs. Sheep or cattle used for each sacrifice sometimes numbered three or four hundred. The method of offering them, whether it was burning in open flames, drowning in rivers, or burying underneath the ground, varied according to occasions; even the color and sex of the animals were carefully prescribed. Sometimes prisoners-of-war were slaughtered as sacrifices. It was believed that the spirits, carefully attended to, would make their wishes known through the oracle bones. To conjure oracles, a priest drilled a turtle shell or a piece of animal bone with a hand piercer on one side and then placed the hollowed points on top of a flame. The other side of the shell or bone began to crack, and the cracks formed various patterns. The priest would then interpret the meaning of the patterns according to a magic formula; his interpretations were the alleged oracles. Thousands of these oracle bones have been unearthed from the Yin ruins.

When these oracle bones were unearthed, the archaeologists were amazed that there were written inscriptions on them. The inscriptions indicated the questions asked by the priest, the answers, and sometimes even the eventual outcome. Before 1899 when the first oracle bones were discovered, there had been two popular theories with regard to the origin of the Chinese written language. One theory traced the language's beginning to the knot-writing of the remote period; unfortunately, we know little about this type of writing. According to the other theory, the early beginning of the language was the Eight Diagrams, supposedly invented by the culture hero Fu-hsi. The Eight Diagrams will be discussed in connection with Chinese philosophy in a later chapter; suffice it to say that the Diagrams, having only simple, horizontal lines, were too simplified a form to generate a complicated language like Chinese. Since the discovery of the Shell-Bone script (chia-ku wen), as the inscriptions on the oracle bones are called, we have been greatly enlightened. More than two thousand written characters of this script have been deciphered, and most of them have been identified with their modern counterparts in the Chinese written system. It is beyond any doubt that the Shell-Bone script was the forerunner of modern Chinese. In fact, the modern script can be traced all the way back to this ancient script through several stages of development. The large number of written characters in the Shell-Bone script implied an advanced and sophisticated society which used it; the number of Chinese characters commonly used today does not exceed more than five thousand. The period during which this ancient script flourished is placed between 1700 and 1100 B.C.; since it had already reached an advanced stage by then, it is reasonable to assume that the rudiments of a written language first appeared in China around 2000 B.C., if not earlier. Perhaps we are not in great error when we say that China entered the historical period four thousand years ago.

The Chinese language, the oldest surviving language in the world, is unique in the sense that it is non-phonetic. Interestingly, it is still used by the largest number of people in the world. It began with pictographs and ideographs, and after 4,000 years they still constitute a sizable portion of modern characters, even though they have been stylized, simplified, or both. The words "sun" and "moon" were written ⊙ and 𝕯 respectively in the Shell-Bone script; today they are written 日 and 月 . The words for "one" and "two" have been written — and 二 throughout Chinese history because stylization and simplification are not necessary in these two cases. On the other hand, more complicated characters have passed through a long process of stylization and simplification. Here the words "turtle" and "horse" are used as examples.

Shell-Bone Script	Great Script	Small Script	Scribe Script	Modern Script
Shang Dynasty	Chou Dynasty	Ch'in and Former Han	Later Han	

One might notice that Small-Script characters are sometimes (such as in the case of "turtle") more complicated than the Great-Script characters that antedated them. The reason is that the Ch'in state which used the Small Script dictated its adoption by all Chinese after Ch'in had unified China in 221 B.C. The decision, politically motivated, might have deterred the simplification process for the time being. Both characters, even in their present forms, do not seem simplified enough to a Westerner. The present Communist regime apparently shares this sentiment, and since its establishment in 1949 has further simplified the more complicated characters. Today in all works published in Communist China, these two characters, "turtle" and "horse," are written respectively as follows:

龟　　　马

Most Chinese characters are not simple pictographs (such as in the case of "sun" and "moon") and ideographs (such as in the case of "one" and "two"); they are compound characters. A large number of compound characters are combinations of significs and phonetics. Both significs and phonetics are simple pictographs or ideographs and are characters themselves. However, when they become a part of compound characters, they lose their original meanings, except in an incidental sense. Take the word "village" which is written 村 . It is a compound character, composed of the signific 木 and the phonetic 寸 . The character 木 was originally written 米 which meant "tree" as it depicted a tree with branches on the top and roots at bottom. The character 寸 means a Chinese inch which obviously has nothing to do with a village. It is a phonetic and indicates that the compound character "village" should be pronounced the same way as the phonetic 寸 (*ts'un*). Why should the character "village" have the signific "tree"? Presumbly, because there are trees around a typical village. There are other compound characters which cannot be so easily explained. Take the character 李 as an example. Besides being a surname, it means a plum tree and is pronounced *li*. It is a compound character, composed of the characters 木 and 子 . The character 子 ("son") is pronounced *tzu* and is therefore not a phonetic in this particular case. Most Chinese characters are of this type; they defy explanation or even rationalization because they have advanced too far from their beginnings. There could have been a logic in the composition of each of them, but that logic has been by and large lost.

When it is pointed out that each character can serve the purpose of an English letter or syllable besides being an independent word, it is easy to see what a versatile language Chinese is. On the other hand, since the language is not phonetic and since each character has to be memorized independently with regard to its pronunciation as well as its variety of meanings, Chinese is acckowledgedly one of the most difficult languages in the world. While a great deal could be said about the disadvantages of a non-phonetic language, the fact that in the Chinese language the written form (as contrary to pronunciation) counted most enabled it to spread to faraway places where it was adopted even though the pronunciation of the same item as indicated by a Chinese character was entirely different.

In other words, after foreigners had adopted the written characters, they pronounced the characters not as the Chinese pronounced them but as they had been pronouncing those words which they then began to write in Chinese. Today, a Japanese, a Korean, and a Chinese might not be able to communicate with each other orally, but they could do so with a piece of paper and a pen, because a written Chinese character conveys the same (or approximately the same) meanings to all of them. The same is true of a southern and a northern Chinese who write the same characters but pronounce them differently. Had the phonetic part of the language not been detached from its written part to a considerable extent, many written languages would have been developed in China in view of the difficulties in communication and transportation of the ancient years. The sharing of a common written language meant a common heritage and a common identity for all Chinese despite great distances between them. When it is pointed out that the word *Chinese* is more a cultural than a racial term, we can easily see what an important role the language has played in the development of China as a nation.

CHOU

In the twelfth century B.C. a western tribe called Chou replaced Shang as the common sovereign of all Chinese tribes in North China. The word "sovereign" is used deliberately, because during the early stage of the Chou dynasty there was a great deal of power concentrated in the hands of the central government. The ancestry of Chou's royal house was cloaked in mystery, and according to the legend, its founder, Hou-chi, was born of virgin birth after his mother had inadvertently stepped on a huge footprint in the field and thus become pregnant. During the Shang dynasty the Chou tribe pledged allegiance to the Shangs. Half nomadic and half agricultural, the tribe had moved from place to place until it settled down in the Wei River valley in modern Shensi. The Chou capital, Hao, was located near modern Sian. The fertility of the Wei valley and the bumper crops it yielded strengthened the tribe economically, while living among the "barbarians" maintained its martial spirit and fighting ability. During the twelfth century B.C. the royal house produced in succession several able leaders, notably King Wen (Wen Wang) and his two sons, King Wu (Wu Wang) and Duke Chou (Chou Kung). Before King Wen died in 1120 B.C. it was reported that more than two-thirds of the Chinese tribes had switched their loyalty from Shang to Chou. Two years later his son and successor, King Wu, formally declared war on Shang and led those tribes that had pledged allegiance to him for a final campaign against its king, Cheo. The declaration of war accused Cheo, among other things, of having been under the undue influence of wine

CH'ÜAN-JUNG
(barbarian)

HSIEN-YÜN
(barbarian)

YELLOW RIVER

•Yen

•Huo

Han•
•Tsin
•Hsün
□Hao
•Hsikuo
•Kuo
•Kuan
•Wei
•Lu
•Ch'i
•T'eng

Yellow
Sea

•Sung

•Yupao

•Yung
•Shen
•Ts'ai
•Chiang

YANGTZE RIVER

SI RIVER

MAP 8
WEST CHOU
(C. 1100 B.C.)
• Capital of Feudal State
□ Capital of West Chou

0   150   300   450
Scale of Miles

and women in his political decisions, of having failed to perform religious services in honor of his ancestors, and of being cruel to his subjects. The debauched monarch committed suicide ("burned himself to death") after his army had been defeated. The Chou dynasty formally came into being in 1122 B.C.

The new dynasty was destined to be the longest in Chinese history, from the twelfth to the third century B.C. However, after the eighth century the Chou sovereignty was largely nominal; local states were essentially independent countries. Many historians call the period 722–481 B.C. the Spring and Autumn period, a period covered by the famous history, *Spring and Autumn Annals*. From 403 to 221 B.C. was the period of Warring States which ended in the latter year with the grand unification of China by the Ch'in state. Generally speaking, the first four centuries of the Chou dynasty was an era of peace and prosperity. The last five centuries witnessed a decline of central authority, the rise of local states, and the prevalence of anarchy and interstate warfare.

At the time when the dynasty was established, it was full of vigor and vitality. At the helm of the government were two of the greatest statesmen of ancient China, King Wu and Duke Chou. After the former's death in 1115 B.C. the Duke served as regent to King Ch'eng, his nephew, who was then a minor. Traditional historians credited the Duke with the suppression of a rebellion, the establishment of a central bureaucracy, and

BRONZE TIGERS   These two tigers, weighing 47 pounds each, were cast during the Chou dynasty (c.1122–249 B.C.). Each has an open hollow chamber in the center, and its surface is decorated with low relief.

the introduction of a variety of institutions, including a nation-wide school system. Besides, he was a man of literary and artistic ability, and many of his achievements are recorded in *Chou Institutions* (*Chou kuan*), a book which was written several hundred years after his death. Though he was greatly idealized by Confucians, all evidences seem to indicate that he was a man of integrity and outstanding ability.

Among the Chou institutions none was perhaps more important than *feng-chien* or feudalism. At the time when it was instituted, it was a centralizing rather than a decentralizing process. The Shang dynasty, Chou's predecessor, left the conquered tribes to manage their own affairs so long as they recognized the Shang suzerainty. The Chou, on the other hand, annexed or otherwise relocated many tribes and imposed a feudal order on all of them. A new theory was advanced that "all land belongs to the king and all men are the king's subjects," and the king could grant land to whomever he wished. Except areas around the capital which were under the king's direct management, all territories in China were distributed among the newly created lords. These feudal lords were either the descendants of the former royal houses (including Shang), the close relatives of the king, or the generals and statesmen who had helped the king in winning the war. Among the most notable of the feudal states thus created were Lu, Ch'i, and Tsin, which received the largest and the best arable land in North China. Five feudal ranks were instituted corresponding roughly to the English duke, marquis, earl, viscount, and baron. To avoid uncertainty and rivalry after the death of a lord, a new rule of succession was devised, covering the succession of all nobilities, including that of the king. The rule stated that legal wives were superior to concubines and that the elder sons were superior to the younger. After the king died, for instance, the eldest son of his legal wife (namely, the queen) would inherit the throne. This son might be younger than the oldest son of a concubine, but that did not make any difference in succession, because legitimacy had priority over seniority. This was contrary to the Shang practice wherein the dead king was usually succeeded by his next younger brother. With the Chou feudalism the other sons of the dead king were awarded the rank of duke. A duke's eldest son born to his legal wife would eventually succeed him as duke, while the rest of his male children would become marquises, and so on. As a baronate was the lowest feudal order, all the baron's sons, with the exception of one, had to step down as commoners. By this device the majority of noble descent would wind up as commoners eventually, and in numbers the nobility would not be overburdened. It was hoped that through the rigid enforcement of the succession rules internecine strife could be avoided.

Accompanying feudal ranks were feudal fiefs and feudal obligations. Feudal fiefs were land granted by the lord to his vassals in return for feudal obligations which consisted of tributes and services performed by the vassals for the lord. Fiefs varied in size. While a feudal state might be larger than New York state, some of the small fiefs were smaller than a large ranch in Texas. Relations between the lord and his vassals were carefully prescribed. Whenever he wished to, the king could inspect the administrative details of his vassalages; the vassals in return had to make periodic trips to the capital to pay tribute and to report personally to the king on the state of affairs within their domains. Failure to do so on the part of the vassals entitled the king to take retaliatory measures such as the suspension or deprivation of ranks and fiefs, and in more serious cases, sending troops against them. In many larger states key ministers were even appointed by the king. In time of war, the vassals were required to contribute troops at the king's disposal, whether or not the king's enemies were barbarians or insubordinate vassals. They were obligated to defend the king, whenever and by whomever the king was attacked.

This, of course, represents an idealized stage of feudalism when practice more or less followed theory during the early period of the Chou dynasty. As time went on, some vassal states had become too strong to allow this theory to function effectively. After the eighth century B.C. the king's sovereignty became largely nominal, and each state pursued whatever courses it devised for itself.

Opposite the nobility and at the lower level of the social structure stood the commoners. They were the merchants, the artisans, and the peasants who produced things to support the entire society. The nobility constituted the governing class, the commoners the governed. The overwhelming majority of the commoners were peasants. Since land ownership was vested in the nobility, the peasants had only the right of utilization for which they paid the lord produce as rent plus labor. In a more or less typical situation a tract of land was divided into nine sections of about fifteen acres each. Each family tilled one of the eight surrounding sections, while all eight families tilled the central section in common. The harvest of the central section went to the lord as rent; the crops raised in each surrounding section belonged to the family which tilled it. Under feudal law the eight families should plow, seed, water, weed, and harvest the lord's common first before they could do the same with their own sections. Whenever this arrangement was found inconvenient, nine families, instead of eight, would till the nine sections as described above, and each family was responsible for its own assigned section. In this case each family gave one-tenth of its harvested crops to the lord as rent. Feudal obligations, however, did not end here. A portion of whatever the peasants produced, be it silk or wine, was customarily presented to the lord as gifts. Corvée could be imposed whenever necessity arose, such as repairing roads, building bridges, dredging rivers, or constructing dams. These obligations varied from place to place and from time to time, very much depending upon the kind of lord the peasants happened to have.

A poem in the *Book of Odes* describes vividly the life of a peasant who lived in Shensi in the early Chou period when feudalism was in its prime. According to this poem, the peasant started to repair his farm implements in the first month of the year for the seeding season ahead. In the second month he plowed the land; his wife prepared the food and carried the food basket to him at meal time. Meanwhile, his daughter went to the mulberry groves to pluck leaves for the hungry silkworms at home. Sometimes the lord's steward strolled by smiling and inquired how the work was going. In the eighth month harvesting began. His daughter was busy at home weaving silk cloth and dying it black, yellow, or flashing red to make clothes for the lord's children. In the tenth month when harvesting had been completed, the peasant began to brew wine so that he could present it to the lord as a birthday present sometime in the next spring. Then he went to work in the lord's house cutting reeds in the daytime and making ropes in the evening. Occasionally, there was a feast when all gathered in the lord's house, ate roasted lamb, and drank to the lord's health, shouting happily, "Long live the lord!" In the eleventh month the peasant hunted for foxes whose skins would be used to make the lord's winter coat. In the twelfth month, military training was conducted under the lord's supervision. The pigs which had been fattened were then presented to the lord. It was also the time to store ice underneath the ground to be used by the lord in the next summer or spring. All in all, the peasants seem to have existed only for the comfort of the lord. However, this poem also paints a picture of peace and prosperity, an orderly country life, and a warm relationship between the lord and his peasants. Though the peasant's life under feudalism was anything but enviable, the fact is that it was never bettered afterwards. After the eighth century B.C. when the country drifted into chaos and war, the peasants simply wished that they could have lived some centuries earlier.

Below the peasants and at the bottom of the social scale were the slaves. Slavery existed as early as men could recall, or at least as early as the Shang dynasty. After each battle the Shangs condemned most of their prisoners to slavery, no matter whether the prisoners were Chinese or barbarians. Slaves were employed in a variety of ways, as laborers in the farm, as household servants, or sometimes as expendable fodder on the battlefield. With the establishment of an orderly society in the twelfth century B.C. when warfare had become less frequent, the supply of slaves fell off. Fortunately for the slave owners, there were other sources. One source was provided by former freemen who, unable to pay their debts, were forced to sell their children or even themselves as slaves. There were also condemned criminals enslaved by the government. After the eighth century B.C. when wars became a normal state of affairs, prisoners-of war again formed a major source of supply, and slave-hunting was sometimes a major motive in waging warfare. After each war, all captives, including the nobles and high-ranking officials, were enslaved. If the warring parties so desired, captives could be exchanged and so saved from enslavement. On other occasions the state which held them asked for ransoms, the amount varying according to the worth of individual captives. In one case, the ransom was "five sheets of sheep skin." In other cases, ransom prices could be very high. In 611 B.C., for instance, the state of Sung was willing to pay a ransom of "one hundred chariots and four hundred horses" to the state of Ch'u to free a high-ranking official. If a person became a slave, his life was miserable indeed. His master not only monopolized his services but controlled his body as well. He could be bought and sold and was sometimes used as collateral for securing loans. In one instance, a lord commanded his slave to taste poisoned food even after it had been tested by a dog which died immediately. Cruelty like this might be an exception rather than a rule; it nevertheless shows the absolute control the master had over his slaves.

THE TURBULENT AGE OF WAR

King Yu, the ruler of Chou between 781 and 771 B.C., was not unlike the last monarchs of Hsia and Shang. He raised taxes, squandered them for his personal comfort, and was unconcerned with the welfare of his subjects. The immediate cause of his downfall, however, was his neurotic infatuation with a favorite concubine named Pao-ssu, according to traditional historians. When Pao-ssu gave birth to a son, he deposed his crown prince and named the infant as his heir apparent. The crown prince's mother, the queen, was the daughter of a powerful lord who, learning what had happened to his grandson, made a secret alliance with the barbarian tribe Ch'üan-jung for possible military action against the king in order to reinstate his grandson as the crown prince. Meanwhile, King Yu, not knowing of the conspiracy against him, sank even deeper in his infatuation with his favorite concubine. Despite her great beauty, Pao-ssu rarely smiled and the king tried in vain to induce her to smile often. Finally, he ordered the lighting of beacon fires which under normal circumstances signified a barbarian invasion and the urgent request for vassals' help to defend the king. The vassals arrived at the head of their armies, but there was no enemy. Amused by their bewilderment and awkwardness, Pao-ssu smiled. Having found a sure way to make her smile, the king lit the beacon fires repeatedly and often.

We do not know how much truth the above story contains, but it is recorded as history in one of the earliest writings. In 771 B.C. Ch'üanjung, in alliance with the queen's father, invaded and quickly surrounded Chou's capital, Hao. The king ordered the lighting of beacon fires, but none of his vassals arrived as they obviously thought that the king was playing another practical joke upon them. The barbarians captured the capital and sacked it thoroughly, besides killing the captured king. Meanwhile, with the help of his maternal grandfather and the barbarians, the deposed crown prince ascended the throne as King P'ing. As the old capital was too close to the barbarians to be safe, the new monarch moved his capital eastward to Loyang. From then on the dynasty was never the same. Since Loyang was east of Hao, the Chou dynasty after 771 B.C. was often referred to as East Chou. The period East Chou (771–249 B.C.) overlaps with the Spring and Autumn period (722–481 B.C.) and the period of Warring States (403–221 B.C.). The Chou dynasty before 771 B.C. is sometimes called West Chou.

The five centuries after 771 B.C. were years of turmoil, war, and also social and economic changes. The central authority weakened, then became nominal, and finally ceased to exist. The weakening of central authority was accompanied by increasing frequency of foreign and domestic wars. The large states invaded and conquered the small states; the king had to confirm whatever had been accomplished, by naked aggression or otherwise. One king, trying to punish one of his subordinate vassals and thus to reassert his authority, found his army defeated and himself wounded on the shoulder (707 B.C.). As all states were free to conquer and annex one another, their total number decreased steadily. There were about two hundred states in the eighth century B.C.; towards the end of the fifth century B.C. and at the beginning of the Warring States period only seven major states remained.

During the Spring and Autumn period, efforts were made to bring some order out of chaos. Since the king was powerless and thus helpless, the leadership had to come from rulers of individual states. Among them Duke Huan of Ch'i (Ch'i Huan-kung, 686–643 B.C.) and Duke Wen of Tsin (Tsin Wen-kung, d. 629 B.C.) were the most prominent. Both pledged "the respect of central authority and the repulsion of barbarians" and claimed that their leadership would lead to the implementation of both principles. The real purpose, however, was to reach a *modus vivendi* among the major powers in North China and to prevent the barbarians and the less Sinicized powers such as Ch'u from threatening their dominant positions. From time to time force was used to compel small states to acknowledge such leadership. Duke Huan was said to have gone to war twenty-eight times during his reign of forty-three years; some of the wars were waged against the barbarians who had invaded the Chinese states, but the purpose of most of them was to make the other Chinese states his allies. Outside of North China he was greatly concerned with the rising power of Ch'u and in 656 B.C. he sent an army to invade that southern state on the ground that the latter had failed to pay tribute to the king of Chou, the nominal sovereign. This action earned him the reputation of protector of Chinese states against barbarians.

CH'ÜAN-JUNG
(barbarian)

HSI-JUNG
(barbarian)

TI
(barbarian)

SHAN-JUNG
(barbarian)

YEN

TSIN
Hsint'ien

Hantan

CH'I
Lintzu

WEI
chaoko

LU
Ch'üfu

Yellow
Sea

CH'IN
Yung

CHOU
Loyang

SUNG
Shangch'iu

Hsincheng
CHENG

CH'IANG
(barbarian)

Tanyang

Laichou

PA
(barbarian)

CH'U
Ying

TS'AI

Wu
WU

Kweichi
YÜEH

MAP 9

CHINA IN THE
SIXTH CENTURY B.C.

• State Capital

0   150   300   450

Scale of Miles

To strengthen his leadership among the Chinese states, time and again (twenty-six times altogether) Duke Huan of Ch'i invited them to attend interstate conferences. Some of these conferences were called to deal with a particular emergency such as a barbarian invasion; others were convened to find some general principles to govern the relations among the Chinese states. In one of these conferences four major principles were adopted. First, the king's authority should be respected, though everybody knew that this was only a nominal gesture. Second, whenever there was a barbarian invasion against any state, all other states should hold consultations among themselves and should cooperate to repel the invader. This principle sounds like our modern concept of collective security. Third, if an internal revolt resulted in the assassination of the reigning prince and the establishment of a new regime, the regime would not be recognized, and all the states would send a joint force against the usurper until a legitimate ruler was installed. To prevent such an eventuality, each state promised, among other things, that it would not change its crown prince "casually" and would not "let women interfere with state affairs." Obviously, the conferees believed that these were the two major causes of internal revolt. Lastly, all states pledged non-aggression among themselves. In case of dispute among them, the leader state (Ch'i) would be called to arbitrate and to render judgment. Though these principles were often violated, the fact that efforts were made to bring a semblance of order among the northern states was a great achievement in itself. Without such efforts there would have been complete chaos. One hundred years after Duke Huan's death Confucius spoke highly of his achievement.

After Duke Huan's death in 643 B.C. Ch'i began to decline and the leadership of the northern states was later assumed by Duke Wen of Tsin. By then the potential enemies of the northern states were not the barbarians further north but the semi-Sinicized state Ch'u. In a ferocious battle fought in 632 B.C. (Battle of Ch'engpu) the advance of Ch'u was checked, and Duke Wen was proclaimed as the new leader of the northern states. The Duke died in 629 B.C., but Tsin, under a succession of capable leaders, continued to be the dominant power in North China. In 598 B.C. Ch'u defeated Tsin in the Battle of Pi (Honan), but it was unable to exploit its victory as it had overextended itself from its base in the Yangtze Valley. When Ch'i proceeded to challenge Tsin's leadership after the battle, Tsin quickly defeated it, and Ch'i was forced to acknowledge Tsin's leadership. The last of the three great battles between Tsin and Ch'u was fought in 567 B.C. (Battle of Yenling, modern Honan) when Tsin avenged its former defeat and was victorious. If the three battles indicated anything, they meant that neither side was able to challenge successfully the other's leadership in its own sphere of influence.

Tsin was the leader in North China, and Ch'u continued to be the dominant power in the south.

The stalemate produced one of the most interesting interstate conferences in ancient China. The small states had been victimized by the repeated warfare among the major powers, a warfare over which they had no control, and they were hoping for some kind of arrangement whereby the major powers would renounce war as an instrument of foreign policy. Sung, a small state between Tsin and Ch'u which had suffered greatly in the wars between the two giants, took the initiative in arranging a non-aggression conference. At its invitation the delegates of eleven states, including Tsin and Ch'u, gathered at its capital Shangch'iu in the summer of 546 B.C. There were numerous diplomatic maneuvers behind the scene, not unlike those which occur so often in our modern international conferences. A multilateral agreement was finally reached, and each signatory pledged non-aggression against its neighbor. The agreement paved the way for a peace of more than forty years, a remarkable achievement in view of the existing chaotic situation. When the peace was finally breached, it was breached by the southern state of Wu which had not been a signatory of the agreement in the first place.

So far we have been concerned mostly with North China, as this was the area where Chinese civilization was born and where the most important events took place. The rise of Ch'u indicated the increasing importance not only of an individual state but of the entire south as well. Ch'u's challenge of the dominant position of the northern states was more than political; it was also cultural and economic. It meant that the south which was customarily referred to as barbarian territories had become more and more Sinicized and that the southerners had been gradually absorbed by the Chinese culture as originated in the north. The southerners not only learned the northerners' written language but also adopted their institutions on a large scale. Though politically separated from the northern states, the south had become a part of the Chinese cultural system. Economically, it was intensely developed and was challenging North China in population and wealth. By the fourth century B.C. it had become so far advanced that it was able to produce such men as Ch'ü Yüan and Sung Yü whose poetry could be compared favorably with the very best written by the northerners.

The middle Yangtze, the home of Ch'u, was traditionally referred to as a barbarian territory. Early during the Chou dynasty when the king proposed to confer a feudal title on a Ch'u prince, the latter declined the honor on the ground that he was a barbarian and had no use for Chinese titles. In 706 B.C. the reigning Ch'u prince requested a feudal title, but this time Chou refused, because by then Ch'u had repeatedly invaded Chinese states in the north. Rebuffed, the prince of Ch'u proclaimed himself king two years later. Ch'u's power continued to grow throughout the seventh century B.C.; it conquered and annexed many Chou states and expanded northward to modern Honan province. Meanwhile, it held sway from the middle to the lower Yangtze valley. Time and again its troops penetrated deep into the North China Plain and at one time (598 B.C.) defeated Tsin in one of the most bloody battles in ancient history. It remained the strongest power in South China throughout the sixth century B.C. At the beginning of the fifth century B.C. Ch'u began to decline, as it had been weakened by repeated warfare with the northern states. Moreover, its rulers had slowly lost their martial vitality; and, exposed to the northern influence, they had succumbed to an easy, luxurious life as common among the northern rulers.

With the decline of Ch'u, others states emerged as contending powers in the Yangtze region. Among them Wu and Yüeh were the most prominent. Both states were located in the lower Yangtze; Wu in modern Kiangsu and Yüeh in Chekiang province. The lower Yangtze, being further away from the North China plain than the middle Yangtze, was exposed to Chinese culture at an even later date than Ch'u. While North China had advanced to a high stage of civilization early in the Chou dynasty, the people of the lower Yangtze were said to have such "barbarian" customs as "tattooing their bodies, cutting their hair short, and clearing the jungle to build cities." Progress, though slow, was nevertheless steady. Towards the end of the sixth century B.C. when Wu and Yüeh emerged as powerful states, the people of lower Yangtze had been greatly Sinicized, though the more advanced northerners still referred to them as barbarians. The emergence of the two southern states was followed by an interstate struggle which began in 506 B.C. and did not end until 473 B.C. At one time Wu not only defeated Yüeh; it almost wiped out Ch'u. Wu's supremacy, however, turned out to be short-lived. Flushed with victory, it sent its troops northward to attack Ch'i and Lu. This gave Yüeh a golden opportunity. In 473 B.C. it attacked Wu's home base and succeeded in conquering the entire state. From then on Yüeh dominated the lower Yangtze for seventy-three years. In 346 B.C. a revitalized Ch'u won a decisive victory against Yüeh. Soon Yüeh disintegrated into a number of small states and was no longer an important factor in interstate politics.

THE RISE OF CH'IN

In 403 B.C. Tsin disintegrated into three separate states, Han, Wei, and Chao. The disintegration marked the beginning of the Warring States period. After three centuries of conquests and annexations now only seven major states remained. These were Ch'in, Ch'i, Ch'u, and Yen, plus the three states that were the former Tsin. During this period military force

MAP 10
THE WARRING STATES
(c. 300 B.C.)
• State Capital

0   300   600
Scale of Miles

YEN

•Chi

CHAO

WEI   CH'I

Hantan   •Lintzu

P'ingyang   •Ch'üfu

CH'IN   CHOU   Taliang   LU

Loyang   SUNG

Hsienyang   HAN   Hsincheng   •Shangch'iu

Yellow
Sea

•Ying   CH'U   YANGTZE RIVER

YANGTZE RIVER

SI RIVER

South China Sea

LIAO RIVER

alone decided interstate issues—gone were the days of interstate confer-ences and sophisticated diplomacy. Agreements were made to be broken, and diplomats were experts in treachery and deceit. Every prince was bent on conquest, and might had become right. Prior to this period the value of human lives was often taken into consideration even on the battlefield. In one case the invading force of Ch'u, having heard that the long besieged city of Sung was so starved that "people were forced to exchange their children for food," voluntarily lifted the siege. The military commanders during the period of Warring States would not give much thought to moral scruples. Casualties ran to hundreds of thousands in each of the many military campaigns, and no mercy was shown to prisoners-of-war who were often slaughtered *en masse*. In this age of madness, gen-erals were rated and rewarded according to the number of enemies they killed. Bloodshed increased by the improvement in weapons and methods of warfare. Cavalry and infantry replaced war chariots, and the wide use of iron had made the new weapons more deadly. Besides, military strat-egy had become a specialized science. Top strategists like Wu Ch'i and Sun Pin not only showed their talent on the battlefield but also wrote books for the benefit of future generals. Each of the two large states, Ch'in and Ch'u, boasted of an army of more than one million men; even a smaller state like Han, Wei, or Yen was said to have several hundred thousand men among its military rank and file.

Eventually the western state Ch'in was able to conquer the other six states, and it unified China in 221 B.C. Located in the Wei River valley, Ch'in was a comparative newcomer in the interstate community. For centuries it was regarded as backward and semi-barbarian, and it exer-cised no great influence in the east where the more advanced states were located. The attitude of the eastern states towards Ch'in was not unlike the attitude of the Greek city-states towards Macedonia. As late as the seventh century B.C. Ch'in's expansion towards the east was blocked by Tsin and it had to be satisfied with being "the leader among the western barbarians." In the long run, however, the unique advantages it enjoyed enabled it to become the most powerful state and eventually to unify China. First, it rose up among nomadic tribes and was surrounded by them; it possessed a primitive vitality not shared by the more advanced states in the east. Second, its home base, the Wei River valley, was per-haps the most productive area in the entire Yellow River basin. Besides, the Ch'in people were known to be hardy, diligent farmers. Third, it was bordered by high mountains in the east and in the south, and these mountains were broken only by narrow passes. Behind its mountain shield it could move to attack whenever opportunities presented them-selves and shut itself behind its natural barriers when confronted with a superior enemy. Moreover, being isolated in the west, it could exploit whatever differences existed among the eastern states and even promote such differences. Though these states knew about Ch'in's ambition, they were hopelessly divided among themselves.

Ch'in's supremacy was of course not achieved overnight. In addition to the natural advantages as described above, it benefited, time and again, from the presence of great leaders at the helm of its government. One of them was Shang Yang, who was Ch'in's chief minister before he died in 338 B.C. An interesting story tells us of his rise to power. Born in Wei, he became a protégé of Wei's chief minister at an early age. When the chief minister was about to die of old age, the reigning prince asked him whom he would recommend as his successor. The chief minister suggested Shang Yang, saying that he was the ablest man in the country for the position. Having noticed the prince's reluctance to accept his advice because of Shang Yang's youthfulness, he urged the prince to kill Shang, because, if the king could not use him, the young man would be employed by some other sovereign to Wei's great disadvantage. After the prince departed, the chief minister summoned Shang Yang to his death-bed, and advised the young man to flee for his life. Shang Yang was unruffled and replied calmly: "If the prince cannot accept your advice to appoint me as chief minister, how can you expect him to accept your advice to kill me? I am very safe indeed." Shortly afterwards, Shang Yang went to Ch'in and was granted a series of audiences with its prince, Duke Hsiao (Ch'in Hsiao-kung). The prince was so impressed that he soon appointed Shang Yang as his chief minister.

Historians classify Shang Yang as a follower of the Legalist school; the philosophy of this school will be discussed in the next chapter. For our immediate purpose, suffice it to say that the Legalists believed in the sanctity of law and the complete subservience of individuals to the state. Once a law was enacted, it should be obeyed by everyone in the state, including members of the royal household. Shortly after Shang Yang became the chief minister, the crown prince violated the law, whereupon Shang Yang announced his intention to punish him as if he were a commoner. Others protested on the ground that the dignity of the heir apparent should be maintained, and finally the chief minister agreed to accept the prince's tutor as a substitute, and the latter was branded accordingly. Presumably, the tutor had not taught the prince how to behave and should therefore accept the blame. After this incident, "all Ch'in people learned to obey the law" and became "brave in public warfare and cowardly in civil strife." The observance of law was of course not an end itself; the real purpose was to channel each individual's energy to the service of the state. To mobilize manpower, Shang Yang ordered that all households in the state be organized into small groups and that each household be held responsible for the words and deeds of other households within the same group. Civil strife was strictly forbidden, while bravery on the battlefield in the service of the state was abundantly rewarded. Economically, the goal was the maximization of production, especially the production of the two basic branches of the economy, farming and cloth-making. Every acre of land was to be tilled; the strength of every man was to be utilized. Those who were not engaged in useful occupation and those who suffered poverty because of their own laziness were condemned to slavery. As Ch'in was sparsely populated, Shang Yang offered favorable terms to attract immigrants from the east. These new immigrants were exempted from military service, so they could concentrate on opening up virgin land and forests. To provide more incentive, feudal land tenure was abolished; land transaction between individuals was legalized; and land enclosure was even encouraged to provide more efficient cultivation. Efforts like these did not fail to yield results. Ten years after Shang Yang began his tenure of office, it was said that every family was economically sufficient, banditry and thievery were completely eliminated, and Ch'in became one of the best governed states. Domestically strong, it was just a matter of time before Ch'in made its power and influence felt abroad.

By the second half of the fourth century B.C. Ch'in had become the most powerful state in China. Such being the case, it was clearly to the advantage of the other states to form a common alliance for defense. Such an alliance, sponsored by Chao's chief minister Su Ch'in, came into being in 330 B.C., and for a period of fifteen years it successfully stopped Ch'in's advance towards the east. The alliance, however, could not be maintained indefinitely. For one thing, while all the six states were afraid of Ch'in, they hated each other even more. There was the deep-seated hatred between Ch'i and Yen which resulted in two major wars in three years (314 and 312 B.C.). The hatred between Ch'i and Ch'u was equally bitter. While each state was debating about its foreign policy, Ch'in did not remain idle. It sent its own chief minister Chang Yi (who, incidentally, had been Su Ch'in's classmate and best friend at one time) to exploit the differences between the six states and to persuade them not to form a common front against the Ch'in state. Chang, an articulate man, combined persuasion with threat and coercion. Well equipped with gold, he distributed it generously to make the persuasion even more convincing. His strategy worked well. Su Ch'in's alliance collapsed, and the six states kept on quarrelling and fighting among themselves, much to Ch'in's gratification.

As the third century progressed, interstate warfare became more and more vicious. For each war, hundreds of thousands of fighting men were mobilized by each of the belligerents, and casualties reached many thousands at the end of each battle. Quarter was rarely given, and captured prisoners-of-war were often slaughtered in cold blood, as has been said before. In 274 B.C. a Ch'in general defeated Wei and reportedly killed 150,000 enemy soldiers. Fourteen years later, another Ch'in general, Pai

Ch'i, was said to have slaughtered 450,000 Chao soldiers in one single battle (Battle of Ch'angp'ing). These numbers were unquestionably exaggerated. It is nevertheless true that military commanders had become increasingly brutal and inhuman on the battlefield. After the Battle of Ch'angp'ing, it was clear that none of the eastern states could stop Ch'in's march towards final victory. Ironically, one of the last efforts to stop Ch'in was made by King Nan of Chou who led a hodgepodge force to attack a Ch'in stronghold in 256 B.C. As expected, he was defeated. After his defeat, he handed over his domain (30,000 people and 36 towns and villages) to his victorious enemy. Subsequently, another Chou prince claimed the throne. He was in turn defeated and forfeited his territory. In 249 B.C. the Chou dynasty formally came to an end.

Beginning in 230 B.C. Ch'in conquered one state after another, starting from its neighbors and working towards its neighbors' neighbors. Finally, there were no more neighbors left. The following table shows how quickly Ch'in moved.

	CONQUERED
230 B.C.	Han
228 B.C.	Chao
225 B.C.	Wei
223 B.C.	Ch'u
222 B.C.	Yen
221 B.C.	Ch'i

SOCIAL AND ECONOMIC CHANGES

As wars were frequent after the eighth century B.C., territories changed hands often. The common practice of a victorious state was to bring conquered territories under central or bureaucratic control instead of sorting them out as feudal fiefs. As this process continued, the territories under central administration increased while those under feudal control steadily declined. A state, large or small, might or might not have a feudal relationship with the reigning Chou king. Even if it had such a relationship, its allegiance to the king was nominal. In the territory within its control it was supreme and sovereign. It had officials who were familially related to the reigning prince and who bore feudal titles, but they were not different from other bureaucrats who served the state in an assigned capacity. A commoner, upon becoming a government official, might be given a feudal title, but this title indicated nothing except that he was a high-ranking official. For his service he might be assigned a certain number of households administered for his benefit. But the income he received from these households was in fact his salary, and the area in which they were located was not a fief in the true sense of that word. It could be taken away from him once he ceased to be a government official. Within each state the power of the prince was supreme and all people were his subjects. To be sure, feudal fiefs still existed as late as the third century B.C., but they constituted only a small part of the prince's territory. Moreover, the people within the feudal fiefs owed absolute loyalty to the prince as subjects rather than to the feudal lords as peasants. When there was a conflict between the two loyalties, the loyalty to the prince prevailed, as the feudal lord himself owed allegiance to the prince. The development of a centralized government took a long time to complete. In fact, before the fifth century there had been times when there was a decentralizing tendency within individual states, notably in Ch'i and Lu. The over-all tendency, however, was towards centralization. By the beginning of the fourth century B.C. such a development had been largely completed. In summary, while there was a power deconcentration after the eighth century B.C. as far as the king was concerned, there was an increasing concentration of power in the hands of individual states. Though moving in opposite directions, both processes contributed to the decline of feudalism.

Together with the political factors described above, there were social and economic causes that slowly undermined the feudal structure. One of these was the rise of the merchant class and the growth of cities. Feudalism thrived best in a self-sufficient economy within a small area, but geographical specialization in production was bound to destroy such self-sufficiency and eventually feudalism as well. While basic crops such as rice and wheat were raised practically all over China, different sections specialized in producing different products: "lumber, bamboo, and precious stones in Shansi; fish, salt, lacquer, silk and musical instruments in Shantung; fruits in the Yangtze River valley; and copper and iron in the mountainous regions in Szechuan." As society became more advanced, people desired more and better goods. This was especially true with the nobles who, being wealthy, could afford and consequently demanded luxuries produced in other areas. As such demands increased, each area, besides producing for its own needs, had to produce a surplus to exchange for what it needed and did not have. Hence there arose the merchant class which shipped goods from one place to another by performing a necessary economic service. Barter was no doubt the earliest form of trade, but as trade increased, money had to be used. Money in various forms was in use as early as the Shang dynasty, but it was not until the seventh or the sixth century B.C. that governments began to mint metallic coins. They came to different states at different times. The comparatively backward state of Ch'in, for instance, did not coin money until the fourth century B.C. After the fifth century B.C. gold began to circulate in large quantities. While the princes used it for rewarding their own ministers as well as bribing the ministers of other states, the merchants employed it as a medium of exchange. The use of precious metals as money unquestionably facilitated trade.

Trade also benefited from the increasing mobility of the people. Despite the fact that China was politically divided, there was no restriction of movement across state lines. A merchant could move freely from one state to another without encountering harassment from government on

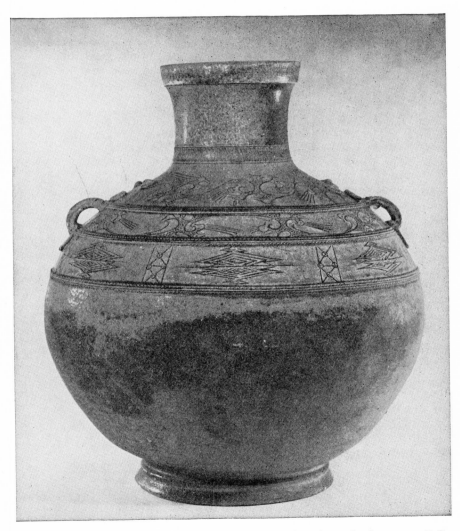

PORCELAIN VASE This vase was produced in the fourth or third century B.C. Notice the symmetrical designs and the balanced lines.

either side of the border line. No state would persecute a merchant simply because he came from another state; nor would it discriminate against him on behalf of its own merchants. It seemed that all governments had recognized the importance of his services. Under this benevolent atmosphere, many merchants became powerful and wealthy, so wealthy that in many cases they outshone the feudal lords in the display of luxuries. Often they doubled as moneylenders and even had kings and princes as their regular customers. One of the Chou kings, we are told, was so much in debt that he rarely chose to emerge from his palaces because he was afraid that he might bump into his creditors. As wealth increased, influence increased proportionally. The big merchants were granted audiences and were treated as equals by reigning princes in whichever states they happened to be. Often they exercised great influence over domestic and interstate affairs. It was said that Tzu Kung, a powerful merchant and also a former student of Confucius, in one trip, "saved Lu, deranged Ch'i, destroyed Wu, strengthened Tsin, and raised Yüeh to a position of supremacy." His feats were no doubt exaggerated. The fact nevertheless remains that the merchants were a powerful group to reckon with during this period.

The increase of commercial activities was reflected in the growth of cities. Cities became larger and more numerous, especially those located along the trade routes or chosen as state capitals. In North China four cities stood out prominently above others; they were, from west to east, Hsienyang, Hantan, Loyang, and Lintzu, each being a distribution center in its own area. In the fourth century B.C. Lintzu had a population of about 350,000; Loyang had a population of 500,000 toward the end of the third century B.C. In the south some cities were even larger. The outer wall of the capital of Wu, for instance, covered an area almost as large as present Peking (17 miles versus 18 miles in circumference), though statistics regarding its population are now unavailable. Cities with a population of almost 100,000 were common all over China. This booming scene was particularly noticeable in South China. Through the efforts of the southern states, Ch'u, Wu, and Yüeh, the Chinese frontier was extended steadily southward to the modern Fukien province and the southern portions of the modern Kiangsi and Hunan provinces. Here natural environment was more rewarding, land was more productive, and people were generally more spirited and carefree. All these, of course, were favorable conditions for the growth of commercial activities. There was the famous merchant Fan Li who, after retiring from an official career as Yüeh's chief minister early in the fifth century B.C., amassed a huge fortune in a period of nineteen years. He distributed much of his wealth among his friends and relatives, still leaving a large amount to his descendants. Today his supposed image is still hung in many Chinese stores whose owners are no doubt hoping to duplicate the achievement of this ancient financial wizard.

In the cities life was lively and interesting. Whenever a large number of people congregated, community activities existed; some of them were secular and others were religious. In the northern city of Lintzu, one of the most important events was the annual spring festival in honor of the Earth God. On that day all were dressed in their best, and the city provided a variety of entertainments including songs, dances, dramas, and acrobatics. Country people flowed into the city for the occasion, and many young maidens could enjoy overt flirtations without being criticized. After all was over and when evening drew near, there was plenty of wine for people to get intoxicated. The temple of the Earth God was perhaps the most important building in the city besides the palaces. Before a military campaign, meat and wine were offered to the Earth God to bring about good luck. After the campaign, victory was reported to him; sometimes the captured enemy commanders were killed in the temple as sacrifices. Natural disasters like flood and drought had also to be reported so he could give counsel with regard to the best of possible remedies. In a lawsuit when the judge was unable to render a judgment because of the lack of evidences, both sides were required to swear before the Earth God and wait for miracles to happen. Whenever there was an eclipse of the sun or the moon, people gathered in front of the temple, beating drums loudly to scare off the evil spirit who was about to swallow up the heavenly body.

As feudalism declined, land ownership was no longer confined to those who had inherited it as a hereditary right. It could be bought and sold like any other commercial product. Consequently, there was a growing tendency towards the concentration of land ownership in the hands of a few. The new landlords held no high sounding feudal titles; they were the powerful bureaucrats, the princes' favorites, and the wealthy merchants. This process of land concentration had gone on for a long time in North China. When the state of Ch'in formally abolished feudal land tenure and permitted the buying and selling of land ownership in the fourth century B.C., it only legally confirmed an existing practice. However, once legalized, this process of land concentration gathered additional momentum. For the farmers who had been until then under feudal protection, this was ominous enough. Either they were forced to sell their land because of incurred debt or they had to fight for subsistence against great odds. In either case, life was hard.

Chinese historians have preserved for us the budget of a typical farmer in Wei who lived in the fourth century B.C. He was the head of a family of five, and he cultivated 100 *mou* (15 acres) of land. His harvest averaged 1.5 piculs of grain per *mou* and his total harvest was 150 piculs

(1 picul = 133 lbs approximately). Each person consumed an average of 1.5 piculs per month; total yearly consumption for the whole family was 90 piculs. According to the market price, each picul was worth 30 standard coins; when he sold them, the remaining 45 piculs would bring him 1,350 standard coins in cash. After contributing 300 coins to the temple of the Earth God and for rites for deceased ancestors and festivities, he had 1,050 standard coins left. For a family of five, the minimum expenditure for clothes was 1,500 coins. So in a normal year he would wind up with a deficit of 450 standard coins. If additional taxes were collected, which occurred often, or if there were births, sickness, and deaths in the family, the annual debt would be even larger. When the accumulated debt became too large, he had to sell his land, and in sadder cases, sell his children or even himself as slaves. All in all, the decline of feudalism brought him only woes and misfortune. Under feudalism a peasant might not have plenty, but at least he had security. So long as he fulfilled his feudal obligations, he could keep his land and could count on a tolerable return for his labor. His more personal relationship with the lord forestalled oppressive extortions; it also entitled him to protection from his lord in time of need. With the decline of feudalism he was on his own. He was exposed to direct pressure from the big landlords, the money lenders, and worst of all, the impersonal government. There was no shield between him and forces bigger than his own. Sooner or later he might have to give up the struggle.

Disadvantageous though it might be to the peasantry, the decline of feudalism was not without its compensating effects. One of these was the spread of learning and education which, in turn, resulted in the increase of social mobility. When feudalism was at its prime, education was a monopoly of the nobility because feudalism thrived best on the rigidity of social stratification and the absence of social mobility; the spread of education to the lower strata of the population would have destroyed both. After the eighth century when wars were carried on almost incessantly, each state was in a constant struggle between survival and oblivion. It was ability rather than birth which could benefit a state and brought a man to power and wealth. With a good education, a man could rise above his humble background through sheer intelligence, ability, and an ambition to succeed. This emphasis on education was duly reflected in contemporary writings. Education rather than birth was hailed by many writers as the dividing line between the governing and the governed. To use the language of Mencius, there were two classes of people in a society: the gentlemen and the mean men. The gentlemen were the educated who specialized in mental work and who were the governing class. The mean men were the uneducated engaged in physical labor and were the governed. Although Mencius was describing an ideal society where this division of labor existed, he nevertheless pointed out a direction in which the society was then actually moving. As education was expanded, a new elite man arose who was more proud of what he had in his mind than what he had in his blood.

The importance of education did not mean that everybody could have an education. For the most part, the privilege of enjoying it was confined to a small group. Though he was not legally restricted from obtaining an education, an average peasant was simply too busy in tilling his field and trying to make both ends meet to be seriously concerned with it. As has been noted earlier in this chapter, under Chou feudalism the great majority of the noble descent would eventually wind up as commoners. As time went on, a new class gradually emerged. The people of this class were of noble descent, but they were not nobles. They were commoners; yet, they had nothing in common with other commoners such as the peasants. They were *shih,* sometimes translated as gentry scholars. Two factors made them different from other commoners. First, they owned enough land or other means of support which spared them from the necessity of doing physical labor. Second, they had an education which provided them with the ways and means of acquiring leadership. Having enough to live by and yet not enough to discourage ambition, they were the most dynamic group during this period. But they were neither revolutionaries nor idealists. The aim of most of them was a worldly and selfish one, namely, winning the confidence and favor from a reigning prince and thus gaining power and wealth. As long as China was divided, they tried to exploit the existing situation to their own advantage. Many of them roamed from state to state and would serve whoever chose to hire them. They felt no patriotism or loyalty towards any state; they pledged allegiance only to those who hired them. Generally speaking, they were an unprincipled group and would not hesitate to use any means to achieve their selfish ends. During the period of Warring States their influence had become so great that many powerful princes made a habit of extending patronage and competed with one another in winning the allegiance of the roaming scholars. Prince Meng-ch'ang of Ch'i, for instance, supported three thousand roaming scholars from various states at one time. In other cases, roaming scholars held high-ranking and responsible posts in state governments. In Ch'in where feudalism was not so deeply rooted as in the eastern states and where innovations could be adopted with comparative ease, many able ministers came from this group. Shang Yang and Chang Yi were the two leading examples. Both were natives of Wei but served capably the Ch'in state. It was people like them who built a strong Ch'in regime which eventually unified China.

ii

The Philosophers

THE IDEOLOGICAL PATTERN

The five centuries after 771 B.C. were a period of paradoxes. On the one hand, it was marked with incessant warfare, political anarchy, and moral degeneration. On the other hand, it was an era of dynamic social and economic changes and of great masters of new ideas. In fact, from the point of view of ideology, there has never been a period so constructive. The positive and negative aspects of this paradoxical age were not entirely unrelated. As the existing society degenerated further, there was more incentive to think in terms of an ideal society that could have existed but did not. After peace and justice had slowly disappeared, the longing for them became more intense. The great philosophers of this period were metaphysicians only in the most incidental sense; rather, they were overwhelmingly concerned with the imperfect world and the imper-

66

fect man. They were not interested in the supernatural forces either, because they believed that man's problems could only be solved by man himself. They were in this world, and they wished to make it a better place to live. They dealt extensively in politics, economics, and most importantly, ethics. Their interest in metaphysics and religion was confined to applying them if possible to the more mundane, worldly affairs. Theirs was a "man-centered" ideology to which all branches of knowledge must submit themselves.

The overwhelming concern about man marked distinctly the difference between Chinese philosophers and philosophers of other countries. The Greek and Indian philosophers of ancient times were also interested in man, but man's affairs formed only a part of their philosophical system. To the Chinese, man was the measure of all things, and without human values philosophies lost their basic meanings and could not even justify their own existence. There was no such thing as speculation for the sake of speculation; all learning was related, directly or indirectly, to human affairs. As theologians in medieval Europe believed that no knowledge was meaningful and worthy unless it contributed to the salvation of the soul, the Chinese philosophers of the classical age were equally scornful of pursuits that did not in any way help the physical man and his relationship with other people. The medieval theologians emphasized the importance of the other world, and the Chinese were occupied with this world. Both groups, seeing the universe from man's point of view, tended to neglect the universe as the universe was. In other words, they neglected to study our physical environment as an objective science. The European trend was reversed early in the modern period, and such a reversal paved the way for the advancement of modern science and technology. The Chinese, on the other hand, did not change their sense of values until the twentieth century.

This "man-centered" Chinese tradition is sometimes referred to as humanism. This term, however, should not be interpreted in the sense as Renaissance humanism in Europe. For one thing, the man in the tradition of Chinese humanism was an ethical being, and in that sense he had more in common with the man of medieval theologians than with the man in the spirit of the Renaissance. Secondly, the Chinese humanism emphasized man's relationship with other men rather than man as an independent, free individual. While Renaissance humanism freed man from his bondage to other men, especially his superiors in a manor, guild, or monastery, Chinese humanism, stressing human relations, strengthened that bondage. Chinese philosophers like Confucius were not interested in establishing a society composed of equal, independent individuals, but a society where man's position was clearly and carefully prescribed. Whereas Renaissance humanism led man out from medieval feudalism, Confucian philosophers wished to reestablish Chou feudalism which was then in the process of disintegration. The European humanists looked forward towards the future; the Chinese leaned back towards the past. Instead of freeing man from social control, Chinese humanism made such control even more formidable. Politically, it strengthened authoritarianism, in contrast to Renaissance humanism which, emphasizing individualism, might be said to have paved the way for modern democracy.

Such being the case, how could the Chinese system be still called humanism? It was humanism in the sense that it emphasized human welfare as man's most important concern and that man was the worthiest topic of all learning. By man was meant man as a social being rather than an independent individual. His relationship to other men was more important than he in himself. To the Chinese mind, the collective welfare of a group had priority over the well-being of individuals who composed it, and the enhancement of group welfare would presumably enhance individual well-being as well. Theoretically at least, human relations were more important than human beings. Such emphasis tended to degrade individuals rather than elevate them, because it made them mere points of conjunction in the intricate pattern of human relations.

Some of these relations were biological such as those between father and son and among brothers and sisters; others were nonbiological such as those between king and his ministers and among friends and neighbors. There were rules governing each of these relations, and altogether they constituted the moral code. Throughout centuries Chinese philosophers strove to find the rule that underlay all individual rules in the same spirit as our modern scientists strive to find the universal law that governs all natural laws. Their conclusions were of course different, and they debated among themselves throughout history. However, they did agree on one thing. Were human relations to be harmonious, individuals had to be virtuous, because it was impossible to establish a harmonious society if its members were woefully lacking in the basic attributes of worthy constituents. The improvement of individual character was therefore the first step towards the betterment of society. All ancient philosophers advocated the cultivation of personal virtues, though the definition of virtue might be entirely different. Those who failed to live up to the expectation of society were to be severely punished, by social or legal methods and often both. Thus, despite their humanistic beliefs, the ancient philosophers, with rare exceptions, showed little concern over the inhumanity of the penal code enforced in their times, which provided such diabolical punishments as branding, foot-amputation, and castration. The rules that governed relationship among men had to be maintained at all costs, including occasional but harsh punishment of individuals. These philosophers saw no contradiction in the advocacy of morality and ethics on the one hand and the inhuman punishment of individuals on the other. In fact, the latter was regarded by many of them as a necessary means to achieve the former.

According to Confucian philosophers, there were five cardinal relationships among men: those between king and his subjects, father and son, husband and wife, elder and younger brothers, and among friends. All these relationships were between superiors and inferiors, and even among friends the older were supposedly superior to the younger. The relationships did not cease with the death of the party involved; theoretically at least, they lasted indefinitely. The ancestors of a reigning emperor were revered by the nation as a whole, and the greatest men of the past such as Confucius were worshipped throughout history. This may account for the unique historical mindedness of the Chinese and their strong sense of identity with an ageless past. Within a family or a clan such sense of identity was even stronger. Ancestors were worshipped long after their death; the older the generation to which they belonged, the more they were honored. A man's mischiefs on earth were conveniently forgotten after his death, while his achievements, often exaggerated, were glorified. As a common practice, his eulogy was inscribed on his tombstone for the eyes of posterity, and a long time ago the Chinese had invented a literary style for the sole purpose of writing eulogies. When such style was followed, it was almost impossible to write anything derogatory of the dead man. The tablet that bore his name would appear in the family temple in due course, to be worshipped by his descendants for generations to come. The family register was one of the holiest books carefully preserved, and today many Chinese claim that they can trace their family beginnings to the time before the Christian era. The extension of human relationship to the deceased gave rise to the custom of ancestor worship which had been practiced by the Chinese from time immemorial. By the time that Confucius was born (551 B.C.) it was already a common practice.

The emphasis on human relationship personalized even the impersonal institutions such as government. The rulers were to rule by example, and they were "fathers and mothers" of the people. The moral calibre of those who enforced the law was more important than the law itself. Good government meant virtuous rulers, not necessarily good laws and sound institutions. In the Chinese thinking, the words in a legal contract were useless unless the parties who had concluded such a contract were morally strong enough to abide by it regardless of eventualities. A business agreement of bygone times was often an oral promise; to suggest otherwise would be regarded as an insult to the integrity of the contracting parties. Whenever difficulties arose, they believed that they could count on each other's sense of fairness to resolve their differences. In other words, they placed trust on the adherence by both parties to an unwritten moral code that governed human relations rather than an impersonal legal document. When a man pledged the hand of his baby daughter to his friend's baby son, he was not supposed to violate his pledge no matter how unworthy his prospective son-in-law turned out to be. When the children grew up, he and his friend relied on their filial obedience to carry out the arranged marriage. The parties directly involved might suffer from this alliance, but the rules that governed human relationship—the inviolability of promises among friends and the obedience of children to parents—had to be observed at all costs.

The observance of the ethical code came from no other consideration except that man, being a social being, had to live by certain rules. Rewards or punishments, either in this world or in the next, were immaterial. Man was unique among animals because he alone did not need inducement to be good. Otherwise, said Mencius, he could not have been different from other animals. Thus, most of the philosophers in ancient China based their hope of mankind on the essential goodness of man, and the ethics they taught was a "man-centered" ethics, totally devoid of the otherworldly connotations. A good man had no Heaven to look forward to; nor should a bad man be afraid of punishment after death. Religion and ethics were two separate fields, and they should be kept separate. An ethical man was not necessarily religious; nor was a religious man necessarily moral. Confucius said: "Worship the spirits, but keep them at a distance," because the spirits were not human and therefore had nothing to do with the rules that governed human relations. If a man was good simply because he expected reward or was afraid of punishment after his death, he would have lived a life of hypocritic pretensions. Was he really a good man in the first place? What would have happened to morality and ethics if he became an agnostic or atheist? What would have happened to society if all its members became agnostics and atheists? A man was expected to be good because he was a man, not a wild animal. He was born with goodness, said Mencius. He only needed to be taught to transform his innate goodness into righteous conduct.

How could immortality be achieved if a man's behavior in this world bore no relation to his life in the next? The ancient philosophers were not greatly concerned with this problem and did not regard it as particularly important. People like Confucius frankly admitted that they did not know the answer. "Not yet understanding life, how can you understand death?" said Confucius. When the question had to be answered, it was answered in the context of human relations. A Confucian classic, written perhaps in the fourth century B.C., said that there were three ways of achieving immortality. They were, in the order of importance: the establishment of virtues, the accomplishment of good deeds, and the writing of books. In other words, a man's immortality lay in the memory of his fellow men. The more his life on earth benefited his fellow men and the longer his influence was felt, the more immortal he would become. It was not an immortality in the spiritual sense. As to spiritual immortality, the ancient philosophers provided no answer.

The separation of ethics from religion, a unique feature of the Chinese cultural system, was not without its blessing. In the Chinese mind, ethical standards were more important than religious standards, and in case of conflict between them, the former should always prevail. As the Chinese looked at it, these two standards were not necessarily the same and were sometimes contradictory. A religious sect that did not believe in wine-drinking had no right to condemn those who were convinced of the harmlessness of such habit, unless intoxication disrupted peace and order and affected adversely the relationship among men. In such case, the issue was a moral, ethical issue instead of a religious one. While religious standards were peculiar to a certain religion or religions, ethical standards were universal and should be applied to all men. One should not impose his own religious standards upon others who did not belong to his religion. To do so might be regarded as religious from his point of view; certainly it was not ethical. A religious fanatic bent on the condemnation and destruction of all other religions by whatever means he possessed was a social degenerate, deserving no mercy from his fellow men. Above religious beliefs was an ethical standard which all religions must abide by if society were to survive. Such a standard governed the relations between groups of individuals (such as religious sects) as well as individuals themselves. As ethics was separated from religion and was regarded as superior to religion, the Chinese were remarkably free from religious bigotry, and persecution on religious grounds, while not absent altogether, was noticeably mild compared with that of many other countries.

CONFUCIANISM

When we mention the Chinese cultural system, we inevitably associate it with Confucianism, and for more than two thousand years the word "Confucianism" was almost synonymous with the word "Chinese." Who was this man Confucius who exercised such a strong influence over so many people for such a long period? Throughout the centuries there have been so many words and deeds attributed to him that it is often difficult to differentiate the man from the myth. He was born in 551 B.C. or thereabouts and died in 479 B.C. Yet, a biography was not written about him until the second century B.C. Meanwhile, a legend had been built up, and his alleged words and deeds were scattered in many ancient writings. Fortunately, there is the book *Lun-yü* or *Analects* which was compiled by his disciples shortly after his death. The more cautious historians rely heavily on this book for a better understanding of this man, perhaps the greatest China has ever produced.

Confucius was a native of Lu which was located in modern Shantung province. By the time that Confucius was born, Lu had passed its prime as a political power and, located between three giants, Tsin, Ch'i, and

IMAGE OF CONFUCIUS This image of Confucius was painted by Prince Ho-shuo-kuo in the year 1735 A.D. On the top are Chinese characters of an ancient script which, roughly translated, read: "Confucius, the Sage and the Teacher." The small characters on the right read: "Respectfully painted by Prince Ho-shuo-kuo on the day of the full moon, in the ninth lunar month of the year of Chia-yin, during the reign of Emperor Yung-cheng." Below these characters are the prince's official seal which shows his name in Manchu on the left and Chinese on the right.

Ch'u, it had great difficulty in maintaining its precarious independence. Culturally, however, Lu had no peers. Originally the fief of Duke Chou, the state had been known for its cultural refinements for centuries. Both Confucius and Mencius, the two architects of Confucianism, were born in this state. As a child, Confucius was described as unusually inquisitive and showed great interest in rituals. Like other educated men of his time, he aspired to a governmental career and was reported to have served in various capacities in the Lu government. However, it was his teaching career that made him famous; what he taught became the basic tenets of what was later known as Confucianism. Accompanied by his students, he travelled a great deal, forever seeking the right prince who would give him a position of authority so that he could carry out his own teachings. In this matter he was bound to be disappointed because every prince he approached regarded his teachings as impractical at best. At one time during his travels he and his students lost their means of support and almost starved to death. At another time he was mistaken for a hated local politician because of physical resemblance and was almost mobbed. The Master, as he was generally called, took these ordeals in stride. Away from Lu for many years, eventually he returned home at an advanced age. It was then that he gave up any hope of a political career and concentrated on teaching. According to tradition, he wrote the *Spring and Autumn Annals,* besides commenting and editing many other works. Modern historians are more skeptical and even question whether he wrote anything at all.

Outwardly, it seems that he was a complete failure. Yet, in his unspectacular, prosaic way, he exercised the greatest influence over a large section of mankind for more than two thousand years. What was his secret? He succeeded by simply being himself. To millions of Chinese for centuries he represented perfection, a perfection which was expressed in human terms and was therefore easily comprehensible. He was unpretentious and honest, and he could be easily identified as one of the best among men, a good friend and a kind neighbor. He did not advise people to do the extraordinary and the impossible; he set up a standard which could be attained if they really tried. He had no use for pretension, whatever purpose it was meant to achieve. "When you know, say that you know; when you do not know, say that you do not know. This is the secret of knowledge." This advice came from Confucius; it could have come from any good school teacher.

This story is told of Confucius. A man was short of ginger and went to Wei-sheng Kao to borrow some. Instead of telling him that he did not have any himself, Wei-sheng Kao went out his back door without his friend's knowledge and borrowed some from his neighbor in order to lend it to his friend who had come to borrow. After Confucius heard this story, he criticized Wei-sheng Kao for being dishonest on the ground that he should have told his friend the truth. When his student Yen Yüan died, Confucius was overwhelmed with grief. Yet, when the dead man's father suggested that Confucius should sell his chariot to raise money to buy his son an outer coffin, the Master refused, saying that he had not sold his chariot on behalf of his own dead son and that he needed his chariot for travelling. We use these two examples to illustrate the humaneness of Confucius' moral standards, a touch of common sense which was ignored by later Confucians. They were never meant to be rigid and ritualistic as later they did become.

As a person, Confucius was gay, pleasant, and vivacious. He loved to sing, and according to the *Analects,* he stopped singing only when he heard that some one he knew had died. He liked outdoor life and one of his best recreations was to swim with his friends in a nearby river. He loved the art of archery and chariot riding. Though he complained that he had not met a man who loved virtue more than sex, he did not regard sex as evil. In fact, a Confucian classic said explicitly that food and sex were the two basic, natural desires of man. When one of his students complained after Confucius had consented to meet a female admirer and famed beauty, Confucius was clearly irritated: "If I have done anything improper, let Heaven punish me, let Heaven punish me!" A sound and workable code of ethics had to be based upon the humanness of man. Deprived of its humanistic elements, it became inflexible, harsh, and penalizing and would do more harm than good. Virtue was to be enjoyed, not to be feared. Unattainable virtues ceased to be virtues because they became a source of fear rather than love. They contributed nothing to the well-being of man.

What were the Confucian virtues? Time and again the word *jen* appeared in the *Analects,* and each time Confucius gave it a different interpretation. The word has been variably translated as benevolence, love, and the like; it was the basic principle that governed the relationship among men. It was derived from man's innate goodness, though outwardly it was manifested in a variety of forms.

"When Fan Ch'ih asked about *jen,* the Master said: 'Love people.'

"When Yen Yüan asked about *jen,* the Master said: 'If you can control your selfish desires and subject them to the rules of propriety and if you can do this for a single day, it is the beginning of *jen* for the entire world. *Jen* is self-sufficient and comes from your inner self; it requires no outside help.' Yen Yüan asked for more details. The Master said: 'Don't see the improper; don't hear the improper; don't talk about the improper; and don't act improperly.'

"When Chung Kung asked about *jen,* the Master said: 'When you meet a person outside of your house, greet him as if he were a great noble. If, as a government official, you have to impose corvée duties on the people, you should approach your task with the same seriousness that you would use in performing a religious ritual. Don't do to others what you yourself do not desire.' " [1]

When a person was not sure whether he had done the right thing, he simply asked himself whether he would wish the same thing be done to him. He should be strict with himself as he had been strict with others. Goodness was implied in manhood; it needed no outside inducement. If a man performed good deeds for ulterior purposes, whether they be fame or wealth, his motives were not pure and there was little goodness in his deeds. In fact, motives were more important than results. Through vigorous self-discipline, a man would eventually reach a status in which he could do whatever he pleased without ever doing anything wrong. When such status was reached, he became a *chün-tzu,* or a morally superior man.

A superior man was not satisfied with his own perfection, because virtue, in order to survive, had to be contagious. There was an element of

[1] Fan Ch'ih, Yen Yüan, and Chung Kung were Confucius' students. All these passages appear in Chapter VI of the *Analects.* The translation is the author's own.

goodness in every man, and in such goodness lay the hope of mankind. "Among any three men walking in the street, there is one who could be my teacher," declared Confucius; "I shall follow their good traits, while correcting my own weaknesses which I have also found in them." A superior man, seeking perfection in himself, also tried to induce the best from others. For maximum results he could choose the career of a government official or that of a teacher because in either of the two capacities the people whom he could influence were large in number. As a government official, he influenced people by his own example; he could not achieve his purpose by instituting harsh laws and severe punishments. "The virtue of a superior man is like wind and the virtue of the people is like grass," said Confucius; "the grass bends towards the direction where the wind blows." He had no use for law, as law involved compulsion, and its observation arose from fear. A good government relied on morality to prevent wrong-doing instead of law to punish the wrongdoers. A student asked Confucius about the nature of good government. The Master said that there were three essentials that constituted a good government: sufficient food, adequate defense, and faith. If one of these three had to go, which one should go first? asked the student. The Master said defense. If one of the remaining two had to be abandoned, which one should be abandoned? The Master said food. "All men have to die," concluded Confucius; "without faith no nation can survive." By faith was meant the moral values of a nation that differentiated civilized men from wild savages.

Generally speaking, Confucius was a conservative in government and politics. He attributed the existing social ills and political anarchy to the disruption of authority and advocated return to the early form of Chou feudalism. He believed that only when authority was properly instituted and carefully observed could peace and order prevail. Society was composed of a variety of individuals and each individual had a special function to perform. However, authority did not and should not imply despotism. With each name, according to Confucius, there was a reality; without reality a name would be deprived of its meanings. Thus a prince (name) could not be rightly called a prince if he did not perform the functions (reality) assigned to him. If, for instance, he used his authority for selfish purposes instead of the welfare of his subjects, he was a prince in name only, but not a real prince. There was a heavenly imposed duty on the ruler as well as on the ruled. A ruler should set an example to his subjects. Only when the ruler was wise and virtuous could the people be expected to be loyal and obedient. The same principle was also applied to the household. Though the husband was superior to his wife, parents superior to children, and elder brothers superior to the younger ones, there were mutual obligations governing each other: love and protection on the part of the superiors and loyalty and obedience on the part of the inferiors. The respect and obedience a superior received was not auto-matic by any means. Only when a king treated his ministers with *li* (propriety), said Confucius, could the ministers reciprocate it with *chung* (loyalty). By the same token, a cruel, unloving father forfeited all rights of demanding filial piety from his son. A correct relationship imposed obligations on both sides; those who were not willing to give should not receive either.

Confucius was never given the opportunity to carry out his teachings as a government official; as a teacher, however, he was superb. He be-lieved in the educability of man, whatever his natural endowment. The achievement might not be the same, but each man became better off after the educational process. The purpose of education was not merely the acquirement of knowledge or skill, however important that might be. The real purpose was the cultivation of virtues and the purification of personal character. According to the *Analects,* Confucius emphasized four main items in teaching his own students: literature, conduct, sincerity, and faith. Of the four items only the first one can be classified as academic learning. In another instance, the Master grouped his students into four categories in accordance with their attainments. They were: personal vir-tue, speech, politics, and literature. There is no question as to which category he emphasized most. As far as academic learning was concerned, it seems that he used the *Book of Odes,* the *Book of Rites,* and the *Book of Changes* as the standard texts, especially the first two whose importance was repeatedly emphasized in the *Analects.* As to teaching technique, the Master used the informal, conversational method. A question was raised, and the students tossed it around and expressed their own opinions. From time to time the Master came in and offered his ideas. There was no set answer or answers to each question. Like Aristotle, Confucius believed in the influence of music in refining a man's character. Archery and char-iot-riding also formed a part of the curriculum. In short, the purpose of education was the cultivation of an all-round, versatile gentleman, setting a moral example to other people in private life and serving them ably and conscientiously whenever he was given an official post to hold.

Besides *jen,* the other virtue mentioned most often in the *Analects* was *li. Li* has been variably translated as propriety, ceremony, ritual, rite, mannerism, etiquette, etc.; it could have been any one of these, depend-ing upon the context in which it was used. If *jen* was the manifestation of a man's innate goodness in acts that materially benefited his fellow men, *li* was the rule of conduct that reflected a person's goodwill which might not benefit the other party materialistically. To present a bag of rice to a hungry neighbor was an act of *jen;* to express sympathy and concern without providing material help was *li.* On the other hand, if one could help in a material way and yet chose to do nothing except express per-functory sympathy, the outward *li* became meaningless because in that case it was devoid of content which should have been goodwill. If *li* were addressed to living beings, it could be translated as propriety, etiquette and so on; if it were addressed to deceased ancestors, spirits, and gods, it became religious rites and rituals. In short, it was a code of conduct that governed relations among men and also men's relations with gods and deceased ancestors.

One hundred and fifty years after the death of Confucius, Confucianism found its great champion in the person of Mencius. According to tradition, Mencius owed much of his fine character to his mother who, among other things, changed residence three times in search of a proper neighborhood for the boy to grow up. If the style of his book (*Book of Mencius*) indicates anything, he was forcible, aggressive, and uncompromising and was an expert in the art of speech and debate. Like Confucius, he aspired to a position of authority to carry out his own teachings and travelled from state to state for that purpose. He failed in his mission as Confucius had done so before him. For one thing, his program of "love and righteousness" was considered impractical in an age of political anarchy when the fate of a state depended upon the outcome of each conflict on the battlefield rather than the moral virtue of its rulers. However, wherever he went, he was received with consideration and respect, because by then the honoring of roaming scholars had become the fashion of the time as we have said in the preceding chapter. Unlike Confucius who travelled under conditions of extreme hardship, Mencius was at the head of "scores of chariots and hundreds of followers" wherever he went, and he chastised reigning monarchs like school children for their "evil" ways of governing their people. They listened attentively but discarded his suggestions once he had left.

What did Mencius teach? He elaborated and strengthened Confucius' basic beliefs and advanced some new ideas of his own. While Confucius only implied the natural goodness of man, Mencius said emphatically that human nature was good.

"Human nature is like water current," said Kao-tzu (a contemporary of Mencius). "If it is led to the east, it flows eastward; if it is led to the west, it flows westward. Like water which can be led to either of the two directions, human nature is neither good nor bad. It depends upon the direction towards which it is led."

"While it is true that water can be led eastward or westward, is it also true that it knows no difference between 'upward' and 'downward'"? asked Mencius. "The goodness of human nature is like water's natural inclination to move downward. As water is inevitably moving downward, there is no man in the world who is not good. If you beat water hard, it jumps up and can rise higher than your forehead. If you channel it and push it upward, it might even reach the top of a mountain. But, is this the nature of water? It acts contrary to its nature because it is given no other choice. If a man does bad things, he, like water, has been forced to do them and has not been given a better choice. His wrongdoing has nothing to do with his inherent nature which is good." [1]

Had Mencius never written or said anything else, the above passage alone would have made him one of the greatest thinkers in history. It elevated the dignity of man and raised the hope of mankind. More than two thousand years ago he anticipated our modern environmental theory. Enunciating his political theory, time and again he emphasized the importance of the people. While he did not challenge the hereditary right of monarchs to rule, he said that they should rule for the benefit of their subjects. Should a monarch fail to do so, his subjects had the right of rebellion because in that case he forfeited his own right as a monarch. During a time when casualties ran to many thousands in a single battle, Mencius maintained that no prince who mercilessly took away human lives could win the war and unify the country. Who could unify the country? It was the prince who practiced the "policy of love" (*jen cheng*). The prince who "humanizes his penal code, reduces taxation, promotes agriculture, and teaches people the virtue of filial piety, humility, loyalty, and faith" would eventually succeed. In any case, he should not exact more than ten percent tax of his subjects' produce. Unlike Confucius who had no use for material wealth ("Wealth is like floating clouds to me," said the Master), Mencius maintained that only when people were economically sufficient could they be expected to conduct a virtuous life.

An enlightened monarch should see to it that people should produce enough to support their parents and their wives and children. In good years they should have enough to eat, and in bad years they should not have to be starved to death. In such a case, it would be easy to lead them to as virtuous a life as they would be happy to follow. Nowadays people do not have the means to support either their parents or their wives and children. They suffer even in good years and cannot escape death in bad years. When they are confronted with possible death everyday, how can you expect them to have time to engage in rites and righteousness? [2]

While Confucius talked a great deal about *jen*, Mencius spoke often about *yi*. What was the difference between these two virtues? According to Kao-tzu (as quoted by Mencius), *jen* was the goodness within a person and *yi* was the righteous action that was derived from the innate goodness. Every action that benefited other people had to be motivated by goodwill, otherwise such action was meaningless and ceased to be righteous. The opposite of righteousness was profit, because profit was meant to benefit oneself instead of others. A virtuous man measured every step he took against a simple standard: was it profitable or was it righteous? Needless to say, he should reject the profitable and follow what was right.

---

[1] Translated from the *Book of Mencius,* Chapter VI.
[2] Translated from the *Book of Mencius.* Chapter I.

THE BASIC WORKS OF CONFUCIANISM 79

What kind of ideal society did Mencius visualize for mankind? It was a society where "men will not only honor their own parents and love their own children but will do the same with others' parents and children as well." It was a society where "all men are brothers." The first step towards that direction was of course the cultivation of personal virtues. When every person did the same, idealism would be eventually translated into reality. When that day arrived, peace and goodwill would prevail and war and injustice would be gone forever.

So far we have defined Confucianism as it was originally expounded by Confucius and Mencius. It was an ethical system, dynamic and humanistic. It deviated from its original meanings in later centuries as it became more rigid and formalistic. The Confucianism vigorously attacked by the twentieth-century liberals as a handicap to progress was not the Confucianism taught by Confucius. As Confucianism was a philosophy and a way of life, it did not have a priesthood or hierarchy; various schools interpreted it differently in their own ways. After the twelfth century the Sung School emerged as the most influential and dominated the intellectual scene for the next seven hundred years. It was then that Confucianism became more doctrinaire and dogmatic and consequently less humane. We shall have more to say about this in the coming chapters.

THE BASIC WORKS OF CONFUCIANISM

The basic works of Confucianism were those that were written before the second century B.C. when Confucianism was proclaimed as the state philosophy, as against those that were written afterwards. Some of them were so highly regarded that they were called *ching* or classics. By classics was meant more than masterpieces; they were also sacred. To an orthodox Confucian they contained the cream of all knowledge and wisdom, their words were to be memorized by heart, and their teachings were to be followed literally. What were the classics? Usually we say *Five Classics*, though occasionally the terms *Nine Classics* and *Thirteen Classics* were also used. In either of the latter case lesser works were added to the *Five Classics* to make the required number. The *Five Classics* were: *Book of Odes, Book of History, Book of Changes, Book of Rites,* and finally, *Spring and Autumn Annals.* The *Book of Music,* one of the original *Classics,* was lost in the third century B.C. during Ch'in Shih Huang-ti's book-burning campaign (see Chapter III). The *Five Classics,* however, have survived the long years.

The *Book of Odes (Shih ching)* was one of the oldest written works in history, dating from the tenth to the seventh century B.C. At one time it contained more than 3,000 poems; after Confucius' editing, said tradition, only 305 of them were allowed to remain. Of the 305 poems that constitute the present version, some are folksongs (*feng*), and others are political poems (*ya*), and ritual hymns (*sung*). The most charming and best known are the folksongs that have universal appeal regardless of time and space. The following is the conversation between a newly married couple who, according to Chinese tradition, lived under the same roof with the groom's parents.

> The cock is crowing;
> Oh, dear, it is already morning.
>
> It is not the cock crowing;
> It is only flies' droning.
>
> The east is brightening;
> The morning is here, my darling.
>
> It is the moonlight, not the sun;
> You must be mistaken.
>
> My head is dizzy;
> The flies are droning.
> I love to lie beside you longer
>   Sharing our unfinished dream.
> But what would others say,
>   When they come home from their gathering?
> Get up, sweet;
> Their scorn is frightening.[1]

What kind of moral could traditional Confucians derive from this piece of literature which was a love poem? To squeeze out a moral, they had to twist the meaning of the poem. This poem showed a virtuous wife, said the moralists, who urged her husband to get up early to attend the morning audience with the king. The "others" in the poem meant the "other ministers," and the "gathering" meant the "daily audience with the king early in the morning." The moral was: "Thou shalt not let passion blind your sacred duty to the king." Many other poems were given moral meanings in the same manner.

The *Book of History* (*Shu ching*) consists of historical and semi-historical documents dating from the early period of the Chou dynasty. During Ch'in's book-burning campaign, this book, like many other Confucian works, was ordered to be burned. After the establishment of the Han dynasty a search was made for the lost text, but in vain. As a last resort, the government invited a Confucian scholar named Fu Sheng (c. 180 B.C.) to reconstruct the lost text. Fu had memorized the entire work; now, more than ninety years old, he dictated what he had memorized

---

[1] Translated by the author from "The Folksongs of Ch'i" in the *Book of Odes*.

to his daughter who then transmitted the reconstructed text to the government. Since this text was written in the Han script, the same script as the Chinese are using today, it was called the *Book of History* in the "modern text." Later, when the old residence of Confucius was destroyed, a copy of the *Book of History* written in an ancient script was found inside a broken wall, and it contained sixteen more essays than the "modern text." Many scholars claimed that this was the original text, the text that had existed before Ch'in's book-burning campaign. Since the circumstances under which it was found were not exactly known, there were others who doubted the authenticity of the "old text." The debate regarding the comparative merits of the two texts has been going on for the past two thousand years. Generally speaking, the "modern text" is more reliable than the "old text" which contains a sizable portion of later forgeries.

The *Book of Changes* (*Yi ching*) is the only Classic that deals with the supernatural. As such, it was claimed by both Confucians and later Taoists as a part of their heritage. We know that Confucius read this book with great diligence and once remarked that he would be less subject to error if Heaven gave him more years to study this book more thoroughly. Why should it take him so many years to read a book which was small in volume? Obviously, readers like Confucius saw more meanings between the lines than the terse text contained. It is in fact a diviner's book, dealing with the meanings of the various combinations of the Eight Diagrams. A Diagram is composed of either two unbroken lines and one broken line or one unbroken line and two broken lines with two exceptions that are composed of either three unbroken lines or three broken lines. The unbroken line — symbolizes *yang*, the positive force in the universe, and the broken line - - symbolizes *yin*, the negative force in the universe. Their interactions, said the ancient diviners, created the universe and the things in it. Some scholars claim that the unbroken and broken lines represented the male and female sexual organs respectively and were therefore adopted as symbols for the two opposite but complementary forces in the universe. By arranging any three of the broken and unbroken lines in different positions, the ancient diviner obtained eight possible combinations which were called the Eight Diagrams.

The diviner, by doubling any two of the Eight Diagrams, could make a total of sixty-four possible combinations. As an illustration, we shall draw some of them as follows:

This may look like child's play to us, but to the ancient Chinese each of these combinations represented a particular form in which the cosmic forces expressed themselves. Each form foretold the future and the eventual outcome of prospective events. This was of course a different kind of divination from that practiced by the Shangs and perhaps did not come into wide use until the early period of the Chou dynasty. The terse, ambiguous text in the *Book of Changes* was traditionally attributed to King Wen and Duke Chou, the founders of Chou dynasty. It is more likely that they had nothing to do with it. The text was intentionally ambiguous to provide room for the individual diviner's own interpretations. Appendixes and comments were added to the text by later scholars and diviners; some of them were attributed to Confucius who, in this case, might have earned a reputation which he did not deserve.

The origin of the *Book of Rites* was even more ambiguous. We know that Confucius listed rites as one of the most important subjects in his curriculum. Was the present version of the namesake used at the time of Confucius? A portion of it might have been, but most of it was the creation of later scholars. The compilation, in its present form, did not come into being until the second century B.C. In the twelfth century A.D. two chapters of this book, *Great Learning* (*Ta hsüeh*) and *Doctrine of the Mean* (*Chung yung*) were taken out to form two of the *Four Books*. The other two books were the *Analects* and the *Book of Mencius*. After the twelfth century the *Four Books* and the *Five Classics* have been regarded as the basic texts of Confucianism.

The last of the *Five Classics* is a history of the state Lu entitled *Spring and Autumn Annals*. Tradition credited Confucius with its authorship. Thanks to its association with the great sage, its text has been carefully preserved. Its brief, terse remarks enabled Confucian scholars of succeeding centuries to read into them moralistic meanings.

In addition to the books described above, there were lesser works that were also a part of Confucian tradition. Closely related to the *Book of Rites* were *Ceremonies and Rituals* (*Yi li*) and *Chou Institutions*. The former appeared in the second century B.C.; the latter, also titled *Rites of Chou* (*Chou li*), was an idealized picture of Chou institutions. Though Duke Chou has been credited by tradition with its authorship, it was in fact a much later creation (second century B.C.?). Traditionally associated with the *Spring and Autumn Annals* were three other independent works: *Commentaries of Tso* (*Tso chuan*), *Commentaries of Kung-yang* (*Kung-yang chuan*), and *Commentaries of Ku-liang* (*Ku-liang chuan*). They were called commentaries (*chuan*) because they were supposedly to complement the *ching* which, in this case, was the *Spring and Autumn Annals*. They were variably dated from the fifth to the second century B.C. Among the three the *Commentaries of Tso*, attributed to a man named Tso Ch'iu-ming, was the most widely read during the later centuries as it contained many historical episodes lyrically written. Tso Ch'iu-ming was said to have also written *Conversations of the States* (Kuo yü) which was a description of events in the various states. *Documents of the Warring States* (*Chan-kuo ts'e*), by an anonymous author, was a book of similar nature dealing with a later period. The *Bamboo Annals* (*Chu-shu chi-nien*), a history of Tsin, was discovered in an ancient grave in the third century A.D. It bore that title because the text of the discovered copy was recorded on bamboo slips, an ancient material for writing. The original copy was subsequently lost, and the existing work, bearing the same title, is a reconstructed copy and contains mere fragments of the original. Finally, there was the *Book of Filial Piety* (*Hsiao ching*) which, since its composition in the third or second century B.C., had been a standard text used to indoctrinate school children on that virtue until the twentieth century.

The discussion of ancient Chinese literature is incomplete without mentioning the works of two southern poets, Ch'ü Yüan and Sung Yü, though their works did not form a part of the Confucian tradition. Ch'ü Yüan (343?–277 B.C.), according to a biography written in the second century B.C., was "broad in knowledge and clever with words." He had been a high-ranking official in Ch'u until the king listened to other people's slanderings and dismissed him. In despair, he eventually committed suicide. He left us several works among which are *Sorrows* (*Li sao*) and *Nine Songs* (*Chiu ko*). His poems were imaginative and lively, and his style was so unique that it was widely copied during succeeding centuries. The copied form, fully developed during the Han dynasty, was known as *fu*. Sung Yü was said to have been a disciple of Ch'ü Yüan, but we have no way to ascertain this tradition. We know little about his personal life except what he said about himself. If we can believe literally what he said, he was extremely handsome and was very popular with young damsels (a good indication that Confucian morality, the term as we understand today, was not yet known to the southerners in his life time). A dozen of his *fu* have survived, and they generally followed the same style as that of his alleged teacher.[1] The works of both writers are collectively referred to as *Elegies of Ch'u* or *Ch'u Tz'u*. They differed from the works of northern writers in content as well as in form.

TAOISM

In terms of influence over the life and thought of the Chinese people for the next two thousand years, Taoism was second only to Confucianism. As the Chinese did not regard philosophies (or religions) as mutually

---

[1] *Fu* is a literary form or style, but it is also the poem or poems written in such a form or style.

exclusive, the same person could be influenced by both philosophies without consciously identifying them. Both philosophies constituted a part of the Chinese cultural heritage, and a Chinese was a follower of the entire Chinese heritage rather than a particular school of philosophy. Since Confucianism was the dominant school of thought since the second century B.C., a Chinese before the twentieth century inevitably identified himself as Confucian, even though he also believed in other philosophies or religions such as Buddhism. This is very confusing to a Westerner who is brought up to believe that if a person follows one religion he cannot follow the other and that he has to leave his own church in order to join another church. As an average Chinese did not belong to a church organization in the Western sense of that term, there was no higher authority than himself with regard to religious matters. Such being the case, he wound up in believing a little of every major philosophy or religion as existed in China; he himself selected whatever he wished to believe. A Chinese intellectual might be said to be a synthesis of the entire Chinese heritage rather than a follower of a particular school of thought or religion. Since he was a recognized leader in his community, his approach and attitude towards different philosophies and religions were also shared, by and large, by his fellow countrymen who might not be able to read or write.

According to tradition, the founder of Taoism was a mystic figure named Li Erh, better known as Lao-tzu which means, literally, the Old Master. As a matter of principle, Lao-tzu was opposed to activity, not to speak of any intention, to found a school of philosophy. However, Taoism came into being despite Taoist philosophy and has influenced Chinese life and thinking ever since. According to Ssu-ma Ch'ien, the great Han historian who lived in the second century B.C., Lao-tzu was born in Ch'u early in the sixth century B.C. He served as a librarian in the Chou Archives and was reported to have received and conversed with Confucius when the latter was a young man. After the interview, said Ssu-ma Ch'ien, Confucius was greatly impressed and compared Lao-tzu to a flying dragon who "rode the wind and cloud up in the sky." Seeing that Chou had begun to decline, Lao-tzu decided to leave his post for good. On his way to the west he was recognized by a warden on a mountain pass who begged him to write a book. The book was written in short order, amounting to some five thousand words. The biography ends by saying: "He (Lao-tzu) then went away, and nobody knew what had become of him." The book Lao-tzu is supposed to have written was later known as *Tao-te Ching*, or *Book of Taoist Virtue*.

Modern historians wonder whether Lao-tzu in fact ever existed, let alone the correctness of these details of his life. The present version of the *Book of Taoist Virtue* was definitely a later creation, written in the fourth or third century B.C. Its authorship has not been determined and perhaps

never will be. If it was written in the Warring-States period, as is generally assumed, it may be regarded as another form of reaction (as distinct
from that of Confucianism) to the incessant warfare and political chaos
of contemporary China. When a man becomes intensely dissatisfied with
the existing situation, he either attempts to take positive steps to correct it
as in the case of the Confucians, or resigns himself to his fate, takes a
negative attitude towards the entire world, and resorts to drawing whatever comfort he can from an extremely disagreeable situation. The author
who wrote the *Taoist Virtue* belonged to the second category. Like the
Confucians, he condemned war, but in much stronger terms. What was
the sense of this endless slaughtering? he asked. Every general was a
murderer in disguise, because his glory was built on the dead bodies of
thousands of innocent men. Every hero was an evil man by definition
because his heroism indicated nothing except that he knew how to kill
more people with better efficiency. Therefore, " a man of Tao avoids and
loathes weapons as tools of bad omen" and "views every victory celebration as a funeral rite." A hero was to be pitied because he did not know
his own guilt and ignorance.

The same kind of argument permeated the entire work. It condemned all values which contemporary society held dear. It subjected to
scrutiny all conventions and traditions that men had long taken for
granted. Its attack was as sweeping as it was intensive. What was the
value of power, fame, and wealth? it asked. Had they done any good to
the men who possessed them, not to mention the harm they did to others?
If a government had to exist, let it govern the least. The best rulers were
those who did not rule, and the less effective a government was, the
better it would be. "The more there are laws, the more there will be
thieves"; and mankind was much better off without any of them. Wisdom
and knowledge contributed nothing to human welfare except discontent
and unhappiness, and "the most ignorant is always the wisest." "By abandoning wisdom and discarding knowledge, the people will benefit a hun-
dredfold." Education was worse than useless; as long as people were not
taught to be good, they would not know what was bad and consequently
would not become bad. A simple, primitive society was much more preferable than a complicated, advanced one where "luxury breeds envy and
envy brings strife," and no one was happy in the end. An ideal society was
economically self-sufficient and should produce nothing except necessities
to satisfy the basic needs. No one envied another, as no one had more than
the other had. As envy ended, so would rivalries and strifes. Wars would
cease, since no state could gain anything by invading others. In such an
ideal society, "there is no use for boats and vehicles, nor arms and soldiers. . . . While neighboring states are so close that people can hear the
crowing of a cock or the bark of a dog in other states, they will not visit
one another for the entire duration of their lives."

If all existing values were discarded, what would be the values a man of Tao should adhere to? His values were those of an infant, unspoiled by the existing society. He did not know gains or losses; honor or shame; ambitions or disappointments. He should be weak and meek; he should be withdrawing and submissive. Nothing was weaker than water; yet, it could destroy the hardest mountains. Nothing was lower than the ocean; yet, it received the mightiest rivers. The more we tried, the less we would succeed. A man of Tao, therefore, preferred a constant state of inactivity. What was Tao? Tao was formless and shapeless; it could not even have a name because a name presupposed a form. It could not be discussed because what could be discussed was beyond the sphere of Tao. Tao, in fact, was nothing, and "nothingness" was the essence of Tao. Why was "nothingness" so important? Because without "nothingness" nothing in the world could have existed. "Nothingness" was the "mother of all things," including the universe. From "nothingness" the universe had arrived and to "nothingness" it would eventually have to go. In the physical universe which "nothingness" had created, "nothingness" pervaded in everything and was the most useful thing of all existences. How could stars move without "nothingness" in between? Could they exist in the first place? What was the usefulness of a bowl? It was useful because it was hollow and contained "emptiness" within itself. A window or door was useful because "nothingness" dominated its existence. We could not exist one day had there been no "nothingness" around us. For one thing, we could not even breathe.

Thus, Taoist "mysticism," when reduced to common sense terms as the author of *Taoist Virtue* attempted to do, was nothing mysterious at all. The book did not attempt to explain the inexplainable; nor did it deal with the supernatural. It was in line with the secular, humanistic pattern as we have discussed earlier in this chapter. Besides *Taoist Virtue* the other important work in Taoism is the *Book of Chuang-tzu* whose author, Chuang Chou, was believed to have lived in the fourth century B.C. *Chuang-tzu* was a more substantial book, and its present version, edited and commented on by Kuo Hsiang (d. 312 A.D.), contains thirty-three separate essays. Generally speaking, it followed the same basic beliefs as those of *Taoist Virtue;* its style, however, was more biting and incisive. Its author was witty and humorous; invented conversations between ancient sages to strengthen his own argument; and was good with a tale or fable to bring home a particular point. Like *Taoist Virtue*, its major purpose was to smash conventional values, including those in morality and ethics. As expected, it singled out Confucianism as its main target of attack.

Confucian morality, argued Chuang Chou, benefited only those who were satisfied with what they had and discriminated against those who sought change. It glorified the mighty and the powerful, and it kept the lowly in their proper place. Take thievery as an example. Those who stole nations became kings and dukes, and those who stole such small things as "fishing hooks" were condemned as thiefs and were punished accordingly. Who were worse thieves, the kings and dukes who killed thousands of innocent people to steal a nation or the small man who was forced by hunger to steal a fishing hook? The bigger the crime, the more people glorified it. A crime ceased to be a crime and became heroic instead if it was big enough and involved the lives of thousands of people. The Confucians, by glorifying the bigger crimes and condemning the smaller ones, committed a hypocritic act. Moreover, the kings and dukes whom they glorified might not have the virtues as possessed by a common thief. Chih, one of the most notorious thieves of ancient times, was asked whether a thief had any virtues. "Certainly he has," Chih replied. "To know where the valuables are hidden indicates high intelligence. To enter into a house first shows bravery. To leave it last is an act of righteousness. To know whether to enter a house or not is wisdom. And to divide spoils according to merits is justice. It is impossible to become a great thief without possessing all of these five virtues."

If a thief could conceivably possess more virtues than the more respectable members of a society, the society might do well to reexamine its own sense of values. The continuous existence of fixed ideas and accepted conventions did not necessarily mean that they possessed irreparable, intrinsic values; it might have resulted simply from long usage. Did usage itself constitute a value? Should mankind subject itself to the bondage of convention simply because it had been hallowed by time? Man would have done a great service to himself if from time to time he stopped to reappraise his own beliefs. To illustrate, Chuang Chou invented a story about himself. Chuang Chou was about to die, he said, and his students were thinking of purchasing the best coffin in town when the inevitable arrived. "Why should you buy any coffin for me at all, not to mention a good coffin? I prefer to use the whole universe as my coffin," he protested. "We are afraid that your body would be eaten up by hungry vultures," replied his students. "It is true that without a coffin my body will be eaten up by vultures. But do you realize that with a coffin my body will be eaten up by ants? Now you are proposing to take my body away from the vultures and give it to the ants. Is that fair to the vultures? Why should you favor the ants and discriminate against the vultures?"

Being skeptical about Confucian rites, Chuang Chou was equally merciless in his attack on other Confucian virtues such as *jen* and *yi*. Moral standards were invented by man; they were superficial and superfluous. There was an inherent futility in man's endeavors, including his search for moral values. A wise man, knowing such futility, adhered to the principle of inactivity. What could be done would be done spontaneously by nature. The more man interfered with the function of natural order, the worse the situation would become. The futility of human endeavors did not stem from the incapacity of the human mind to acquire knowledge and ability; rather, it resulted from the very nature of reality itself. Reality was by definition contradictory, ironical, and uncertain. Its natural uncertainty was totally beyond man's control. A reality might be an illusion, and *vice versa*. What was the difference between these two anyway? They might be the same thing. To illustrate, Chuang Chou again invented a story about himself. He said that once in his dream he had become a butterfly, fluttering hither and thither, to all intents and purposes a butterfly. After waking up, he was confused. "Did I dream of becoming a butterfly or is the butterfly now dreaming of becoming me? Was the butterfly in my dream or am I now in the dream of the butterfly?" Such was the irony of life, the irony of all existences. "What it is" might be "what it is not," and *vice versa*. A crooked tree, said Chuang Chou, might live a long life because it was not good enough for making anything and was consequently spared by woodsmen. On the other hand, a goose that could not cackle ("has no virtues") would have to go to the kitchen table first. As far as he was concerned, Chuang Chou concluded, he preferred to live like an old tortoise "dragging my tail in the mud," rather than going around, trying to save mankind.

Why was Taoism so appealing to the Chinese? Its political and social theories were impractical, and its advocacy of returning man to his natural primitiveness was clearly an exercise in impossibility. To understand the appeal of Taoism, we have to understand the nature of man. Because Taoism was not merely an abstract philosophy, it was also a mental attitude, a sense of values towards life and things in general. Was a man really happy when he had acquired all elements that constituted wordly happiness: power, wealth, fame, etc.? Even during his "happiest" moment, there was a sense of sadness and he missed something which he could neither name nor describe. Man alone possessed such sensitivity which no other animals possessed. While a Westerner might renounce the worldly cares and seek comfort in religion, a Chinese might retreat to a mode of negativity in which all values, worldly or spiritual, became blurred and insignificant. Spiritual values were still values and were therefore not Taoist, because Taoism was the negation of all values, religious or otherwise. It was against any efforts, including efforts to attain a better life in the next world. If we have to use an analogy to drive home our point, Taoism was a state of drunkenness without being intoxicated. To be sure, not all men wished to adhere to the principle of Taoism at all times, because, whatever intrinsic merits it might possess, it was simply impossible to do so in the physical world. Yet, when it arrived, it provided great strength and comfort.

The appeal of Taoism might also have been related to China's social and economic environment. Life was extremely uncertain in China where one's fate was often beyond his own control. A prospective harvest might be suddenly ruined by a heavy storm, and a high ranking official might unexpectedly lose favor and be summarily dismissed. By recognizing the Taoist contention that one extreme was bound to be followed by another extreme in the opposite direction, one was more inclined to be moderate in success and acquiescent in failure. The recognition of the inevitability produced a Stoic indifference during the time of distress, engendered great courage to face what had to be faced, and provided cheer during even the most unhappy moment. It compelled modesty from the most proud and injected dignity into the most humble. Taoism was likely to be most popular during trying times: natural disasters, wars, and governmental oppressions, about which an ordinary mortal could do nothing except submit. Knowing the inevitability and facing it with resignation were in themselves a source of strength.

So far we have confined our discussion to Taoism as a philosophy (*Tao chia*). There was also Taoism as a religion (*Tao chiao*). The standardized English translation makes no distinction between these two, and consequently there is a great deal of confusion. As to the Taoist religion, it developed along independent lines and will be discussed in a later chapter.

"A HUNDRED SCHOOLS CONTEND"

The ancient philosophers made no distinction between philosophy as a speculative science and philosophy as a way of life. As their major concern was human relations, a philosophy was meant to be lived by rather than to be discussed in abstract terms. How a philosopher conducted his personal life spoke more eloquently of his philosophy than anything he might have said or written. In other words, he was a living manifestation of his philosophy. Aside from Confucianism and Taoism there were numerous other schools during the period under discussion, and each of them came into being as it sought the best remedy against the background of a turbulent, disorganized society. Confucianism and Taoism have survived, but most of the other schools did not. It is a matter of debate whether survival was a reflection of merit. Perhaps not. Since the other schools exercised less influence on later Chinese than the two main streams of thought, we shall discuss them more briefly.

Among the various schools one of the most outstanding was unquestionably the philosophy of Mo Ti, or Mo-tzu, which means Master Mo. He was born to a humble family in North China about the time that Confucius died. One hundred years later, his philosophy had become so widely accepted that it challenged Confucianism as the leading system of thought in the fourth century B.C. The main themes of his philosophy were two, universal love and non-militarism, the latter being a supplement to the former. While Confucians defined love as emanating from man's inner self and extending towards the outward world in different degrees according to the closeness of the receiving persons, Mo Ti believed in universal love, the same in intensity for all men under Heaven. Confucius emphasized the importance of filial piety, but Mo Ti ridiculed it on the ground that to place priority on family was clannish and selfish and that family welfare was often advanced by Confucian believers at the expense of the welfare of the whole society. It was the welfare of the whole society, said Mo Ti, that should be a gentleman's first concern. The welfare in Mo Ti's mind was a material welfare, as contrary to the moral welfare expounded by Confucius. As universal love implied equal well-being, not until the humblest man in the nation acquired a satisfactory standard of living could any one else have the right of enjoying the same. Customs and conventions that presupposed wasteful spendings with no real increment of material well-being should not be condoned, and they should be in fact abolished. In this respect, Mo Ti singled out Confucian rites as the target of his strongest criticism because he regarded them as purely wasteful. There was no sense of spending so much for a funeral, argued he, when one had not enough to eat; nor was it a sound logic to favor the dead at the expense of the living. To oppose waste, he urged the practice of thrift and the finding of ways and means to increase production. This utilitarian approach led him to elevate Yü above all China's past heroes, as Yü was the hard-working, legendary engineer who many centuries before had dug canals and built dams to protect North China from future floods. Emphasizing the importance of basic, material needs, Mo Ti spoke for the poor and the humble. An ideal society in his mind was a welfare state of material sufficiency rather than a moral commonwealth with emphasis on intangible values.

No mere theorists, Mo Ti and his followers substantiated what they believed with concrete actions. Coming largely from the lower strata of society, most of them artisans and engineers, they were deft in technical and manual work. Mo Ti led them to tasks which he believed would bring about a better human relationship. In order to love, one had to learn first not to hate. Of all the forms of showing hatred, warfare was unquestionably the worst. Hence non-militarism was the first step towards universal love. Non-militarism, however, was not synonymous with non-violence; nor did it mean "turning the other cheek." While violence was deplorable, sometimes one had to use it to prevent further violence because persuasion, however convincing, yielded only slow and often ineffective results. As wars were frequent then, Mo Ti mobilized his followers to help the defense of a city or state which had been unjustifiably attacked. Being engineers and artisans, they were expert in defense and in making defensive weapons, and they often gave a good account of themselves. More than once were the invaders stopped when Mo Ti sided with the defenders. This organized group of soldiers and engineers pledged no loyalty to any sovereign or state but only to a principle as interpreted by Mo Ti himself. To this principle his followers were willing to commit anything, even their own lives.

Despite many differences, Mo Ti and Confucius had much in common. Both were motivated by a sincere interest in human welfare and in taking positive steps to advance it, and both accepted the existing form of government, monarchy, as the best kind of government. Like Confucius, Mo Ti insisted that the ruler should be virtuous and should set examples to his subjects, so that "his rule would be in harmony with the wishes of Heaven." The difference was on the emphasis regarding the attributes of a good sovereign. While Confucius talked in moral terms, Mo Ti was more practical and utilitarian. In the treatise *Universal Love* he said:

> I have heard that a man of gentle character loves his friend as if his friend were he himself, and treats his friend's relatives as though they were his own relatives. . . . I have also heard that a good prince places the welfare of his subjects above that of his own. He feeds them when they are hungry, clothes them when they are cold, nurses them when they are sick, and buries them when they die.

Another school of importance was Legalism. There were no conscientious efforts on the part of the Legalists to form an independent school; it came into being as a result of grouping together the writings of those who emphasized the importance of law as the sole means of attaining efficiency in government and orderliness in society. One of these works was *Kuan-tzu*, attributed to Kuan Chung, the chief minister of Ch'i under Duke Huan. It was, however, the creation of a later age. Another work was the *Book of Lord Shang* (*Shang-chün shu*) which, traditionally attributed to Shang Yang, was actually written by an anonymous author in the third century B.C. The leading thinker of the Legalist school was Han Fei (d. 233 B.C.) who wrote *Han-fei-tzu*, the most comprehensive presentation of the Legalist philosophy. Han Fei was a disciple of Hsün Ch'ing, a Confucian philosopher who, unlike Mencius, believed that human nature was basically bad. Hsün Ch'ing's other disciple, equally famous, was Li Ssu who served as Ch'in's chief minister before he died in 208 B.C. If Han Fei was the theoretician, Li Ssu was the practitioner who, as the chief minister, put the Legalist theory into practice. However, there was a strong personal rivalry between these two. Eventually, Li Ssu threw his former schoolmate into jail and forced him to commit suicide. The Legalists, like the modern Fascists, did not believe in such things as love and compassion; power was to be maintained and secured at any cost, including murder.

While Hsün Ch'ing believed in education as a sure means to improve the evil nature of man, his disciple Han Fei proposed the enactment and enforcement of law to prevent his evil nature from running its wild course. To expect goodness from people of their own accord was unrealistic and wishful, said Han Fei. The so-called virtues proposed by Confucians were at best hypocritic pretensions, readily utilized by the pretenders for their own selfish purposes. In fact, no virtue existed without some selfish motive behind it. To build society on virtues, false, fleeting, and unreliable, was like building a house on sand which, being unstable, would collapse eventually. The Confucian *li*, the outward manifestation of virtues, was as superficial as it was wasteful. Confucius' admonition of returning to the golden past was an outmoded thought because the times were different and the need was also different. No institution had a permanent value; the best was such as most fitted each historical period. Therefore, let no one admire any longer "the virtues of Yao, Shun, Yü, T'ang, Wen, and Wu"; new sages should come forward to devise new means for a new age.

What was the current need? The Legalists said that it was law. To use Han Fei's analogy, law was like measures to a carpenter. As a carpenter could not build without the help of measures, a prince could not rule without laws. Law should be just and fair; but whatever the law was, once instituted, it should be equally enforced upon all, for the nobility as well as the peasants. Law should be made exact and clear so that people would know what to do and what to avoid. The offenders should be severely punished, and abiders richly rewarded. In fact, reward and punishment were the two basic weapons in the hand of a prince. Emphasis on law spared the necessity of searching for motives which simply could not be known. Motives unknown, it was the external conduct of which the prince should take account. Virtue could only be measured by external conduct, and laws should be the standard of measurement. What was inside a person was not the prince's business.

The enforcement of law necessitated a strong government and government should be strengthened at all costs. In order to create a centralized and all-powerful state any means was justifiable regardless of moral or ethical considerations. Machiavelian methods were definitely advisable, as long as they could bring results. Every prince had to face the fact that the conflict between the rulers and the ruled was an inevitable and uncompromising one. To safeguard his own superiority, he should employ the inducement of fame and wealth to win him supporters, and coercion and punishment to compel obedience from others. Genuine gratitude never existed, and it was all to the good that it did not exist, since no man would do anything without expecting something in return. A man became moral or law-abiding only when he had no other choice. This kind of cynical argument permeates all of Han Fei's writings.

In an ideal society of the Legalist image, material welfare was definitely more important than the cultivation of virtues. "Only when people are well fed and clothed can they be expected to know the difference between honesty and shamefulness," as Kuan Chung was reported to have remarked. When Shang Yang was the chief minister of Ch'in, he organized the whole state to the last man for the purpose of increasing agricultural production. In Han Fei's thinking, man's virtues should be expressed and judged in two fields only: diligence in work and bravery in warfare. An ideal society was a society composed of well-organized farmer-soldiers governed and controlled by an all-powerful state headed by an omnipotent prince. All men should be good farmers in peace and brave soldiers in war. In peacetime military training went side by side with the tilling of the soil. In such a society there was no need for philosophy or literature, said Li Ssu. Law was the sole subject of learning; government officials were alone the teachers. Conventions and traditions were untrustworthy, however good once they might have been. The most important was the present, and the urgent need of the present, argued Han Fei, was a centralized state wealthy and powerful enough to unify China so to bring back order from chaos. After a copy of Han Fei's work reached Ch'in's reigning prince, later known as Ch'in Shih Huang-ti, he sighed with regret that he was not fortunate enough to have lived in the same age as the author, thinking that Han Fei must have been an ancient sage. He did not know that the author's schoolmate was his own chief minister Li Ssu who was then doing his very best to carry out Han Fei's philosophy.

Confucianism, Taoism, Moism, and Legalism constituted four major schools of thought prior to Ch'in's unification of China in 221 B.C. There were, of course, the lesser schools. The Agriculturalists believed that all material values were derived from land and that farmers alone were producers. They regarded people of other occupations as exploiters and proposed that even kings and princes, to justify the material support they received to maintain their livelihood, should till the field side by side with other farmers. There were also the Dualists (*Yin-yang chia*) who believed that the essence of the universe was the two opposite but complementary forces, *yin* and *yang*, and that all things in the universe were made of varying combinations of the five primary elements: metal, wood, water, fire, and earth. The basic theory of the Dualists was later incorporated into Taoism and was also accepted by many Confucians.[1] Finally, there was the School of Names (*Ming chia*, often translated as School of Dialecticians) whose philosophers, like the Greek Sophists, loved a good argument for the sake of argument. They debated on such matters as whether a white horse was a horse or a hard rock was really a rock. To people of other schools this kind of debate was an exercise in futility. Since it bore no relation to man and his relationship with other men, it was regarded as trivial and insignificant. This school of thought which might have devel-

[1] For a detailed description of Dualism, see Chapter VII.

oped as a basis for our modern logic died shortly without an heir. The overemphasis on human relations in China's intellectual heritage killed off the potential growth of a pure, impersonal science.

SCIENCE

Though science was not emphasized in ancient China, there were individuals whose natural inquisitiveness carried them beyond the ordinary confines of human relations. They never received the attention accorded to humanistic philosophers, and most of their contributions remained anonymous. Like many other ancient peoples, the Chinese believed that the revolutions of heavenly bodies had a direct bearing on human affairs. It was not surprising that their major interest should be in astronomy and its related field mathematics. The *Book of History* mentioned one of the earliest solar eclipses on record which was placed at 2137 B.C. Modern archaeologists examined the Shell-Bone inscriptions and found that the total eclipse of the sun in 1137 B.C. as well as the total lunar eclipse in 1311 B.C. were duly observed and recorded. The *Spring and Autumn Annals* recorded thirty-seven solar eclipses of which thirty-three have been positively identified as actual occurrences. In 28 B.C. sun spots were first observed, more than sixteen centuries before Johannes Kepler made his discovery in 1607.

The greatest Chinese work on mathematics before the Christian era was the *Chou-pi Mathematics* (*Chou-pi Suan-ching*), written perhaps in the third century B.C. It contained the Pythagorem theorem ($a^2 + b^2 = c^2$), computations of the distance between the sun and the earth as well as the sun's orbit, quadratic equations, and formulae for prisms, cones, and cylinders. It was stated in this book that a mathematician named Shang Kao was told by Duke Chou (twelfth century B.C.) to measure the "height of the sun." Shang Kao placed three rods of equal length at three different cities with a distance of 1,000 *li* (c. 333 miles) between any two of the three cities. All the three cities were located on a straight line running from the north to the south. On the day of summer solstice (c. June 21) when the sun reached its northernmost point and began its southward journey, the sun shadow of each of the three rods was measured. Knowing the differences between the lengths of the three shadows, continued the story, Shang Kao had no difficulty computing the "height of the sun." The concept of π seemed to have antedated the writing of *Chou-pi Mathematics;* however, it was not until the third century A.D. that the Han mathematician Liu Hui came out with a nearly perfect answer, 3.1416.

The ancient Chinese of the pre-Ch'in period used the frequency of a musical tone as the standard of determining correct measures and weights, just as modern scientists use the velocity of light for the same purpose. The standard tone was that of Yellow Bell (named after the legendary ruler Huang-ti or Yellow Emperor), a pitch pipe which, according to modern scientists, yielded a sound frequency of 348. One-ninth of the Yellow Bell was a standard Chinese inch (*ts'un*); the internal space of the Yellow Bell which contained 1,200 standard grain was the smallest unit of volume, *sha*; and the total weight of 2,400 standard grain (which filled up two Yellow Bell pipes) constituted the basic weight, *liang*. *Liang*, literally, means "double" or "two." Applying the principle of sound frequency, the ancient scientists were able to make different kinds of pitch pipes as music instruments. Lengthening or shortening the Yellow Bell pipe by one-third of its existing length repeatedly, they were able to produce a variety of harmonious, melodious notes. It was reported that as early as the sixth century B.C. they had discovered the seven pitch notes which we are using today. Of course, they called these notes by different names (*kung, shang, chüeh,* etc.) instead of do, re, mi, etc.

In the field of applied science the Chinese paid great attention to irrigation work and flood control as dictated by circumstances. We know little about the engineering details that accompanied the construction of numerous dams and dykes in North China before the Warring-States period. However, by the third century B.C. hydraulic engineering had become an advanced science. The Ch'in engineer Li Ping built one of the most intricate irrigation systems in western Szechuan which, after more than two thousand years, is still in working order. The soundness of his engineering seems to indicate that the basic principles of hydraulics must have been known to his predecessors. Another example was the Great Wall. As early as 500 B.C. individual states began to build long walls as a defense measure against northern nomads. However, it was not until the third century B.C. that the Ch'in regime connected them to form what was later known as the Great Wall. Crawling a distance of 1,700 miles, it was an engineering feat of first magnitude.

Though overwhelmingly concerned with humanities, the ancient Chinese did not seem to have done badly in the field of science. Unfortunately, the Chinese achievements were individual, isolated events. There was no such thing as a scientific community in which different scientists could exchange each other's findings and inspire and stimulate their common interests. This contrasted sharply with the lively activities of philosophers. Nor was there a conscientiously accumulated knowledge in a particular discipline which enabled a scientist to follow up what his predecessors had achieved and eventually reach a new height in his own field of specialization. Practically every discovery or invention was the work of an individual genius. There was no precedent to follow; nor was a man sure that his efforts would be appreciated by his contemporaries, let alone posterity. Any scientific or technical invention was regarded as a "small skill" (*hsiao chi*), unworthy of the attention of great statesmen and scholars. Brought up in the Chinese sense of values, a discoverer or inventer tended to look down upon his own achievement. If historians bothered to record his contribution at all, they did so more out of curiosity than out of appreciation. Moreover, being scholars rather than scientists, they could only describe the outward phenomena instead of the underlying principles. Their recordings would not help people of succeeding generations who might have a similar interest. Many new discoveries and inventions must have come into being during each generation, but most of them disappeared with the death of the scientists involved because there were no follow-ups. The few inventions that possessed commercial value (such as drugs) were carefully guarded as family secrets and passed through one designated male member of each succeeding generation. If he died suddenly or prematurely before he had the opportunity to transfer the family secrets to a member of the next generation (usually his oldest son), the invention was lost to the society as a whole. Daughters were not allowed to share such secrets, because they would be married and would carry the secrets to other families. Behind all these impediments to a continuous growth of scientific and technological knowledge was of course the traditional contempt the Chinese held for such knowledge. Confucian scholars had successfully convinced their countrymen of the trivial nature of "small skills" as compared with the overwhelming importance of morality and ethics that governed human relations. If China lacked a tradition in science and technology, these scholars were at least partially responsible.

꩜ *iii*

The Grand Unifications

THE UNIFICATION OF CHINA

Though of short duration, Ch'in was one of the most dynamic regimes in Chinese history, and it exercised much stronger influence on later generations than its short span of life tends to suggest. Not only was China unified, but its territory was also considerably enlarged. The northern barbarians were pushed back to their desert homes, and in the south Chinese settlers built their homesteads as far as the modern Kwangtung province. More significant, however, were Ch'in's domestic policies and the philosophy behind them: they left an imprint not to be erased for many centuries to come.

The man responsible for all this was Ch'in Shih Huang-ti, one of the greatest yet most controversial men China ever produced. A person of unusual vitality, he pursued relentlessly the goal of unifying China, and in

97

MAP 11
THE CH'IN EMPIRE
• Cities   □ Capital
⊔⊔⊔⊔ The Great Wall

0   150   300   450
Scale of Miles

YELLOW RIVER

LIAO R.

Liaohsi
Liaotung

Yǔyang

Yenmen

Taiyuan

Hantan

YELLOW RIVER

Lunghsi

Hotung

L'angyeh

YELLOW SEA

Hsienyang

Yingch'uan

Tunghai

Hanchung

Nanyang

Shu

Pa

YANGTZE RIVER

Nanchǔn

YANGTZE RIVER

Changsha

Minchung

Kweilin

SI RIVER

Nanhai

Hsiangchǔn

SOUTH
CHINA SEA

221 B.C. he had the satisfaction of seeing the entire country firmly under his control. The price of unification was a heavy one: millions of lives had been lost and much property destroyed or damaged, not to mention the moral degeneration that resulted from an almost continuous status of war. Such a price, however, mattered little to him since in his opinion a war to unify China was a war to end all future wars: from thence onward all men under Heaven would live in peace under his and his successors' benevolent rule. Accordingly, he assumed a new title, Shih Huang-ti, or the First Emperor. It was hoped that "the imperial line will last for thousands of emperors, with no ending whatsoever."

The strong personality of Ch'in Shih Huang-ti was not the only factor that determined his success. After centuries of intermittent warfare people would accept any regime, as long as it could bring peace. The peasants were naturally the most eager, as they were the first victimized in any war. The merchants had an equal stake in peace; correctly they believed that a unified China would further their interests, since trade could move more easily when political boundaries were eliminated. The prospect of political unity was further enhanced by the fact that though the country had been politically divided, the Chinese had a common cultural background. Despite living in different states, they shared essentially the same language, traditions, beliefs, and even sentiments and aspirations. People could move freely across state lines, and within each state no legal or social discrimination was enacted against residents from other states. The Ch'in state, for instance, made a habit of searching for the best brains in the country to serve as its chief ministers, whether they came from the state of Wei or Chao. Cosmopolitan in outlook, the Chinese believed that even the difference between Chinese and barbarians was culturally tentative. The people of Ch'u and Yüeh who had been looked down upon as barbarians were readily accepted as equals by their more advanced brethern in the north, once they modeled their institutions after the northern states. This cultural assimilation continued, in spite of, or was even accelerated by, the continuance of warfare. All these being considered, it seemed that political unification was merely a matter of time.

Unification achieved, Shih Huang-ti's next concern was the organization of a centralized state and the establishment of an autocratic government. Since the decline of the Chou regime, the decentralization process had gone on for centuries until China was divided into many rival states without a central authority to arbitrate peace. Shih Huang-ti and his chief minister Li Ssu blamed feudalism for all political ills of the past and proposed to organize a strong, centralized government. Consequently in 221 B.C. a decree was issued to abolish feudalism once and for all. China was thereby divided into thirty-six administrative provinces, and all governors were appointed by and responsible to the imperial government. It should be pointed out, however, that the establishment of centrally con-trolled administrative units did not originate with Ch'in. As early as the Spring and Autumn Period, whenever a state felt strong enough, it abol-ished feudalism in areas where local lords were weak and ineffective and replaced it with central administration. The abolition of feudalism on a nation-wide scale and the introduction of a bureaucratic administration proved to be a measure of great significance in the long run. In whatever forms feudalism did reappear during the later dynasties, its existence was generally brief. Since the precedent created by Ch'in, the establishment of a centralized, autocratic government with jurisdiction over all of China was the goal every succeeding regime strove to achieve, and its absence was considered as temporary and abnormal. Such a government would be headed by a theoretically omnipotent prince to whom all Chinese owed allegiance, and the loyalty to him was supposedly higher than any other loyalties, including filial piety which had been so much emphasized by the Confucians. Many political theorists anxiously pointed out that only under a unified, centralized state could peace and order prevail, and they saw no good alternative to a bureaucratic, autocratic rule.

After the goal had been set up, the Ch'in regime took concrete meas-ures to eliminate local influence so as to discourage any decentralizing tendencies. Natural fortresses and local fortifications were ordered to be destroyed to enable imperial troops to move in quickly, when and if rebel-lion occurred. Military weapons hitherto scattered over the country were collected, melted, and cast into huge bells and statues, and nobody was allowed to possess any kind of weapons without government authoriza-tion. To eliminate local leadership, the very wealthy were ordered to take residence at the capital, Hsienyang, where their actions could be easily observed. It was said that no fewer than 120,000 families actually moved. To consolidate the empire around the imperial government, trunk roads were built to link major cities with the capital. These roads were unusu-ally wide and were planted with trees along both sides at regular inter-vals. Moving along these roads imperial troops could quickly appear on the scene, wherever trouble started. Hsienyang was rebuilt to inspire awe and to serve as a symbol of imperial strength. Two hundred and seventy palaces were lined up for a distance of many miles, and the magnificent Afang Palace towered over them all. The emperor himself made regular inspection trips to the four corners of his empire; one trip, for instance, took him all the way to modern Chekiang province.

Not satisfied with consolidating and strengthening his empire in a physical sense, Shih Huang-ti introduced a series of programs aimed at cul-tural regimentation and thought control. The four centuries prior to the establishment of the Ch'in dynasty had been one of the most creative eras of Chinese cultural history. Books were written; scholars and philosophers vied with one another in expounding new ideas on government and ethics.

After the Ch'in regime was established, many continued their traditional ways of advocating their own ideas and criticizing what they did not believe. Shih Huang-ti and his advisers concluded that if different schools of thought were allowed to contend and criticisms of government policies were left unchecked, they would soon become seeds of dissension and discontent which in turn might weaken government control over its subjects, induce revolts, and eventually break up the empire. Accordingly, they took strong measures to suppress the so-called heretical ideas, punish severely the critics of the government and its officials, and direct the people along what was regarded as the correct line of thinking. At the suggestion of Li Ssu, the government decreed that all books of political significance, with the exception of the authorized version of Ch'in history, were to be burned, and those who possessed the forbidden books or who discussed clandestinely their contents were to be severely punished according to law. In this book-burning campaign particular attention was directed at the *Book of Odes* and the *Book of History* which, according to the Ch'in authority, had been too often quoted by Confucians "to extol the past and criticize the present." Books specially exempted from the burning list were works of a technical nature, such as books of medicine, divination, and forestation. While reading in general was disapproved, the study of law was encouraged. Following the Legalist tradition, the government decreed that those who wished to study law could do so under the guidance of government officials.

Whatever temporary success the government might have achieved in its thought control programs, great damage had been done to China's cultural heritage. When learning was again revived early in the Han dynasty, many books had to be rewritten from memory, thanks to the thoroughness of the Ch'in censors. Other books, unfortunately, had been permanently lost. Moreover, by pursuing a policy of anti-intellectualism, the Ch'in regime made itself an avowed enemy of the country's intelligentsia who as community leaders commanded great respect and following among local population. The policy of thought control, designed to strengthen the regime, was actually to backfire against the regime itself. Later when revolts flamed and spread far and wide, the intellectuals swarmed to the standard of the rebels and speeded up the downfall of the Ch'in dynasty; and ever since few historians have had much good to say about China's first totalitarian regime.

To be sure, not all of Ch'in's policies were as nonconstructive and useless as thought control. During the period of Warring States, each state had its own legal and economic system. Law codes, weights and measures, and even scripts for writing were altogether different from one state to another. Differences in weights and measures hampered the movement of trade; variance in statutes caused confusion in law enforcement. After the country had been unified, the Ch'in regime ordered the standardization of weights and measures as promulgated by the imperial government. State laws prior to the unification were declared invalid, and a new code was formulated based upon the old Ch'in statutes. The new code followed the Legalist emphasis on reward and punishment, and it covered everyday life so thoroughly that it was said to have served the purpose of "a fishing net through which even the smallest fish cannot slip out." From hindsight the most beneficial of Ch'in's reforms was perhaps the standardization of writing script. The existence of various forms of scripts prior to the unification was not only a source of confusion and misunderstanding but also made the learning process an extremely difficult one. In 221 B.C. the government proclaimed that from then on Ch'in's Small Script was to be the standard for all writing and that the use of other scripts would be punishable by law. While this measure no doubt facilitated communication within the empire, the government also was able thereby to erase the last excuse for misunderstanding and misinterpreting the law, since all statutes were to be written in the same script. In its eagerness for standardization, the government even decreed that all vehicles were to be equipped with standard axle lengths. We have no way of knowing how successful this was, since no extant materials have shed any light on this matter.

Ch'in's other achievements were equally remarkable. Its military might enabled it to defend China successfully against the northern nomads and to keep its northern frontier peaceful and secure throughout its existence. The Great Wall, built by Shih Huang-ti as a defense measure, stands today as a witness to the vigorousness with which Ch'in conducted its foreign policy. In the south the Chinese frontier was extended steadily southward until it reached the South China Sea. Moreover, it was for the first time that China was truly unified, feudalism abolished, and a central government with authority over all China established, thus ending centuries of interstate strife and warfare. Roads and bridges were built to facilitate the movement of merchants and soldiers; coinage was made uniform; and commerce and industry were also encouraged. Public works were carried out on a large scale: today the Chengtu irrigation works in Szechuan province bear ample witness to the ingenuity of Ch'in engineers. All these were truly remarkable in view of the brief existence of the Ch'in regime after it had unified China.

Needless to say, tremendous sacrifices had been exacted from the people for these achievements. Taxes of various forms were many times higher than before, and corvée was the most intolerable of all exactions. Though corvée had been an old practice prior to Ch'in, conscripted workers were mostly used locally to repair bridges, build roads, and to do whatever local needs necessitated. The number of conscripted workers was generally small and their working period short, usually in winter after harvest when farmers had more time to spare. The Ch'in regime, however, changed the entire picture. Thousands of miles of roads had to be built in addition to thè construction of the Great Wall. Farmers were conscripted from all parts of the country and were often sent hundreds of miles away to work on public projects. To be more exact, it was said that a regular force of 300,000 worker-soldiers were maintained along the northern frontier to guard against the nomads; 500,000 were sent to the deep south to open up virgin fields; and the construction of the Afang Palace alone engaged some 700,000 coolies. Farmers were taken away from their home whenever the government thought it needed them, whether summer or winter. The working period was indefinite; many of the conscripted workers did not expect to return and never did. The Ch'in regime showed its ugliest face in the abuse of corvée which turned out to be the immediate cause of its downfall.

In 209 B.C. two obscure farmers, Ch'en Sheng and Wu Kuang, were ordered to report for work at Yüyang, many miles away from their home. There was a heavy storm; the roads were destroyed by the flood; and they knew that they could not possibly arrive in time. According to Ch'in law, the penalty for late arrival in corvée assignment was death. Choosing between certain death and rebellion to stay alive, they did not hesitate. They persuaded their fellow conscripts to do the same and started a revolt which spread like wildfire. In 207 B.C. the Second Emperor, son and successor to Shih Huang-ti, died at the hands of a group of conspirators. Shortly afterwards the capital, Hsienyang, was stormed by bands of rebels, the Afang Palace was burned to the ground, and the empire collapsed.

FEUDALISM BRIEFLY REVIVED

After a short period of peace, China was again plunged into civil war. Local dissenters who had been under Ch'in's rigid control now saw an opening crack and were eager to exploit it. Soon there was fighting all over China. The rebels not only fought against the Ch'in but among themselves as well. After a few years of warfare two rebels emerged as the leading candidates for the vacated Ch'in throne. Seldom in history have two contenders for one prize been so different in personality. Hsiang Yü was born to an aristocratic family; for generations his family had served with distinction in the state of Ch'u. Possessed of an impressive physique, he was a warrior of the first order, strong, brave, though often reckless. Frank and generous, he could be soft-hearted even to his bitterest enemy, though he could become extremely brutal on occasion. Liu Pang, his opponent, was born of an ordinary farmer whose only achievement in life was to have fathered an illustrious son. In his younger days, Liu Pang was known as a loafer, a man without any trade or skill. Later, however, he did manage to obtain a position as a village chief. Arrogant and mischievous, he nevertheless had a way of making friends and influencing people. Totally unappreciative of intellectual activities, he was not much of a military man either. He was defeated in every battle except the last one which happened to be the most decisive. He won the war and became the first emperor of the Han dynasty, the first commoner ever to reach that lofty position. How did this happen? After the war was won, he answered this question by saying that though he himself was not much of a strategist or general, the best strategists and the ablest generals had been willing to serve under him. "While you generals know how to command soldiers, I know how to command generals," said he happily to his chief lieutenants. Simply stated, he was a superb politician.

The Han dynasty, the first dynasty founded by a commoner, was destined to be one of the longest and greatest in Chinese history. Except for a brief interruption early in the first century A.D. it lasted more than four hundred years. Before the interruption it was called the Former Han or West Han (202 B.C.–8 A.D.); after it, it was called the Later Han or East Han (25–220 A.D.). The interruption was caused by Wang Mang whose Hsin dynasty lasted only fifteen years (8–23 A.D.).[1]

Having been convinced that Ch'in's quick collapse was largely due to the absence of support from members of the royal family during the time of distress, Liu Pang decided to revive feudalism, hoping that the newly created dukes and counts selected from his closest relatives would rally to the support of the royal house whenever it was threatened by outside intruders. To safeguard the royal house, he took steps to eliminate those who he thought were most likely to challenge the position of the crown. He sent to death some of his ablest lieutenants on charges of treason; many others chose voluntary exile and obscurity so as to escape the wrath of the new emperor. Favored by many sons, he granted them the titles of dukes and counts and placed them in the most strategic and richest areas in China. These duchies and counties were autonomous regions that appointed their own officials, levied taxes for their own support, and maintained independent armies. However, they were under the over-all supervision of the imperial government. If the imperial government so chose, it could call upon a feudal lord to explain a policy it regarded as unorthodox or unusual. In exceptional cases the lords could be summoned to appear in person at the capital, Ch'angan (Map 12). Failure to appear if called could be considered as an overt act of treason. After a lord had

[1] Though Han is the name of a dynasty, it also means the Han government or China during the Han dynasty. This is a Chinese usage which is followed throughout this book. Thus, a Sung philosopher means a philosopher who lived during the Sung dynasty, or, in rare cases, a philosopher who followed a school of thought most popular during the Sung dynasty. A chronological chart of Chinese dynasties appears at the end of this book.

appeared in the capital and if the emperor considered him unfaithful or disloyal, he could order his detention and might punish him according to his offense. Secret dealings among the lords were strictly forbidden to prevent conspiracies against the crown. If the emperor was at any time threatened by foreign invasion or domestic revolt, all lords were required by law to provide troops and supplies to come to his rescue. As long as a lord was loyal and met his feudal obligations, the imperial government would not interfere with his domestic affairs.

The revival of feudalism, however, proved to be only temporary. By the time of Emperor Han Wen-ti (179–157 B.C.) some lords had already become too strong for imperial comfort. Chia Yi (201–168 B.C.), then a young and precocious scholar, suggested to the emperor in a memorial that the larger duchies should be broken up to create small ones, on the ground that feudal lords with smaller territories would pose a less effective challenge to the imperial position. But the suggestion was ignored. When Emperor Han Ching-ti (156–141 B.C.) took this suggestion seriously, it immediately provoked a revolt as had been generally expected. Thanks to its able generals, the imperial government quickly crushed the revolt, thus ending the so-called Seven States' Rebellion (154 B.C.). After this, feudalism underwent a complete change. Powerful lords were ordered to divide their domains among their offspring, and as territories became smaller, the power and influence of their successors were considerably reduced. Whenever possible the crown replaced feudal with central administration. With the lapse of time, areas of central administration continued to expand at the expense of feudal domains, and appointed governors, instead of feudal lords, became the real local authority. Having been deprived of their political power, the lords' sole privilege as men of rank consisted of "deriving a livelihood from their land estates."

However, it was Emperor Han Wu-ti (140–87 B.C.) who dealt the final blow to Han feudalism. He decreed that feudal rank ceased automatically for those who passed away without legitimate heirs and, in such cases, their fiefs were to be returned to the imperial government. Those who allegedly committed "offenses" against the crown also lost their feudal titles and fiefs. Some of the so-called offenses were specious enough. According to a Han custom, each year in the month of the eighth moon the emperor conducted the grand ceremony of offering sacrifices to Heaven, and the nobles by tradition were required to make contributions, usually in gold. By the pretext that the gold contributed was either impure or underweight, many nobles were found to have committed offenses and were penalized by having their feudal titles taken away. In the year 112 B.C. alone, for instance, the government penalized 160 nobles this way. Once deprived of his title, a noble became a *shu-min* or commoner, and he lost his feudal rights and privileges. After Han Wu-ti feudalism was abolished *de facto,* if not *de jure.*

MILITARY CONQUESTS

Dynamic and full of vitality throughout his life, Han Wu-ti has been described by historians as a man who "loved greatness and enjoyed military deeds." In this respect he was not unlike Ch'in Shih Huang-ti. His long reign of fifty-three years marked the apex of Han power. Domestically, he introduced many innovations destined to affect Chinese society for centuries to come. In foreign affairs he was particularly noted for his daring and aggressiveness. While the country was at peace, he started a series of military campaigns aimed at the destruction of the military strength of the northern nomads. He conquered Korea in the northeast and pushed the Chinese frontier to the border of Tibet in the southwest.

Of the northern nomads the most formidable were the Hsiung-nu, a Mongolian tribe. The Hsiung-nu were a simple yet warlike people. As nomads, they were constantly on the move, always seeking new pastures for their herds and flocks. They carried their tents with them; where their tents were, there they were at home. They counted animals as their wealth, mostly cattle and sheep, but also horses and camels. Whenever travelling, they rode on horses, while camels carried their heavy belongings. Meat was their food, milk their drink; animal skins were processed to make clothes. A man's status in society depended upon his youth, courage, and ability as a warrior; the aged and the weak were despised. Horsemanship and archery were the required training as soon as a child learned how to walk; the Hsiung-nu's expertness in these skills was legendary. Being nomads, they had no settled towns worth mentioning. Whenever they needed things which they could not produce, they obtained them by trading with the Chinese who had always valued highly the Mongolian horses. There were no elaborate government organizations; the so-called law was largely custom and tradition together with orders issued by tribal chiefs.

For centuries the Mongolian nomads posed a constant threat to the agricultural Chinese to the south; the economic abundance in China proper had always been an irresistible temptation. If an able leader emerged who could unify the nomadic tribes and if at the same time China happened to be militarily weak, an invasion was sure to come. With great mobility the nomads could retreat as fast as they could strike. They chose the weakest point to attack; but upon encountering a stronger Chinese force, they disappeared as fast as they had appeared. During the Ch'in dynasty the best the Chinese could do was to push them back to their steppe home and then erect the Great Wall to discourage future incursions. As civil war was renewed after the collapse of the Ch'in regime, the Hsiung-nu again became strong; sometimes they penetrated as far as the modern

MAP 12

THE HSIUNG-NU EMPIRE

Original Home

Under King Mao-tun 210-174 B.C.

Around 100 B.C.

Scale of Miles

0   400   800   1200

Shansi province. In his efforts to repulse them, Liu Pang himself was once besieged at an isolated city in northern Shansi and was almost captured. Two years after this incident, with the security of his northern frontier in mind, the founder of the Han dynasty found it necessary to appease the nomads by marrying one of his princesses to the Hsiung-nu chief, sending him silk, wine, and rice as gifts, and calling him "brother." After Liu Pang's death, the invasions were renewed with eagerness; the nomads attacked wherever the defense was the weakest, looted, and then disappeared. With Han Wu-ti on the throne, the Han government concluded that the best way of stopping these incursions and invasions was a large-scale counter-offensive, seeking the enemy's main forces and destroying them. In 127 B.C. a major expedition was sent northward; as a result, most of the modern Inner Mongolia was brought under the Han control. Again in 121 B.C. an even larger force was organized under the famous general Huo Ch'ü-ping who defeated the Hsiung-nu repeatedly, cleared Outer Mongolia of their forces, and reached as far as Lake Baikal. After this military feat, the western tribes of the Hsiung-nu surrendered themselves to the Han authority. In their place the Han created four administrative provinces along the present Hohsi Corridor of Kansu province. One conquest led to another, and before the century was over, Han extended its jurisdiction not only to the Tarim basin but to part of what is today known as Russian Turkestan as well.

In the long run, however, these impressive victories only provided a temporary relief. This process of attacks and counterattacks was to be repeated throughout the Han dynasty. While the Chinese might be able to defeat the nomads on the battlefield, they were unable to maintain a sustained occupation of the steppe and desert territory. As an agricultural people, they could only make permanent settlement in areas where soil, rainfall, and other geographical conditions made agriculture productive. If relocated in a desert, their hoes and plows taken away, they ceased to be Chinese. For centuries they had been able to expand steadily to South China where agriculture was rewarding. This expansion made South China invariably Chinese. On the other hand, they were totally unable to expand further beyond the Great Wall. This salient fact made the grassland belt between the desert north and the agrarian south a zone of contention between the nomads and the Chinese. Instead of attempting the impossible task of occupying the desert, the Han emperors tried the next best thing and what was then regarded as the more feasible. This called for the conversion of the grassland belt into farm land which could be divided among the frontier soldiers for their own support. Were this successful, not only would a defensive army be readily available when attacked, but the government would be also saved from the great expenses of maintaining such an army. Though this program was more than once put into practice, it was not as successful as had been

Yellow
Sea

South
China
Sea

YELLOW RIVER

YELLOW RIVER

☐ Ch'angan

YANGTZE RIVER

SI RIVER

HSIUNG-NU

Lake Balkhash

WU-SUN

Bay of
Bengal

ARAL SEA

SOGDIANA (KANG-CHIH)

FERGHANA (TA-YÜAN)

KUSHAN
(YÜEH-CHIH)

Arabian
Sea

MAP 13

THE HAN EMPIRE
Circa 100 B.C.

☐ Capital
——→ Chang Chien's Routes to
the "Western Regions"

0   400   800   1200

Scale of Miles

hoped. For one thing, rainfall was too little and too unreliable to sustain agriculture on a permanent basis. Furthermore, the program required irrigation projects on a large scale which, even when they were started, were often neglected during the time of war.

A by-product of the Hsiung-nu campaign was the Han government's exploration of the west. Seeking allies for a joint offensive against the Hsiung-nu, Han Wu-ti sent Chang Ch'ien to Central Asia to explore such possibilities. The emissary's first trip ended in failure, as he was detained by hostile tribes for more than thirteen years. His second trip, however, culminated in an alliance with the Wu-sun, a nomadic tribe living in the Ili valley (modern Sinkiang). Through diplomacy, threats, and outright coercion, he was able to win most of the states in Central Asia as Han's allies. The allies, attacking from the west, helped Han to defeat the Hsiung-nu in the north. The economic significance of Chang Ch'ien's trips was even greater. As a result of these trips, an overland route was opened for trade and commerce. As long as Han's authority was maintained and peace secured, trade flourished and was beneficial to all nationals. The Chinese valued highly the thoroughbreds of Central Asia; the nomads were equally anxious to obtain Chinese silk, tea, and handicrafts. Some of the Chinese products found their way as far as Rome; Chinese silk, for instance, was a prized article among the Roman ladies.

Contrary to its subjection of the nomadic tribes in the north and the northwest, Han's conquests of other areas had a more permanent result. In the northeast the Koreans had been influenced by Chinese culture from time immemorial. During periods of civil wars which frequently occurred, many Chinese went to Korea to seek refuge, and attracted by the abundance of farm land, settled down as permanent residents. Early in the Han dynasty, due to the chaotic conditions along the border, the number of immigrants became even larger. Frictions between Han and Korean authorities flared up from time to time and often led to the clash of arms. In 109 B.C. Han Wu-ti sent two expeditionary forces, one across the sea from the modern Shantung province and the other overland through southern Manchuria for the conquest of Korea. The Korean army was defeated, and its king was killed. The country was then annexed to create four administrative provinces in 108 B.C.

But in what is now Southwest China, Han's conquest proved to be more difficult. The area was larger, mountainous, and almost inaccessible. Many tribes in various stages of culture inhabited this area; some organized themselves as independent kingdoms. Though agriculture was their main occupation, the tribesmen were skillful in making handicraft products, some of which found a ready market in China proper. While all they desired was to be left as they were, Han Wu-ti decided to bring them under Chinese jurisdiction. After several years of intermittent warfare, the entire region was pacified by 109 B.C. New administrative units were created, which were the forerunners of modern Yunnan and Kweichow provinces.

Territorial expansion on this scale had to come from internal strength. When Han Wu-ti came to the throne, the country had experienced an unprecedented prosperity for many decades. The conservative policy of Emperors Wen-ti and Ching-ti "to rest with the people" had achieved its desired result. According to historian Ssu-ma Ch'ien, a contemporary of Han Wu-ti, "Imperial granaries were filled to capacity with grain. There was so much of it that it overflowed its containers, rotted, and was inedible. The imperial treasury had an abundance of money in reserve. It was so abundant that a large number of coins had not been in circulation for a long time. Consequently the strings used to hold them together were often found broken and it became extremely difficult to count them." By the end of Han Wu-ti's reign, the picture completely changed. A half century of wars and expansions had imposed a tremendous burden on the nation's economy. The government's treasury was now empty; taxes had been so heavy that even diligent people could not make both ends meet. The price paid in terms of lives lost and social disorganization had been immeasurable. Even Han Wu-ti's admirers wondered whether the gains resulting from the building of a great empire were not more than offset by the tremendous social and economic losses.

Under the government's stringent economic control, business men suffered with the rest of the nation. In a previous chapter we have traced the rise of the merchant class, as feudalism declined after the eighth century B.C. The Ch'in regime, long before it unified China, had adopted a pro-business policy; it abolished feudal land tenure, encouraged private entrepreneurs to open up natural resources, and rewarded successful business men with ranks and titles. The momentum of business growth was carried over to the Han dynasty. Early Han emperors, believing that business men had become too strong, reversed the Ch'in policy and started to persecute them. Liu Pang, for instance, subjected them to social humiliations, such as forbidding them to ride in vehicles and wear silk clothes, besides increasing taxes on their income. Decrees were also issued barring them from taking part in politics and becoming government officials, though the rigidity of their application was relaxed shortly afterwards. These political and social discriminations, however, did not have much effect on economic growth, as the business group continued to enhance its power and influence. Early in the reign of Han Wu-ti, industrial and mercantile families amassed great fortunes by engaging in their specialized businesses. One of the most profitable was the iron-mining and smelting business, as the demand for iron products continued to grow in the countryside where farmers used iron to make farm implements. There were also financiers such as the Wu-yen family which made a reputation for itself by lending money at high interest to the often bankrupt members of the royal house. Others made money by operating ranches; Pu Shih, for instance, accumulated a great fortune through sheep raising, contributed his gains to the royal cause, and was rewarded with the position of chief censor in the imperial court. Sang Hung-yang, another self-made business man, rose to become the finance minister under Han Wu-ti. Even businesses of a dubious nature, such as gambling and grave-robbing, were large operations. Since profits were also large, more and more people abandoned their regular occupations to participate in trade. Ch'ao Ts'o, a statesman and scholar of the second century B.C., once remarked: "The law honors farmers, yet farmers have become poorer and poorer; the law degrades merchants, yet merchants have become richer and richer." Even law could not stop the momentum of economic forces.

As the reign of Han Wu-ti progressed, the situation began to change. To raise funds for foreign wars necessitated higher taxation. Many new taxes were introduced, most of which were aimed at business men. Among the newly introduced taxes, the property tax turned out to be the most damaging. At the beginning it seemed harmless enough. A decree issued by the imperial government required the periodical report of business assets; the property tax was assessed on the reported assets. The tax rate was not high; nobody showed great alarm about it. However, as financial needs mounted due to the continuance of foreign wars, the government took full advantage of this decree to squeeze out whatever it could from the business group. The crucial provision of this decree was that "those who fail to report or make false reports will be exiled to the frontier for one year and their property confiscated, with half of the confiscated property awarded to the informer." Greed, jealousy, and rivalry sent the unscrupulous to inform on one another. Sometimes A informed on B, simply because B had informed on A. A nation-wide hysteria ensued; even the best families were involved. The government stood by and was not altogether unhappy about the outcome. All those with a more than average income became the targets of informers; once accused and brought to trial, seldom did they come out without losing all they had. After the dust had finally settled, practically all wealthy and well-to-do merchants became bankrupt. The government confiscated and acquired large quantities of movable and immovable assets, including land and hundreds of thousands of slaves. Throughout the Former Han dynasty, business men never recovered from this terrible blow.

In addition to his various ways of raising revenue, Han Wu-ti made two basic industries, salt and iron, government monopolies in 119 B.C.

Among the reasons advanced for the monopolization were, first, to discourage the so-called non-essential occupations such as manufacturing and trade, and to encourage what the government regarded as the essential occupation, namely, farming; and second, to prevent monopolistic control from developing among private business. The ostensible purpose was to reduce prices so as to benefit consumers. After the government monopoly had been established, it was found convenient to retain former owners as managers, as government officials knew little about running this kind of business. The government monopoly, however, was much less a success than had been hoped. There was much waste and inefficiency in government-operated businesses. Prices, instead of becoming lower, rose. Even the quality of products deteriorated. Under such conditions many business men chose to defy government orders and produce salt and iron in private, despite heavy penalties if they were caught. The farmers whom the monopoly was supposed to benefit often refused to purchase government products and preferred the better quality though illicit products of private business. Since a boycott would certainly affect public income, the government introduced a quota system, forcing consumers to buy its products at regular intervals of time. This naturally caused resentment and distress on the part of the farmers.

In spite of stringent measures aimed at raising revenue, still the government was unable to meet the mounting expenses. Other methods had to be devised. On the one hand, it started to sell offices, instead of merely ranks and titles that had been occasionally offered for sale in the past. On the other hand, it debased currency to create more and cheaper money. In 119 B.C. the standard coin was debased, with a metal content of only 60 per cent of its face value. In a more shameless case, square pieces of white deer skin, with trappings along their edges, were declared worth 400,000 standard coins each, though they were not convertible into cash. As prices soared, many people found their savings wiped out overnight. Despite heavy penalties, counterfeiting was widespread; the counterfeiters and the government flooded the market with cheap money, chasing good money out of circulation and thus aggravating the already grave situation. As money became more and more useless, prices became higher and higher. Many people simply refused to accept government-issued currency and resorted to barter trade instead.

EDUCATION AND LEARNING

While there is much to criticize about Han's economic policy, its encouragement of learning has been universally acclaimed. In this respect it was fortunate that the Ch'in regime lasted only for a short period. Though Liu Pang was too busy consolidating his new empire to pay

PAINTED SHELL The hunting scene on this shell was painted in red and black during the period of either East Chou (770–249 B.C.) or Former Han (202 B.C.–9 A.D.). There are no words on it; the painter is unknown.

much attention to cultural activities, his son Han Hui-ti (194–188 B.C.) formally abolished the long out-dated Ch'in law which prohibited the ownership and traffic of forbidden books. As learning gained more prestige, great emphasis was laid on education. A central university was founded in the capital Ch'angan and local schools were established all over China. Entrance to the central university was strict and competitive. Students were chosen among youths who were high in native intelligence and had shown an eagerness to learn. Curriculum consisted mostly of Confucian classics, though individual students might become advanced enough to learn other subjects, such as government and law. The professors (*po-shih*) were selected from the best scholars in the nation, who allegedly "know all about the past and the present"; most of them, however, were authorities on Confucian classics. To enroll in the university, a prospective student must be first recommended by his local magistrate. He must be a young man at least eighteen years of age, good in appearance, dutiful towards his parents, and sound in character, besides having good native intelligence and a propensity to learn. The number of students varied. When the university began during Han Wu-ti's reign, there were only fifty students; but enrollment kept on increasing until at the end of the Former Han dynasty the number reached more than three thousand. Besides doing research and teaching students, the professors had additional functions. They could be called by the government to deliberate and advise on foreign and domestic issues; and as learned men, they were often consulted on rituals and ceremonies for important occasions. Sometimes they were appointed by the emperor as his roving envoys, visiting provinces and reporting on local conditions. Being men of indisputable integrity, they were counted on by the emperor to make impartial and objective evaluations. Encouraged from above, local officials established their own schools and took great pride in them. Provincial governors enjoyed great prestige if they were actively interested in the promotion of education and learning. Theoretically, these schools were open to all; actually, only the comparatively well-to-do could take advantage of the opportunity.

Though Han's encouragement of learning deserved much praise, Han differed greatly from earlier regimes in its attitudes towards different schools of philosophy. Prior to the Ch'in dynasty, many schools of thought contended and thrived, though at one time or another one school of thought might be more popular than others. Learning was free and unconventionalized, as the governments of various states did not intervene on behalf of one philosophy or another. After Ch'in unified China, the government elevated Legalism as the official cult and banned all others. Early in the Han dynasty, Taoism was the most popular, since it was the philosophy most favored and patronized by the royal house. During the reign of Han Wu-ti, at the suggestion of the Confucian scholar Tung Chung-shu, the government proclaimed Confucianism as the state cult. This was a step of monumental importance, because from that time on Confucianism was the official philosophy for more than two thousand years. However, other schools of thought were allowed to compete with Confucianism, though they were not officially encouraged. The Han government promoted Confucian learning by creating professorships of Confucian classics and by providing employment for students who had done particularly well in this field. As time went on, proficiency in Confucian philosophy became a prerequisite to administrative appointment. Influenced from above, the people followed the trend with eagerness. Not only were there experts on each Confucian classic; different schools developed for its interpretation. A great master might have a new interpretation which was handed down and further developed during later generations, thus forming a new, independent school. Within the Confucian framework, all these schools contended side by side.

Under this atmosphere great academicians emerged from time to time. None, however, showed more originality and exercised greater influence than Tung Chung-shu. An authority on the *Spring and Autumn Annals,* he built his philosophical theme on the dual existence of nature (literally Heaven) and man and the necessity of maintaining a harmonious equilibrium between them. As nature was always perfect, man's duty was to accommodate and adjust himself to it, so the desired harmony could be achieved. This was true not only for maintaining one's internal peace, but for the creation of an orderly, peaceful society as well. However, nature was not stationary; it changed constantly. As change was essential to nature's functions, all human devices, society included, should be changed from time to time, so the harmony between nature and man could always be preserved. Applying this theory to government and politics, Tung Chung-shu further observed that no regime should and could stay in power forever. As summer came on the heel of spring, a new regime was bound to replace the old one, whenever the right time arrived. Before an old regime was replaced, there were unmistakable signs indicating its coming end, such as flood, drought, famine, and epidemics, the same as twilight signified the rising sun and falling leaves marked the coming of winter. When natural calamities repeatedly occurred, it was clear that the old regime had lost the mandate of Heaven. Then the reigning monarch, facing the inevitable, should elect the wisest and most virtuous man to replace him, so to make the change of dynasties a peaceful transformation. Failure to do so would provoke revolt which, in this case, was clearly justified. In the end the old regime would be overthrown and replaced by a new dynasty, which in turn had to pass through the same process. The theory of the mandate of Heaven, in its many modified forms, was accepted and believed by practically all Confucian scholars. For many centuries to come, it would impose moderation on all monarchs whose extremely tyrannical acts could be interpreted as the withdrawal of the mandate of Heaven, thereby giving their subjects the right to revolt. Whenever a serious revolt took place, it was a matter of heated debate whether the symptoms were such that the existing regime had lost Heaven's favor. As expected, the rebels argued for the affirmative answer, while the supporters of the existing regime were just as sure that it was not so. The issue had to be decided on the battlefield; whoever won the war usually won the argument.

In the spirit of the Confucian adage that "only the most learned serve," education and learning were closely linked with the pursuance of a governmental career. In the early years of the Han dynasty top-ranking officials were usually military leaders who had helped Liu Pang in winning the war and unifying the country. As peace prevailed, more civilians were appointed to higher positions. Ability was the criterion; it mattered not whether the prospective official was a military man, a merchant, or a scholar. However, with the lapse of time education and learning were more emphasized and scholars were generally preferred for government employment. In the time of Han Wu-ti, even some military leaders were polished men of letters, such as Su Wu and Li Ling, the two famous yet tragic commanders who once headed a disastrous expedition against the Hsiung-nu forces. In seeking government positions, not only the knowledge of classics and law was universally required; sometimes the prospective employee had to show proficiency in a specialized field such as history, astronomy, mathematics, music, languages, medicine, or even alchemy. Once a candidate was accepted, appointment would be made according to his specialization. Local magistrates had the duty of reporting to the imperial government any special talents within their jurisdictions. When necessity arose, the imperial government held special examinations under the emperor's personal supervision. One of these examinations held in 134 B.C. produced two famous men, Tung Chung-shu and Kung-sun Hung, both of whom rose to become high-ranking officials later in their careers. Students in the central university were examined yearly. Successful completion of their studies entitled them to administrative appointment.

As men of letters, Han scholars developed a new style of prose writing which was noted for its clarity, conciseness, and vigor. They wrote on a variety of subjects, with philosophy and political issues as their most favored topics. The essays of great masters like Chia Yi, Ch'ao Ts'o, and Tung Chung-shu have been required reading in Chinese schools for more than two thousand years, not so much for their content as for the beauty of their expression. However, in terms of versatility, none exceeded the historian Ssu-ma Ch'ien whose *Historical Records* (*Shih chi*) is not only a primary source of historical information, but a masterpiece of literature as well. The book is divided into sections of biographies, treatises, and chronological charts, with comments by the author whenever necessity required. Such division created a precedent for later historians to follow. The book covers a long span of time from the very beginning of China to the reign of Han Wu-ti, with more reliable and more detailed information on the later periods. Part of this monumental work was written by the author's father, Ssu-ma T'an, though we do not know which part it was. For the expression of emotion and sentiments, poetry was generally preferred. Han poets were the first to use extensively the five-character form. Each line consisted of five characters and the last character of every first, second, and fourth lines rhymed. Most of the verses deal with the eternal topic of man's unhappiness, such as the departure of the beloved and loneliness. A typical example and also one of the best written is the *Nineteen Old Poems*, written by an anonymous author or authors. *Fu*, a generally lengthy and more adorned form of poetry, was also popular with Han writers. Ssu-ma Hsiang-ju (179–117 B.C.) and Yang Hsiung (53–18 B.C.) were two of the most famous *fu* writers.

WANG MANG AND HIS REFORMS

Between the third and the first century B.C. autocracy was firmly established in China, with all its merits and demerits. A successful autocracy relied on the performance of a successful autocrat. Unfortunately, the concentration of power in the hands of one person only too often led to its abuse. If an autocrat was wise, intelligent, and capable, he raised the country's prestige and brought peace and prosperity at home. If he was not, he plunged the country into chaos and misery. As the blue blood was not always the best blood, sooner or later mediocre autocrats were bound to appear under monarchy's hereditary rule. In such case, either power was badly abused, or it fell into the hands of those who could control the monarchs. After Han Wu-ti, a succession of mediocre monarchs succeeded to the Han throne. While they indulged in horses, women, and other dissipations, their maternal and conjugal relatives fought for the control of the state. The fate of one emperor was so pathetic that after his death he was officially titled Ai-ti, or Emperor Sadness (6 B.C.–2 A.D.). The deterioration continued until the reins of government were finally taken over by Wang Mang, a relative of one of the empresses.

The Wang family, by supplying the reigning monarchs with empresses, was the dominating power toward the end of the Former Han dynasty. While the female members of the Wang family controlled the royal weaklings, its male members occupied the highest positions in the imperial government. According to the standard of those days, they were not altogether bad ministers: they served the government as well as their family interest to the best of their abilities. Wang Mang, the last member of the Wang family to achieve great power, was particularly reputed for his proficiency in Confucian learning, modesty, and hard work. He had built his reputation so well that once when he was forced into temporary retirement by his political enemies, hundreds of Confucian scholars petitioned for his reinstatement. On another occasion after he had refused to accept a high honor out of professed modesty, a petition of half a million signatures urged his acceptance. As he became more popular, his power and influence increased proportionately. In 6 A.D. Baby Emperor Ying, aged two, ascended to the throne, and Wang Mang was appointed as the regent, with the title of Acting Emperor. Many Confucians openly opined that the Han dynasty had lost its mandate of Heaven and that Wang Mang was the new sage destined to found a new dynasty. In 8 A.D. Wang Mang took the advice; Hsin was the title of the new dynasty.

When Wang Mang made himself emperor, his prestige had never been higher. Yet in a short period of fourteen years his regime collapsed and he himself was killed. If he had had merely his throne in mind, his dynasty might have been a long one. Instead he decided to solve many social and economic problems in a drastic manner and, in doing so, aroused the anger of many powerful elements in the country. His efforts failed and he earned the unflattering appellation "The Usurper."

In order to appraise Wang Mang's reforms, we have to know what the problems were. In an agricultural society like China, land was the major wealth, and landowners were the most powerful section of the population. Farming was acclaimed as an essential occupation, while others, like trade and industry, were regarded as secondary and were sometimes denounced as nonproductive or even exploitive. Since the amount of land was limited under the system of private ownership, some landowners were bound to expand at the expense of others. Small, independent farmers could not compete successfully with great landlords who could easily force them out of their holdings by more efficient cultivation and by exercising political and economic pressures. This state of affairs was further accentuated by the fact that official policy was often in line with the aspiration of the great landlords, as the policy-making officials came mostly from this class. Peasants could not afford to give their children an education which would lead them to a governmental career. During the Ch'in regime the government encouraged the enclosure of small farms to promote efficiency and urged great landlords to open up new fields for cultivation. The process of land concentration continued with the coming of the Han dynasty. Land-grabbing, legal or otherwise, had become a common practice; government officials were just as anxious to join the game. As the rich became richer, independent farmers were hard put to retain their small holdings. Taxes were high; requisitions were numerous. Often in debt, sometimes they had to sell their crops immediately after the harvest when prices were low. Then in the spring they had to borrow money at high interest to start the sowing season and thus incurred an even larger debt. This vicious circle continued until the day when they might have to sell their land. Once they became tenant farmers, they paid about one half of their produce to the landlord as rent and kept the rest to pay taxes and to support their families. Needless to say, they were worse off than they had been before.

As had been the case during the previous dynasties, the most unfortunate of the landless wound up as slaves. There were two kinds of slaves: public slaves owned by the government and private slaves owned by individuals. Public slaves were either convicts condemned into slavery or private slaves confiscated by the government after their owners had been convicted of crimes. Since slaves were regarded as property, they could be bought and sold and could be employed in whatever callings the owners chose, be it farming, trade, industry, or household service. Though no reliable figures are now available, their number seemed to be large. Domestic slaves alone, we are told, constituted about one percent of the total population. We know that in the second century B.C. one family in Szechuan had more than one thousand slaves, and public slaves numbered perhaps hundreds of thousands. How slaves fared varied a great deal; it largely depended upon individual owners and the kind of work in which the slaves were engaged. By the time of the Han dynasty the institution of slavery had been so firmly established that even the most liberal-minded statesmen saw nothing morally wrong with it, and none had ever advocated its abolition.

However, Han statesmen were greatly concerned with the fate of small farmers. To them the sharp contrast between the extremely rich and the very poor was not only an injustice; it also created serious social problems. The very poor, when denied the barest subsistence, were often driven by desperation to lawless activities such as banditry. During Han Wu-ti's reign, Tung Chung-shu once proposed that land holdings be limited to forestall land aggrandizement, but nothing came out of this suggestion. Towards the end of the first century B.C. a more concrete program was formulated whereby the amount of land and the number of slaves owned by each individual was made proportional to his rank and position in the government. But this program was never implemented, as powerful interests connected with the royal family successfully sabotaged it before it could be carried out. Shortly after making himself emperor, Wang Mang, relying on the popularity he enjoyed then, took drastic measures to reverse the trend of many centuries and started a series of reforms.

The ultimate ownership of land, said an imperial edict, belonged to the nation as a whole, and no buying and selling would be allowed. The amount of land allotted for each farmer should be sufficient for the maintenance of a decent livelihood and should be proportionate to the size of his family. A family with a male membership of less than eight and owning land more than one *ch'ing* (c. 15 acres) should distribute the excess amount among his relatives and neighbors. Nor could slaves be bought and sold. Farmers who allowed their land to lie idle and uncultivated should be triply taxed. However, if the loss of employment could not be attributed to personal fault, the local magistrate should see to it that they were clothed and fed. To prevent the exploitation of farmers by merchants, the government stepped in to regulate prices, and for this purpose government agencies were established in all major cities. As long as commodities were sold below the regulated prices, the agencies would not intervene. However, if they were sold above price ceilings, the agencies would investigate and could compel the merchants to sell them to the government at cost, if the merchants were found guilty of violations. Whenever prices were depressed because of over-supply, the agencies would buy commodities at market price and store them in government-operated warehouses. These commodities would be resold in the open market at market or below market price, if prices soared as a result of strong demand. By manipulations like this it was hoped that price fluctuation would be reduced to a minimum and that farmers who often had to sell when price was low and had to buy when price was high would not be taken advantage of by ruthless merchants. To prevent usury the government operated banks to finance small loans. Whenever a man needed money for legitimate purposes such as starting a small business, improving farm estates, and performing funeral and religious services, he could borrow from these banks by paying an annual interest of 10 percent, instead of going to private money lenders who usually charged 20 to 30 percent for their investment. Important enterprises such as the liquor, salt, iron business, and coinage of money were government monopolies upon which the government relied for raising revenue to meet its administrative expenses.

However good the motives were behind these reforms, they never achieved the results that Wang Mang had hoped. For one thing, they were thrust upon the ill-prepared nation without adequate planning. No sound organization was ever established for their implementation, and the officials bungled them from the very beginning. In many localities wealthy merchants were employed as regulation agents, though they were more interested in enriching themselves than serving justice. Whenever a law encountered opposition in its enforcement, the government quickly changed it, instead of giving it adequate time to yield results. As the law was changed often, people had no idea what the law was; this was especially true in remote areas where communication and transportation were more difficult. The outcome was confusion and anarchy. The farmers whom the reforms were supposed to benefit suffered with the rest of the population. When Wang Mang finally realized the futility and called an end to the whole reform program, enough damage had been done and revolt had already begun. Moreover, the powerful landowners had never reconciled themselves to the new regime which proposed to confiscate their land. When the first discontent was heard, they lost no time in exploiting it. Once started, the revolt against Wang Mang soon spread over the entire country. The landlords provided the leadership; the peasants filled up the rank and file. It was this combination which overthrew the shortlived Hsin dynasty.

THE LATER HAN

Amidst the turmoil and confusion the rebels fought among themselves as well as against the government, a situation not unlike that at the end of the Ch'in dynasty. Some of the rebels were descendants of the former royal family of Liu; they carried more prestige and enjoyed a greater following than the others. Now that Wang Mang's reforms had been fully discredited, a new theory began to gain ground: that Wang Mang had unjustifiably usurped the throne and that the Liu family should be restored to its former position. The eventual victor among the Lius who had raised the standard of revolt was Liu Hsiu, a remote descendant of Liu Pang. He successfully exploited the general discontent that resulted from a local famine and collected enough followers to start his revolt in modern Honan province. He was described as a modest and conservative person, with none of the impudence and flamboyance which characterized his more illustrious ancestor Liu Pang. In 25 A.D., after he had brought two-thirds of China under his control, he assumed the title of emperor. Thus the Later Han dynasty began with its capital at Loyang (Map 10). Since Loyang was located east of Ch'angan, the capital of Former Han, the Later Han dynasty is often referred to as East Han.

During the interval of dynastic change when the Chinese were again occupied in fighting among themselves, the barbarians were left unhampered to consolidate and expand at the expense of the Chinese border provinces. The most formidable were still the Hsiung-nu whose marauders raided as far south as the modern Shensi province. Fortunately for the Chinese, they soon split into two hostile groups, the north and the south, as a result of the rivalry of two powerful chiefs who sought the same throne. The northern group was more aggressive and warlike; the southern group, pressed by its northern neighbors, had to seek protection from the Chinese. The Chinese settled them in Inner Mongolia, hoping to erect a bulwark against the more warlike northerners. After peace was finally restored within China itself, the Later Han regime decided to take the offensive. Allied with the southern Hsiung-nu, it twice sent armed expeditions to Outer Mongolia, once in 73 A.D. and again in 88 A.D., and pushed the enemy all the way to the Altai Mountains. The Hsiung-nu forces were so decisively defeated that for more than a century the northern frontier was secure and peaceful. A more spectacular adventure, however, was the exploits of Pan Ch'ao. By sheer daring and ingenuity, he and his small group of select warriors subdued all the hostile tribes in the Northwest. Having brought most areas of Central Asia under control, he sent his lieutenant Kan Ying westward, who then travelled through the desert roads of the Near East for the avowed purpose of getting in touch with Rome. Kan Ying went as far as the Persian Gulf where he was advised not to advance further by native sailors who warned him of the great danger of sailing on the uncharted Arabian Sea. In the southwest Han troops marched as far south as Annam and annexed that country to the Han Empire.

In domestic politics and administration, the Later Han regime had a similar experience as its more illustrious predecessor. In both cases, the first half of the dynasty was characterized by capable and energetic emperors, increased prestige abroad, and general peace and prosperity at home. The second half witnessed the decline of imperial prestige and a succession of weak sovereigns. This situation was particularly acute during the Later Han. Many emperors came to the throne when they were children; their mothers, as a rule, served as regents. While in rare cases a capable empress dowager might actually rule in behalf of her child, most of them relied on their relatives for making important decisions. This situation can be easily visualized in view of the fact that women of those days lived in seclusion and had to depend upon the men they trusted for necessary information before rendering judgment. There were six female regents during the Later Han dynasty; each of them placed her relatives in high government positions. Of course, not all empresses' relatives were power-seeking, influence-peddling oligarchs. Some were statesmanlike and did what they regarded as best for the nation's interest. However, the institution itself was fraught with misfortunes. After the emperor came of age, he found himself surrounded and forcibly advised by his mother's relatives. To keep themselves in power, these relatives had to keep him secluded and isolated. This, of course, caused great resentment, especially if the emperor was a man of pride and strong character.

Denied contact with the outside except through these intermediary relatives, the emperor found no one he could trust except his personal servants whom he relied on for advice and counsel on state as well as personal affairs. These personal servants, called eunuchs, were an ancient institution. They came into wider use as monarchy became more absolute. A reigning monarch always had a harem of concubines; the number sometimes ran to thousands. Since their number was large, many never had an opportunity of meeting their supposed spouse for their entire lives. To prevent scandal, all male servants were castrated before they were employed in the palaces. Without much education, they were just as noted for their ignorance as for their lack of principle and any sense of public responsibility. Yet the young emperor, in his eagerness to assert himself, would have to take them as his allies. The leaders of the eunuchs were consequently appointed to high and responsible posts in order to counterbalance the power of the dowager's relatives. Two factions were thus formed; they soon clashed against each other. With the emperor's blessing the eunuchs often won out and the dowager's relatives were either executed, exiled, or sent to prison. This was especially true if the dowager no longer lived. Having purged their opponents and gained the reins of government, the eunuchs eventually became too powerful even for the emperor who by then had found himself a mere puppet of his nominal servants. They with their followers built their own political machines from the imperial to the local level with no other objective in mind except maintaining themselves in power. This situation continued until a new child emperor came to the throne. The new empress dowager would serve as regent, purge the eunuchs, and elevate her relatives to high positions. And then the whole process would be repeated. Though greatly simplified in its description here, this tragic sucession of events occurred repeatedly during the Later Han dynasty.

Both the eunuchs and the empresses' relatives had a third force to contend with, namely, the scholar-gentry. Since the second century B.C. Confucian teachings had become a universal subject of learning among the country's educated. As only the leisurely rich could devote full time to the many subtle interpretations of the Confucian classics, the educated were largely confined to the landowning class. Consequently a distinct group emerged from the countryside, who because of their learning and wealth assumed local leadership and enjoyed respect and prestige among the masses. As the masses were illiterate and inarticulate, the gentry scholars represented whatever public opinion there was, for they lived among the peasants and were familiar with local conditions. Whenever the government became too oppressive, it was they who stood as a bulwark between the bureaucrats and the masses. Earlier it was this group who rallied behind Liu Hsiu in his successful revolt against Wang Mang and in his administration of the empire during the best years of the Later Han dynasty. As the dynasty progressed in time, their influence with the imperial government became less and less effective. For by then personal relationship with the emperor and his relatives was more an important factor in winning appointment to high positions than personal character, learning, and ability. The decline in influence of the gentry scholars generally coincided with the rise of nepotism, corruption, and incompetence.

Towards the end of the Later Han dynasty, the conflicts between the three groups, especially that between the eunuchs and the scholar-gentry, became more intense. As offices of all levels were by appointment, the party in power invariably placed its followers in important offices throughout the nation. Factional feuds were thus extended to the provinces and were carried on with a bitterness which had seldom been seen before. The eunuchs, with the imperial authority behind them, were often the winners. Their followers took full advantage of their positions to enrich themselves. Wherever they went, they made a mockery of justice. They often resorted to murder to eliminate their political opponents and invoked governmental authority to conduct mass purges. In 156 A.D. and again in 169 A.D., hundreds of gentry scholars were arrested and sentenced to death and others were exiled to the frontier on the ground that "they conspired to organize parties, criticize government policies, and abuse good customs." In 172 A.D. several thousand students at the Central University in Loyang were arrested on similar charges. The misuse of power by the eunuchs finally forced an alliance between the party of the empresses' relatives and the leaders of the gentry scholars. However, with the imperial seal in their hands and occupying important positions in the government, the eunuchs were hard to dislodge. In desperation, Ho Chin, the brother of Empress Dowager Ho, decided to take a step which was as drastic as it was grave. In 189 A.D. he invited a military governor named Tung Cho to send his troops to the capital to help him to eliminate the abusive eunuchs. But the plot was discovered; Ho Chin was murdered in his official residence. However, Tung Cho's troops soon arrived and forced themselves into the palaces. The order of the day was to kill all the beardless; more than two thousands were slaughtered on the spot, including many innocent ones who were not eunuchs but happened to be beardless!

The arrival of Tung Cho ushered in a period of warlordism and civil war. The Later Han regime was considerably weakened. It lingered on for thirty more years and finally came to an end in 220 A.D.

CULTURAL ACTIVITIES

In the cultural field, the emphasis on Confucian learning continued throughout the Later Han dynasty. Liu Hsiu, a former university student, made a habit of discussing Confucian theories with learned scholars even during his military campaigns. Another emperor Han Ming-ti (r. 58–75 A.D.) sometimes took the professor's role and lectured on Confucian subtleties among scholarly academicians. Encouraged and patronized by the government, learning was the fashion of the day. While students during the Former Han dynasty had to travel to the capital for the best kind of instruction, education during the Later Han dynasty became so widespread that great masters could also be found in the provinces. A center of learning was a place where a great master taught; students came from all parts of the country to wherever a learned man located his school. In the capital, facilities in the Central University were continually improved to accommodate more professors and students. At one time early in the first century A.D. it was said that the University had 30 professors, 360 instructors, and 10,800 students. Toward the end of the Later Han dynasty, total enrollment exceeded 30,000. Close to the political scene, the students were activists in politics. Through petitioning and demonstration they advocated what they believed to be the right policy on important issues. Because of their gentry background, often they regarded themselves as the avowed enemies of the eunuchs. Impractical as they were, they were noted for their patriotic fervor and their uncompromising position towards what they regarded as evils.

According to a Confucian adage, a learned man was a gentleman in retirement and an incorruptible official in service. By the Later Han dynasty an institution had been established whereby local magistrates had to make a yearly recommendation of the best talents within their jurisdiction to the imperial government for possible employment as government officials. The number of nominees varied in direct proportion to the size of population within each locality. In making recommendations particular attention was paid to such qualities as filial devotion and personal integrity along with academic learning, qualities presumably only known to local magistrates after years of observation. In other cases, appointments to high offices were made through special invitations, an honor reserved only for the most famous and most outstanding. With the passage of time this emphasis on Confucian virtues was carried to such extremes as to border on ridiculousness. As personal character was the key to social prestige and possible political appointment, many people went to extremes to make a reputation for themselves. While most of them were doubtless sincere, others committed extravagances for the simple purpose of making themselves known. An atmosphere was thus created to outdo one another in the name of good conduct. One man might undertake a mourning of three years after the death of his superior in the government, even though such an extreme form of mourning was generally reserved for one's own parents. Another man, who was told by his dying friend that the only regret he had in his life was that he was unable to take revenge against the man who had killed his father, walked out immediately, killed the offender, and brought the man's head to his friend. Actions like these might not meet our approval today but were considered as noble deeds then. A more comical example was provided by a man who, after the death of his parents, underwent an unusual form of mourning by living inside the tomb of the dead for twenty years. While his reputation as a filial son soared, the magistrate in the end had to punish him, after it was discovered that during these twenty years his wife had borne him five children, an intolerable phenomenon during the period of mourning. Even among the well-known gentry scholars there were those who were inclined to be dogmatic in their beliefs, eccentric and noncooperative in their conduct, and more concerned with their personal reputations than with larger issues such as social welfare. Self-centered and self-righteous, they often let Confucian dogmas blind them to facing social and political reality. Critical of others and yet devoid of constructive ideas of their own, they became easy targets for the eunuchs who murdered hundreds of them under legal pretenses.

Of course, not all gentry scholars were pedantic academicians or self-centered fame seekers. An outstanding example of intellectual excellence was Pan Piao and his son Pan Ku and his daughter Pan Chao. Rarely had there been so many geniuses concentrated in one family. Another son of his, Pan Ch'ao, almost single-handedly brought much of Central Asia under the Han control, as has been mentioned before. Pan Piao began the writing of the *History of the Han* (*Han Shu*) but did not complete it when he died. Pan Ku (32–92 A.D.) continued the work, and after twenty years, finished most of the book. After his death, the reigning emperor Han Ho-ti (r. 89–105 A.D.) ordered his sister Pan Chao to the palace to complete the unfinished work. She was credited with the eight chronological charts and the treatise on astronomy in the completed work. The *History of the Han* (Former Han) was the first dynastic history and set a precedent for the writing of such works for later historians to follow. It was more adorned in style than the *Historical Records* by Ssu-ma Ch'ien. Both books, however, are regarded as two of the greatest works

China has ever produced. Both authors, incidentally, had sad personal lives. Pan Ku was convicted on a trumped-up charge and died in jail. Ssu-ma Ch'ien was punished by castration after he had protested to Han Wu-ti the innocence of his friend Li Ling. After such humiliation, he said that he did not choose to commit suicide because he wished to complete his monumental work. Li Ling, as one recalls, suffered disastrous defeat in a military campaign against the Hsiung-nu, and being completely sur-rounded, he surrendered instead of committing suicide as he would be expected to do. The tragic story of the two of the greatest literary gen-iuses in Chinese history gave ample evidence of the autocratic nature of the Han regime.

Another example of academic excellence was Chang Heng (78–139 A.D.) who was not only a famous *fu* poet but a great scientist as well. He constructed an armillary sphere to locate planets and stars and traced their movements with remarkable accuracy. More impressive, however, was a seismograph he invented. It was described as composed of a bronze cylinder of eight feet in diameter with the central opening "bulging up like a wine cup." Surrounding a central column in the middle of the cylinder were eight sculptured dragons which represented eight different directions. Whenever an earthquake occurred, one of the dragons would eject a small ball which was then received by a carved toad attached at the base. It was said that by using this device an earthquake taking place several hundred miles away could be easily detected and located. Unfor-tunately, we know nothing about the underlying principles upon which he built this remarkable instrument. His fellow scholars, while impressed, did not attach much importance to his invention.

Finally, there was Wang Ch'ung (died about 100 A.D.) who showed great originality in an entirely different field. Skeptical of his fellow schol-ars' efforts in tracing the many subtle meanings of Confucian classics and critical of their so-called virtuous conduct, he doubted whether Confu-cianism was the universal truth. Having dismissed the harmony theory between Heaven and man, he maintained that Heaven was no more than a blind, mechanical force and that there was no observable relationship between the movement of heavenly bodies and human events. Nor was the existence of a spiritual world possible, said he, because its existence was contrary to sound logic and good reasoning. As a healthy society could not be created on false assumptions, a man could not be true to himself if he simply followed the popular, established conventions without using his own reasoning and knowledge to guide himself. Throughout his book, *Critique of Opinions* (*Lun heng*), he tore into pieces what he regarded as false values. Like many Taoist philosophers before him, he called man to return to nature, though his "naturalism" (*tzu-jan*) was not clearly de-fined anywhere in his book. Being vastly different from the orthodox Confucian philosophy, his ideas may be viewed as a belated reaction against the seemingly endless pursuit of Confucian dogmas which had been the prevailing trend after the second century B.C. On the other hand, it may also be regarded as an indictment against many of his fellow gentry scholars whose great concern with Confucian virtues carried them to ridiculous pretensions. Although Wang Ch'ung did not know it, a growing tendency towards Taoist skepticism started with him which was to dominate China's intellectual scene for centuries to come.

iv

Disintegration
and Amalgamation

The massacre of eunuchs in 189 A.D. ushered in a long period of turmoil and wars. Except for the West Tsin regime (265–317) which unified China for a short period, China remained politically disunited until late in the sixth century when unification was again achieved under the Sui dynasty. The four hundred years from the second to the sixth century were not only noted for China's military and political weaknesses, which in turn invited barbarian invasions, but they were also noted as a period of political and social disintegration, mass migrations, and culturally, as the time of the reappraisal of traditional values. On the more constructive side, this period witnessed a continuous process of Sinicization among the non-Chinese and the rise of South China as a political and cultural equal of the North. Ideologically, Taoism gained new adherents among the scholar-gentry class as the strength of Confucianism declined. Buddhism had been introduced earlier and now spread far and wide. It became a strong spiritual force and even challenged the supremacy of Confucianism in the field of morals and ideals. Taoism, Buddhism, and Confucianism remained the main spiritual and ethical forces in China until modern times.

Towards the end of the Later Han dynasty, nominal sovereignty was still vested in the emperors, but actually they were puppets of whichever ministers or governors were in a position to control them. As rumor gained ground that the Han dynasty had lost the mandate of Heaven, rebellions sprang up like bamboo shoots after an early spring shower. Some had noble, well-defined purpose; others were simply organized banditry. Among the rebels the most destructive was a group called Yellow Turbans, a religious sect which claimed the ability to cure bodily ills through the use of charms and incantations. It was sometimes called "the Sect of Five Bushels," because initiation into membership cost five bushels of rice. As Han prestige continued to decline, the Sect began to exploit popular discontent and transformed its religious functions into those of a political conspiracy; it even had some powerful eunuchs as its allies. In 184 A.D. it raised the standard of revolt; its members wore yellow turbans to distinguish themselves from others. Organized first in the modern Hopeh province, the revolt soon spread to other areas, from Manchuria in the north to as far as Fukien province in the south. City after city fell before the looting and marauding rebels. Governors and magistrates fled as fast as they could. If they were captured, they might be conveniently used as sacrifices for the rebels' "Heavenly God." Powerful as they were, the Yellow Turbans had no appealing ideology nor any constructive programs. Their followers soon became disillusioned and the rebellion collapsed as speedily as it had arisen. By 190 A.D. it had already run its course, after devastating eight provinces for six years. Its leaders were either killed or captured, and most of its followers simply disappeared.

To defend themselves against rebels like the Yellow Turbans and to combat wide-spread banditry in the country, provincial governors were authorized by the imperial government to organize their own fighting forces. Sometimes great landlords took the initiative in mustering large followings for similar purposes, with or without authorization from the imperial government. In such cases, the imperial government usually confirmed the *fait accompli*, granting ranks and titles to local leaders in accordance with their military and political strength. As localism increased, the whole country was divided among military governors and local leaders who owed a nominal allegiance to the crown but who were actually independent warlords fighting one another to expand their own territories. One of them, Tung Cho, marched into the capital and liquidated all eunuchs, as has been described in the preceding chapter. With his army stationed near the capital and his opponents eliminated, Tung Cho could do whatever he pleased. He deposed the reigning sovereign and placed on the throne a young prince, Han Hsien-ti, who turned out to be the last emperor of the Han dynasty. After the imperial authority had all but disappeared, military governors lost their last scruples and one after another declared their independence from central control. In 192 A.D. Tung Cho was murdered by one of his own men. Amid the confusion that ensued, the capital Loyang became a looting ground for soldiers and bandits alike, who enjoyed "burning palaces and starving government officials." This situation continued until the arrival of Ts'ao Ts'ao who managed to restore some kind of order in North China.

Of all the warlords of this period, Ts'ao Ts'ao (d. 220 A.D.) was perhaps the ablest and certainly the most colorful. As his father was an adopted son of a eunuch, he had no family prestige to be proud of and had to depend upon his own ingenuity for his drive towards power. He first became nationally known when, as a military governor, he successfully defended his province against the Yellow Turbans who had run wild in other areas. Through a series of conquests and successful manipulations, he became the new strong man and took over the reins of the imperial government as prime minister. With the imperial authority behind him, he defeated and eliminated one warlord after another until he brought North China under his control. However, he was stopped short in his attempt to annex the south and the southwest. In the south the house of Sun Ch'üan had long established itself as the rallying point of the southerners against the more aggressive north. In 208 A.D. Ts'ao Ts'ao marched his victorious army southward with the explicit purpose of eliminating the last block to the unification of China. The ensuing battle was one of the best known in Chinese history, immortalized in the famous novel *The Romance of the Three Kingdoms*. Though the northerners seemed invincible in land warfare, they were not so skillful in handling warships. Sun Ch'üan and his generals out-maneuvered Ts'ao Ts'ao and forced him to fight a river battle at Ch'ihpi along the Yangtze River in the modern Anhwei province. The northerners were decisively defeated and were forced to withdraw, and Ts'ao Ts'ao had to forget about the unification of China for the time being. After the battle, Liu Pei, an ally of Sun Ch'üan, went westward to conquer the modern Szechuan province. In 220 Ts'ao Ts'ao died, and his son Ts'ao Pi succeeded him as prime minister. Ts'ao Pi lost no time in deposing the last Han emperor (Han Hsien-ti), assumed the imperial title, and named his new dynasty Wei. In the following year, Liu Pei also proclaimed himself emperor and named his regime Shu. Soon Sun

Ch'üan did the same and called his state Wu. Thus China entered the period of Three Kingdoms, Wei in the north, Shu in the southwest, and Wu in the southeast. Of the three kingdoms, Wei was by far the strongest. Yet she was unable to conquer the other two as long as the latter cooperated in their defense. A stalemate ensued and lasted about half a century. After the death of Liu Pei and Sun Ch'üan in their respective countries, Shu and Wu underwent a process of deterioration and were no longer able to resist the more powerful north. Meanwhile the house of Ssu-ma, endowed with able and vigorous leaders, replaced the house of Ts'ao as the real ruler of North China. In 263 Wei conquered Shu. Two years later Tsin Wu-ti (d. 290 A.D.), a member of the Ssu-ma family, deposed the last Wei monarch and proclaimed himself emperor. He changed the dynastic title from Wei to Tsin, sometimes referred to as West Tsin. In 280 Tsin conquered Wu, and China was again unified for a brief period.

BARBARIAN INVASIONS

While the Three Kingdoms were fighting for supremacy in China proper, events of great importance developed in the grassland belt below the Gobi Desert. Towards the end of the Former Han, a precedent was established whereby Mongolian tribesmen who had either voluntarily surrendered themselves or sought protection from Han authorities against their enemies, were granted right of residence within the Chinese border provinces and lived side by side with native Chinese. As the number of these tribesmen grew over the years, Han began to fear that in case of an internal upheaval within China proper they might be incited to revolt by ambitious leaders and become military vanguards to invade China proper. Early in the third century Ts'ao Ts'ao divided them into five tribes, resettled them in the northern parts of the modern Shensi and Shansi provinces, and appointed a Chinese official who resided with each tribe to supervise its activities. After the establishment of the West Tsin regime, this policy of settling nomadic tribesmen within Chinese provinces was continued, despite repeated warnings that in case they revolted, the capital Loyang would be within their easy march. While this policy was originally motivated by the desire of winning goodwill from the otherwise hostile tribes and of bringing them under closer supervision by Chinese authorities, it backfired badly when it became evident that succeeding Chinese governments had neither the tact to win their friendship nor the strength to command their respect. To make the situation worse, both Wei and Tsin habitually looked southward in their struggle for the conquest of China proper; they were negligent in their defense against the northern nomads. Moreover, in their dealings with the barbarians, they

MAP 14

THE THREE KINGDOMS

□ *Capital*

0   150   300   450

Scale of Miles

Sea of Japan

Yellow Sea

East China Sea

South China Sea

WEI

WU

SHU

□Loyang

□Chienyeh (Nanking)

□Chengtu

YANGTZE RIVER

SI. RIVER

YELLOW RIVER

had no historical lessons to guide them and to enable them to see the forthcoming danger, for until then no barbarian tribes had ever been able to maintain a permanent occupation of China proper. By the time the danger was recognized, it was already too late.

Of course, the invasions could at least have been postponed if there had been no internecine strife within Tsin itself. Even before he unified China, Tsin Wu-ti had unwisely revived a semi-feudal system by dividing large areas of his kingdom among his close relatives. Most of these newly created dukes and counts lived in the capital, even though their fiefs were outside in the country. No sooner had Tsin Wu-ti died than intrigues and conflicts began to develop. To make the situation worse, his son and successor, Tsin Hui-ti, was one of those royal weaklings who had an intelligence no better than that of a child. Once when he was told that people had no rice to eat because of a bad famine, he allegedly retorted, "Why do they not eat meat instead?" His wife Queen Chia, a strong-willed but stupid woman, took over the reins of government and started to arrest and execute those whom she regarded as her enemies. This precipitated a series of murders, assassinations, and even open wars, with the high rank-ing dukes and counts fighting on one side or another at different times. By 306 A.D. when the strife finally ended, Queen Chia, Tsin Hui-ti, and several dukes had all been murdered in cold blood, not to mention thou-sands of their followers who had been slaughtered in open warfare. As a result, Tsin was greatly weakened and so there was an excellent opportu-nity for the barbarians to march southward.

The designation "barbarians" was given by the Chinese to cover all nomadic tribesmen living in a grand semicircle extending from Tibet in the southwest to Manchuria in the northeast, for a distance of more than 2,500 miles. They were barbarian in the sense that first, contrary to the agricultural Chinese, they were pastoral and nomadic; and second, they lacked many refinements generally characterizing a more advanced, sed-entary society. During the fourth century many barbarian tribes partic-ipated in the invasion of China proper at one time or another. In the north it was the Mongolian and other related tribes that played the lead-ing role; in the west it was the Tibetans who made frequent incursions along the border provinces. In 311 A.D. one of the Hsiung-nu groups, later known as Ch'ien Chao, captured Loyang, sacked the city thor-oughly, murdered more than 30,000 government officials, and carried away the rest, including the reigning monarch and an empress dowager. No sooner was a new sovereign proclaimed on the throne than another Mongolian tribe marched southward and captured him too. Meanwhile all North China fell into the hands of the barbarian invaders. With the capture of the last emperor in 316 A.D. the West Tsin dynasty came to an end. Those who managed to escape migrated southward to establish the East Tsin regime south of the Yangtze River.

In the north political power was in a continuous state of flux. One tribal chief made his claim to an imperial title only to be overthrown and replaced shortly afterwards by another chief of a more powerful tribe. Altogether five major tribes established sixteen kingdoms in a period of less than one hundred years; some of them lasted only a few years. Many of the so-called kings were among the worst of their kind: even the worst Chinese tyrants looked like angels compared to these barbarian chiefs. Together they created a Dark Age of one century for future historians to remember. Caring little for moral scruples, they killed and burned wherever they went; sometimes they did this merely for the fun of doing it. By the middle of the fifth century the modern Shensi, Shansi, and Honan provinces were completely devastated. According to one eyewitness, one could walk miles without seeing one house standing or hearing one dog barking. According to another, for every one hundred households less than one had survived the disaster. These were the same provinces that had been the cradle of Chinese civilization for more than two thousand years. Ch'-angan, once the capital of mighty Han, had about one hundred households left. The whole city of Loyang was described as looking like a gigantic garbage dump. The worst among the barbarian chiefs was unquestionably Shih Hu (literally Shih the Tiger) who ruled North China for a brief period during the first half of the fourth century. Among the many outrageous things he did was the conscription of 260,000 farmers to build his palaces in which he kept an official harem of 30,000 concubines and a nonofficial harem of 20,000 more, temporarily recruited from his subjects' wives and daughters. He found great enjoyment in tortures, such as pulling out people's hair, cutting tongues, and gouging out eyes. Fortunately, his reign lasted barely a decade. Shortly after his death, one of his generals ordered all city gates closed, and murdered all people who were directly or indirectly related to the Shih clan. Few survived this massacre.

SINICIZATION

In time even this primitive savagery could be mollified. First, to maintain a permanent occupation, there was the necessity of restoring order and establishing governmental institutions. Since no institutions of their own were capable of coping with the many problems of an agricultural society, the alien rulers had to rely on their Chinese subjects for advice and counsel. It gradually became clear to them that it was much more profitable to tax than to rob and that killing would certainly reduce the number of taxpayers. Eventually they adopted Chinese institutions, ways of life, and even ideologies, and operated their governments within the Chinese framework which had been refined for many centuries. This process of Sinicization was also carried on on the lower level. Though mass Chinese migrations to the south occurred under the immediate impact of barbarian invasions early in the fourth century, the majority of native inhabitants remained and they lived side by side with the invaders. In such broad contacts the backward were invariably inclined to learn from the more advanced in a variety of fields, from language, philosophy, and literature to custom, habits, and even mores. One manifestation of this voluntary assimilation was the mass adoption of Chinese names which made the Chinese and the aliens eventually undistinguishable after two or three generations. Furthermore, there was no bar to interracial marriages, which became a common occurrence, especially among the upper class. The alien rulers took great pride in collecting Chinese beauties. The offspring of these interracial marriages, raised under the Chinese cultural atmosphere, were more inclined to identify themselves as Chinese. All these, of course, helped in speeding up the process of Sinicization. Many of the alien rulers were so Sinicized that they patronized Chinese learning and even read Confucian classics themselves. By the fifth century, barely one century after the armed invasions, the so-called barbarians were in every respect Chinese, and barbarian only when one took pains to trace their genealogy.

The first Sinicized monarch of any importance was Fu Chien who came from a tribe racially related to the modern Tibetans. He unified North China in the 370's and built an empire with territories extending from South Manchuria to modern Sinkiang province in the northwest and southward to the Yangtze River basin. Chinese leaders in the north gave him substantial support and many of them served his government as high ranking officials. In time the regime was Sinicized enough to consider itself a direct descendant of the many Chinese kingdoms of the past, such as those of Yao and Shun, the ideal rulers in Confucian ideology, and regarded as barbarian other nomadic tribes in the north and the northwest which had not been brought under its rule. With broad support from both the Chinese and the non-Chinese after it had unified North China, it seemed logical that it should attempt to conquer South China, then under the East Tsin regime. In 383 Fu Chien mobilized one million men for his southward march, 270,000 in cavalry and the rest in infantry. The East Tsin, his opponent, could only muster 100,000 men to face him along the Fei River in modern Anhwei province. The Tsin army, though small in number, was a well-disciplined group and was under the command of an able general, Hsieh Hsüan. Fu Chien's one million men, on the other hand, was a motley army of green troops most of whom had only recently been conscripted. The battle was one of the most dramatic in military history. After an initial setback the northerners became panicky; everyone took to his heels, including the generals. Men and horses ran into each other; thousands were trampled to death, as the Tsin troops followed them in hot pursuit. Fu Chien himself was wounded in the shoulder by a flying arrow. After his return, he found his empire rapidly disintegrating. The various tribes which had been subject to his rule took the opportunity of his defeat to reassert their independence. The North was again divided and was plunged into intertribal wars for many more decades. The Battle of the River Fei was one of the turning points in Chinese history. Had the North won, South China would have been conquered, and the whole of China would have been unified under a non-Chinese regime for the first time in history.

About half a century after the Battle of River Fei another powerful Mongolian tribe emerged from the grasslands in the North. Endowed by a long succession of capable rulers, it conquered one kingdom after another until in 439 it unified the entire north. The dynastic title of this regime was Wei, but more often it was referred to as North Wei, Later Wei, or Topa Wei, to distinguish it from the Wei dynasty established by the Ts'ao family some two centuries before. It was an energetic and enlightened regime; during its prime it was unquestionably one of the best regimes ever established by a non-Chinese group in the north. The man most responsible for raising it to such high standard was Wei Hsiao-wen-ti who ascended the throne in 471.

Hsiao-wen-ti's contribution as a statesman lay more in his success in domestic reforms than in any achievements he made in military conquests. Realizing the impossibility of conquering the south without running the risk of political disintegration and economic bankruptcy, he concentrated his energy upon consolidating his empire and creating economic prosperity for his subjects. In this respect he continued the policy of his predecessors by promoting agricultural production, reforming the tax structure so as to reduce taxes and other requisitions, and simplifying and making more efficient his administrative apparatus. He periodically sent roving envoys to the provinces to report on local conditions, to reward the honest and punish the guilty.

Hsiao-wen-ti's most significant achievement, however, was his success in carrying out land reforms. After the collapse of the West Tsin regime, North China had been in a state of intermittent warfare for two centuries. The farmers who bore the direct brunt of war suffered the most. In each village many perished and others left their homes and never returned. Farms were abandoned and deteriorated into patches of wilderness. For those who had returned, there were the unending lawsuits involving land titles, for deeds had been lost and official records had been destroyed during the wars. Many claimed ownership to land which might not rightly belong to them. While good farms continued to lie idle, many bona fide farmers found no available land to till. In 485 the government made a drastic move and enacted a law to arrest waste and to rationalize land ownership. According to the law, every male subject was entitled to receive seven acres of land from the state after he reached the age of fifteen; he could receive more if he possessed additional capacity of production as measured by the number of people in his household. This land would be returned to the state for redistribution after he died or when he became too old to carry on agricultural activities. Besides, an adult male was granted an additional 3.5 acres of land which did not have to be returned to the state even after he reached old age, and which could be inherited by his children. This additional land provided the necessary means of support for the aged. In addition, there were lands granted for specific purposes, such as the construction of households, the growing of mulberry trees and flax, and vegetable gardening. The lands of convicted criminals, together with the lands of those who voluntarily left their homes without expressing a desire to return or who died without heirs, would be returned to the state for redistribution among the needy farmers. In return for land granted, the grantees paid tax in produce, which was generally light. A married couple, for instance, had to pay a yearly rate of only one bolt of silk and two piculs of grain; for a boy of premarital age, it was only one-fourth as much. However, tax rates would be proportionally increased if the taxpayer owned male or female slaves. Of the total amount of tax collected, two-thirds went to the imperial treasury; the other third was left with local authorities to meet administrative expenses, including the salary of governmental employees.

On the village level, village chiefs were chosen from local leaders who collected taxes and carried on many other administrative functions. While they were not paid salaries, they did receive exemption from taxation and military services. Besides mediating local disputes and punishing offenders for small crimes like thievery, they saw to it that the needs of the aged, the sick, the orphaned, and the destitute were taken care of by the entire village.

The Later Wei thus achieved what many reformers had failed to achieve during the previous centuries. In this respect, Hsiao-wen-ti was particularly fortunate; he did not encounter the same strong opposition as Wang Mang had encountered previously. His reforms were less drastic and consequently more enforceable. Though there was a minimum amount of land granted to each individual male, the amount increased in direct proportion to the number of people in the grantee's household (including females). Two-thirds of the land was to be returned to the government for redistribution upon the death of the grantee; his heirs were nevertheless allowed to inherit the other one-third. By this device the wealthy could keep the land they owned and the poor, in the meantime, could be assured of a minimum means of support. Moreover; since the disintegration of the Later Han regime, there had never been a time more propitious for land reform than the time of Later Wei. After two centuries of intermittent warfare, large tracts of land were unclaimed, either because the original owners had perished during the wars or because they had left their homes as war refugees and never returned. The mass migration towards the south under the initial impact of barbarian invasions alone left millions of acres of unclaimed land, for those who could afford to migrate southward were generally the wealthy. Throughout the years much of the abandoned land was uncultivated; in other cases, deserted land was cultivated even though the tillers could not show certificates indicating their ownership. As ownerless land was available for distribution among the landless, the government did not have to take land away from the rich in order to give it to the poor. While Wang Mang's land reforms provoked strong opposition from the landlords and precipitated a revolt which resulted in the downfall of his regime, a similar measure adopted by the Later Wei was carried out peacefully without causing a social upheaval.

A more difficult task, however, was the implementation of a Sinicization program. Though assimilation of nomadic tribes into the Chinese cultural system had begun when the first contact of the two groups was made, it was Wei Hsiao-wen-ti who first made it an official policy enforced by legal measures. To show his determination to Sinicize his regime, he moved his capital southward from P'ingch'eng (modern Shansi) to Loyang which was not only a trade center but also an ancient Chinese capital for many centuries. He could move the capital only after he had successfully crushed a rebellion among his own followers who feared that movement of the capital would mean the destruction of the hardy, nomadic tradition and the acquirement of Chinese "softness" which might eventually weaken the regime. The tribesmen became more alarmed when it was clear that in the formulation and implementation of governmental policy the emperor relied on the advice of Confucian scholars, while showing an undisguised contempt for the nomadic fighters. As opposition was strong and widespread, he even found it necessary to order the execution of his own son, the crown prince, who had refused to go along with his Sinicization program. By royal decrees, not only was nomadic costume to be discarded and replaced by Chinese dress, but the Chinese language was proclaimed as the official language and had to be learned by all persons under the age of thirty. All family names were to be Sinicized, including the name of the royal family which from then on was to be known as Yüan instead of its original form Topa. Interracial marriages were encouraged. The emperor himself took Chinese wives and asked his ministers and subjects to do the same. Confucian learning was made a requirement for the educated. Scholars with special contributions were rewarded with fame and position.

The policy initiated by Wei Hsiao-wen-ti was generally followed by other alien dynasties which succeeded Later Wei in the north. Thus by conquering North China wave after wave of nomadic invaders were absorbed into the Chinese cultural system. Eventually, they all became Chinese.

THE SOUTHERN AND NORTHERN DYNASTIES

When the first wave of barbarians swept down on the North China plain and captured Loyang in 311 and again in 316, it was the signal for a mass migration to the south. The emigrants came mostly from the upper classes because first, they alone had the means of moving for such a long distance and second, they had more to lose if they ever fell into the hands of the invaders. According to one record, six or seven out of every ten gentry families joined the southward march. In many cases, entire clans including neighbors and servants left their homes and travelled hundreds of miles to establish new homes south of the Yangtze River. Millions of people moved southward, probably the largest migration ever recorded in history. By the time they reached their destination, they found that a new Chinese regime had already been established. In 317 the military commander in the south, a member of the royal family, formally proclaimed the creation of a new regime, after news came from the north that the last emperor of West Tsin had been killed by the invaders. The new regime was known as East Tsin (317–420) and the new emperor was Tsin Yüan-ti (r. 317–322). To accommodate the newly arrived refugees, the government set up administrative provinces south of the Yangtze River for their settlement. As members of the upper class, the refugees brought to the south their wealth, experience, and technical skills which benefited their adopted homeland greatly in cultural and economic matters.

The sudden arrival of a large number of northerners caused great resentment among the native inhabitants. At the beginning the southerners refused to cooperate with the new government. But Tsin Yüan-ti was tactful and patient. Eventually, he was able to persuade the southern leaders to cooperate with his regime. After the leaders had given in, others soon fell in line. Frictions between northerners and southerners flared up from time to time, but they never reached major proportions. From the southerners' point of view, there were genuine reasons for complaint. For one thing, the northerners were preferred as office-holders; rarely were the southerners given high and responsible posts in the imperial government. To minimize their complaint, the government was careful enough not to interfere with the privileged position and the vested interests of the leading southern families. They were the original leaders of the south; as long as they did not choose to lead a revolt, the government was safe. Generally speaking, these families kept aloof from the northern orientated government, neither actively supporting it nor openly hostile to it. When the government decided not to interfere with their vested interests, they did not see the necessity of openly defying it at the risk of losing whatever they had. Throughout the long period of northern domination there was never a revolt organized on regional issues.

When the northerners first came to the south, they thought that their stay would be only temporary and that soon they should be able to reconquer the north and return to their ancient homes. Throughout the East Tsin dynasty this hope was kept alive by the division among the alien kingdoms in the north and by the prospect of revolt organized by the northern Chinese who were then living under alien rule. No sooner was the East Tsin regime established than an expedition was sent northward to recover the lost territories. But this attempt, like several others that followed, ended in failure. On the surface it seemed strange that these expeditions should fail, as the alien kingdoms fought among themselves and none had any popular support. But the Chinese regimes in the south were even weaker. The southern Chinese showed no enthusiasm in supporting the reconquest of the north for the northerners; moreover, there was not a single leader in the south who could inspire confidence and trust from both the northerners and southerners and mobilize all the resources for a sustained campaign in the north. In fact, practically all expeditions were organized by individuals on a personal or clan basis. They were supported by the government only reluctantly, for it feared that a successful and popular general would become unmanageable and would pose a threat to the government itself. The nearly successful campaign was made by an East Tsin general named Liu Yü who conquered the modern Honan province and captured Loyang and Ch'angan in 417. His success, however, proved to be short-lived. After he returned to the south, his subordinates began to quarrel among themselves. The reconquered territories again fell into the hands of the alien invaders.

After 417 Liu Yü became the strong man in the south. Three years later, he forced the last emperor of East Tsin to abdicate on his behalf. He called his regime Sung, sometimes referred to as Liu Sung to distinguish it from the Sung dynasty of a later period. Meanwhile in the north, the alien regime Later Wei was conquering and consolidating its gains in the Yellow River basin; it eventually unified North China in 439. The year 420, when the Liu Sung regime was established, marked the beginning of the period of Southern and Northern Dynasties. As far as the north was concerned, this period was ended in 581 when Sui replaced North Chou. In the south this period ended eight years later when Sui conquered the last of the southern dynasties, Ch'en, in 589.

The northern and southern regimes are listed as follows:

Yellow Sea

South China Sea

Chienkang (Nanking)

EAST TSIN

LATER WEI (NORTH)

Loyang

Changan

Lake Balkhash

TARIM RIVER

GANGES R.

Bay of Bengal

CEYLON

Aral Sea

INDIA

INDUS RIVER

Arabian Sea

Caspian Sea

MAP 15
CHINA around 400 A.D.
FA-HSIEN'S JOURNEY
TO INDIA, 399–412 A.D.

□ Capital   ● City
...... Fa-hsien's Routes to
and from India

0   400   800

Scale of Miles

NORTH CHINA	SOUTH CHINA
Wei (220–265)	Wu (222–280)
West Tsin (265–317)	East Tsin (317–420)
Later Wei (386–535)	Sung (420–479)
West Wei (535–556)	Ch'i (479–502)
East Wei (534–550)	Liang (502–557)
North Ch'i (550–577)	Ch'en (557–589)
North Chou (557–581)	

The six southern regimes with their capital at Chienk'ang (modern Nanking) were sometimes referred to as the Six Dynasties.

After Liu Yü's northern expedition, there were no more serious attempts to reconquer the north throughout the period of the Southern Dynasties. Meanwhile the north, under the regime of Later Wei, was more interested in consolidating its gains than in making new conquests. When the north was again divided into rival kingdoms after 535, it was too disunited to attempt to conquer the south. Thus a period of peaceful co-existence endured for about one hundred and seventy years. Ambassadors were often exchanged between the northern and the southern regimes, as the northern kingdoms after the Later Wei were no longer viewed as barbarian by their southern counterparts. Though their boundary line fluctuated, it divided the land into roughly the same areas which are today termed North and South China. Loyang in the Yellow River basin was the administrative center for the northern dynasties; Chienk'ang on the southern bank of the Yangtze River was the capital of the southern regimes.

PERSONAL LOYALTY AND THE FAMILY ELITE

Since the unification of China by Ch'in, the disintegration of the Later Han marked the beginning of the longest period during which China was politically divided. The divisive tendency began long before the barbarian invasions, though the barbarians, by occupying North China, prolonged it. The grand unification of the Former Han had as its theoretical basis one of the cardinal principles of Confucianism, namely, loyalty to the monarch as the symbol of the entire state. As the Later Han progressed, such loyalty slowly weakened and eventually became only nominal. After the Yellow Turbans' rebellion, it all but disappeared. The loyalty which had hitherto been expressed to the emperor as the symbol of the state was now transferred to local strong men who received such titles as governors and governors-general after they had acquired a large following through their own initiative. As national loyalty to the emperor was replaced by local loyalty to individual strong men, localism replaced nationalism as the focus of political ideals among the educated elite. National loyalty to the emperor could be justified on the ground that the emperor embodied the will of the state; such loyalty, consequently, strengthened power concentration and political unity. Personal loyalty to local strong men, on the other hand, served exactly the opposite purpose.

Since personal loyalty was hailed as one of the greatest virtues, it in due time degenerated into a blind faith, bearing no relation to the principles of the man to whom such loyalty was addressed. In other words, if a man was hired as a government official, he was socially and morally bound to obey and support his superior, even though the actions of his superior could not be morally or legally justified. It was expected that such loyalty would continue even after the official superior-inferior relationship had long been terminated. Once a personal loyalty was established, it was supposed to last forever. Sometimes such loyalty was expressed in the most abject terms. We know that one official resigned from his post in order to enter a period of mourning after the death of a former superior, when such an extreme form of mourning was customarily reserved only for one's parents. Towards the end of the Later Han, the warring governors fought constantly among themselves, and each of them, pursuing his own selfish purposes, could always count on the support of his subordinates. After a process of elimination among the warring governors, this personal loyalty eventually became centered on the three most successful regional leaders, Ts'ao Ts'ao in the north, Liu Pei in the southwest, and Sun Ch'üan in the southeast. Even after West Tsin had unified China, localism was as strong as it had been before. It weakened the regime so much that West Tsin became an easy prey to the invading barbarians. After the barbarians had twice captured and sacked Loyang, the Confucian concept of a unitary government was damaged beyond repair, and for the following centuries the Chinese had to learn to live under a new system of divided rule. This passive acceptance of political division was particularly remarkable in view of the fact that most of the northern kingdoms were non-Chinese regimes. In the south, personal loyalty to local leaders was continually emphasized and was partially responsible for the quick succession of dynasties.

This overemphasis on personal loyalty came into being partly because the normal avenues to a governmental career no longer existed. A person, to enter governmental service, had to rely on the goodwill of an official in power who could extend to him the benefit of patronage. In a society where the only way of winning power and prestige lay in employment with the government, the avenues to a governmental career were extremely important. During the golden years of the two Han dynasties, there were normal ways of entering governmental service, and theoretically, it was possible for men of humble origin to attain the highest positions in the nation. In due course this remarkable system deteriorated.

Towards the end of the Later Han, great emphasis was laid on Confucian virtues, especially filial piety, in the selection of prospective officials. Hoping to be elected, a sizable number of the intelligentsia went to great extremes to show that they were "virtuous." After the establishment of the Wei dynasty it was thought that a better defined system was needed for the recruitment of governmental personnel. Consequently in 220 the nine-rank system was adopted at the suggestion of the Minister of Personnel, Ch'en Ch'ün. Under this system all gentry scholars in the country were rated and grouped into nine grades in accordance with their "virtues and abilities," from the highest first to the lowest ninth. In each province or district, officials appointed by and responsible to the imperial government were stationed for the specific purpose of rating and evaluating personnel within their jurisdiction, elevating them to higher ranks if they followed a Confucian pattern of virtuous life and degrading them if their behavior was regarded as unbecoming to the status of the scholar-gentry.

While the original motive for the establishment of the nine-rank system was doubtless sound, this system too deteriorated after it had been consistently abused. First, only the outward and often superficial "virtues" were appreciated, and no attempt was made to appraise a person in a more profound manner. Filial piety was the virtue most revered, and many prominent men (such as the famous historian Ch'en Shou) suffered degradation either because they did not resign from their official posts after the death of their parents or because they did not perform the ritual of mourning in an approved manner. With such emphasis on outward and often superficial conduct, this system promoted conformity at best and encouraged hypocritical acts at worst. Second, not all evaluators were impartial and objective. Impartiality and objectivity were even harder to obtain when members of influential families became subjects of evaluation. Even when evaluators were conscientious and unbiased, the great number of people to be judged within their respective jurisdictions made the task too huge to yield trustworthy results. So they would not antagonize the powerful and the wealthy, but ingratiate themselves with them, most of the evaluators, ignoring the so-called virtues, simply rated persons in accordance with the power, position, and wealth of the evaluated. By the early West Tsin dynasty, it was found that "there are no poor families among the higher ranks; nor can the old elite be found among the lower rated."

Despite its original purpose, the nine-rank system had thus become a device of providing additional luster and prestige to a small group of elite families called *shih chia* or old families. It should be noted, however, that these families did not come into being because of the system; they had existed long before it. We can trace their origin to many sources, and one of these sources was the emphasis given to Confucian learning after the second century B.C. when Confucianism was proclaimed as the state philosophy. As time went on, traditions developed in certain families as the recognized authorities on the interpretation of a Confucian classic after its interpretation had become a specialized affair which required the undivided attention of a lifetime. As Confucian learning was closely related to office holding, the families that produced prominent Confucian scholars were the same families that had power and influence with the government. Even out of office, they were the recognized leaders in their own communities. Once a family had reached such an elevated status, it enjoyed great prestige regardless of whether at a given time it had among its members any scholars or government officials. Its social standing did not change with the change of dynasties. In fact, monarchs of each succeeding regime had to ingratiate themselves with the old families in order to win their support. Generally speaking, the old families cooperated with any successful political leader so long as he did not initiate measures to change the status quo which they had long enjoyed.

The power and influence of the old families further advanced as a result of the political and social disintegration after the second century A.D. For self-protection against marauding soldiers and bandits, powerful landlords took the initiative in organizing local militias, recruiting supporters from the lesser landlords and independent farmers since the imperial authority could no longer be counted on to maintain peace and order. Sometimes the lesser landlords and independent farmers had to send their children or relatives to live with the great landlords as hostages to guarantee their unswerving loyalty. A psuedo feudal relationship was thus established in which the lesser landlords became *pu-ch'ü* or subordinates to the most powerful of the local landlords. During the barbarian invasions, most of the old families moved southward with the East Tsin, taking their subordinates with them. In the south their lofty position was recognized as it had been in the north; they enjoyed more social prestige than even the leading families in the south. Those which chose to stay in the north cooperated with the non-Chinese regimes which were anxious for their cooperation and support. In fact, the non-Chinese monarchs considered it a social honor to be able to marry their children into some of these old families. Even a liberal-minded emperor like Wei Hsiao-wen-ti made a habit of choosing his officials from this group.

In the south the old families enjoyed even greater prestige and influence throughout the Southern Dynasties. In selecting officials the government invariably checked with genealogies; members of the old families practically monopolized high positions regardless of individual merit. As genealogy was a key to office holding, the government made special efforts in correcting and editing the genealogies of the old elite, for falsifications of family origins, as would be expected, had become a common practice. The oligarchic control of governmental positions accounted partially for the complacency with which the government regarded China's political division into the Southern and Northern Dynasties, for the old families had more to lose than to gain in a renewal of warfare with the north. There was no reason to change the status quo, when its maintenance was to their own advantage.

Social differentiation existed even among the old families themselves. They were grouped into different classes, according to the various degrees of prestige they commanded; Hsieh, Ts'ui, and Lu were acknowledged as highest. Under such circumstances, snobbishness and prejudice were bound to occur. Families of the upper classes did not even try to conceal their contempt for those socially below them, and the families of the lower classes were just as anxious to be accepted by those socially above. This was shown poignantly in the matter of marriage. The upper class families customarily intermarried with families of their own standing, while the lower class families considered it a great honor to be able to marry their children into the upper classes. Social status was achieved through tradition; power and wealth were only contributory factors. During the Ch'i dynasty, upon the decision of a Wang family to marry one of its daughters to an extremely wealthy man of lower standing, a court censor thought it was a good case for judicial indictment. When Hou Ching, a high ranking official, asked for Emperor Liang Wu-ti's good office to secure a wife from the Wang or Hsieh family, the emperor replied that the prospective groom should not aim so high and that he should seek his bride among families below those of Chu and Chang. Later, when Hou Ching started a rebellion and captured Chienk'ang, he murdered in cold blood many of the old elite, probably in revenge for a past social slight. The old families and their prestige, however, survived his massacre. A man of humble origin might occasionally rise high in governmental service, but he would be still looked down upon as an upstart, with whom the old elite would have nothing to do socially. Sometimes social snobbishness was carried to such an extreme that two persons of different social standing were not supposed to ride in the same carriage or sit on the same bench. Family classification according to prestige existed throughout the Southern Dynasties and persisted as late as the seventh century. When the T'ang Emperor T'ai-tsung ordered a codification of family registers throughout the empire, the royal family Li was rated third in prestige, two ranks below the leading family Ts'ui.

It should be noted, however, that the social differentiation described above was applicable to the gentry families only. It did not affect the majority of the population, namely, the peasants. As far as the peasants were concerned, they had always been on one of the lowest levels of the social strata, and they still were.

REACTIONS AGAINST CONFUCIANISM

During the golden years of the two Han dynasties Confucianism was not only a system of government but also a code of personal behavior. As long as the basic teachings of Confucianism were observed, they provided an aim and a purpose for society as well as for individuals. Towards the end of the Later Han dynasty, the perversion of Confucianism in the name of "virtuous" conduct gave rise to skepticism and cynicism which led to the renunciation of Confucian values. A reaction had thus set in and lasted more than four centuries. The new cynical attitude was best shown in the famous *Three Decrees* issued by Ts'ao Ts'ao in which he asked anyone with extraordinary ability to join his staff, even if "he had once stolen his sister-in-law, accepted bribes, murdered his wife, or failed to return home for his mother's funeral." This kind of statement would have been unthinkable one century before. As Confucian virtues were discredited, Confucian learning was given even less emphasis. It is interesting to note that during the period of Southern and Northern Dynasties whatever Confucian learning was left was promoted more in the north under the alien dynasties than in the south under the Chinese regimes.

As Confucianism declined, Taoism won new adherents among the country's intellectual elite. In an age when life was most uncertain and rewards, either of social recognition, power, or wealth, did not necessarily follow talents and hard work, the best brains sought refuge in a philosophy of resignation and escape. Unwilling to submit to a world they could not change, they built a world of their own and shut themselves off from unpleasant realities. In this small world of their own they met friends of similar inclinations, conducted philosophical conversations, and found self-satisfaction in their own speculations. Confucianism had lost its appeal partly because it had failed to meet the challenge of a disorganized world. This new elite of intellectuals repudiated completely the traditional Confucian virtues such as loyalty, self-discipline, and filial piety, and advocated instead a code of behavior based upon natural inclinations rather than established conventions. They believed in self-expression unfettered by old dogmas and popular beliefs. They themselves did not favor any set of principles either as a philosophy or code of behavior except the cardinal principle of being honest and true to oneself. It was natural that they should seek refuge in the teachings of Lao-tzu and Chuang-tzu, as these teachings repudiated established values and emphasized naturalism and non-activity as the most important virtues. The *Book of Changes,* though generally considered as a Confucian classic, was singled out as the most praiseworthy, largely because of its mystic and metaphysical attractions. Despite their principle of non-activity, the new intellectual elite did a remarkable work in editing and commenting on the writings of Lao-tzu and Chuang-tzu and the *Book of Changes.*

In the pursuance of truth and wisdom, the Taoist philosophers of the Wei-Tsin period attached great importance to verbal exchange. During the course of verbal exchange, truth and wisdom came into being not through logical reasoning but as a result of sudden flashes of insight. The answer to a question was likely to be concise in words and broad in implication, leaving much room for individual speculation and interpretation. Even the tone and placement of voice contributed to the most propitious atmosphere; the best voices were often described as "golden" or "cool," or as "sounds from a harp." Argumentative statements during the conversation had to be avoided, as they would destroy the very purpose of Taoist passivism. In fact, the manner of expressing an idea was just as important as the idea itself. Even clothes worn by the conversationalists should be appropriate for the occasion, generally described as wide, loose, and comfortable. Besides, there was the indispensable horsewhisk in the hand of the conversationalist as a symbol of detachment and non-involvement. The purpose was not so much to convince as to express, leaving individual listeners complete freedom to digest and infer for themselves.

This new vogue of *ch'ing t'an,* or "purified conversation," was begun in the 240's during the Wei dynasty and reached its apex of popularity during the West Tsin dynasty. Its architects were Ho Yen (d. ca. 250), Wang Pi (226–249), and Kuo Hsiang (d. 312), all of whom were not only expert conversationalists but also writers of considerable originality. However, their basic ideas did not exceed the confines set up by Lao-tzu and Chuang-tzu several centuries before. Like those two masters, they emphasized such key teachings as "nothingness" (the beginning of the universe), "non-activity" ("everything will be done when nothing is being done"), and "naturalism" (the right path to genuine behavior). They ridiculed all efforts aimed at the improvement of personal conduct and the betterment of political and social institutions. The Taoist attitude was an attitude of perfect detachment from worldly endeavors, and they conducted their personal life according to what they called natural inclinations, with little or no regard for conventional restraints. While most of their personal behavior might be simply amoral, there were others who interpreted the new teachings as a form of sensual escapism. A treatise of anonymous authorship entitled *Yang Chu,* probably written during the Former Han dynasty, enjoyed a sudden popularity, as it neatly filled the gap left in the writings of Lao-tzu and Chuang-tzu. In this treatise the author advocated the avoidance of pain and the pursuit of pleasure, as he assured his reader that life was short and most uncertain and that the other world was unknown. Once this path was followed, Taoism, originally interpreted as a means of achieving personal purification, was now perverted into a teaching advocating sensual self-satisfaction.

In practice, the patterns of behavior on the part of its adherents varied a great deal, from conduct which was highly moral and purely ascetic to that which was downright absurd. On a higher level, we may cite T'ao Ch'ien and Wang Hui-chih as examples. T'ao Ch'ien (376–427) was a noted poet and prose writer whose works have been universally praised for their aesthetic beauty in describing natural environment. During the time he was a magistrate, he decided to "hang up his official seal" (indicating his resignation) on the ground that he could not humiliate himself by bowing to an unworthy superior for the "five bushels of rice" which he had received as his salary. Wang Hui-chih was the son of the famous calligrapher Wang Hsi-chih (321–379). One beautiful moonlit evening, he thought of a good friend who lived many miles away and decided to pay him an unannounced visit. He arrived at his friend's residence early in the morning after a long drunken voyage by boat during the previous night, only to return immediately without making the intended call. Asked by his boatman the reason for his peculiar behavior, he replied that he was enthusiastic to see his friend when he started his journey but that such enthusiasm was gone after he had reached his destination, so there was no sense in then seeing his friend.

While conduct like this might be genuinely "naturalistic," other men, such as the famous Seven Sages of the Bamboo Grove, went to great extremes to prove their point. As a rule, they sought satisfaction in the wine cup, and one of them had a record of being drunk consecutively for sixty days. One of the Sages, Liu Ling, was regularly accompanied by a servant with a shovel wherever he went. He instructed his servant to bury him wherever he should be when he dropped dead. Often remaining completely naked at home, he would protest when surprised by visitors: "The universe is my dwelling place and my house is only my clothes. Why, then, do you enter into my pants?" Behavior such as this could have been dismissed as individual eccentricity and would hardly be worthy of notice by historians were it not for the fact that these people were the elite of the scholar-gentry, and it was this class that traditionally provided leadership and guidance for the entire nation. The point has been raised that in an age of injustice under a corrupt, despotic regime, to shield oneself behind the Taoist philosophy was the best means of achieving survival. It was nevertheless true that the traditional sense of public responsibility generally expected from this class was completely lost in a selfish indulgence which China then could least afford. In this new age, life had no meaning except the pleasure one could derive from it:

> When there is wine,
> There should be a song.
> Life is like morning dew
> That disappears
> Soon after the sun rises.[1]

[1] These are the first lines of a poem written by Ts'ao Ts'ao.

After the fall of the West Tsin regime to the barbarians early in the fourth century when most of the northern gentry families moved to the south, they found that the south, having suffered no major war devastations and being economically more productive, enjoyed such prosperity as had seldom been seen before. The term Six Dynasties often reminds one of a life of ease and plenty. The easy life produced a typical gentleman of this age, weak in limbs, short-sighted in outlook, ignorant of practical matters, but expert in witticism and repartee. Let us look at a description of these gentlemen by a northern contemporary:

> The gentlemen of the Liang dynasty all wore ponderous dresses with wide belts, tall hats, and high-soled shoes. When they went out, they rode in carriages; at home they were waited on [by their servants]. . . . During the Hou Ching rebellion many of them were physically so weak that they could hardly walk. Being bony in body and becoming breathless in the mildest physical efforts, they could stand neither summer nor winter. Many of them simply waited for death, when the rebellion occurred suddenly . . . The ancestors of these gentlemen passed across the Yangtze River when the Tsin dynasty was established in the south. For eight or nine generations they did not participate in tilling the fields, and all depended upon government salaries for their support. Those who owned land relied on their servants for its cultivation; they themselves had never seen the plowing of one spot of earth or the planting of one single tree. Nor did they know the time to sow and the time to reap. Being so impractical as they were, how can you expect them to know the rest of the worldly affairs? They were incompetent as government officials and ineffective as heads of households. This is all due to the fault of having too much leisure.[1]

However, these gentlemen had little difficulty in finding ways to spend their leisure. For the more sophisticated, there were literature, calligraphy, painting, music, and other recreations. The writers of the Six Dynasties developed a new style of writing, called *p'ien t'i* or parallel form. Sentences were constructed in such a way that each phrase or sentence was neatly balanced by a phrase or sentence of equal length (namely, the same number of characters), and the last characters of both phrases or sentences usually rhymed with each other. The result was a literary form lying somewhere between prose and verse, and when recited, it conveyed a flow of sound extremely pleasant to the ears. Since sentence construction had to conform strictly to the parallel form, obscure characters which would not have been used ordinarily had to be employed. The use of obscure characters and the concise sentence structure accounted partially for the difficulty of understanding the composition itself. The parallel form was sometimes called the ornamented form as phrases and sentences were lavishly embellished with flowery, elegant words which were sometimes empty in meaning. Too often content had to be sacrificed to form. As its writing required great knowledge in charac-

---

[1] Translated from *Family Instructions for the Yen Clan* (*Yen-shih chia-hsün*) by Yen Chih-t'ui. This passage appears in the chapter on "Worldly Affairs" (*shih-wu*).

ters and rhythm, it was no mean achievement to be able to write a presentable essay in parallel form. It remained as a mental exercise for the country's gentry scholars for many centuries to come. As for calligraphy, it had long been a cherished art form. Being composed of pictographs and ideographs, the Chinese written language was uniquely fit for calligraphic development. The Tsin dynasty produced Wang Hsi-chih whose style was noted for character and strength and has been emulated ever since. During the Six Dynasties the extremely cursive grass style acquired increasing popularity;[1] expertly executed, its graceful and sweeping lines conveyed a sense of beauty, power, and even mental exaltation. Writing with the grass style, a calligrapher sometimes had to make omissions (and occasionally additions) in each character in order to achieve the desired result. Many contemporaries complained about this corruption of Chinese characters, but to the admirers of the grass style, this was a small price to pay for a superb form of artistic expression. As for music the lute remained the major instrument. Like the ancient Greeks, the Chinese believed that music had a beneficial effect on a person's morale and character. To be able to play the lute was regarded as a necessary refinement for a gentleman. As the Chinese then did not have a system of musical notation but depended on memory for their performances, we have no idea how music was played during this particular period.

Besides literature and art, there were chess and games of chance for the southern gentry to indulge in. From what we can gather, the chess game played was the traditional *wei-ch'i*, or game of encirclement (called *go* in Japan). If they played with the same rules as modern Chinese do, a good game would have taken hours or even days to finish and might be regarded as a mental exercise par excellence. However, it was such a waste of time that Confucius once remarked: "Is there any one who does not like chess? If there is, will he not be rightly said to be wise?" Many contemporaries condemned chess on the same ground, but it remained as popular as ever. Another ancient game which enjoyed a new vogue was the pitch-pot game in which arrows were thrown into a vase placed at some distance. This, of course, required skill as well as luck. One man, we are told, never missed his target, even though his view of the vase was cut off by a screen. Sports of a more strenuous type, however, were not indulged in, for vigorous physical exercise was regarded as vulgar, not becoming the dignity of a gentleman. The same pleasurable life was also enjoyed by the ladies. Since they were not allowed to mingle socially with men or share their activities, they had a world of their own and spent a considerable part of their time in making themselves pretty. Cream, powder, and rouge were widely used, as they had been used before. One

---

[1] It is called "grass style" because the strokes that compose a character are supposedly shaped like grass.

of the fads then was the wearing of high, popped-up wigs, called false heads. The wigs had different forms; some of them, we are told, were shaped like "flying birds."

From the Confucian point of view, the personal life of China's rulers during the Southern Dynasties was anything but exemplary. With the possible exception of Liang Wu-Ti, none of the rulers in the Southern Dynasties could be described as able and conscientious. Many of them were mischievous, malicious, and outright wrongdoers. One crown prince, for instance, murdered his father. Another king tried to poison his mother. Still another used the navel of a fat minister as target to practice archery and stole dogs from a neighboring Buddhist temple to be cooked as food. Nor did the fair sex behave any better. Complaining that her brother the king had thousands of concubines while she had only one husband, a princess asked the king to obtain for her some handsome men as consorts and received thirty of them. One empress dowager received a gift of thirty handsome men from her son (the king) to serve in whatever capacity she chose. In short, these rulers were anything but virtuous and lived a life directly opposed to what would be expected from a Confucian ruler. They could not look beyond their immediate concerns; sensual enjoyments and private feuds occupied most of their time. Even the best of them, Liang Wu-ti, was more concerned with his spiritual salvation than the national welfare for which he was supposedly responsible. Though unimpeachable in private life, he was so enchanted with the other-worldliness of Buddhism that twice he had to be implored not to relinquish his throne to enter a Buddhist monastery as a monk. So the best rulers during this period were so other-worldly as to ignore the welfare of this world, and the worst of them simply made the best of this world by living a life of corruption and immorality. In either case the people did not benefit.

TAOIST RELIGION AND BUDDHISM

So far Taoism has been discussed as a philosophy and a way of life. Quite different from this was Taoism as a religion. Partly due to the paradoxical messages contained in the *Book of Taoist Virtue* and partly due to the traditional belief that Lao-tzu never really died after he had disappeared in the mountainous west, his name had long been associated with alchemy, the magic art of achieving earthly immortality. The fear of death prompted the desire to prolong life indefinitely; this fear was found especially among emperors who had acquired great power and wealth and would like to enjoy them forever. The court of Ch'in Shih Huang-ti, for instance, was frequented by alchemists and magicians. One of them, Hsü Fu, was sent by the emperor to the eastern seas to search for immortal drugs. He left with several thousand boys and girls and never returned. The legend had it that they became the first settlers in Japan from the mainland. The great expanse of the Western Pacific stimulated imagination; many people believed that beyond that great expanse lived immortals whose blessings must be sought before they could attain immortality for themselves. Early in the Han dynasty, the name of the legendary emperor Huang-ti, for reasons never satisfactorily explained, was often combined with the name of Lao-tzu; thence the Learning of Huang-Lao became known as the magic formula of extracting elixir. Even an emperor like Han Wu-ti could not resist the popular fad, and one of the court magicians was said to have been successful in arranging a meeting between the emperor and his long deceased concubine.

In addition, religious Taoism also contained strong elements of animism. The Taoists believed that there was a spirit in charge of every mountain or river whose good grace must be sought to prevent natural disasters and to bring prosperity to the community. To communicate with the spirits, the help of Taoist priests who alone knew the appropriate rites had to be invoked. Their help became absolutely necessary when the emperors made their periodical sacrifices to the greatest spirits of them all, Heaven and Earth.

Taoist mysticism was further enriched by the injection of divination and prognostication which had become very popular towards the end of the Former Han dynasty. The theory that the universe together with its constituent parts was created through the interaction of the two opposite but complementary forces, *yin* and *yang*, was given a new meaning: namely, by watching closely the changing patterns of these two forces at work one might be able to foretell the future. Thus the Taoist priests acquired a role similar to that of an astrologist. Meanwhile, new elements of Taoism were also introduced. While the rulers were interested in the search for immortal drugs, the common people had a more practical concern; after all, alchemy was too expensive a practice for men of ordinary means. Towards the end of the Later Han dynasty a man named Chang Ling (also known as Chang Tao-ling) attracted large followings due to his reputation as a successful magician, curing diseases through the use of charms and spells. He was later proclaimed by his followers as the founder of Taoism as a religion (as distinguished from Taoism as a philosophy), and he is still regarded as such. A pantheon of Taoist gods and goddesses soon developed; some were imaginery divinities and others were historical figures. Throughout later ages Taoist priests continued to practice medicine through charms and spells; they also performed funeral services to assure the deceased a place in the heavenly kingdom of spiritual bliss.

Though Taoism as a philosophy had speculative merit, Taoism as a religion was a medley of mystic practicums. It had no elaborate theology; nor did it provide a system of ethics aimed at the improvement of human relations. Though many books written throughout the ages were generally classified as Taoist, they were most concerned with personal salvation and immortality through meditative retirement, alchemy, and many other such means. The road to salvation was a technical one and bore little relation to personal conduct in this world. Consequently, their impact on social and moral institutions was rather limited. However, Taoism filled a vacuum left in Confucian ideology which provided no spiritual domain for one to look forward to, and it made available a spiritual comfort to satisfy a basic human need. While Confucian scholars might dismiss Taoist religion as a form of superstition and preferred the practical wisdom of Confucianism, the less intellectual masses found this wisdom useless if they had nothing to hope for after death. Throughout the long centuries Taoist religion was a cherished faith in the hearts and minds of the common people in China and was a convenient vehicle through which the masses expressed their emotions and feelings. Perhaps it was no mere coincidence that whenever a rebellion occurred, more often than not Taoism was hailed as a rallying standard, for the government was practically always Confucian in outlook. In this sense Taoism might be said to be a people's religion.

However, a more serious challenge to the supremacy of Confucianism was an alien religion called Buddhism. Buddhism means the teachings of Buddha, or the Enlightened One. The real name of the Enlightened One was Siddhartha, born to the Gautama family in a small country south of Nepal. His birth date was traditionally placed at 563 B.C. or thereabouts. Since the details of his life were not put in writing until several hundred years later, what we know about this man is at best semihistorical. He was said to have been born to a rich, aristocratic family with a loving but perhaps overprotective father. As the boy grew up, his father gave him everything a man's heart could possibly desire, including a harem of beautiful girls. But the old man would not let him go out of the palace ground, because outside of the palace ground there were the unpleasant realities which he did not wish his son to see. Overcome by curiosity, the young man finally sneaked out with his charioteer to the outside world without his father's knowledge. He saw an old man, a sick man, and then a dead man. "Why is it that people have to suffer so much?" he asked. He wanted the answer, but he could not find it. He returned to the palace, but he was no longer the same happy prince. One night he took a last look at his sleeping wife and his infant son and silently left the palace. Outside of the city and at the edge of a forest, he cut off his long hair with a sword, discarded his princely robes and put on those of a beggar, and set out to seek the answer for himself.

He wandered from place to place and sought answers from India's holy men. Their answers, however, were not satisfactory. For six long years, he meditated and he fasted, but the answer was as remote as ever.

Meanwhile, he had been so weakened by self-imposed mortifications that he had all but wasted away. All these efforts, however, were not exercised in vain. One day as he sat underneath a tree in a grove a flash of insight struck him, and all of a sudden the absolute truth about life and death was revealed to him. He knew The Answer and he had become the Enlightened One or Buddha. The stage he had reached was *nirvana*, the "unconditioned world where there is neither time nor space." He could have left the physical world then, but out of infinite compassion for his fellow men he decided to stay longer so that he could transmit his own experience to others. Why was it that human beings had to suffer so much? It was because life was a painful process by definition. One life was merely the reincarnation of a preceding life; while the wheel of births and rebirths rolled on unceasingly, there would be no end to man's sufferings. To liberate oneself from the endless cycle of deaths and rebirths, one needed to recognize that the physical world was illusory and that one should not seek for the fulfillment of worldly desires, whether they be fame, wealth, power, or the opposite sex. Desires were the basic cause of pain, and to stop pain, a person had to eliminate desires. Meanwhile, he should conduct his life in accordance with the Eightfold Path: right views, thought, speech, conduct, livelihood, effort, mind control, and meditation. The Eightfold Path was the Middle Way that led to "pure compassion," the "selfless love for all that lives." Those who followed the Middle Way would of course abstain from killing, stealing, falsehood, unchastity, etc.

Though Buddhism was born in India, it was in countries east of India that it achieved its greatest triumph. Spreading to Southeast Asia was the Hinayana ("Lesser Vehicle") School which was closer to the original Buddhism as taught by Buddha. The school that spread to China and eventually to Korea and Japan was the Mahayana ("Greater Vehicle") School which, recognizing the distinction between absolute and relative truth, was more tolerant of non-Buddhist ideas and was consequently more welcome to the Confucian Chinese. In due course Mahayana Buddhism developed a pantheon of deities: the Bodhisattvas who dedicated themselves to the saving of weaker souls. The Buddha Amitabha was known to the Chinese as O-mi-t'o-fo, and Avalokitesvara, changing his sex, became the Chinese Kuan-yin, or the Goddess of Mercy. They were two of the most popular deities in China. Once in China, Buddhism adjusted itself to its new environment by emphasizing charity and good works: to contribute to one's own salvation by helping others. Meanwhile, those who followed Buddha's original teaching of celibacy and asceticism could always join the monastic ranks. Mahayana Buddhism appealed to both the clergy and the laity as it provided a path of salvation for both groups.

Until modern times there was never a foreign impact so great and so

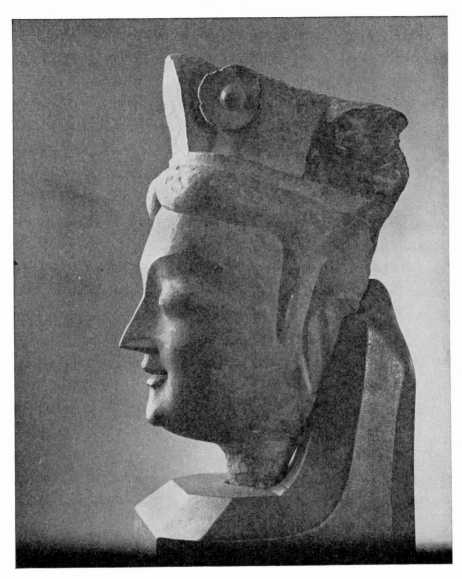

BODHISATTVA, LATER WEI DYNASTY (386–535)   This figure was found in the Lungmen cave (modern Shansi province), a fragment of a large statue. The Chinese copying of Indian works in depicting the Bodhisattvas was perhaps responsible for the clearly discernible Greco-Roman influence in this figure.

influential as Buddhism. There were many reasons for the tremendous success of this imported faith. First, Taoism aside, there was not a native ideology in China which satisfied a universal spiritual need. The Buddhist emphasis on compassion and love contrasted sharply with the selfish motives behind many Taoist practices; it struck a tender response from the best part of human nature. By providing a spiritual substance it substantiated such Confucian virtues as *jen* and *yi* which even at their best were only worldly and human. For the less intellectual the meaning was even greater. It raised hope for the next and better world which Confucianism did not elaborate and which Taoism defined only in the vaguest terms. Furthermore, it was the only religion known to the Chinese which linked ethics in this world and heavenly bliss in the next. Its moral teachings attracted the Confucian intellect and its other-worldliness appealed greatly to the masses. Secondly, it was introduced to China during a period which was most opportune for its growth. Eccentric conduct on the part of many Confucian scholars in the name of filial piety and righteous action during the second century were denounced by many as hypocritical, and Confucianism as a moral force consequently declined. On the other hand, Taoism as a philosophy had come to mean a doctrine of self-protection from cruel, worldly realities, and Taoism as a religion was unfortunately mingled with many superstitious elements. A spiritual and moral vacuum had to be filled, and it was filled by Buddhism. Thirdly, this was an age of political disunity, turmoil, and wars, with their implications of human sufferings. The need for spiritual comfort was never so great. Being able to look forward to a promising unknown helped one forget the unpleasant realities, and the Buddhist theory of reincarnation provided an additional relief. Finally the Chinese under Confucianism were essentially a tolerant people, relatively free from religious prejudice and bigotry. Believing in Confucianism by no means limited them from accepting another faith. In fact, when Buddhism was introduced, many Confucian scholars welcomed it as a supplement to Confucian beliefs. Though persecutions of Buddhists did occasionally occur, they were confined to small areas for short durations; most of them were instigated by Taoists rather than Confucians. For the average Chinese, religions did not need to be mutually exclusive, and he saw no contradiction in holding two or three faiths at the same time.

Through trading with Central Asia the Chinese heard of Buddhism as early as the second century B.C. In 2 B.C. a Chinese scholar travelled to one of the Central Asian kingdoms to learn about this new faith, but nothing consequential came out from this trip. Many decades later Emperor Han Ming-ti (r. 58–76 A.D.) was said to have dreamed of a golden image of Buddha. Curiosity aroused, he sent a Confucian scholar named Ch'in Ching to India with the intended purpose of bringing back Buddhist scriptures. Ch'in Ching returned with two Indian monks, and many

Buddhist scriptures loaded on white horses were transported to China. After his return, the emperor ordered the erection of a Buddhist temple at his capital Loyang, called the Temple of White Horses, the first Buddhist temple in China. Buddhist monks came to visit China and Chinese students and monks went to study in India. From then on a cultural exchange of unprecedented scale followed. One of the most famous monks during this period was Fa-hsien who set out for India in 399 and did not return until fifteen years later. He wrote a book on India, and his observations provide historians with valuable information about the India of this period. Through the joint efforts of Indian and Chinese monks, most of the Buddhist literature was translated into Chinese. The translation was a difficult task, as many Buddhist terms did not have their counterparts in Chinese. In translating, colloquial rather than literary Chinese was preferred, so that the new gospel could reach larger masses.

Although China had never been conquered militarily by a foreign country, she was completely captivated by the Buddhist faith. Because of Buddhism, China learned to respect India; India was perhaps the only country in the world which the Chinese have never called barbarian. Encouraged and patronized by Chinese monarchs, Buddhism spread fast and wide. Buddhist believers multiplied; so did Buddhist temples. Of course, not all the faithful were truly sincere. There were exceptions even among the Buddhist monks. Some joined the monastic ranks because they wished to avoid military service. The tumult and turmoil of a warring age, ironically, helped Buddhism to spread. During the period of the Southern and Northern Dynasties, Buddhism made more converts in the north than it did in the south. In the north, Buddhism claimed more than 40,000 temples and more than three million monastic monks at its peak of popularity, not to mention millions of Buddhist laymen. In the south, Buddhism was most popular during the Liang regime which had within its jurisdiction 2,846 temples and 82,700 monks at one time. Monarchs competed with wealthy laymen in donating funds for the building of temples and the erection of Buddhist statues. One of the Liang monarchs even wished to abdicate his throne for a more meditative, monastic life as has been mentioned before.

The impact of Buddhism was not confined to religious and philosophical fields; its influence was felt in other areas as well. In literature it introduced logic and organization in essay writing; the lack of sound logic and good organization had been notoriously obvious in ancient Chinese writings. It gave prestige to the writing of stories and novels which had been traditionally held in contempt by Confucian scholars, though this effect was not fully felt until several centuries later. Buddhist influence was also felt in sculpture and architecture. When Buddhist statues were in great demand, sculpture, previously neglected as an art form, attracted many new talents. Sculptors and painters commissioned by kings and

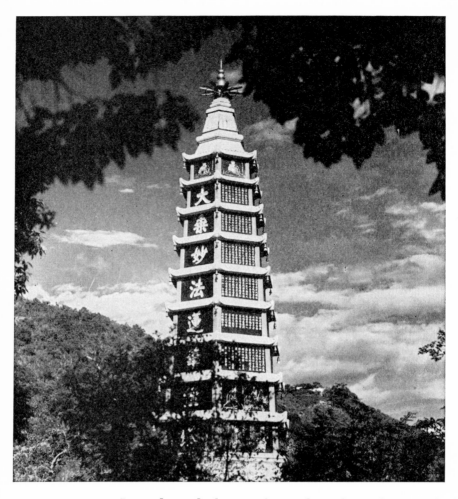

BUDDHIST PAGODA   Located outside the city of Hangchow, this modern pagoda has inscribed on it excerpts of a Buddhist scripture.

wealthy patrons produced numerous Buddhist statues and images of artistic taste. They were made of various materials: iron, stone, wood, or clay. One such statue, we are told, rose as high as 70 feet. Many of them were gilded with gold; historians since then have blamed this expensive devotion for the comparative scarcity of gold in later periods as compared with its apparent abundance prior to the introduction of Buddhism. Many stone statues were carved out of mountain cliffs. Today the impressive Yünkang statues at Tatung, Shansi province, bear witness to the skill of the sculptors as well as to the devotion of their patrons. So far as architecture was concerned, most important was the introduction of an architectural form known today as pagoda. A pagoda during the Later Wei period had either a round or many-sided base and rose several stories high, with a total height of as much as nine hundred feet (a later source, four hundred feet), as in the case of the famous Yungning temple built in Loyang in 516 A.D. While Confucian scholars had traditionally condemned extensive buildings, religious or otherwise, as unnecessary luxuries, the new Buddhist converts spared no expense to build great temples in honor of Buddha and the Bodhisattvas. Many even went bankrupt in doing so.

From China, Buddhism spread to Korea and eventually to Japan. Wherever it went, its triumph was complete.

V

Sui and T'ang

The disunity which began in the second century finally came to an end late in the sixth century when China was again unified under the Sui regime. Sui, however, did not last long. Like Ch'in which paved the way for Han, the Sui regime existed long enough to initiate the golden age of T'ang. While historians might debate the relative merits of Han and T'ang as military powers, there is little doubt that T'ang surpassed all previous dynasties in the overall contributions to a better, more cultured life. It may even be claimed that T'ang surpassed any contemporary civilization of the world. During the days of Han there was Rome. But there was no contemporary culture comparable to the T'ang culture in Europe. Today many Chinese still call themselves Men of T'ang. The Chinatowns in many American cities are called *T'ang-jen Chieh* which, literally translated, means Streets for Men of T'ang.

In an autocratic society like China no factor was more important to the good administration of the country than the ruler himself. This was so because all objective factors in the society, whether they were political, social, or economic, remained substantially the same despite the passage of time, and each ruler had to face and solve the same problems. At home, there were always the problems of irrigation and flood control, famine relief, the maintenance of peace and order, the administration of justice and taxation, the delegation of authority, and the operation of a fair, efficient bureaucracy. In foreign affairs it was the ruler's duty to make China strong enough to discourage incursions and invasions from abroad, but not so aggressive as to overextend Chinese jurisdiction over non-Chinese, nomadic territories. To do so would impose a burden too great for an agricultural economy to bear and would in time disturb the delicate equilibrium between him and his subjects. Once such equilibrium was disturbed, his subjects might rise to challenge his authority. The past shows that the Chinese have not been hesitant to employ the only means they had to get rid of a hated sovereign, namely, revolt. Thus, according to Confucian ideology, a successful monarch not only set an example for his subjects in the cultivation of virtues but also maintained a "harmonious relation between Chinese and barbarians and between rulers and subjects." Of course, not every monarch was able to do do.

The Sui dynasty had a propitious beginning with Sui Wen-ti who conquered the last regime of the Southern Dynasties, Ch'en, in 589. Though not particularly brilliant, he was nevertheless capable and conscientious. He pushed back to their nomadic homes the Mongolians in the north, the Turks in the northwest, and the Tibetans in the west, these being the same peoples who had repeatedly penetrated into China proper during the preceding period and had once established many non-Chinese kingdoms in North China. After the country had been pacified, he turned his attention to domestic construction. Among the most notable was the establishment of ever-ready granaries on a nation-wide scale. During the previous dynasties one of the main causes of local grievances was the fluctuation of farm prices and the unavailability of food during the time of famine. Prices fell sharply at harvest time and rose steadily during the spring sowing season, to the detriment of small, independent farmers. Due to poor transportation, it often occurred that one area was short of food because of flood or drought, while farmers in other areas suffered from depressed prices because of a bumper crop. As nature was most unpredictable, Chinese farmers suffered from the occurrence of alternating bumper and lean years. Good years depressed farm prices and bad years caused famines which, to the dismay of rulers, were often interpreted as a legitimate excuse for open rebellion. As famine repeatedly occurred, revolts were also frequent. One way to remedy this situation, as many believed, was to store away surplus food during good years and make it available at the time of famine. By adopting this measure, fluctuation of farm prices could also be considerably reduced. Thus two birds could be killed with one stone.

Though the ever-ready granary system was introduced in the fourth century B.C. and was put into practice in various degrees during the succeeding centuries, it was Sui which put it on a permanent basis and on a nation-wide scale. In 585 it was first adopted in North China and was later extended to all other areas. Ever-ready granaries were established in the national capital, Ch'angan, in the provincial capitals, and in all local communities. Each year at the time of harvest, every landowner was required by law to contribute a small amount of grain to be stored away in the local granary as a part of his regular tax load; the amount varied in accordance with the size of landownership, the maximum being one picul for each landowner. In a lean year when there was a shortage of food, the granary made available the stored grain to the proved needy free of charge. If the local supply was inadequate, local officials might call on provincial or even imperial granaries for additional help. By 605, the last year of Sui Wen-ti's reign, the program had been so successful that the total amount of stored grain was said to be more than adequate to take care of the nation's needy for at least fifty years.

When Sui Yang-ti, Wen-ti's son, ascended the throne in 605, the country had never looked so prosperous, thanks partially to the ever-ready granary system. Yet in less than a decade, the people revolted in anger. His regime toppled and he was murdered. Historians often compare him with Ch'in Shih-Huang-ti, and there are reasons for doing so. Both were capable but egoistic; both enjoyed luxury and lived in extravagance; both believed in military expansion; both lost their regimes because of the unscrupulousness with which they used the country's labor force. While Ch'in Shih Huang-ti could not foretell his own fate and thought that his regime would last forever, Sui Yang-ti had the cynical satisfaction of knowing what would happen to himself. Even during his best years, he had the ominous thought of the inevitable end and, as the story goes, he once murmured to himself before a mirror: "Such a beautiful head! Who will be the lucky one to take it?" From what we can gather, he was a handsome man.

Though his labor projects have been decried as "torturing people and wasting financial resources," there were some remarkable exceptions. The most remarkable was perhaps the construction of the Grand Canal. Topographically, China slopes down from west to east; with rare exceptions major mountain ridges stretch out eastward like fingers from an opened palm. All great rivers, such as the Yellow River and the Yangtze, flow between these mountain ridges eastward, and after a long and wind-

Khitan

Koguryo

Yellow
Sea

East China
Sea

LIAO R.

YEN

CH'ING

HSÜ

Loyang

YÜ

YELLOW RIVER

East Turks
(Tung T'u-chüeh)

YI

Ch'angan

CHING

YANG

South China Sea

YANGTZE RIVER

SI RIVER

YUNG

LIANG

Nan-chao

T'u-yü-hun

West Turks
(Hsi T'u-chüeh)

MAP 16
THE SUI EMPIRE
(590-618)

o Capital before 605 A.D.
□ Capital after 605 A.D.

0   150   300   450
Scale of Miles

Bay of
Bengal

ing journey, pour into the Pacific Ocean. Thus transportation was made comparatively easy by following the natural courses of rivers along the west-east direction, but was extremely difficult over the land routes from the north to the south and vice versa. Prior to the Sui dynasty, this situation was not too serious, as North China was more or less economically self-sufficient; whatever the northwest lacked in grain and other agricultural produce was usually supplied from areas in the east such as the modern Hopeh, Honan, and Shantung provinces. By utilizing water transportation via the Yellow River and its tributaries, produce paid as taxes could be shipped westward to such capitals as Loyang and Ch'angan. As time went on, the economic position of each geographical region and its relative importance gradually changed. During the four hundred years from the second to the sixth century when North China was under alien occupation, South China was intensively developed agriculturally, thanks to the industriousness of the southerners and the technical knowledge brought in by the northern refugees. By the sixth century South China was a major agricultural producing area and had a surplus readily available to meet the needs of other less fortunate regions. To transport overland bulky products like grain and silk hundreds of miles from South to North China was an extremely difficult task. The problem became even more acute after Sui had unified China. Sui, unlike the preceding dynasties, depended increasingly upon South China for tax revenues, and since taxes were generally paid in kind, these goods had to be shipped to royal storage facilities located in Honan and Shensi in North China. As there was no water route from South to North China, an artificial one had to be built. Thus Sui Yang-ti set out to construct one of the greatest public works in history, the Grand Canal. Its scale was comparable to the building of the Great Wall by Ch'in Shih Huang-ti.

The construction of canals was not begun with Sui Yang-ti, but it was during his reign that they were built on such a grand scale. The first Sui canal was built by his father in 584; its completion provided a water route between T'ungkuan on the present Honan-Shensi border and Ch'angan, a distance of about one hundred miles. This, of course, was only the beginning of a much larger project yet to come. The Grand Canal, constructed under Sui Yang-ti, had three sections, all connected in a general north-south direction. The central section was the T'ungchi Canal which, built in 605, linked the southern tributaries of the Yellow River with the northern tributaries of the Yangtze River. Thus, for the first time in history a water route was provided between the valleys of the two most important rivers in China. The canal was said to be forty paces in width, with state highways along its banks, and these highways were planted with willows on both sides. In 608 the northern section of the Grand Canal, called the Yungchi Canal (from Panchu on the Yellow River to the city of Cho near modern Peking), began to be built. More than one million people

GULF OF POHAI

YELLOW SEA

Hangchow Bay

Cho

Yellow River

YUNGCHI CANAL

Kaifeng

Panchu

Loyang

T'UNGCHI CANAL

Yangchow

KIANGNAN CANAL

Yangtze River

Yühang
(Hangchow)

Kueichi

Tungkuan

Changan

Ching River

Wei River

Yellow River

MAP 17
THE GRAND CANAL
in the Seventh Century A.D.

——— The Grand Canal

were conscripted to work on this project. This project was followed two years later by the construction of the southern section, called the Kiangnan Canal, which began at the modern city Chinkiang on the Yangtze River and extended southward to Hangchow on the Ch'ient'ang River (the lower valley of the Chekiang River). After the Grand Canal had been completed, produce from South China could be shipped by boat to North China for a distance of about one thousand miles. Its importance cannot be overemphasized. More than anything else it fused North and South China as an economic and cultural whole, and their interdependence was greatly increased because of its existence. It was only after the introduction of railroads in modern times that the canal began to outlive its usefulness and deterioration began to set in. Prior to this time, it was the main artery between the north and the south, and each dynasty had always considered the good maintenance and efficient operation of the Grand Canal as one of its primary concerns.

Other public works of Sui Yang-ti, such as the construction of his many luxurious palaces, were much less beneficial to his subjects. Towards the end of his reign, he became more and more unscrupulous in the use of man power for his numerous petty projects, and he lived a life so extravagant that even his finance minister had a difficult time in keeping the accounts. Tax rates had to be raised, and soon they reached a point so high that people could no longer bear them. His pleasure trips to the Yangtze areas were not only an annoyance to his subjects, but often meant financial ruin to the local gentry and officials who had to wait on him. The popular saying was: "People are angry, but dare not speak." They had to wait for a disaster to fall on him before they would speak with a mighty clash of arms. The disaster they awaited did happen when his military campaigns against Korea met with reverses.

Since Han Wu-ti's conquest of Korea in the second century B.C. the Hermit Kingdom had been an off-and-on tributary state to the Celestial Empire for more than seven centuries. During the period between the second and the sixth century Korea was most of the time independent with little or no interference from China, as China herself was divided. After Sui Wen-ti had unified China, Korea, being afraid that China would intervene in her domestic affairs again, took defensive measures on the Sino-Korean border. The fear was soon realized. In 597 Sui Wen-ti sent an ultimatum to the Korean king, enunciating a number of reasons why he had to declare war: that the allied tribes of Sui on the northeastern border had been repeatedly attacked by Korea; that many skillful Chinese archers had been tempted away to Korea through the offering of better salaries; that Chinese envoys sent to Korea for the investigation of Korean affairs had been either refused entry or did not receive cooperation from Korean authorities; that Koreans had often passed across the border to murder Chinese; that Korea had frequently sent spies to China to obtain information; that Korea had shown openly her displeasure when Sui unified China and so on. The following year an expeditionary force was sent to subdue Korea but failed to achieve its purpose. During Sui Yang-ti's reign, three times the emperor personally led military expeditions against Korea, but each time the brave Koreans fought the invading forces to a stalemate. Because of the tremendous difficulty in shipping supplies over the rugged mountains in eastern Manchuria, a large portion of Chinese troops died of starvation before they could even reach the front. It did not help that the defenders adopted a delaying technique by fortifying themselves behind well-built strongholds and refusing to give battle. The invaders, frustrated and eventually exhausted, had to give up the siege, once their supplies were no longer adequate. It was not until 668 that Korea was finally conquered, when the T'ang dynasty under T'ang Kao-tsung threw in all its resources and captured Korea's capital of Pyonyang.

By the 610's all signs indicative of a dynasty's downfall were clear for everybody to see: foreign adventures had failed; taxes and labor conscription had been increased beyond endurance; the emperor continued to be insolent and callous; and to trigger the rebellion, famine again raised its head after a devastating flood had raged over Shantung and Honan provinces, when "people sold themselves as slaves in countless numbers." As expected, the revolt was begun in Shantung and Honan where people had previously suffered the most during the Korean campaigns because of their geographical proximity to Korea. What followed is too familiar to repeat. Warlords and bandits sprang up all over the country, and sometimes it was difficult to distinguish between them. In 618 Sui Yang-ti was murdered by a rebel leader, when he was in the gay city of Yangchow. Two months later Li Yüan, another rebel leader, assumed the imperial title at Ch'angan and called his dynasty T'ang.

THE T'ANG RULERS

The man instrumental in the establishment of the new dynasty was Li Shih-min, the second son of Li Yüan. He is better known by his imperial appellation, T'ang T'ai-tsung. Historians regarded him as one of the most enlightened rulers China ever had, and his reign (627–650) was among the best people could recall. He was a warrior, a statesman, and, if we can believe all the legends about him, a man almost perfect. According to a popular story circulated soon after his death, one of his arch-rivals, after stealing a look at him in a prearranged meeting, immediately conceded defeat, because Li Shih-min "has an irresistible air of being great." This personal magnetism enabled him to gather around himself the best brains of his time and delegate to them authority according to their individual capacities. Rarely had so many conscientious men served so ably under one ruler. Following Confucian teaching, he believed in setting the example for his subjects and "shared the sorrows of his subjects as if they were his own." An episode which occurred during his reign has been often cited to show what a benign monarch he was. About three hundred criminals were tried, sentenced to death, and were to be executed on the fifteenth day of the eighth moon, the customary day of execution each year. Having thought that people committed crimes because the ruler was not virtuous enough, the emperor ordered the prisoners to be set free so they could join their families, on the condition that they would voluntarily surrender themselves to the executioners before the scheduled execution. To everybody's surprise, every one of the three hundred returned of his own accord on the scheduled date. According to another story, once the emperor was very upset by his chief censor because the latter had criticized the emperor severely in front of his ministers. Though he was able to hold his temper in public, he gave vent to his intention to seek revenge after he had retired to his private chamber. His wife, having heard the story, went to her room and then emerged in ceremonial dress to congratulate him. Asked for the reason, she replied: "Only the best kind of rulers have courageous, frank censors. I am glad that I have the best kind of ruler as my husband."

T'ang T'ai-tsung was succeeded by T'ang Kao-tsung (650–684), a capable, though less colorful monarch. It was during his reign that Korea was conquered and converted into administrative provinces; the northern border was pacified after the various Mongolian and related tribes had been brought under control; in the West, Chinese jurisdiction was extended to Central Asia near the Persian border. Those kingdoms in Central Asia that were not conquered nevertheless considered themselves tributary states, addressing the T'ang emperor as "Celestial King" or "King of All Kings." Towards the end of his reign T'ang Kao-tsung was continuously in ill health, half incapacitated, and eventually he became a captive of his ambitious wife, the famed Empress Wu. Empress Wu, formerly a harem official during T'ang T'ai-tsung's reign, went to the nunnery after her master's death but soon was called to become empress after T'ang Kao-tsung had ascended to the throne. After the death of her imperial husband, she installed her son Chung-tsung as the emperor, soon found him too independent, dismissed and exiled him, and placed a more pliable child of hers on the imperial throne. Six years later she assumed the imperial title herself, thus ruling China in name as well as in fact. Young men of unusual sexual capacities were openly recommended and accepted for her royal pleasure, and scandal, once made open for all to see, somehow ceased to be scandal. But to her these lovers were merely "white faces"; she would not hesitate to order their death if they

Sea of Japan

Yellow Sea

East China Sea

South China Sea

Lake Baikal

RIVER

Changan

YELLOW

YANGTZE RIVER

Lake Balkhash

TARIM RIVER

INDIA

Bay of Bengal

Sthanesvara

Kapilavastu

Aral Sea

Caspian Sea

MAP 18

THE T'ANG EMPIRE
Circa 700 A.D.

□ Capital
......Hsüan-tsang's Routes
   to and from India

0   500   1000

Scale of Miles

ever tried to meddle in political affairs. [1] She entrusted governmental affairs to the very best men she could find, and they proved to be unswervingly loyal to her. Thus despite what might be said about her personal life, she was a capable, enlightened ruler, and her reign (690–705) was among the best during the T'ang dynasty.

The elegance of T'ang court life reached its most refined stage during the reign of T'ang Hsüan-tsung, also known as Ming-huang (713–756). The country had been at peace for more than a century, and people, both high and low, had experienced an unprecedented prosperity. To the T'ang court came China's ablest statesmen, renowned artists, famous writers, and talented poets, among whom were the immortal Li Po and Tu Fu. To posterity the best known episode during this period was the romantic story of the emperor and his favorite, Yang Kuei-fei, a story which was indicative of the easy, pleasant life during a period of abundance. Many poems (including one writen by Li Po) were written in praise of the unsurpassed beauty of this commoner's daughter with whom the emperor had fallen in love at first sight. Enchanted by her charm, the emperor did all he could to keep her happy and amused. A music and dance troupe of several hundred persons was kept in the court to entertain her, and horses and riders, we are told, ran around the clock from Canton to Ch'angan to carry fresh litchi—her favorite fruit—to the royal court, a distance of more than 1,500 miles. Her male relatives were all made dukes and counts, and there was a saying in Ch'angan: "Don't grieve when the new born is that of the female sex." In 755 news arrived in Ch'angan that An Lu-shan, a military governor in the northeast, had revolted. This came as a shocking surprise, for the emperor and his favorite had placed complete confidence in his loyalty for the defense of the northeastern border. On the battlefield the royal garrisons were outfought and out-maneuvered by the rebel leader who, though a barbarian and an illiterate, was nevertheless a capable general. Soon the rebels knocked at the front gate of Ch'angan, and the emperor and his favorite had to flee. In a mountain pass leading to Szechuan, the dispirited and half-starved soldiers refused to march forward, unless, said they, the culprits responsible for this miserable state of affairs were punished. Yang Kuei-fei's brother who was then the prime minister was cut into pieces by the mob of soldiers, and still they demanded more blood. With tears in his eyes, the emperor ordered his favorite to be led away, and she hanged herself on a nearby tree. Throughout the rest of his life, the emperor was a sad, depressed man, "washing his face everyday with a fountain of tears."

[1] A "white face" or *pai-mien* was a man who was sexually attractive but otherwise useless. This term is only occasionally used today.

Yen-p'ing Gate   Chin-kuang Gate   Ming-yüan Gate

West Market

Kuang-hua Gate

Fang-lin Gate

An-hua Gate

Yi-t'ing Palace

Imperial City

Ta-chi Palace

Ming-te Gate

Ting-wu Gate

Ch'i-hsia Gate

East Palace

Ta-ming Palace (Emperor's Summer Residence)

East Market

Lake Chü-chiang

Yen-hsing Gate   Ch'un-ming Gate   T'ung-hua Gate

W
S   N
E

MAP 19
T'ANG'S CAPITAL: CH'ANGAN
Total Area: 972 ch'ing or 14,752 acres

)(City Gate
Famous Churches and Temples: B Buddhist;
N Nestorian; T Taoist; Z Zoroastrian
---- Walls of modern city of Sian

GOVERNMENT AND INDUSTRY

During their prime, the strength of Sui and T'ang lay not only in the personalities of their great emperors but more so in the institutions which they helped create. With modifications here and there, the governmental structure established during this period was retained by later dynasties. The emperor, as the head of the state, ruled as well as reigned. He was assisted by *San Kung*, or Three Dukes, who were usually chosen from the country's most respected elder statesmen and served as advisers to the sovereign in connection with the formulation and implementation of policies. The daily administrative duties were carried out by three separate departments: two secretariats and one executive department. The first secretariat, called *Chung-shu Sheng*, was in charge of drafting decrees, orders, and proclamations issued in the name of the emperor, and the second secretariat, called *Men-hsia Sheng*, was responsible for screening and examining reports and petitions from lower governments or private citizens. The second secretariat could return the reports of local governments to their senders, if it regarded these reports as improper or unnecessary. As an order or decree had to be officially proclaimed by the second secretariat before it could become law, the latter was given the authority to return the same to the emperor, if it regarded such order or decree as too rash or unwise. In general, the two secretariats worked closely together to assure speedy communication between the central and the local governments.

The main responsibility for the enforcement of law and the implementation of policy was entrusted to the executive department, called *Shang-shu Sheng*, which had within its jurisdiction six ministries, namely, the Ministries of Rites, Finance, Personnel, War, Justice, and Public Works. Besides all these there was the Bureau of Censors independent of the departments described above, and its duty was to criticize and censor policy or personnel, if it regarded such policy as being harmful or injurious to the people or the state, or if an official was thought unfit for his work. On the local level, there were provinces and districts, the latter being the subdivisions of the former. Local officials were appointed by and responsible to the imperial government which kept a detailed record of each officeholder as a basis for recommending promotion or demotion. Roving envoys and inspecting generals were sent periodically from the capital to check into local conditions and to report on the merit of provincial and district officials; some of them were given the authority to promote or dismiss local officials on the spot.

One institution which accounted much for T'ang's military might was the militia system called *Fu-ping chih*. The origin of this system was remote and obscure; it did not reach perfection, however, until the T'ang dynasty. Its basic principle was to "reside soldiers among farmers" and to make the two occupations interchangeable. In peace time every soldier was a farmer, and when war came, every farmer became a soldier. During the reign of T'ang T'ai-tsung (627–649), the country had 634 militia units, each headed by a divisional commander. The divisional commander not only commanded his men on the battle field but was also responsible for their training during peacetime. Training was usually conducted in winter, after the autumn harvest and before the spring sowing season, so that training would not interfere with farmers' agricultural activities.

This militia system had many advantages. First, the country had an army that was always prepared, but without carrying the financial burden of supporting a standing army. Second, a divisional commander, by living together with his men through peace and war, presumably knew each of them well and would utilize each according to his fullest ability. Third, relatives and friends generally belonged to the same unit. It was hoped that they would emulate each other in achievement and that on the battlefield they would fight courageously to protect one another. During the time when this system functioned at its best, a T'ang army would never surrender under any circumstances, even though it might be defeated.

The system of land tenure during the T'ang dynasty was generally the same as introduced and implemented during the time of the Later Wei some three centuries before. Each male, after reaching adulthood, was given about fifteen acres of land. One-fourth of the portion was hereditary; the rest was to be returned to the state for redistribution after the grantee had reached the age of retirement when he could no longer work in the field. Widows and widowers, as well as the crippled and the disabled, were granted land as a relief measure, which could be rented out for cultivation and was redistributable after the death of the grantees. For land received, each farmer paid taxes in produce which consisted of grain and silk (or cloth). Besides, he had to perform labor service which, under normal circumstances, amounted to about twenty days a year. If he chose not to pay taxes in produce, he could substitute extra working days on whatever public projects the government assigned to him.

This system worked fairly well early in the T'ang dynasty. It began to deteriorate in the latter part of the eighth century. The reasons were many. First, there was a continuous increase in population as a result of a long period of peace and prosperity, while the total amount of arable land remained substantially the same. In 755 the official register listed the nation as having 8,919,309 households with a total population of 52,909,309. The actual population was considerably larger, for many households either failed to report or reported smaller numbers to evade taxes. As the population continued to grow, eventually there was less land available for distribution. Second, the land distribution system had never been universally enforced. From the very beginning, court and government officials were exempt from the control of the land distribution agency. Many of them owned hundreds or even thousands of acres of land which was not subject to distribution. Moreover, the number of officials was not small. According to one estimate, court and government officials on all levels, civilian and military, reached a total of 368,000 at one time. The effectiveness of this system was hampered by the fact that one could be free from its control simply by securing a position with the government. Third, the proper operation of this system relied on the availability of accurate census of both land and people, but an accurate census was hard to obtain in those days. When China was again plunged into war and chaos after An Lu-shan's rebellion, the taking of an accurate census was virtually impossible. People moved more frequently during the war years, and many people, having left their homes, never returned. Amidst the turmoil of wars, land and population registers were often destroyed, and births and deaths were no longer recorded. The land distribution system which had once functioned so effectively now completely collapsed. Tax collectors roamed the countryside using whatever ingenuity they had to collect as much as possible, with little or no regard to the principle of equity. The old tax system had become too elaborate for a turbulent era, and changes had to be made.

Confusion continued until the 780's when a new tax system was devised and put into practice. According to this system, the government at the beginning of each year estimated its expenditures and using this as a basis decided how much tax would be levied for that year. Tax was assessed on the ability to pay rather than age and other considerations. All taxes hitherto paid in produce and labor service were now combined into one single tax to be paid in cash. However, if a taxpayer chose to pay in produce, he could do so by paying an amount equivalent to his cash assessment, the conversion rate varying according to market prices. Payment was to be made twice a year, once before the end of the sixth moon month and once before the end of the twelfth. Because of its simplicity, this new system—called *liang-shui fa*, or semiannual tax system—was a great improvement over the previous one. It continued in force throughout the rest of the T'ang dynasty.

In industry, T'ang made continuous progress in the manufacturing of silk, tea, porcelain, and handicraft products. Sericulture had been an ancient industry, but due to the increase of demand both at home and abroad, it assumed greater importance in the people's economic life. The technique of dyeing had been greatly improved, and the quality of colored silk had thus become better. Tea was a popular drink, and new skills were introduced in making and preparing it. A book on tea written by a contemporary not only discussed its manufacture, but went into such details as the boiling process and the utensils to be used. Porcelain was made all over the country, but certain areas were particularly noted for their skill and fine products. In the north it was Loyang which specialized in making different kinds of chinaware for the royal house. In the south it was Yüeh (modern Chekiang province) whose dishes, according to a contemporary description, "look like ivory, but are as delicate as thin layers of ice." Handicraft products were made of different materials, such as wood, bamboo, leather, metal, ivory, and precious stones. Those made of ivory and precious stone were the most highly valued. Artisans who made them taught their skills only to their children, in order to keep professional secrets within their own families. Often they sent their best products to the emperor as tribute.

Most of these industrial products were for domestic consumption. Some, however, were destined to be exported abroad. During the T'ang

EWER IN THE
FORM OF A
COURT LADY,
T'ANG DYNASTY

dynasty the traditional silk routes across Central Asia were again open for trade. Many cities along these routes both east and west of the Pamirs became exchange centers for Arab, Turkish, Persian, and Chinese merchants. In addition, Arab and Persian traders arrived in large numbers on the east coast of China via the sea routes. The four most important trading centers were Chiaochou, Canton, Ch'üanchou, and Yangchow, all located along the south and the southeast coast. Many of the foreign traders became extremely wealthy, took up permanent residence in China, and were a power to be reckoned with in local politics. In the 880's it was estimated that in Canton alone there were more than 120,000 Muslims, Jews, and Persians. Even in faraway Yangchow there were several thousand Arabs and Persians. It was not until the tenth century when China was again plunged into civil wars that foreigners ceased to come, and the once lucrative trade became a dream of the past.

CULTURAL EXPANSION

The extensiveness of international trade resulted partly from T'ang's cosmopolitan attitude towards foreigners. The early T'ang emperors regarded China as the civilizing center of the world, and as such, China thought it had a moral obligation to educate and civilize the "benighted barbarians." Foreigners in China were not persecuted or discriminated against; they were given every right and privilege enjoyed by the Chinese themselves. It was hoped that foreigners, having been exposed to Chinese civilization, would inevitably abandon their barbarian ways, due to the very superior nature of the Chinese cultural system. During the golden age of T'ang, hundreds of foreign students came to China to learn about religion, philosophy, the arts, and political institutions. Most of them came from Korea and Japan. After returning to their own lands, as recognized leaders in their fields, they helped mold cultural developments in their own countries. From then onward Chinese culture remained the strongest foreign influence in Korea and Japan until the coming of the Europeans in modern times.

Recent discovery of Chinese coins on Japanese soil seems to indicate that relations between the two countries existed as early as the fifth century B.C. After Han Wu-ti's conquest of Korea in the second century B.C. more Japanese came to China via Korea, and Korea from then on became a natural bridge over which Chinese culture passed to Japan. Early Chinese historians discussed Japan only in the most desultory manner, either because there was little known, or because they did not think Japan deserved more attention than the most casual remarks, such as "they sent tribute to China each year, including occasionally slaves." It was not until the third century A.D. that Chinese historians began to write in some detail about Japan and the Japanese people. By then Japan was already a culturally advanced country, even though it was politically divided. According to one description, "the dwarfs (Japanese) are expert divers, skillful in catching fish and clams. They grow rice, flax, and their sericulture is also quite advanced. Their climate is temperate and warm.

AN ANCIENT MAP SHOWING THE CHINESE CONCEPT OF THE WORLD   China is located at the center of the map (white area) surrounded by water (black area) dotted with island kingdoms including Japan. Further beyond is an enveloping ring of land (white area) on which are located countries with such odd names as "Country of Giants" and "Country of Gentlemen." Beyond this land is the universal ocean (black area) which extends outward indefinitely. On the upper right is the explanation which reads: "There are one hundred nations in the world: twenty-five surrounded by the Seas, forty-five on the Seas, and thirty beyond the Seas." The four Chinese characters around the map indicate directions: "East" in the right, "North" on the top, etc. The calligraphy on this map is embarrassingly poor, indicating perhaps that the map was an amateurish production.

People eat vegetables raw regardless of summer or winter." "Men, old or young, tatoo their bodies. . . . Women let their hair loose over their shoulders. Their clothing looks like a bed sheet: an opening is made in the middle through which the head emerges." But the Japanese were a polite people. "Whenever an inferior meets a superior on the road, he steps aside, squats or kneels down, to show his respect."

Of all the things Japan learned from China, none was more important than the Chinese written language. By adopting it Japan conditioned herself to learning many facets of Chinese culture of which language was the most eloquent symbol. Chinese written language was probably introduced to Japan towards the end of the third century A.D. Soon it became the standard means of communication among the country's educated, as Japan had then no written language of her own. The Japanese learned so well that by the fifth century Chinese court officials were amazed at the elegance of style in letters which Japanese rulers sent to their Chinese counterparts. From the latter part of the sixth to the last decade of the ninth century Japanese envoys, monks, scholars, and students arrived in increasing numbers at Ch'angan. Early during this period they came to China via the traditional Korean route, but later, as ships and navigation skill improved, they sailed directly across the East China Sea and landed on the east coast near modern Shanghai. After their return, their influence was immeasurable in shaping Japan's cultural development along the Chinese pattern. For instance, Chinese philosophy and political institutions were transplanted to Japanese soil without much modification. Even the Japanese capitals, Nara and Kyoto, were built as small replicas of T'ang's capital, Ch'angan. Japan also learned the more advanced methods in sericulture, textile manufacturing, paper making, woodworking, and printing. Buddhism and Confucianism gradually replaced animism as the popular beliefs, and moral and cultural values also underwent a profound change. Even in the field of recreation, the impact was just as great. More sophisticated Japanese were no longer satisfied with the traditional sword-swinging; they learned to appreciate Chinese music and dance; they sculpted and painted after the Chinese style; and they played games of intellect, such as the popular game *go*.

As China headed for another periodical decline early in the tenth century, the Japanese ceased to come. By then they had already learned what they wished to learn from China. Culturally the Japanese child had grown to a man; there was no more to learn from the parent.

EDUCATION AND CIVIL SERVICE

T'ang, as the civilizing agent in the East, drew its strength partly from a remarkable educational system. In the capital there were the famous Six Colleges (*Liu hsüeh*), controlled and operated by the government. The first three were colleges of general education and were reserved for children of higher officials. Their purpose was to provide students with a broad background of liberal arts, especially the classics and history, with the hope that they would serve the state more intelligently if they were called on after their graduation. Children of lower officials and common citizens could be admitted to the other three colleges: the Colleges of Law, Calligraphy, and Mathematics. In addition there were two exclusive schools, called study institutes, that were attended by members of the royal family and the families of top ranking officials, such as the prime minister. Later, two other schools were added, the School of Medicine and the School of Metaphysics. The former, besides teaching the students how to feel the pulse and how to massage, also taught them how to exorcise the evil spirits. The latter concerned itself with the study of Taoist philosophy; Lao-tzu and Chuang-tzu were the standard texts. On the local level, schools were established in provinces and districts, though they were of a lower quality than those in the capital. Students who did well in local schools were allowed to go to the capital for advanced studies. In all schools, central or local, the teaching of Confucian philosophy and ethics was required for every student.

For most students learning was not an end in itself; it prepared them for a governmental career. For them taking the civil service examination was one of the most important events in life. It climaxed the learning process, and their whole future might well depend upon it. The civil service examination system was introduced earlier by Sui Yang-ti, but it was not perfected until the T'ang dynasty. Students who took this examination were either the graduates of regular schools or those who had been specially recommended by local magistrates. In either case they had to be screened for moral character before they were allowed to take the examination. Hope ran high before each examination, but for most of them it was one disappointment after another. Under T'ang rule no more than one from every hundred examinees was allowed to pass, simply because the government was obligated to provide those successful with positions, and positions were few. It was not uncommon that father and son took the same examination, and while one passed, the other failed. Early during the T'ang regime, there were many kinds of examinations classified according to subject matter. As time went on, one category, called *chin-shih* or advanced scholarship, became the most esteemed and the most popular. The country's brightest young men usually chose this category, as it was more a test of native intelligence and comprehension than a test of memory. Having chosen this category, the students took two separate tests, one in poetry composition and the other an essay test on philosophical or contemporary problems. If they failed to compose satisfactory poems on specified topics, they automatically failed and were not allowed to take the second test. For the scant few who had passed both tests, the honor was great and the prestige enormous. They were called *chin-shih*; their names were made known throughout the empire; and they became candidates for government positions. Their descendants would proudly mention their names for generations to come.

The civil service examination system marked a sharp departure from the general practice prevalent during the preceding period with regard to the recruitment of bureaucratic personnel. While the governments of Wei, Tsin, and the Southern Dynasties emphasized family background, the governments of Sui and T'ang placed great importance on a candidate's knowledge and ability. Recognizing that the political disunity of the preceding period resulted largely from localism and partly from the obsession with family prestige, the governments of Sui and T'ang tried to cultivate a national purpose and strengthen national solidarity. It was hoped that the successful functioning of the examination system would not only bring the best men to serve the government but would also destroy localism, since the most talented young men in the provinces, instead of serving a local or family cause, would look beyond their provincial borders for patronage and advancement. Thus provincialism would be replaced by a national allegiance. As the examination system took no consideration of family or professional background, the glamor hitherto attached to the old families would disappear, and the government would be the sole dispenser of fame, power, and wealth. By dangling rewards constantly in front of the country's educated, the government obtained the unswerving loyalty of the country's most powerful group, and those who had been rewarded abundantly after passing the examinations could be counted on to support the existing regime. It is no wonder that with modifications and occasional interruptions the civil service examination system continued in force for the next twelve centuries—it was not completely abolished until the twentieth century.

Like all other systems, the examination system had its advantages and disadvantages. On the positive side, it might be said that it had broadened the government's base by drawing officials from all levels of society and thus introduced a democratic element into an otherwise oligarchic society. Theoretically at least, it was entirely possible for a man of the humblest origin, by passing the specified examinations, to rise in power, wealth, and prestige. More than anything else, the examination system accounted for the absence of a caste system in China and the large degree of social mobility denied to many other authoritarian societies. Second, to find the right man for the right task, nothing could be more objective than a test impartially administered, and the civil service examination system was adoped precisely for that purpose. Many great statesmen in China were a product of this system. Third, the examination system brought to mind the importance of education and learning and thus indirectly raised the cultural level of the country as a whole. While in other countries landlords, merchants, or industrialists might be men of the greatest prestige, in China the most respected had always been the scholars.

However, those who criticized this system could point out that the examination which at best was a test of literary learning should not be used as the sole criterion to judge a man's true ability, since a good administrator was more often a man of the world than a man learned in Confucian classics or skillful in writing poetry. Moreover, while the examination system might have increased social mobility, it did not end social stratification. A barber's son might pass the examination and thus be accepted as one of the social elite, but this did not help the rest of the barbers who were still regarded as the "mean" people. Furthermore, except for the wealthy few, who could afford to spend years of study just to prepare for the examinations? The so-called democratic outlook of the examination system was perhaps more apparent than real. Critics of this system were anxious to point out that the overemphasis on literary learning at the expense of other intellectual pursuits had done great damage to other areas of learning of equal importance. This accounted for, at least in part, China's lag behind some other countries in the field of science and technology, despite its achievement in the humanities. Individual scientific talents did occur from time to time, but as society did not attach much importance to the study of natural science and offered no reward for its development, and as people generally looked down upon manual work, there was no intellectual tradition outside the study of humanities. Last, perhaps the most serious indictment against the examination system was its contribution to the development of despotism. After this system was adopted, a man could no longer attain political authority or social recognition through any channel but one, which was controlled by the government. Forever looking for favor and patronage from the central government, the country's educated lost their political initiative and independence and became the ardent defenders of the status quo. As the educated class went, so went the country as a whole.

RELIGION

While Confucianism was the required learning for all students and officials, other schools of thought continued to prosper under the T'ang government's benign policy towards all ideologies and religions. Nestorians, Zoroastrians, and Muslims quietly built their temples and churches in Ch'angan with no interference from the government. Many T'ang emperors, such as T'ang T'ai-tsung, not only took religious toleration for granted, but even encouraged the spread of alien ideologies, in order to "show the world the benevolent policy of the Celestial Empire towards all barbarians." Of all alien ideologies, the most influential was still Buddhism which embraced within its fold people of all walks of life. Monasteries and temples continued to translate Buddhist scriptures into Chinese; some of the translations were done under government sponsorship. Indian and Central Asian monks were invited to China to teach, and Chinese pilgrims travelled to India, over almost impassable mountains and deserts, to obtain more authentic copies of Buddhist scriptures. During the T'ang dynasty the most famous of the pilgrims was Hsüan-tsang who left Ch'angan in 628 and did not return until seventeen years later. The number of Buddhist monasteries and nunneries continued to increase throughout the seventh, the eighth, and the first half of the ninth century. In the 710's there were 3,245 monasteries and 2,113 nunneries in China. By the middle of the ninth century, the total number had reached 44,600, and there were about 260,500 monks and nuns.

Conditioned for centuries by Confucian worldliness, the Chinese from the very beginning showed more interest in the practical aspect than the theological aspect of Indian Buddhism. Therefore, it was the Mahayana School, with its emphasis on achieving personal salvation, which eventually won the heart of the nation's faithful. In time the Mahayana school split into many sects since different masters emphasized different aspects of Buddha's teachings. During the T'ang dynasty, three sects emerged as the most prominent, Ching-t'u (Pure Land), T'ien-t'ai, and Ch'an (known as Zen in Japan). Of the three, Ch'an, due to its simple yet philosophical teachings, had great appeal to Chinese intellectuals. It de-emphasized book learning and gave priority to meditation as the means of achieving the ultimate, *nirvana*. One great master, we are told, faced a wall for nine years before enlightenment was finally obtained. Ch'an's seemingly contradictory, incoherent explanations of all existence engendered a mystic fascination of its own. The followers of Ch'an left the questioner much room for his own answer besides whatever information the answerer himself had already provided. In fact, true Ch'an could never be explained; it could only be felt and understood. The role of the master was to provide the road, but not the destination. Understanding came as a result of intuition, insight, rather than logic and reasoning. Here is an example:

> Monk: Who knows the meaning of the apricots?
> Master: The Buddhists know.
> Monk: Can a monk know?
> Master: I don't know Buddhism.

The last statement was the most important. Both the monk and the reader could make their own interpretations.

Of course, not all Chinese were happy with the popularity of this imported faith. Many Confucian scholars, led by the famous essayist Han Yü, attacked Buddhism on both theoretical and practical grounds. On the side of theory, they regarded Buddhism, with its relics, prayers, and the teaching of heavenly bliss, as pure superstition, incompatible with the good common sense which had characterized the development of native Chinese thought. On the practical side, they pointed out the disadvantage of having such a large number of monasteries and nunneries. The monks, said they, living on other people's toil, were no better than parasites. No doubt influenced by the latter line of thinking and further instigated by Taoist priests, one of the T'ang emperors, T'ang Wu-tsung (r. 841–847), ordered the reduction of the number of Buddhist temples and the forced return to laity of many monks and nuns. But the effectiveness of this order was short-lived because no sooner had his successor ascended the throne than a decree was issued to restore all rights and privileges to the formerly dispossessed Buddhist establishments. This turned out to be China's last persecution against Buddhism. It lasted only two years (845–847) and does not seem to have anything to do with the decline of Buddhism after the ninth century. Buddhism remained one of the popular faiths in the succeeding centuries, though it had lost official patronage.

LITERATURE AND FINE ARTS

A long period of peace and prosperity enabled T'ang writers to produce a large number of scholarly works. There were books on religion, philosophy, history, and science, together with books in a lighter vein, like poetry, painting, calligraphy, and short stories. For the first time all books were classified into four major categories: (Confucian) classics, history, philosophy, and miscellaneous, a classification which was followed by later Chinese librarians. The governments of Sui and T'ang maintained excellent libraries. The imperial library of Sui, for instance, had a holding of more than 370,000 rolls. In the 710's when the imperial library at Ch'angan catalogued its holdings, it had 53,915 entries written by writers prior to T'ang and 28,469 entries written by contemporary authors. To secure accuracy in book copying, the T'ang government established a special bureau staffed by copyists, proofreaders, and calligraphers, and each copy was checked and rechecked for accuracy before it was deposited in the imperial library for safekeeping. Individuals had their own private holdings. One scholar, we are told, had a private collection of 20,000 rolls. Another man had to hire thirty oxcarts to ship his books when he changed his residence. As demand for good ink and paper increased, the techniques of making them were considerably improved during the T'ang period.

Though the government patronized only works of a more serious nature such as Confucian classics and philosophy, the T'ang writers who became famous to posterity were the historians, poets, and writers of short stories. *The Understanding of History* (*Shih t'ung*), written by Liu Chih-chi (661–721), underscored a new method in which analysis and evaluation played roles equally important as the narrative of historical events. Another historian, Tu Yu, who wrote *The Study of Institutions* (*T'ung tien*), was perhaps the world's first institutional historian. In prose writing, Han Yü (768–824) and Liu Tsung-yüan were regarded as the most outstanding. Their writings covered a variety of subjects, from serious discourse on political issues to casual observation of a particular incident in life, always, of course, with a moral to teach. However, they are read today not so much for their contents as for their style which, contrary to the parallel form popular during the Six Dynasties, is noted for its audacity and forcefulness, like "the mighty roaring of river torrents." Short story writers of the T'ang period (all men) found a popular theme in the faithfulness of women and the fickleness of men. Sometimes the guilty males repented and thus a happy ending ensued. Other times they let power and wealth cover their conscience; their ever faithful lovers or wives either died of longing or committed suicide. The wronged spirits came back to haunt the guilty, to make sure that the latter received what they deserved, and thus, finally, justice was served. The best written short story during the T'ang dynasty, however, did not follow this popular theme. *The Story of the Curly Whiskers* (*Ch'iu-jan ke chuan*), written by Tu Kuang-t'ing, is a romantic story with strong political connotations. Its moral is that great leaders, like the T'ang emperors, are born, not made, and that to attempt the impossible can only result in one's own frustration and unhappiness.

During the T'ang dynasty the most prolific literary output was in the field of poetry. Li Po (701–762), who has been hailed as a true genius of all times, wrote beautiful poems "as easily as water flows out from a fountain." His poems deal with emotions and sentiments; their style is lively and spontaneous. A habitual drunkard, he refused to write a poem to praise Yang Kuei-fei's beauty until the emperor made him dead drunk. He died of natural causes at a fairly advanced age, though according to a popular tale, he died by drowning when, having drunk too much one evening, he tried to embrace the moon by diving into a river. Tu Fu (712–770), another great poet, was more serious. He used his pen as the voice of the masses to tell of their undeserved fate and of their untold sufferings. The tragic figures in his poems often appeared whenever there were wars and famine. Following the same line, a later poet, Po Chü-yi (772–846), described the tragedy of wars and the sadness of the poor and the deserted. Because his poems strike a responsive chord whenever they are read, he has been called a people's poet. Other poets, especially those of a later period, found a theme in "wine, women, and song." The women whose beauty they praised so lavishly were the professional dancers and singers who lived in the demimonde, and the poets had no scruple in putting down the most intimate affairs with them in the most readable terms. Many of these verses became so popular that music was composed to accompany them. T'ang emperors patronized both poets and musicians. One emperor in the ninth century was said to have had 6,500 professional musicians on the royal payroll at one time, of which 1,500 were "popular" dancers and singers.

The fact that T'ang produced more masters of painting than any previous dynasty was partly due to royal patronage. T'ang Hsüan-tsung, a lover of fine arts as well as beautiful women, invited to the court many prominent painters of his time, notably Li Ssu-hsün (651–720) and Wu Tao-tzu. Wang Wei (699–759), who was as famous in painting as in poetry, was said to have injected poetry into his painting as he had injected painting into his poems. While painters of previous dynasties were more interested in painting religious subjects, T'ang masters were particularly versed in the painting of people, still life, animals, and landscape. The familiar theme of misty mountains, tranquil waters, and a hermit in his pagoda-shaped abode was no doubt due to the influence of Taoism which advocated the return to nature and a life of seclusion, peace, and meditation. Some of the paintings of this period have survived. These surviving examples prove the remarkable quality of the painting materials used at that time. Though calligraphy continued to be a popular art form, practiced by all men of learning, none seemed to be able to exceed Wang Hsi-chih of an earlier period. T'ang T'ai-tsung loved Wang Hsi-chih's calligraphy so much that when he was about to die, he requested to be buried with one of the latter's masterpieces.

In general, Chinese achievements in science and technology during the T'ang period were far behind those in the humanities. T'ang astronomers were most concerned with the relative position of the sun and the earth, as such knowledge was essential to the making of an accurate calendar. Map making was another emphasized field. While these maps were fairly accurate with regard to China proper, they became vague and inaccurate when they tried to cover the so-called barbarian territories.

THE DECLINE

After 755, the year of An Lu-shan's revolt, the T'ang regime underwent a steady decline. To suppress the revolt, the reigning T'ang emperor made the short-sighted move of inviting military help from barbarian tribes beyond the northern and the northwestern frontier. The most powerful group among them was a nomadic, Mongolian horde called Huiheh (Wigours) which had its base of operation in the modern Kansu

province. Primitive, warlike, and eager for material gain, it agreed readily
to the T'ang government's offer, on the condition that all the wealth of
recaptured cities should be regarded as its war booty and that it had free
disposal of all captured persons, including women and children. Thus a
gate was open to a new influx of barbarians, much to the government's
later regret. When Loyang was recaptured from An Lu-shan, the Hui-heh
sacked the city thoroughly and burned whatever they could not carry,
only stopping when the elders of the city offered their leaders "ten thousand bolts of silk." The T'ang government's woe did not end even after An
Lu-shan's rebellion had been suppressed. Hui-heh soldiers roamed freely
in Shensi and Honan, "torturing people and insulting local officials," besides carrying on the customary looting. They conducted their lawless
activities even in the capital, Ch'angan. One day early in 766, a Hui-heh
envoy was busy directing the kidnapping of Chinese civilians right in
front of the Bureau of Barbarian Affairs, and Chinese officials looked on
and did not dare to intervene. Each year the Hui-heh sent to the T'ang
court thousands of horses to trade for silk, at the stipulated rate of one
horse for forty bolts of silk, even though "most of these horses were so old
and weak that they could not even walk." Sometimes this trade became so
one-sided that Chinese officials decided to give the silk anyway, without
bothering to ask for horses. Corrupted and softened by Chinese luxuries,
the Hui-heh began to decline by the 780's and T'ang emperors, following
an ancient custom, supplied its rulers with Chinese princesses as consorts.

The T'ang government's appeasement of the Hui-heh was partly due
to its fear of another powerful tribe of Tibetan origin, namely the T'u-fan.
Several times it had to call upon the Hui-heh for help to stop the T'u-fan's
invasions from the southwest. As Chinese troops moved eastward to combat An Lu-shan's rebels in the 750's, a power vacuum was created along
the southwestern border, and the T'u-fan quickly moved in. Each year
they raided and looted areas deep within China proper, until in 765 they
captured their biggest prize, Ch'angan, which they sacked for fifteen days
before finally retreating. This miserable state of affairs continued for several decades. It was not until the middle of the ninth century that the
T'ang government recovered from the T'u-fan the last of its lost territories. By then the T'ang dynasty had been so weakened by foreign invasion and domestic rebellion that it never really recovered.

While barbarian invasions were an important factor contributing to
the decline of the T'ang regime, the basic cause seemed to be internal.
Both the Hui-heh and the T'u-fan, despite their warlike activities, were
interested only in looting and in making temporary material gains and
had neither the ambition nor the capacity to occupy China proper on a
permanent basis. From the middle of the eighth century on, the T'ang
emperors were mediocre almost without exception, during a time when
strong leadership was badly needed. Real power fell into the hands of

corrupt, selfish eunuchs whose only interest was to acquire power and retain it. Once they were entrenched, it was almost impossible to dislodge them. Their power was so great that throughout the ninth century they murdered two emperors and installed seven, every one of whom was their puppet. The T'ang court, once the center of elegance and culture, at this time became a hotbed of intrigues, feuds, and assassinations.

As the court lost its dignity, the people lost their respect for it. Discontented elements in the provinces took full advantage of local grievances engendered by corruption and injustice to organize revolt. After the middle of the eighth century, rebellions repeatedly occurred. The most damaging was the Huang Ch'ao rebellion which devastated the country for more than nine years. Huang Ch'ao (d. 884) was a former salt merchant who, after amassing a fortune, decided to try his luck in the civil service examinations. Poorly educated and inadequately prepared, he repeatedly failed to pass. Instead of blaming himself, he blamed the whole of society for his misfortunes. During a famine in 875 when a bandit group swept across his native district in Shantung, he decided to join forces with the bandits. As he led his followers southward, the rebel rank snowballed; local officials either fled in advance or surrendered themselves. For a nine-year period, his hordes marched up and down the eastern half of China proper without encountering much resistance. They indulged in mass massacre after the capture of each city, with officials, intellectuals, and wealthy families as their favored targets. It was said that in 878 after Canton had been captured, 120,000 foreigners (Christians, Muslims, Jews, and Persians) were slaughtered in cold blood, presumably because they were "too wealthy." While he was robbing the rich, Huang Ch'ao gave some of his loot to the poor, with whom he was quite popular. His success culminated in the capture of Loyang and Ch'angan in 880; he sacked both cities thoroughly, as the barbarians had done before. However, without the support of the scholar-gentry class which he looked down upon with utter contempt, he was never able to organize an efficient government, even though at one time most of China proper was under his control. In 884 after his hordes had been repeatedly defeated by a T'ang general, he asked one of his devoted friends to kill him and to take his head to the T'ang headquarters for a reward. When his friend refused to do so, he committed suicide.

To cope with rebellions like this, provincial governors were given extraordinary powers; often several provinces were put under the jurisdiction of one man to achieve more efficient military campaigns. Eventually these governors or governors-general became too powerful for the imperial government to control after the rebellions had been suppressed. They collected their own taxes, appointed their own officials, and maintained their own armies. Theirs were independent kingdoms in all except name. To perpetuate the independent status of their provinces, they often appointed their successors (usually their own children) before they died, and the imperial government could do nothing except confirm these appointments. Thus the most powerful provinces were not only independent but also governed by hereditary rulers. The governors fought among themselves and annexed territories at each other's expense. It often happened that when a T'ang emperor decided to punish the most recalcitrant governors, being militarily weak he had to seek help from other governors. By becoming a partner in the wars between the governors, he degraded himself in the game of annexing territories which nominally belonged to him anyway. Eventually he wound up on the loser's end, as the governors whose help he had asked gained most of the territories conquered from the defeated and consequently became even more unmanageable. Were he on the losing side, he found himself in the most embarrassing position of having to issue a decree publicly denouncing himself and apologizing to his nominally inferior subordinates. In either case, he could not win.

With invasions from abroad and disunity and rebellions at home, it was only a matter of time before the T'ang dynasty would come to an end. In 907 the last T'ang emperor abdicated in favor of one of his generals named Chu Ch'üan-chung. The latter called his dynasty Liang, known as Later Liang to historians. Following this change in dynasties, five dynasties rose and fell in quick succession; it was a matter of one strong man replacing another. The five dynasties were known as the Later Liang (907–923), the Later T'ang (923–936), the Later Tsin (936–947), the Later Han (947–950), and the Later Chou (951–960). Under none of these dynasties was China unified. The many warlords in the provinces continued their independent or semi-independent status. This shifting situation finally ended in 960 when Chao K'uang-yin, a scholarly general, conquered most of the warlords and founded a new dynasty called the Sung.

vi

The Two Sungs (*1*)

CHAO K'UANG-YIN

On Chinese New Year's Day, 960, Loyang was alerted by urgent dispatches from two governors in the northern frontier that the Khitan Tartars, a nomadic tribe in Inner Mongolia, were about to march southward towards China proper. An emergency meeting was called, and it was decided that Chao K'uang-yin should head an expeditionary force to meet the invading enemies. Two days after the alarm was sounded, the commander and his troops were speeding northward.

The rise of Chao as the most powerful man in Loyang was no less than phenomenal. Only a year before he was one of those young generals who had plenty of ambition but was quite uncertain of what the future would hold. It was a surprise to him and to everybody else that all of a sudden the reigning emperor, Chou Shih-tsung (954–959), decided to promote him to the rank of Commander-in-chief of All Armed Forces, by-passing the older and better known generals, including the emperor's closest relatives. Chou, however, had his own reason for the appointment. He was suffering from an incurable disease and his days were numbered; he wanted a conscientious, dependable man to take care of his seven-year-old crown prince after he could no longer do so himself.[1] Among the candidates he had in mind he finally decided on Chao K'uang-yin. First, Chao was incorruptible during a time when practically everyone used his position to enrich himself. Second, he loved learning. In the mind of the emperor, a man genuinely interested in books could not possibly be bad. Once Chao was accused of having accepted bribes and of having shipped large trunks of gold and precious stones to his home after a successful military campaign in the south. The emperor ordered an investigation, and the investigators found nothing in those trunks except books which Chao had carefully collected and preserved from the devastation of war. Then and there the emperor decided that this was the man for whom he had long been looking.

On the third day of the first lunar month, the expeditionary force reached Ch'ench'iao where the soldiers stayed overnight after a long day's march from the capital. In the early morning of the next day, Chao K'uang-yin was waked from his sleep by repeated sounds of shouting in the inn where he stayed. Opening his bedroom door, he saw hundreds of soldiers swarming into the inn, and some of his generals, their swords unsheathed, stood on both sides of the inner court. The noise reached its apex when the soldiers spotted the emergence of their commander. When the commotion finally subsided, the generals voiced in unison: "Be our commander, the emperor of China!" Before Chao had time to answer, one of the generals put a yellow robe—symbol of imperial authority—on his back, and all the soldiers knelt down immediately, shouting at the top of their voices: "Long live the emperor!" Subsequently the soldiers carried him to his horse, and the entire expeditionary force moved southward towards Loyang.[2] In Loyang the child emperor abdicated, and Chao K'uang-yin formally assumed the imperial title as the first emperor of the new Sung dynasty. The capital was moved eastward to Kaifeng.

Though there had been instances of emperors installed by soldiers during the Five Dynasties, the mutiny at Ch'ench'iao turned out to be the most consequential, for the Sung dynasty lasted almost three centuries. Outwardly humble and modest, Chao K'uang-yin had won many influential friends long before the mutiny. There was little opposition when he and his soldiers returned to the capital. Though most of the residents had

[1] Upon the death of his father, the crown prince, known as Chou Kung-ti, ascended to the throne in the summer of 959.

[2] Meanwhile the Khitan Tartars retreated after they had achieved their goal of looting some of China's border provinces.

no doubt that the mutiny was voluntary and spontaneous, Chao's mother, after hearing the good news, was said to have commented calmly: "I knew my son would make it." [1]

The way the dynasty was founded affected greatly the forthcoming events of the new regime. After most of China had been brought under his control, Chao did not forget that he had become emperor only through a mutiny engineered by his subordinates, and he was fearful that he himself might be deposed in a similar manner. What followed was one of the most curious episodes in Chinese history, the famous "disarmament beside the wine cups." As the story goes, the emperor one evening invited his top lieutenants to a banquet in his palace. In the midst of joyful drinking he dismissed all attendants and then remarked that he was thankful to his generals for their support and that he was nevertheless worried and often sleepless ever since he had ascended to the dragon throne.

"Why?" asked the generals.

"This is not difficult to see. Who does not wish to occupy my place?"

Upon hearing this all the generals present knelt. "The mandate of Heaven has already been bestowed upon Your Majesty. Who can and dares to be different?" said the generals.

"You might not be. But how can you control your subordinates who wish to acquire power and wealth as once you did when you proclaimed me as your sovereign? If and when they put the yellow robe on your back, how can you refuse?"

Then the emperor gave them a lecture on the meaning of life, saying that the purpose of life was pleasure for oneself and one's descendants, and that it would be better for all concerned if the generals would relinquish their military authority and retire to their private estates, so that no suspicion could possibly exist between the sovereign and his generals and that everyone present, with God's help, would live a long span of life. The next day the generals resigned from their posts, all on account of "sickness." [2]

[1] The mutiny at Ch'ench'iao, which led to the establishment of the Sung dynasty, is recorded in the *History of the Five Dynasties* (*Wu-tai shih*) by Hsieh Chü-cheng (d. 981), as well as many other books. However, the most detailed description of this incident appears in *Su-shui Records* (*Su-shui chi-wen*) by Ssu-ma Kuang (1018–1086). While most historians believe that the mutiny was "voluntary and spontaneous," some have raised doubt, in view of the alleged remark made by Chao K'uang-yin's mother. Whatever the truth was, it should be noted that the installation of emperors by soldiers was a common practice during the Five Dynasties. After Chao's accession to the throne, Chou Kung-ti, the deposed child emperor, was granted the title of Cheng Wang, or King of Cheng. He died in 973 when he was twenty-one years old.

[2] One of the most detailed descriptions of this incident, "disarmament beside the wine cups," appears in *Source Materials Compiled As a Sequence to History*

The "disarmament beside the wine cups" formally ended a long period of warlordism and political disunity which had plagued China since the eighth century and paved the way for a prolonged era of internal peace. Anxious to correct past abuses, the founder of the Sung dynasty made it a rule that only civil officials could be appointed as governors; that military men, regardless of rank and position, should always be subject to civilian control; and that all officials, from those in the imperial government to those on the lowest administrative unit, the county, were directly appointed by and responsible to the emperor. To check the power of local authority, to each province was assigned a resident-adviser whose signature, in addition to that of the governor, was necessary to validate any official document. To deprive the governors of their financial independence, the privilege of levying and collecting tax was transferred to a newly created independent officer, the *chuan-yün shih,* or transport envoy, who, after seeing that local expenses had been disbursed, shipped all surpluses to the imperial treasury. To conserve the military strength of the imperial government, able-bodied and better-trained recruits were assigned duties in the capital and its environs, while the weak and the aged were left in the provinces. Military commanders were regularly transferred from one post to another to forestall any personal loyalty which might develop between generals and soldiers. Military units moved periodically from one garrison duty to another so that no military unit would acquire a local attachment detrimental to the imperial interest. In carrying out these measures Chao K'uang-yin had the help of his prime minister, Chao P'u, a Confucian scholar who once boasted that he could easily rule the world with half of the knowledge he had acquired by reading the *Analects of Confucius.*

LIAO

While these measures strengthened the central government and corrected the tendency toward decentralization prevalent in the preceding centuries, it soon became clear that by bending too far in one direction danger was encountered from another. When these measures were adopted, the Sung government desired to eliminate the uncontrollable, independent or semi-independent warlords whose prevalence had plagued China since the beginning of An Lu-shan's revolt in 755. And in this respect it was very successful. As the central government was strengthened, the fear of warlordism diminished. In fact, the new policy was so success-

As A Mirror (Hsü Tzu-chih t'ung-chien ch'ang-pien), roll 2, by Li T'ao who lived in the twelfth century. The incident is also recorded in "The Biography of Shih Shou-hsin" in the *History of the Sung Dynasty (Sung shih)* by T'o-t'o who lived in the fourteenth century.

ful that throughout the dynasty few revolts occurred and the challenge
to central authority was never really serious.

The new policy, however, was not altogether an unmixed blessing.
Complete dependence on the imperial government discouraged local initiative and eventually deprived local authorities of the ways and means to
meet a local situation. This problem became particularly serious in the
border provinces where the governors were often denied adequate
means to defend themselves against foreign incursions. The deliberate
degradation of military personnel unfortunately occurred at a time when
the nation's survival depended upon the successful outcome of military
operations. The subjection of military personnel to civilian control was
carried to such an extreme that often a man whose talent lay more in
composing poetry than in military strategy was made the commander of
an armed force for the defense of a frontier. During the golden years of
Han and T'ang, civil and military careers were considered of equal status
and prestige, and young men chose their careers in accordance with their
temperament and natural ability rather than the dictation of social approval. Thus the two dynasties produced men of valor as well as men of
letters, and their societies benefited from an equitable distribution between them. The Sung government, on the other hand, degraded military
personnel so much that young men of talent inevitably avoided the military and sought a civil career. The safety of the nation suffered as a result.

In foreign relations Sung inherited most of its difficulties from the
defunct Five Dynasties. The Five Dynasties were called dynasties only
through a strict adherence to "legitimacy" by historians. They were all
weak regimes of short duration, and none of them had control of all
China. Their existence was made more precarious by the mounting pressure of the northern nomads who had taken advantage of a weaker China
to expand. The most powerful among the northern nomads were the
Khitans, a Mongolian tribe originally located along the Liao River of
Manchuria. Early in the tenth century a great leader named Apaochi
conquered neighboring tribes and soon brought Inner Mongolia and part
of South Manchuria under his control. To strengthen his regime economically, Apaochi promoted agriculture by granting land on liberal terms to
immigrant Chinese farmers; he built towns and cities, opened salt and
iron mines, coined money to facilitate trade, and established exchange
centers along the border to barter with the Chinese. Chinese scholars
were invited to serve his government, and a new written language was
invented by simplifying Chinese characters. To encourage Chinese immigration a dual system was devised under which resident Chinese would
be governed by their own law and customs. By 927 when Apaochi died,
the foundation of a rising state had been firmly established, and this state
was ready to test its strength with the Chinese dynasties in the south.

In 928 the Khitans invaded China proper for the first time, looted, and then withdrew. In 936 a Chinese garrison surrendered without a fight what was known as the Sixteen Yen-Yün Districts, which covered modern Chahar and the northern portions of modern Shansi and Hopeh provinces, including Peking. The occupation of areas south of the Great Wall exposed all of North China to the Khitan encroachment, and efforts aimed to recover the lost territories were never successful throughout the Sung dynasty. In 947 the Khitans changed their national title to the more Sinified name of Liao, and adopted Chinese ideas and institutions. Agriculture, instead of herding, had become its major occupation.

The founding emperor of Sung, Chao K'uang-yin (also known by his posthumous title Sung T'ai-tsu), was too busy in unifying and consolidating his regime to pay much attention to the northern threat. After his brother, Sung T'ai-tsung (976–997), had ascended to the throne, an effort was made to recover the Sixteen Yen-Yün Districts. In his first attempt to recapture Peking, his troops were routed, and two flying arrows struck his shoulder while he was fleeing southward. Two more attempts were made during his reign, one in 980 and again in 986, but in each case the result was humiliating defeat. In the winter of 1004 Liao took the offensive, and as the troops marched southward they met little resistance. Kaifeng, the capital, was in a panic, and many Sung ministers openly advocated the abandonment of the city and the transfer of the capital either southward to Nanking or westward to Chengtu. When the panic finally subsided, Emperor Sung Chen-tsung (998–1022) was persuaded to take personal command of the army and met the invading troops in the north. Around the city of Shanchou and near River Shan a battle was fought with no decisive victory for either side. A stalemate ensued and both sides were ready for a negotiated peace. The peace agreement consisted of notes exchanged between the Sung and the Liao emperors. The Sung note read in part:

> To help disburse military expenses, the Sung Government agrees to deliver to Liao each year 200,000 bolts of silk and 100,000 taels of silver. . . . Garrisons on each side defend their respective territories along the frontier, and trespassing by civilian or military personnel is strictly forbidden. Thieves and bandits who escape from one side should not be given quarters by the other [and should be extradited]. Farmers on both sides should be left alone to live in peace; they and their farms should not be interfered with. The cities and their fortifications are to remain the way they are; no additional walls or canals are to be built by either side [to strengthen defense]. May the above agreement be witnessed by Heaven, Earth, the gods, and the spirits, and be reported to the temples of our ancestors. Be it observed by our descendants until eternity to come. He who violates it—may he not live long to enjoy his country, and Heaven be the witness, he shall die a violent death.[1]

---

[1] The original appears in *Hsü Tzu-chih t'ung-chien ch'ang-pien.*

The Liao note, after repeating in full the Sung note, added: "Untalented though I (the Liao emperor) am, I wish to observe this agreement. I have reported it to Heaven and Earth and sworn its observance on behalf of my descendants. May gods punish him by death who chooses to violate it."

The above agreement, known as the Agreement of River Shan, paved the way for a peace of 118 years between the two countries. During this

MAP 20
CHINA around 1000 A.D.
□ Capital   • Cities

0   300   600
Scale of Miles

period envoys were exchanged to attend the inauguration, funeral, or birthday celebration of an emperor or empress, and, occasionally, New Year festivities. Sung agreed to open markets along the border for Liao merchants to trade with the Chinese. Though militarily stronger, Liao rulers after 1004 were generally moderate and conservative in temperament and were not interested in new conquests. Sung, militarily weaker, was in no position to claim the lost territories. When hostility was resumed one century later, it was Sung which broke the peace, to its profound regret shortly afterwards.

WEST HSIA

The Agreement of River Shan enabled Sung to have a freer hand with many of its other enemies. During the best years of T'ang, the nomadic tribes and kingdoms beyond China's northwestern frontier acknowledged T'ang's suzerainty and sent tribute missions regularly. Among them was a small and comparatively insignificant Tibetan tribe called Tangut which was noted, according to an official statement, for "its friendliness towards the Chinese and its high degree of Sinicization." During the reign of T'ang T'ai-tsung, its hereditary ruler was given the surname Li (the same as that of T'ang's royal house), an honor traditionally reserved for the heads of friendly tribes. During the Huang Ch'ao rebellion the Tanguts sent military help to the reigning T'ang emperor, and after the suppression of the rebellion its ruler was granted a high title and was made a governor along the northwestern border. The same good relations were generally maintained during the early period of Sung despite the occasional turbulent behavior on the part of the Tanguts. By then the surname of its rulers was changed to Chao, as Chao was the surname of China's new reigning house. Hostility, however, finally broke out early in the eleventh century.

A study of Sung-Tangut relations will throw much light on the basic difficulties between an agricultural and a pastoral society. Economically, they were complementary and mutually dependent. China as an agricultural society imported from the nomads furs, skins and hides, and above all, horses, which were the single largest item of import and were demanded by both military and civilian groups. The nomads, on the other hand, had to import from China agricultural and industrial products, notably grain, silk, cloth, and tea. As pastoral products were not essential to the maintenance of daily life in the sense that grain and cloth were and since they (like horses) could be domestically raised or imported from other sources if the need became too great, the Chinese had an economic advantage not enjoyed by the nomads. Whenever there was a population pressure in the pastoral areas, a situation almost unavoidable if peace persisted for a relatively long time, the need for agricultural and industrial products from China became larger and more pressing. Since physically it was impossible for the nomads to produce these products in their own land, they had to trade to obtain them. If trade was denied to them or if it became unfeasible because they could not offer goods of equal value in exchange, they might decide that war was the only means by which they could obtain whatever they needed from the Chinese. This increasing demand for agricultural and industrial products was partially met, in the case of Liao, by an annual tribute (called gifts) from the Chinese government, as long as the nomads were strong enough to impose such a condition on the Chinese. This, however, only alleviated the gravity of the problem; it did not solve it. Sooner or later the nomads found it necessary to acquire these products by force. This need accounted for the frequent and periodical raids on China's border provinces even in time of peace. When a strong leader was able to organize a large fighting force among the nomads, a formal war with China was almost inevitable.

The above generalization applied particularly well to the Sung-Tangut relations. In the case of Liao, it had occupied agriculturally rich areas north and south of the Great Wall as early as 937, and its demand for products from China was not particularly great. This situation made possible the Agreement of River Shan and a prolonged peace of 118 years. In the case of the Tanguts, their land was poorer and their need for trade was greater. Before the opening of hostilities they had been subsidized by Sung through periodical gifts. Even then Sung did not hesitate to apply its economic weapons, either by withholding subsidies or by forbidding trade, to "punish the barbarians for their misdeeds or unbecoming behavior," which is to say, for their occasional raids and unauthorized incursions into China proper. But retaliations of this sort only achieved the opposite results. The Tanguts, deprived of peaceful trade to obtain the goods they needed, resorted to the use of even more force and this, from Sung's point of view, warranted the closing of more markets. This vicious cycle continued until the whole issue had to be settled by a war of major proportions.

Early in the eleventh century the Tanguts produced two great leaders in succession. The first was Li Te-ming (notice the change of his surname from Chao back to Li, after Sung had "disowned" his father because of the latter's "misdeeds") who unified neighboring tribes and brought under his control modern Suiyuan province and the Kansu area west of the Yellow River. By 1004 he had become so strong that Sung found it necessary to confer on him a new title, the King of Great Hsia. However, it was not until the accession to the throne of his son Yüan-hao in 1032 that open warfare on a large scale began. Among the great leaders who emerged from the northwestern grassland, Yüan-hao was doubtless one of the most talented. The official history of the Sung dynasty described him as "a vigorous and persevering leader versed in military strategy." "He was also proficient in painting and in the creation of artistic objects. He knew well both Chinese and the nomadic languages and was thoroughly familiar with Buddhist ideology." He even devised a written language for his people, and under his direction many Chinese and Buddhist books were translated into the new language. Though an admirer of Chinese culture, he warned his people against the undiscriminating mimicry of everything Chinese. He extolled the virtue of a rugged, nomadic life and advised his people not to rely on Chinese products, such as silk and cloth. A superb organizer, he boasted of a fighting force of 500,000 men when open hostility occurred.

Among the Sungs there were two schools of thought on how to deal with Hsia's invasions. One school called for the organization of a strong expeditionary force to seek the enemy and destroy him, thus settling the problem once and for all. The other school, led by a man named Fan Chung-yen (990–1053), took a more cautious approach. It recommended strong fortifications along the frontier and the avoidance of pitched battles in the hope that the invading force would be eventually worn out and forced to retreat. During the early stage of the conflict, the Sung generals followed the first strategy and the result was disastrous. For in open warfare, the Chinese were inferior to the nomads, as the latter were strong in cavalry and were more familiar with local geography. The strategy of seeking the enemy and destroying him had been regularly followed by the Han generals in their campaigns against the Hsiung-nu, but it could not be profitably applied by a weaker regime like the Sung. Resigned to defensive warfare of long duration, the Sung commander Fan Chung-yen cut off all trade with the Hsia allies but rewarded others with trade and gifts if they remained neutral or allied themselves with the Sung government. When the Hsia army attacked, the Sung forces scorched the earth before they retreated and then shut themselves behind well-built fortifications. This Fabian strategy eventually paid off. Though Hsia won victory after victory on the battlefield, continuous war took a heavy toll upon its limited manpower and financial resources until it could no longer afford further loss. There was widespread discontent, and Yüan-hao could not hold his people together for a sustained effort. In 1044 he proposed peace and Sung readily accepted. The annual grant of silver, silk, and tea was resumed, and trade was reopened for merchants of both sides. Four years after the peace Yüan-hao came to an inglorious end when he was assassinated by his own son, after the old hero had taken an unusual interest in his daughter-in-law and refused to surrender her to his newly married son.

SUNG SCHOLARS

Thanks to men like Fan Chung-yen the Tangut war was confined to China's northwest, and the 118 years after the Agreement of River Shan stood as the most glorious of the Sung dynasty. Cultural activities were encouraged, and the learned were respected and abundantly rewarded. In the capital the government-sponsored university and colleges, staffed by prominent scholars, opened their doors to the country's most talented persons. On the provincial and district levels land-grant schools were established to accommodate local talents. More famous than the government-subsidized schools were some of the private institutions that taught subjects according to the specialties of their instructors instead of a prescribed curriculum. The most famous were the so-called Four Colleges, Yingt'ien, Polutung, Shihku, and Yolu. All of them were situated in scenic mountains far away from the noisy cities, so that students could concentrate better in their scholarly pursuits. That three—the last mentioned three—of the Four Colleges happened to be located on or south of the Yangtze River indicated the increasing importance of South China as a cultural area.

Side by side with an extensive school system was the examination system for civil service. Graduation from school did not guarantee employment with the government; a student had to pass the civil service examination to qualify for government position. Though Sung inherited the examination system from the T'ang dynasty it enlarged its scope and gave it greater importance. It was so successful that during its best years practically all men of importance in public life were the products of this system. To be eligible, candidates had to be nominated by local magistrates on the basis of character and scholarship. As in the T'ang dynasty many categories of tests were offered and the most popular and most honored was the "advanced scholarship." Early in the Sung dynasty the imperial examination was held every other year and after 1064 it was held once every three years. The change was made to "spare the students the hardships of making too many journeys to Kaifeng," for students who failed could try as many times as they chose. According to the T'ang practice, successful candidates had to undergo a period of apprenticeship before they were eligible for government positions. The Sung government, however, followed a more generous policy and gave successful candidates pecuniary compensation immediately after the result of examinations was made known. Moreover, throughout Sung the number of candidates permitted to pass in each examination continued to increase. While during the times of Sui and T'ang no more than two or three dozen candidates were permitted to pass each time, Sung raised the number to several hundreds after 977. This, of course, did not mean that the examination had become easy. In 991, for instance, more than 17,300 candidates participated in the imperial examination, but only a few hundred passed.

The difficulty of the examination gave added prestige to the successful candidates. To be able to score the highest in these examinations was the fondest dream of every young man in the kingdom. After the result had been officially proclaimed, a special messenger would speed to the home of a successful candidate to announce the good news. Overnight his family became one of the most celebrated in the community, however humble it had once been. In the capital Kaifeng, a big celebration was duly held. The man who had received the highest honor in the examination would ride at the head of a parade along the main streets, receiving the adulation and admiration of thousands of onlookers like a conquering hero. One of the Sung emperors, while watching the parade, remarked that he would be happy to give up his throne if like that young man he could ride at the head of that parade himself.

The fact that education was prized and that the educated were honored and rewarded did not mean that education was conducted on a mass scale. A pre-industrial society like China could not afford universal education; nor was universal education regarded as desirable. Throughout Chinese history the privilege of having an education was confined to a few. As a privilege reserved for a few, education imposed upon those who had acquired it a moral obligation towards society as a whole. Theoretically at least, the purpose of acquiring an education was neither for material gain nor for self-glorification; education merely enabled a person to serve better and well his fellow citizens. He and his fellow intellectuals constituted the intelligentsia who were the recognized leaders in the nation and in each of the communities where they lived. Culturally, they were responsible for the transmission of a vast heritage to the next generation. Politically, they should serve as loyal civil servants whenever their service was needed, and when in retirement from public office they should be personal examples to their fellow citizens. Thus a Confucian scholar should be a gentleman, scholar, and statesman all in one, always mindful of the great responsibility that the acquirement of education had imposed on him. During the Sung period we see again the emergence of this Confucian ideal, and the personal achievements of "Sung Scholars" (*Sung ju*) had become an inspiration to Chinese intelligentsia for centuries to come. In personal life, the Sung scholars varied a great deal, ranging from the austere Ch'eng brothers (Ch'eng Hao, 1031–1085, and Ch'eng Yi, 1032–1107), who lived and glorified a Spartan type of ideal, to the gay genius Su Shih (1036–1101), whose known fondness for wine, women, and song could best be described as amoral, if not immoral. While varying in personal preference insofar as a good life was concerned, they were all inspired by a great devotion to the state and to the welfare of their fellow citizens as they interpreted it.

This self-imposed responsibility as a member of the educated elite can be best illustrated by citing the example of Fan Chung-yen. Left an orphan after his father had died and his mother remarried, he was anything but happy in his childhood. Determined to pursue an academic career, he took residence at a Buddhist monastery in Shantung, and there he educated himself with a vast amount of Confucian literature. He then passed successfully the civil service examinations and in due time rose to be one of the most respected members of the Sung bureaucracy. While in office, he repeatedly urged political, economic, and educational reforms, but Emperor Jen-tsung (1023–1063) and his ministers chose not to take any action. During the Tangut War, he was called to head an army to defend the northwestern frontier after many Sung generals had failed. He stopped the Tanguts' advances, and in due time was able to impose on them a peaceful settlement. As a person he was incorruptible. His own ideal that "an educated man should suffer before anyone suffers and enjoy after everyone has enjoyed" was the criterion he used to measure himself and his fellow intellectuals. Finally, in retirement after a long, distinguished governmental service, he was a good friend and neighbor to all who knew him, always humble, kind, and helpful. As a writer, he was prolific in poetry as well as in prose. His extant poems are noted for a rugged manliness; they resemble "mountains and deep gorges" rather than "flowers and the moon."

While as individuals most Sung scholars could be said to be good men, the inevitable result of mixing scholarship with politics was to make them potential or real political enemies. The Confucian obsession with "learning for the purpose of application" (hsüeh yi chih yung) could not but transform academic differences into those in practical politics, and scholars of different philosophies soon found themselves political enemies as well. Various philosophical and political cliques emerged, though more on an informal than on a formal basis; each clique centered around an eminent scholar who more often than not was deeply involved in politics. Their mutual distrust and constant bickerings weakened further a hopelessly weak government. It seemed that honest differences between men of highest principles sometimes could be as dangerous as private feuds among the most selfish persons, especially when there was no higher authority able and willing to arbitrate those differences. Normally the arbitrators were the emperors; but unfortunately most of the Sung emperors were not strong leaders.

Factional strifes among Sung scholars culminated in the formation of the so-called Old and New Parties during the 1060's. The rivalry of these two parties was caused largely by the New Party's proposed reforms.

From a socioeconomic point of view, these reforms were among the most significant events during the Sung dynasty. First, the disagreements on these reforms reflected two different social and economic philosophies. Second, these reforms revealed the many social and economic problems which the Sung government had to face. Lastly, factional strifes over these reforms weakened the Sung regime so much that it never recovered. Before discussing the reforms, it is necessary to describe the problems that prompted these reforms.

MILITARY AND ECONOMIC PROBLEMS

Militarily, Sung was one of the weakest regimes in Chinese history. Ever since the decline of T'ang, China's military weakness continued through the Five Dynasties, and the situation did not improve when the Sung regime was established. Throughout its existence, the Sung government faced repeated invasions from the northern and northwestern barbarians. Its founding father, Sung T'ai-tsu, was no military genius; nor could his brother and successor, Sung T'ai-tsung, do any better in improving Sung's military strength. Their humiliation at the hands of the Khitans were rightly regarded as a national disgrace. The Sixteen Yen-Yün Districts had been lost and their recovery was regarded as a matter of moral principle as well as economic necessity because these districts had always been Chinese. But with the existing military capacity, the Sung government could not hope to achieve its purpose. Worse still, if Liao decided to march southward, the outcome could be disastrous.

This military weakness resulted partially from a national policy of "emphasizing the importance of civil personnel while degrading that of the military" (*chung wen ch'ing wu*) as previously discussed. A more important factor, however, was Sung's anarchic, irresponsible attitude regarding financial matters. It invited constant bankruptcy by spending more than it could afford, and the vast amount of money it spent was often unnecessary and wasteful. To begin with, Sung's territory was comparatively small. It did not have a large empire, and half of North China was never brought under its jurisdiction. Though South China had by then been intensively developed and proportionally provided the largest revenue for the government's treasury, the financial resources of the nation as a whole were clearly limited.

To be sure, some of the expenditures were unavoidable. The unusually large military budget was necessitated by the foreign wars and the constant threat of powerful enemies. As foreign danger mounted, the size of the standing army continued to increase until by the middle of the eleventh century its fighting men numbered more than 1,250,000. Not only was agricultural production curtailed when able-bodied men were taken away from their farms, but the support of such a large army imposed a heavy burden on the nation's limited resources. Being militarily weaker, Sung repeatedly had to accept whatever peace terms its enemies chose to impose, and those terms worked further to its financial disadvantage. In the Agreement of River Shan, for instance, Sung promised to pay Liao a yearly tribute of 100,000 taels of silver and 200,000 bolts of silk. The payment was later increased to 200,000 taels of silver and 300,000 bolts of silk, after Liao had demanded additional territories and threatened a mass invasion if Sung did not make financial accommodations. Even in dealing with the weaker Hsia, Sung often found it necessary to offer financial payments to secure peaceful settlements. In 1044, for instance, it offered to pay yearly a vast amount of silver, silk, and tea, if Hsia would promise not to raid its border provinces. Needless to say, these annual tributes were a heavy drain on Sung's financial resources.

The supporting of a large army and the paying of annual tributes might be said to have been dictated by circumstances and therefore unavoidable. Sung's other expenditures, however, could not be so justified. Considering "generosity towards the intelligentsia" as a dynastic policy, Sung took the unprecedented role of subsidizing the intellectual elite. In each civil service examination the number of candidates permitted to pass was many times larger than in any previous dynasty, and each successful candidate was immediately put on the government's payroll regardless of the availability of governmental positions. A huge bureaucracy was thus created, and a large portion of it was paid for doing nothing, for there were always more officials than positions. To make the situation worse, each succeeding emperor tried to outdo his predecessor in liberalizing remunerations. According to Sung practice, a government official was not only paid salaries, allowances, and bonuses; he was given additional payments in kind, including silk, cotton, rice, heating and cooking fuel, wine, and tea. If he served in the provinces, he derived additional income from public land granted to him during his tenure of office (maximum: 40 ch'ing, or 605 acres). His salaries and allowances were further increased, if for any reason he could not bring his family to his post. Whether serving in the capital or provinces, all his personal servants were on the government's payroll; the higher his position was, the more servants he could have. To carry generosity to a ridiculous degree, the government might allow him to designate a certain number of persons (children, relatives, or sometimes friends) to succeed him in receiving annuities even after he had passed away. In the beginning this particular honor was reserved for officials of unusually distinguished service, but later any official with a long tenure of office automatically enjoyed this privilege. When an emperor performed the ritual of "Heaven Worship" (chiao t'ien) once every three years, all officials expected extra pecuniary awards.

One Sung emperor was so generous that he willed a million taels of silver to each of his ministers before he passed away. While these liberal treatments of government officials might achieve the purpose of "cultivating the virtue of honesty" (*yang lien*) and discouraging corruption, their wastefulness was rather obvious. In all history there had never been so many paid so much for doing so little.

Such large expenditures had to be met by increased revenues. Early during the Sung dynasty, the total receipts of the imperial government were twice as much as those of T'ang, and by the 1060's they were more than twenty times as much. As Sung's territory was much smaller than that of T'ang, the increased revenue had to come from a much heavier taxation. The regular land tax, for instance, was seven times as much as that of T'ang, besides newly imposed taxes, including taxes on farm implements, oxen and ox skins, salt and flour, and even clothes and shoes. As had always been the case, small, independent farmers suffered most from the increased taxation. Many Sung scholars, recognizing the inequity of the tax structure, advocated retrenchment as the first step to tax reform. But any retrenchment would affect adversely the vested interests of the intelligentsia, and most intellectuals preferred to let things stand the way they were. Even such an ardent reformist as Wang An-shih (1021–1086) did not advocate retrenchment; the opposition was simply too strong for anybody to face.

The inarticulate, illiterate farmers resorted to the only way they knew to express their grievances—revolt—whenever their lot had become too miserable to bear. Revolt they often did. Poorly organized and poorly led, practically all revolts were local in character and were quickly suppressed before they could spread. No internal revolt during the Sung dynasty was extensive enough to threaten the existence of the Sung regime.

The most extensive and perhaps most significant revolt occurred early in the 1120's and was known as the Fang La rebellion. It was triggered by the excessive corvée and other forms of governmental oppression in connection with the gay emperor Sung Hui-tsung's search for "rare flowers and stones" in South China. The real cause, however, was the long-standing grievance that the southerners had been excessively taxed and unjustifiably exploited to support the imperial government in the north. Fang La, addressing his followers, expressed the south's grievances this way:

> The nation should operate on the same principle as that of a family. What kind of a family would it be if the sons worked hard all year round, to till and to weave, yet receive little to eat and little to wear, while their father took away all the fruits of labor and wasted them, brutally lashed them according to his whims, and often lashed them to death without showing any mercy? If you were one of the sons, could you stand continuously such wanton brutality? . . . . The government exacts from us everything it can and presents it

to the northern barbarians. Our enemies have become richer each day, and not showing gratitude, they have become more aggressive and more insulting instead. Why does not the government stop paying them annual tribute, in view of the fact that it is constantly insulted? . . . . The wasteful luxuries the government enjoys and the annual tribute it pays to the enemies are made of the blood of the Southeastern Chinese. Yet the more the enemies get, the more contemptuous they become, and the paying of annual tribute has not deterred them from invading the Central Kingdom repeatedly. . . . Though we work hard all year round, we have never had a full stomach, and our wives and children suffer constantly from cold and hunger.[1]

At one time the rebels controlled modern Chekiang and the southern third of Anhwei province. But without the cooperation and support of the country's intelligentsia, the revolt was doomed to fail. It lasted four years, and, according to an official estimate, resulted in the death of more than two million innocent persons.

WANG AN-SHIH'S REFORMS

The Fang La rebellion was a result, rather than a cause, of Sung's social and economic ills. The basic weaknesses of the degenerate society had been obvious for a long time. The process of degeneration was gradual and slow, and as long as the barbarians could be bought off, none of the Sung emperors bothered to stir himself. With Sung Shen-tsung (1068–1085), however, it became a different matter. He visualized himself as another T'ang T'ai-tsung and wished to build up a strong regime, to be remembered as among the greatest in Chinese history. Looking around, he found no one ambitious and capable enough to share his vision of grandeur. One day somebody mentioned Wang An-shih. He summoned Wang for an interview, and after one conversation he decided that this was the man whom he could trust and from whom he could expect greatness. Wang was soon promoted from a comparatively obscure position as magistrate of Nanking to that of Prime Minister. To the literary elite, however, Wang was no stranger. He had passed the imperial examinations with the highest honors, and his writings, both prose and poetry, had been widely acclaimed as the work of a true genius. He was said to have a photographic memory and a bad temper, never avoiding an argument or debate whenever he thought the issue involved was important. His personal life was frugal to the greatest extreme: he cared little for good food and good clothing, and it was even said that he seldom

---

[1] Translated from a quotation that appears in Chou Ku-ch'eng, *A History of China* (*Chung-kuo t'ung-shih*) (Shanghai: The Kaiming Book Company, 1947), Vol. II, p. 732. According to Chou, the original is contained in *The Story of the Ch'ing-hsi Rebels* (*Ch'ing-hsi k'ou-kuei*) by Fang Shao.

bathed. He had served with distinction as magistrate of Ningpo (modern Chekiang) before his appointment in Nanking. Once he sent a long petition to the reigning emperor urging sweeping reforms, but the petition was rejected and ignored. It was not until the accession to the throne of Sung Shen-tsung that he was given the opportunity to carry out his reforms.

The purpose of these reforms was to build up Sung into a strong, powerful regime which could fight and win against the northern barbarians or negotiate peace with them on equal terms. Whatever benefits they might have brought to individuals were of secondary consideration. A Confucian with Legalist leanings, Wang An-shih believed that the interest of the state was always superior to that of individuals and that whenever conflict occurred, the interest of the state should prevail, though at all times he strived to make both interests parallel. What he tried to achieve was not a socialist or welfare state, but a society composed of physically strong, economically well-to-do, but well-disciplined, individuals who happily and willingly served the interest of the state at all times.

Wang An-shih's reforms conveniently fall into three main categories: economic, military, and educational. Though facing an empty exchequer, he did not advocate retrenchment. In fact, the reforms he suggested necessitated the enlargement of the bureaucracy and consequently a much larger expenditure. The purpose of his economic reforms was to open up new revenues by a combination of two methods: first, the increase of taxable income through strengthening the economic position of taxpayers, and second, governmental participation in economic enterprises. Since the overwhelming majority of the Chinese were farmers, it was not surprising that most of Wang An-shih's economic reforms were farm programs.

Among the farm programs, perhaps the most significant and also most controversial was the green sprouts program (ch'ing miao fa). It required the government to provide easy credit at low interest rate to needy farmers. Before its adoption the prevailing interest rate on borrowed money from private sources ranged anywhere from 60 to 70 percent per year, and such a high interest rate had bankrupted many small, independent farmers. Under the new program, the government lent money twice a year to needy farmers at a semiannual interest rate of 20 percent, with capital drawn from the government operated ever-ready granaries in each district or province. The borrowers were required to pay both principal and interest twice a year when they paid their regular land tax, usually in spring and autumn. In case of a bad harvest the borrowers might be granted a moratorium in payment for a one-year period. It was called the green sprouts program because each year the first loan was made in the spring when rice sprouts were green and when farmers needed money most.

To protect the interest of consumers and to stabilize prices, the marketing and exchange program (*shih yi fa*) was introduced in 1072. Under this program the government established more than twenty marketing agencies in the capital and other large cities for the purpose of buying and selling commercial products. These agencies would buy products when their prices had been depressed during the time of oversupply and would sell them in the open market when their prices had been bid up too high during the time of strong demand. In selling to the marketing agency, a producer at his own option could waive cash payment and request instead the exchange of his overstocked merchandise for goods that had been in short supply in the market and therefore commanded better prices. In other cases, when certain merchandise was in short supply, merchants might be allowed to borrow such merchandise from the marketing agency by paying a semiannual interest of 10 percent and then sell it in the open market. By applying devices like these it was hoped that supply and demand would be well-balanced, that prices would be stabilized, and that consumers would not be exploited by ruthless merchants. Furthermore, the government would make a handsome profit through all these transactions.

The least controversial of Wang An-shih's reforms were those dealing with irrigation, flood control, and the reclamation of waste land. While large projects were undertaken by the government, farmers were encouraged to proceed with projects of their own, and in such cases the government would grant loans on easy terms with capital procured from the ever-ready granaries. In 1077, seven years after this measure had been adopted, the result was so encouraging that 361,178 *ch'ing* (c. 5.5 million acres) of waste land were said to have been reclaimed. To secure a more equitable system of taxation, all land was reclassified into five grades so that land of higher productivity would pay higher tax regardless of its ownership.

In military matters, Wang An-shih's reforms were aimed at the strengthening of Sung's military capacity. Among the most important were the draft exemption program (*mien yi fa*), the *pao-chia* system, and the horse conservation program (*pao ma fa*). Though universal conscription had been Sung's policy ever since its establishment, it became less and less effective as time went on. By the middle of the eleventh century, it was rampant with abuses. For one thing, farmers were often drafted for military or semimilitary duties (such as collecting taxes and catching thieves for the local government) at times when they were badly needed on their farms. Since rich landlords could often use their influence to evade military duties, the supposedly universal conscription worked further to the disadvantage of middle and small farmers. In 1070 the conscription system was abolished, and a new tax, called the draft exemption tax, was imposed. The amount of tax to be paid by each household varied in accordance with its ability to pay, and the government would use the revenue to hire mercenaries, thus making soldiery a full-time occupation. Under the new program those who had been traditionally exempted from military service, such as the underaged, women, Buddhist and Taoist priests, and government officials, were required to contribute financially to the maintenance of a professional army. It was hoped that by replacing conscripted soldiers with a professional army the continuation of agricultural activities would be secured since farmers would no longer be drafted while engaged in farming. Meanwhile, a better fighting force would be created.

A far more revolutionary program was the *pao-chia* system. Under this system all villages and villagers were organized on a semimilitary basis. Ten households constituted a basic unit called *pao,* and all able-bodied men in each household, with the exception of one, were required to join the militia. Each *pao* was headed by a *pao* captain, chosen from among independent farmers or landlords. Five *pao* formed a larger unit called *ta pao,* and ten *ta pao* were organized as a *tu pao.* On each organizational level officials were chosen among constituent members to carry on daily administrative duties. Whenever crimes were committed or any other irregularity occurred, each household was responsible for reporting them to the *pao* captain. Within each *pao* everyone was responsible for the conduct of the others, and all were duty bound to inform on one another. Those who failed to report, whenever they should, would be charged with conspiracy and regarded as accomplices; they would be prosecuted accordingly. The militiamen were taught the fundamentals of warfare and were drilled at times when farming activities were at a minimum, usually in winter time after the harvest had been collected. Their duty was to maintain peace and order in the countryside during peace time and to contribute to the strength of the regular army at the time of war. Thus soldiery and farming became interchangeable occupations, and the same person was a soldier in war and a farmer in peace. The cardinal principle of the *pao-chia* system was "to reside soldiery among farmers" (*yü ping yü nung*).

The purpose of the horse conservation program was to provide an abundant supply of horses for military use. Under this program farmers might either borrow horses from the government or take cash payment from the government to purchase horses from private sources. In either case the ownership of horses resided with the government, while the farmers, having promised to take good care of these horses, had the right to use them. To encourage participation in this program, the government provided special tax relief for the participants. Once each year government-appointed veterinarians would inspect and examine horses under private care to see to it that they were not being abused. If a horse died, all households within a *pao* were held jointly responsible for making adequate compensation. It was hoped that when this program was successfully carried out, not only would the farmers have adequate animal power, but the government would also have a steady supply of horses in case of war. Moreover, the government would not have to rely on the grasslands in the north, a source of supply which would be curtailed or cut off in time of war against the northern nomads. To standardize and improve the quality of military weapons, a new office was created in the capital to supervise the manufacturing of all weapons within the empire.

In education Wang An-shih's proposal called for a reappraisal of the civil service examination system and the reorganization of the Central University at Kaifeng. To him the civil service examination system had not produced men of the best quality, and he attributed this to the over-emphasis on memory in the examinations and the impractibility of the subjects tested. At his suggestion all categories of tests with emphasis on memory were thereafter abolished, and only the category of "advanced scholarship" was to be maintained. In "advanced scholarship" the candidates would be tested on their knowledge of Confucian classics and practical topics, and the test on poetry was no longer required. Though he did not advocate the abolition of the civil service examinations, Wang An-shih believed that men of great quality could be better cultivated in schools. Accordingly, he reorganized the Central University with the hope that supervised studies leading to degrees would eventually replace the civil service examination system. In his new plan all students in the university were grouped into three grades in accordance with their academic achievements, low, middle, and high. Students were carefully screened before they were admitted. Once in, they were tested in their assigned work every month, and each year there was a final examination covering the entire year's assignments. Those who successfully passed the examinations were promoted to a higher grade and were given rights and privileges corresponding to those on the similar levels of the civil service examination system. For instance, the high grade students who completed their work at the top of their class would be recommended to the Ministry of Personnel for assignment as government officials, as if they had passed the civil service examinations with the highest honors.

As long as Sung Shen-tsung remained as emperor and Wang An-shih as his prime minister, the reforms were carried out with thoroughness and speed. With the death of Sung Shen-tsung in 1085 died all of Wang An-shih's reforms. The opposition, as represented by the Old Party, came to power and spared no time in undoing what had been achieved during the previous twenty years. During the process of a sweeping reversal, even the commonly recognized good programs (such as the draft exemption program) were discontinued. The members of the New Party were summarily dismissed from office and fell into disgrace. But thanks to Sung T'ai-tsu who had dictated to his successors that "under no circumstances shall cabinet ministers and censors be executed," the change of administration was devoid of bloodshed. Furthermore, the leaders of both parties were men of high principle and were above the pursuance of private vengeance. Thanks again to Sung T'ai-tsu who had established as a dynastic policy that eunuchs should never be allowed to participate in politics and that their position should always remain as that of servants, one of the most sinister elements in Chinese politics was notably absent. The disagreements between the Old and the New Parties were those among gentlemen; they were not resolved by violence.

The Old and the New Parties were respectively led by Ssu-ma Kuang (1018–1086) and Wang An-shih, two of the most respected Sung scholars. Their difference was a difference in basic beliefs as well as in personality. Ssu-ma Kuang, a northerner and conservative, was a Confucian of the most orthodox type. He placed the importance of personnel above that of institutions, and he believed that only good men could make good government, not *vice versa*. The role of government was primarily a moral and ethical one, and it should never interfere with people's economic activities. A ruler should set a moral example for his subjects, and he became intolerable indeed if he "competes with his subjects in making profits" (*yü min cheng li*). A wealthy nation was a nation where wealth was scattered among the people, rather than concentrated in the hands of the government. The less a government interfered with private pursuits, the better that government was. Wang An-shih, a southerner and reformist, believed just the opposite. He called attention to the fact that this was no ordinary time and that if the Sung regime was to meet successfully its dangers from abroad, it had to rise above its own inertia and complacency. His reforms, he contended, were the answer to Sung's problems.

Wang An-shih's reforms were the last attempt to arrest the dynastic decline. After his death in 1086, the decline continued until the dynasty met its pre-destined end. Though the New Party was again in power early in the twelfth century, it had neither the leadership nor the capacity to carry out the reforms. Then its standard bearer was a comic figure named Ts'ai Ching who seemed to believe that the only way to become wealthy was to spend; he spent so wastefully that by the end of his premiership of almost twenty years the country was totally bankrupt. The Kaifeng regime became so weakened that it took only a single push by the northern barbarians to bring about its collapse.

CHIN

The barbarians who eventually ended the Kaifeng regime were the Nuchens. Before they began their career of conquest, they lived in Manchuria and the area known today as the Maritime Province of Russia. A nomadic people, they moved from place to place during summer months, but always returned home in winter time. The so-called home was a simple affair, made of log and covered with clay, usually built over a hollow in the ground to protect its occupants from the bitter wind of Siberia. Wealth consisted of horses and cattle, and cattle were often used as presents in marriage proposals. The basic social unit was the family, and the highest political organization was the tribe. Each tribe was headed by a hereditary chieftain, and at one time (fifth century) the Nuchens had altogether seven major tribes. Without the benefit of a written language, their law was a matter of custom and tradition, and in the enforcement of law the entire family was held responsible for any crime committed by one of its members. For instance, if a man was killed, the family of the offender was required by law to surrender one of its members to be at the disposal of the injured family, plus ten horses, ten cows, and six taels of gold. Less serious offenses were usually compounded into a fine, paid in horses or cattle.

Before the twelfth century, the Nuchens were practically unknown to the outside world. They had never produced any great leaders and had never won any important battles. Early in the seventh century, they were subject to Korea, and after the T'ang China had defeated Korea, they changed their allegiance accordingly. With the decline of the T'ang dynasty they regained their independence. Throughout centuries they maintained their own way of life, and culturally speaking, they were little influenced by the Chinese. Early during the Sung dynasty, the Nuchens were split into two groups. Those who lived closer to China proper and were more or less Sinicized were called the assimilated Nuchens; those who lived beyond the assimilated group continued to maintain their nomadic existence. It was the unassimilated group which early in the twelfth century produced a great leader named Wenyen Akuta, who, in a short lifetime, materially changed the power structure in North China.

Though we know little about Akuta as a person, he seemed to possess two important qualities of a successful conqueror. First, he had the best of all nomadic virtues: ambition, courage, and organizational ability; and second, he was flexible, wise enough to adopt sedentary institutions to secure the smooth functioning of a permanent political organization. While admiring Chinese culture, he warned his followers against mimicking everything Chinese. If the Nuchens were ever to become a great nation, said he, they had to maintain their nomadic vitality, and Sinicization would dilute their fighting ability. The Chinese way of life, while comfortable, was truly dangerous. Once the Nuchens became Sinicized and assimilated, said he, they would lose their separate identity and would be easily conquered by the Chinese without ever losing a single battle to them. For him the task was how to maintain the ruggedness of his nomadic tribesmen while taming them enough to be the rulers of a highly civilized people.

In Liao under whose rule the Nuchens had been subject hitherto, what Akuta was warning against on behalf of his people had already taken place. By occupying part of China proper and ruling Chinese subjects, Liao rulers had become completely Sinicized, and the dynastic cycle of prosperity followed by a period of decline inevitably occurred. The last Liao ruler was typical of many last rulers of Chinese dynasties. He sought personal pleasure at the expense of national welfare; taxes were constantly increased until they became unbearable; and the once vigorous government was beset with corruption and incompetence. Though he carefully camouflaged his ambition, Akuta could not fail to see the opportunity offered to him, and he calmly and unobtrusively exploited the grievances which his people had against their Liao overlord. In 1115 he led his people along an independent course and staged an open rebellion. He called his regime Chin (which literally means gold) on the hopeful assumption that *chin* was stronger than *liao*, as *liao* literally means iron.

After declaring his independence, Akuta won one battle after another and was pressing hard on the disintegrating Liao forces. As Liao was greatly weakened, Sung, against its better judgment, thought this was a golden opportunity to recapture the Sixteen Yen-Yün Districts. In 1122 Sung and Chin concluded a military alliance. Sung was to attack Liao from the south and Chin from the north, with the Great Wall as the dividing line between the two zones of operation. Sung agreed that once Liao was conquered the annual tribute that had been regularly paid to Liao would be instead paid to Chin, and under this condition, Sung was to be allowed to recover the Sixteen Yen-Yün Districts, including Peking. After hostilities had resumed, Chin forces marched victoriously southward, encountering little or ineffective opposition, while Sung, on the other hand, failed miserably in its repeated efforts to capture the prized city of Peking. As the last resort, Sung sought Chin's help. Thus invited, Chin forces quickly defeated the remaining Liao army, passed across the Great Wall, and captured Peking. Sung, throughout its existence, was never able to dislodge them. Early in 1125 the fleeing Liao king was captured by a pursuing Chin army, and the Liao regime, after nine rulers and 210 years, came to an end. One of the Liao generals named Yeh-lu Ta-shih managed to escape from the encircling Chin forces, led his men westward, and after subduing hostile tribes along the way, established a new kingdom in modern Russian Turkestan. The new kingdom, called West Liao, lasted a considerable time before it was finally conquered by the Mongols.

Having achieved little in the conquest of Liao, Sung was in a poor position to bargain, when the time arrived for dividing the spoils. At the beginning Chin refused to honor the territorial arrangement as agreed in the military alliance on the ground that Sung had done nothing material to bring about the victory. When an agreement was finally reached, Sung was allowed to keep Peking on the condition that the annual revenue normally collected in the Peking district would be handed over to Chin. Besides, Sung agreed to pay Chin an annual tribute of 200,000 taels of silver and 200,000 bolts of silk and consented to the opening of markets along the border for Chin merchants to trade with the Chinese. No sooner had the agreement been reached than it became clear that neither side intended to honor it as a permanent arrangement. For Chin the rich south was too tempting to be left alone, while Sung could not forget the treaty's humiliating terms. It took only a few border incidents for war to break out again. Unfortunately for Sung, instead of facing a decaying Liao, it was with a vigorous Chin that it now had to contend.

Sung Hui-tsung (1101–1125), Sung's reigning emperor, was a talented artist, a poet of excellence, and a great lover, but an incompetent, hapless ruler. A look at any of his extant paintings should convince us of his artistic ability, and his alleged romance with a famous prostitute in Kaifeng has been immortalized in many beautiful poems. Fancying himself as a living Taoist deity, he squandered the treasury on the building of temples, on charity, and on religious festivities. His search for "rare flowers and stones" triggered the Fang La rebellion previously discussed. A political imbecile, he did not know how to find good men to whom he could delegate authority, and the only men he could trust as prime ministers were such mediocrities as Ts'ai Ching and T'ung Kuan. Talented in the six arts, he would have been a great man indeed, if he had not unfortunately become a king.

In 1125 Chin invaded Sung on two fronts: one army based on Tatung attacking Taiyuan (both in modern Shansi province) in the west and another army moving straight southward towards Kaifeng. In the bitter winter of early 1126 the east wing of the attacking force passed across the Yellow River and quickly surrounded the capital. The Sung garrison was decisively defeated, and distress and panic took over the besieged city. As expected from a Chinese monarch under such circumstances, Sung Hui-tsung issued a series of decrees to condemn himself, as he had failed in protecting his people. Orders were sent out to provincial armies to come to the emperor's rescue; but once they arrived, they were easily dispersed by the seemingly invincible Chin army. Facing an untenable situation, Sung Hui-tsung abdicated in favor of his son and sued for peace. The peace terms, as dictated by the victorious enemy, were very harsh indeed. Not only had Sung to surrender three strategic areas (including Taiyuan) along the border, it also promised to pay a heavy indemnity: five million taels of gold, fifty million taels of silver, one million bolts of silk, and ten thousand head of horses and cattle. Sung's prime minister and many princes of royal blood were to be unconditionally surrendered to Chin as hostages and were not to be returned until the indemnity was paid. To add insult to injury, the Sung emperor was forced to address the Chin ruler as "elder uncle" in all state communications.

The peace, however, turned out to be brief. The Chin commander on the western front, having heard the heavy indemnity exacted from Sung by his colleague in the east, demanded the same treatment. Sung, rightly regarding the indemnity as paid to Chin as a nation, refused the demand, and pending further negotiations, ordered local commanders not to surrender the three strategic areas as had been previously agreed. Chin accused Sung of bad faith and ordered a new invasion. Kaifeng was again besieged, and as a price for lifting the siege, the enemy demanded ten million taels of gold, twenty million taels of silver, and twenty million bolts of silk. But nowhere could this much treasure be found. After searching for twenty-three days from private as well as public sources (even the pockets of prostitutes and entertainers were emptied to meet the demand), the Sung government could not come up with the amount demanded. The enemy renewed the attack, and Kaifeng, after serving Sung as the capital for more than one and one-half centuries, fell into barbarian hands. The nomads sacked the city as had been expected. What they could carry away was carried northward, including the entire royal house of more than three thousand persons. Even emperor Sung Ch'in-tsung and his father Hui-tsung were not spared. In his new capital, Peking, the Chin ruler celebrated his victory by ordering the two former emperors to appear before him in blue robes (commonly worn by servants), and to show his contempt for the two hapless prisoners, bestowed upon the father the title "Duke of Confused Virtues" and upon the son that of "Marquis of Recurrent Confusions."

One of the Sung princes who was fortunate enough not to have fallen into Chin's hands was Prince K'ang. In 1127 when it became clear that the two former emperors would not be returned by the enemy, he was duly proclaimed the new emperor, later known by his imperial title, Kao-tsung. The Sung dynasty before 1127 with its capital at Kaifeng is generally referred to as North Sung. South Sung, with its capital eventually settled at Hangchow in South China, lasted another century and a half before it was conquered by the Mongols.

ᚱ vii

The Two Sungs (2)

South Sung came into existence under the most inauspicious circumstances. No sooner was the new emperor Kao-tsung inaugurated than Chin launched an all-out attack. For three years after 1127 the invading force swept over China proper without meeting much resistance. At one time it penetrated deep into South China and captured such famous cities as Nanking and Hangchow. At this point it had apparently over-extended itself and spread too thin. Early in 1130 a Sung general named Han Shih-chung cut off its logistic support by blocking the crossing points along the Yangtze River. At a ford called Huangt'ien Tang a battle was fought, and the invading force was for the first time defeated. The Battle of Huangt'ien Tang in all likelihood saved the Sung dynasty for another century and a half. In the newly conquered territories in North China,

217

Chin set up a puppet regime called Ch'i and installed a former Sung official as "emperor." South in Hangchow Sung eventually managed to stabilize itself and hopefully began an offensive of its own. By then Chin was just as exhausted as its opponent in the south, after so many years of incessant fighting. Sung recovered part of North China, and the puppet regime Ch'i, without full support from its overlord, collapsed in 1137. A stalemate was reached, and once again it seemed that the time had arrived for a negotiated peace.

Meantime in Hangchow there was a great debate on the basic issue of peace and war. Now that much of China proper was under alien occupation, many believed that as a matter of principle war had to be continued until the last lost territories were recovered. Others, however, took a different point of view and a more conservative approach. Realizing their country's economic and military weaknesses, they doubted that Sung could win in a prolonged war against a more powerful enemy. A negotiated peace would preserve the nation, while an adventurous war might jeopardize its very existence. The group that advocated the continuance of war was called the Idealists (Yi-li p'ai); most military commanders, intellectuals, and university students belonged to this group. Their opponents were the Realists (Shih-shih p'ai), composed largely of politicians in power. They were the people the emperor trusted, and their policy eventually prevailed. The Idealists, arguing for the continuance of war, emphasized the "difference between Chinese and barbarians" (Hua yi chih pien), and the impossibility of compromise between them. How could one seriously talk about peace, asked they, when the lost territories had not been recovered, when millions of Chinese were living under alien rule, and when the two ex-emperors were still captives and not returned? While the Idealists were appealing to people's patriotic emotions, the Realists, being the men responsible for the formulation and implementation of policies, could not do more than what an unpleasant reality had already dictated. That Sung was so much weaker than Chin was a fact which they could not ignore.

The first major conflict between the two factions concerned the trial and execution of a famous general named Yo Fei. Yo Fei, one of the ablest generals Sung ever produced, had won many battles against the Chin and Ch'i forces in the 1130's. As a military man, he saw no other solution to the Chin problem except the military conquest of the lost territories and the elimination of Chin as a state, and to compromise with the enemy sounded treasonous and immoral indeed. In the capital many intellectuals shared his opinion; a high official named Hu Ch'üan, for instance, wrote an eloquent essay in defense of this militant position. Prime Minister Ch'in Kuai, however, urged a negotiated peace despite popular opposition. There was a strong fear among the men around the emperor that many military commanders in the field had become too

MAP 21
CHINA around 1200 A.D.
□ Capital

0   300   600
Scale of Miles

MONGOL

LIAO RIVER

WEST
HSIA

□ Tahsing
(Peking)

C H I N

YELLOW RIVER

Yellow
Sea

T'U-
FAN

S O U T H

•Chengtu

YANGTZE   RIVER

□ Linan
(Hangchow)

T A L I

S U N G

SI RIVER

South
China Sea

strong and independent and that the continuance of war would enhance their power and make them uncontrollable. The arrogant behavior of many field commanders did not help in alleviating such fear. In 1141 while on a successful campaign in the north, Yo Fei was called back by twelve consecutive orders to face a charge of alleged conspiracy. With Ch'in Kuai's henchmen sitting as judges, he was pronounced guilty, even though there was little evidence to substantiate the charge. Subsequently, he and his young son were put to death. Today his body lies in a scenic spot outside the city of Hangchow, and the temple built in honor of him has become a national shrine.

The death of Yo Fei was followed by the conclusion of a new peace treaty. Besides the customary annual tribute and the cession of territories, Sung agreed to acknowledge Chin as its suzerain and call itself a vassal state. The boundary line between the two states generally followed the Ch'inling Mountains in the west and the Huai River in the east. The agreement continued in force until 1164 when Sung, taking advantage of an internal dissension within the Chin government, pressed for the betterment of the terms. As a result, the amount of annual tribute was somewhat reduced, both states regarded each other as equals, and the Sung emperor would address the Chin ruler as "younger uncle" instead of "lord" in all state communications. The boundary between the two states, however, remained the same as it had been before.

Early in the thirteenth century a political opportunist named Han T'o-chou became Sung's prime minister. Facing opposition at home because of the unpopularity of his domestic policies, he thought he could change public opinion by waging a successful war abroad. Without preparing adequately for a major offensive, the invading Sung force soon retreated on all fronts under heavy pressure after winning a few insignificant battles. The pursuing enemy passed across the Huai River and soon occupied all areas north of the Yangtze River, including the famous gay city Yangchow. As Hangchow was within the enemy's easy march, Sung once again sued for peace. As a price for peace, Sung promised to pay an annual tribute of 300,000 taels of silver and 300,000 bolts of silk, in addition to a lump sum of three million taels of silver paid to the invading troops as an "award." The Sung emperor would address the Chin ruler as "elder uncle" instead of "younger uncle" as had hitherto been the case. As the enemy demanded the punishment of war criminals, Han T'o-chou was conveniently murdered by imperial order, and his head was delivered to the Chin court by a special messenger. The war of 1206–1207 was the last major conflict between the two states. Soon they were to be replaced by a more dynamic, more barbarian regime rising further in the north.

Politically one of the weakest regimes in Chinese history, Sung was nevertheless one of the most productive in cultural achievement. The achievement covered practically all humanistic fields; it was a cultural renaissance in the truest sense. In philosophy, Sung scholars showed more originality than philosophers of any other period, with the exception, of course, of the pre-Ch'in era when great men like Confucius and Mencius dominated the academic scene. The Sung school of philosophy, generally referred to as the Rational School (*Li hsüeh*), was more than philosophy in its metaphysical sense; it was a way of life. The personal life of the philosopher, theoretically at least, should be more indicative of his philosophy than any book or books he might have written; he himself was his philosophy. On the other hand, this new trend of turning away from bookish learning to the examination of oneself might be regarded as a belated reaction against the Han School with its emphasis on the commentary and interpretation of Confucian classics. To a Sung scholar it was the content of Confucian classics, rather than their literary aspect, which was all important. A good Confucian was a person who lived according to Confucian precepts; it was secondary or even immaterial whether he was a learned scholar. Thus the Rational School attempted to go back to the simple form of Confucianism as Confucius originally taught, bypassing voluminous comments and interpretations of more than one thousand years. On the other hand, the popularity of this school might also be attributed to Sung scholars' disillusionment with the Wei-Tsin skepticism. To them life was real and earnest, and the deliberate violation of Confucian ethics, the advocation of "naturalist" behavior, and the passive resignation to fate were not only irresponsible but also immoral, because such an attitude could neither contribute to personal well-being nor benefit society. A true Confucian, in fact, was a dynamic moral being who desired to improve himself and to enlighten others.

How could one improve himself and eventually reach the goal of moral perfection (*chih sheng*)? The answer, according to Sung scholars, lay in the careful cultivation of an element within oneself called *ch'i*. While all men were born with goodness, no man was naturally endowed with moral perfection, and it required constant, conscientious endeavor to improve one's ethical well-being. Even Confucius admitted that he did not reach a state of beatitude until he was sixty years old. While no two Sung scholars completely agreed to its definition, *ch'i* might be regarded as a person's moral vitality born with him and imbedded in his personality. It was uniquely human because no animal except human beings had a moral conscience and could "tell the right from the wrong, and the good from the bad." A man's moral conscience was inevitably reflected in his outward conduct. If his *ch'i* had been improved or changed (*pien ch'i-chih*), his outward behavior would improve accordingly. As *ch'i* continued to improve, the time would eventually come when he "can do whatever he pleases without ever doing anything wrong." He had no false pride (*ching*) which, according to Sung scholars, was among man's worst enemies. He was above worldly temptations, whether they be fame, power, or wealth. Yet he was neither otherworldly nor passive or fatalistic. He believed that this was the best of the possible worlds, and he would do his share to better it still. The first step to that goal was to better himself as an ethical being because no world could be better than the individuals who composed it.

As the cultivation of *ch'i* was the road to moral perfection, the question arose how and by what means it could be cultivated. One effective way, according to many Sung scholars, was through personal contacts with men of moral perfection themselves. By constantly exposing oneself to an atmosphere which only such men could generate, one imperceptibly absorbed the greatness which was imparted to him. This process was like, to quote a Sung scholar, a plant "bathing in the wind of spring" which made the plant grow without the plant's ever realizing its own growth. The purpose of education, therefore, was not merely the acquirement of knowledge; it was the imperceptible change of *ch'i* that an educator should strive to achieve. A teacher could not teach unless he was morally sound and was capable of setting an example to his students. Through education a moral elite would be created to set examples for the entire nation.

While book learning should not be an end in itself, many Sung scholars saw the close link between virtue and intellectual achievement. The twelfth century philosopher Chu Hsi (1130–1200), for instance, believed that the acquirement of knowledge was a prerequisite to wisdom and virtue. Knowledge, according to him, could be acquired in a variety of ways, such as travelling, personal contacts with men of wisdom, observation of physical surroundings and things in them, and above all, the study of written records, whether they be history, geography, political science, astronomy, mathematics, or even books of divination. There was a hidden truth in every subject, and the understanding of such truth would help a man to understand the truths in other subjects. As a person continued his studies conscientiously and diligently, said Chu Hsi, a time would come when all truths would appear in their proper places and the universal truth of which individual truths were only constituent parts would be "suddenly" revealed to him. He would begin to know the innermost secrets of nature and man, and for the first time he would be truly "enlightened." He would not only be wise; he would be free. His would be moral perfection without the slightest effort and despite himself.

The way to moral perfection, as explained by Chu Hsi, raised more questions than it answered. Even if moral perfection came from intellectual achievement, how could a person, with a short lifetime, possibly master all knowledge? Second, what was the true relationship between the mastering of all knowledge and the "sudden enlightenment," and how did one lead to the other? The mystic link was never adequately explained. Third, if "the acquirement of knowledge comes from the observation and investigation of things" (*chih-chih tsai ke-wu*), how did one proceed to do so? A story was then told that a man who wished to know all about bamboo went to a bamboo grove everyday "to observe and to investigate" but came back with no more knowledge about bamboo than what he had had before.

Due to the many difficult problems posed by Chu Hsi's theory, other Sung scholars advocated a different approach. "The truth of the universe is within myself, and there is nothing to investigate outside of my own mind," said Lu Chiu-yüan (1139–1192), Chu Hsi's contemporary and academic opponent. Lu maintained that to investigate outward, objective matters was to pursue the unlimited by the limited means; it was wasteful and fruitless. There was no close relation between the physical world and oneself, he continued, and the knowledge of one's surroundings had nothing to do with his inner conscience. In fact, the physical world did not exist unless man's mind existed, and there was no truth other than what was contained within oneself. To acquire truth and therefore virtue, said Lu, all a person needed to do was to examine himself and rectify his own mind. The rectification of mind was the first step to moral truth. Whenever in doubt, a person should search his conscience and ask himself whether such action he proposed to do was "righteous" (*yi*) or "profitable" (*li*), and he should not profit himself at the expense of righteousness. To discipline oneself was therefore more important than to right outside wrongs. The world outside of oneself would rectify itself if one's own mind had been rectified. To do otherwise, said Lu Chiu-yüan, was to "confuse end and means" (*pen mo tao chih*) and could not yield good results.

Later in life Chu Hsi recognized the limitation of a man's intellectual pursuit. While all knowledge was desirable, there were certain works, according to him, that contained the basic truth and should be studied with great diligence. Besides the *Analects of Confucius* and the *Book of Mencius*, he added the *Great Learning* and the *Doctrine of the Mean*, both taken from the *Book of Rites*, as the basic works of Confucianism. Together they were the *Four Books*. The impact of this selection was enormous. For the next seven hundred years, the *Four Books* were the first taught in schools and the standard texts from which questions for the civil service examinations were drawn. Whatever advantages it might have, the selection unfortunately compelled students to be unoriginal and conforming and often made them mere echoes of stereotyped ideas.

Chu Hsi's "sudden revelation" and Lu Chiu-yüan's emphasis on inner self contained a speculative interest which had not characterized the ancient Confucian tradition. While condemning Buddhism and Taoism on practical as well as ideological grounds, Confucianism as interpreted by Sung scholars was unquestionably influenced by them. The new speculative interest led to the examination of the hitherto less emphasized and more speculative works, notably the *Book of Changes* and the *Book of Taoist Virtue*. As elaborated by Chou Tun-yi (1012–1073) and many others who followed him, Sung cosmology presupposed a rational universe that functioned according to well-defined rules. The universe began with The Infinite (*wu chi*), the invisible vital force which was the very essence of its being. Once it acquired form, it became The Absolute (*t'ai chi*), the beginning of the physical universe as could be known through our senses. Though The Infinite preceded The Absolute, they were in fact inseparable. The former provided content (*chih*), and the latter gave form (*hsing*). Without content form could not exist; without form content would remain unknown. The monolithic Infinite-Absolute multiplied itself and created things through the interaction between two opposite forces within itself, namely, *yin* and *yang*, or the negative and the positive. Things thus created could be either *yin*- or *yang*-dominated. The sun, for instance, being *yang* dominated, was *yang;* the moon, being *yin* dominated, was *yin*. Likewise men were *yang*, and women were *yin*. By things were not only meant concrete objects, but also abstract concepts. South and brightness were *yang*, and north and darkness were *yin*. Though the two forces maintained their separate identity, each existed in the existence of the other. There would not have been men without women, and the concept of darkness was impossible unless there had been brightness.

Yin and *yang*, being forces, were not things themselves. Most things in the universe, whether they be trees or clouds, were the final, rather than the immediate, products of their creations. The immediate products of the *yin-yang* interactions were the five primary elements, namely, metal, wood, water, fire, and earth. The five primary elements were the simplest forms of physical existence and were the essense of the physical universe which we human beings recognized through the use of our five senses. They, through their various combinations, in turn created the more complicated things such as trees and clouds. In each of the things they created, one of the five elements had a more dominating position than others. The trees, for instance, had a "wood virtue" (*mu te*), and the clouds, water. While maintaining their separate identities in each given instance, the five primary elements successively produced and destroyed each other, and no element could maintain its present status indefinitely. Their mutual relations are indicated in the following graphs:

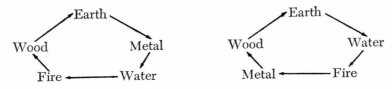

THE GENERATION CYCLE   THE DESTRUCTION CYCLE

In the left graph, earth generated metal, metal generated water, etc. In the right graph, earth destroyed water, water destroyed fire, and when wood destroyed earth, the cycle was completed. It should be noted that during each generation or destruction process, each or any of the five elements was not lost; it only changed its form. In both cycles nothing could be ever gained or lost.

Thus the universe maintained its dynamic existence through the continuous interaction between *yin* and *yang* and the incessant permutations of the five primary elements as they successively produced and destroyed each other. The law of the universe was the law of change; it was change that kept the universe living and dynamic. Was it not clear, Sung scholars asked, that day followed night and summer followed spring? The universe was eternal; so was change. Change, however, did not go on in a random, blind fashion. It followed a definite pattern, the pattern of the Eight Diagrams. The two opposite forces, *yin* and *yang*, interacted in accordance with the form as provided by one of the Eight Diagrams.

In the first two diagrams one force so completely dominated the other that the latter simply did not appear. They were the purest *yang* and *yin* diagrams (*ch'ien* and *k'un*), representing Heaven and Earth respectively. The other six diagrams had either two *yin* and one *yang*, or two *yang* and one *yin*. In the former case the diagram was a *yin* diagram, and things created through this kind of combination were *yin* things, such as the moon. In the latter case it was a *yang* diagram, and things thus created were *yang* things, such as the sun. As has been said in a previous chapter, in each diagram a broken line was used to denote the *yin* force, and an unbroken line the *yang* force. As a reminder, two typical *yin* and *yang* diagrams are drawn as follows:

Yin Diagram   *Yang* Diagram

Through a continuous process of combination, dissolution, and recombination *yin* and *yang* destroyed and created the constituent parts of the universe. Whenever they combined to create things, they always followed one of the Eight Diagrams.

In summary, the whole cosmology may be pictured as follows:

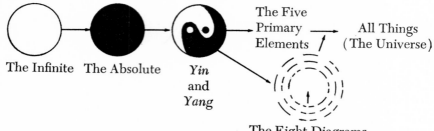

The Infinite   The Absolute   *Yin* and *Yang*   The Five Primary Elements → All Things (The Universe)

The Eight Diagrams

Before we leave the subject, it should be pointed out that the basic ideas of Sung cosmology did not originate with Sung scholars. The concept of The Absolute first appeared in the *Book of Changes*, and the idea of The Infinite was introduced in the *Book of Taoist Virtue*. The concepts of Eight Diagrams and five primary elements were equally old. Moreover, Han scholars like Tung Chung-shu had written a great deal about the *yin-yang* reactions. The contribution of Sung scholars was the coordination and systematization of the existing ideas; they made these ideas appear in their proper places and incorporated them into a rational, logical system. As the universe was rational and harmonious, they, like many Confucian philosophers before them, emphasized the necessity of conducting human relations along the same line. Men should strive for harmony among themselves as they had to do so with regard to nature. Only when harmony was established among men could there be peace and good will.

HISTORY

Few peoples were more historically minded than the Chinese. To them history was not merely a written record of the past; it taught ethics and good government. Whatever lessons had to be learned, they learned from the past, and the past was relied on as the guide for the future. History described the rise and fall of dynasties, the success and failure of each monarch, and the joy and sorrow of the people, so that succeeding generations might profit by avoiding past mistakes and by pursuing policies that had been proven successful. In the academic tradition of China there were no separate disciplines of government, economics, or any other branch of what we today call social sciences except history. It was history that taught the Chinese practically everything that had to be learned, including morality and ethics. It showed, for instance, how a conscientious monarch was rewarded with a successful reign and how a debauched ruler ended his infamous life by a premature death. With facts at their command, historians praised and condemned as they saw fit, always, of course, more subtly than openly. To them history was not merely an objective record of the past; it was meant to serve a moral purpose. It was said that when Confucius wrote the *Spring and Autumn Annals*, "rebellious ministers and unfilial sons trembled." They trembled because Confucius' book was meant to condemn both.

Because of the great importance attached to history, the Chinese gave history and historians a position unique among the civilized peoples in the world. The post of official historian was said to have been established as early as the Shang dynasty; such a post was maintained practically throughout the entire course of Chinese history. The great historian Ssu-ma Ch'ien held that post during the second century B.C., as his father had done before him. Since his recording had to be objective to be useful, tradition made the post of official historian politically independent. His personal integrity should never be in doubt, and he should record events as they occurred, even though the recording of such events might displease the men in power who in a rage might punish him severely.

The independence of the official historian was best illustrated by an incident which occurred in the seventh century B.C. In the feudal state of Tsin a minister assassinated the unpopular king and proposed to install on the throne a prince of his own choice. The prime minister was then in hiding because the dead king had previously demanded his own death on an alleged offense. Since the king was dead, the prime minister returned to the capital, but he did nothing to bring the assassin to justice. Displeased with his inactivity, the official historian recorded: "The prime minister murdered the king." Asked why he recorded what he did when obviously this was not the truth, the historian replied: "As the prime minister, you have the duty to bring the assassin to justice. When you do not, you are as guilty as the assassin." More than a century later when Confucius heard this incident, he praised the Tsin historian highly and asked every other historian to follow his example.

Ever since the Han dynasty it was customary for a new regime to write an official history of the preceding dynasty, and the resulting work would be regarded as the final and the most authoritative of the history in question. Since so much importance was attached to this work, the historian (or historians) who volunteered or had been assigned to its writing approached the task with a sense of mission almost sacred. Groping through mountainous materials that had not been consumed by time, he sifted and winnowed until they were reduced to a manageable portion. He selected and discarded in accordance with his own judgment and conscience. He should write factually and objectively; any slant or distortion would be a reflection on his personality and scholarship. He should not let personal feelings and contemporary considerations play a part in his writing because he had in mind not only contemporaries but readers for many centuries to come. But being human, he was not altogether faultless. With due allowance for personal preferences (though perhaps unknown to him), under the dictation of circumstances and being involved in the contemporary atmosphere, he often became less objective when writing about the last monarch or monarchs of the preceding dynasty whom the reigning emperor or his immediate predecessors had replaced. He was as inclined to exaggerate the "vices" of the past regime as he was happy to praise the virtue of his own sovereign. However, he could be counted on to be conscientiously accurate concerning most of the period he was describing; his impartiality was somewhat tarnished by his loyalty towards his own government when he came down to record events that led to, or became a part of, the conflict between the preceding regime and the new administration. But even then his sense of duty towards intellectual integrity and the overwhelming concern and pride in writing a masterpiece intended for posterity prevented him from indulging in any considerable measure in purely transient or ephemeral considerations.

It is generally agreed that Ou-yang Hsiu (1007–1072) and Ssu-ma Kuang (1018–1086) were the most outstanding Sung historians. Ou-yang Hsiu came from the same area (modern Kiangsi province) in South China as Wang An-shih and had been a patron and friend of the future reformer until the latter's radicalism turned them into political opponents. Active in politics, he nevertheless found time to write two monumental works, the *New History of the Five Dynasties* (*Hsin wu-tai shih*) and the *New History of the T'ang* (*Hsin T'ang shih*). The former was an independent, private undertaking. The latter, however, was done under government sponsorship and was written jointly with another scholar of equal fame named Sung Ch'i; it took them seventeen years to complete it. Both works were entitled "New" because books on the same topics had been written before. In collecting materials for his undertakings, Ou-yang Hsiu used private sources extensively as well as official documents. His works were written in a style noted for its conciseness and simplicity.

Insofar as impact on later historians was concerned, a far more influential work was *History As A Mirror* (*Tzu-chih t'ung-chien*) written by Ssu-ma Kuang. The book was so titled because it was intended to serve as a reminder to future emperors to avoid the mistakes of the past and to follow the virtuous path of the great. Whenever appropriate, the author added comments at the end of each event he described, so that his readers would not miss the significance of such events and might profit from them morally. With a total of 294 rolls, the book covered 1,362 years

(403 B.C.–959 A.D.) in chronological order, and took seventeen years (1067–1084) to complete. Though recognized as one of the greatest works ever undertaken, it had the obvious disadvantages of all chronicles. For one thing, it was difficult for a reader to follow an event from the beginning to its end, as the description of a certain event spread over several rolls, interrupted by other events that occurred in the same year or years.

In the twelfth century a man named Yüan Shu (1131–1205) regrouped all entries in Ssu-ma Kuang's work in accordance with "events" instead of "years." Originally compiled for the convenience of his own reading, the new work, entitled *Events in History As A Mirror* (*Tzu-chih t'ung-chien chi-shih pen-mo*), set a new precedent for historical writing, as no Chinese history had been written in this way before. Immediately it became popular because it was much easier to read than the original.

Equally important as those mentioned above were two other works written according to "topics." One was *General Records* (*T'ung chih*) by Cheng Ch'iao (fl. 1120's) in which the entire Chinese heritage was discussed under the headings of twenty main topics, including astronomy, etymology, phonetics, geography, arts, famine, and criminology. It was intended to cover the history of all important subjects in one work. Towards the end of the Sung dynasty another historian named Ma Tuanlin, though praising highly Cheng Ch'iao's work, thought that its coverage was not extensive enough. He began to write a topical history of his own, and the result was *A Study of Cultural Heritage* (*Wen-hsien t'ung-k'ao*). Altogether twenty-four topics appeared in the book, including taxation, money, population, education, and divination. Each topic was covered in considerable detail, and the book was particularly strong on Sung institutions. According to the author, more than twenty years were spent in its preparation, and the authenticity of each source was checked and rechecked before it was used. The importance of these two works cannot be overemphasized. Generally speaking, dynastic histories (*tuan-tai shih*) were most concerned with government and politics; the social and economic life of the people was given only secondary consideration. On the other hand, topical histories (*t'ung shih*) covered a much wider range of subjects, social, economic, as well as political. Institutions, rather than personalities, were the topics of their discussions. Both types of history, however, supplemented each other, and one became richer because of the existence of the other.

LITERATURE

Throughout Chinese history it was literature to which the greatest talents of each generation devoted themselves. The Chinese written language, composed of characters with rich but shadowy meanings and devoid of grammar in the Western sense, provided the most challenging ground for literary exercise. Refined by time, it possessed a delicacy and a subtlety that few languages in the world could ever hope to match. Written in classical Chinese even a declaration of war sometimes sounded like a pastoral poem, and history was not without precedents in which an enemy commander surrendered simply because the letter requesting his surrender was too emotionally beautiful to refuse.[1] In the seventh century when Empress Wu received a public denunciation from a group of rebels condemning her for her immorality and lack of virtue, she, impressed by the unsurpassed beauty of its style, inquired about its author and, instead of being angry, blamed the prime minister for not having recruited a man of such talent to her service. In the Chinese mind no man could be considered truly great if he could not write prose or poetry with classical beauty. On the other hand, the evil of the most evil man was somewhat forgotten (if not forgiven), if he knew how to put together beautifully any combination of the commonly used 10,000 characters. The civil service examination from which the most talented men in China were chosen to run the government was by and large a literary test, and no man could ever pass the examination if he did not write classical Chinese well. The mastery of literature was in fact one of the achievements prized most by the Chinese.

The two standard ways of literary expression were prose and poetry. In prose Sung continued the trend pioneered by the two T'ang essayists Han Yü and Liu Tsung-Yüan. The new style of prosewriting, often referred to as the "ancient" style, represented the style of Han writers with such characteristics as conciseness, forcefulness, and fluidity. It was in direct contrast to the so-called "parallel form" which had been most popular among the writers of the Wei, the Tsin, and the Southern Dynasties. The return to the "ancient" style might be said to be a belated reaction against the artificial ornamentation of the "parallel form." To seek new inspiration in style, T'ang and Sung writers went all the way back to the Han dynasty when such masters as Chia Yi, Tung Chung-shu, and Ssu-ma Ch'ien reigned supreme. A piece of good writing, as one critic dramatically put it, "should sound like gold whenever it was dropped on the ground." While it has been repeatedly debated whether the T'ang-Sung writers ever came close to the Han masters, they did pioneer a new style eagerly followed by writers of many centuries to come.

Among the Sung writers the most talented and most versatile was unquestionably Su Shih (1036–1101), also known as Su Tung-p'o. Su Tung-p'o came from China' s Southwest in the modern Szechuan province and

[1] The author has in mind the letter which Ch'iu Ch'ih (d. 508), a literary genius during the Liang dynasty, wrote to Ch'en Pai-chih, a military commander of the Later (North) Wei. The letter is still in existence.

was compared with history's greatest men of letters by his contemporaries. With a variety of lively interests, he divided his time successfully among government desks, scenic mountains, wine cups, and "moth-eyed" prostitutes. Ideologically broad-minded, he found many of his best friends among the Buddhist monks. As a writer, he was equally versatile in prose and poetry. Universally praised for the beauty of his style, he did not care to go through the routine of being modest. In a letter to his brother Su Ch'e, he described the style of his writing as follows:

> My essays are like thousands of fountains shooting with a violent burst from an uncharted wilderness. When the water reaches the plain, it becomes a roaring torrent, sweeping thousands of miles with complete ease. When it encounters rocks and mountains, it changes its shape and course and adjusts itself to its surroundings. It is completely unpredictable. It goes wherever it should go and only stops whenever it should stop.

The best known among his extant essays is the *Song of Ch'ihpi* (*Ch'ih-pi fu*), a sentimental review of a battlefield where some eight hundred years before the mighty Ts'ao Ts'ao had met his first major defeat. As a prose writer scarcely less famous was Su Tung-p'o's friend and patron Ou-yang Hsiu whose name has been mentioned before in his role as a historian. An extant example of his writing is the *Introduction to the Old Drunken Man's Pagoda* (*Tsui-weng t'ing hsü*) which for hundreds of years school children had to commit to memory as an example of the best literary style.

Great though its achievement was in prose, the Sung period was even better known as a golden era in poetry. By then poetry had developed into two distinct forms, *shih* and *tz'u*. In *shih* each line had the same and equal number of characters, and since each character had always one syllable, all lines provided even rhythm throughout the entire poem. It was the general practice for each poem to have either five-character or seven-character lines, though many of the very ancient poems like some in the *Book of Odes* had four-character lines. Though poetry in the form of *shih* reached its most glorious age during the time of Li Po and Tu Fu, Sung poets like Su Tung-p'o and Wang An-shih could not be said to be much inferior without causing a heated debate. Usually it was the personal taste, rather than the inherent merit of the poems themselves, that made rating different. Whatever the opinion might be in the case of *shih*, there was a consensus that in the other form of poetry, *tz'u*, Sung surpassed all other periods, before or after, in the number of great masters and in the quality of poems they produced.

Nobody knows for sure when *tz'u* first began. It began perhaps no earlier than the seventh century because no *tz'u* before that period, if it ever existed, has survived. As with all forms of literary expression, it passed through a long revolutionary stage before it reached its final form.

It was first found in the houses of entertainment where the songs sung by female entertainers were arranged in such a way that each succeeding line contained a definite number of characters (syllables). The singing of these songs was usually accompanied by musical instruments. The line and metric arrangement in each song was called *p'ai*, and the words were *tz'u*. Today few people know how these songs were actually sung; but since the words have survived, modern poets can still compose *tz'u* by following the same line and metric arrangements (*p'ai*). It was and still is customary to entitle each poem by the name of an original *p'ai* which it followed, rather than the content of the poem itself. Since the number of *p'ai* was limited, theoretically there could have been thousands or even millions of *tz'u* with the same title. But, as only the very best have survived the test of time, the actual number of extant *tz'u* with the same title is comparatively few. At the beginning the *tz'u* as sung by the girls in entertainment houses were perhaps no better than those found in similar places in today's Hong Kong or Macao; but quality improved once the great poets took an interest in composing them.

As has been noted in an earlier chapter, it was customary in those days for men to visit houses of entertainment which were in fact disguised brothels. Until modern times the professions of female entertainer and prostitute were practically the same, and the Chinese often mentioned them in the same breath. During the T'ang-Sung periods the better entertainment houses provided well-educated girls as their customers' companions. These girls were versed in music, art, and literature, and some of them even wrote poetry. The most celebrated example was the ninth century Hsieh T'ao who had among her friends the most distinguished poets of her time and was said to have written about five hundred poems herself, though very few of them have survived.

It was not difficult to understand how these houses prospered. In a society where every aspect of outward conduct was strictly regulated according to well-defined rules and where all marriages were arranged, the houses of entertainment provided an emotional outlet such as no other institution could. Here alone could a man become uninhibited, discard his respectability, and do whatever his true self dictated. He left his Confucian propriety behind when he entered a house of "wild flowers." Sometimes genuine friendship or even romance developed between the "wild flowers" and their customers, and such romance appeared in numerous novels and short stories. If the customers happened to be talented poets, there was no reason why they should not write lyrics for the songs sung by their favorites.

Though it had its beginning in the houses of ill repute, *tz'u* became a respectable form of literary expression once the famed poets took a hand in composing it. As time went by, it was divorced from its original purpose of singing; people wrote it merely to express their sentiments and emotions. The major difference between *shih* and *tz'u* was that while the former had an equal number of characters (syllables) in each line, the number of characters in each line of *tz'u* varied, usually from two to nine. As such, *tz'u* was a much freer and more convenient vehicle of expression than *shih,* and perhaps because of its background it fitted better with lighter topics such as love and romance. T'ang *tz'u,* as represented by the works of Wen T'ing-yün (818–872?) and Li Shang-yin (813–858), were flowery and artificially ornate; they lacked depth and conviction. It was not until the tenth century that *tz'u* found its great champion in the person of Li Yü (936–978), sometimes referred to as Li Hou-chu. Li Yü was the last ruler of a small kingdom called South T'ang in the lower Yangtze River valley which was eventually conquered by Sung. As a king he was a miserable failure. He spent most of his time with dancing girls and musicians when he should have been with his cabinet ministers. His earlier works were good, but not exceptional. It was only after he had lost his kingdom and was living in captivity that his literary talent fully bloomed. His later works were written with deep feeling and were full of pathos. While he wrote them only to quench his emotional thirst, many of his immortal lines were on the lips of his countrymen for a thousand years to come.

   Tz'u as a form of poetical expression continued to be popular throughout the Sung dynasty. There was a Liu Yung (fl. 1030's) who had written so many *tz'u* for the brothel girls that it was said that "wherever there is drinking water there are girls who know how to sing his poems." His popularity was partly due to the fact that he preferred more commonly used words, and consequently his poems could be better comprehended by the less educated singers. Having passed successfully the imperial examination, his experience with a bureaucratic career was not a happy one, partly because, to use his own words, he "prefers to exchange illusory fame for some light drinking and low singing." When he finally died after a turbulent, libertine life, he was so poor that his admiring brothel girls had to contribute funds for burial expenses.

   About one century after Liu Yung's death, there was another great *tz'u* poet named Hsin Ch'i-chi (1140–1207) who differed from him both in temperament and in the nature of *tz'u* produced. By then the golden age of peace and prosperity had passed, and the Chin horsemen had swept down as far as the Yangtze River. Being a war veteran himself, Hsin wrote poems to express his patriotic sentiments. As one critic put it, his poems were not meant to be sung by brothel girls; they were to be shouted aloud by marching soldiers.

   Between Liu Yung and Hsin Ch'i-chi there were many poets whose *tz'u* have survived. Perhaps the greatest of them all was the poetess Li Ch'ing-chao (b. 1081) whose achievement in *tz'u* could be well compared with that of Li Po in *shih.* She came from an intellectual family in Tsinan (modern Shantung province), and she had been well tutored in the best of China's cultural traditions before she was married to a university student named Chao Ming-ch'eng. The marriage was a happy one. She said many years later that she and her husband had spent many happy evenings in matching wits and in outdoing each other in guessing the sources of famous literary quotations, recalling not only the names of books but also the volumes and page numbers. After her husband had been assigned to an official post far in the south and had to leave home, she sent him one poem after another, expressing the sadness of separation and the hope and the joy of reunion. A story was told that her husband was so impressed with her poems that he tried to surpass her by writing many himself. Without identifying their sources, he showed both their poems to a friend, and the friend, without the slightest hesitation, pointed out the best lines, all of which happened to be hers.

Unfortunately this happy life did not last long. The Chin forces marched southward, and Li's home, together with the rest of North China, fell into the enemy's hands. Li's unhappy refugee life was further saddened by the early death of her husband. For the rest of her life she lived in poverty and sorrow, but with a beautiful memory. As far as her poems were concerned, they were a happy combination of superb techniques in the choice of rhythms and words and a deep feeling which only a born poetess knew how to express. They sounded like murmuring streams, never loud and yet seemingly audible even at a great distance. They opened before the reader a new horizon of elevated emotions, neither of sadness nor of joy, but of an indescribable kind that seemed to have existed in a totally different world.

Popular though it was, poetry, in the form of either *shih* or *tz'u*, was written by and addressed to the literati. As it demanded conciseness and strictly followed a prescribed form, both in rhyme and in words, it had to be written in literary Chinese, which could only be understood by the well educated. The cultural needs of the illiterate masses were met by other means. During the Sung dynasty the masses found entertainment in the increasingly popular *p'ing hua*, or vernaculur tales. Throughout the centuries professional storytellers travelled from town to town, from village to village, relating the great stories of the past. In the teahouses and in the market places, for a small fee they made their audiences laugh and cry, and they stopped at the moment of suspense so that their listeners would come back the next day. The stories they told were vernacular tales which, contrary to stories written in literary Chinese, could be easily understood by the masses. At the beginning they told their stories from memory, and their stories were handed down orally from generation to generation. Considerable time had elapsed before some of the popular tales were put down in written words. Their writers were generally anonymous, either because no person could really claim credit for them, or because they did not care to claim authorship on account of the traditional contempt for anything written in vernacular form. Such authorship would in no way enhance the writer's literary prestige.

Many of the vernacular tales written during the Sung period have survived and are available today. Some were fictional and others claimed to be historical. In either case, the heroes were exalted and the villains condemned; at the end of each tale the good men were always rewarded and the bad men could in no way escape punishment. Written by inferior authors and perhaps to satisfy a mediocre taste, most of these tales were poorly organized and crude in expression. It was no surprise that traditionally they had been looked down upon by the country's intellectual elite. From a historian's point of view, however, they are extremely valuable. They provide firsthand reports about the life of the common people during the Sung dynasty, information which is unobtainable in dynastic histories where only the great and the mighty receive attention. Though they did not possess much literary value, some of the vernacular tales did provide inspiration for later writers. For instance, the great novel, *The Marsh Heroes* (*Shui-hu chuan*), drew most of its basic material from a vernacular tale written during the Sung period.[1]

PRINTING

What fascinates the historians is the fact that many of the surviving vernacular tales were actually printed during the Sung dynasty. Their publication suggests not only the popularity of vernacular tales; it also shows the comparative advancement in printing. Though the printing of books was not widely practiced until the Sung dynasty, its basic techniques had been known for a long time. It is not known when the first printed book came into being, but like other inventions of historical importance it must have undergone a long, evolutionary process. The use of stone and bronze seals and inscriptions could be dated at least as early as the fifth century B.C., and rubbings on stone carvings had been a common practice many centuries before the invention of printing. Due to the great similarity between them, the rubbing process must have been the immediate predecessor of block printing. Rubbings were done on carved stones, and stone carving was a very ancient art form. Late in the third century B.C., for instance, the Ch'in emperor Shih Huang-ti ordered stone monuments to be erected in the "four corners of the earth," and on them were inscribed eulogies of the emperor and his regime. During later dynasties the government often sponsored the inscription of Confucian classics on stone slabs so as to standardize the texts and to popularize Confu-

[1] For a detailed description of *The Marsh Heroes*, see Chapter X, p. 330.

cian teachings. After Buddhism had been introduced to China, the same thing was done with regard to Buddhist scriptures. Sometimes pictures used to illustrate the text were also inscribed. The process of rubbing was a simple one. The rubber placed a piece of damp paper on the stone, pressed it into the inscriptions, applied ink on the plain surface of the paper, and then rubbed it gently with a brush. As his brush swept across the paper, the words and pictures soon appeared on the paper as exactly as they were on the stone. By binding together successive rubbings, one would have a book of considerable size.

Rubbing, however, was still not printing. The first mention of print-

RUBBING This rubbing was made from a stone monument on which one of the earliest known images of Confucius was inscribed. The image was painted by the great T'ang painter Wu Tao-tzu who lived in the eighth century, but was not cast into stone, however, until 1107 A.D. The Chinese text on the top, also inscribed in stone, was written by a Professor Shang in the same year. The purpose of casting this image into stone, said Professor Shang, was to preserve for posterity the best image of Confucius then known. The man on the right was believed to be Tseng-tzu, one of Confucius' disciples. In ancient times a student habitually walked a few paces behind his teacher, to show his respect.

ing was in an imperial decree of 593 in which Sui Wen-ti ordered the printing of Buddhist images and scriptures, but no details with regard to this enterprise were ever given. If printing had been invented then, it must have been in its most rudimentary stage, for as late as the eighth century hand copying was still the common method of producing books. Toward the middle decades of the ninth century printed books first appeared in quantities in Shu (modern Szechuan province) and could be purchased from private dealers. The art of book printing soon spread to other provinces, and by the end of the ninth century it was common all over China. By then printed materials had covered a much wider range, including not only Confucian classics and Buddhist scriptures but also dictionaries, books of mathematics, and others.

It was long after book printing had become a successful private business that the government decided to use it for its own purposes. In 932 the government of Later T'ang, acting on the recommendation of prime minister Feng Tao, ordered the printing of the *Nine Confucian Classics* for wide circulation. The Department of Cultural Affairs (*Kuo-tzu chien*) was made responsible for the selection and editing of texts, for the employment of hand carvers and other personnel, and for the printing operation itself. Consisting of one hundred and thirty volumes, the entire work took some twenty years to complete. While the government was sponsoring the publication of more serious works, there were individuals who were so proud of their own writings that they published them at their own expense. We know that in 953 a man named Ho Ling printed several hundred copies of his own poetry and distributed them among his friends and relatives.

So far only block printing was involved. In the 1040's the art of printing was further advanced through the invention of movable type. Block printing, whether it was done on stone or wood, was a costly and time-consuming process, for each carved block could only be used for a specific page of a particular book. The invention of movable type was attributed to a man named Pi Sheng about whose life, unfortunately, we know very little. The invention was simple but ingenious. Each piece of movable type had on it one Chinese character which was carved in relief on a small block of moistened clay. After the block had been hardened by fire, the type became hard and durable and could be used wherever that particular character was required. In the process of printing a certain page of a book, the movable type bearing different characters were placed on an iron plate and were arranged in accordance with the text of the book to be printed. The type was glued together and to the plate by a mixture of turpentine, wax, and burned paper ash. The pieces of movable type could be easily detached from the plate and from each other by placing the back of the plate over a gentle fire, whenever this type had to be used somewhere else. Some of the books printed during this period by this device have survived, and amazingly they are still in fair condition. Printing by movable type, however, did not replace block printing. Throughout the centuries they existed side by side until our own time. When Marco Polo visited China in the thirteenth century, he must have seen printed books. It is possible that he or some other European traveller brought that knowledge to Europe, a knowledge which later inspired such men as John Gutenberg.

FINE ARTS

In the field of fine arts, the Sung period was most noted for its achievement in painting. A cultured gentleman of those days had to be versed in the four arts: the lute, chess, calligraphy, and painting, though their relative importance did not necessarily follow that order. Like calligraphy, painting was done more for the expression of one's inner self than for the depiction of physical objects. Theoretically at least, whatever appeared in the painting, whether landscape or flowers and birds, was merely a vehicle through which the artist communicated with the invisible unknown. A Chinese painting, therefore, should not be judged according to its realism; it was the presence or absence of such communication which made a painting a good or bad one. It was neither the form nor the content that mattered; all important was a mystic quality called *shen yün*, or divine harmony that signified the existence of such communication. While a great master could achieve this by a few quick strokes of bamboo leaves, a less endowed person could paint an object to its exact outward likeness and was still regarded as a mediocre novice because his painting had not in it that mystic quality.

As taught by great masters, a man should paint according to what he had conceived in his mind rather than what he saw with his eyes. A good artist would never look at an object while he was painting. He interpreted nature, instead of copying it. A landscape painter might spend days in the mountains and along the streams, feeling rather than seeing his environment. He would not paint until what he felt had been crystallized into a presentable form. Since such an inspiration could disappear as suddenly as it had occurred, he tried to project it on a piece of paper or silk as quickly as possible, lest his inspiration fail him in the midst of his effort. What he painted was not what he had seen with his eyes but what he felt at that moment. Once the ink was on the paper, under no circumstance should there be erasures or corrections. Describing the technique of painting bamboo, Su Tung-p'o once remarked: "To paint bamboo, the painter holds the brush steadily, looks intently at the paper, and visualizes the broadest outlines of the proposed painting. When the vision flashes, he follows it quickly, and with his brush sweeping across the paper, he

馬遠松陰玩月

A CHINESE PAINTING This painting is attributed to Ma Yüan of the Sung dynasty. The Chinese characters on the upper right read: "Ma Yüan plays with the moon in the shade of a pine tree."

pursues it as a falcon chases an elusive rabbit. If he slackens his pace, his vision escapes and may never return."

In subject matter, Sung painters preferred landscapes, animals, and plants to paintings of a religious nature. This secular tendency began as early as the T'ang dynasty, though religious paintings were supposedly more important at all times. The best of Sung painters were experts on secular subjects. Huang Ch'üan, for instance, specialized in the painting of flowers, Li Kung-lin (1049–1106) in the depicting of "human affairs," and Mi Fei (1051–1107) and his son Yu-jen were best known for their landscapes.

Early in the twelfth century the painters found their best patron in the person of Sung Hui-tsung; it was during his reign that all fine arts, including painting, received the warmest encouragement from the government. A royal institute of calligraphy and painting was established in the capital Kaifeng where famed painters were commissioned to paint and

LANDSCAPE BY AN ANONYMOUS PAINTER OF THE TWELFTH CENTURY Taoist influence plays an important part in practically all landscapes of the traditional style. Notice the dominance by mountains and water in this picture and the comparative insignificance of man. Man accommodates himself to nature; he does not change it.

were salaried to teach. It was then that the *Hsüan-ho Catalogue of Painting* was compiled under the personal direction of the emperor. It contained 6,396 paintings by 231 artists and was divided among ten different categories according to subject matter. The ten categories were: (1) Taoism and Buddhism, (2) "human affairs," (3) palaces and other buildings, (4) barbarians, (5) dragons and fishes, (6) landscapes, (7) birds and beasts, (8) flowers and plants, (9) ink bamboo, and (10) vegetables and fruits. With the exception of the first category, all were secular subjects, and their collection far outnumbered the collection on religious matters. Sung Hui-tsung himself was an expert painter of flowers and birds. Some of his paintings are believed to have survived today.

Compared with painting, Sung's achievements in other fields of fine arts were minor and less spectacular. For reasons that have never been adequately explained, the Chinese, especially during later periods, looked down upon sculpture, ceramics, and bronze-casting as art forms. They were dismissed as mere crafts, whereas painting and music were regarded as a more orthodox pursuit for cultural refinement. As craftsmen, the sculptors and the makers of ceramics and bronzes rarely received the credit they deserved, and practically all works in these fields remained anonymous. However, enough works have survived to enable us to appraise their accomplishments. As far as sculpture was concerned, it suffered a steady decline after the Shang dynasty. It was not until the introduction of Buddhism in the first century A.D. that sculpture began to become an important art form, largely due to the increasing demand for Buddhist images. During the next centuries religious themes practically dominated the entire field, and being largely an imported art, the sculpture of Buddhist statues as created by the Chinese showed unmistakably Central Asian and Indian influences. Perhaps because of their religious nature, there was little originality in these statues, and the art of making them had long become highly conventionalized. The Buddha, for instance, always looked placid, serene, and contemplative, and even his posture, whether sitting or standing, changed little from one statue to another. The T'ang artists tried to make these statues more lifelike, but the improvement was too little to be really noticeable. It does not seem that the Sung artists did any better.

However, in secular art, especially in the field of ceramics, the Chinese were much more imaginative and original. Fine figures of people and animals made of pottery have been found in Han tombs, and for two thousand years after the Han dynasty potters created art objects of unsurpassed beauty without ever receiving any recognition from the historians. Ceramic art reached a great height during the T'ang dynasty. The T'ang potters left us many small statues of dancing girls, horses, and the like, and one piece of work, showing a lady riding a galloping horse, was particularly noteworthy because of the graceful and lively lines the artist created of both the horse and its rider. Further advances in pottery were made during the Sung dynasty. The Sung potters, unlike their T'ang predecessors, were best known for their porcelain wares. The extant Sung porcelains have a variety of colors: crimson, purple, blue, and brown; and all colors were applied with care and good taste. Some have a delicate cream or ivory tone and their color glaze appeals to the touch as well as to the eye. They are highly rated as collectors' items.

As far as bronze art was concerned, the apogee was reached as early as the Shang dynasty. The technical skill of Shang craftsmen and the beauty of their creations have never really been equalled. The Sung, like any of the later dynasties, never produced anything which even remotely resembled the greatest works of the past.

THE FALL OF SUNG

What amazes historians is not Sung's eventual downfall but the fact that Sung lasted as long as it did. We have discussed in some detail Sung's weaknesses. The real cause of such weaknesses was much deeper than what appeared on the surface; it seemed to be deeply imbedded in and originated from the popular mentality and the ethical concepts of the Chinese. The ancient Chinese were perhaps no less warlike than other peoples in the world, and we have noticed in an earlier chapter how ferociously battles were fought. Emerging successfully from the interplay of brutal forces was the Ch'in regime which, once established, adopted Legalism as its state cult and emphasized fighting as an invaluable virtue for all its citizens. The Ch'in regime, however, did not last long. After the downfall of Ch'in, Legalism and all it stood for were fully and completely discredited. For more than two thousand years after Han Fei had finished writing the last sentence of his book, no Chinese philosopher ever glorified war. To the popular mind war was an evil by definition. Chinese sages said time and again that under no circumstance should war be waged for military conquest, and war, if it came, should be conducted for extremely compelling reasons and for self-defense only.

Chinese pacifism was further strengthened during the second century B.C. when Confucianism was officially proclaimed as the state cult. Confucians denounced war as a matter of principle, even war for the defense of Confucianism. They glorified "the way of peace" (*wang tao*) and condemned in unequivocal terms "the way of war" (*pa tao*). While revolt might be justified under extraordinary circumstances, there should never be war for the conquest of foreign territories. Their prescription for the best way of conducting foreign relations was a simple and perhaps naive one: the Chinese, especially their rulers, should cultivate their virtue (*te*) diligently so that the barbarians, overwhelmed by the cultural and ethical greatness of China, would voluntarily submit themselves. By submission they meant that the barbarians would send tribute missions to the Chinese emperor, adopt the Chinese calendar, and acknowledge China as their suzerain.

History shows that this Confucian theory rarely worked. While the barbarians might adopt many facets of Chinese civilization for their own purposes, they were nevertheless not impressed with Chinese virtue, and the only way of preventing them from marching southward was to station a strong garrison along the border. When the barbarians raided and looted, the Confucian theorists attributed these unfortunate happenings to the unchangeable and brutal nature of the barbarians, and under no circumstance would they doubt or reappraise the soundness of their theory. This theory, originating from a strong sense of cultural superiority, might be argued as a mere rationalization of a political reality which will be discussed presently. For better or worse, it dominated Chinese thinking with regard to the so-called "barbarian affairs" (*yi wu*).

The application of this theory, however, had to vary from time to time. There were times when the Chinese army marched into enemy territories and forced the barbarians to pledge allegiance to the Chinese. This happened during the reign of Han Wu-ti and again during the reigns of the early T'ang emperors. But in each case the real objective was more defensive than offensive in nature; it was an offensive operation aimed at the defense of Chinese territories. There was never any thought of permanent occupation of enemy countries. The invading force withdrew after its former enemies had promised to send tribute (which was often trade in disguise) and pledged nominal allegiance. There was no colonialism or imperialism in our modern sense. Perhaps the Chinese could not do otherwise. Culturally sedentary and economically agricultural, they could not survive as Chinese in arid or semi-arid regions. If physically they did survive, they could no longer be rightly regarded as Chinese, for the word "Chinese" was a cultural and to a lesser extent an economic rather than a racial term. It could be strongly argued that Chinese pacificism was really dictated by geographical factors. Within China proper practically all virgin lands suited for agriculture had been occupied as early as the Ch'in dynasty, and by the time of the Han the frontier of agriculture was quickly disappearing. For the next two thousand years agricultural China was a have-nation, and the barbarians, living in less productive areas, were the have-nots. China had everything to gain in peace and much to lose in war.

Dictated by circumstances and solidified by Confucian ideology, Chinese pacificism was a strong force in the modeling of personal life as well as the conduct of foreign relations. In the hundreds of novels, short stories, and dramas that have survived, a hero was usually a delicately built, pretty-faced, and sophisticated scholar. If in rare cases he happened to be a soldier, he was a scholarly one, versed in Confucian classics and literature, and he was perhaps less proud of his military achievement than of his literary talents. That "Good men should never become soldiers as good iron should not be used to make nails" stood true as a popular Chinese concept throughout centuries. Children were taught by their parents not to play "wild games" that required physical exertion, and that they should always be polite, gentle, and unaggressive. To be healthy was all right, but to have muscles was downright disgraceful. In schools physical education had no part in the curriculum, and archery, which was occasionally practiced, was more an art than a sport. Throughout the dynasties there were many great universities and colleges, but not a single outstanding military academy had existed until modern times. Military commanders were often chosen from among civilian scholars, and amazingly they sometimes won battles.

In a Confucian sense, there was never a better regime than Sung. By and large the Sung rulers were conscientious and just, and did what they regarded as right and proper in the sense of Confucianism. Among them one finds no brutes or outright debauchees such as one often finds among the rulers of other dynasties. They entrusted state affairs to the country's intellectual elite, and the influence of eunuchs and empresses' relatives which had plagued the Han and the T'ang governments was notably absent. Cultural activities were encouraged and promoted, and the educated were abundantly rewarded. As a result, Sung stands in history as one of the greatest eras in cultural achievement and was perhaps the best of all Confucian states. From hindsight it seems that what was wrong with Sung was that it applied too well the orthodox concepts of Confucianism. It was antimilitary when its very existence was constantly threatened by foreign invasions. It was extravagant and wasteful when the treasury could not meet its payments. When Wang An-shih called for "the enrichment of the nation and the strengthening of the military" (*fu-kuo ch'iang-ping*), his opponents scorned him for having betrayed an ancient Confucian tradition. Sadly for Sung, they were correct. As long as enemy conquest was not imminent, the Sung people and their rulers were happy enough to enjoy the moment. Marco Polo, the Venetian who visited Hangchow towards the end of the thirteenth century, when the Sung spirit still survived under alien rule, described the people of that city in the following words:

The inhabitants take such delight in ornaments, paintings, and elaborations that the amount spent on them is something staggering. The natives of Kinsai (Hangchow) are men of peace, through being so cosseted and pampered by their kings (the emperors of South Sung), who were of the same temper. They have no skill in handling arms and do not keep any in their houses. There is prevalent among them a dislike and distaste for strife or any sort of disagreement. They pursue their trades and handicrafts with great diligence and honesty. They love one another so devotedly that a whole district might seem, from the friendly and neighborly spirit that rules among men and women, to be a single household. This affection is not accompanied by any jealousy or suspicion of their wives, for whom they have the utmost respect. A man who ventured to address an unseemly remark to any married woman would be looked upon as a thorough blackguard. They are no less kind to foreigners who come to their city for trade.[1]

With regard to the people of South Sung as a whole, he remarked as follows:

[1] *The Travels of Marco Polo,* tr. by R. E. Latham, The Penguin Classics, 1958, p. 191.

I give my word that the men of the province of Manzi (South Sung), if they were a war-like nation, would conquer all the rest of the world. But they are not war-like. I can assure you rather that they are capable merchants and skilled practitioners of every craft, and among them are wise philosophers and natural physicians with a great knowledge of nature.[1]

The strong and the weak points of the Sung regime were eloquently expressed in the words of an impartial observer. Liao could have conquered Sung in the tenth century but it did not. Chin could have done the same in the twelfth century but it chose not to. In 1279, 320 years after the founding of the Sung dynasty, the Mongol emperor Kublai Khan, whom Marco Polo once served and greatly admired, drove the last claimant to the Sung throne to the sea and ended the Sung regime. Previously, Kublai had ascended to the dragon throne in Peking, and all China, for the first time in history, came under foreign domination.

[1] *Ibid.*, p. 183.

🦋 viii

Yüan

THE MONGOLS

The Mongol Empire of the thirteenth century was the largest the world had yet seen, covering most of the Eurasian continent and extending from the Pacific to the Mediterranean Sea. Within its jurisdiction were peoples of many nationalities, religions, and cultural backgrounds. They were the subjects of the Great Khan, the world conqueror to whom they owed allegiance and paid tribute. The rise of the Mongols was spectacular indeed. Throughout history no other people had built such a large empire in such a short time. It had taken the Romans almost four centuries to bring within their control the territories around the Mediterranean; it took the Mongols less than one century to build an empire much larger than that of the Romans. The total Mongol population was estimated to be somewhere between 1,000,000 and 2,500,000, and the number of their fighting

246

men, at the top of their strength, probably did not exceed 250,000. Yet, besides slaughtering millions on their warpath, they brought under their control, directly and indirectly, several hundred millions. In all history rarely had so many been conquered by so few.

What made the Mongols so powerful? To begin with, the very nature of nomadic life bred a warlike spirit, and until the invention of firearms the nomads had always been among the world's best fighters. Life was extremely hard in the arid and semiarid regions, and to live the nomads had to struggle successfully against fellow men as well as their natural environment. The amount of usable land was limited in nomadic regions, and the population increase of one tribe could only be accommodated by depriving other tribes of their holdings. Besides, a slow change of climatic conditions might render marginal land unusable, and a sudden burst of animal epidemics could strike terror among the nomads. In either case, the nomads had to move or die, and when they moved, war began. Thus the precarious conditions of steppe life made war a common occurrence, and the nomads had to prepare for war while living in peace. In fact, the difference between life in peace and life in war was never a clearcut one. A nomad made his livelihood on horseback and fought on it too. He killed wild animals with arrows from his strong bow and shot his enemies in the same way. Hardiness, endurance, and bravery were as much required in peace as in war. Since war frequently occurred, the nomad was used to it. He changed his life from peace to war with complete ease, and there was no such problem as adjustment.

North of the Great Wall and south of the Arctic Circle the basic pattern of nomadic life had changed little from time immemorial. From pasture to pasture the nomads moved on their camels and horses, thrived on meat and milk, and slept at night in portable tents. Outwardly peaceful, they turned into ferocious warriors whenever their leaders asked them to do so. From time to time battles were fought, and emerging from each battle was a great hero, only to be eclipsed in time by even greater ones. Savagery accompanied each battle, and no mercy was shown towards the vanquished. As a normal practice, men captives were put to the sword, and women and children were condemned to slavery. While such battles could not achieve any purpose in the long run, temporarily they did have the benefit of easing population pressure. The sad fact was that the steppe land, unfit for cultivation, could not support a dense population, and survival of the militarily fittest had always been the steppe law. Chinese historians have recorded time and again barbarian brutality towards the Chinese. It should be remembered that the barbarians were no less barbaric towards their fellow barbarians.

Whenever a tribe had successfully defeated its neighbors and unified a considerable portion of the grassland, it was inevitable that it would cast an envious eye on the rich agricultural land to the south. Its objective could be either temporary raiding and looting, or the looting might be part of a grandiose plan for the conquest of China proper. Only when China was strong could she stop the nomad hordes short of the Great Wall.

In fact, the history of China's external relations, until modern times, was largely a history of peace and war with her nomadic neighbors. Such relations began as early as history. During the second millennium and the first half of the first millennium B.C., the Chou people called all the northern nomads Ti, and those who lived west and northwest of their border were differentiated as Jung. One of the Jung tribes captured the Chou capital Hao in the eighth century B.C., sacked the city, and killed the reigning king. The Chou government, forced to move its capital eastward to Loyang, never really recovered from this defeat. During the Ch'in, Han, Wei, and Tsin dynasties, the most formidable nomads were the Hsiung-nu, a Turkish-speaking group who dominated the northern grassland for almost a millennium. From the fourth century A.D. on, other tribes began to play a more important role. The Mongol Topa tribe established the first Sinicized regime in North China in the fifth century. With its decline in the sixth century, other groups reasserted themselves. During the Sui and T'ang dynasties, the most powerful tribes were the T'u-chüeh (Turkish) in the north, the Uighurs (Turkish) in the northwest, and the Tanguts (Tibetan) in the west and the southwest. They were held in check as long as T'ang remained strong. After T'ang's decline in the eighth century, the nomads were again on a rampage. Throughout the Five Dynasties they fought among themselves as well as against the Chinese. When the dust finally settled, the Khitan Tartars (Mongolian) emerged triumphant and established a Sinicized regime called Liao. Liao was eventually replaced by a more vigorous tribe from the northeast, a Tungusic group called Nuchens who, on the Liao ruins, established another Sinicized regime called Chin.

Thus the balance of power shifted time and again in the northern grassland; the change of overlordship was as frequent as dynastic change in the south. Whatever Chinese regime happened to rule the rich, agricultural south, one of its greatest concerns was its relations with the more warlike nomads in the north. The past showed that while Chinese domination of the grassland, whenever it infrequently occurred, was indirect and temporary, the nomads, with the help of their Chinese collaborators, had been able to maintain a more direct and more permanent rule in the south. The balance of power seemed to have been in favor of the nomads. However, until the thirteenth century the nomads, at their very best, had been able only to bring part of China proper under their control, and no alien regime had ever extended its jurisdiction beyond the Yangtze River. The situation changed with the arrival of the Mongols. The Mongols not only subjugated China; they went beyond, conquered much of Burma and Vietnam, and brought many South and Southeast Asian kingdoms under their tributary system.

The accomplishment of the Mongols was no less than sensational. Less than a century before their conquest of China they had been among the least promising of all nomadic tribes. They lived in the arid wastes of what is known as Mongolia, and life was as hard then as it is today. Good pastures were few and far between, and the Mongols had to move from one pasture to another so that there would be enough grass for their multitude of flocks. Like seasonal birds they migrated southward during the winter months, and with each approaching summer they began their northward journey, grazing their beasts as they went. Each man's house was a portable, circular tent, supported by wooden rods and covered with felt. To set it up was as easy as tearing it down, and whenever its owner moved, it was transported on an ox-pulled or camel-drawn wagon. The Mongols lived on meat, milk, and game, and they had "no objection to eating the flesh of horses and dogs and drinking mares' milk." Wealth was measured by the number of beasts that one owned and was expressed by the better clothing (silk and rich furs) he wore or the number of wives he had. Polygamy was an accepted custom, though women were held in high respect by men. While men's major interests were hunting and warfare, less strenuous tasks, such as buying and selling, the care of children, and the maintenance of households, were within women's jurisdiction. Men and women both believed in a supreme High God who resided in Heaven. The most popular deity, however, was an earthly god who watched over their beasts, crops, and children.

What made the individual Mongol a formidable opponent on the battlefield was his ability as a horseman and archer. He was taught to ride a horse as soon as he learned to walk. As a scout and hunter, he rode his horse as a matter of daily routine. When war turned him into a fighter, he could ride his horse during the day and sleep on it at night, while his mount fed itself with whatever grass it could find on the ground. If need be, he could go or stay for a whole month without provisions, drinking mare's milk and eating wild game. If no water was available, he cut a vein of his horse and drank its blood. There was no supply problem, as far as a Mongol warrior was concerned. He was able to endure exertion and hardship as few men could. As an archer, he was equally unsurpassed. Constantly using his bow and arrows against wild animals, he had no difficulty in switching his target to one of the human species, and to the dismay of his enemies, he was deadly accurate. Riding hard and aiming constantly he and his colleagues dropped their enemies before the latter could come close to them. They could often win even though they were far outnumbered. Fighting alone or jointly with others, a Mongol warrior possessed a mobility unsurpassed before the invention of motorized vehicles. He struck quickly when he was sure to win and disappeared equally fast if, in his judgment, the odds were heavily against him. To begin a career of conquest, all he needed was a great organizer to lead him. Early in the thirteenth century he found such a leader in the person of Temujin, later known as Genghis Khan.

Temujin was born to a Mongol tribal chieftain, and historians have not yet agreed on the year that he was born. A Chinese source says that he was born with his right hand holding a lump of blood which looked like a red stone and that the name of Temujin was given to him because his father was then celebrating his victory over a rival chieftain of the same name. Temujin's father died when Temujin was young, and the boy attached himself and his tribe to On-Khan, the chief of the Kereit tribe. He was so successful in defeating the many enemies of the Kereit tribe that On-Khan eventually felt uneasy himself because he was not sure that an ambitious man like Temujin would be satisfied to be his vassal permanently. Having sensed On-Khan's suspicion and distrust, Temujin decided to strike first, and without warning he marched toward his former lord and decisively defeated him. He annexed the Kereit tribe and thus enlarged his base of operation. From then on it was one victory after another, and by 1206 all Mongol tribes had been brought under his control. In that year he called upon all his vassals to gather in the upper valley of the Onon River, and in a solemn ceremony he was proclaimed the Almighty Emperor, or Genghis Khan.

Though there was nothing unusual about tribal warfare, Genghis Khan's victory was different in the sense that for the first time in history the Mongols had produced a true conqueror of rare proportions. While information about him as a person is meagre, he seems to have been a conqueror in the truest sense of that word. He conquered for the glory of conquest, and the benefit of material gain, if it was in his mind, was secondary and unimportant. He made a life of conquest, lived it, and would not leave it until his breath failed him. "Man's highest joy," he is believed to have said, "is in victory: to conquer one's enemies, to pursue them, to deprive them of their possessions, to make their beloved weep, to ride on their horses, and to embrace their wives and daughters." While this advice had nothing to recommend it to a more civilized society, it expressed the highest ideals of a nomadic warrior. The purpose of conquest was victory itself, pure, simple, and therefore noble. Such purpose allegedly justified the most wanton brutality that human beings ever committed: the slaughtering of the entire populations of cities, the enslavement of women and children, and the senseless destruction of many ancient centers of civilization. As the Mongols galloped, the world trembled.

Having unified all Mongol tribes, Genghis Khan began his conquest of non-Mongol tribes and kingdoms. From Manchuria to the Black Sea one victim fell after another. Southward he sent his hordes across the

Great Wall and captured modern Hopeh, Shantung, and Shensi provinces, including Chin's capital, Peking. The Chin ruler was forced to retreat southward to Kaifeng. In the fall of 1227 Genghis died of a battle wound suffered in the siege of Hsingchungfu, the capital of West Hsia. Several days later West Hsia surrendered, and in accordance with the dead Khan's wish, the entire city was put to the sword. Ogodei, the third son of Genghis, succeeded his father as the Great Khan. Under him continuous conquests were made:

1. Kaifeng, the new capital of Chin, fell in 1233, and the former Chin territory, most of North China, was annexed.

2. Korea was conquered in 1231–1232.

3. Ukraine and South Russia had been previously conquered by Genghis Khan. In 1235 the famous Mongol general Batu pushed northward and eventually occupied what is known today as Great Russia, including Moscow. One column captured the ancient city Novgorod, not far from the Gulf of Finland.

4. In 1240 Batu invaded Poland, Bohemia, Hungary, and the Danube Valley. One column advanced as far as Venetia. All of Western Europe might have fallen to the Mongol hordes had it not been saved by an unexpected incident. In the spring of 1242 news arrived that the Great Khan Ogodei had passed away, and Batu, eager to participate in the election of a new supreme ruler, called off further invasions. Thus Western Europe was saved by Mongol domestic politics.

After several years of internal struggle during which foreign expansion was temporarily suspended, Mangu, a grandson of Genghis, was proclaimed as the supreme ruler in 1251. During his reign of eight years the Mongol Empire expanded southwestward to Persia, Mesopotamia, and Syria. His brother, the famed Kublai Khan who ascened the throne in 1260, finally conquered South Sung. Thus the Mongol Empire, begun with Genghis' military exploits two generations before, was completed during the reign of Kublai. The empire, because of its huge size, was divided into four khanates:

1. The Khanate of the Great Khan, extending from Eastern Siberia southwestward to Tibet. It included Mongolia, Korea, Manchuria, China, and the northern sections of Burma and Vietnam.

2. The Khanate of Chaghadai (Ili) which covered Afghanistan and Russian and Chinese Turkestan.

3. The Khanate of Persia (Il-Khans) in the Near East, including modern Iraq, Iran, and Southern Caucasus.

4. The Khanate of Kipchak (Golden Horde), extending from Chinese Turkestan to Eastern Europe. It included Western Asia, Russia, and Ukraine.

Theoretically, the Great Khan who sat on the dragon throne in Pe-

Lake Baikal

Karakorum

Tatu □ (Peking)

china Sea

KHANATE OF THE GREAT KHAN

Bay of Bengal

Lake Balkhash

KHANATE OF KIPCHAK (GOLDEN HORDE)

•Samarkand

KHANATE OF CHAGHADAI (ILI)

ARAL SEA

Arabian Sea

•Moscow

KHANATE OF PERSIA (IL-KHANS)

CASPIAN SEA

•Kiev

•Bagdad

PERSIAN GULF

BLACK SEA

RED SEA

MEDITERRANEAN SEA

MAP 22
THE MONGOL EMPIRE
□ Capital   • Cities

0   400   800   1200
Scale of Miles

king had jurisdiction over all three other khans. However, due to the great distances between them, such jurisdiction was more nominal than real, and each khanate was virtually independent.

THE CONQUEST OF SOUTH SUNG

The Mongol conquest of South Sung turned out to be more difficult than the relative strength of the two countries would have warranted. While the Mongols swept across Central and Western Asia with comparative ease, it took them more than a generation to subjugate their southern opponent. The reasons were not difficult to find. To begin with, the Mongols were better fighters on the desert and the steppe than in the agricultural areas where the performance of the cavalry, wherein their strength lay, could be considerably hampered by the paddy fields and the undulating forest hills. Secondly, the existence of numerous cities and the high density of population in China proper slowed down conquest and made it more difficult, for a city could not be taken unless the city leading to it had been taken previously. This was contrary to the situation in Central and Western Asia where population centers were few and far between. Thirdly, and perhaps most important of all, the Mongol invaders aroused a strong sense of nationalism among the South Sung Chinese. Under good leadership such nationalism could be harnessed into an iron will of resistance which in turn slowed down the victorious march of even the seemingly invincible Mongols. A case in point was the heroic defense of the twin cities Hsiangyang and Fanch'eng (modern Hupeh province) which, although completely surrounded, managed to hold their own for five years (1268–1273). In the long run, however, the military superiority of the Mongols foretold the final outcome. They might be slowed down, but they could not be stopped.

Previously, when the Mongols attacked Chin, South Sung made the mistake of allying itself with the rising Mongols against a much weakened neighbor. It did so because it hoped to recover its lost territories south of the Yellow River. For a while it did occupy Kaifeng and Loyang after Chin's defeat. In 1234, when Chin was finally conquered, South Sung found itself face to face with a ferocious horde. In the following year the Mongols attacked South Sung along several fronts. The western column, under the able general Kublai, soon captured Szechuan province. Meanwhile Kublai's fellow generals on the eastern front ravaged the area between the Yellow River and the Huai. In 1252 Kublai invaded Yunnan and extinguished a small kingdom called Tali (former Nanchao). One of his generals continued southward and invaded northern Vietnam. By 1259 the entire Southwest fell into Mongol hands, and the Mongol control of the upper Yangtze Valley extended eastward to include Wuchang

TEMPLE OF HEAVEN The temple, dating from the thirteenth century, is located in Peking. The emperors used to worship here.

(Hupeh province). Then Kublai received the news that the Great Khan Mangu had died. He quickly arranged a truce with Sung commanders in the field and hurried back to Karakorum, the capital of all Mongols. In the following year Kublai, dispensing with the formality of being elected, assumed the title of Great Khan. It was not until 1271, however, that on the recommendation of a Chinese scholar the national title was changed from Mongol to a Sinicized name Yüan. By adopting a Sinicized national title the Mongols considered themselves legitimate heirs to the fast disappearing Chinese Sung dynasty. Thus Kublai and his successors assumed a dual role, one as a Chinese emperor and the other as the Great Khan for all Mongols.

After Kublai became the supreme ruler, the invasion of South Sung was renewed with eagerness. The heroic defense of Hsiangyang and Fanch'eng upset the conqueror's schedule, but after the fall of the two cities in 1273 other cities were captured with comparative ease. In 1276 Hangchow surrendered without a fight, and the Mongol invaders, spearheaded by their Chinese collaborators, pushed hard against the remnants of the disheartened Sung forces. Since then many historians have contended that the Sung forces could have held much longer on the rugged terrain of the Southeast had it not been for the "treacherous betrayal" of an Arab merchant. The Arab merchant, known by his Sinicized name P'u Shou-keng, came to China in his boyhood and rose to become a Sung official in charge of the Superintendency of Merchant Shipping at the flourishing port of Ch'üanchou in modern Fukien province. For thirty years he monopolized the lucrative trade between Fukien and Southeast Asia and grew in wealth, power, and influence. Under his control were not only the merchant marine but also powerful battleships. Many people contended that if he had supported Sung's cause, the Southeast would not have fallen so fast, because the Mongols, despite their invincibility on land, were quite inadequate in sea warfare. But P'u Shou-keng chose to surrender his ships to the Mongols on the ground that "continuous warfare is bad for business." Under his supervision, hundreds of warships were constructed at Ch'üanchou for the invaders. As an admiral under his new overlord, he cleared up the remnants of Sung's naval force along the southeastern coast and was partially responsible for the breakdown of Sung's last resistance. In 1279 the last claimant to the Sung throne, caught between the pursuing enemy and the blue sea, chose the latter and drowned himself.

Though triumphant on the Chinese mainland, Kublai was not successful in his attempt to subjugate Japan. He had repeatedly sent envoys to demand Japan's acknowledgement of his overlordship but each time he was haughtily refused. In 1275 he dispatched from Korean ports 25,000 troops for the invasion of the island kingdom. The invading force, after winning an initial victory, was forced to re-embark by foul weather and return to Korea with heavy losses. The second and much larger invasion occurred six years later, after Kublai had conquered South Sung and had brought the captured Sung navy to strengthen his invading armada. The invaders managed to establish a beachhead in North Kyushu but were unable to penetrate much beyond. For the second time the weather came to Japan's rescue. A typhoon struck and destroyed or disabled most of the invading ships. Having been deprived of their ships, those invaders who had been stranded ashore were easily liquidated by the Japanese. Of 140,000 men who began the invasion less than half returned home.

From their bases in southwestern China the Mongols repeatedly invaded Vietnam and Burma, ravaged the country side, and caused great damage. In the 1280's Mongol envoys were successful in persuading many small kingdoms in South and Southeast Asia to acknowledge Yüan's overlordship and send tribute to China. However, Mongol influence was never substantial in the tropical regions.

CHINA UNDER MONGOL RULE

From the year 936 when a Chinese garrison surrendered the Sixteen Yen-Yün Districts to the Khitan Tartars, China proper was not unified under one regime until 1279. What the Sung emperors had vowed to accomplish but had failed to do was attained by the alien ruler Kublai

MAP 23

CHINA UNDER MONGOL
RULE, Circa 1300 A.D.

□ Capital
● Provincial Capital

0   150   300   450

Scale of Miles

SUNGARI RIVER

Sea of JAPAN

LINGPEI

Holin
(Urga, Ulan Bator)

LIAOYANG

● Liaoyang

CHUNGSHU SHENG

Tatu
□ (Peking)

Kaicheng
● CHENG
TUNG

Yellow
Sea

East China
Sea

YELLOW RIVER

KANSU

● Kanchou

SHENSI

● Fengyüan

Pienliang
● (Kaifeng)

HONAN

Wuchang
●

Hangchow
●

KIANGCHE

Lunghsing
● (Nanchang)

KIANGSI

HUKUANG

SI RIVER

SZECHUAN

Chengtu
●

YANGTZE RIVER

YUNNAN

Chungching
● (Kunming)

CHINSHA RIVER

Khan, known to the Chinese as Yüan Shih-tsu. Shih-tsu was perhaps the ablest and the most enlightened among Yüan rulers, but most Chinese did not take kindly to him and regarded him as no better than half-barbarian. There were reasons for this. Other alien rulers, such as Hsiao-wen-ti of North Wei or later the Liao and Chin rulers, had been thoroughly trained in Chinese ways before they ruled Chinese subjects. Yüan Shih-tsu, on the other hand, was basically a nomadic warrior, and he never "dismounted to rule" as his Chinese subjects thought he should. His major interest was conquest, and when he needed recreation, he found it in hunting and falconry. From the Chinese point of view, he should have devoted more time to the patronage of art and literature and to the cultivation of Confucian virtues. In this respect his successors were regarded as worse than he, for none of them was ever Sinicized in the real sense. In the Chinese mind, to be civilized meant to be Sinicized, and the Yüan rulers, in their efforts to maintain a separate identity, remained outsiders forever to the Chinese. The Yüan dynasty was one of the most unpopular in Chinese history, and the eighty-nine years of Mongol rule were regarded by many Chinese as among the worst China had ever encountered. Despite its military grandeur, the Yüan dynasty was nevertheless a period of cultural recession.

Overwhelmed by a superior military force and betrayed by many of their own leaders, the Chinese were slow in acquiescing to the Mongol rule. Marco Polo, travelling in China in the 1280's, commented repeatedly on Chinese resentment against their new rulers. Mongol garrisons were stationed in all sizable cities to prevent revolt and to crush it if and when it occurred. The authority of the garrison was supreme, and if it were challenged, the whole city would have to pay dearly for its defiance. The Venetian said that the entire population of Chinkiang (east of Nanking on the south bank of the Yangtze River) was slaughtered, after a party of madly drunken Mongol soldiers were slain by some irresponsible local citizens. People resented the garrison soldiers residing among them. "They cannot bear the sight of a soldier or of the Great Khan's guards," remarked Marco Polo. Thanks to the Mongols' iron hand, few revolts occurred, and whatever resistance there might have been was soon driven underground. It was not until the 1340's when the Mongol rule had been considerably weakened that Chinese revolts met with some degree of success.

Culturally backward and numerically outnumbered, the Mongol rulers realized that they could not rule China indefinitely unless they could devise and adopt a system whereby their Chinese subjects would never be in a position to challenge their supremacy. Out of this consideration came a caste system in which people of lower groupings were discriminated against in favor of those of higher groupings. Discrimination was practiced in all fields of human activities, political, legal, and socio-economic. There were four castes altogether, and a person's enjoyment of rights and privileges, or the lack of it, varied in accordance with the caste to which he belonged. However, the emperor, sitting at the pinnacle of the hierarchy and being the sole dispenser of all favors, could at any time, if he chose to, grant exceptions; theoretically he could raise even the humblest to the noblest regardless of the caste system. For instance, he could appoint a Chinese as his prime minister if he wished to, though under normal circumstances he was not expected to take such an unusual step. The highest caste was the ruling oligarchy to which all Mongols belonged. It was followed by *se-mu jen* (literally, "color-eye" people), or people whose skin colors and eye shapes were different from those of the Chinese and the Mongols. They were what the Chinese called *hsi-yü jen*, or "people from the western regions," whether they be Persians, Uighurs, or any of the Central Asian groups. Religiously they were predominantly Muslim; many of them, however, were Buddhist or Nestorian. Northern Chinese belonged to the third caste, and Southern Chinese were at the bottom of the caste system. Northern Chinese were the former subjects of Chin who, having lived under alien control before, were not so resentful of the Mongol rule as their southern brethren who, before the Mongol conquest, had been the citizens of the Chinese dynasty, Sung.

Discrimination was most pronounced in the selection of government officials. Practically all high posts were occupied by Mongols, assisted by their Muslim collaborators. Rarely could a Chinese rise to cabinet rank, and few Chinese were appointed as governors. Throughout the Yüan dynasty all but three prime ministers were Mongols. Of the three, one was a Uighur and two were Northern Chinese. At local levels Chinese could serve as staff assistants, but they could not become the head of a department or an office. This differentiation in official appointment created much confusion in local administrations. At one time it was reported that in the Yangtze area none of the provincial officials knew how to read or write. Towards the end of the Yüan dynasty, the government, hard pressed by financial needs, began to sell offices of lower ranks to whoever wished to buy them regardless of caste origin. Few Chinese, however, took advantage of this offer. Those who did buy them were characterized by local population as "scoundrels" (*wu-lai*).

The enforcement of law also took into consideration caste differences. One of Genghis Khan's famous orders was that if a Mongol murdered a Muslim, he should pay 40 *palishi* of gold, but if the victim happened to be a Chinese, he should hand over to the injured family a donkey or its equivalent. Judicial discrimination was extended to all of China after the Mongol conquest of South Sung. Under no circumstances were Chinese allowed to do physical harm to Mongols, but the law did not say that Mongols could not harm Chinese. For the same crime Chinese were punished more severely than Mongols. Chinese were not allowed to possess arms or to learn military skills, and in 1289 an imperial decree ordered them to hand over to the government all their horses. In cities they were forbidden to walk in the streets at night, and they could not gather in any large numbers, whether for religious worship or for commercial purposes. While discrimination was applied to all Chinese, the Mongol rulers were somewhat lenient with craftsmen and artisans, such as blacksmiths, goldsmiths, carpenters, and the makers of bows and arrows. Whenever a city was captured, they made a point of sparing the lives of artisans. According to one story, the entire city of Kaifeng would have been put to the sword after its fall if the Mongols had not been afraid that they might kill by mistake many artisans whom they needed.

Culturally the Yüan dynasty was one of the most sterile periods in Chinese history. By all counts it was an anticlimax after the brilliant era of the two Sungs. The Mongol rulers singled out intellectuals for the worst repression, partly because they neither appreciated nor understood cultural activities and partly because they distrusted intellectuals as loyal subjects. Intellectual activities were looked down upon as a profession. In the Mongol concept of the relative importance of different professions, intellectuals were placed a little above beggars and were much below prostitutes (another source says "common people"). Teachers and beggars were considered the most useless and they were often mentioned in the same breath. Though they learned quickly to appreciate the services of artisans and physicians, the Mongols, at the beginning, had no use for farmers. When Genghis Khan entered China proper for the first time, he had hoped to turn North China into empty pastures. Later when the Mongol conquerors learned that farmers could pay more taxes than nomads, they went to great lengths to promote agriculture. However, they never thought highly of intellectuals. During their conquest of China, they condemned all captured intellectuals to slavery, if they chose to spare their lives. Later, when it was apparent that government could not function without literate clerks, they allowed many of them to buy their freedom. By then intellectuals had become a necessary evil to be tolerated. Most of the Yüan emperors did not know how to read or write and did not care to learn.

This mixed feeling of contempt and distrust was reciprocated by Chinese intellectuals who regarded the Mongols as the worst kind of barbarians China had ever encountered. The best among them boycotted the new government. Those who had illusions learned fast. The famous Sung historian Ma Tuan-lin, for instance, served under the new regime for a while and quit as quickly and as graciously as he could manage it. The civil service examination system which had been the traditional way of selecting government personnel was not revived until 1315. The government did not attach much importance to it and it never produced men of any prominence. Among the Yüan bureaucrats less than one percent was the product of the examination system. The best among Chinese intellectuals did not participate in it, even though the examination was held as frequently as once in every three years. In each examination two tests were given, one for Chinese and one for Mongols and "people of western regions." The test for the Chinese was much stiffer, and the test for others was often a formality. Many Mongols and "westerners" who had passed the examination were later found to be illiterate. Power, fame, and wealth, which under the Sung could be obtained through academic excellence and ability to serve, were now based upon race and nationality. Many intellectuals, denied their traditional outlet for advancement, busied themselves with their own petty projects, such as the verification of an ancient text or the editing of an old classic. Without government sponsorship, schools were established and maintained through local initiative. There were students but few scholars, and among scholars few were original thinkers.

By virtue of conquest the Mongol rulers regarded China as their private domain and thus revived a feudal concept which had been abandoned by the Chinese many centuries before. The purpose of ruling China was to enjoy what China could offer: land, population, and natural resources, and governmental policy was formulated with that purpose in mind. The Mongol conquerors, knowing nothing about financial matters and distrusting their Chinese subjects, often turned over the execution of such policy to their Muslim collaborators. When Ogodei first entered China, he sold the right of collecting taxes to a Uighur merchant. Even a monarch like Kublai had no better appreciation of fiscal policy than the collection of the largest tax revenue. Those who knew how to collect the largest amount with the least expense were regarded as able and were promoted fast. Tax revenue continued to increase so that by the 1330's the total yearly amount was said to be one hundred times as much as that collected during the 1280's. After South China was pacified, large tracts of farmland together with Chinese households were awarded to Mongol princes, princesses, and others who had unusual military deeds to their credit. The number of households awarded to each person varied, from scores to more than 100,000. Other Mongols took over Chinese land on their own initiative, and some of them, wishing to be surrounded by a more familiar scene, turned rich agricultural land into empty pastures. The existence of pastures side by side with paddy fields caused frequent frictions between Mongol cattlemen and Chinese farmers.

Ironically, the group singled out by the world conquerors for preferential treatment was the professionally religious. In the Mongol concept of the relative importance of different professions, the priests were ranked second highest, next to government officials. Within their empire the Mongols followed a policy of religious toleration. Different faiths existed side by side, and within one city could be found the religious establishments of Buddhism, Taoism, Islam, and Nestorianism. The Mongols themselves, however, preferred Lamaism, a mixture of orthodox Buddhism and a Tibetan faith called Bon. Lamaism was given extensive royal patronage, and millions of acres of land were granted to leading Lamaist monasteries. A leading monastery in Shantung, for instance, was granted land amounting to 323,000 *ch'ing* (about 4,887,000 acres), and another monastery was given 37,059 farm households for support besides 100,000 *ch'ing* (about 1,513,000 acres) of land. Each year government expenses for Buddhist and various religious services accounted for more than one-half of its total expenditure! In 1292 it was said that altogether there were 42,318 Buddhist temples and monasteries and 213,148 monks and nuns.

To speculate as to what might have made the warlike Mongols so religious is beyond the field of a historian, but any historian knows that not all religious men practiced what they taught. While most of these Buddhist monks were doubtlessly pious and sincere, many joined the monastic rank simply because it was the easiest way of making a living. The behavior of some others was anything but exemplary. One government censor reported in 1310 that many monks were married and had children, and another censor reported in 1324 that often monks invaded private homes, chased out the male residents, and raped the wives and daughters. According to a widely circulated story, one Mongol prince did not wish to have anything to do with Lamaism until he was advised by his father, the emperor, to experience it personally. Accordingly, a lama was assigned to teach him "the secret way of attaining great joy in Buddhism." After one instruction, the prince remarked happily: "Mr. Li has taught me Confucian classics for years and I don't understand a thing about them. The great lama from the West taught me the Buddhist way to great joy and I understand everything about it in one evening." This incident allegedly occurred towards the end of the Yüan dynasty, almost one century after the Mongol conquest of China. Even then the Mongol rulers seemed to be no less barbarian than their forefathers who had founded the Yüan dynasty.

MONGOL ACHIEVEMENT

It would be an oversimplification to say that all was darkness under the Mongol rule. When they first entered China proper and knew nothing about governing a sedentary people, the Mongols had to rely on Chinese and Sinicized non-Chinese for advice and counsel. One of the greatest men serving in this capacity was a Sinicized Khitan named Yeh-li Ch'u-ts'ai who served both Genghis and Ogodei with distinction. It was he who advised Genghis not to turn North China into empty pastures, and he was also credited with having saved millions of lives from the Mongol sword.

During the early reign of Kublai Khan efforts were made to secure Chinese cooperation, and many Chinese did join his government. Unfortunately, this policy was not followed by his successors. What Chinese influence there was moderated somewhat the naked barbarity of the nomadic warriors. Though Chinese were never allowed to play any substantial role in the Yüan regime, as time went on there were Mongols Sinicized enough to promote peaceful pursuits. Under their direction there were many outstanding achievements.

Foremost among Yüan's achievements was its transportation system. The Mongols, maintaining the world's largest empire, depended upon efficient transportation to hold the empire together. Roads were built through the length and breath of the empire, and all of them, directly or indirectly, were linked with the nerve center, Peking. In peace time traders and travelers used them, and in time of war, troops could be sent with dispatch to trouble spots. An efficient postal system was maintained, mostly for the transmission of messages from Peking to the provinces and vice versa. Marco Polo gives us a vivid description of Kublai Khan's postal service. According to him, courier stations were built along the roads, and there were both mounted and unmounted couriers. The unmounted couriers could "travel a ten days' journey in a day and a night," and "in the fruit season it often happens that this means fruit gathered in the morning in the city of Khanbalik (Peking) is delivered on the evening of the next day to the Great Khan in the city of Shang-tu, ten days' journey away." The Great Khan's mounted messengers, of course, travelled even faster. "They ride 200 miles in a day, sometimes even 250; indeed, in extreme urgency, they can achieve 300 miles," says the Venetian. During the reign of Kublai, more than 200,000 horses were regularly maintained for courier service.

The Yüan regime also improved river and sea transportation substantially. All major rivers in China ran from west to east; how to ship food from the rice producing areas in the Lower Yangtze to North China had been a problem faced by many dynasties in the past. To solve this problem, Sui constructed the Grand Canal which was later improved by Sung. Since both regimes located their capitals along the southern bank of the Yellow River, the Grand Canal as then completed was adequate to meet their needs. But it was a different matter with Yüan which chose Peking as its capital. To feed the swelling population in the new capital, Yüan ordered the construction of two canals: Chichou and Huit'ung, both running northward through western Shantung. Boats carrying farm products could thus sail from the Lower Yangtze all the way to the Peking area. Two and a half million coolie laborers were employed in this project, which was not completed until 1289.

Side by side with shipping through the Grand Canal was a sea transport service whereby ships loaded at Shanghai sailed northward along the

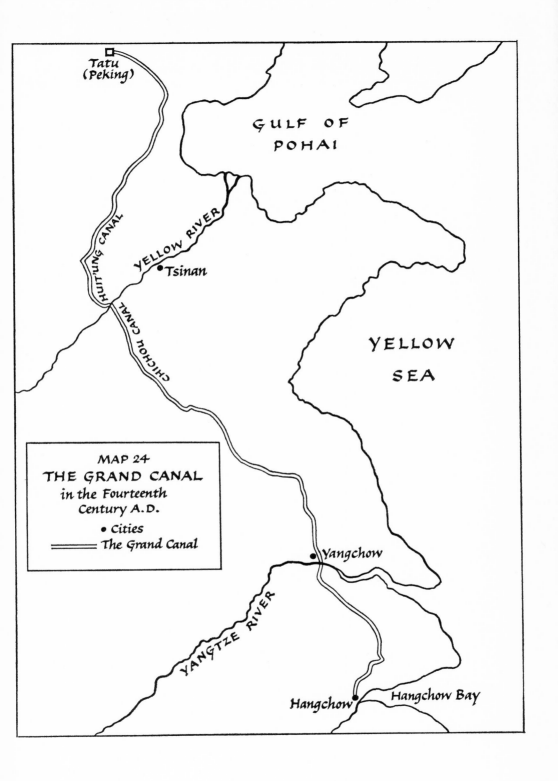

Tatu
(Peking)

GULF OF
POHAI

HUI-T'UNG CANAL

YELLOW RIVER

• Tsinan

CHI-CHOU CANAL

YELLOW

SEA

MAP 24
THE GRAND CANAL
in the Fourteenth
Century A.D.
• Cities
═══ The Grand Canal

• Yangchow

YANGTZE RIVER

Hangchow •   Hangchow Bay

sea coast until they reached Takuk'ou at the mouth of the Ku River. This sea route, however, was much more hazardous and therefore less practical.

Equally as important as the improvement of transportation facilities was Yüan's promotion of agricultural activities. Though Genghis never thought much of agriculture, his grandson Kublai, upon assuming the role as a Chinese emperor, soon recognized its importance. Among the many new measures he adopted, the most far-reaching was perhaps the commune system. In a decree issued in 1286 he ordered the organization of every fifty to one hundred farm households into a commune. The purpose of the commune, said the decree, was mutual help and better farming among constituting households so as to increase farm production. Each commune would be captained by an elderly, experienced farmer whose duty was to reward the diligent and punish the laggard, besides teaching and advising on better farming methods. Within each commune was an elementary school where children were taught the fundamentals of reading and writing during times when they were not needed in the field. There was also an ever-ready granary to which each household contributed a small amount of its harvest during good years and from which the poor could draw relief during the years of famine. While land was individually owned, each commune member had the obligation to help others, especially when they could not till their land themselves on account of sickness, death of family members, or other legitimate reasons. In case of a major disaster such as an epidemic when the resources of one commune could not cope with the situation, other communes were obligated to help on a basis of reciprocity. Judging from available evidence, the commune system seems to have functioned fairly well.

More controversial than the commune system, however, was Yüan's wide use of paper currency. The use of paper currency had not originated with Yüan. Its origin could be traced back to the ninth century when the T'ang government, considering the inconvenience of shipping cash to distant areas where government purchases were made, paid local merchants with money certificates called "flying cash." These certificates bearing different amounts of money could be converted into hard cash on demand at the capital. Since they were transferable, they were exchanged among merchants almost like currency. However, "flying cash" was not meant to be currency and its circulation was rather limited. Real paper currency was not introduced until early in the Sung dynasty, when it was utilized by a group of rich merchants and financiers in Szechuan, the same province where the art of printing had been invented. Each banknote they issued had printed on it pictures of houses, trees, and people. Red and black inks were intermittently applied; the seals of the issuing banks were affixed; and confidential marks were made on each bill. All these devices made counterfeiting extremely difficult, if not impossible. These banknotes could be converted into hard cash at any time in any of the issuing banks. Widely circulated, they were readily accepted for the payment of debt and other financial obligations. Later, however, some of the banks apparently printed too many notes without adequate backing. When the bearers went to them for cash, they were unable to honor their obligations. Lawsuits resulted and there was considerable confusion. Eventually the government decided to prohibit the issuing of banknotes by private banks and made it a government monopoly. Government issues made their first appearance in Szechuan and, because of their success, were later introduced in other areas as well. After Chin entered China proper, it followed Sung's practice. In 1154 it established a Bureau of Paper Currency in Kaifeng as the central agency in charge of all issues. Two kinds of paper currency were issued, one of large denominations, consisting of one to ten strings (each string was worth 1,000 standard coins) and another of small denominations, bearing the amounts of one to seven hundred standard coins. The validity of each issue was limited to seven years.

There was nothing wrong with paper currency as long as it had sufficient backing and, on demand, could be readily converted into hard money. When the government printed too much paper money and these two principles could no longer be practiced, inflation resulted and the whole paper structure eventually collapsed. That was exactly what happened during the Yüan dynasty. In 1260 Yüan's first paper currency was issued. Various denominations were printed, ranging from a face value of two standard coins to the highest denomination of two strings. Excessive printing year after year soon flooded the market with depreciated paper money until the face value of each certificate bore no relation whatsoever to its counterpart in silver. In 1272 a series of new issues was put in circulation, and the old issues were converted into the new ones at the ratio of five to one. The new issues were printed with copper plates instead of wood blocks, as had been the case before. As the printing press was overworked, a new round of depreciation began, and by 1309 another conversion became necessary. The 1272 issues were converted into the new issues again at the ratio of five to one. Thus in fifty years (from 1260 to 1309) Yüan's paper money was depreciated by 1,000 percent. As the value of paper money came down, prices of commodities moved up. Counterfeiting was widespread despite severe penalties. To make the situation worse, the government often refused to exchange for new issues old certificates that had been worn out through a long period of circulation. This legalized robbery, naturally, did not endear the government to its people.

From hindsight, the greatest achievement during the Yüan dynasty was neither its transportation system nor its paper currency, but its music drama. Musicales began at least as early as the fifth century, but it was not until the eighth century that they reached their most glorious age under the patronage of T'ang Hsüan-tsung. Musicales, however, were not music dramas. They could be sung and danced to, but each piece of music stood independently and there was no story linking all of them together. Music drama, in fact, did not begin until the Sung dynasty. Even then, men of literary fame did not bother to write them, and no outstanding works appeared. The situation changed early in the Yüan dynasty. Music drama became a popular form of literary expression and attracted many men of talent. Some historians attribute this phenomenon to the fact that Chinese intellectuals, denied their traditional outlet of advancement in government, applied their talents to the less consequential fields, such as music drama. Whatever the real cause, Yüan's achievement in this field was superb and has never been surpassed.

There were dozens of drama writers during the Yüan dynasty. However, only 116 of their works have survived. The greatest of the writers were Kuan Han-ch'ing, Ma Chih-yüan, and Wang Shih-fu, all living during the middle decades of the thirteenth century. We know little about their personal life, and all seem to have been unsuccessful as government officials. Kuan Han-ch'ing left us ten of his dramas, the best known of which is the *Butterfly Dream* (*Hu-tieh meng*), a story about the philosopher Chuang-tzu and his unfaithful wife. Among Ma Chih-yüan's six extant dramas, it is commonly recognized that the best is *Autumn in the Han Palace* (*Han-kung ch'iu*), a story describing the sorrow of the Han emperor Yüan-ti after his beloved concubine had left for a Hsiung-nu prince in the northern desert.

None of the extant Yüan dramas, however, is more popular than *The Romance of the West Chamber* (*Hsi-hsiang chi*), written by Wang Shih-fu. Some critics regard it as the best music drama ever written. According to an unsubstantiated story, Wang often lay flat on the ground whenever he was thinking hard to find the right words for his songs. One day in writing a departure scene between the hero and the heroine in *The West Chamber,* he searched so hard for the words most appropriate to the scene that finally when he found them, he rose up, wrote them down, fainted away and died. The unfinished portion was later completed by Kuan Han-ch'ing. The drama tells the story of a student who, while studying in a Buddhist temple in preparation for the imperial examination, was attracted to a young lady who was living next door with her family. Through the aid of the young lady's maid, they met and their love was consummated. One month later, when the secret affair was discovered, the girl's mother refused to give her consent for marriage until the young man could establish himself by passing the imperial examination. With his departure for the capital to take the examination, the story ended.

While stories varied, all Yüan dramas followed a commonly accepted pattern. All persons who appeared in them fell into three categories, *mo* who were the male leaders, *tan* who played the leading females, and *tsa* who played supporting roles, including the ubiquitous jesters. When an actor appeared on the stage, the audience could immediately identify the role he played because the make-up and the dress he wore were highly conventionalized. Each drama began with an introduction which was followed by the standard four acts. The story of each act was told by singing, acting, and dialogue. Besides the songs, the words of the dialogue and each of the actors' movements were all recorded as part of the drama. The songs were written in semiliterary form, and when sung, were perhaps difficult to understand. But there was no question about understanding the dialogues which were written in colloquial and even slangy Chinese. Thus the drama appealed to the illiterate as well as the intellectuals.

THE FALL OF THE YÜAN REGIME

Sung, a militarily weak regime, lasted more than three hundred years; Yüan, the most powerful dynasty in Chinese history, collapsed in less than a century. How can this be explained? First, as we have noted, the Yüan regime never had popular support. Second, the regime began to deteriorate soon after the death of Kublai Khan, and such deterioration resulted largely from the degeneration of the Mongol ruling class.

When Kublai died in 1294, all the territories which the Mongols had intended to conquer had been conquered. The only exception was of course Japan. As conditions of peacetime replaced the state of war, the Mongols had no more use for their greatest asset, their fighting ability. Peace, ironically, turned out to be their unconquerable enemy. Living in peace, the Mongols slowly lost what had made them fearsome and great on the battlefield. Meanwhile, they had not yet acquired qualities that would have made them successful rulers in peace. Having dispensed with bow and arrows and not yet learned to use the pen, the Mongol emperors after Kublai Khan were ludicrous misfits on that dragon throne in Peking. They did not possess the same valor and vitality as their nomadic ancestors; yet, they were unwilling or unable to master the arts of peace. Corrupted by power and wealth, they acquired many Chinese vices (such as love of luxuries) without at the same time acquiring some of the Chinese virtues (such as love of literature and learning). This was true not only of the Mongol emperors but of the entire Mongol hierarchy as well. From lofty princes and princesses to lowly garrison soldiers in a remote city—they were all softened by the wealth of the nation which they conquered. The once simple, hardy Mongol princes, no longer needed on the battlefield, had now become parasitic, and they had no other desire except to enjoy the material best which China could provide. The garrison soldiers, once the backbone of Mongol strength, were corrupted by an easy life from which they seemingly had no way to escape. With no check or restraint, nepotism and corruption were rampant from top to bottom. To make the situation worse, the Mongols, as the ruling class, were neither required nor allowed to learn any useful profession. As there was no more fighting to do, they were completely lost in the labyrinth of civilization. As they were corrupted, they were no longer the same invincible Mongols.

Undisputed power tended to corrupt itself. Since their authority was no longer challenged from the outside, dissensions soon developed among the Mongols themselves. Intrigues, conspiracies, and strifes which had been common in Chinese politics reappeared in the Mongol court as well. Power struggles intensified themselves during the time of succession when each powerful faction within the Mongol hierarchy attempted to place its own candidate on the throne. This, however, was not the situation before Kublai Khan when the Mongols had a remarkable system of choosing imperial successors. After a Great Khan died, an election was held among the Mongol princes, and theoretically everyone related to the dead khan was eligible to be elected to succeed him. This system worked very well during the period of Mongol expansion because the man elected was usually among the ablest of the electors. These were the years when the Mongols were engaged in their conquests, and the Great Khan had to be a man of character and valor to command the respect of his fellow princes and inspire the entire nation to a continuous war effort. Kublai was the first man to violate the tradition of election, as he assumed the imperial title without bothering to be elected. However, he was so highly regarded by his fellow princes that there was only ineffective opposition to his assumption of the title.

Once it was violated, the election system was never revived. Immediately after the death of an emperor, the struggle began among the Mongol princes to seize the throne. According to a Mongol custom, every prince related to the dead emperor could succeed him, whether he were an uncle, a brother, a nephew, or a son. Though normally the strongest candidate succeeded, it often occurred that the leaders of powerful factions blocked each other's chances, and often they had to compromise on a less prominent and less forcible person. In such a case, the new emperor became a mere figurehead, and the real power was in the hands of his supporters. If a reigning emperor chose to designate a crown prince (as some did), such designation would be challenged by his other relatives. Often they backed up their verbal challenge with the threat or the actual use of military force. In the latter case, civil war began. The problem of succession first appeared after the death of Kublai Khan and continued to plague the Yüan regime throughout its existence. More than anything else, it sapped the strength of the Mongol ruling class.

Contrary to the Mongol custom, the Chinese system called for the oldest son of the first legal wife (the empress) as the logical successor, unless the reigning emperor had expressly designated some one else as the crown prince. Due to the emphasis the Chinese placed on filial piety and ancestor worship, rarely was the dead emperor's wish defied, once he had made it known. Whatever disadvantages the Chinese system might have, it provided an orderly transmission of power from one generation to the next, and it lessened, though it did not prevent, the intensity of the power struggle generally following the death of an old emperor.

Despite internal differences, the Mongol ruling class presented a united front insofar as their Chinese subjects were concerned. Living in a hostile land and numerically outnumbered, perhaps they could not do otherwise. They enforced strictly the separate identities between themselves and their Chinese subjects because they knew that any relaxation on this score would eventually lead to their Sinicization and assimilation, a situation which they did not wish to see arise. This emphasis on separate identities, arising from political necessity, antagonized further the Chinese who concluded that their rulers could not be Sinicized, and in their opinion, civilized. Though there had been alien regimes in China before, with the Mongols the gap between the ruling and the ruled seemed to be unbridgeable. While they could do nothing about unuttered resentment, the Mongols took extreme measures to prevent potential revolts; some of these measures have been described earlier. By degrading intellectuals they hoped to deprive the Chinese of their traditional leadership, and by concentrating all military power in their own hands they tried to prevent the development of warlordism which had toppled many Chinese dynasties before. When the Yüan regime was finally overthrown, it was overthrown by popular revolts, led by neither intellectuals nor warlords.

While the Mongol rulers kept an watchful eye on the intellectuals, Chinese nationalism was driven to reside within the lower strata of the population where it remained dormant. Toward the end of the Yüan dynasty when the Mongol power began to show weakness, this nationalism revived and emerged. When it emerged, it took the form of religious propaganda, organized banditry, and popular uprisings. The uprisings which eventually crystallized into mass revolts were led by people of the humblest origin, with little or no education. What triggered the uprisings, however, was the classical case of famine. When famine occurred, people were no longer their rational selves. Driven by hunger, the usually submissive peasants became overnight a massive wave of defiance. Ambitious leaders were quick to exploit the situation. When they called for a revolt against all injustices, real or imaginary, the peasants followed them in a blind fashion.

The first revolt against the Yüan regime was organized by the White Lotus Society, a secret religious sect. It took its beliefs liberally from Taoism and Buddhism, and its leaders claimed the power of communicating with the spiritually unseen. Through the use of magic formulae, they said they could cure the sick, predict the future, and do numerous other miracles. The White Lotus Society first appeared in the area north of the Huai River (modern Anhwei province), and with the passage of time it attracted a large following among the ignorant, superstitious peasants. From time to time it was prosecuted by the Yüan government, and many of its leaders were exiled from their homes as a form of punishment. However, the more the government prosecuted it, the more influential it became. Governmental prosecution, in fact, turned it into a symbol of resistance against an unpopular, alien regime and converted it into an underground nationalist movement. Early in the 1350's repeated famines hit the Huai River area, and the White Lotus Society confidently predicted a major social upheaval and a dynastic change. Because of its pseudo-religious nature, Confucian intellectuals wished to have nothing to do with it, and it was led by poorly educated, mass agitaters. Acting according to its prediction, the Society secretly prepared a revolt. To exploit the nationalist sentiment and to rally popular support, Han Shan-t'ung, its leader, claimed that he was a direct descendant of the Sung emperors. However, the plot of revolt was discovered before it could be carried out, and Han was arrested and subsequently executed. Liu Fu-t'ung, one of Han's top lieutenants, installed Han's son as the figurehead "Sung emperor," and vowed to drive the Mongols out of China. The once invincible Mongols retreated before the hastily organized peasants, and the rebels captured city after city until they had practically the entire Yellow River basin under their control.

For a while it seemed that the Mongol regime would fall at any moment. This, however, was not to be the case. While Liu Fu-t'ung and his generals were ravaging North China, other rebel leaders emerged in the Yangtze River basin. In the Lower Yangtze was Chang Shih-ch'eng who, as a lowly salt merchant, had long held a grudge against the rich "aristocrats" who had either insulted him openly because of his occupation or refused to pay him the debts which they owed. In 1353 he and his small band went on a rampage, killed all the rich men they could find, and burned their mansions. Knowing that he faced certain death if he were captured, he called all men of discontent to join his revolt. His call did not go unheeded, as thousands of salt coolies, worked to exhaustion by their superiors, were happy to find a leader who promised to lead them out of their miseries. After 1353, consecutive famines hit northern Kiangsu, and the rebels' ranks were swelled by starved peasants. For more than ten years Chang Shih-ch'eng remained as the unchallenged rebel leader in Kiangsu and West Chekiang.

Beyond the Southeast coast was another rebel leader named Fang Kuo-chen who chose to rule the ocean waves. Also a former salt merchant, he became a pirate in 1348 after he had been accused of having piratical connections. He and his fellow pirates pillaged the Chekiang and Fukien coasts and intercepted grain ships that sailed along the coast northward to Peking. Time and again the Yüan government sent their best generals against him, only to be decisively defeated. For nineteen years (1348–1367) Fang Kuo-chen was the pirate king.

In the middle Yangtze valley one rebel leader after another proclaimed his independence. One was a former cloth peddler named Hsü Shou-hui who from 1351 to 1358 ruled modern Kiangsi and parts of Hupeh and Hunan provinces. After 1358, however, his position became untenable after repeated defeats at the hands of other rebels. In due time his army was taken over by Ch'en Yü-liang, a former subordinate. Ch'en, a fisherman's son, controlled the middle Yangtze from Hupeh to Anhwei during his prime of power and at one time even proclaimed himself an "emperor."

Ruling the upper Yangtze was Ming Yü-chen who in 1357 conquered Szechuan and established an independent regime at Chungking. He was perhaps the most enlightened of all rebel leaders. He reduced the taxes in the areas which he controlled, opened schools, and even gave civil service examinations. But his neglect of military affairs turned out to be his undoing. After he died in 1366, his son and successor was easily conquered by other rebels.

The rebels fought among themselves as well as against the Yüan government. Corrupted by an easy life, the Mongols offered little resistance to the hard-fighting peasants. Towards the end of the 1350's the Mongols were no longer an important factor in the struggle for supremacy, and the rebel leaders were more concerned with eliminating one another than with fighting against the Mongols. By then it had become clear that whoever emerged as the most successful rebel leader would overthrow the Yüan regime and become the new ruler of China. While the top rebel leaders were busy slaughtering each other, little did they know that their true rival would emerge from an unexpected corner.

In northern Anhwei consecutive famines produced two unusually capable rebel leaders, Kuo Tzu-hsing and Chu Yüan-chang. Kuo's father, a listless peasant, had previously struck it rich by marrying the blind daughter of an extremely wealthy man. The family's wealth increased with the passage of time. Early in the 1350's when revolts sprang up like wildfire all over China, Kuo distributed his wealth among the able-bodied, discontented men in his native county. Having successfully built up a following, he attacked and captured the strategic city of Haochou (northern Anhwei) from the Mongols and raised the standard of revolt. It was then that Chu Yüan-chang went to join him. Small successes in conquering neighboring cities were soon followed by feuds among the rebel leaders. For a while it seemed that this band of rebels would follow the footsteps of so many others into elimination or oblivion. In 1355 Kuo died and Chu inherited the leadership. It was then that the situation changed materially better for this group of rebels.

In Chu China again encountered a true leader of rare proportions. With Anhwei as his base of operation, he successfully defeated his rebel opponents, one after another. By 1367 practically all areas south of the Yellow River had been brought under his control. In that year he dispatched 250,000 of his battle-proven veterans northward to capture Peking. The Mongol military machine, once the best in the world, collapsed overnight. The last Yüan emperor left Peking for Mongolia in the summer of 1368, and with his departure the Yüan dynasty formally came to an end. Earlier in the same year Chu Yüan-chang assumed the imperial title at Nanking and called his new regime Ming.

ix

Ming

CHU YÜAN-CHANG

Chu Yüan-chang (1328–1398), the founder of the Ming dynasty, came from a very humble background. Even by the low Chinese standard, the family was exceedingly poor, and rarely could it maintain itself above the starvation level. Born the youngest of four sons in Fengyang (Anhwei province), he had a harsh life during his childhood. In 1344, when he was sixteen, a severe drought hit his native province, and whatever crops had remained in the fields were soon destroyed by swarms of locusts. A famine ensued, and his parents and brothers perished in the widespread disaster. He was so poor that he did not even have the money to buy a small lot to bury them. Having lost his home, he was taken in by a Buddhist monastery as a novice. He left the monastery shortly afterwards and wandered aimlessly for three years. During this period he was beset with sickness and hunger and had to beg for food to keep himself alive. Finally he returned to the monastery for more regular meals.

Early in 1352 the revolts against the Mongol regime spread to his native province. The commander of the local Mongol garrison, not daring to attack the rebels, chose instead to capture thousands of innocent farmers as prisoners of war and reported this to Peking as great victories in order to win rewards. Not knowing what to do under the circumstances, Chu asked a diviner for advice, and the diviner, invoking the power of the spirits, replied "no" to his inquiry about whether he should continue to stay in his native city or leave to avoid being captured by the Mongols. Asked again whether he should join the ranks of the rebels, the spirits answered with an emphatic "yes." After this alleged incident, Chu went to see Kuo Tzu-hsing, and the latter, taking a look at him, was greatly impressed with his unusual appearance; reportedly he was one of the ugliest men ever to appear on earth. The young man was awarded an orphaned girl as his wife, who was later to be the first empress of the Ming dynasty. He soon proved his worth by defeating repeatedly the Mongols and their collaborators. By 1355 when his old patron died, he was the logical successor, and with an increased following he was ready to contend for the highest prize in the kingdom. How he succeeded has been briefly described in the preceding chapter. Thus in sixteen years (1352–1368) a former beggar rose to become the emperor of China.

Though there was more than a millennium between them, Chu Yüan-chang and Liu Pang are often compared as the two commoners in Chinese history who founded new dynasties. Both came from the most humble backgrounds and rose to supreme power through native ability, personal magnetism, and the uncanny gift for doing the right thing at the right moment. With little or no formal education, both were contemptuous of the intellectuals who, they believed, could only be used but should never be trusted. Both were shrewd, calculating, and ruthless; when power was at stake, they forgot even the most common decency. Both were outrageous for ingratitude to their lieutenants who had helped most to put them on the throne. Once the regime was established and stabilized, the new emperors liquidated them one by one, fearful that these lieutenants, with their increased power and prestige, might threaten the security of the imperial line. However, in the eyes of most Chinese they were heroes because they successfully overthrew two of the most tyrannical regimes in Chinese history. Chu Yüan-chang was perhaps the more heroic, for the Yüan regime was not only tyrannical but also alien.

As with every success story, sheer luck was as important a factor as personal ability. Certainly Chu was not dreaming of becoming the future emperor of China at a time when he had to beg for food from door to door. Many years after he had ascended the dragon throne, he was still sensitive to any mention of his humble background, especially of his brief experience as a Buddhist monk. At least two Confucian scholars were found guilty and were sentenced to death when inadvertently they used the word "birth" (*sheng*), which seemed like a possible pun for "monk" (*seng*), in their congratulatory memorials. According to a widely circulated story, one day the emperor visited one of his palaces under construction, and, pleased with himself and thinking that nobody was nearby to hear him, he said to himself: "Who would believe that a humble monk could have a day like this!" Raising his head, he saw a workman on one of the beams, who had obviously heard what he had just said. The workman was ordered to come down, and after finding that he was both mute and deaf, the emperor decided to spare his life. Later, when it was learned that he was neither, nowhere could the workman be found. He never reported again for work; in fact, he completely disappeared. This incident may or may not have occurred, but it does say a great deal about Chu Yüan-chang, the commoner who had become an emperor.

Moreover, this story speaks eloquently of the absolute power Chinese monarchs enjoyed. Though Chinese monarchy had always been absolute, monarchic absolutism reached new heights under the Ming regime. With reference to autocratic rule, a history student cannot fail to notice the continuous growth of monarchic power throughout Chinese history. In other words, Chinese monarchy became more absolute with the arrival of each succeeding dynasty. This trend began as early as recorded history began and did not end until the monarchical system itself ended in 1912. While this was the general trend, it should be quickly added that the actual power exercised by each individual monarch varied a great deal, and it varied in accordance with his personality (strong or weak), ability, and the circumstances under which he ruled. Generally speaking, the first emperors of each dynasty were more powerful than the last ones, for the power of monarchs declined as each dynasty declined. However, it was still true that over the long run, monarchic power increased and that the monarchy of each succeeding dynasty was generally more absolute than that of the preceding dynasty. For instance, Ming monarchy was more absolute than Yüan; Yüan was more absolute than Sung; and so on.

The continuous increase of monarchic power did not result from any change in political theory; rather, it came as a result of innovations and accumulated usage. In theory the emperor was the Son of Heaven, and being responsible to nobody on earth, he enjoyed absolute power by definition. The checks on the exercise of that power could only be imposed by the emperor himself, *e.g.*, his own willingness to observe custom and tradition, his fear of potential revolts, and the conviction, if he chose to have it, that he should always rule for the benefit of the ruled. There was no way of getting rid of a bad government except by successful revolt, and if a monarch abused his power, revolts were justified in theory as had been done often in practice. But revolts, even successful ones, were extremely costly and time consuming, and as both monarch and his subjects agreed, they should not be indulged in lightly. Until modern times, China had never practiced any other form of government except absolute monarchy because to the Chinese the alternative was anarchy, which should be avoided at all costs.

Since absolute monarchy was the accepted form of government, the only way to avoid its abuse lay in the betterment of the monarch himself: he should be intelligent, wise, and able, and he should rule not for his own self-glorification, but for the welfare of his subjects. As taught by Confucians, the education of monarchs was the most important education in the realm, for they believed that a good government was impossible unless the monarch was virtuous and that the prerequisite to an orderly society was the "cultivation of virtues" among the rulers. Thus in Chinese politics personnel was always more important than institutions since the basic institution, that of absolute monarchy, remained the same throughout centuries.

When Chu Yüan-chang emerged as the emperor of China, one of his major concerns was the security of the imperial line and the best way to preserve it. A man of commanding personality and unusual ability, he had no fear of any challenge to his own authority, but he was greatly concerned with what could happen when he was no longer in charge of state affairs. His eldest son, the crown prince, was a weak figure. After the early death of the crown prince, Chu Yüan-chang designated the crown prince's eldest son, then a child, as his heir apparent. To secure the throne for his successor, he thought that before he died he had to eliminate all potential enemies of the future emperor. Two purges (in 1380 and again in 1393) were conducted, and each was a bloodbath. The two purges were centered on two prominent figures, Hu Wei-yung, the prime minister, and Lan Yü, a marshal and field commander. Both had been his top lieutenants in overthrowing the Yüan dynasty and in establishing the new regime. The two main characters might or might not have been guilty of treason as charged (the prime minister, for instance, was accused of having communicated secretly with the Japanese and of having invited them to land on the eastern coast of China for a common effort to topple the Ming regime), but there was no question about the innocence of thousands of others who had to perish because they were directly or indirectly, personally or otherwise, associated with the two accused. After the two purges, all political figures who could be remotely considered a threat to the throne were liquidated. With the comforting thought that the crown had been secured for his grandson, Chu Yüan-chang died in peace in 1398. Little did he realize then that the danger to his grandson's crown would come from an unexpected corner.

Rejecting the revival of feudalism on a large scale and yet entertaining the hope that the royal house in Nanking would be defended by its own members in case of need, Chu Yüan-chang placed three of his eldest sons in three strategic areas of North China in command of concentrations of troops, while his other sons were given rank, title, and wealth, but little real power. The role of the three was twofold: to come to the rescue of Nanking whenever help was needed and to defend North China against possible Mongol invasion, since the Mongols, though driven out of China proper, were still a potential threat. When Chu Yüan-chang's grandson, Ming Hui-ti, inherited the throne in 1399 at the age of sixteen, he was greatly concerned with the semi-independent status which his three uncles enjoyed, and he proposed to reduce their power which, he believed, threatened his own security as emperor at Nanking. His real target, however, was third uncle, Chu Ti, who was by far the ablest and the most powerful of his numerous uncles. Declaring that his nephew was badly advised by evil elements and that there could be no peace until they were removed, Chu Ti personally took command of his troops and

MARBLE STATUES OF ANIMALS   These statues, erected in the fourteenth century, line the tomb of Chu Yüan-chang, founder of the Ming dynasty. The tomb is located outside of Nanking and is a major tourist attraction. The names of some of the tourists are scratched on the bodies of the two elephants in the foreground, a destructive way of achieving immortality practiced everywhere in the world.

marched southward from his base at Peking. The resultant war lasted three years, and while the fortunes of war changed from time to time, the uncle's greater ability decided the final outcome in the end. Nanking fell in 1402, and the boy emperor disappeared when his palace caught fire and was burned to the ground. It was not known whether he had been burned alive or had managed to escape. In the following year Chu Ti ascended the throne and was then known by his reign title Yung-lo. The capital was moved northward to Peking.

The reigns of Hung-wu (Chu Yüan-chang's reign title) and Yung-lo, which jointly covered more than a half century, were the most dynamic of the Ming regime. Hung-wu was regarded as one of the ablest monarchs China ever produced, and his innovations were followed without question by his successors. He disregarded all limitations on his power imposed by custom and tradition, and his reign was marked by a despotism unprecedented in Chinese history. Angered by Hu Wei-yung's alleged treason, he decided to abolish the institution of premiership once and for all, and "anyone who dares to petition for its reëstablishment will be ordered to perish immediately together with the rest of his family." The Six Ministries (Rites, Finance, Personnel, War, Justice, and Public Works), which formerly had been headed by a prime minister, were now made directly responsible to the emperor alone. Thus the institution of premiership, which was almost as old as Chinese politics itself, came to an end, and it was not reëstablished throughout the Ming dynasty.

The abolition of premiership strengthened further the power of Chinese monarchs. Though appointed by and responsible to the emperor, a prime minister enjoyed a certain degree of independence as the head of the government, as against the monarch who was the head of the court as well as the head of the state. He was usually promoted from the rank and file of a professional bureaucracy, and being raised up among the people, he presumably knew "the people's sickness and sorrows." The monarch, on the other hand, was usually a product of palace life and had no personal experience with the life of his subjects outside the palace. Generally speaking, the prime minister, being one of the people, had in mind the welfare of the nation as a whole, while the monarch was more concerned with the security of his crown and the welfare of the royal household. A monarch inherited his throne through no virtue of his own, while a prime minister earned his position by academic excellence and personal ability. Against an impulsive or capricious emperor, a conscientious and upright prime minister upheld the principles he stood for. Respecting his position and prestige, even the most despotic monarch would think twice before he inflicted upon his prime minister undeserved punishment. Thus a good prime minister always served as an effective check on the absolute power of the supposedly omnipotent prince.

The emperor Hung-wu, by abolishing the premiership, created a

SEA OF JAPAN

East China Sea

Yellow Sea

South China Sea

MAP 25

CHINA PROPER
around 1400 A.D.

□ Capital
• Provincial Capital
˄˄˄˄˄ The Great Wall

0   150   300   450
Scale of Miles

LIAOTUNG
•Liaoyang

Shanhaikuan

CAPITAL
□Shuntien (Peking)

SHANTUNG

•Tsinan

SHANSI
•Taiyuan

HONAN
•Kaifeng

SHENSI
•Sian

NANKING
(Yingtien (Nanking))

CHEKIANG
•Hangchow

FUKIEN
•Foochow

KIANGSI
•Nanchang

HUKUANG
•Wuchang

YANGTZE RIVER

YELLOW RIVER

SZECHUAN
•Chengtu

KWEICHOW
•Kweiyang

KWANGSI
•Kweilin

KWANGTUNG
•Canton

YUNNAN
•Yunnan (Kunming)

CHINSHA RIVER

MEKONG RIVER

SALWEEN RIVER

most unfortunate precedent for his successors to follow. Though able monarchs like Yung-lo had no difficulty in carrying out a prime minister's duties, the less fortunate ones, with tremendous power in their hands and yet not knowing how to use it, turned to their personal favorites for guidance and counsel. Surrounded in the Forbidden City by concubines and eunuchs, they increasingly turned to the latter for consultation on state affairs. To be sure, the Board of Censors was allowed to function even after the abolition of premiership. But the censors, being officials of lower ranks, could only remonstrate with their superiors at their own peril. They were neither supposed to nor did they actually serve as an effective check on the omnipotence of absolute monarchs.

Ming despotism was vividly demonstrated by a new custom, the corporal punishment of government officials. The ancient tradition that "a gentleman could be ordered to die, but he should never be humiliated" was no longer observed under the new regime. Though corporal punishment had been frequently used against common criminals, it was for the first time legally sanctioned by a Chinese regime against intellectuals. In Chinese thinking, the intellectuals, as the standard bearers of the Chinese heritage, should always be held in respect and should never be humiliated in public. If a member of the intelligentsia committed a crime of an unforgivable nature, tradition called for him to commit suicide; and, if he were true to his Confucian principles, he should do so without complaint even though he might be fully convinced that he was innocent. The Ming regime dispensed with this honorable custom and introduced instead corporal punishment. Whether the new regime inherited this practice from the Mongols is a matter of conjecture, but Chu Yüan-chang would have started it even if there had been no precedent. For the founder of the Ming dynasty was an unusually cruel man, and coming from a humble background with no formal education to speak of, he might have subconsciously enjoyed the humiliation and tormenting of the seemingly self-centered intellectuals. Whatever the real motive was, he made the flogging of public officials a court routine, and those who died of injuries included a duke and a Minister of Public Works. The floggings became so indiscriminate and deadly that it was said that court officials bid farewell to their wives every morning when they left for the imperial conference and congratulated each other for having lived another day if they came home alive. One court official who dared to petition the emperor for some relief from this cruel practice was thrown into jail and never came out alive.

Once the precedent of corporal punishment was established, later Ming emperors followed it as a matter of common usage, and none of them ever questioned its advisability and wisdom. In fact, "court floggings" (t'ing chang) developed into ritualistic affairs and were done with well-defined, specified rules. Whenever a public flogging occurred, all court officials were required to wear ceremonial robes and to be present to observe in the emperor's audience hall. Once the victim was brought in, his guilt was publicly announced by an imperial guard. He would then lie flat on his stomach, with both arms and legs tied tightly so he could move neither left nor right. A wooden rod was used to flail his exposed buttocks after his underwear had been publicly stripped off. The number of blows he would receive depended upon the seriousness of his offense. Usually he died before the last blow could be delivered.

Barbaric though it might be, the severe punishment of government officials did yield one good result: the elimination of bribery and corruption. Early during the Ming dynasty the law stipulated that any official who accepted bribes exceeding sixty taels of silver was liable to capital punishment, and those who had accepted less would be flogged and then condemned to an indefinite period of hard labor. Meanwhile, able and conscientious officials were honored and abundantly rewarded. The imperial government periodically sent inspectors down to the provinces, punishing the guilty and rewarded the deserving. Rarely in Chinese history had government officials been so honest.

MARITIME EXPEDITIONS

If Chu Yüan-chang could be compared to Genghis Khan in foresight and personal ability, Yung-lo was certainly another Kublai Khan. In both cases their successors were far behind them in performance as vital, capable rulers. The reigns of Hung-wu and Yung-lo were not only marked by a new height in autocratic rule at home, but they were also characterized by the implementation of a vigorous foreign policy abroad. In this respect the first few decades of the Ming dynasty have been often compared with the expansion years of the Han and T'ang regimes. Chu Yüan-chang not only drove the Mongols out of China but repeatedly sent his troops deep into the enemy's territories. Twice the Ming forces captured Karakorum, and the Mongol chieftains were forced to sue for peace. The fact that Yung-lo located his capital only forty miles south of the Great Wall indicated an extremely confident regime which felt strong enough to be face to face with China's traditional enemies from the northern steppes. Like many Han and T'ang emperors, he took offensive actions to achieve an essentially defensive goal: time and again his men invaded and penetrated deep into the grasslands, seeking out the enemy's forces and destroying them. Throughout the Yung-lo reign the nomads were forcibly kept within their own boundaries. But for reasons we have discussed before, the very nature of the grasslands prohibited any permanent success of an agricultural ruler. When the Ming regime began to show signs of decline after the 1430's, China's traditional enemy once again threatened her northern frontier.

Believing that all peoples on earth should be brought under the benevolent influence of the Son of Heaven, the first Ming emperor sent envoys overseas demanding the acknowledgement of his overlordship shortly after his accession. For reasons of their own, many of China's peripheral states and some in faraway South and Southeast Asia allowed themselves to be persuaded to join Ming's tribute system. Korea, Japan,

A MAP OF CHINA MADE DURING THE MING DYNASTY   The Great Wall is shown on the upper part of this map. The two heavy tree-like lines indicate the Yellow River in the north and the Yangtze in the south. Within the large circle on the upper right is the Chinese word "Peking." The black area on the right and lower side is, of course, the ocean.

Liu-ch'iu, Annam (Vietnam), Cambodia, Siam (Thailand), Borneo, Java, Sumatra, several Malay states, and some small kingdoms on the southeast coast of India, directly or by implication, acknowledged Ming's overlordship at one time or another. Hung-wu's efforts along this line were continued by his son Yung-lo. It was during the latter's reign that Chinese influence was expanded overseas in a manner never before accomplished.

Under Yung-lo and his two immediate successors the Chinese launched a series of maritime expeditions on an unprecedented scale. From 1405 to 1431 Chinese armadas led by the court eunuch Cheng Ho made seven voyages to the "Western Ocean" (a term used during this period to cover the general area of South and Southeast Asia) for the ostensible purpose of "glorifying Chinese arms in the remote regions and showing off the wealth and power of the Central Kingdom." In 1405 when the first expedition began, a powerful fleet of 62 vessels carrying 27,800 men sailed from Fukien, visited many Southeast Asian countries, and went as far as India. In the places it visited, it "proclaimed publicly the decree of the Son of Heaven" (of demanding their submission), and "if they refused to submit, force was used to coerce them." On the other hand, if the local chieftains decided to cooperate, gold, silk, and other valuables were showered on them as rewards. The first expedition, successfully accomplished, was followed by six others, and most of them went as far as the Persian Gulf or Aden at the southeastern end of the Red Sea. In at least two of the voyages Chinese vessels personally commanded by Cheng Ho called on some of the small kingdoms on the east coast of Africa. As a result of these expeditions it was reported that altogether thirty-six countries in the "Western Ocean" sent tribute missions to China and acknowledged Ming's overlordship. These thirty-six countries included eight from the East Indies, eleven from India and Ceylon, five from Persia and Arabia, and five from the east coast of Africa.

Cheng Ho's voyages were the most spectacular maritime expeditions the world had yet seen. From a historian's point of view, they raise more questions than have ever been satisfactorily answered. First, what were the motives behind this adventure? What did it try to achieve? Second, what seamanship did the Chinese then possess which made these expeditions not only possible but also remarkably successful? Third, why did not the Chinese follow up their initial success, as later the Western Europeans did, with the establishment of a commercial and perhaps a political maritime empire? Lastly, what was the true meaning of the tribute system which, the Chinese insisted, was the only proper basis in their relations with non-Chinese countries?

Chinese sources give two reasons for this unprecedented maritime adventure: first, to trace the whereabouts of Ming Hui-ti who was believed by some to have escaped from Nanking and who might be some-

Liuchia Kang

Foochow

Canton

South China Sea

MING

Peking

YELLOW RIVER

YANGTZE RIVER

Palembang

Bay of Bengal

Lake Balkhash

Aral Sea

Colombo

Calicut

Indian Ocean

Caspian Sea

Arabian Sea

Hormuz

PERSIAN GULF

To Aden

To Malindi

MAP 26
THE VOYAGES OF CHENG HO

□ Capital   ● Cities
⋯⋯⋯⋯► Routes

0   400   800
Scale of Miles

where in Southeast Asia, and second, to "impress people overseas with Ming's power and wealth" and to "bring ten thousand nations to bear tribute missions to the Central Kingdom." The first reason might have had something to do with the first voyage, but even then it was secondary at best, for there were no extensive efforts made during any of the seven voyages to find the ex-emperor. If this were a genuine reason, there would have been no need for these voyages to go as far as the Near East or Africa. The second reason was more plausible, since so far no other motives have been found. In other words, these expeditions were launched for ideological reasons and prestige. The material or commercial motive which prompted European expansion at a later date was notably absent.

Ideologically, the Ming emperors regarded themselves as the Sons of Heaven, thus representing all people on earth. Once such an assumption was made, it seemed logical that they should wish to bring as many foreign nations under their overlordship as they physically could. While the Han and T'ang emperors looked northward and overland for the extension of their pretensions, the Ming emperors looked southward and overseas for the same purpose. Perhaps by then history had shown them the futility of expansion across the grasslands and deserts on account of geographical and cultural factors. If a southern expansion was to be equally unprofitable, as later it did turn out to be, they had no historical lessons to guide them at that time. The word "profit," of course, should not be interpreted in its material sense, since the Chinese did not believe that material profit should be a primary factor in governing the relationships among nations. Traditionally against commercialism which seemed to be the only practical reason for such an adventure, they undertook one of the most costly operations in history for nonmaterial purposes.

Despite the basic attitude of anticommercialism on the part of the Chinese government and most of the Chinese people, the fact that China had a long coastline indented with many fine bays and harbors should explain why a certain portion of its people became orientated to the sea and depended on the sea to earn a livelihood. Regardless of what other people thought of them and their activities, the people on the southeast coast had long been engaged in commercial endeavors overseas. Since they lived far away from the Yellow River basin where more important history was made and since the Chinese had traditionally looked down upon trade and commerce, what they did in the faraway areas of Fukien and Kwangtung was only scantily recorded by the agriculturally minded historians. On the southeast coast where the rugged terrain dropped abruptly into the sea to form an irregular coastline with many bays and harbors, the land was poor and arable areas were few. As the pressure of population increased with the passage of time, people were forced by necessity to look beyond the blue horizon for a livelihood. With or without government approval, they sailed abroad with Chinese products and brought home goods of exotic origins. Many perished on the high seas or on remote islands; others brought back uncountable wealth. For every family that succeeded, many others mourned the loss of their beloved ones. Merchants who had found a more rewarding existence overseas settled down there permanently and never returned. Early in the 1560's it was reported that tens of thousands of Chinese resided in Luzon, and a Chinese community of several thousand families had been established in the city of Palembang (Sumatra).

As overseas trade expanded, numerous trade ports on the southeast coast flourished. The most important among them was Ch'üanchou (Map 1) which remained the leading shipping and trading center throughout the Sung, Yüan, and Ming dynasties. Government posts in charge of merchant marine and shipping were so lucrative that they were eagerly sought after, and officials who occupied them grew in power and wealth. One of them, P'u Shou-keng, became so powerful that his change of loyalty shortened the life of the South Sung regime, as has been mentioned before. Despite a basic anticommercial attitude, overseas trade was so profitable and prosperous that both government and people benefited from it. The large amount of wealth that could be acquired from overseas trade and the great risk involved in it gave birth to a new custom in Fukien province, the adoption of foster children. Abandoned children and orphans were adopted by families even when they had children of their own. They were sent abroad for commercial enterprise after they had grown up, while the true sons were generally kept at home. If they made good, the whole family benefited; if they were lost forever, their families would be somewhat comforted by the thought that they were not true sons in the first place.

Since seafaring had a long history on the southeast coast, seamanship improved with the passage of each generation. The merchants who roved the seven seas for profit could be easily converted into naval captains for manning warships, once their government demanded their service. When Kublai Khan decided to invade Japan again in 1281, enough seamen and ships to transport 140,000 troops were gathered in short order. When Yung-lo ordered his men to venture into the south seas, the people on the east coast were equally ready to provide what he needed. Generations of experiments and improvement enabled the Chinese to manufacture ships that were among the most seaworthy the world had yet seen. Some of the vessels used in Cheng Ho's first voyage, for instance, had a length of 44 *chang* (c. 517 feet), and a width of 18 *chang* (c. 212 feet), built with four decks and watertight compartments. With favorable winds they could make as fast as six knots an hour. The compass, which had been used for centuries to locate proper burial places for the dead, was now an indispensable instrument in navigation. Early during the fifteenth century when

Cheng Ho made his voyages, the Chinese had the men and the skill to undertake such feats of seamanship as had never before been seen in world history.

Despite their monumental success in seamanship, the maritime expeditions of the Ming dynasty were discontinued as suddenly as they had been launched. Cheng Ho goes down in history as an earlier Columbus who was not followed by a Cortes or a Pizarro, and his overseas voyages turned out to be the first and the only large-scale maritime adventure ever undertaken by a Chinese government. If the Chinese had continued his efforts, the economic and political structure of the world in the subsequent centuries, or at least that in Asia, would have changed considerably. The immediate causes of their discontinuance were rather obvious. First, these maritime expeditions were extremely costly, and yet they brought back nothing except dubious prestige. The Ming regime simply could not continue them indefinitely. Second, other areas began to demand more attention from the government after the 1430's, especially the northern frontier where the Mongols again threatened an invasion. The real causes, however, went much deeper. Had the maritime region on China's southeast coast constituted an independent state acting in observance of its own interests, it could have been another Portugal or Spain, one of the first maritime nations in the world. Its sailors, having touched the east coast of Africa early in the fifteenth century, could conceivably have reached the Cape of Good Hope later, and eventually might have been able to "discover" such strange places as England and France. This, however, was not to be the case. China remained land-centered and anticommercial. Instead of discovering more new territories, China and its tributary states were "discovered" by Western Europeans in a later age.

The reasons for the failure to follow up Cheng Ho's initial success with sustained interest and effort can be found in the nature of Chinese culture itself. In other words, the sense of values contained in the Chinese cultural system would not allow maritime success on a sustained basis. The Chinese lacked the motivations that prompted Western Europe to discover and explore new areas in a later period. First, as a people the Chinese were unusually self-centered. Separated from other centers of civilization by oceans and almost impassable mountains and deserts, the Chinese developed their culture independently. They had been little affected by foreign influence, except Buddhism from India, until modern times. The result was a self-centered "culturalism" which regarded the Chinese culture as the most unique and incomparably great. While foreigners were welcome to come to China to be Sinicized and, in the opinion of the Chinese, civilized, it was considered improper for the Chinese to go overseas for the sole purpose of propagating Chinese beliefs. Active proselyting was to be avoided because it could not serve any purpose except to place doubt on the advocated beliefs. In the Chinese mind, true values needed no persuasion, and if the Chinese culture were truly great (as they believed it was), foreigners would follow it of their own accord. Throughout Chinese history individual Confucians might go to foreign countries to teach if they were invited, but there were no organized efforts on the part of the Chinese or their government to send missionaries overseas. Thus the missionary zeal which played such an important role in Europe's discovery and exploration of new territories during the age of commercial revolution was singularly absent so far as the Chinese were concerned. Second, there was the traditional anticommercialism in China. Ever since the Han dynasty the merchants had been regarded as exploitative and parasitic, and despite the useful functions they performed, they were discriminated against socially and occasionally even persecuted. During the Ming dynasty the fact that the seafaring merchants generally came from the lower strata of the population and were the least cultured in Confucian learning strengthened further an ancient prejudice. In the minds of most Chinese, the merchants who voluntarily left their parents and their ancestors' graves to seek fortunes overseas were the most contemptible because by doing so they neglected to observe two cardinal virtues of Confucianism, i.e., filial piety and ancestor worship. Third, rightly or wrongly the Chinese believed that they were economically self-sufficient and that they needed nothing from foreign lands. That Cheng Ho's expeditions brought back nothing remarkable except such curiosities as ostriches, zebras, and giraffes further convinced them that while foreigners depended upon trade with China for the improvement of their livelihood, China had nothing to gain in trading with foreigners. This belief was strengthened in a later period by the insistence of Western Europeans on opening China to trade.

Spectacular as Cheng Ho's expeditions were, they did not represent a basic need from the Chinese point of view. Many Confucian scholars regarded this maritime adventure as being wasteful and unnecessary and merely "a eunuch's enterprise" with which they would have nothing to do. Though they had no objection to bringing many foreign lands into the tribute system, they believed that this should be done on a voluntary basis and that no coercion or "persuasion" should be applied for that purpose. The tribute system, as they saw it, was based upon a cultural relationship between superior and inferiors. China, being culturally superior, extended its benevolent influence to its neighbors, and its neighbors sent tribute missions to China out of gratitude and appreciation. Foreign countries that sent tribute missions should be given Chinese products in return that were worth more in monetary value than the tributes they sent in order to show "the generosity and abundance of the Central Kingdom." There should not be any motive for material gain in the operation of the tribute system. The tribute system, enshrined in tradition and history, was the only basis of international relations Confucian scholars would recognize. Clearly they did not believe in equality among sovereign nations because in their mind no nation except China was truly sovereign. This self-centered "culturalism," as one might call it, had worked fairly well throughout Chinese history until modern times when China was brought into contact with Western Europeans.

The actual performance of the tribute system fell far short of the ideal as conceived by Confucian scholars. The material motive, theoretically absent, played an important role as early as the tribute system began. The gifts given by Chinese emperors to foreign rulers and their emissaries were often subsidies and bribes in disguise; the Chinese hoped that foreigners, given the choice of obtaining what they needed by peaceful means, would not resort to the use of more violent methods. On the other hand, foreign countries perhaps had no objection to being considered as inferiors so long as the manifestation of inferiority did not extend beyond the nominal, ritualistic gestures such as the adoption of the Chinese calendar and the receiving of Chinese ranks and titles. Moreover, tribute embassies were often foreign trade missions in disguise and brought material benefits to the countries that sent them. Thus the tribute system rationalized foreign trade and gave it an aura of respectability which otherwise it would not have had. Traditionally anticommercial, the Chinese government would have been hard put to sanction foreign trade if it were not disguised as tribute missions. During the Ming dynasty the so-called tribute bearers were often the representatives of foreign trade interests. In many cases these representatives were Chinese exiles who had been chosen by foreign traders to represent them because of their expert knowledge of Chinese affairs. Oftentimes, the Chinese government threw these exiles into jail or even executed them, once their identity was established. From the government's point of view, the fact that these exiles left their ancestors' graves for foreign lands spoke eloquently of their rascality for which, it believed, they deserved no mercy. Needless to say, the government did not favor Chinese emigration overseas.

JAPANESE PIRATES

Like many dynasties before it, the Ming dynasty underwent a familiar dynastic cycle. The first stage of the cycle was the stage of exuberant energy characterized by expansion abroad and peace and prosperity at home during the reigns of Hung-wu and Yung-lo. Then followed the stage of stability during which a power equilibrium existed between China and its "barbarian" neighbors. While there were occasional clashes of arms between them, neither side was able to advance decisively against the other. Domestically, as population increased following a period of peace and prosperity, the balance between food supply and demand had become marginal and delicate, and a serious drought or flood would tip the balance and cause a famine and possibly an internal revolt. From 1424 when Yung-lo died to 1628 when the last Ming emperor, Ch'ung-chen, ascended the throne, there were several serious revolts, not to mention riots of a more local nature. The government, however, was able to suppress each revolt after considerable bloodshed. The rebels could challenge the imperial authority, but they could not threaten its existence. The last years of the stage of stability merged imperceptibly with the first years of the stage of decline. The decline was a gradual and continuous process, and it is difficult to say exactly when it began. During the period of decline, as the scope and the frequency of internal revolts became increasingly larger, the government was less and less able to cope with them. Meanwhile, the non-Chinese tribes beyond the Great Wall became stronger and bolder; they invaded, or threatened to invade, border provinces. At home, corruption, incompetence, and factional strife continued to sap the strength of the government. The Ming regime finally ended when it was too weakened to last any longer.

The first indication that all was not well with the state was its inability to suppress Japanese pirates on the east coast in the 1520's. Since 1401 when Japan had sent its first tribute mission to China, extensive trade had been conducted between the two countries under the guise of tribute missions. Ningpo (Chekiang province) was designated as the port of entry, and both sides seemed to benefit greatly from the exchange. However, problems soon developed, and there were constant bickerings and wranglings between traders of both sides. To simplify the matter, the Ming government decided in the 1430's that the Japanese could send only one tribute mission every ten years, that each mission should not consist of more than two ships and two hundred persons, and that only authorized representatives of the Japanese government would be recognized as members of the mission. This policy, however, did not work so well as the Ming government had hoped.

Trade being exceedingly profitable, the competition to send tribute missions was intense. Since Japan was not unified at that time, different feudal lords sent their own missions to China, each claiming to represent Japan. When the tribute missions arrived at Ningpo, the Chinese government had to decide whom to recognize. It often occurred that Chinese officials in charge recognized the mission that offered the largest bribe and turned back the rest. With so much at stake financially, the Japanese who had been turned back simply would not accept the Chinese decision. Since they could not trade legally, they resorted to smuggling. When engaged in smuggling, they had no difficulty in finding Chinese collaborators who were eager to help for a commission. Thus the rejected tribute bearers transformed themselves into smugglers overnight, and with the help of their Chinese collaborators they were remarkably successful. As their success story spread, other Japanese merchants followed suit. Together they made smuggling a widespread affair on the east coast of China. When the Chinese authorities set out to suppress them, they fought back and ravaged the coastal villages and towns in retaliation. The very same Japanese would be tribute bearers, legitimate traders, smugglers, or pirates, depending upon when and where they made their appearance.

In 1523 when again it was time to send tribute missions to China, many Japanese lords competed for the prized privilege. When two rival delegations arrived at Ningpo, the Chinese official in charge (a eunuch) violated the principle of priority—"first come, first served"—by inspecting first the goods of the delegation that arrived later but had offered a large bribe to the Chinese. The rival delegation led by a Buddhist monk attacked the delegation which the Chinese had favored. Chinese officials, instead of offering their good offices, secretly helped the side they favored with military weapons. Learning about this, the rival delegation and its auxiliary warriors retaliated by burning and looting Chinese towns and cities. When peace was finally restored, the Ming government ordered the suspension of trade with the Japanese "now and forever," and all Japanese were ordered to leave China immediately. Recognizing the weakness of its defenses along the coast, the government thought that this was the best policy to follow; but it was to backfire shortly afterwards.

As long as trade was legalized and officially supervised, it benefited both Chinese and Japanese merchants, despite friction and occasional outbursts of violence. Once it was suspended, the legitimate trade went underground and became a clandestine operation. By then trade had become so prosperous that merchants of neither side wished to abandon it. While the government had in mind coastal defense and consequently prohibited trade, the merchants on the east coast were so anxious for profits that they continued to trade with the Japanese despite the government's prohibition. Unwilling or unable to check the illicit trade, local officials adopted an attitude of "salutary neglect." Well-bribed, they could be counted on to close their eyes.

Without government supervision and regulation, trade became a private affair between Chinese and Japanese merchants, and they had to settle whatever difficulties that arose by themselves. One of the recurring difficulties was the inability or unwillingness on the part of many Chinese merchants to pay their debts to the Japanese exporters after they had received goods. Refusing to go home empty-handed, the Japanese took temporary residence on the nearby islands off the coast and waited and demanded to be paid. When their food and other provisions were exhausted, they found it necessary to raid coastal villages to obtain the means of livelihood. The Chinese debtors would then accuse them of piracy and demand the local garrisons to chase them out. Meanwhile, they secretly informed their Japanese creditors of the coming raid to make sure that they would leave safely for Japan before the arrival of Chinese troops. By these devious maneuvers these Chinese merchants hoped to achieve a double purpose: they did not have to pay the debts they owed, and the Japanese merchants, once safely home, could be expected to return with more goods next time. If they did return, the same scheme would be again used. Though most Chinese and Japanese merchants were honest in their dealings, there were among them enough such black sheep to cause constant friction between the two groups.

While honest Japanese traders could not find redress for their legitimate grievances, the dishonest ones resorted to illegitimate means to achieve their purpose. They would trade when they were allowed, smuggle when legitimate trade was denied to them. They resorted to piracy if they believed that the returns could be even larger. The long coastline and Ming's weak defense made piracy extremely difficult to suppress, and once one piracy went unpunished, others followed suit. Piracy being so profitable, the entire coast from the Liaotung Peninsula to Kwangtung was soon infested with pirates. From 1523 when trade with Japan was officially suspended to 1564 when piracy was finally suppressed, the merchant-pirates from Japan went up and down the coastline, looting, burning, and killing, encountering little or no opposition. Ming's defense was so weak that on many occasions pirates not only ravaged the coastal areas but penetrated deep into the interior. In one instance, a small band of Japanese pirates went as far as South Anhwei and then turned northward to attack Nanking.

While officially they were lumped together and were called "dwarf (Japanese) pirates," most of these pirates were actually Chinese. From the very beginning, Chinese took an active part in these lawless activities. At one time it was estimated that they constituted about 70 percent of the pirate force. These Chinese came from various walks of life, and all of them, for one reason or another, had become dissatisfied with their previous occupations. Among them were dismissed government officials, students who had failed in the civil service examinations, jail-breaking prisoners, runaway Buddhist monks, and professional ruffians. Many of the local gentry either connived at or were actually involved in this lawless but profitable occupation. Though these pirates ravaged the entire coast, it was Kiangsu and Chekiang provinces that suffered most, partly because there were many islands off the coast of these two provinces which conveniently served as jumping-off places for piratical raids. The Chushan Islands, for instance, were notorious as pirate strongholds. After 1558, however, the pirates moved southward and concentrated their efforts on Fukien and Kwangtung provinces. It was not until the 1560's that their energy was spent and they were finally suppressed.

INTERNAL DECLINE

The fact that bands of pirates could devastate such large areas for such a long time was a clear indication of Ming's decline as a military power. Military commanders were usually political appointees who knew little or nothing about warfare. They fled before the arrival of the enemy and left towns and cities wide open to the invaders. In 1555, for instance, a band of sixty-seven Japanese pirates swept across three provinces for several hundred miles, looted in a dozen cities, and killed more than four thousand persons in a period of three months. More than anything else, this incident reflected an almost unbelievable bureaucratic incompetence. More than a century of unchallenged, autocratic rule had created such complacency among government leaders that minor rebellions and piratical raids could not even create a stir of urgency and arouse them to a better effort. During this period the emperors were all products of an easy palace life, and most of them knew or cared little about state affairs. Two of the emperors shared a notorious record for not having received any of their ministers for twenty years. Instead of delegating power to legally constituted authorities, the emperors turned over the reins of government to their personal servants, the eunuchs. As eunuch power increased, the Ming regime slowly declined.

A combination of circumstances made eunuchs a unique factor in Chinese politics. They were: (1) the seclusion of emperors from the outside world, (2) the emperors' unlimited power and unchallenged position, (3) the great size of the imperial harem, (4) the daily contact between emperors and eunuchs, and (5) the general acceptance by the Chinese people of the above practices. The special privileges reserved for an emperor alone were also a handicap which he must overcome if he wished to become a successful ruler. He had to be unusually wise not to be corrupted by the power he enjoyed. But monarchs, like any other group of people, had their share of mediocrities. The soft, femininized palace was no place to breed hardy, strong leaders. During his daily routine, an emperor saw only women and eunuchs. He could not venture into the outside world without causing great alarm among court officials since his safety was their most important concern. He knew little about his subjects except whatever information his ministers and eunuchs chose to give him. Yet his power was so great that he could order the death of anyone who, in his opinion, had shown "disrespect" or had personally offended him. Under such circumstances it took an unusually courageous minister to be frank, and courageous ministers were only too few. The Ming record shows that time and again ministers trembled with fear in an emperor's presence, and when pressed to speak, spoke what they thought the emperor would like to hear. They were anxious to keep bad news from his knowledge, lest in a sudden burst of anger they might be punished more severely than they deserved. For instance, the last Ming emperor Ch'ung-chen had no idea where the rebels were until they began to climb the walls of the Forbidden City and attack his palace. Pampered by women and eunuchs and cut off completely from the outside world, an emperor had to be an exceptional man to govern successfully the largest nation on earth. But most emperors were not exceptional. Many of the Ming emperors, for instance, relied on their eunuchs for information and judgment, since the eunuchs alone saw them everyday and could perhaps talk with them on a personal basis. In some cases, an emperor simply turned over the whole government to a head eunuch, while he could enjoy "wine, women, and song" without being disturbed by state affairs.

With the possible exception of the Sung, practically all major Chinese dynasties were plagued with the usurpation of power by eunuchs in various degrees. After the establishment of the Ming regime, Chu Yüan-chang took extra precautions to prevent eunuchs from acquiring power and formulated strict rules to govern their lives. The number of eunuchs was limited to one hundred, and they were not allowed to read and write. They served in the palaces only, and under no circumstance would they be allowed to become government officials. To remind the eunuchs of their place, Chu Yüan-chang ordered that an iron plate be placed on one of the palace doors, on which was inscribed: "Eunuchs should not meddle in governmental affairs. Let those who violate this rule be punished by death." Though this rule was meant to be permanent, it was soon violated by Chu Yüan-chang's son, the emperor Yung-lo. To reward the eunuchs who had helped him win the war against his nephew Hui-ti, Yung-lo appointed them to high positions with great responsibilities. Some were sent to foreign countries as his personal envoys. The most prominent of them was Cheng Ho whose maritime expeditions have been discussed earlier. Yung-lo, a strong ruler, could use the eunuchs according to their talents and ability without prejudicing his own power as a sovereign. His successors, however, were not so fortunate. They often handed over the power of government to the eunuchs and shut themselves off from outside contact. While they enjoyed the various forms of dissipation within the Forbidden City, the eunuchs ran the government.

The apogee of eunuch power was reached during the reign of Ming Hsi-tsung (1621–1627) when the head eunuch was a man named Wei Chung-hsien. Wei was described as a listless loafer during his boyhood, and he reportedly castrated himself in a sudden burst of emotion after he had lost a great deal in gambling. Subsequently selected for service in the imperial palace, he ingratiated himself to the wet nurse of the crown prince. When the crown prince, a boy of fifteen, ascended the throne as Ming Hsi-tsung, he showed his gratitude to his former nurse by appointing her friend Wei to high offices in the government. Though an illiterate who could not even write his own name, Wei was a shrewd, crafty man with an extraordinary memory. When it became clear that he was the emperor's favorite who could dispense favors, all officials, high and low, sought his patronage and competed to join "the eunuch's clique." As his power increased, he rewarded and punished government officials in accordance with their loyalty to him. Meanwhile, he kept the young emperor happy and content with "prostitutes, entertainers, good horses, and fast hounds." At the height of his power, all high-ranking officials, from cabinet ministers to provincial governors, were his personal followers, and no man could hold office long if he were considered the eunuch's enemy. Many governors, only too eager to please the new strong man, launched a shameless movement of temple building to honor the "grand" eunuch. The building of temples to honor great men of the past such as Confucius and Chu Hsi was a common practice in China, but to build temples to honor a contemporary was a rare occurrence. The temples of Wei Chung-hsien went up all over China; in Confucian temples sometimes the "grand" eunuch's name was placed side by side with that of Confucius. Of course, not all gentry scholars joined "the eunuch's clique." Those who opposed the "grand" eunuch formed their own clique called Tung-lin, named after an academy at Wusih (Kiangsu province) where many of the anti-eunuch Confucian scholars taught. But as long as the emperor placed confidence in eunuch Wei, there was nothing these Tung-lin members could do. It was not until 1627 when Ming Hsi-tsung died that the eunuch's political machine finally collapsed.

What made eunuch rule particularly objectionable was that whenever it occurred, it was inevitably accompanied by nepotism and corruption. Most of the eunuchs were either illiterate or poorly educated. Usually they came from families of dubious background, for obviously no decent family would allow its members to pursue the career of a eunuch. This lack of education possibly explains why it was that, as a group, they were the most unprincipled in Chinese politics. To them power and wealth were an end, not a means. They had no interest in national welfare; nor could they stand political opposition. They rated government officials according to their loyalty rather than their performance and, as a result, the incompetent and morally degenerated occupied the key positions in the government. These people had no other desire except to stay in power and to enrich themselves further. Early in the sixteenth century when one of the eunuchs was sentenced to death on the ground that he had "peddled influence, dismissed upright scholars, and conspired to commit treason," he was found to have possessed, among other things, 2.5 million taels of gold and 50 million taels of silver. The confiscated valuables of Wei Chung-hsien were said to have been even larger. Whenever it appeared, eunuch rule was always one of the worst in Chinese history.

However strong it was, eunuch power was basically transitory and unstable because it had no theoretical or constitutional basis. Confucian theorists had always condemned it on principle and denounced eunuchs in power as usurpers. A eunuch might rise quickly, but his power could also collapse at any moment. During the Ming dynasty, for instance, a eunuch could enjoy power as long as he enjoyed the emperor's confidence. The withdrawal of favor meant not only political oblivion but very likely death as well. Most of the Ming eunuchs who had exercised great power died an unnatural death. After an emperor died, his successor invariably found it politically wise to punish the eunuchs severely for real or imaginary crimes they had committed. Wei Chung-hsien, for instance, was forced to hang himself soon after the new emperor Ch'ung-chen ascended the throne.

As the Ming regime declined, nepotism, corruption, and incompetence were found in local as well as the imperial government. The first century of honest and efficient rule was now past. In the provinces, local officials and big landlords often worked together to advance their respective interests. These officials were appointed by and responsible to their bureaucratic superiors, and they could, if they chose, completely ignore local opinion. As long as their superiors were satisfied, there was little the local populace could do, unless they wished to express their grievances in a violent manner such as riots and revolt. These officials could hardly be expected to be virtuous when their superiors in the capital were the even less virtuous eunuchs. The officials enriched themselves as fast as they could and by whatever means they could find before a shift of power in the capital sent them home jobless and powerless. As all government officials were appointed, they, in turn, rewarded their own henchmen with governmental positions within their jurisdiction. When there were no positions, they created new ones. In fact, many officials were paid salaries even though they had nothing in particular to do. In some areas the office of superintendency of rivers was maintained long after such rivers had changed courses and when there were no more rivers to supervise. This expanded, wasteful bureaucracy necessitated higher taxation which placed an additional burden on the taxpayers.

The big landlords, on the other hand, were interested in enlarging their estates. During the Ming dynasty private landholdings of large size were called *chuang-t'ien,* or plantations. Among them the royal plantations (*huang-chuang*) owned by the imperial household were by far the largest. Most plantations were created by royal decree. After the founding of the Ming regime, Chu Yüan-chang rewarded his relatives, generals, and ministers with large tracts of land. His successors followed this practice as a matter of usage. These plantations varied in size, from 100 *ch'ing* (c. 1,500 acres) to sometimes 7,000 *ch'ing* (c. 105,900 acres). Once they were created, they were often enlarged by illegal or pseudo-legal methods. Farmers who owned land adjacent to the plantations were often "persuaded" to sell their holdings at lower than market prices to the plantation owners. If they refused to be "persuaded," the plantation managers might decide to use force to evict them from their holdings. To bring complaints before the law was often worse than useless because local officials were in no position to challenge the authority of plantation owners and could only do so at their own peril. With odds heavily against them, small farmers sometimes found it wise to hand over their holdings "voluntarily" to the big landlords without asking for compensation, once they knew that their powerful neighbors had coveted their land for some time. In other cases their holdings were "offered" to plantation owners as "presents" without their knowledge; apparently someone had forged their names to make such a presentation. It was useless to protest when the plantation owners had already expressed their "gracious appreciation for such generous gifts."

The owners of these big plantations lived in the capital or in other large cities; it was their managers who supervised the operation of their estates in the countryside. These managers were so anxious to produce "good" results that often they employed the most dubious means in achieving them. The managers worked closely with local officials who were expected to support them in their various schemes. Whenever their overt actions aroused public anger, these officials were counted on to minimize legal consequences. In 1489 the Minister of Finance Li Min, in a memorial to the reigning emperor, described the situation as follows:

> Within the capital area there are five royal plantations with a total acreage of 12,800 *ch'ing* (c. 193,860 acres). Besides these, there are 332 plantations with a total acreage of 33,000 *ch'ing* (c. 499,290 acres) owned by royal relatives and eunuchs. Plantation managers and their subordinates hire hoodlums and ruffians to do their bidding. They forcibly take over people's land, extort their money and other valuables, and debauch their wives and daughters. If people dare to make the slightest protest, they find themselves being sued on fabricated charges. The sheriff comes to arrest them, and their whole families tremble with fear. This is why people hate the plantation managers to the marrow of their bones.[1]

While plantations represented the largest and perhaps the worst form of land concentration, there were lesser landlords who exercised power and influence in their communities in proportion to the size of their holdings. To be sure, not all landlords were ruthless exploiters; nor were all

---

[1] Translated from the official *History of the Ming* (*Ming shih*). This passage appears in the first section of *Economics* (*Shih-huo chih*) dealing with land tenure.

government officials corrupt. The truth seems to be that as members of the gentry class most of the landlords tried to live up to their reputation as respectable community leaders. They supposedly set moral examples for their peasant neighbors and perhaps most of them did. However, in a country where there was a large population in proportion to the amount of land suitable for cultivation, land concentration intensified the contrast between the rich and the poor, for whatever was gained by one person had to be the loss of somebody else. As bureaucratic corruption became more widespread, small and tenant farmers found an increasingly unsympathetic or even hostile government unresponsive to their complaints. The few government officials who chose to champion their cause could only do so at the risk of their own positions. The Lower Yangtze basin was one of the richest areas in China, but early in the seventeenth century taxes were so heavy that sometimes small, independent farmers "have to sell their children to meet tax payments. When they still cannot pay the amount due, they desert their farmsteads, and their farms are left behind in waste. Meanwhile, the amount of tax due on these farms is piled up year after year." The lot of tenant farmers was even worse. According to Ku Yen-wu, a famous scholar who lived towards the end of the Ming dynasty, nine out of every ten farmers in the Lower Yangtze region were tenant farmers. He described their life as follows:

The fields they till are small in size. In assessing land for tax purposes, the government considers all ditches and roads that run through the farm as taxable areas. A tenant farmer reaps one harvest each year in the fall and collects anywhere from 1 to 3 piculs of unpolished grain for each *mou* of land. From this amount he pays his landlord anywhere from 8 pecks (0.8 piculs) to 1.3 piculs as rent. He works hard all year round, and a considerable time is devoted to the collection of human and animal waste to be used for fertilizers. His cash expenses for each *mou* of cultivated land are about one string of cash. Thus after the expenses are deducted, his harvest amounts to less than 1 picul per *mou*. It is not unusual that after his rent is paid today, he has to beg for food tomorrow.[1]

THE DOWNFALL

In 1628 when the last Ming emperor Ch'ung-chen ascended the throne, the regime had deteriorated to such an extent that nothing except a miracle could reverse the trend. Ch'ung-chen was one of the better emperors, conscientious and hard-working, but he could not stop the accelerating decline of the Ming regime. No sooner was he proclaimed emperor than he heard of a dreadful famine in Shensi province. One of the memorials he read described the situation as follows:

[1] Translated from *Jih-chih lu* or *The Daily Accumulated Knowledge*, roll 10.

Your humble servant was born in Anse subprefecture, Shensi province. I have read many memorials submitted by Your Majesty's officials in connection with the present state of affairs. They say that famine has caused fathers to desert their children and husbands to sell their wives. They also say that many people are so starved that they eat grass roots and white stones. But the real situation is worse than what they have described. Yenan, the prefecture from which your humble servant comes, has not had any rain for more than a year. Trees and grasses are all dried up. During the eighth and the ninth moon months of last year people went to the mountains to collect raspberries which were called grain but actually were no better than chaff. They tasted bitter and they could only postpone death for the time being. By the tenth moon month all raspberries were gone, and people peeled off tree bark for food. Among tree bark the best was that of the elm. This was so precious that to consume as little as possible people mixed it with the bark of other trees to feed themselves. Somehow they were able to prolong their lives. Towards the end of the year the supply of tree bark was exhausted, and they had to go to the mountains to dig up stones as food. Stones were cold and tasted musty. A little taken in would fill up the stomach. Those who took stones found their stomachs swollen and they dropped and died in a few days. Others who did not wish to eat stones gathered as bandits. They robbed the few who had some savings, and when they robbed, they took everything and left nothing behind. Their idea was that since they had to die either one way or another it was preferable to die as a bandit than to die from hunger and that to die as a bandit would enable them to enter the next world with a full stomach. . . .[1]

While starved peasants in northern Shensi ravaged the countryside in search of food, garrison soldiers in South Manchuria and Shensi mutinied because they had not been paid for a long time. To make the situation worse, the government decided in 1629 to cut down some of its administrative expenses by reducing the number of coolie couriers in Shansi and Shensi provinces. These coolie couriers, employed by government posts in carrying mails, were suddenly without jobs, and they too decided to join the rebels. In the same year the Manchus moved southward to attack Peking. Responding to the call from the imperial government for help, the governors from Shansi, Suiyuan, and Kansu led their soldiers eastward, only to see them mutiny on the road before they could reach the capital. These soldiers, like those of the Shensi and Manchuria garrisons, had not been paid for some time and they refused to obey any more orders. Thus the rebellion, first started by bands of starved peasants, was quickly joined by unemployed coolie couriers and soldier mutineers. The number of rebels continued to grow as other dissatisfied elements joined them en masse.

Early in the 1630's Chang Hsien-chung and Li Tzu-ch'eng emerged as the two leaders of the rebel forces. Both were born in Shensi, had a

[1] A copy of the Chinese original can be found in Chou Ku-ch'eng, A History of China (Chung-kuo t'ung-shih) (Shanghai, 1947), vol. 2, pp. 880–881.

common peasant background, and had received little or no education. Before the rebellion Chang was a mercenary soldier, and Li was first a coolie courier and then a Buddhist monk. Both had been once sentenced to death on account of crimes or alleged crimes and managed to escape through some devious methods. When the starving peasants began to revolt in 1628, Li was among the first to join them. Chang joined two years later after he had collected a small following. From 1628 to 1635 the rebels were most active in the Northwest, though occasionally they moved eastward to Honan and Hupeh and southward to Szechuan. In the latter year rebel forces had snowballed to more than 400,000, and at the suggestion of Li Tzu-ch'eng their leaders decided to move eastward to contend for all of China. Government troops that were sent against them retreated or otherwise dispersed before the marauding hordes. City after city surrendered without a fight, and others were captured after a brief engagement. To encourage surrender, the rebels announced that they would not take away a single life if a city surrendered the day they arrived. However, if it chose to defend itself for one day, 30 percent of the city's population would be put to death; 70 percent would be killed if it were defended for two days; and the entire city would be destroyed if it hesitated for more than three days before opening its gates. Among the things they looted they kept for themselves horses and arms; food, cloth, and money were generously distributed among starving peasants. They promised to abolish taxation forever if they won. And many peasants believed in them.

The rebel ranks soon split into two groups. One group led by Li Tzu-ch'eng ravaged the Yellow River basin; the other, led by Chang Hsien-chung, moved up and down the Yangtze River valley, killing and burning as it went. Chang Hsien-chung was one of the most bloodthirsty persons ever recorded in Chinese history and was said to have felt uncomfortable if he did not see somebody killed each day. His favorite targets were the Ming nobility, the bureaucrats, and the intellectuals. In one instance, he called students to take his civil service examinations, but when they arrived, he ordered all of them to be slaughtered in cold blood. His generals were rated according to the number of people they had killed; some of his generals were sentenced to death simply because they had not killed enough to meet the norm. In Chengtu, Szechuan province, there stands a monument believed to have been erected by Chang Hsien-chung. The monument bears the following inscriptions:

> Heaven produces myriads of things to nourish man;
> Man never does one good to recompense Heaven.
> Kill, kill, kill, kill, kill, kill, and kill!

It seems that he sought neither fame nor wealth, but the power to destroy. In one case, he dammed a river and placed millions of dollars' worth of gold, silver, and precious stones on the dried river bed, and then ordered the dam be broken so that all these valuables would be washed away towards the sea. Why did he do this? Because, said he, he wanted these valuables to be denied to posterity. From 1630 when he joined the rebels to 1646 when he was finally captured, millions of innocent people died victims of this psychopath. The most devastated area was Szechuan which at one time was said to have "few" people left. When the Manchus marched towards Szechuan, many people looked to them as their saviors. In 1646 one of Chang's generals deserted him and led the Manchus to his stronghold. Chang was wounded by a flying arrow and the pursuing Manchus found him hidden underneath a pile of firewood in a small village. He was captured and subsequently beheaded.

Equally ferocious but perhaps less brutal was Li Tzu-ch'eng, nick-named "The Dashing King." In the beginning he was no better than other rebels; his hordes plundered, burned, and slaughtered wherever they went. After most of North China was brought under his control, he began to think seriously of being a contender for the Ming throne. He promised to abolish taxation to win the support of peasants and imposed some discipline on his marauding soldiers. His soldiers were no longer allowed to plunder and rape, while money, grain, and cloth which he stole from the rich were handed over to the very poor as relief. In 1643 he declared the establishment of a new regime at Sian (formerly Ch'angan) and organized his government according to the Ming pattern. In the same year his troops entered Peking without encountering much opposition. The last Ming emperor Ch'ung-chen hanged himself on the Coal Mountain behind the Forbidden City, after his wife the empress had committed suicide before him. Fearing that his beloved daughter, the First Princess, would be molested by the rebels if she fell into their hands, he proposed to kill her with a long sword. Sobbing audibly, he said to her: "Why did you have to be born a princess?"

Thus the Ming dynasty came to an end after an existence of 277 years.

INTELLECTUAL AND CULTURAL ACTIVITIES

Though he distrusted intellectuals and often subjected them to public humiliation, Chu Yüan-chang knew that he needed educated men to staff his bureaucracy and assist him in running his empire. In 1375 he ordered the establishment of a nation-wide school system. Schools were to be established in every prefecture and subprefecture, and their maintenance would be subsidized by the government. To enroll in one of these schools, a prospective student had to be a relative of a government official. If he were not, he had to possess additional qualifications: he must be over the age of fifteen, had to show promise as a scholar, and must already have mastered the *Four Books*. The same decree also called for the establishment of village schools, "one in every thirty-five households," though we have no idea how effectively this was carried out. These village schools taught the fundamentals: reading and writing, simple mathematics, and Confucian morality. Students who had shown promise as scholars would be encouraged to continue their education in nearby cities. Besides the government-sponsored schools, there were also private institutions supported by high officials, big landlords, or sometimes rich merchants. There were more than three hundred private academies (*shu-yüan*) in the country, and generally speaking, they were of a better quality than government-sponsored schools. To attend school was, of course, not compulsory. A child of wealthy parents was more likely to be tutored at home, and often his teacher was a disappointed, unsuccessful candidate in the civil service examinations. Tutoring provided the most intensive training and was preferred by parents if they had the financials means, because tutors, in most cases, roomed and boarded in the houses of their employers and had daily contact with their charges. Sometimes two or three families pooled their resources and jointly hired a tutor.

The decisive moment arrived when the student took the lowest level of the civil service examination. According to the Ming practice, a student had to pass the preliminary examination in his subprefecture (*hsien,* sometimes translated as "district" or "county") first before he could take the lowest level of the civil service examination which was held twice every three years in the capital city of a prefecture (*fu*). If he passed the prefectural examination, he received the degree *hsiu-ts'ai* ("flowering talent") which qualified him to take the preliminary test for the second level of the civil service examination. The second level of the civil service examination was held in the provincial capital once every three years, and the successful candidate was called a *chü-jen* ("recommended man"). Only a *chü-jen* was eligible to compete in the imperial or metropolitan examination which, like the provincial examination, was held triennially. Students all over the country gathered in Peking for this occasion, and the successful competitors were awarded the highest degree *chin-shih* ("advanced scholarship"). All *chin-shih* were personally interviewed by the emperor who, after the interview, would decide the order of the top candidates. The person whose name was placed at the head of the list was called *chuang-yüan* ("number one"), the highest goal of every scholar in the nation. He and his fellow *chin-shih* were entitled to appointment to governmental posts. Without much modification, the examination system described above was followed throughout the Ming-Ch'ing period.

Most of the successful candidates in the imperial examinations could look forward to governmental careers on the lower levels of the bureaucracy, and they were sent out to various parts of the empire to be "fathers and mothers" of the people. A selected few who had shown great talent and originality would be appointed as research fellows in the nation's highest academic institution, the Hanlin ("Forest of Culture") Academy. The origin of this institution can be traced back to the T'ang dynasty, but it was not until the Sung dynasty that it was perfected as a purely academic institution. Under the Sung the research fellows were not assigned any particular task to perform; rather, they were paid to read or write whatever they pleased. The institution was referred to by contemporaries as a "talent reservoir" from which, it was hoped, the greatest and ablest ministers would eventually emerge. Generally speaking, the Ming regime followed the Sung precedent with regard to the purpose and functions of the Hanlin Academy, though from time to time the Hanlin scholars would be called to perform such "practical" tasks as drafting decrees for the imperial government or giving counsel on historical precedents. They could also take the initiative to petition the emperor with regard to policy, and in that case they became actively involved in politics. Oftentimes, a government official was assigned to the academy as a research fellow when there was no appropriate opening suited for his talent. When he was given a post to hold, he could expect higher rank and a more responsible position compared to those ordinarily awarded to *chin-shih* scholars. After Yung-lo became the emperor, he enlarged the Hanlin Academy by creating the position of "research associates" (*shu-chi-shih*). As their title implied, the research associates did not command the same prestige as the research fellows. They were chosen from the *chin-shih* scholars who did not score high in the metropolitan examinations. The Hanlin Academy remained the nation's highest academic institution throughout the Ming-Ch'ing period.

As for intellectual achievements, the Ming dynasty lagged behind its more illustrious predecessors, Han, T'ang, and Sung. It did not produce great thinkers of originality with the possible exception of Wang Shou-jen (also known as Wang Yang-ming, 1472–1529). Wang, a holder of the *chin-shih* degree, had a distinguished career as a government official, but he was most famous for his philosophy of "innate knowledge" (*liang-chih*). He maintained that all knowledge existed within one's inner self and that it could not be obtained by investigating outward things. To seek knowledge outside oneself was to place the cart before the horse and was useless and futile, because there could not be any truth if one's mind did not exist. He only needed to look at his own inner mind to obtain the absolute truth, and if his inner mind were rectified, the truth of the outside world would reveal itself. He, in fact, was the center of all truths, and "all things are complete within me." To find truth and knowledge was therefore to find oneself. How to find oneself? He needed to investigate his inner mind and concentrate his thought, and the truth of the universe would ultimately come to him through a sudden flash of insight. He and the universe would then become one, a single entity inseparable.

This sounds like Ch'an Buddhism; in fact, Wang Shou-jen was perhaps influenced by it. However, the truth in Wang's philosophy was not a metaphysical truth as it was in Buddhism; it was a moral truth as it had been advocated for centuries by Confucian scholars. Using Buddhist tools, Wang attempted to achieve an essentially Confucian purpose. To him, knowledge and truth were not ends by themselves. They should lead to right conduct, conduct that would benefit one's fellow men. To use his own words, "Knowledge is merely the beginning of conduct; conduct is the completion of knowledge." Knowledge was meaningless and useless without conduct. In other words, the acquirement of absolute truth was not the attainment of *nirvana* as it was in Buddhism; it merely equipped the enlightened man with the necessary means to enlighten others. The ultimate purpose was not the salvation of individual souls; it was the betterment of society. Wang did not advocate escape from the physical world; on the contrary, he urged people to go deeper into it. In that sense, his philosophy was worldly and humanistic; it was basically Confucian. It was similar to the doctrine that had been expounded earlier by the Sung scholar Lu Chiu-yüan. In fact, this philosophy of emphasizing "innate knowledge" has been referred to as the Lu-Wang School by historians.

Unlike Wang Shou-jen, most Ming scholars were busy with less abstract work, commenting, editing, and compiling existing works. In terms of influence on later generations, few works of the Ming period were more important than *The Outline of Herb Medicine* (*Pen-ts'ao kang-mu*) edited and compiled by Li Shih-chen. Since its completion in 1578, it has been the basic text in the hands of every Chinese doctor who practices the traditional medicine. Remarkable as Li was, the authors of the official *History of the Ming* (*Ming shih*, compiled under the the Manchu government's sponsorship and completed in 1739) devoted only a few paragraphs to him, even though his book had perhaps saved more lives than any other Ming scholar or statesman ever did. His brief appearance in the dynastic history shows the traditional antiscience bent, and to traditional historians the moralists who taught people how to live were always more important than the scientists who taught people how to live longer. According to this brief biography, Li Shih-chen consulted more than 800 existing works, checked and rechecked their possible errors, and worked thirty years before his work was completed. The final work consisted of 16 volumes of 52 rolls. It listed 1,932 different animal, vegetable, and mineral drugs and more than 8,000 prescriptions. All drugs were classified and itemized; each of them was accompanied by an illustration, with detailed information on its origin, color, shape, and smell. It was the most complete medical work China had ever produced.

A POET WANDERING IN THE MOONLIGHT This picture was painted by Tu Chin, who lived in the fifteenth century. The Chinese characters in the picture are a seven-character poem written by the painter to describe the scene. A typical seven-character poem has four lines, each consisting of seven characters. These lines are rarely separated, however; nor are punctuation marks used.

Monumental though it was, *The Outline of Herb Medicine* was a small work compared with the gigantic *Yung-lo Encyclopedia* (*Yung-lo ta-tien*). The compilation of this encyclopedia began in 1403 under the sponsorship of the emperor Yung-lo and was completed four years later. It consisted of all major works in Confucian classics, history, philosophy, and miscellaneous subjects, totalling 22,877 rolls and involving the work of 2,316 scholars. Originally, the government planned to print it, but abandoned its project when the estimated cost proved to be too great. Consequently, only three hand-written copies were made; two were housed in Peking and one in Nanking. The compilation of the *Encyclopedia* was by far the largest literary project ever undertaken by the Ming government.

In the field of fine arts the Ming dynasty was most famous for its painters. Among the painters one of the best known was T'ang Yin who lived in Soochow (modern Kiangsu) early in the sixteenth century. Proclaimed a true genius by his contemporaries, he nevertheless decided to forego a governmental career after he had passed the provincial level of the civil service examination and chose a life of "wine, women, and song" instead. His numerous antics included the impersonation of a humble servant to seek employment in a gentleman's house so that he could be close to a maid whose beauty he greatly admired. He achieved what he had set out to achieve and cared not what other people thought of his personal life. Interestingly enough, his "improper conduct" was dismissed by many of his contemporaries as an unavoidable attribute of a true genius who happened to be a libertine by nature. Though he was described as a prolific painter to whose door "people of all walks of life come daily to beg for paintings," only a few of his paintings have survived. The other famous painter was Tung Ch'i-ch'ang (d. 1636) who, unlike T'ang Yin, lived a virtuous, Confucian life for 83 years and had a distinguished career as a government official. Besides, he was a historian, a calligrapher, and above all, a painter. According to the official *History of the Ming*, even a short note of his was a collector's item, eagerly sought after in the open market and commanding a high price. As a painter, he first followed the style of the Sung painter Mi Fei and eventually established an independent style of his own. He specialized in landscape, and his landscapes were said to have synthesized the best of all paintings since the Sung dynasty. To many of his contemporaries, he was the greatest painter of the Ming dynasty, surpassing all others, including T'ang Yin.

X

Ch'ing

THE MANCHUS

The Great Wall, originally built in the third century B.C., served as a defense shield against northern nomads throughout most of Chinese history. The eastern end of the Wall was the city Shanhaikuan which occupied a narrow level land between the rising mountains in the west and the Gulf of Pohai in the east. Shanhaikuan, literally translated, means "the Pass between the Mountain and the Sea." The pass was so narrow that those who held it controlled the access to or from Manchuria and, once it was taken by an enemy, the road to Peking would be wide open. To defend Peking, the Chinese had to defend Shanhaikuan at all costs. Early in 1644 when Li Tzu-ch'eng and his rebels entered Peking, the Ming garrison commander at Shanhaikuan was a man named Wu San-kuei. After entering the capital, the rebels captured his father and used him as

307

hostage to demand Wu's surrender. Fearing for his father's life, Wu led his troops westward with the intention of complying with the demand. However, he soon learned that his favorite concubine Ch'en Yüan had been kidnapped by one of the rebel generals, and hating the thought that she was now in the arms of another man, he vowed revenge. Instead of surrendering to the rebels, he returned to Shanhaikuan and decided to fight. Yet he knew that the odds were heavily against him if he fought alone. In desperation he sought help from the Manchus. He opened the Pass between the Mountain and the Sea, and the Manchus poured in. The invited "barbarians" not only defeated Li and his rebels but established a new dynasty in China as well. The new dynasty was Ch'ing which lasted more than two and one-half centuries until 1911.

The Manchus sprang from the same Tungusic stock as the Nuchens who at one time occupied North China and founded the Chin dynasty (1122-1234). Their home was the woodlands in southern and eastern Manchuria, east of the Liao River and west of the Manchuria-Korean border. Their economy was largely pastoral, though centuries of contact with the Chinese had converted a considerable portion of them into sedentary farmers. The conflict between the Chinese and the Tungus began as early as written history began, mostly because both sides coveted the rich, agricultural area in South Manchuria. During the period of Warring States (403–221 B.C.) the northernmost state Yen pushed the Tungus deep into the wooded north and forcibly took over the Liao River basin. After Ch'in's unification of China (221 B.C.) Manchuria was incorporated as part of China and governed as an administrative province. Enticed by the cheap, rich farmland, Chinese immigrants came in increasingly large numbers. However, located on the frontier and surrounded by hostile nomads, South Manchuria was difficult for China to hold. Whenever the central authority in China proper weakened, South Manchuria would be conquered by the Tungus or other non-Chinese tribes. The Tungus annexed it during T'ang's decline in the eighth century and created a new kingdom called P'o-hai (713–926). At its height, P'o-hai's territory covered southern and eastern Manchuria and the northeastern corner of Korea. Throughout the Sung dynasty South Manchuria was a part of the Khitan empire of Liao and then a part of the Tungusic empire of Chin. During the Yüan dynasty practically everyone in Asia was either directly or indirectly under the Mongol rule, including the Chinese in South Manchuria and the various Tungusic tribes such as the Manchus.

Thus, after the eighth century South Manchuria had been continuously under non-Chinese rule, and it was not brought under Chinese jurisdiction until the Ming dynasty when again the Chinese extended their military might north of the Great Wall. Chinese immigration to South Manchuria was revived, and the land-hungry Chinese peasants opened the virgin forests as eagerly as their countrymen had done before

the eighth century. As the Chinese relentlessly pushed forward the frontier of agriculture, they ran into difficulty with the non-Chinese tribes
who naturally wished to keep these wooded areas as their pastoral preserve. This difficulty was further compounded by other problems involving
trade. The non-Chinese tribes in Manchuria were not economically self-
sufficient, and they needed trade to obtain agricultural products from the
Chinese. Realizing their need, the Chinese government often used trade
as a political weapon; it suspended or threatened to suspend trade whenever it thought that "the barbarians had behaved in an outrageous manner." As trade was officially supervised, Chinese officials were in a position
to regulate price, and prices of foreign products were often artificially
depressed to the disadvantage of tribal traders. Moreover, tariff duties
imposed on imported and exported merchandise were heavy and unspeci-
fied. This uncertainty of tariff levies provided a flourishing ground for the
growth of corruption on the part of Chinese officials.

Whatever injustices the Ming government might have done to the
Manchus and other non-Chinese tribes in Manchuria, it could always
make its will prevail as long as it remained militarily strong. It could no
longer do so when its military strength declined during the second half
of the sixteenth century. The Ming government, like many of its predecessors, incorporated South Machuria as a part of China. As Ming's military
strength declined, South Manchuria became more and more a military
liability since it was surrounded on three sides by hostile non-Chinese
tribes and was linked to China proper largely through the narrow pass of
Shanhaikuan. Logistical support became extremely difficult if the enemy
could somehow cut off the normal supply line along the northern shore of
the Pohai Gulf. During the second half of the sixteenth century the Chinese settlements in the Liao River basin were subject to increasing pressure from the surrounding nomads who raided and ravaged whenever
these settlements were inadequately defended. Often the Ming government retaliated by suspending trade with the offending tribes, only to see
the raids become more frequent and more intensified because the enemy, denied trade to obtain what he needed, resorted to more violent
means to achieve his purpose. Early in the seventeenth century the government found that it could no longer defend all Chinese settlements in
South Manchuria, and those located on its fringe and close to the nomadic
areas had to be abandoned. Whenever the settlers refused to leave, they
were forcibly evicted and resettled in more defensible regions. The abandoned areas were soon taken over by the non-Chinese tribes.

While the Ming government was making a strategic retreat in South
Manchuria, the Manchus rose steadily to take its place. Nominally they
were Chinese vassals and as such they were allowed to trade at specifically
designated places. Their main exports were horses, lumber, and genseng.
The last-mentioned was a herb medicine believed to have the power of

rejuvenation and had a large market in China proper. As Ming power declined, the Manchus, like other non-Chinese tribes, found it more profitable to raid than to trade. At the beginning the raids were largely economically motivated, but early in the seventeenth century these desultory raids were coordinated and became part of an over-all strategy aimed at military conquest. This shift took place under the great leader Nurhachi (1559–1626), who succeeded his father as a tribal chief and Chinese vassal in 1584. Secretly preparing his tribe and himself for "the great deed," he tried to avoid Ming's suspicion by performing faithfully all the rituals required of a Ming vassal and by repeatedly sending tribute missions to Peking. At one time (1590) he personally led a tribute mission to pay his homage to the reigning emperor. Little did the Ming government know then that underneath his humble appearance was the burning ambition of a powerful opponent.

While Ming's suspicion was in abeyance, Nurhachi annexed and unified all Manchu tribes under his personal control. He organized his own military machinery through the creation of the "banner" system. The banner system was a politico-military organization to incorporate all Manchu tribesmen into new administrative units (first four and later eight) called banners, and all Manchus, including their captives and slaves, were required to register under assigned banners. Each banner was headed by an appointed official personally loyal to Nurhachi rather than the hereditary tribal chieftains. It was called the banner system because each organizational unit was identified by a banner of a specified color. After the Manchus began to expand and brought non-Manchus under their jurisdiction, sixteen more banners were added, eight Chinese and eight Mongol, making a total of twenty-four. Each banner contributed a certain number of fighting men whenever a Manchu ruler was engaged in war, the number varying in accordance with the purpose and scope of the war efforts. By 1644 when the Manchus began the conquest of China proper, the total number of their fighting men was approximately 170,000.

In 1616 when his preparations were complete, Nurhachi raised the standard of revolt and called his newly created regime Later Chin. Two years later he announced his famous "Seven Grievances" against the Ming regime and declared war. The Ming government retaliated by sending 200,000 men to Manchuria, only to see them decisively defeated by the outnumbered but hard-fighting Manchus. Realizing their relative weakness in fighting pitched battles, later Ming generals adopted the Fabian strategy of building strong fortifications at strategic points and shutting themselves behind these strongholds, hoping to wear out the limited resources of the enemy and eventually to force him to sue for peace. However, the Manchus captured the countryside to isolate these strongholds and in due time were able to capture cities as well, such as Mukden. In

1626 Nurhachi died of battle wounds sustained during an attack on a Ming stronghold and was succeeded by his son Abahai, known also by his posthumous title, Ch'ing T'ai-tsung. Abahai attacked and defeated Korea in 1627 and concluded the war with a peace treaty whereby Korea promised to supply the Manchus with grain and open markets for trade. Korea, in fact, became a Manchu protectorate. With his rear safe and secure, he attacked the Ming fortification Ningyüan but was pushed back with heavy losses. With the resources of all China at its disposal, it seemed that the Ming regime could have held South Manchuria indefinitely had it not deteriorated so fast at home.

After 1628 and for almost two decades the regime was beset with nation-wide rebellions. It could no longer concentrate its efforts in the Manchurian campaign. The situation was not helped when it executed some of its ablest generals whenever they suffered a temporary setback. Summary punishments like this inadvertently helped the enemy's cause; several Ming generals surrendered to the enemy because they no longer felt safe. In 1632 the Manchus completed the conquest of Inner Mongolia, and thus the entire northern frontier was subject to the Manchus' direct attack. The same year also saw the Manchus change their dynastic title from Later Chin to Ch'ing. With their rear safely secured, they repeatedly entered China proper and at one time (1638) went as far as Shantung province and captured its capital Tsinan. They withdrew only when they had obviously overextended themselves. Many Chinese generals, tempted by Manchus with offers of higher positions and more responsibilities, voluntarily surrendered; two such generals brought with them Portuguese cannons which greatly facilitated the capture of Ming's walled cities. From the point of morale, the most damaging surrender was that of Hung Ch'eng-ch'ou who had under his command some 130,000 troops at one time. An upright statesman and scholar, he was expected to commit suicide when his army was defeated and he himself was captured. When the news arrived at Peking that he had surrendered to the enemy, the shock was greater than any reverse the Ming regime had suffered. In the minds of many Chinese a man like him symbolized the "national spirit," and when he surrendered, the nation's morale and pride were damaged beyond repair.

In 1643 Abahai died and was succeeded by his six-year-old son Shun-chih (1644–1661). Abahai's brother Dorgon (1612–1650) served as regent. One year later the Ming general Wu San-kuei surrendered Shanhaikuan to the Manchus. Rebel Li Tzu-ch'eng fled westward to Sian and the Imperial City fell into the hands of the Manchus. Once again China was ruled by an alien regime.

However, it took many more years before China was completely pacified. In South China the Ming loyalists continued to fight and installed various members of the royal house as claimants to the Ming throne.

There were Prince Fu at Nanking, Prince Lu at Chekiang, Prince T'ang at Fukien, and Prince Kuei at Kwangtung. But the resistance movement was neither coordinated nor effective. The Manchus pushed relentlessly south-ward, and their Chinese generals such as Hung Ch'eng-ch'ou and Wu San-kuei paved the way as vanguards. In the spring of 1645 the victorious Manchus passed across the Yangtze River and captured Nanking. In the next year the resistance movement centered at Fukien also collapsed. The last claimant to the Ming throne, Prince Yung-ming, moved from Kwang-tung to Kwangsi and then to Yunnan, always with a pursuing enemy be-hind him. In 1659 he escaped to Burma where he established a govern-ment-in-exile for two years. The Burmese, fearing that the Manchus might use his presence in Burma as an excuse to invade their country, attacked and captured him and handed him over to the Manchu garrison com-mander across the border. He was subsequently hanged, and the Ming line was thus exterminated.

CONSOLIDATION AND EXPANSION

In less than three generations a small tribe succeeded in conquering and imposing its rule on the largest nation on earth. How was the success to be explained? First, the Manchus rose at the propitious moment of Ming's decline. Early in the seventeenth century all the classic features indicating the approaching of the dynasty's downfall were in evidence: feeble and effeminate rulers, a corrupt bureaucracy, incompetence and factional strife among government officials, natural disasters, and finally internal rebellions. If the Manchus had not replaced the Ming regime, it was likely that some other foreigners or internal rebels would. On the other hand, the fact that it was the Manchus and not any other group who succeeded in overthrowing the Ming regime spoke eloquently of their intrinsic strength. When Nurhachi succeeded his father as a tribal chief in 1584, he is believed to have had no more than five or six hundred fighting men under his control. With these men as a nucleus he built a strong military machine which enabled him to start his career of conquest. Among the many factors that contributed to the Manchus' spectacular success, none was more important than the fact that they had a long string of capable leaders. Nurhachi was succeeded by the equally able Abahai. After Abahai died, it was fortunate that Dorgon—the Conqueror of China—served as regent while the boy emperor Shun-chih was a minor. This string of capable leaders extended long after China had been conquered. The three emperors after Shun-chih, in the order of succession, were K'ang-hsi, Yung-cheng and Ch'ien-lung. It was during their reigns that the Ch'ing dynasty reached its most glorious age. Thus for six consecutive generations, one able emperor followed another. This had not happened to any other dynasty in the course of Chinese history.

All the early Ch'ing emperors realized that to conquer China and to rule it successfully, they had first, to adopt Chinese culture and Chinese institutions, and second, to win the support of the Chinese population, especially that of the scholar-gentry class. The banner system, first introduced by Nurhachi, was essentially an adaptation of a bureaucratic system to tribal conditions, and as such, there was no difficulty in utilizing it within agrarian China, once the Manchus had conquered Chinese territories. Nurhachi ordered the translation of Confucian works and Ming penal codes into his newly invented Manchu alphabet and adopted Chinese institutions to suit his own purpose. This voluntary Sinicization was continued by his successors. The dynastic title was the Sinicized word Ch'ing (pure), and all Manchu rulers assumed, and were given posthumously, Chinese titles. Chinese scholars were invited to staff the Ch'ing bureaucracy, and Chinese generals were encouraged to surrender. Once they surrendered, they were given higher or better positions in the new government. Sometimes the same generals who had suffered repeated defeats under the Ming regime performed remarkably well once they switched their loyalty and fought for the Manchus. Some of the most famous field commanders who conquered China for the Manchus were Chinese, such as Hung Ch'eng-ch'ou, Wu San-Kuei, Keng Chung-ming, and Shang K'o-hsi. All of them had served the Ming government at one time or another. The decaying Ming could not use fully their talents, but the young, vigorous Ch'ing regime could.

Fortunately for the new dynasty, it had a wise, intelligent statesman to give it direction during the most crucial years after it had entered China proper. He was Dorgon (1612–1650), fourteenth son of Nurhachi and uncle of the reigning emperor Shun-chih. He was learned in Confucian ideals and Chinese institutions, and one of the letters, addressed to a Ming general, that bore his name can still be found, as an example of literary excellence, in many Chinese textbooks. His whole regime was Chinese orientated. The administrative apparatus of the defunct Ming government was adopted without much modification, and Ching regarded itself as the legitimate heir to Ming which, it believed, had lost the mandate of Heaven. After the Manchus' entry into China proper, Dorgon, on behalf of the boy emperor, adopted a series of measures aimed at winning Chinese support. All incumbents of the old regime were encouraged to stay on their jobs and could expect to be promoted by one rank if they voluntarily surrendered themselves to the victorious Manchu army. Local officials were requested to recommend men of wisdom and ability to serve the new regime, and no questions would be asked about their past loyalties. Taxes were to be reduced and all extra levies besides the regular tax load were to be thereafter abolished. The new government vowed to punish severely all incompetent and corrupt officials, and the inspector-generals and censors were instructed to personally visit the populace "to inquire about their sicknesses and sorrows." The Manchus were forbidden to behave like conquerors and to use their privileged position to violate the law and enrich themselves. This policy of winning Chinese support worked well and yielded good results. When the Chinese were ordered to shave part of their heads to indicate their loyalty to the new regime, all Chinese except the staunch Ming loyalists complied. By winning Chinese support, the Manchus, who constituted no more than 2 percent of the population in China, were able to maintain themselves in China for almost three hundred years.

The general cooperation on the part of the Chinese population enabled the Ch'ing government to crush two simultaneous, though not coordinated, rebellions. The leader of the first rebellion was Wu San-kuei who in 1644 had opened Shanhaikuan to lead the Manchus into China proper, and who, together with other Chinese collaborators, was responsible for the elimination of Chinese resistance. The Manchus rewarded him lavishly, awarding him the title of prince and marrying one of the Manchu princesses to his son. He was made a virtual dictator in China's Southwest. He recruited his own bureaucratic personnel, maintained his own army, and strengthened his domains economically by establishing mining and trade monopolies. Meanwhile, the central treasury at Peking subsidized him with a yearly amount of nine million taels of silver.

As his power and wealth increased, he became more arrogant and indiscreet. Obviously this situation could not last indefinitely. In 1673 the Ch'ing government decided to take away his command and ordered him to leave for Manchuria to live in retirement. Facing the prospect of political oblivion, he raised the standard of revolt. He persuaded two other governors-general (one at Kwangtung and another at Fukien) to join his revolt because these two governors-general had also enjoyed a semi-independent status and had been ordered to leave their command. At one time more than one-third of China proper fell into the rebels' hands and rebel influence extended from Kwangtung and Fukien in the Southeast to Kansu and Shensi in the Northwest. But slowly and steadily the Ch'ing government fought back. After Wu San-kuei died in 1678, the rebellion soon collapsed.

Why did this happen? First, the majority of the Chinese population, especially the scholar-gentry class, were on the side of the existing government and against the rebels. The regime was young and vigorous and there was a rising prosperity. The Chinese were in no mood for another change. Second, the cause of nationalism which Wu and his fellow rebels invoked to rationalize their revolt was no longer a valid issue because most Chinese had accepted the new dynasty as legitimately Chinese.

Furthermore, it was not convincing because all of the three rebel leaders had once served and then betrayed the Chinese Ming regime and had led the way to the conquest of China by their Manchu masters. As far as most Chinese were concerned, they should be the last ones to advocate Chinese nationalism.

The other rebellion was led by a man of higher principle named Cheng Ch'eng-kung or Koxinga (1624–1662). Cheng's father was an ex-pirate who surrendered to Ming in 1627 and, then being made a Ming official, came to control overseas and coastal trade in Fukien province. When the Manchus marched to the Southeast, he surrendered his men and ships to ingratiate himself with the new regime. His son, then a boy of twenty-two, regarded his father's actions as disgraceful and decided to go his own way and follow an independent course. He and his small following pledged themselves to the continuous support of the Ming cause when other Chinese generals with thousands of troops had switched to the winning side and surrendered without a fight. From 1651 to 1659 he ravaged the Chekiang and Fukien coast and turned down all Ch'ing's overtures requesting his surrender. In the latter year he felt strong enough to invade the Lower Yangtze valley. His troops landed on the Shanghai coast, captured Chinkiang and laid siege on Nanking. Many garrisons in South Anhwei responded to his call for revolt and joined the rebels. Peking was alarmed and reinforcements were quickly dispatched southward to stop his advance. With odds greatly against him, he left the Lower Yangtze and returned to Amoy in Fukien. As the Manchus increased their pressure, he and his followers sailed across the Taiwan Strait and reestablished themselves on the island of Taiwan.

Taiwan is an island shaped like a drifting leaf, 150 miles off the coast of Fukien province. It is 250 miles in length and 90 miles in width at its widest point, with a total area of some 13,800 square miles. It is also known as Formosa which means "beautiful" in Portuguese. Early in the Ch'ing dynasty, two major ethnic groups were to be found in this island. The first group was the aboriginal Taiwanese who seemed to be racially related to modern Indonesians. Today the Chinese call them Kao-shan Tsu, or High Mountains People, largely because they live in the mountainous regions on the eastern and central sections of the island. The majority of the inhabitants on Taiwan were in the second group, the Chinese. Financially hard-pressed at home where arable areas were few and small, the Chinese on the Fukien and Kwangtung coast found the Taiwan land irresistible and inviting. Since the first immigration began sometime during the Sui-T'ang period, it was continued throughout succeeding centuries. However, it was not until the sixteenth and the seventeenth centuries that Chinese came to Taiwan in increasingly large numbers. Most of the newcomers were farmers; others were fishermen and traders. The farmers opened up the virgin lands and found them so fertile

that they had no difficulty in raising three crops each year. Soil, temperature, and rainfall were all ideal for a rice economy. In the early 1660's it
was estimated that total acreage of paddy fields was approximately
30,000 acres. This acreage was considerably enlarged during the succeeding decades. For the poverty-stricken Chinese peasants, Taiwan was a
bright new haven indeed.

Loosely organized as a Chinese prefecture and separated from the
mainland by the Taiwan Strait, early in the seventeenth century Taiwan
was successively occupied by Chinese pirates, Japanese traders, and in
1623, Dutch adventurers. Though their interest was largely commercial,
the Dutch promoted agriculture by reducing land tax, constructing irrigation works, and even providing small loans to enable the poorest peasants
to acquire oxen, farm implements, and seeds. Their benevolent rule encouraged even more immigrants from Fukien province. In 1659 Cheng
Ch'eng-kung returned to Amoy, after his unsuccessful attempt to seize the
Lower Yangtze Valley. Two years later, hard pressed by the victorious
Manchus, he decided to take over Taiwan and to use it as the last stronghold to rally all Ming loyalists. After he defeated the Dutch and captured
the island, Cheng turned his energy to the establishment of a new government and invited Chinese scholars to staff it. He opened schools, promoted
the opening-up of virgin fields, and encouraged immigrants from the
mainland. Unfortunately, dissensions soon developed among his successors after his death in 1662. Though the island government continued to
maintain its independence for more than twenty years, it was no longer a
threat to Ch'ing's authority on the nearby mainland. In 1683 the Ch'ing
regime took the offensive, and the last Ming stronghold subsequently
collapsed. Taiwan was incorporated as a Ch'ing prefecture and remained
under Chinese jurisdiction until 1895.

The pacification of China proper was followed by a vigorous policy
of expansion towards the grasslands beyond China's traditional borders.
By now the Ch'ing emperors regarded themselves as Sons of Heaven à la
Chinese, and as such, they thought they should bring all "barbarians"
under their "benevolent" influence. A more important motive, however,
arose from a practical, strategic consideration. Throughout Chinese history the danger to China proper had always come from the grasslands in
the north, and to safeguard China proper, the Chinese believed that they
had to neutralize that danger either directly or indirectly by controlling
part or all of these grasslands. The success story of the Manchus provided
additional weight for this argument. The Manchus, upon becoming rulers
of China, thought along the same lines as the great Chinese emperors of
the past. Before their entry into China proper in 1644, they had succeeded
in subjugating Korea and Inner Mongolia as their protectorates. As their
northeastern frontier was thus comparatively secure, their subsequent expansions were directed northwestward. In 1697 the emperor K'ang-hsi

MAP 27
THE CH'ING EMPIRE AND
ITS DEPENDENT TERRITORIES
Circa 1800 A.D.

Scale of Miles
0   400   800   1200

———— Areas under Chinese Influence,
         circa 1800
-·-·-·- Chinese Boundaries, 1900
········· Boundaries of China Proper
         (The Eighteen Provinces)

Lake Baikal

OUTER MONGOLIA

MANCHURIA
LIAO RIVER
S. Mukden
Ninguta
KOREA
SHANHAIKUAN
G. OF POHAI
Peking
Tsinan
Yellow Sea
YELLOW RIVER

INNER MONGOLIA

SHENSI

KANSU

ALTAI MTS

DZUNGARIA

CHINESE

Lake Balkhash
ILI RIVER
PAMIR MTS
TARIM RIVER

TURKESTAN

Lake Balkhash

Aral Sea

CASPIAN SEA

TIBET

Lhasa
Shigatse

NEPAL

BURMA

YUNNAN

KWEICHOW

SZECHUAN

YANGTZE RIVER

HUNAN

KWANGSI

KWANGTUNG

VIETNAM

FUKIEN

Amoy

ANHWEI

CHEKIANG

Nanking

Chinkiang

Yellow Sea

TAIWAN
TAIWAN STRAIT

South China Sea

HELMAND RIVER

Bay of Bengal

Arabian Sea

personally led an expeditionary army to Outer Mongolia and in a crucial battle near Urga, the Mongol power was destroyed. Outer Mongolia became a Ch'ing vassalage and remained so throughout the Ch'ing dynasty.

The conquest of the area west of Outer Mongolia, however, turned out to be a long, protracted process. In this area was located the Mongol kingdom of Dzungaria which at its peak of power in the 1670's covered Chinese Turkestan, the Ili River Valley, and the Altai Mountains. In 1697 and again in 1732 the Ch'ing regime sent expeditionary forces to conquer it, but each time the invaders fell short of their desired goal. One generation later when Ch'ien-lung was the emperor, the Manchus made an all-out effort, and after a military campaign of three years (1755–1757), they finally succeeded in conquering this Mongol kingdom. The conquest was accompanied by a ruthless slaughter which practically wiped out the Dzungars. One year after the conquest of the Dzungars, the Muslims in Chinese Turkestan revolted, as if they had never heard what had happened to their neighbors in the north. The rebellion, however, was quickly suppressed. As a result of these operations the Ch'ing regime extended its jurisdiction north of the Ili River basin and west of the Pamir Mountains. The Greater Northwest was incorporated as a part of the Manchu empire.

The Manchu conquest of Tibet, on the other hand, was complicated by a religious factor, Lamaism. Lamaism, originally developed in Tibet, won its largest following during the Yüan dynasty when the Mongols gave it special privileges and extended patronage. The downfall of the Mongol Empire in the fourteenth century did not in any way reduce its influence among the Mongols. Early in the fifteenth century a reform movement took place within the Lamaist church, and the reformers emphasized a more secluded, meditative life as a way to enlightenment. A new sect emerged from the reform movement, known as the Yellow Hat Sect to distinguish it from the older Red Hat Sect. The founder of the new sect, Tsong-kha-pa, died in 1419, but his branch of Lamaism continued to grow. In time his divinity was supposedly divided among two lines of successors, the Dalai Lamas and the Panchen Lamas, the successors to his first and second disciples respectively. Lama succession was achieved through a process called reincarnation; the new Dalai or Panchen Lama was supposedly the reincarnation of the old ones. When a Dalai or Panchen Lama died, a search was made among the newly born, and the wise men of the Lama court would decide, with divine guidance, on the reincarnated Lama. Theoretically both Lamas shared the same degree of divinity, but historically the Dalai Lama had always enjoyed a greater temporal power.

As Lamaism was deeply rooted in Tibetan life, it seemed natural that the Ch'ing government should wish to use the two grand Lamas to achieve its political control. Even before entering into China proper, the

Manchus made useful connections with the fifth Dalai Lama (1617–1662) at Lhasa, and after moving the capital from Mukden to Peking, they invited the grand Lamas to send tribute missions. However, Ch'ing influence in Tibet was then nominal and it amounted to no more than Tibet's recognition of Ch'ing as suzerain. In an attempt to extend their influence in Tibet, the early Ch'ing emperors had to compete with the Dzungars who had a similar design of their own. In 1717 the Dzungars moved in with a strong force, captured Lhasa, and terrorized the country. Ch'ing responded in 1720 when it sent two armies into Tibet and drove out the Dzungars. It installed the seventh Dalai Lama in the Lhasa palace (Potala) and a Ch'ing garrison was left behind to maintain peace and order. The easternmost part of Tibet was incorporated as a part of Szechuan province. The successful intervention of 1720 was followed by similar interventions afterwards. A Tibetan civil war in 1727–1728 brought another Ch'ing expeditionary force whose purpose was to make sure that the pro-Ch'ing faction in the civil war would remain in power. In 1750 the Ch'ing regime intervened again when there was a general breakdown of order following a series of murders of political leaders and a continuous state of anarchy and confusion. After order was finally restored, the emperor Ch'ien-lung let it be known that the Dalai Lama would be the sole temporal ruler and that a council of ministers would be created to advise him on state affairs. His spiritual rival, the Panchen Lama, would remain at Shigatse, located to the west of Lhasa. A Ch'ing garrison would stay in Lhasa permanently to maintain order, and the Dalai Lama, in exercising his state functions, was to seek advice from Ch'ing ministers in residence. Through these devices China was able to maintain its indirect rule in Tibet, which remained a vassal and protectorate throughout the Ching dynasty.

To strengthen its southwestern frontier, the Ch'ing government decided in the 1720's to bring the various minority peoples in Kwangtung, Kwangsi, Kweichow, Szechuan, and Yunnan provinces under direct control. These minorities were often lumped together and called Miao, but there were numerous sub-groups under that term. They lived in the remote, mountainous regions and there was little or no cooperation among the various sub-groups. It was said that their ancestors were driven out from China proper in ancient times by the Chinese, but historians have not been able to prove or disprove this assertion. Throughout the centuries there had been constant clashes between the Chinese and the Miao minorities. Miao revolts occurred from time to time and each time they were suppressed with considerable bloodshed and vengeance. During the Ming dynasty the government succeeded in instituting a system of indirect rule whereby hereditary tribal chieftains were awarded Chinese ranks and titles and were brought under the overall supervision of Chinese governors. Though this system worked fairly well, it prevented Chinese officials from having direct jurisdiction over the Miao people. This lack of direct jurisdiction created considerable difficulties, especially in areas where Chinese and Miao lived side by side. If a Miao committed a crime, Chinese officials could not bring him to justice without his chieftain's approval. Moreover, Chinese governors could not evaluate, promote, or dismiss tribal chieftains according to their performances as they could with Chinese officials. They could only dismiss them at the risk of inviting a rebellion. In 1726 at the suggestion of the Yunnan governor Oh-erh-t'ai, the system of indirect rule was abolished and all minorities were brought under central administration. Officials in charge of Miao territories were appointed by and responsible to their respective governors and could be promoted and dismissed like any other Ch'ing officials. Oh-erh-t'ai was so successful with his work that he was soon promoted to the rank of governor-general in charge of Yunnan, Kweichow, and Kwangsi provinces. By 1731 he had succeeded in extending bureaucratic administration to all minorities in the Southwest.

Beyond the southeastern border, the Vietnamese pledged their allegiance to the Ch'ing regime soon after the Manchus entered China proper. Succeeding Vietnamese kings were awarded titles and honors. Ch'ing's subjection of Burma, on the other hand, encountered difficulties. Two Ch'ing expeditions (one in 1767 and another in 1770) suffered defeat when they ventured into the inhospitable jungle areas of northern Burma. It was not until 1789 that the reigning Burmese king, facing great difficulties at home, decided to surrender and become a Ch'ing vassal.

THE CH'ING EMPERORS

In contrast to the Mongols of the Yüan dynasty who conquered and ruled China through the use of naked military force, the Manchus attempted to base their rule on some form of popular support. It has been mentioned earlier that they made conscientious efforts to Sinicize their regime before they entered China proper. This policy of winning Chinese support was continued after the regime had established itself at Peking. In the imperial government the Chinese shared power and responsibility with their Manchu colleagues. Each of the Six Ministries had two ministers, one Manchu and one Chinese, and four deputy ministers, two Manchu and two Chinese. On the provincial level, while most governors-general were Manchus, the governors were mostly Chinese. The magistrates in charge of prefectures and subprefectures were of course overwhelmingly Chinese. Only in military commandership were the Manchus given priority and preference. The better-trained banner troops were mostly commanded by Manchus, while Chinese commanders had to be satisfied with the militia-like "green battalions." Except for the emperors, who had to be Manchus by virtue of heredity, theoretically there was no limit for the Chinese in ascending the bureaucratic ladder. Rumor even had it that the great emperor Ch'ien-lung was actually Chinese, though the validity of that statement is generally discounted by serious historians. By and large it is safe to say that the Manchus intended to rule China jointly with the Chinese.

To justify their rule in China, the Manchus had to overcome a tremendous ideological difficulty. Many Chinese scholars, invoking the Confucian teaching about the uncompromising "difference between Chinese and barbarians" (*Hua yi chih pien*), regarded alien rule as an affront to the dignity of the Central Kingdom. This nationalist sentiment was particularly strong in the Yangtze River basin. The three outstanding scholars in this area, Huang Tsung-hsi (1610–1695), Wang Fu-chih (1619–1692), and Ku Yen-wu (1613–1682) all had fought against the Manchus in the past and refused to serve the new regime after it had succeeded in conquering China. It was to the credit of the new regime that these men were left alone to pursue their scholastic interests despite their known antigovernment beliefs. While the government could do nothing to change the opinion of the staunch Ming loyalists, it was very successful with the less staunch ones who were by far in the majority. To be sure, there were occasional purges conducted by the government to eliminate the disloyal elements among the academic ranks, but they were no worse than those conducted by some Chinese emperors in the past such as Chu Yüan-chang.

To combat the sentiment of Ming loyalists about alien rule, the Manchus had to justify their regime in China. In 1727 a plot engineered by a group of Ming loyalists to overthrow the government was discovered and the conspirators were brought to trial. The reigning emperor Yung-cheng decided to use this occasion to refute once and for all the loyalists' contention that barbarians could not rule China and that all Chinese were morally bound to fight against the Manchus. The court proceedings together with the emperor's comments were compiled and published and distributed among Chinese scholars. The book, entitled *A Record of Awakening to Great Righteousness* (*Ta-yi chüeh-mi lu*), contained a key confession by one of the main conspirators. The confession began by saying that sages were not a monopoly of China and that foreign lands would in due time produce their own share of the truly great. In fact, said the document, many Chinese heroes in the past were born in barbarian lands, such as the legendary emperor Shun and the founder of the Chou dynasty King Wen. They were barbarians, but they were hailed in history as legitimate Chinese emperors. The important thing, continued the confession, was not a person's birthplace but the possession of a unique "virtue" which entitled him to rule over China. The document implied that by the 17th century the Manchus had already possessed such a virtue.

The first Ch'ing emperors, as we have already said, were men of outstanding ability, especially K'ang-hsi, Yung-cheng, and Ch'ien-lung. K'ang-hsi inherited the throne at the age of seven and ruled China con-

A WOODCUT SHOWING THE PEACEFUL COUNTRY SCENE The women on the right are unreeling silk fibers. On the left a woman and her child chat with their neighbors over a fence. The Chinese characters in the picture are a five-character poem describing the scene. On top of the picture is a seven-character poem believed to have been composed and written by Emperor K'ang-hsi.

secutively for sixty-one years (1661–1722). It was during his reign that the revolt of Wu San-kuei was crushed, Taiwan was incorporated as part of China, Outer Mongolia and Dzungaria were conquered, and Tibet became a Ch'ing vassal and protectorate. However, he was remembered by posterity not only as a great conqueror but also as a conscientious, enlightened monarch. He advanced agriculture by reducing land taxation and by promoting the construction of flood-control and irrigation projects. His policy of limiting the number of Buddhist monks and nuns especially pleased Confucian scholars. A generous patron of education and academic activities, he was an outstanding scholar in his own right. It was said that as a boy K'ang-hsi was so obsessed with book learning that he would not stop reading even when he was dangerously ill, and the habit remained with him throughout his life. He strove to become a Confucian model monarch and set a moral example to his subjects. In an imperial edict issued during his reign and hung on the walls of all schools in China, he commanded his subjects to do the following:

1. Observe filial piety and brotherly love to improve the basic human relations.
2. Respect your clansmen to promote the virtue of concord.
3. Live harmoniously with your fellow villagers to avoid quarrels and lawsuits.
4. Promote agriculture and sericulture to assure an adequate supply of food and clothing.
5. Practice thrift to save expenses.
6. Exalt schools to rectify the conduct of scholars.
7. Discard heretic ideas to strengthen orthodoxism.
8. Be familiar with the law to avoid ignorance and rascality.
9. Be humble and modest to cultivate good customs.
10. Be diligent in your profession to stabilize your will.
11. Warn your children and younger brothers aginst lawless activities.
12. Stop lawsuits to preserve good will.
13. Do not protect lawless elements in order to avoid involvement in conspiracies.
14. Pay your taxes to ward off tax duns.
15. Strengthen the *pao-chia* system to prevent robbery and thievery.
16. Patch up quarrels to protect your own life.

All teachers and students in each school were ordered to assemble twice a month to recite aloud the above edict, once on the first of the month and once on the fifteenth. The edict, called the *Sixteen Sacred Injunctions*, summarized the basic attributes that a Confucian monarch expected from his loyal subjects.

One thing, however, marred the happy tranquility of K'ang-hsi's old age. He had sired thirty-five sons, and as he grew more advanced in age, intrigues developed among his sons as many of them wanted to be designated as his successor. His personal favorite was Yün-jeng, the first born son of the empress, who under normal circumstances should have been the crown prince anyway. However, the crown prince became mentally unbalanced, conducting himself in such an unprincely manner as to, among other things, bring in country girls to the Forbidden Palace. Much to his grief, K'ang-hsi found it necessary to depose him as the crown prince. After that, intrigues and feuds among his numerous sons became even more intensified. It was not until 1722 when he was on his death bed that he finally decided on his fourth son who, after accession, was known by his reign title Yung-cheng.

In contrast to his father who was known as being tolerant and lenient, Yung-cheng was strict and harsh. To prevent any challenge to his authority, he threw several of his brothers into prison, where they eventually died, and their supporters were liquidated *en masse*. He placed informers and spies in both the palace and the government to warn him in advance of any plot or conspiracy. Remembering well the fraternal strife involving the designation of a crown prince during his father's reign, he refused to let his choice of successor be known while he was living. In the very first year that he became the emperor, he secretly wrote down the name of his successor and placed it in two sealed envelopes, one kept in the Outer Court and the other in the Inner Court. Nobody else knew the designated successor, and he ordered that these envelopes should not be opened until immediately after his death. In 1735 when he died, the court officials opened the envelopes and found the name of his fourth son who, after accession, was known as Ch'ien-lung.

Despite his suspicious nature, Yung-cheng was an able, conscientious, and just ruler. He was shrewd in the management of the nation's finance, impartial in his selection of government officials, and rewarded and punished in accordance with his subordinates' performances. Under him were some of the ablest governors of the Ch'ing dynasty, such as Governor-general Oh-erh-t'ai of Yunnan-Kweichow-Kwangsi provinces. To concentrate imperial power in his hands, he created a new organ called the Privy Council (*Chün-chi ch'u*) which formulated governmental policy under his personal command, bypassing the regular government apparatus. He personally read all important documents and rendered decisions, and he made all governors directly responsible to him, rather than indirectly through the Six Ministries.

Yung-cheng was succeeded by Ch'ien-lung, the last of the great Ch'ing emperors. His long reign of fifty-nine years (1736–1795) marked the apex of Ch'ing power and saw further expansion of the Ch'ing empire. The kingdom of Dzungaria was annexed, the Muslim uprisings in Chinese Turkestan and the Miao uprisings in Kweichow were successfully suppressed, Vietnam and Burma were brought in as Ch'ing vassals, and

Nepal was made a tributary state. At home peace and prosperity continued to prevail. The imperial exchequer was so full of unused money that four times during his reign the emperor ordered cancellation of all tax payments. The unprecedented prosperity was nowhere better indicated than in the tremendous increase of population. From 1749 to 1793 population in China proper was more than doubled. Towards the end of Ch'ien-lung's reign, however, the regime began to show some internal weaknesses. The military campaigns against China's neighboring states, victorious and glorious in appearance, were extremely costly. It was estimated that altogether they cost more than 150 million taels of silver. His six pleasure tours of the Lower Yangtze cost even more, estimated to be 200 million taels. As he grew older and more complacent, he delegated authority to a favorite of his called Ho-shen. Ho-shen served as his Grand Chancellor for twenty years, and through various corrupt means amassed a great fortune. When he was finally brought to trial after the death of Ch'ien-lung, he was found to have possessed more than 800 million taels of silver, equivalent to ten years' revenue of the Ch'ing empire! Most of this money was found in his mansion, including 260 million taels hidden inside the walls.

CULTURAL ACTIVITIES

Both K'ang-hsi and Ch'ien-lung prided themselves on being grand patrons of learning and literature. Though the Manchu written language was still one of the two official languages in the government, it remained mostly a formality, and with the passage of time even many Manchus did not bother to learn it. On the other hand Manchu intellectuals—including the above-named emperors—found great challenge and enjoyment in the literary tradition of China. Militarily China was conquered by the Manchus, but culturally China's conquest of its conquerors had never been so complete. Both emperors were literary men of considerable talent and were versed in Chinese philosophy and literature. Ch'ien-lung reportedly wrote more than 100,000 poems and was a discriminating critic of painting and calligraphy. K'ang-hsi was even more versatile: he studied astronomy, geography, mathematics, and music, besides Confucian classics and traditional literature. He was even said to have had a smattering of the Latin language. During his reign he personally supervised the printing of twenty-six items on Confucian classics, sixty-five items on history, thirty-six items on philosophy, and twenty items on miscellaneous subjects. The famous *K'ang-hsi Dictionary* was also compiled under his patronage.

The most significant literary task during K'ang-hsi's reign, however, was the compilation of an encyclopedia entitled *A Collection of Books*

and Illustrations of Ancient and Modern Times (*Ku-chin t'u-shu chi-
ch'eng*). In this effort the emperor obviously attempted to vie with another great patron of learning in the past, *i.e.*, the emperor Yung-lo of the
Ming Dynasty, who, as we have said in the preceding chapter, sponsored
the compilation of the *Yung-lo Encyclopedia* (*Yung-lo ta-tien*). During
the change of dynasties all but one copy of the *Encyclopedia* had been
destroyed, and even the extant copy was incomplete. The compilation
of *A Collection of Books* was undertaken in 1700 and was not completed
until 1725. Its size was comparatively smaller than the *Yung-lo Encyclopedia*, but it was the largest work ever printed to that date anywhere in
the world. Two generations later when Ch'ien-lung was the emperor, an
imperial decree ordered the collection of all major works on all subjects,
whether they be printed, out-of-print, or hand-copied. This gigantic task
took nine years to complete (1773–1782) and the resulting collection was
entitled *The Complete Library of the Four Treasuries* (*Ssu-k'u ch'üan-
shu*), consisting of 3,457 entries in 93,556 fascicles. The *Four Treasuries*
was even larger in size than either the *Yung-lo Encyclopedia* or *A Collection of Books*. Seven hand-written copies were made, housed in seven
newly built libraries, four in North China and three in the Yangtze
River basin. Those in the north were open only to selected scholars;
the three in the south, however, were open to the general public.
Though historians since then have universally praised Ch'ien-lung's foresight in undertaking this gigantic task, critics pointed out that many
works of great value had been destroyed during the compiling process.
Any work that described the Manchus in terms that were only slightly
derogatory was ordered to be destroyed. Censorship was also extended to
Sung works criticizing Liao and Chin, and to Yüan and Ming works
criticizing the Mongols. In other cases, books were destroyed simply because they did not appear "literary" enough to the censors or because they
allegedly dealt with "trifles" or "nonsense."

Among the different Confucian schools the early Ch'ing emperors
singled out the Rational School of Chu Hsi for emphasis. The emperor
K'ang-hsi, for instance, regarded Chu Hsi as the greatest philosopher since
Confucius and Mencius. The elevation of Chu Hsi was not new; the Ming
emperors had honored him before. Obviously his teachings were more
appealing to Chinese monarchs than those of other Confucian scholars.
First, he believed that the building of moral character among individuals
was the first step to the betterment of society. To discipline oneself was
therefore more important than to criticize others. Second, he taught the
importance of using reason to combat human desires, whether they be for
fame, wealth, or power. He maintained that within every man there was a
perpetual conflict between "Heavenly reason" (*t'ien li*) and "human desires" (*jen yü*), a battle between the good and the evil, and that a person
could eliminate the evil by conscientiously cultivating the good. Every

man had to make his own choice because between the good and the evil there could not be any compromise. Third, the purpose of academic learning was its practical application, and a Confucian scholar should serve his government whenever the opportunity presented itself. In a Confucian sense, the nation (*kuo*), the government (*cheng*), and the monarch (*chün*) were almost synonymous, and to serve the nation was by implication to serve the monarch. Loyalty to the monarch was one of the greatest Confucian virtues. Fourth, Chu Hsi, like many other Sung scholars, advocated government by legitimate rulers. By legitimacy was not meant legitimacy in its hereditary sense; legitimacy came into being through the possession of a traditional virtue (*tao t'ung*). This traditional virtue supposedly began with the legendary emperors Yao and Shun and passed through many great dynasties of the past such as Chou, Han, T'ang, and Sung. Though such virtue was never adequately defined and was only vaguely understood, its possession was regarded as the prerequisite to legitimate government. By elevating Chu Hsi the Ch'ing emperors believed that they had followed the great emperors of the past in the possession of that virtue which entitled them to the ruling of China.

Finally, Chu Hsi proposed the dual existence of "form" (*hsing*) and "reason" (*li*), the two inseparable elements of everything in the universe. Form was what we know through the application of our senses, and reason was the law that governs the existence of the form. To use Chu Hsi's own example, a boat has a form which enables us to know its physical existence, but a boat is not really a boat if it cannot sail. The capacity to sail is the "reason" for its being a boat and this capacity existed before any particular boat existed. "Reason" was *a priori*, and "form" was *a posteriori*. Chu Hsi, like all other Confucian scholars, was interested in the application of his theory to human relations. The correct relations between fathers and sons and between monarchs and their subjects, said he, existed before the existence of the parties involved. The virtue of fathers and monarchs was "benevolence" (*jen*) towards their sons and subjects respectively, while "reverence" or "respect" (*ching*) should be the virtue of the inferior parties. The law ("reason") governing the relationship among men existed before particular men existed and was superior to the parties involved. It was eternal, while men themselves were ephemeral. An orderly society could be established only when each individual knew his assigned role and respective place in the society.

In view of what Chu Hsi advocated, it is not difficult to see why his philosophy appealed greatly to monarchs. Both the Ming and the Ch'ing emperors ordered that in Confucian temples his name should be placed beside that of Confucius, to be honored by all students and scholars. The *Four Books* originally selected by him as the basic works of Confucianism were the standard texts which students who wanted to pass the civil service examinations must master thoroughly.

Influential though it was, Chu Hsi's philosophy was not altogether unchallenged. Since it was sponsored by the government, such a challenge, as expected, came mostly from unofficial circles and independent thinkers. Early in the Ch'ing dynasty, Ku Yen-wu attacked the Rational School on the ground that the followers of this school, emphasizing the cultivation of personal virtues, tended to cut themselves off from the outside world and that they failed as leaders of society when they did not recognize and find a remedy for social and economic ills. The metaphysical speculation of the Rational School served no useful purpose, and its overemphasis tended to take a scholar away from a more important concern: the welfare of the society and its people. A true gentleman, said Ku Yen-wu, "should regard social well-being as his own private end to strive for," and knowledge failed to be true if it could not advance human welfare in a practical way. Following his own philosophy, Ku Yen-wu wrote two books, both on "practical" matters: *Problems and Challenges of Various Areas in China* (*T'ien-hsia chün-kuo li-ping shu*) and *The Daily Accumulated Knowledge* (*Jih-chih lu*).

A more vigorous and systematic attack on the Rational School came from another Ch'ing scholar named Tai Chen (1724-1777). Tai Chen was born to a poor family in South Anhwei, the same region which had produced Chu Hsi more than seven centuries before. It is said that he was inquisitive and critical about everything he read when he was a child and that he often asked questions which even his teacher could not answer. When he was sixteen, he reportedly had committed to memory all the Confucian classics and their major commentaries. Talented though he was, he failed repeatedly in the civil service examinations. He earned a living by teaching, and through his writings he was regarded by his contemporaries as one of the greatest Confucian scholars. His most important work was *A Commentary on the Words and Meanings of Mencius* (*Meng-tzu tzu-yi shu-cheng*). During his declining years he was invited by the emperor Ch'ien-lung to help in the compilation of the *Four Treasuries*. He died of overwork at the age of fifty-four.

Tai Chen, like many other critics of the Rational School, attempted to bypass the Sung period in his search for the meaning of Confucianism. These critics believed that one had to go to the writings of the Han dynasty and before in order to ascertain the true intention of the great Confucian masters. Because of their emphasis on the Han writings, their school of thought was called the Han School or Han Learning, as opposed to the Rational School represented by Chu Hsi. They maintained that post-Han writings, especially those of the Sung scholars, were influenced by Taoism and Buddhism and could not be relied on in understanding Confucianism. What was wrong with "human desires?" asked Tai Chen. Had not the *Book of Rites* said that food and sex were man's two basic, indispensable desires? Was it not true that the elimination of desires was originally a Taoist and a Buddhist teaching? The sages taught a person to channel his desires along the right direction, and there was no mention in the ancient texts that he should suppress them with "reason." Moreover, what was the definition of "reason"? What one person regarded as "reason" might not be "reason" for others. "Reason" being such a loose term, every one used it to advance his own interest. "The haughty use it against the humble, the elders use it again the young, and the aristocrats use it against the common people." But, if the inferiors used it in front of their superiors, "they are accused of being rebellious even when they are right." "How many injustices have been done under the disguise of 'reason'?" asked Tai Chen. "Harsh and cruel officials kill people by invoking the law, and later [Sung] scholars killed people by invoking 'reason.'" "The sad thing is," he continued, "that while people might feel sorry for those killed by law, none expresses sympathy for those killed by 'reason.'"

Wishing to have nothing to do with metaphysical speculation, Tai Chen and other "Han School" scholars applied themselves to "practical" research. They made great contributions in the fields of phonetics, philology, etymology, and textual criticism. Theoretically, these studies were not ends in themselves. They were meant to contribute to the understanding of Han and pre-Han writings.

POPULAR LITERATURE

The debate between the Han and the Sung Schools was confined to the highly sophisticated intellectuals. The majority of the Chinese people did not understand and cared little about it. When they read, they wished to be entertained and amused, and certainly they could not find entertainment in philosophical works that were written in a classical style. Fortunately there were many works with popular appeal, and among them novels stood as the most outstanding. Historians call them Ming-Ch'ing novels, though some of them (such as *The Romance of the Three Kingdoms*) were actually written during the Yüan dynasty. Chinese intellectuals looked down upon novels as a form of literary expression, and some of these novels did not even bear the name of the author. Presumably they were not proud of their own works, and they wrote them simply because they wished to "kill time." Unshackled by this ancient prejudice, today we are perhaps better equipped to judge their works than they themselves were. Modern scholars agree that the best Ming-Ch'ing novels are among the greatest literary creations of all countries.

There must have been a long evolutionary process between the plain vernacular tales of the Sung dynasty and the superbly written novels of the Ming-Ch'ing period. Whether written in classical or vernacular form, the Ming-Ch'ing novels, at least the best among them, possessed a refinement which the Sung tales had never attained. They appealed to learned intellectuals as well as to those who heard them retold by professional story-tellers in the tea houses. They were the popular literature, appealing to people of all walks of life and of all social standings.

Among the novels in question one of the best written and most popular was *The Marsh Heroes* (*Shui-hu chuan*), translated by Pearl S. Buck as *All Men Are Brothers*. It was originally written by Shih Nai-an and subsequently completed by Lo Kuan-chung, both authors living in the fourteenth century. It was a work of historical fiction, the story of Sung Chiang and his fellow bandits who early in the twelfth century had ravaged the countryside and captured many cities before they were finally suppressed. In *The Marsh Heroes,* however, they are portrayed as the victims of oppression and injustice and as Robin Hoods who robbed the rich and aided the poor. Altogether there were 108 "heroes" in this book, but the author concentrated on a dozen or so of the most colorful figures. There was the runaway monk whose hate for all evil was as strong as his love for good wine and tasty food. There was the ex-captain of the imperial guards who had to forego a promising career to become a bandit because a powerful official coveted his unusually attractive wife. There was also the tall, handsome Wu Sung who spurned the overtures of his brother's wife, only to find himself accused of having seduced her. After the woman had found a great lord as her lover and poisoned her husband, Wu Sung took the law into his own hands and slaughtered her in cold blood right in front of his brother's dead body. Thus he became a wanted man and joined the bandits. The leader of these bandits was the ex-clerk Sung Chiang. He became an outlaw because he was forced to murder his wife who had threatened to expose his underworld connections. Throughout the book the author's sympathy was with these bandit-heroes.

Scarcely less popular was another work of historical fiction, *The Romance of the Three Kingdoms* (*San kuo yen-yi*), reportedly written by Lo Kuan-chung. The book begins with the ominous remark that "an empire is founded to be broken, as a broken empire is bound to be reunited in the course of time." The broken empire described in this book was the Later Han which early in the third century was broken into Three Kingdoms (see Chapter IV). While the book covers a long period from the time of the Yellow Turbans rebellion to the reunification of China by Tsin Wu-ti, its central figure was a man named Chu-ko Liang who served as an adviser and then prime minister to the King of Shu, Liu Pei. His ingenuity and cleverness, according to *The Romance,* enabled South China to successfully resist Ts'ao Ts'ao, who was singled out as the villain in this work. Written in a semiclassical style, *The Romance* was easy to read, and reportedly many Chinese, by reading this book and imitating its style, learned to write their first presentable letters. Its numerous episodes were adapted in many plays and operas of succeeding centuries. There was hardly anyone in China who did not know some of these stories.

Less popular but perhaps of greater literary value was *The Dream of the Red Chamber* (*Hung-lou meng*), by Ts'ao Hsüeh-ch'in who lived in the eighteenth century. It is a story of love between two cousins, Chia Pao-yü (Precious Jade) and Lin Tai-yü (Black Jade). The story ends with the death of the heroine and the insanity of the hero who subsequently joined the monastic ranks. Pao-yü could not marry his true love because his grandmother had her eyes on a more wholesome and less clever girl named Hsieh Pao-ch'ai. The day he married Pao-ch'ai was also the time when his true love departed from the earth. The romance of the two cousins was conducted on a platonic level; they exchanged notes and poems and made subtle, remote remarks whenever they saw each other. Physically delicate and emotionally oversensitive, Tai-yü would cry for days and vow never to see him again if he made some remarks that could be remotely construed as offensive. Meanwhile, she might write long, sad poems of self-pity and murmur them while "collecting and burying fallen flowers." The love story itself might be regarded as over-sentimental, but the book throws much light on the life of the leisurely rich and the operation of a scholar-gentry family of high standing. It is still one of the best books to read for anyone who wishes to study the Chinese family system. Most Chinese, however, read it for the story.

Another book, beautifully written in a classical style, was a collection of 431 short stories entitled *Strange Stories from a Lonely Studio* (*Liao-chai chih-yi*), by P'u Sung-ling (1640–1715). The heroes in these stories were mostly men, but the heroines were usually either ghosts or fox-fairies. The love and romance between them make interesting, if weird, reading. Almost without exception, the ghosts and fox-fairies described in this book were more honest and trustworthy than human beings. Did the author mean to satirize the imperfections of human beings? According to Chinese hearsay, foxes, once transforming themselves into human beings, were sexually irresistible, and when approached, their victims were completely helpless to maintain their chastity. How did this superstition begin? One explanation is that even in a society where males and females were strictly segregated and their private meetings were socially taboo, cases of unwed mothers did occasionally occur; and that to save the family of an unwed mother from social disgrace, there had to be a face-saving formula to explain the supposedly unexplainable. "This is not her fault," her parents would like to hear people say when their unwed daughter became unexpectedly pregnant, "because you could not expect her to resist a male fox who came in through a window crack and made her unconscious by the waving of a hand." In such a case, her parents might be persuaded not to punish her too severely (as by putting her to death) in order to save the family's reputation. The Chinese being a practical people, even the most intelligent among them did not bother to attack this superstition as long as it served a useful purpose.

Among other interesting novels is *An Unofficial History of the Literati* (*Ju-lin wai-shih*), by Wu Ching-tzu (1701–1754). It is a well-written satire attacking the hypocritical behavior of many shallow, worldly scholars. *Flowering Plum in a Golden Vase* (*Chin p'ing mei*), which first appeared in printed form in the 1570's, was an anonymous work describing the amorous adventure of a man named Hsi-men Ch'ing. Hsi-men the Lord, as he is called in this book, captured one beautiful woman after another until he debilitated his health and died of exhaustion at an early age. The moral of the book, which appears on the last page, is that overindulgence does not pay, but the book's chief attraction has been its pornographic details.

Another popular novel, written in a different vein, was *Journey to the West* (*Hsi-yu chi*), by Wu Ch'eng-en. It describes the successful journey of the Buddhist monk Hsüan-tsang to India in the seventh century and the colorful exploits of his escort, a monkey, who, among other things could "cover eighteen thousand *li* (about 6,000 miles) in one jump." Less well-written but equally popular was *The Romance of Deification* (*Feng-shen yen-yi*), by an anonymous author of the Ming dynasty. It describes the war between Chou and Shang in the twelfth century B.C., with all gods and goddesses fighting on one side or another. Some of the gods travelled in the sky and others did so underneath the ground. Chou won because all good deities happened to be on its side.

We cannot leave the topic of popular literature without mentioning the charming autobiography of Shen Fu who lived in the eighteenth century. The present version of the autobiography, *The Six Chapters of a Floating Life* (*Fou-sheng liu-chi*), has actually four chapters, the other two chapters having long been lost. It describes the life of an unsuccessful, impoverished gentry-scholar, enjoying what he had and accepting what he could not change. It is permeated with Taoist and Buddhist influences. The most charming chapter is perhaps the first which deals with the author's domestic life. Though Shen's marriage was arranged, rarely has there been a happier couple. To show what an understanding wife he had, the author mentioned the fact that his wife had been looking for a good concubine for him for a long time without his knowledge. Their happy life, however, was marred by the misunderstanding between his wife and his parents and by the recurrent poverty that beset them for their entire lives. But as long as money lasted, they enjoyed boat rides under the moonlight and the flowers they planted in their small garden. The story ends tragically when his wife died at an early age.

DYNASTIC CYCLE

The internal strength of the Ch'ing regime reached its apex during the middle decades of the eighteenth century, and the decline began to set in towards the end of Ch'ien-lung's reign. The revelation of Ho-shen's grand larceny in 1799 was a great shock to the nation. To many who believed in the dynastic cycle, it signified the end of a glorious era and the beginning of a downward trend. No sooner was the new emperor Chia-ch'ing installed on the throne than a mighty rebellion swept across the Upper Yangtze basin. The rebellion, led by the White Lotus Society, lasted nine years and was not suppressed until 1804. Thus weakened, the Ch'ing regime continued to decline throughout the first half of the nineteenth century. Once a regime began to decline, very likely it would deteriorate to the very end. Like a river seeking an outlet towards the sea, there might be some reverse currents, but the general direction was unmistakably downward. This has been noticed with regard to the Ming dynasty, and the Ch'ing dynasty provides another excellent example for studying the dynastic cycle. During the stage of decline there were domestic rebellions and foreign invasions. What made the Ch'ing situation different was first, that foreign invasions came overseas from the south instead of overland from the north as had been traditionally the case; and second, that the new "barbarians" were of a different kind and were by far the most sophisticated China had ever encountered. They were not only superb warriors, but they possessed a highly advanced, though quite different, culture. That the Chinese made no distinction between these new "barbarians" and those with whom they had had experience before worked only to their own disadvantage. More will be said about this in a later chapter.

Internal rebellions, foreign invasions, and the inability of the government to cope with them characterized the declining stage of a dynastic cycle. Chinese historians long realized the existence of the dynastic cycle, and they explained it in terms of Confucian and Taoist philosophy. Dynastic change, said they, was as inevitable as any other change in the universe, and the permutation of the five primary elements was equally applicable to dynastic successions. The Ch'in regime, for instance, believed that it possessed the "water virtue" (*shui te*) and was therefore entitled to succeed the Chou regime which was said to have possessed the "fire virtue" (*huo te*). After the Han regime was established, its historians maintained that the new regime possessed the "earth virtue" (*t'u te*) which enabled it to succeed the Ch'in regime. Towards the end of the Former Han dynasty, some historians contended that the Ch'in regime was too short to be considered a regular dynasty and that the entire "virtue" system should be rearranged. In the new arrangement, the Chou dynasty was said to have possessed the "wood virtue" (*mu te*), and Han, the "fire virtue." When the Wei regime succeeded Han, it believed that it possessed the "earth virtue," which destroyed and replaced the "fire virtue."

What interests us most is that this theory of dynastic permutation presupposed the organic development of a political regime. A political regime, like a living organism, grew, matured, decayed, and finally ceased to exist. Then it would be replaced by a new regime which would pass through the same process. When a new regime was born, it was said that it had received the mandate of Heaven to rule; when it declined, allegedly Heaven had withdrawn its mandate and was in the process of designating a successor. Natural disasters, famines, incompetence and corruption in the government, internal revolts, and foreign invasions— these were indications of Heaven's displeasure with the existing regime. What should a ruler do under such circumstances? He should repent and should cultivate his virtue more diligently, said Confucian moralists. Tradition dictated that whenever a national disaster occurred, whether it were natural or man-made, the emperor should take full responsibility for its occurrence and issue proclamations to condemn himself, with the hope that Heaven, taking into consideration his repentance, would not punish him further by sending more disasters. The past shows that Heaven rarely intervened in those matters and that once decay set in, it continued until the existing regime was extinguished. Under the most auspicious circumstances the decay might be arrested for a short span of time, but rarely could it be stopped. During the Ch'ing dynasty, a dynastic regeneration occurred in the 1860's, but the decline continued beginning with the 1870's. The "cultivation of virtue" on the part of emperors contributed little in reversing the downward trend, once a dynasty reached the stage of decline. Though most emperors during the declining stage of a dynastic cycle were weaker leaders compared with their predecessors, it cannot be said that all of them were not "virtuous." The last Ming emperor Ch'ung-chen, for instance, was a strong, conscientious monarch, and few of the Ch'ing rulers had tried so valiantly to rejuvenate a deteriorating regime as Kuang-hsü, one of the last Ch'ing emperors.

It seems that there were forces beyond human control that worked to effect the rise and fall of each succeeding dynasty. Chinese scholars traditionally explained the existence of the dynastic cycle in abstract and philosophical terms and moralized upon it for the benefit of posterity. Modern historians, on the other hand, view it from a more rational angle and explain it in social and economic terms. We have mentioned in an earlier chapter that in China the frontier of agriculture had virtually disappeared as early as the Han dynasty and that the amount of land available for the production of food did not increase by any substantial amount for more than two thousand years. As the Chinese remained predominantly agricultural, they could not establish permanent settlements on the grasslands beyond the northern and western frontiers, and as they were land-centered, they were either unwilling or unable to expand overseas. Thus the geographical size of China was naturally limited by the grasslands and deserts in the Northwest and the Pacific Ocean in the Southeast. The increase of population throughout Chinese history had to be accommodated within the natural confines of China, and such an accommodation became increasingly difficult with the passage of time.

Chinese historians recorded land shortage as early as the fourth century B.C., and by the time of the Former Han dynasty, population pressure had become an acute problem. Population increased at an accelerated rate during the rising stage of a dynastic cycle when peace and prosperity prevailed. Sooner or later a point would be reached when the fixed amount of land could no longer support even the barest existence. When natural disasters struck, widespread famines would ensue, and open rebellions against public authority often came in the wake of widespread famines. The country was then plunged into chaos and war, and the barbarians, taking advantage of the situation, raided the border provinces and sometimes occupied part of China proper. This situation would continue until a strong man or a succession of strong men emerged, defeated all opponents, and reunified the country. Normalcy returned when all China was brought under the new leader's jurisdiction, barbarians were repelled, and he himself was installed as the founding emperor of a new dynasty. In the case of Ch'ing, the new emperor was a barbarian himself, but once he had come to the throne of China as a Chinese monarch, he regarded it as his duty to repel other barbarians as strong Chinese rulers would. During the period of dynastic change, famine, war, diseases, and a high death rate helped to reduce the population. When a new dynasty was established, again there was enough land to support a much reduced population. Population pressure thus eased, the rising stage of a new dynastic cycle began, and once again there was peace and prosperity. As the amount of land was not enlarged, and farming techniques remained the same, peace and prosperity again brought about population pressures which in turn prompted another dynastic decline.

These, of course, are much simplified statements about a complicated phenomenon. Nevertheless they are basically valid. The Chinese of old were not very statistically minded and they left us few figures to work on. However, whenever statistics are available, they tend to support this land-population theory. The following is a list of population figures:

1575 (Ming dynasty)		60,692,000
1661 (Ch'ing dynasty)		19,138,000
1749		177,495,000
1783		284,030,000

1793	307,460,000
1812	361,690,000
1842	413,021,000
1860	360,925,000
1885	377,636,000
1910	438,425,000

These were the population figures of China proper as they appeared in tax registers, and they are at best approximations. The comparatively small figure for 1575 reflects the declining stage of the Ming dynasty. By 1661 population had been reduced to the almost incredible nineteen millions, less than one-third as large as that in 1575. What a heavy toll the change of dynasties had taken! Once the Ch'ing regime was established, population increased at an accelerated speed. The increase was so fast that it can best be described as an explosion. From 1842 to 1885 population actually decreased, indicating that the dynasty was in a stage of decline.

Land shortage and population pressure were duly reflected in the increase of land prices. On the Lower Yangtze basin the best farm land was sold for about two taels per *mou* (0.15 acre) in the 1640's.[1] It rose to ten taels per *mou* in the 1730's and went further to sixty taels in the 1780's. Thus the price of farm land rose thirty times as much in 140 years and six times as much in fifty years. The rising price for land speeded up the process of land concentration, as only the very wealthy could then afford to acquire additional acreage. Small farmers, once forced to sell their land on account of accumulated debts, became tenant farmers or unemployed. Moreoever, as population swelled and the unemployed increased, the competition to obtain tenancy became more intense, and the landlords were in a good position to drive a favorable bargain for themselves. This often left the tenants very little once they paid their rent and fulfilled their contractual obligations. Those who were rejected by the landlords as tenants joined the rank of the rural unemployed. Thus, the increase of population caused land shortages which in turn caused higher land prices. As prices rose, land became more concentrated in the hands of a few and the rural unemployed became even larger in number. All these resulted in one thing: increasing poverty among the rural population. The increasing poverty among the peasants and the existence of a large army of the unemployed combined to create a potentially explosive situation for all concerned.

As long as there was no immediate danger of mass starvation, the traditional Confucian values which emphasized correct relationship and mutual help among neighbors, friends, and relatives kept in check the

[1] Unless otherwise indicated, a tael is always a tael of silver. It is equal to one ounce approximately.

dissatisfied elements and prevented a precarious situation from deteriorating into mass violence. Once a natural disaster struck and famine ensued, such values could no longer hold people within their normal confines, and the once scattered bandit groups soon coalesced and rose up in open rebellion. Whatever cause the leaders might have used to rationalize their revolt, so far as most peasants were concerned, hunger was the only reason for joining a rebellion. As China entered the stage of civil war, war itself generated more famines which further swelled the rank and file of the rebels. Farms were deserted and production slackened as able-bodied men were either drafted into the army or joined the rebels. When a social upheaval of such magnitude occurred, life meant little or nothing, and millions died as a result of war, starvation, and disease. By then most people were convinced that the existing regime had lost the mandate of Heaven.

℞ xi

Traditional Chinese Society

THE COMING OF THE WEST

So far we have discussed Chinese history as an independent development, little affected by outside influences. This independent development was largely due to geographical isolation, as has been said before. During the past four centuries, however, the situation has completely changed. The Commercial Revolution which began with Columbus' historical voyage to the New World affected China as well as the rest of the world. The oceans which had been viewed as insurmountable barriers to men's contact and knowledge of one another now became international highways over which travelled traders, missionaries, and adventurers. The expansion of European influence during and following the Commercial Revolution was unprecedented in scope, and as such expansion continued, many of the hitherto unknown or inaccessible parts of the world were either occupied by Western powers outright or were subject to strong Western

338

influences. By the nineteenth century there was no inhabited part of the world which had not felt the Western impact.

For the first time in its history China faced a cultural rival and was presented with a cultural alternative with which it had never been confronted before. The impact of the West was so great that its full meaning and scope will perhaps not be understood for a considerable time to come. Before modern times the only major foreign influence on Chinese culture came with the introduction of Buddhism from India. But the impact of Buddhism could not be compared with the pervasiveness of modern Western influence. Even at its prime, Buddhist influence was largely religious and philosophical. Chinese institutions, ethical values, and traditional loyalties and beliefs were little affected, and the basic structure of Chinese society remained the same as it had always been. Though Buddhism enriched Chinese life, it did not change it. The West, on the other hand, presented to the Chinese not only a new religion

LANTERN FESTIVAL   This tapestry panel of the eighteenth century depicts the scene of a lantern festival, traditionally celebrated on the fifteenth day of the first lunar month. There are the familiar dragon dance, the firecrackers, and the loud band, besides the lanterns. The Chinese characters on the flag behind the dragon read: "Peace on Earth" (literally, Peace within the Four Seas). The Chinese character *hsi* or "happiness" appears on the two lanterns on the right. Notice that all the people in this picture are male children or boys.

DRAGON BOAT FESTIVAL   The dragon boat festival depicted in this tapestry panel (eighteenth century) is celebrated on the fifth day of the fifth lunar month. The most important event on this day is the dragon boat race, pitting sometimes one wealthy family against another. There are four dragon boats in this picture, each of which has a boy riding on the dragon's head. Notice also the Chinese type of houses on the lower right, the pagoda on top of a bridge on the upper left, and the dresses of the people on the lower part of the picture.

(Christianity), but also a new political institution (that of representative government), new economic theories (capitalism, socialism, etc.) and, in short, a new way of life. Rejecting Western culture at the beginning, eventually China had to modify its institutions and sense of values in order to survive in a fast-changing world. Whatever the future holds, certainly China will never be the same as it has been before. Presently many forces are at work, some traditional and others foreign in origin. Will traditional values survive in the long run? Or, will they become completely submerged under the pervasive Western influence? Or, will a synthesis of Eastern and Western cultures come into being eventually? China is in a period of transition, a period which goes back to the time when its doors were forced open for normal Western trade in 1842 (Treaty of Nanking). Beginning with the middle decades of the nineteenth century, all major events in China have been related to the Western impact, in one way or another. Before we proceed with the discussion of the Western impact, it is only proper that we should devote one chapter to an analysis of the traditional Chinese society, as a summary of the preceding chapters and as a prelude to the coming ones.

THE ECONOMIC SCENE

Economically, China is agricultural and has been agricultural for more than four thousand years. This simple fact conditioned to a great extent the nature of the traditional Chinese society. The agrarian civilization of China was one of the oldest in the world, and like an elderly man who had enjoyed a long life, it suffered inevitable weaknesses. The amazing thing is not that these weaknesses existed; it is amazing that the agrarian civilization of China continued to flourish without basic changes despite these weaknesses. Obviously there must have been intrinsic values within the civilization itself to remedy or correct these weaknesses, even though they could not be eliminated. The survival of the traditional Chinese society depended upon the continuous functioning of these corrective devices. Before we discuss the corrective devices, we have to know what the weaknesses were.

Of all the problems China had to face, perhaps none was more important than the perennial problem of land shortage and population pressure. It is difficult to say when this problem began; but in any event it became more serious with the passage of time. Such a problem did not exist during the Shang dynasty, because it is known that even in the most densely populated area (the North China Plain), there was still virgin land to be opened up, and forests could be found even in the suburb of Shang's capital Yin. In the twelfth century B.C. Chou conquered Shang. Chou, being more advanced agriculturally, quickly opened up the North China Plain, and tempted by the rich land in the south, extended its control southward to the Yangtze Valley. As new land was still available, there was no land shortage. The comparative abundance of arable land enabled the Chou regime to impose a feudal structure on all China, extending it to the lowest level, the peasants. Under Chou feudalism, each peasant family received one hundred *mou* (fifteen acres) for cultivation in return for feudal services which included the tilling of the lord's "common." Though a farm of fifteen acres is not large in the West, it was enviable in China. It may be said without exaggeration that Chinese peasants have never been so well off as they were under Chou feudalism. Subsequently, Confucian scholars (Confucius included) spoke constantly of the golden age of Chou.

Feudalism had to be destroyed eventually, because, among other reasons, there was simply not enough land to be distributed among the peasants as population continued to increase. While Confucians were still dreaming about the golden past, the Legalists were looking towards the future as they proposed the abolition of feudalism. When the Ch'in regime formally ended feudalism by declaring land to be private property subject to trade, it did what circumstances had clearly dictated. Since feudalism was abolished, it has never been successfully revived.

The two ancient conquerors, Ch'in Shih-huang and Han Wu-ti, enlarged China's "living space" through military conquests. Using South Manchuria (which had been settled by the Chinese previously) as the base of operation, they annexed Korea. Southward Chinese jurisdiction was extended to the shore of the South China Sea and included the modern Kwangtung province. Even the unproductive Yun-Kwei Plateau did not escape Han Wu-ti's attention. Beyond the southwestern frontier only the rugged terrain and the inhospitable jungle prevented the Han army from marching into the Salween and the Mekong valleys. In the north, land was intensively cultivated as long as there was enough rainfall, and this included the semi-arid, marginal land on the southern fringe of the Mongolian deserts. Of all the territories that constitute arable China today, only a small enclave on the Fukien coast and the island of Taiwan were not brought under Han control. (The former, hilly and unproductive, was spared for the time being, and the latter was protected by the 100-mile-wide Taiwan Strait.) Thus by the second century B.C. practically all land suitable for agriculture had been brought under Chinese control. The frontier of agriculture had virtually disappeared.

The importance of the disappearance of the agricultural frontier cannot be overemphasized. It means that subsequent increases in population had to be accommodated within the limited amount of arable land in China. Land shortage and population pressure was the main cause of the dynastic cycle, as has been stated in the preceding chapter. It is no coincidence that after the unification of China by Ch'in, major dynasties usually lasted two or three hundred years, enough time to reduce food production per capita to a dangerously low level. With the exception of Ch'in Shih-huang who in an enthusiastic mood predicted that his regime would last "thousands of emperors," no Chinese ruler ever believed that his dynasty would continue indefinitely. Sooner or later, there would be famine, rebellion, and war, and his dynasty, like so many before, would collapse in a mass social upheaval.

Since the amount of arable land was limited, the logical solution to the production problem seemed to be the increase of yield per unit area. Unfamiliar with the Chinese situation, many people blame the lack of technological advances for the Chinese inability to raise total production. While it is true that no major technological advance has occurred since the invention of the iron-shod plow in the sixth or fifth century B.C., the result would not have been materially different even if there had been such improvements. The fact is, the manual farming as conducted by the

Chinese has been and still is one of the most efficient in the world, as far as yield per acre is concerned. For instance, in the production of rice or wheat, a Chinese farm produces more per acre than a mechanized European or American farm. The introduction of machinery would have aggravated rather than alleviated the Chinese problem. The same farming method, highly efficient and suited particularly well to the Chinese situation, has not been changed for more than two thousand years. The prospect of reduced yield would have discouraged any prospective inventor of labor-saving devices. This might account for, partially at least, the lack of technological advances in Chinese agriculture. In short, the Chinese problem has been and still is the problem of land shortage.

All factors considered, it seems that there only could be two solutions to this problem: to reduce population pressure by practicing birth control and to make equally available to all what the land produced. Birth control was out of the question because, in addition to social and cultural considerations (such as the glorification of large families), the Chinese had no such knowledge and could not practice birth control even if they wished to. The second solution was not a true solution, but it was the best available to the Chinese. Because of the lack of a better term, we shall call it the principle of equalitarianism. The spirit of this principle was: no man should have too much at the expense of others.

The translation of this principle into practical policies met with varying degrees of success throughout Chinese history. Chou feudalism was perhaps the most successful in this respect because land was then comparatively plentiful, and the distribution of fifteen acres of land to each peasant family caused no practical difficulty. When Wang Mang attempted a similar arrangement, he failed miserably (Chapter III). His failure, however, did not discourage later rulers. Equal land distribution among peasant families was revived by subsequent regimes, notably Later (North) Wei and T'ang (Chapters IV and V). It could be carried out at the beginning of each of these regimes because dynastic change had substantially reduced population pressure and there was enough land available. The system deteriorated and eventually had to be abandoned as the central authority weakened and population continued to increase. None of these regimes practiced land distribution for any prolonged period, and beginning with the Sung dynasty it was abandoned altogether. Moreover, there were in each dynasty vested interests that were unaffected by the equalitarian principle, including the landholdings of members of the royal household and high-ranking government officials. Since land was subject to buying and selling, the tendency towards land concentration remained a serious, recurrent problem ever since the abolition of feudalism. However, the equalization of land ownership was one of the fondest dreams of all Chinese idealists who condemned land concentration whenever it occurred. In modern times it reappeared as one of Sun

Yat-sen's economic programs and in Mao Tse-tung's collective farms and communes.

Though it was difficult to translate the principle of equalitarianism into the equalization of land ownership, the principle was nevertheless built into Chinese customs. Contrary to many European countries where primogeniture was the rule, in China the property of the deceased was divided equally among his male children. However large the original size of a landholding, it would be eventually fragmented among a number of owners. Thus, land concentration never reached the same proportion as in historical Europe, and landholdings of plantation size were infrequent. The infrequent occurrence of large plantations might account for the absence of a large slave population such as could be found historically in many other countries. Landholdings being small, there was no need for slave workers. Those who have visited rural China must have noticed the crisscrossing footpaths that separate small, garden-like plots, most of which are a fraction of an acre in size. An old Chinese proverb says, "No family can be rich or poor consecutively for three generations." Though to become rich in three generations was more an expression of hope than a statement of fact, for a wealthy family eventually to become poor was in fact a commonplace.

Within a family the application of the equalitarian principle meant that all family members should have the same standard of living despite differences in earning power. A Chinese family was more like a clan in the Western sense, consisting of three or four generations and including brothers, cousins, and their wives and children. It was not merely a biological relationship; it was an economic unit, the members of which protected one another in financial matters. Men being unequal in natural endowment, their achievements in society (and in earning power) were bound to be different, and the Chinese believed that the strong had a moral obligation to help and protect the weak. Since the family came into being through a natural, biological relationship, it seemed to a Chinese that it was the most logical place to fulfill such moral obligations. In reality, of course, he did not rationalize in this matter; he was brought up to believe that a family was a closely knit unit and he acted on that premise. In theory and often in practice, all income of a family, including the earned income of its various members, would go into a common treasury, and each member would receive a certain amount for expenses regardless of the amount he had contributed to this common treasury. The actual amount he received usually varied in accordance with seniority (generation and age) rather than earning power. If the family prospered, all members benefited; if the family fortune declined, all suffered the same. Thus, a Chinese family served the same purpose as many of our social inventions put together—the insurance company, the Social Security Act, the unemployment compensation, and all other socialistic features of a modern society. The Chinese system was less costly, because it did not create so many middlemen.

The assumption of mutual obligations was extended beyond the immediate family members, to the clan, the neighborhood, and relatives and friends in general, though the extent of such assumption was steadily reduced as the relationship became less close. In other words, one's obligation towards his immediate family was higher than his obligation towards clan members, the obligation towards clan members prevailed over the obligation towards his neighbors, and so on. Nevertheless, all these obligations existed. A person was morally obligated to take care of his third or fourth cousin who became destitute, even though he had never met this cousin who was now seeking his help. One day opening the front door, one could also face a total stranger with a suitcase in his hand, who announced that their fathers had once been great friends and that he needed a place to stay for a few days (which often lasted a few weeks or months) until he could find employment. The prospective host did not have to invite the stranger in, but he would encounter social disapproval if he did not. Once coming in, the caller would be treated as a member of the family rather than as a guest, and he would undertake whatever tasks inside and outside the house he was capable of doing. He received no pay and did not expect any. When famine arrived in a village, the rich were morally bound to help the poor. When the rich men's last bit of grain was gone, they, rich and poor, all moved out to other towns and villages that, following an established custom, provided relief for the travelling refugees. The refugees came back early in the spring before the sowing season began.

One of the great institutions in China was the ever-ready granaries, another example of the equalitarian principle. The landowners were assessed to contribute a small portion of their harvests to the ever-ready granaries in good years, and the accumulated grain would be distributed among the poor as relief in time of famine or, in some cases, sold on the open market at below-the-market prices. The prosperity of the nation was often measured by the degree of fullness of its ever-ready granaries. If the grain they contained became rotten, prosperity must have lasted for a long time and historians duly recorded it with great jubilation. If the amount of grain continued to decline as a result of the lack of replenishment, there was a genuine cause for alarm.

Unable to escape the limitations imposed by nature, the Chinese incorporated into their custom and tradition many safeguards against economic hazards. Even social and moral values reflected the same concern. The Chinese, for instance, glorified thrift and condemned waste in unequivocal terms. Though thrift has been a virtue in practically every culture, the Chinese carried it to an almost unbelievable degree. Two stories might suffice to elaborate this point. A man described in *An Un-*

official History of the Literati (Chapter X) continued to raise his two fingers while lying on his deathbed speechless, and his relatives were at a loss to understand his last instruction in connection with the two fingers. Finally someone grasped what he meant and removed one of the two wicks in the oil lamp, and the man nodded his head and died in peace. The other story is in connection with the Ch'ing statesman Tseng Kuo-fan who turned down an applicant for a position despite high recommendations because in an interview over a dinner table the applicant had carefully picked up the unpolished rice in his rice bowl and set it aside on the table, instead of eating it indiscriminately with the good, polished rice. In Tseng's eyes a man so wasteful could not be trusted to rule the people. In this matter of thrift, the emperor and his officials were supposed to set the example. Historians praised Han Wen-ti, because, among other things, "the empress' skirt did not touch the ground" (it was cut short to save cloth); on the other hand, they condemned with vigor the luxurious habits of Ch'in Shih-huang and Sui Yang-ti who had built elaborate palaces for their personal comfort. Wang Mang won great admiration from the gentry-scholars partially because both he and his wife, despite great wealth at their command, were extremely thrifty people.

From the point of view of a modern society, the equalitarian principle had its obvious shortcomings. The implementation of such a principle necessitated an authoritarian organization, on the family as well as at the national level, because only an unchallenged authority could enforce it. Moreover, the principle discouraged individual incentive and enterprise, especially in connection with economic and financial matters. It took away a man's independence and made him a silent conformist to the status quo. These, of course, are all justifiable criticisms. However, it should be pointed out that individualism and independence are modern Western values and that they did not apply to historical China. In historical China conformity was a virtue and individualism was denounced in unequivocal terms. Criticism loses much of its validity if it does not take into consideration differences in social and economic environment. It is debatable whether the traditional Chinese society would have been better off if it had embraced modern Western values.

THE POLITICAL SCENE

The Chinese believed that a nation should be conceived as a huge family, and like a family, each member had his assigned privileges and responsibilities. At the head of this national family was the emperor who, like a father, should love and protect his subjects. He should see to it that flood control and irrigation works were in good order, famines would be relieved whenever they occurred, and justice would prevail within the empire. Moreover, he should by words and deeds set a moral example to the nation and possess the same virtues (such as filial piety) as he expected from his subjects. In performing his state functions he was assisted by a professional bureaucracy and, like him, all his officials should be "fathers and mothers" to the people whom they ruled. In return for his service, the emperor demanded unswerving loyalty and absolute obedience. Treason was punishable by death not only for the person directly involved but also for all his relatives. At least in one case, the death penalty was also extended to the accused's teachers who presumably had forgotten to teach their pupils to be loyal subjects. In addition, he demanded the payment of taxes to support his court, government, and army, and he could call his subjects to perform military service or corvée labor whenever the necessity arose. He would not interfere with their private lives as long as they complied with his basic demands. A subject could worship the way he wished, choose his own occupation, and move freely within the empire. Generally speaking, there was a great deal of personal freedom within the authoritarian state. Joyfully an ancient peasant sang:

> I begin to work when the sun rises;
> I rest when the sun sets.
> I dig a well for my drinking water;
> I plow the field to provide my food.
> Powerful as the emperors are,
> What has that power to do with me? [1]

The imperial power was hereditary, and the emperor was responsible to no one except the inscrutable Heaven. Accepting these two premises, the Chinese nevertheless built into their political system checks on imperial power expressed in theories and traditions. First, there was the ancient theory that people were more important than kings and that the government existed for the benefit of the governed only (Chapter II). If a king abused his power to the detriment of the people, the people were justified in revolting against him and in overthrowing his regime (Chapter III). Second, there were the unwritten customs and traditions which an emperor had to abide by if he wished to act legally. During the T'ang-Sung period, for instance, custom dictated that imperial decrees could take legal effect only after they had been approved by the prime minister. This custom caused a political crisis in 946 when the incumbent prime minister and his two deputies simultaneously resigned, and Emperor Chao K'uang-yin could not appoint a successor because there was no incumbent minister legally qualified to give approval to the appointment. There were numerous cases in which prime ministers returned imperial decrees back to the emperors on the ground that they were contrary in

---

[1] This anonymous folksong is one of the oldest on record and is dated at least 1,000 B.C.

letter and in spirit to the established custom or tradition. In one case the prime minister contemptuously burned an imperial decree, because in his opinion the woman whom the emperor had wished to promote to the lofty position of imperial concubine through this decree was clearly unqualified. Third, there were the dynastic rules formulated by the founding fathers of each dynasty and legally binding with regard to all their successors. During the Sung dynasty, for instance, one of the dynastic rules was that "under no circumstances should capital punishment be inflicted upon ministers and censors." This rule was dictated by Chao K'uang-yin and was faithfully observed by his successors. Lastly, the institution of censorate which empowered certain officials to criticize and remonstrate with the emperor also helped in preventing the abusive use of imperial power.

The basic weakness of these checks on imperial power was that they could be effective only as long as the emperors wished to observe them. A conscientious emperor like Chao K'uang-yin would abide by them voluntarily, but there was nothing anyone could do if a ruler chose to ignore them. Despotic rulers honored them when it suited their convenience and ignored them when it did not suit them. That eunuchs could not participate in government was clearly a dynastic rule of the Ming. Yet, when Yung-lo came to the throne and felt that he had to reward his eunuch friends, he threw this rule overboard (Chapter IX). Generally speaking, emperors of the later periods in Chinese history were more despotic than earlier ones (Chapter IX), and they were more inclined to violate customs and traditions which restricted their power. In China theoretical and institutional guarantees were not effective means to check the abuse of power; the best guarantee was the inherent and acquired goodness of the rulers. Good rulers made good government, not vice versa (Chapters II and V).

In administering his empire, an emperor was assisted by a huge army of bureaucratic personnel. Before the abolition of feudalism in the third century B.C. little distinction was made between the government and the royal household, and all officials were regarded as the king's personal servants. The situation changed during the Ch'in-Han period when the territory to be administered was a large empire instead of small, independent kingdoms. The government was then separated from the royal household and made solely responsible for the administration of the empire. During the Han dynasty the head of the government was the prime minister (*shang-shu*) appointed by and responsible to the reigning emperor. Under him were thirteen ministries, including war, personnel, transportation, and postal offices. The thirteen ministries were merged into six ministries during the Sui dynasty, and the new arrangement remained unchanged throughout subsequent regimes. The Six Ministries, headed by a prime minister, were often referred to collectively as the cabinet (*nei-ko*). The institution of premiership, however, was abolished early in the Ming dynasty, and the Six Ministries were put under the direct jurisdiction of the emperor (Chapter IX). For the first time in Chinese history, the emperors became their own prime ministers.

As the affairs of the Six Ministries had to be coordinated, the Ming regime created a new post, the Grand Secretariat of the Cabinet (*Nei-ko ta-hsüeh-shih*). The official duty of the Grand Secretary was somewhat of a clerical nature; he could not make policy decisions which belonged exclusively to the emperor. However, with the passage of time he was delegated more authority; if he was able and if he enjoyed the emperor's confidence, he became prime minister *de facto,* if not *de jure.* The Ch'ing dynasty followed the same arrangement until 1729 when the emperor Yung-cheng superimposed on the Grand Secretariat a newly created office, the Privy Council or Office of Strategic Affairs (*Chün-chi ch'u*) over which he personally supervised. Originally created to plan and execute military campaigns, it soon became the policy-making organ of the nation, largely because the emperor personally supervised it. The Grand Secretariat, still in existence, handled the routine, administrative matters. This arrangement persisted until towards the end of the Ch'ing dynasty.

To a Westerner, perhaps the most interesting aspect of the traditional Chinese government was the institution of the censorate. It was an institution as old as the premiership, but it persisted even after the premiership had been abolished. Its official functions varied with different regimes, but its main duty remained the same: to criticize and impeach government officials. The censors were generally low-ranking officials but were empowered to speak candidly on their superiors, including the emperor. Their criticisms extended to an official's private life as well as his official competence because government officials were expected to set examples to the people they ruled.

The institution of the censorate was well developed as early as the Han dynasty. The highest official in charge was the Grand Censor (*Yü-shih ta-fu*), with the rank of deputy premier. Under him were two officials, one in charge of the censorship of government officials (*Yü-shih ch'eng*) and the other keeping a watchful eye on the conduct of the royal household (*Yü-shih chung-ch'eng*), including the emperor. Assigned to each province (*chou*) was a provincial censor (*tz'u-shih*) who visited all districts under his jurisdiction beginning with the eighth moon month each year and reported his findings to the imperial government once every three years. He was a comparatively low-ranking official (annual salary: 600 piculs of grain); yet, upon his recommendation, the high-ranking governor (annual salary: 2,000 piculs of grain) could be rewarded or punished, promoted or demoted. His roving duties familiarized the imperial government with the lastest local conditions, and his independence of the provincial governor enabled him to speak freely on what he had observed. Sometimes he was given the power of promoting or dismissing local officials on the spot.

During the T'ang dynasty the institution of censorate was further strengthened by the establishment of the Board of Censors (*Yü-shih t'ai*). The duty of the censors was to scrutinize government policies and decisions and to criticize and impeach unfit or incompetent officials. Even the prime minister was not immune to their criticism. Independent of the Board of Censors were the imperial counsellors (*chien-kuan*) whose sole duty was to admonish or remonstrate with the emperor. They were chosen by the prime minister from men of highest integrity and broad knowledge, and theoretically at least, they should never be punished for their opinions. In reality, they often served as the mouthpieces of the prime minister and criticized the emperor as the prime minister himself would have criticized him. They acted as a cushion between the two most powerful offices in the nation, so that the emperor and the prime minister were able to maintain a harmonious relationship despite differences of opinion. An enraged emperor could summarily dismiss an imperial counsellor, but the prime minister's office was usually too lofty to suffer a similar indignity.

After the T'ang dynasty the influence and prestige of the censorate declined as monarchy became more absolute. By the Ming dynasty the office of imperial counsellors was abolished altogether, and replacing it was a low-ranking examiner (*chi-shih-chung*) whose sole duty was the examination of royal decrees before they were issued. He could send these decrees back to the emperor if, in his opinion, they were "improper" or "unconstitutional." His delaying action helped prevent unpopular measures from being enacted in haste and gave the emperor additional time to think them over. The regular Board of Censors was maintained, but their independence was greatly reduced. The censors could criticize and impeach their superiors, but they did so at their own peril. Those who wished to become martyrs could of course do whatever they pleased, including remonstrating with the emperor. As autocracy reached its historical apex under the Ch'ing regime, the influence of the censorate was also reduced to a minimum. The office of the examiner was incorporated as a part of the Board of Censors, and imperial decrees could no longer be delayed on "constitutional" grounds. One Ch'ing censor, in order to convince the then empress dowager (Tz'u Hsi) of the correctness of his point of view on a matter of imperial succession, presented his memorial and then ended his life by drinking poison. When a censor had to commit suicide to enable his opinion to be given adequate attention, the status of the censorate had become very sad indeed.

The local administration of different dynasties varied in details, but the basic structure and the spirit behind it remained substantially the same. Its relationship with the administration above and its duties with regard to the people below did not change. The local administration of the last dynasty, Ch'ing, will be discussed here as an example. China proper was then divided into eighteen provinces, each headed by a governor (*hsün-fu*). Two or three provinces were combined to form a viceroyalty, headed by a viceroy or governor-general (*tsung-tu*). To prevent a governor-general from having too much power over a large territory, the Ch'ing regime made the relationship of these two offices a parallel instead of a jurisdictional one. Both governors and governor-generals could petition and had direct access to the emperor. In case of conflict over business matters only the emperor (or whoever controlled the emperor, such as the empress-dowager) could render the final decision. Below the provincial level were the circuits (*tao*), each headed by an intendant or *tao-t'ai*. Each circuit was in turn divided into prefectures (*fu*) and districts (*chou*), prefectures generally being larger than districts. At the bottom of the administrative ladder were subprefectures (*hsien*), the grass-roots units of government. The head of a subprefecture, often translated as magistrate, was the people's immediate ruler; he collected taxes, administered justice, and was responsible for the maintenance of peace and order within his jurisdiction. Though his rank was one of the lowest, he was perhaps one of the most important officials in the nation. If he were wise and incorruptible, the people benefited; otherwise they would suffer. Below the subprefectural level, there was no organized government as such. Village affairs were taken care of by village elders or local gentry, in a rather informal manner. As a general rule, they settled disputes by negotiation and compromise. Only important issues, such as murder and armed robbery, were referred to the magistrate for decision.

All officials, high or low, received their positions through appointment. They were responsible to their superiors who appointed them rather than to the people whom they governed. In recruiting personnel to staff governmental positions, the Chinese invented a fairly objective, impartial procedure. The purpose was to find the most qualified men; birth, religion, and occupation were not supposed to be considerations. There were two major systems in recruiting governmental personnel, namely, selection (*hsüan-chü*) and examination (*k'o-chü*). The first system was more widely used during the earlier periods of Chinese history, and the latter system did not come into being until the seventh century. Many dynasties, however, used a combination of both.

The selection system was developed and perfected during the Han dynasty when the centralized government required a large army of civil servants to administer the affairs at the various levels of the empire. One aspect of this system was the selection by local officials of young men of sound character and good native intelligence to be educated at the central university in the capital. Upon graduation these young men would be appointed as the lowest-ranking officials with the local or central government. Moreover, local administrators could at anytime select those whom they regarded as the most talented (*mou-ts'ai*) or the most virtuous (*hsiao-lien*) to be interviewed by the imperial government for possible appointment to governmental positions. The neglect of selection duties on the part of local officials was punishable by law. During the Later Han dynasty the selection system was more institutionized, and the number of persons to enter civil service each year was made proportional to the total population of each province, usually one for every 200,000 persons. To prevent influence peddling, all selectees were required to take a written examination, and only those who passed could enter the civil service.

The examination system per se was introduced during the Sui dynasty and was not fully developed until the T'ang dynasty. The candidates could be either graduates from public or private schools or those who had been selected by local officials (Chapter V). By the Sung dynasty the examination system had become so prestigious that in the eyes of the public it was the most honorable way of becoming a government official (Chapter VI). When the Mongols conquered China, even they had to conform partially to this tradition (Chapter VIII). It was in force throughout the Ming-Ch'ing period.

Like other systems, the examination system deteriorated with the passage of time, and the question frequently arose as to whether it was the best way of recruiting governmental personnel. Most of the controversies centered on the subject matter of the examinations. The T'ang and early Sung regimes emphasized the composition of poetry which, as has been pointed out in an earlier chapter, was no way of measuring a person's administrative ability. The emphasis on the interpretation of classics (*ching-yi*) during later periods did not improve the situation either. Chu Hsi, for instance, was so dissatisfied with the entire system that he once remarked that the nation would be better off if it stopped giving civil service examinations for thirty years. Ironically, it was his philosophy and the *Four Books* according to his interpretations that became the basic texts of all questions given in the examinations during the Ming-Ch'ing period. Candidates could no longer think and write freely and independently; if they did, their papers would be automatically rejected. Though unsatisfactory as a measurement of a man's true ability, the composition of poetry reflected to some extent his basic intelligence and literary training. Many people wondered whether the formalized expression of popularly accepted ideas could even serve that purpose.

The examination system further deteriorated when not only ideas but also the way to express them became highly conventionalized. The way officially approved was the so-called eight-legged form (*pa-ku*) which required parallel phrases or sentences (balanced like a person's legs) and the rigid observance of a well-defined structural style. First developed during the Ming dynasty, it remained the standard form throughout the

Ch'ing dynasty. That it could not serve the examination purpose was rather obvious, and as early as the seventeenth century, Ku Yen-wu denounced it as worse than Ch'ing Shih-huang's burning of books and burying scholars alive insofar as the promotion of new ideas was concerned. Despite severe criticisms like this, the eight-legged essays remained with the examination system, and the government was either unwilling or unable to find a better substitute. The examination system was finally abolished in 1906.

Serious as these shortcomings were, we should not let them deceive us when considering the basic merits of the examination system. Its shortcomings were those of a technical nature, and its advantages were fundamental and basic. Though much can be said about its unreliability, it cannot be denied that those who had passed the examinations were generally brighter and more intelligent than those who had failed. Whatever disadvantages education might have as a determining factor to judge a person's worth, it was still better than other personal attributes, whether they be birth or wealth. Before modern times China was the only country (except those countries that were under Chinese cultural influence such as Korea) in the world that had an objective, institutionalized method of recruiting governmental personnel. Within the examination system, power and wealth made no difference and only the level of education as measured by the examinations mattered. Attempts to evade the impartiality of the examination system by any sort of dishonest means were major crimes under Chinese law and were often punishable by death. Though much has been said about Chinese corruption, the examination system was one of the least corrupt of all Chinese institutions.

Moreover, the system provided a great deal of social mobility since even the humblest (except the "mean people" for some dynasties) could become a member of the ruling class by acquiring an education and passing the examinations. The absence of clear-cut class divisions might explain partially why parliamentary government never developed in China. As one recalls, parliamentary government developed in Western Europe as a result of the successful challenge by the middle class of the king's monopoly of government. Since in China the people had access to governmental positions through the examination system, there was less need to struggle against the king for the control of the government. With the exception of the throne itself, all offices were open to the public. The Western Europeans, unable to participate in the king's government, overthrew that government and replaced it with one of their own, known as parliamentary democracy. The Chinese, on the other hand, strengthened and prolonged absolute monarchy by joining it. By making all offices open to the people except their own, Chinese monarchs were much more clever than their European counterparts.

THE SOCIAL SCENE

Customarily the Chinese spoke of their society as composed of four classes: the scholars, the farmers, the artisans, and the merchants. The scholars were given the highest status because they performed what the Chinese regarded as the most important function: the transmission of an ancient heritage and the personification of Chinese virtues. The farmers' standing was second only to the scholars because they were the primary producers, feeding and clothing the nation. The artisans processed what the farmers had produced, and their function was not regarded as so essential as that of the farmers. At the bottom of the social scale were the merchants whom the Chinese regarded as outright exploiters, making profits from what others had produced or processed and contributing nothing themselves. Two other classes were often added to the four described above. One was the soldiers, whose expected role of burning and killing was very distasteful to the Chinese. Inasmuch as they took away the most valuable things from society, their standing in society was inferior to that of the merchants. Their image in the eyes of the public was not improved during modern times when the idle and adventurous swarmed to their ranks as mercenaries. The other class was the so-called "mean people" (chien-min), consisting of domestic slaves, prostitutes, entertainers, and members of lowly professions such as barbers. Though the contempt shown for this group could be explained historically, it was nevertheless a prejudice. It should be added, however, that the total number of this group was very small at any given time.

A more accurate classification of the Chinese people was perhaps the one advanced by Mencius some 2,300 years ago. He believed that in an ideal society there were two kinds of people: the educated who ruled and the uneducated who were the ruled. Though Mencius was only speculating on what an ideal society should be, the Chinese applied his theory almost to the letter until modern times. If we transcribe the customary division of classes (scholars, farmers, etc.) into his classification, all but the scholars would belong to the ruled category. Among the ruled it was difficult to say which group actually had a higher standing. Though traditionally the farmers were exalted and the merchants were condemned, such an evaluation of their comparative worth was done more in principle than in fact. It did not affect to any large extent the estimation of each class in the eyes of the general public. With the exception of the Former Han dynasty, discrimination against merchants was more theoretical than actual, though this discrimination, even on a theoretical plane, did discourage young men of talent from pursuing a commercial career. While it is true that a great landlord enjoyed more prestige than a rich merchant, it is not correct to say that a shopkeeper was regarded as inferior to a small, independent farmer. In the eyes of most people he was definitely superior to a tenant farmer. In China as in other societies, income crossed over the established social boundaries to become an important factor in determining social prestige. What made the traditional Chinese society seem unique was that income played only an auxiliary rather than a dominant role in the matter of social standing.

While the difference between farmers, artisans, and merchants was comparatively minor insofar as social standing was concerned, there was no question that scholars towered above them all in social prestige and general esteem. A number of reasons can be advanced to explain their exalted position. First, without an established religion (Confucianism was not a religion), China did not have a clerical hierarchy. On the other hand, some of the essential, useful functions traditionally carried on by the clergy in the West had likewise in China to be performed by someone. The teaching of morals, for instance, was such a function. Under the circumstances no one was in a better position to perform such functions than Confucian scholars. Second, the ultimate goal of practically all Confucian scholars (including Confucius) was to secure a position with the government, and in China as in many other agricultural societies, there was no higher prestige than that of becoming a king's minister. Since government officials were selected from scholars as a matter of principle, the prestige generally ascribed to government officials was also shared by scholars. Third, there was the difficulty of the Chinese written language. Though to learn colloquial Chinese (*pai-hua*) was perhaps no more difficult than to learn the English or Russian languages, it was definitely much more difficult to learn to read and write literary or classical Chinese. This required not only the mastering of more than 10,000 separate characters and their numerous combinations but also a fair knowledge of the great accumulation of Chinese literature. Unless the learner was a born genius, it would take a considerable part of his life just to learn to write in a presentable style. His style could always be improved no matter how good it was, and to improve it would be a life-long process. Most Chinese just could not afford the time. Thus, true mastery of a literary education was bound to be limited to a few. Knowledge, like commodities, commanded a high price when it was difficult to obtain.

The dividing line between the educated and the uneducated, the ruling and the ruled, was not a fathomless abyss unbridged. As education was an acquired attribute, class distinctions were earned, not hereditary. The nobility was noble partly because all noblemen were educated. The same thing can be said concerning the "old families" of the Wei-Tsin period. The only major exceptions were the Mongols during the Yüan dynasty who were noble despite the fact that they might be illiterate. But the Yüan regime was a non-Chinese regime, and its noblemen were never regarded as truly noble in the Chinese sense. Many of the Chinese eunuchs were also uneducated, but they were denounced as usurpers whenever they acquired power as a result of the emperor's abdication of authority. By and large the Chinese used education as a criterion to measure a man's worth. The emphasis on education made China one of the most mobile societies until modern times. Few pre-industrial societies had a faster turnover of the social and power elite, and such a fast turnover kept the Chinese society vital and dynamic. The constant absorption of new blood from the lower strata kept the elite in a state of continuous flux. The knowledge that one would be accepted as a member of the ruling group if he had clearly demonstrated his worth by passing the civil service examinations smoothed over the natural antagonism between the ruling and the ruled. There were no class struggles in the Marxist sense of that term because there were no definite, unchangeable classes.

The lack of class antagonism may have been partially responsible for the unchanged nature of the traditional Chinese society despite changes in political regimes. Dynastic changes meant little more than changes of royal households and should never be interpreted as the triumph of one class over another. With the establishment of a new regime, the same social structure remained intact and people moved between classes as freely as before. As social mobility was high, there was a general satisfaction with the social structure as it was, and no political regime ever wished to alter it. Such a state of contentment may partially explain the Chinese distrust for social innovations and their constant reference to history as the best guide and counsel. Confucius prided himself upon having faith in the ancient sages, and Wang Mang and Wang An-shih, two of the greatest reformers in Chinese history, quoted copiously from Confucian classics to justify their reforms. The reformers wanted to bring China back to its golden past, instead of building a new society for the future. As late as the nineteenth century scholars and statesmen, even when agreeing that reforms were essential, insisted that such reforms should be carried out only within China's historical framework. Since they kept on looking backward, there must have been many things in the past which, in their opinion, deserved to be preserved.

Recognizing that man's distinction in society depended upon earned and acquired attributes, the Chinese viewed with a broad mind religious and racial differences. Religion and race were not factors in class differentiations. Twice in history China was completely conquered by foreigners, and it was only then that race became a dominant factor in social divisions. In both cases, Yüan and Ch'ing, it was the ruling aliens who discriminated against the Chinese. As defined by Confucius, the difference between Chinese and barbarians was a cultural rather than a racial difference, and those who had accepted Chinese culture were regarded as Chinese regardless of their racial backgrounds. The Chinese pointed out with pride that the founders of some of their dynasties were alien in origin. The founder of the Chou dynasty, for instance, rose from a "barbarian" land, and the ancestors of T'ang's royal house could be traced back to a variety of "barbarian" blood. Yet Chou and T'ang were two of the greatest dynasties in Chinese history. The Manchu "barbarians" were accepted as Chinese rulers once they accepted and adopted Chinese culture. One of the diplomatic maneuvers frequently used by ancient emperors was to marry their princesses to "barbarian" chiefs, and no Chinese ever questioned the wisdom of such marriages on racial grounds. The absence of racial discrimination served the Chinese well: it enabled them to expand slowly and steadily until they occupied the geographical area we know today as China. At one time all peoples outside of the North China plain were regarded as barbarians. They became Chinese once they were culturally assimilated. The Roman Empire eventually split into many independent, quarrelling kingdoms; China, on the other hand, remained unified for the most part of her written history.

The absence of racial discrimination extended beyond the Mongoloids, people whose physical features were similar to those of the Chinese. During the historical past, Caucasoids (Persians, Arabs, Jews, and Europeans) were known to have taken permanent residence in China. It is even possible that at one time there was a sizable Negro population. Since historians failed to record exactly how they looked except the casual remark that they were dark, it is still debated whether they were Negroes. Whether they were Caucasoids or Negroids, there is no indication that they were discriminated against on account of race. When racial discrimination was introduced during the modern period, it was the Europeans in China who discriminated against the Chinese.

Unlike Europe where religious differences were a major factor in social cleavage, China did not attach much importance to religion as a determinant in social differentiation. There were Buddhist and Taoist priests, but they did not constitute a distinct class in the sense that they were higher or lower than the rest of the population. China had no established religion, and religion was left to families and individuals. Individual emperors might prefer one religion or another, but no Chinese emperor ever compelled the nation to follow his own example. There was nothing in Confucian ideology which prohibited the existence of other ideologies, and to be intolerant for the sake of intolerance was definitely anti-Confucian. Though from time to time there were individual zealots (Han Yü, for instance) who wrote inflammatory essays condemning Buddhism, the people as a whole were remarkably tolerant in religious matters. There were "Three Persecutions of Buddhism" in Chinese history, and the most severe persecution was conducted by T'ang Wu-tsung. Yet, the most severe persecution, which consisted of the reduction of the number of Buddhist monasteries and monks, was based upon economic rather than ideological reasons, and lasted only two years (Chapter IV). No Buddhist was put to the sword simply because he was a Buddhist. We should never read into these persecutions the same meaning as the Roman persecution of Christians and Christian persecution of heretics. In a typical Chinese household of modern times, the father was likely a Confucian and his wife was in most cases a devoted Buddhist; it was not unusual for them to decide to send their children to Christian missionary schools. In the minds of the Chinese, all religions taught people to be good: a religion defeated its basic purpose if it taught its followers to discriminate or hold hatred against other religions. Like farmers and artisans, the priests (Buddhist, Taoist, etc.) performed an essential, useful service, but they were not entitled to preferential treatment in the eyes of the Chinese. They did not possess the power of reward or punishment, either in this world or in the next. Their conduct and behavior would be judged on the same basis as the rest of the population.

Since education was the primary avenue to power and influence, it would seem that every Chinese family would have sent their children to schools. This, of course, was not the case. There were many considerations against what outwardly seemed to be the most logical decision to make. Most Chinese were small or tenant farmers, and they did not have the economic means to educate their children. A boy in school would not only mean the deprivation of one worker in the field; it would also mean that he would be taken away from farm production permanently once he was an educated man because an educated man was not supposed to do any manual work. Financially, education could be justified only when the educated man passed the civil service examinations and acquired a governmental position, and his chance of passing them, as we have said before, was very small indeed (Chapter VI). Failing to pass the examinations, his other alternative of making a living was to secure a position with small financial returns, such as school teaching or serving as a secretary-adviser (mo-liao) to some other official. In most cases he became an unemployed intellectual and had to be supported by his family for the rest of his life.

In view of the great risks involved, it was not surprising that educated men came mostly from the well-to-do families that had independent income from land or other sources. Though there were cases in which a peasant's son rose to become prime minister, most prime ministers came from the landlord class. In a more or less typical situation, a farmer would encourage the most promising of his children to acquire an education, and the whole family (including his other sons) would work to support him. If he succeeded in passing the civil service examination, the joy and the financial reward would belong to the entire family. If he failed, the family's prestige was nevertheless enhanced by the presence of an educated man, even though his intellectual capacity might not go much beyond the writing of a presentable letter and the composition of badly rhymed poems.

THE FAMILY SCENE

Like the Chinese nation, a traditional Chinese family was an auto-cratic organization. It was organized on two well-defined, unwritten rules: the superiority of the older over the younger generation and the superiority of males over females. In case of conflict, the first rule prevailed over the second. It could be compared to an army, each mem-ber receiving orders from his superiors and giving them to his inferiors. In a family of three generations the chain of command would look something like this:

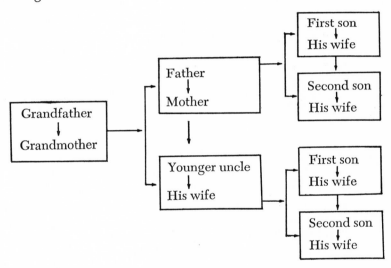

Within each generation the oldest son had authority over his younger brothers and sisters, though this authority was not so absolute as that of the parents. In case of disobedience on the part of a younger brother, the elder could appeal the case to the parents, who under normal circum-stances were expected to support his stand. Since boys and girls were often segregated at an early age, the elder brother's commands—if he had any —to his unmarried sisters were first approved by his mother and then transmitted through her. All these, of course, were done in an informal manner.

These rules worked because they were based upon mutual responsi-bilities and obligations: love and protection on the part of the superiors and respect and obedience on the part of the inferiors. When the head of a family made a decision affecting each member, he took into consideration the family interest as a whole, and it was the absolute trust in his impartiality that made each member obey without complaint, no matter how adversely it would affect him personally. If a father decided that his second son was to be sent to school and the rest of his sons were to work at the family farm or shop, his decision had to be obeyed by all family members unless the father allowed himself to be persuaded to change his mind. Because of his broader knowledge, an educated son might be able to make more suggestions and command more attention with regard to family affairs, but education could not raise his status within the family circle. Theoretically, final decisions could only be made by the father, and in the absence of the father, the mother, even though both parents might be illiterate. Each member was held responsible for the behavior of his section of the family, his wife and children. To an outsider, the head of the family (father or grandfather as the case might be) was responsible for the actions of all members of the family, from his sons to his great grandsons.

Of course, there were individual variations from the pattern described above. A father might decide to abdicate his authority in favor of one of his sons (usually the oldest), and the mother, being out of touch with the outside world, might choose to stand on the sideline with regard to family decisions. But their authority was there, if they chose to exercise it. Generally speaking, the more "gentry" a family was, the stricter the chain of command. An emperor might be the Son of Heaven before his subjects. Yet within the family circle he was his mother's son; he should wait on her and obey her commands at all times and under any circumstances. Filial piety was the first virtue of the nation to which all must subscribe and from which even an emperor could not claim exemption. In the eyes of the public, a father was within his rights to put his daughter to death to save the family from disgrace if, for instance, she were found pregnant while unwed. But the son committed the greatest crime indeed if he took the law into his own hands against his father, no matter how much his father deserved the punishment. The Chinese believed that the father-son relationship was the most important of the five cardinal relationships among men (the other four relationships were between king and subjects, husband and wife, older and younger brothers, and friend and friend), and that the superiority of father over son had to be maintained at all costs.

Like other institutions, the traditional Chinese family had its advantages and disadvantages. It provided psychological and economic security; it created a sense of belonging. Its emphasis on mutual responsibility and family honor helped prevent wrongdoings among family members. Its disadvantages, on the other hand, were many and obvious. The Chinese glorified large families, and often three or four generations lived together. No matter how much each member was supposed to love the others, jealousies and resentments were bound to occur, especially among members of the same generation. Quarrels flared up from time to time, and harmony was often achieved only through the iron-handed suppression by the family elders. The inferiority of the female sex made the female role the least enviable, especially females of younger generations. The in-law difficulties, though universal, were greatly intensified in the Chinese situation. To avoid them was nearly impossible because a Chinese could not easily leave his parents and take away his wife to set up a new household. To do so would bring disgrace to the family, and the son would be universally condemned. To make the situation worse, he was expected to side with his mother against his wife in any disagreement between them, regardless of the merit of the case. The Chinese compared spouses to clothes which could be changed when necessity arose, but parenthood, being a biological relationship, could never be changed. Faced with a nonunderstanding mother-in-law, a young wife could have a miserable life.

Family tragedies often arose from difficulties between mothers and daughters-in-law, and almost without exception it was the latter who had to make the sacrifice. The sorrows of daughters-in-law were lamented by ancient poets and have been recorded in their poems and epics. The most famous epic in this regard is *The Peacock Flies Southeast* (*K'ung-ch'üeh tung-nan fei*), written by an anonymous writer of the third century. It is the story of a talented girl who learned to "weave at thirteen, tailor at fourteen, play the guitar at fifteen, and recite the *Odes* and the *History* at sixteen," and was married to a government clerk at seventeen. The couple were very devoted to each other, and this devotion apparently aroused the jealousy and resentment of the groom's mother. Maintaining that her daughter-in-law did not know how to please her, she insisted that her son should divorce his young wife. His mother's insistence left him no choice; however, he promised his wife that he would bring her back if somehow he could make his mother change her mind. After the girl went home to her parents, her mother and elder brother soon arranged to marry her to a son of a prefectural magistrate. Unwilling to break the promise she had made to her former husband and yet unable to disobey her mother and brother, she decided to drown herself. When the news arrived that she had committed suicide, her former husband joined her by hanging himself on a tree. According to the author, the event had actually occurred, and to those who are familiar with the traditional Chinese family, it is plausible. The Sung poet Lu Yu (1125–1210) had a similar experience, though it ended less tragically. He had to divorce his wife as ordered by his mother, but the couple maintained their affection for each other throughout the rest of their lives.

In the traditional Chinese family practically all marriages were arranged; only the lowest of the low would marry for love and romance. Today it is still fashionable to begin an engagement or wedding announcement by such an august remark as "By the order of our respective parents," even though the parents might have little or nothing to do with the happy occasion. In bygone days the sexes were segregated, and a maiden was not supposed to see a male stranger under any circumstances. The higher the family standing was, the stricter the segregation. Such being the case, marriages had to be arranged. In looking for a prospective wife or husband for their son or daughter, the parents had to consider a number of factors, and the most important factor was the other family's reputation and standing. The personal attributes of the prospective groom or bride came second: the boy should be talented and promising (for gentry families) or strong and hard-working (for peasant families), and the girl should be even-tempered, know her household work (such as sewing), and look wholesome, preferably on the plump side. The interested family revealed its intention to a go-between who approached the other family in the most casual manner; it had to be casual to avoid embarrassment. For a gentry family of high standing, the marriage procedure consisted of "six rituals" (*liu-li*), from the initial inquiry to the wedding itself. Most families, however, could not afford the expenses and passed over most of them. One ritual they could not pass over was the exchange of birth information: the hour, day, month, and year the prospective groom or bride was born. A fortune-teller was called in, and he would decide whether the proposed marriage was an auspicious one. A girl born in the Year of the Tiger would have a much more limited choice. She could not marry a man born in the Year of the Lamb because she would surely swallow him. But it would be all right for her to marry a man born in the Year of the Monkey because the monkey could always jump up to the back of the tiger. Needless to say, many prospects of happy marriages were ended right there.

In the Chinese thinking, a marriage was as much a marriage of two families as it was between the two persons directly involved. Its major purpose was the propagation of the male family line. Children bore their father's name, never their mother's. Individuals submitted themselves to their family's decisions, and rarely were they consulted about their prospective mates. Two great friends, learning that each other's wives were pregnant, might decide right then that their unborn babies were engaged if they turned out to be opposite in sex. Instead of seeing anything wrong with this kind of arrangement, the traditional Chinese society glorified it. Since marriage was arranged, the groom would be an ingenious man indeed if he had seen his wife before the wedding night. A woman performed her function well as a wife if she had borne her husband a son: it was then that her position with the family became absolutely secure. If she failed to perform such a function, her husband would be strongly pressed to take a concubine, mostly by his parents and sometimes by his wife as well. Socially and legally, a man could take as many concubines as he could afford. Since few could afford it, concubinage was confined to a small fraction of the population. Chinese emperors, who could best afford it, had scores or even hundreds of concubines.

Grim as Chinese marriage might seem, there is no indication that it was less happy than marriages arrived at any other way. Even though divorce was socially disapproved, it was legally permissible, and divorced persons could remarry if they chose to. Yet there were few cases of divorce. The concubine system may have saved many marriages, but it did not seem to be the main factor in the scarcity of divorce cases. Social disapproval was definitely a deterrent, and the families involved would normally exercise great pressure to prevent marriages from breaking up. Strange as it may seem, the fact that marriages were arranged might have been beneficial in some respects. A good family background as emphasized by the Chinese was perhaps a more important factor in happy marriages than a prospective mate's physical appearance. The customary subservience of wives to husbands and the Chinese attachment of great importance to children might be another contributing factor. It is not known, however, how many people remained married though unhappy. It will remain unknown, because the Chinese, as a matter of principle, did not believe that they should reveal to outsiders their feelings towards their spouses. Outward affection was taboo, even towards one's own wife. When a man and his wife had to appear together in public, the woman customarily walked ten paces behind.

How did sexual segregation come into being? Certainly there was no such thing at the beginning of recorded history. Then boys and girls enjoyed each other's companionship as much as they have under any other culture. Here is an example:

> You, shy, beautiful lass, my beloved,
>   Failed to meet me in a city corner you'd promised.
> Here I came; nowhere could you be found.
> Should I leave or should I have waited?
> For a long time I hesitated.
>
> You, shy, beautiful lass, my beloved,
>   Gave me a river reed flashing red;
> I love the river reed,
> I love more my beloved.
>
> I love the river reed, beautiful and enchanting;
> What beauty would it possess,
> Had it not caressed my beloved? [1]

[1] Translated from a poem in the *Book of Odes*.

In those ancient years a woman could be equally romantic:

> Are you thinking of me?
> Your love I cannot see.
> What prevents you from crossing the stream
>   That separates you and me?
>
> If you stay your adoration for me,
>   Others will not, certainly!
> Oh, how stupid you can be,
>   How stupid you can be! [1]

As late as the second century B.C. it was still possible to conduct courtship. The Han poet Ssu-ma Hsiang-ju (179–117 B.C.) courted a rich widow with his lute and succeeded in persuading her to elope with him. Four centuries later the handsome P'an Yo (247–300) was reported to have been mobbed by women every time he went out. Such an occurrence would have been unthinkable in a later period. The indications are that sexual segregation became more and more rigid with the passage of time and was strictly enforced after the Sung dynasty. What caused the change? The acceptance of Confucian moralism was unquestionably one of the major reasons, especially the Sung School of philosophy. Chu Hsi, for instance, not only advocated strict sexual segregation but glorified widowhood as well; he thought he did society a great service by encouraging widows to join their dead husbands at the earliest possible moment. As his philosophy dominated the intellectual and ethical scene for the next seven hundred years, his bleak, puritanical ideas began to be accepted as the lofty goal which every gentry family strove to achieve. With the popularity of his ideas, the status of women declined.

Nothing can illustrate better the decline of women's status in society than the custom of foot-binding. It is not known exactly when or how this custom began. One reputable source maintains that it began in the court of Li Yü (Chapter VII) where a court dancer "bent her feet with silk so they were shaped like a crescent and whirled around as if she were dancing in the clouds." By the Sung dynasty foot-binding was widely practiced among the gentry families. The binding process began when a girl was four or five and continued until the desired result was achieved. The net result was a pair of crippled feet, only half the normal size. (Many mothers did such a thorough job that their daughters could barely walk.) Why did this inhumane custom ever get established and moreover persist for almost 1,000 years? Men, for unknown reasons, prefer small feet on women. A Western woman responds by squeezing her feet into shoes of smaller size, and Chinese women, perhaps more eager to please, bound their feet so they could walk forever as a modern

[1] Translated from a poem in the Book of Odes.

ballerina dances. Chinese gentlemen of older generations would not consider a woman attractive unless she had a pair of bound feet. However, it should be pointed out that this custom was by and large confined to a small portion of the population: the gentry families. The peasant women who had to work in the field neither desired nor could they afford such a painful luxury. The custom remained a major curse of the traditional Chinese society until the twentieth century.

THE INTELLECTUAL AND MORAL SCENE

The Chinese believed that the purpose of education was to make man a better man and that this moral purpose was inseparable from the learning process. In fact, moral indoctrination began as soon as the educational process began. A schoolboy of five or six might encounter the following assignment the first day he was in school:

When a man is born (*Jen chih ch'u*),
His nature is basically good (*hsing pen shan*).
Human nature is similar (*hsing hsiang chin*);
Only environment makes it diverse (*hsi hsiang yüan*).

These are the opening statements of the thirteenth century *Three-character Classic* (*San-tzu ching*), the chief primer for school children for almost seven hundred years. Needless to say, the schoolboy did not understand them, but he memorized and recited them like a song as his teacher had commanded. For the time being, the most important thing was to recognize and write the twelve characters that composed the two sentences. After he finished the *Three-character Classic*, his next book assignment might be the *Analects of Confucius*. The first paragraph of the *Analects* reads as follows:

Confucius says, Is it not a great pleasure to learn and to review constantly what you have learned? Will you not be pleased when a friend comes afar to see you? Is he not a gentleman indeed who shows no annoyance even though nobody knows his goodness?

By the time he was nine or ten the pupil should have covered the *Four Books*. If he was intelligent and his memory was good, he might have gone beyond the *Book of Odes* and the *Book of History*. Of course, he did not understand all that was said in these books, partly because of the nature of the subject matter and partly because they were written in a literary, classical style. However, he had acquired a large vocabulary, and it was then that he and his teacher would explore the hidden meanings of the ancient passages. When he reached the age of eleven or twelve, he was expected to write in an understandable manner. Once every ten or fifteen days he would be given a theme to write on: the theme was usually taken from one of the *Four Books* or *Five Classics* and consequently had a strong moral tone. One theme might be: "Confucius says, Do not travel afar while your parents are living. Elaborate." Another theme might be: "Mencius emphasizes the difference between righteousness (*yi*) and profit (*li*). Why?" Needless to say, all themes had to be written in a literary, classical style. Once he knew how to read independently the commentaries as well as the texts, the student's dependence on his teacher was lessened and he was practically on his own. How far he could advance depended upon his native ability, his ambition (or rather, the ambition of his family), and the economic status of his family. The decisive moment would arrive when he took the lowest level of the civil service examination.

It is easy to see that the traditional Chinese training was heavily one-sided, and little room was provided for other studies besides ancient classics and literature. Though Confucius himself believed that an educated man should master the "six arts" (rites, music, archery, chariot riding, calligraphy, and mathematics), academic learning was practically the only thing emphasized by all the later Confucian schools, especially those on the local level. After the civil service examination system was introduced, the students had little incentive to learn anything besides the classics and poetry because the examinations tested primarily these two fields. Thus the best product of the Chinese school system of old was a Confucian scholar, well-learned in Chinese philosophy, literature, and related subjects, but inadequately prepared in more practical fields. He knew nothing about technology and science, and his knowledge of what we today call social sciences was shallow and unsystematic. His sense of values was completely Chinese, as he had no way of knowing anything outside the cultural confine of China.

Of Confucius' "six arts" calligraphy was the only art form given great attention during the latter periods. Calligraphy supposedly taught the virtue of patience and perseverance because long and constant practice was required before the writing would look even presentable. A child began to practice on his calligraphy as early as he learned to read, and usually he began by following the style of one of the great masters. The master could be, say, the ninth century Liu Kung-ch'üan (noted for his "bony" strokes), the thirteenth century Chao Meng-t'iao (famous for his graceful lines), or others; and the pupil's teacher would help him to select the style to follow in accordance with his natural inclinations. He practiced with brush and ink two or three hours a day; very likely he would continue to practice whenever he found time for the rest of his life. A man's calligraphic achievement, like a lady's face, was open for all to see, and too often it was regarded as a measurement of his cultural attainment. The incentive to improve it was enhanced during the Ch'ing dynasty when a paper written for the civil service examination would be automatically rejected if its author's calligraphy was judged as below standard. Well-executed pieces of calligraphy were hung in the most conspicuous places in a gentleman's house as if they were great paintings. Even in paintings there were accompanying poems (a practice developed during the later periods) which indicated unmistakably the painters' calligraphic achievements. A man whose calligraphy was poor would encounter a great deal of inconvenience. It was a severe handicap if he had to look for employment.

Since educational and moral purposes were considered inseparable, every branch of learning had to serve a moral purpose. Music refined a man's character; chariot riding and archery, two of the ancient subjects, taught the learner "the precedence of the seniors over the juniors" rather than physical fitness or military skill. The love poems in the *Book of Odes* were twisted to teach moral lessons, and history was written primarily to "punish the wicked and reward the virtuous." The writers of novels, short stories, and plays had in mind the same purpose. Even the author of *Flowering Plum in a Golden Vase* had to insist that the real purpose of his book was to teach a lesson against sexual indulgence (Chapter X). While the educated received their ethical teaching from works of old, the uneducated learned it from the examples set by the educated and from stories and plays they heard and saw in the tea houses and theatres. Since the basic standards of behavior were those recorded in the ancient classics, there was a moral code familiar to all and universally accepted. Its inviolability was strengthened through custom and usage.

The penalty for violating the moral code was severe and immediate. A thief would be lashed in public, and a murderer would have to pay with his own life regardless of the provocation. Chinese prisons were among the most inhuman places ever created for human beings; they vied with medieval dungeons as possible hells on earth. Though the educated were supposedly above corporal punishment, they received penalties perhaps even more severe if they ever committed crimes. The penalty was more severe because they had been expected to set examples for others. They were regarded as a disgrace to society and were perhaps ostracized forever. The sense of shame would be shared by their entire families and by their descendants for an indefinite time to come. They could no longer participate in the civil service examinations, and their chance for social recognition or any advancement would be gone forever. For practical purposes they would live as "living corpses" for the rest of their earthly terms. The severity of punishment was a strong deterrent to any wrongdoings.

The Chinese drew no subtle distinction between moral and legal codes. A moral offense was often dealt with as if it were a legal crime.

Filial disobedience was a moral offense; it was also punishable by law if the magistrate chose to enforce it. However, as long as an offense was of a minor nature and involved members of the same family, the law would refrain from intervening, trusting that the principle of equity could be better served without intervention. The law would intervene if different families were involved and if they could not settle their disputes through negotiation and compromise outside of the court. Society regarded a family, instead of an individual, as a moral unit. A family was held responsible for the conduct of its members, and the entire family was punishable if any of its members had committed a crime against society. Family members emulated one another in good behavior, and the restraining power of the entire family could usually prevent an individual from going morally astray. When Chang's child fought with Li's child, Chang was socially obligated to punish his child, and he could reasonably expect that his neighbor would do the same with his, because Chang was responsible for his child's behavior, not his neighbor's. It was ungentlemanly to blame others, and it was unthinkable for a father to give such "unfatherly" advice as "Hit him back." A child should be taught to criticize himself before he learned to criticize others, and he should never be allowed to shift the blame. He should be constantly reminded that people judged his family according to his behavior and conduct.

The families that supposedly set examples to other families were the gentry families. The definition of the word "gentry" was rather obscure, and it was more a product of public image than a combination of tangible factors. It varied from place to place: the same person whose status was too low to be considered a man of the gentry in a large city might be a leading member of the gentry class in his native village. However, there were things in common among the members of the gentry class: education, independent income, and a favorable public image. Education made one a member of the intelligentsia, a transmitter of the Chinese heritage; and an independent income freed him from the necessity of seeking undesirable employment. Since most Chinese derived their income from the land, an independent income usually meant the possession of a landholding. A favorable public image resulted from careful cultivation and came only with the passage of time, and a person was well situated indeed if his family had belonged to the gentry class for several generations. As there were numerous degrees within each of the three factors, there were numerous degrees of "gentility." Therefore, an ideal member of the gentry was a person whose intellectual capacity had been confirmed by his successful passing of the civil service examinations, whose income was large, and whose moral character was above reproach. The situation would be most ideal indeed, if he were a great landlord and a holder of the highest academic degree (*chin-shih* or "advanced scholarship"), and especially if his family had produced scholars and government officials for many generations. In such a case he belonged to *kao-men* (literally, high doors) or *shih-chia* (old families), the most enviable of all gentry families.

The gentry were the recognized local leaders. An appointed magistrate, who usually came from another province, had to secure their cooperation if he wished to govern successfully. Living in the same community for generations, if not centuries, the gentry had a deeper concern with local welfare than the temporarily appointed government officials. How a community thrived depended to a great extent upon their efforts and leadership. They financed and supported public works, schools, orphanages, and other useful projects. They were the guardians of public morals, and in moral matters they were expected to be more strict with themselves than with others. Within the Confucian confine, their private life could vary a great deal, depending upon not only individual inclinations but economic status as well. A gentry family of high standing might have a life such as that described in *The Dream of the Red Chamber,* while a less well-to-do person might encounter the same difficulties as the author of *The Six Chapters of a Floating Life* (Chapter X). However, as a personal embodiment of Chinese culture, they all loved poetry, calligraphy, and good paintings. They regarded themselves as superior, and their superiority was admitted by the general public.

SUMMARY

Those Chinese who came from rural areas where the Western influence was the least felt must remember the life described above, and perhaps remember it with a great deal of nostalgia. But for better or for worse, the traditional Chinese society is gone, and it does not seem that it can be revived. Its undermining began more than a century ago and has been virtually completed since the Communists took over the mainland in 1949. Perhaps its disappearance was inevitable. The traditional Chinese society was built on two major pillars: a sedentary, agricultural life and the ancient Confucian heritage. Industrialization would have undermined the former, and the pervasiveness of the Western culture would have broken down the latter. The presence of the Western culture may provide China with new answers to old problems and may direct it to a new path which it has never thought possible before. Of course, many ancient values will have to be sacrificed. It is still too early to tell into what kind of society China will eventually evolve.

ᚚ xii

The Western Impact (1)

THE EARLY INTERCOURSE WITH THE NON-CHINESE WORLD

Until the last century the Chinese had shown little interest in foreign countries. This lack of interest was due partly to the belief that China was culturally superior and had no need to learn anything from the outside world and partly to the fact that China looked down upon trade and was not interested in proselytizing, the two major motives that have brought foreigners to China in modern times. A man who went abroad and left his parents behind and the family cemetery unattended was universally condemned because he had violated a cardinal virtue of Confucianism, filial loyalty. To go abroad was often a legal as well as a moral crime and was punishable by death or long imprisonment. Thus, in the intercourse between China and the non-Chinese world, China had been largely passive. To be sure, there were times when an exuberant China sent out expeditions to learn about the outside world, such as Chang Ch'ien's "exploration of the West," the pilgrimages of Chinese Buddhists to India, and Cheng Ho's "seven voyages to the 'Western Ocean.'" These, however, were isolated cases, and each of them lasted for a comparatively short period. There were many Marco Polos who informed Europe about China, but there had been no Chinese Marco Polo in Europe until the nineteenth century. Western Europe emerged about 1500 and began to dominate the world; but of this fact, and of the profound changes brought about because of it, the Chinese knew nothing. For their ignorance they had to pay dearly, as we shall see later in this chapter.

In bringing China and the non-Chinese world together, foreigners played a much more active role. The Koreans, the Japanese, and the Indians had come to China at one time or another. Beginning with the Wei-Tsin period (220–420) there was also a steady inflow of Near Easterners who came to China as traders or missionaries. A Chinese book (*Loyang chia-lan chi,* or *A Story of Buddhist Temples in Loyang*) written in the sixth century records that there were more than ten thousand alien households in Loyang alone, and a sizable portion of them seems to have been Arabic and Persian. With the establishment of the Islamic empire in the seventh century, the inflow increased, and the newcomers, as one might expect, were mostly Arabs. With the passage of time the sea routes to China became more important, as ships were better built and became more seaworthy. Some of the foreigners came to trade, made a profit, and returned home; others settled permanently in the cities of the coastal areas, such as Canton, Ch'üanchou, and Yangchow. Within each of these cities, foreigners lived in segregated quarters (*fan-fang*), and from them the city government selected a respected or influential man as their chief. During the T'ang-Sung period (618–1279) Arabs constituted the largest number of foreigners in residence, and more often than not the chief was an Arab. If a foreigner committed a crime against his own countrymen, the customary law of his native land would apply; if the crime were committed against a man of a different nationality or a Chinese, the Chinese law would prevail. Foreigners often married Chinese women; they were not allowed, however, to take their Chinese wives back to their home countries.

After many years in China, many of these foreigners acquired Chinese names, learned the Chinese language, and even participated in the civil service examinations. In 848, for instance, an Arab named Li Yen-sheng passed the examination and became a holder of the highest academic degree ("advanced scholarship"). Foreigners like Li Yen-sheng would be eventually Sinicized; they would lose their Caucasoid physical features too, as they kept on intermarrying with the Chinese. However, some of them continued to hold their original religion despite assimilation in every other respect. A story was told during World War II that an

American soldier of Jewish faith went to visit a Chinese synagogue, only to be reminded of his "mistake" at the entrance. "Sir, this is a Jewish synagogue, not a Christian church," said the Chinese usher, bowing and smiling. As far as he was concerned, the fact that the American soldier was a white man automatically ruled him out as a Jew.

Besides the traders, other foreigners came to China to preach and proselytize. Among the most active were the Manichaeans, the Nestorians, and the Muslims. Manichaeanism was introduced to China by Persians towards the end of the seventh century and began to spread one century later. By the twelfth century it was strongly rooted in the Southeast where numerous Manichaean communities could be found. Several Chinese books which describe the Manichaeans have survived, and most of them treat their subject matter in a derogatory manner. The Manichaeans are described as "demon worshippers" and their activities as "incomprehensible." For one thing, they dressed differently. "Their leaders wear purple headwear and loose shirts, and their women cover themselves with black hats and white robes." "Their holy book deals with the two opposites, brightness and darkness, and it speaks of the three worlds, the past, the present, and the future." The Manichaeans would not touch liquor nor eat meat, including milk and cheese. However, "men and women gathered at night to engage in licentious activities and would not disperse until daybreak." They helped one another whenever the need arose; "a new convert is supported by the entire congregation until he becomes established." "They call themselves members of one family and provide room and board for a travelling Manichaean even though they have never met him before." "They worship neither Buddha nor ancestors, and when a Manichaean dies, they bury him naked." Their deviation, in habits and beliefs, from the general cultural pattern, together with their clannishness, caused much misunderstanding and frequent friction between them and the rest of the Chinese population. Local governments occasionally persecuted them. After the twelfth century Manichaeanism declined steadily as a religious force, and many of its followers began to attach themselves to Buddhist or Taoist sects. It was not revived during the subsequent centuries.

The most important source on Chinese Nestorianism is a stone stele unearthed near Sian in 1623. The stele, bearing a cross in the middle of coiling dragons, was erected by a T'ang emperor in 781. The text on the stele, *The Spread of Syrian Nestorianism in China* (*Ta-ch'in ching-chiao liu-hsing Chung-kuo pei*), describes Nestorian activities in China in the seventh and eighth centuries. In 635, says the document, a Syrian priest named A-lo-pen brought to China the Nestorian Bible, and the emperor (T'ang T'ai-tsung) ordered one of his ministers to receive him in the western suburb. "The emperor had carefully examined its teachings and concluded that they were beneficial to men and the world and that they should be made known to all Chinese within the empire." In 638 the first Nestorian church in China, with twenty-one newly converted monks, was established at Ch'angan. During the reign of T'ang Kao-tsung (650–683), says the document, "Nestorian churches were established in all provinces . . . and its gospel was heard within the four corners of the empire." The Nestorian Bible had twenty-seven chapters, and the church was active in educational and philanthropical endeavors. "They fed the hungry, clothed the poor, medicated the sick, and buried the dead." The ability of Nestorian monks as medical doctors was verified by other sources. "The Nestorians are experts in eye diseases and diarrhea," says one source; "they can see illness before it occurs and they even undertake head surgery." In 683, says the Sung historian Ssu-ma Kuang, Emperor T'ang Kao-tsung complained of a severe headache and the loss of eyesight. A Syrian doctor was called in, and the emperor was saved from blindness. "Nestorian monks shaved their heads but grew long beards," says another historian. "They were not allowed to own slaves, nor could they have private property. They worshipped once every seven days and sang hymns seven times a day. They performed a ritual called baptism and they revered the cross."

It is doubtful whether the T'ang emperors who patronized the Nestorian church knew what it was about. A T'ang emperor (T'ang Te-tsung, 780–804) ordered a Nestorian monk to cooperate with Buddhists to translate Buddhist scriptures, even after the Buddhists had pointed out that there was a difference between these two religions. To the emperor, however, there was no reason why they should not cooperate, since both claimed that they knew so much about the next world. Emperor T'ang Hsüan-tsung ordered his four brothers to worship in the Ch'angan Nestorian church, and at the same time he decreed that his image and the images of his four predecessors be kept in the church, to be admired by all Nestorians. Nestorian monks were awarded governmental ranks and titles, and on Christmas Day, they received special incense for their church and a special dinner for themselves. There is no indication that the church ever resented the "pagan" behavior of Chinese emperors.

During T'ang Wu-tsung's persecution of Buddhists, Nestorian monks, together with Manichaeans and Zoroastrians, were ordered to return to civilian life. It is not known whether this persecution was the main cause of the decline of Nestorianism. In any case, this religion had only a small, scattered following even during its prime, and even its minor success seemed to have been due to government patronage. In the public mind, it was associated with the T'ang royal house. When Sung replaced T'ang, Nestorianism practically disappeared from the national scene.

Of the three minority religions described here, Islam proved to be the most enduring. The religion was founded by Mohammed in 622, and one generation later the first Muslim missionary had reportedly arrived in China. In the middle decades of the eighth century when T'ang's power began to decline, the Islamic Arabs gained control of Central Asia and extended their control eastward to include eventually the Tarim Basin. Islamic power continued to advance during the subsequent centuries; when it finally receded, it left behind millions of converts. Today the Muslims are one of the largest minorities in China, and most of them, as one would expect, live in the Northwest. During the T'ang-Sung period Muslims were found in the coastal cities as well as in the Northwest. These Muslims were either Arabic or Persian in origin and came via the sea routes as traders. Chinese historians described them as "abhorring pork and loving cleanliness"; few of them gave many details. One historian, however, was more explicit:

The "sea barbarians" (hai-liao) lived side by side with the Chinese in Canton and the most powerful of them was a man named P'u [believed to be the transliteration of the Arabic word Abu]. . . . The P'u family had been in the city for a long time, and being wealthy, lived a life of luxury far exceeding the level permitted under the law. However, since the local government was interested in encouraging more traders to come and since the family involved was not Chinese, it did not wish to concern itself with the violation. Thus, the P'u house became bigger and more luxurious as its wealth continued to grow at a fast rate. In 1192 when I was ten, I followed my father to Canton and had the opportunity of visiting the P'u house. The house was several stories high and covered a large area, though I can no longer remember the details. . . .

The barbarians worshipped spirits and loved cleanliness; it seemed that they had nothing to do all day long except to worship and to pray for better fortunes. The deity they worshipped sounded like Buddha but there was no image of him in the place where he was worshipped. Frankly, nobody knows what kind of deity he really was. In the place of worship there was a stone stele several *chang* high on which were carved strange, cursive words, and all worshippers prostrated themselves before it instead. . . . Behind the place of worship was a high, slender pagoda protruding skyward towards the clouds. It did not really look like a pagoda, and viewed from a distance, it looked more like a silver brush. It was made of earthen tiles and was painted with white powder. At the ground level was a door which led to a flight of circular stairs, and a person ascended the stairway to reach the top. The stairway, however, was invisible from the outside. Before ships arrived from the sea in the fourth or fifth moon month, these barbarians went up and down the pagoda, making strange, unintelligible noises and praying for southern winds to come. Often the winds responded. At the pinnacle of the pagoda was a golden rooster which turned around with the change of wind. As I understand, one leg of the rooster has been missing.[1]

[1] A copy of the Chinese original appears in Fang Hao, *A History of Intercourse between China and the Non-Chinese World* (*Chung hsi chiao-t'ung shih*). (Taipei: The China Publishing Society, 1959), vol. 2, pp. 37–38.

Throughout the T'ang-Sung period most of the foreigners who came to China were peoples of the Near East: the Persians, the Arabs, and the Jews. With the establishment of the Mongol empire in the thirteenth century also came the Europeans. For a long time Europeans had been fascinated by the possible existence of a "Prester John" in the Orient who, they believed, could be persuaded to attack the hated Saracens from the East if he could ever be reached. When the Mongols rose from the northern deserts and before they became a threat to Europe, many Europeans thought that their prayers had been answered. The Mongols, however, conquered people of all faiths indiscriminately, and Europe was consequently disenchanted. The sentiment of Europe, as expressed by the Bishop of Winchester in 1238, was: "Let us leave these dogs (Mongols and Saracens) to devour one another." Later when the fear of Mongol conquest had subsided, Europeans again entertained the hope of making an alliance with the Mongols. King Louis IX of France sent ambassadors to the Great Khan; so did the papacy. Though no military alliance was made, a Catholic outpost was established in Peking. The outpost was later elevated to an archbishopric, after several thousand converts had been made.

After the Mongols had conquered Central and Western Asia, the Arabs who had blocked the land and sea routes to China were no longer a barrier between Europe and China. With the arrival of the first Roman Catholic missionaries came also the first European merchants. Among them none exercised greater influence on later generations than Marco Polo, whose name has been mentioned in another connection (Chapter VIII). He came to China as a young man, and during his stay of seventeen years (1275–1292) in China, he served Kublai Khan in various capacities. After his return to his home city Venice, a war broke out between his city and Genoa, and he was captured as a prisoner-of-war. In a Genoese prison he dictated to a writer of romances named Rusticiano what he had observed in China and many other countries he had visited. The result was the *Description of the World* or *Travels of Marco Polo*. The information he provided on thirteenth century China was generally accurate, though here and there one notices some exaggerations, perhaps unintended. He described what he saw; there was no attempt to explain it in a more profound manner. His objectivity was sustained as long as the Saracens were not involved; he spoke highly, for instance, of the good customs of the Buddhists and Confucians (called "idolators" indiscriminately in his book). His book is of great value to Chinese historians, as it helps them understand better some of the most important events of the thirteenth century, such as the siege of Hsiangyang, the massacre of Ch'angchou, and the attempted conquests of Japan. The extant Chinese sources on these events are not comprehensive enough.

While Marco Polo could hardly be considered an important personality in China, the impact of his book on contemporary Europe was tremendous. That a more advanced society existed simultaneously with Europe was hard to believe, and most of the Europeans dismissed the book as mere fable. When the book finally won credence, it aroused great interest in China among the literate Europeans. Its readers included such men as Christopher Columbus. To the religiously devoted, there was a huge pagan world to conquer, and to the worldly merchants, there were enormous profits to be realized. The book was the most influential travelogue on China ever written in a European language, and it paved the way for the arrival of thousands of Europeans in the centuries to come.

As a result of the increasing contact between the East and the West, many of China's great inventions were brought to Europe. Among them were printing, paper making, the compass, and gunpowder. Even though Marco Polo might not personally have brought the art of printing to Europe, there were others who could have done it. It is inconceivable that this important invention could have eluded the attention of such an observant person as Marco Polo. There is also the possibility that Europeans learned the art of printing indirectly through the examination of Chinese paper currencies which were either obtained in Western Asia during the Yüan dynasty or had been brought back from China by travelling Europeans. Was there any relation between Gutenberg's movable type and the Chinese movable type which was invented some four centuries earlier? This question remains unanswered. There is no doubt, however, that the Chinese first invented the movable type as well as block printing.

When making books, the ancient Chinese wrote on bamboo or silk, and it was not until the first century B.C. that cloth rags were mixed with silk to strengthen it as a writing material. This rag-silk mixture, however, was not "paper" in the modern sense of that word. Chinese written records indicate that the first true paper, made of discarded fishing nets, appeared in 105 A.D. Recent findings seem to have pushed the date back a little further. Shortly afterwards paper was being made in all parts of China, and among its raw materials were tree barks, hemp dust, and cloth rags. By the eighth century the Arabs had learned the paper-making process from the Chinese, and the paper produced at Samarkand was acclaimed as the best outside of China. Towards the end of the century paper factories were also set up at Baghdad, and Chinese technicians were employed as supervisors. From the Near East the knowledge of paper making spread to Egypt, and then to France and Italy. Slowly this new paper replaced the traditional sheepskin as the writing material for most Europeans.

Though the invention of the compass was attributed to the legendary Yellow Emperor (Huang-ti), it did not appear in written records until the third century B.C. By the Han dynasty it was used by military commanders on the battlefield as well as by magicians (*ying-yang chia*) who depended upon it to locate the most propitious sites for burying the dead and erecting buildings. It does not seem that it was used as a navigational instrument then, because the earliest written record ever mentioning it in that capacity did not appear until 1119. The Arabs learned to use it as "a sailor's friend" towards the end of the twelfth century or early in the thirteenth century. The Europeans, in turn, learned its use from the Arabs, and soon it became standard equipment in every seagoing vessel.

Mention of sulphur and nitrates, two of the materials used to make gunpowder, appeared in written records as early as the Han dynasty. However, they were then used by alchemists to make elixirs, and it was not until the tenth century that they were mixed with carbon to make military explosives. The words "fire cannon," "rocket," "missile," and "fire ball" appear time and again in the official Sung history as well as two other books written during the same period. The first detailed description of using "fire cannon" in warfare was in connection with a battle fought in 1126 when the Sung army used it against the invading Nuchens. The so-called fire cannon was a tube made of bamboo filled with gunpowder which, when fired, threw a flaming missile towards the enemy. Since the barrel was made of bamboo, the flying missile could not cover a long distance. According to a description of a battle scene in 1132, it took two persons to carry a "fire cannon," and the cannons were fired from a moving platform after it had been moved close to the wall of the besieged city. Their effectiveness as a military weapon does not seem to have been great; Sung, which possessed this new weapon, was nevertheless unable to resist the invading army of the Nuchens. The Chinese invention of gunpowder never went much beyond its crudest form, and it was abandoned as a military weapon shortly afterwards. Since it could create a great deal of noise, the Chinese used it to make firecrackers for chasing out evil spirits and celebrating New Years. Today they still make the best firecrackers in the world market.

The Arabs improved gunpowder for military use, and by the thirteenth century Europeans like Roger Bacon had heard of its existence. One century later the Arabs used it to attack the Spanish city of Baza, and the very next year (1326) the city of Florence ordered the manufacturing of cannon and cannon balls. From Italy the making of gunpowder soon spread to other European countries, and by the 1350's it had become an effective weapon on the battlefield. In the seventeenth century both the Chinese and the Manchus had Portuguese cannons in the battle for the control of China.

In this cultural exchange the Chinese also learned a great deal from the non-Chinese world, such as the calendar, medical science, architecture, and music. Generally speaking, China contributed more to foreign cultures than it gained from them. Nevertheless, both sides benefited.

Beginning with the fourteenth century China remained static, whereas Europe surged ahead, not only technologically but in a variety of cultural activities. China was left behind, and in due time had to learn from Europe.

THE MISSIONARIES

Early in the modern period no group played a more important role in the cultural exchange between Europe and China than the Roman Catholic missionaries. We have noticed that the first Catholic missionaries came to China as early as the thirteenth century. Their impact, however, was not great then. The Latin community consisted of several thousand members (missionaries and converts), and the Church never made sustained efforts to enlarge it. When the Ming regime replaced the Yüan in 1368, the patronage hitherto extended to Christianity was withdrawn, and missionary activities all but ceased. They were renewed and intensified after the Reformation when the Church felt that it could more than compensate for its losses in Europe if it could conquer new territories for the faith in the non-European, pagan world. In the Society of Jesus the Church found one of its greatest proselytizing agents, and in training and in devotion to their assigned task, the Jesuits were superb. China, which had the largest population in the world and had more souls to be saved than any other country, was logically the greatest prize to win. If it were won, it would be the greatest victory for the Church since the conversion of the Roman Empire.

There were, however, numerous obstacles which seemed to be insurmountable at the beginning. In entering China the missionaries encountered one of the most advanced societies then known, and they had to establish for their religion some aspects of superiority before it could compete equally with other religions, some of which were older than Christianity and were deeply rooted in Chinese society. That the new faith recognized no other faith except its own was an added disadvantage because it aroused the resentment and anger of other religions. Its claim to the monopoly of truth in religious matters and its exclusiveness in its relationship towards other religions antagonized many Chinese who had long since learned the wisdom of compromise, even in religious matters. Regardless of the comparative merits of different religions which were highly partisan and perhaps impossible to determine, the religion that began its existence in a new territory by condemning all others would conceivably encounter more difficulties. Yet, in the matter of faith, the Roman Catholic Church could not and did not compromise. The uncompromising attitude taken by the Church concerning what it regarded as basic matters was the immediate cause of the banning of Christianity in 1724, as we shall see shortly.

In view of the difficulties involved, the fact that the early Jesuits could make a great impression upon the high officials in Peking attested to their devotion, tact, and ability. Among the Jesuit missionaries the Roman Catholic Church sent to China, Matteo Ricci was unquestionably one of the greatest. Ricci had studied mathematics and astronomy in Rome before he came to Macao in 1582, and with an understanding of the Chinese which had seldom been revealed among Europeans of his time, he plunged himself into the study of the Chinese language, literature, and philosophy. He first wore the garb of a Buddhist monk; but finding that Confucian scholars commanded more prestige, he changed to a mandarin robe. By such tact and by the knowledge he had acquired about Chinese culture, he won respect and esteem from Chinese scholars and officials. He wished to detach himself from European state power, the exercise of which, he believed, would do his mission more harm than good. In 1601 he arrived at Peking and was allowed to reside and preach. He concentrated his efforts on high governmental officials, with the hope that if they were converted to the new faith, the entire nation would follow. In less than five years, more than two hundred people had been baptized, including some high officials.

In retrospect, the contribution of Ricci and his fellow Jesuits lay more in their role as cultural ambassadors than in their mission as religious proselytizers. The total number of Chinese converts at the end of the seventeenth century, one hundred years after Ricci's arrival in China, was estimated between 100,000 and 250,000, a figure far from being impressive in a vast country like China. The lack of sensational success was not due to the lack of devotion and ability on the part of Christian missionaries; it resulted from the strong cultural resistance China could offer. As cultural ambassadors, however, these missionaries were unsurpassed. They enlightened Europe on China and informed China on Europe.

Arriving in Peking, Ricci presented to Emperor Ming Sheng-tsung (r. 1573–1619) an image of Christ, an image of the Virgin Mary, a Bible, a pearl-studded cross, two clocks, a world atlas, and a clavichord as "tribute." The emperor and his court officials were greatly impressed with the atlas and the clocks, but not much with any of the other presents. The atlas showed that there were five continents in the world and that "China is the greatest country in Asia and Italy is the greatest country in Europe." The clocks, as one Chinese official put it, showed the great ingenuity of "foreign devils." From the very beginning a tacit understanding seemed to have been reached. The missionaries would serve as advisers on science and technology in order to gain permission to preach and proselytize, and the Chinese tolerated or even encouraged their stay in

China so long as they could serve China in some useful yet worldly capacity. To the Chinese they were more scientists and technicians than missionaries.

The Jesuits had their first opportunity of showing their mathematical superiority in 1611 when the Ministry of Rites recommended the reform of the old calendar which had erred repeatedly in the prediction of the eclipse of the sun. Subsequently, at the urging of the Confucian scholar Hsü Kuang-ch'i who had been converted to the Catholic faith, the imperial government entrusted a group of Jesuits, headed by Joannes Adam Schall von Bell, to revise the calendar. The resultant calendar was regarded as superior to both the Chinese calendar and the frequently used Muslim calendar (*Hui-hui li*), and the Board of Astronomy in which many Jesuits served became the key position from which the missionaries extended their influence among the Chinese literati. When the Ming dynasty was overthrown in 1644, the new regime, Ch'ing, adopted the Jesuit calendar without much change. After the death of Schall in 1666, another Jesuit, Ferdinand Verbiest, served as an astronomical specialist with equal distinction. Despite occasional attacks by the defenders of the old calendars, the Shih-hsien calendar, as the Jesuit calendar was then called, was used throughout the Ch'ing dynasty. The Jesuits served the new regime as capably as they had served the old one.

Other Jesuit activities included map making, the translation of scientific works into Chinese, and the casting of cannon. Some Jesuits served as medical doctors, and others were called to become translators and consultants when China negotiated a treaty with the Russians (Treaty of Nerchinsk, 1689). Previously, the Chinese literati had been greatly impressed with Ricci's world atlas because this was the first time that the Chinese had ever heard of many foreign countries located on the atlas. As cartographers, the Jesuits' reputation continued to grow, and many Chinese were eager to learn from them. The Ch'ing government decided to take advantage of their talent, and from 1708 to 1715 they were sent by the emperor K'ang-hsi to all parts of China to make a geographical survey and record their findings on maps. The work was completed in 1717 and was entitled *The Complete Atlas of the Empire* (*Huang-yü ch'üan-lan t'u*). It was the first set of maps of China ever made by Western, scientific methods.

The books translated into Chinese were religious as well as technological, but it was the scientific and technological works that attracted the greatest attention among Chinese scholars. Some of these works were ancient classics such as Euclid's *Geometry,* translated jointly by Ricci and his Chinese friend Hsü Kuang-ch'i. The findings of Galileo were also rendered into Chinese. Other works were written by the missionaries themselves. One of the best-received books of this kind was *An Illustrated Explanation of Wonder Instruments* (*Ch'i-ch'i t'u-shuo*) by Joannes

Terrenz, the first systematic treatment of mechanical engineering ever to appear in China. The tremendous amount of knowledge these missionaries possessed amazed most Chinese and overwhelmed others. The following comment made by a Chinese scholar of the seventeenth century was perhaps typical of the reaction of the Chinese intelligentsia at that time:

The Westerners seem to be a hundred times more ingenious than the Chinese. Is it because they have been specially favored by Heaven? On the other hand, many of my friends know as much as they do; it does not seem that the Chinese are inferior to them in basic intelligence. The difference is that in China a man cannot achieve fame through technology and he spends all his time and energy in seeking wordly fortunes. He has no time for technical matters and is consequently inferior to a Westerner in this respect.[1]

Inspired by the Western missionaries, the Chinese then wrote a large number of scientific and technical books themselves. On mathematics alone there were seventy-six known works written during the seventeenth century. Had such inspiration continued, would the Chinese intellectual life have been markedly different from what it was in the eighteenth and nineteenth centuries? After the departure of the Jesuits, the Chinese intellectuals went back to their old routine of practicing calligraphy and writing eight-legged essays to prepare for the civil service examinations. The intellectual curiosity, temporarily stimulated by the Jesuits, soon disappeared.

In addition to map making, translation of books, and a variety of other secular activities, the Jesuits were often called upon to make military weapons. It may seem strange that the Church's representatives should even think of doing such a thing. However, if they had any scruple about their new duty, there was no indication of it. In fact, the close relationship between the acquirement of secular knowledge and warfare was very much in the mind of early Jesuits. Said Ricci in the introduction to Euclid's *Geometry:*

While the use of geometry in various fields is too large a subject to be treated here, it is clear that in warfare upon which a country's survival rests, the knowledge of geometry is absolutely essential. Therefore, a wise, brave general should first learn geometry, otherwise his wisdom and bravery would be exercised in vain. How can a general be considered good if he knows nothing about astronomy and other related sciences? A good general should be first familiar with the geography of the place where the battle is to be fought as well as his supply and logistic problems. Secondly, he should deploy his troops in accordance with the terrain of the battlefield. He could deploy them in a circular fashion if he wishes to deceive the enemy with regard to the size of his command, an angular shape if he wishes to impress his enemy with his own strength, and a formation shaped like a crescent if he intends to encircle his

[1] Fang Hao, *Chung hsi chiao-t'ung shih,* vol. 4, p. 84.

foe. If he proceeds to attack, he marches his soldiers like a sharp sword right through the enemy's ranks with the intention of routing them. Thirdly, he has to make sure that his offensive and defensive weapons are the newest available and that his soldiers are proficient in using them, as old weapons become obsolete with the arrival of new ones. I have read the history of various countries and all of them depend upon the perfection of new machinery [weapons] for offensive and defensive purposes. . . . The various kingdoms in the West had conquered and annexed one another before they were converted to Roman Catholicism some 1600 years ago. There were cases in which a small army could defend a besieged city successfully against an attacking force ten times as large, from land and sea. How did it manage to achieve the almost incredible? It was because its commanders were proficient in geometry.[1]

The use of geometry in warfare as described by Ricci seems to have been far fetched; nor was his interpretation of European history flawless. The motive behind this and similar writings was nevertheless clear: to gain the confidence of the Chinese literati in the practical application of the sciences in which the missionaries were experts and to use such influence as they would thus acquire for the eventual goal of converting China to Christianity. On the other hand, the Chinese government would use the missionaries' talents as well as it could, and it had no objection to their proselytizing activities. It had been tolerant of other religions before, and there was no reason why it should make Christianity an exception.

In 1623 the first group of Portuguese artillerymen arrived at Peking, accompanied by the Jesuit Joannes B. Rodrigues who served as a technical adviser as well as translator. The cannons they brought exploded during a demonstration and killed one of the party; the rest of the group was sent back to Macao. The second group arrived in North China with more and better cannons in 1629 and saw action against the Manchus in northern Hopeh near Peking. Meanwhile the Jesuits in Peking were busy designing and casting new and better weapons. Some of the Jesuits brought their creations to battlefields, and at least one Jesuit was injured in action. In 1640 Schall was ordered by the Ming emperor Ch'ung-chen to cast five hundred cannons, after he had successfully produced some twenty-nine. However, the Ming dynasty was overthrown before the project could be completed.

The Manchus, Ming's enemy, soon learned the use of cannon to good advantage. Some of the Jesuit cannons were brought to them by Ming generals who had surrendered, and others were captured on the battlefield. In 1631, improving upon the Jesuit model they had captured, they began to manufacture their own cannon. The new weapons, nicknamed "the red-barbarian generalissimos," were a major factor in the Manchus' successful campaign in South Manchuria. During the reign of K'ang-hsi

[1] A copy of the Chinese original appears in *Chung hsi chiao-t'ung shih*, vol. 4, pp. 87–88.

time and again Verbiest was called to supervise the casting of cannon. These cannons were reportedly better than any that had been in use before and were partially responsible for the success of the emperor's numerous campaigns. As a reward, Verbiest was promoted to the rank of deputy minister in the Ministry of Public Works in 1682.

The friendly relationship between the Chinese government and the missionaries did not last indefinitely. Ricci and his fellow Jesuits understood Chinese custom and tradition, and they knew that if Christianity were to make headway in China, it had to make some concessions to such ancient Chinese practices as the reverence for Confucius and ancestors. With great tact, Ricci emphasized the similarity between Christianity and Confucianism, and in a letter to a Buddhist layman who had challenged him in a debate, he said that one of his major purposes in coming to China was to teach filial loyalty. He found in ancient Chinese classics evidences to support Christianity, and he maintained that T'ien (Heaven) and Shang-ti were in fact the same as the Christian concept of God. The worship of Confucius and ancestors, said he, was not incompatible with the teaching of Christianity. While Chinese scholars were greatly pleased, his compromise with Confucianism antagonized his fellow Christians, including many in his own mission. Nicolaus Longobardi, Ricci's successor as head of the China mission, did not agree with many of his predecessor's beliefs, but he was too wise to press his point at the risk of losing China for the Church.

The success of the Jesuit mission in Peking encouraged the arrival of missionaries of other religious orders, notably the Dominicans and the Franciscans. With their arrival came also the sectarian rivalries so familiar in Europe. The disagreement between the Jesuits and other orders ranged from the purely academic, such as the meaning of the Chinese word T'ien, to a matter of vital concern, which was whether they should allow their Chinese converts to continue their worship of Confucius and ancestors. The so-called rites controversy split the Catholic missionaries in China into two rival camps. The Dominicans and Franciscans regarded such worship as pagan in nature and prohibited it, and the fight was on. While the Jesuits were spreading the Word among Chinese scholars in Peking and other large cities, the other two orders were active in proselytizing among the poor and the uneducated, especially in Fukien and Kwangtung provinces. Not only did they differ in the interpretation of Chinese customs and beliefs; their approach towards proselytizing was also different.

The controversy had to be resolved eventually by the papacy. Throughout the seventeenth century the papacy did not take a definite stand, and by implication each order was allowed to practice what it believed. However, the Dominicans continued to press their case, and in 1704 Pope Clement XI decided against the Jesuit stand and sent Cardinal

Tournon to China as papal legate to enforce the decision. So far the Chinese government had been content to stand on the sideline, and the emperor K'ang-hsi would have let the rivalry reach its own conclusion in good time if the decision had not been thrust upon him. The Jesuits appealed to him for help, and he, as expected, ruled in their favor. The legate was sent back to Macao where he died in 1710. The Pope, finding that his decree had not been obeyed, sent another legate to Peking in 1715 and issued the bull *Ex illa die* to reaffirm his decision with regard to the rites controversy. Now the issue was not merely a quarrel between two rival sectarian groups; it was a question of the supremacy of either the Church or the Chinese state. The Pope had spoken, and all missionaries must obey. On the other hand, it was unthinkable that K'ang-hsi, who prided himself on being a model Confucian monarch, would prohibit the worship of Confucius and ancestors among his subjects. After reading the papal bull, the emperor, who had been known for his even temperament, nevertheless made the following comment:

Reading this proclamation [papal bull], I have concluded that the Westerners are small indeed. It is impossible to reason with them because they do not understand larger issues as we understand in China. There is not a single Westerner who can read Chinese books, and their remarks are often incredible and ridiculous. Judging from this proclamation, it seems that their religion is no different from other small, bigoted sects of Buddhism or Taoism. I have never seen a document which contains so much nonsense. From now on Westerners should not be allowed to preach in China, so there will be no trouble.[1]

However, missionaries were allowed to preach in China as long as they did not attack the very foundation of the Chinese society, and many Jesuits continued to find ways to evade the decision of Rome and were thus allowed to stay. In 1742 Pope Benedict XIV issued the bull *Ex quo singulari* and cleared up whatever doubts the Jesuits might still have or pretended to have. The controversy came to an end, and one generation later the Society of Jesus itself was dissolved. Though its work in China was continued by other orders, it could not be replaced. The prohibition against the worship of Confucius and ancestors continued in force until 1939 when the papacy, after two hundred years, reversed its stand. However, there was no clear instruction insofar as the interpretation of *T'ien* and *Shang-ti* was concerned.

The rites controversy stunted the growth of Roman Catholicism in China for one hundred years. Chinese Catholics were allowed to worship the way they chose, but the size of their community (about 150,000) remained substantially the same throughout the eighteenth century. In the long run, perhaps the most unfortunate result was the dissociation of the Chinese intelligentsia from the Roman Catholic Church, and the

---

[1] *Chung hsi chiao-t'ung shih,* vol. 5, p. 140.

Church, without the intellectuals' cooperation, not only found its work difficult, but had to confine its activities to the uneducated. During the days of the early Jesuits, many Catholic scholars passed the civil service examinations and became respected and influential members in their communities. During the one hundred years after the rites controversy, there was not a single Catholic in China who could debate with Buddhist or Confucian scholars, as Ricci once did, on a convincing, intellectual basis. This was a serious setback for the Church in a country which honored scholarship and intellectual competence. To become a Catholic was now a mere matter of ritual rather than intellectual conviction, and the Church could appeal only to the less sophisticated section of the population. Often the Church was unjustifiably compared with the White Lotus Society and was characterized by such adjectives as ignorant, superstitious, and seditious. In a generally hostile atmosphere, the life of a Chinese convert was very difficult indeed. He was considered a disgrace to his family since he no longer honored his ancestors; his name would be taken away permanently from the family register; and he was not allowed to enter the family temple. Cut off from his family, he was ostracized by the entire society. Dissociated from the intellectuals, the Church was hard pressed even to find people who knew how to write. The Confucian scholars, looking at its poorly composed or crudely translated religious treaties, were doubly sure of their own superiority. This tendency was not corrected until the last few decades. Meanwhile, two hundred years of potential growth had been lost forever for the Roman Catholic faith.

THE TRADERS

Simultaneously with the missionaries came the traders, the other and worldly arm of the Western civilization. The Portuguese admiral Alfonso d'Albuquerque conquered Malacca in 1511 and was curious about the areas beyond. "Are the Chinese Christians?" he asked; "if not, what do they believe and what kind of deity do they worship?" Six years later (1517) a group of his countrymen arrived at Canton as traders. A Chinese official [1] who was then in charge of maritime affairs in Canton described them as follows:

One day there arrived suddenly two oceanic ships sailing straight towards the Huai-yüan harbor of Canton. Their owner was a man named Chia-pi-tan [*sic*, captain] and announced that he bore tribute to China from Fu-lang-chi [Portugal]. These men all had high noses and deep-set eyes. They wore white turbans and dressed up like Muslims. . . . As they knew nothing about proper

[1] The official was Ku Ying-hsiang who later rose to become the Minister of Justice of the imperial government. A copy of the Chinese original appears in *Chung hsi chiao-t'ung shih,* vol. 3, pp. 241–242.

manners, they were ordered to learn them at the Kuang-hsiao Temple for three days before they could be granted an audience. Since Fu-lang-chi was never a tribute-bearing country, the decision as to whether they should be received was referred to the imperial government. The imperial government consented to receive them, and these men were escorted on their way to Peking. When the present emperor [Ming Shih-tsung, 1522–1567] came to the throne, he was greatly annoyed at these men's lack of respect. He ordered that the Chinese interpreter be punished according to law and that these men be escorted back to Canton where they should be expelled from the country. Thus the matter came to a conclusion.

But the matter did not come to a conclusion. Other Portuguese traders continued to arrive, and their relation with the Chinese government continued to be unpleasant. They traded whenever it was convenient and robbed whenever there was nobody to stop them. The impression they made on the coastal Chinese contrasted sharply with the impression the Jesuits made on the Chinese intelligentsia a generation later. At the risk of their lives on the stormy seas, they came to China for one purpose only: to make the largest profits in the shortest time. They were professional adventurers, and they did not care whether they robbed or traded, as long as there were profits to be realized. Their consciences would not bother them since their victims were pagans. As one Portuguese trader (or pirate) put it, "Why should I be afraid of going to hell, as long as I have faith? The Almighty's mercy is unlimited." That the first Westerners the Chinese met happened to be people like these was extremely unfortunate. That they did not represent Europe or even Portugal is rather obvious. Nevertheless, the wrong impression had been created, and it persisted for more than two centuries afterwards. It remained a major handicap to normal relations between Europe and China long after the moral fiber of the traders had changed for the better. Moreover, it made the work of the missionaries all the more difficult. The Chinese reasoning was: if the missionaries were to teach morality and ethics, they were definitely more needed at home than in China.

The Chinese, on the other hand, were not completely without blame. Their contempt for trade as a profession and traders as a group made normal trade relations difficult, if not impossible. While the Chinese were not allowed to go to foreign countries to engage in trade, there was no national policy with regard to foreigners who came to China for such a purpose. Generally speaking, foreign trade was allowed as long as it was disguised as tribute missions. However, local officials were given the authority to determine whether the prospective traders were legitimate or only troublemakers, and these officials, like officials everywhere, were not immune from the pressure of vested interests, or even bribery. Moreover, they insisted that in a meeting with them, foreigners should behave in the same manner as the Chinese over whom the officials ruled. The Chinese demand, seemingly reasonable, was difficult to comply with. Imagine a rowdy sea captain performing Confucian rituals before a Chinese mandarin![1] Time and again this demand became a major point of controversy between China and European countries in the conduct of trade and diplomatic relations.

While the Portuguese went up and down the seacoast, trading or looting, the Chinese tried to confine their activities to as small an area as possible. In 1557 when a group of Portuguese merchants informed the Chinese that they needed a place to dry their goods before they could be respectably presented to China as "tribute," the local official in charge, heavily bribed, was happy to oblige. The place happened to be Macao, "lent" to Portugal on a permanent basis. The Chinese hoped that the Portuguese trade could be more easily controlled if it were confined to one port of entry and that the undesirable aliens could be isolated in a small area. Interestingly enough, Macao turned out to be the only territory that China ceded to a foreign country on a voluntary basis; it stands today as the last vestige in Asia of the once prosperous Portuguese empire.

As the Portuguese prospered, traders of other nationalities followed suit. The Dutch arrived early in the seventeenth century, and their presence was greatly resented by Portugal, which wished to preserve the lucrative trade for itself alone. Thinking that the Portuguese were already one group too many, the Chinese twice (in 1604 and again in 1607) refused the Dutch request for trade. The Dutch, unable to trade legitimately, resorted to smuggling, and operating from an island in the Pescadores, they carried on in a clandestine manner with the lawless elements of the coastal areas. Subsequently chased out by the Chinese authorities, they retired to Taiwan where, as we have noticed in a previous chapter, they ruled until 1662 when they were driven from the island by Cheng Ch'eng-kung. The Dutch fortunes took a definite turn towards the better in 1683 when the Ch'ing government rewarded them with four trading ports on account of their assistance in conquering Taiwan. Of the four ports only Canton turned out to be of great significance in a later period. Once the concession was made to the Dutch, the government decided that it might as well be made to all European countries that sought trade with China. By the beginning of the eighteenth century both England and France had sent ships to Canton. It should be added, however, that China regarded the opening to trade as a special favor granted to foreigners and that it was subject to revocation if "foreigners behaved in an uncontrollable, barbarian manner." The Ch'ing government did not believe that it had much to gain by trading with foreigners.

The trade as conducted at Canton reflected to a great extent the power flux of contemporary Europe. As the eighteenth century pro-

[1] One of these rituals was kowtow. For more details, see pp. 389–390.

FOREIGN FACTORIES AND TRADING STATIONS AT CANTON   The city wall of Canton is in the background.

gressed, Great Britain slowly emerged as the greatest maritime power of the world, and it also became the largest trading nation in Canton. The East India Company maintained a regular staff at Canton and Macao, as the size and value of the trade increased. As Canton continued to over-shadow other trading ports in importance, the Chinese government de-creed in 1757 that all foreign trade was to be confined to that city alone. In 1784 when the first American ship, the *Empress of China*, sailed for China, the British monopoly had been virtually established. Other coun-tries continued to send ships to Canton, but it was to Britain that they looked for leadership in their dealings with the Celestial Empire.

Though large profits were made, the British traders were not satisfied with the semi-official status upon which the trade was conducted. With-out an official treaty, the trade could be suspended unilaterally. Since Britain had no diplomatic representation in Peking, whatever complaints the merchants might have could not be presented directly to the imperial government. Of complaints the merchants had plenty. They were con-fined to a secluded area outside of Canton during the time that a busi-ness transaction was made, and they had to retire to Macao after it had been completed. Their movements were restricted, and they could not bring to Canton their wives who had to reside at Macao. They could not see any Chinese official in person, and any business they might have with him had to be channelled through the Co-hongs. The Co-hongs were the twelve (and later thirteen) Chinese trade associations franchised by the Chinese government to deal exclusively with foreign traders. They bought all imports and sold all exports, and a foreign merchant could not deal with anyone else except them. They had a monopoly, and they did not hesitate to use it for their own advantage.

Whatever justifications the Chinese government might have had, the situation as described above was hardly satisfactory to the British. To find a remedy, England sent its first diplomatic mission to China in 1792. Lord George Macartney, the head of the mission, arrived in China in the summer of 1793. He sought, among other things, British representation at Peking, the opening of more ports for trade, and the reduction of tariff. To the Chinese, however, he was merely one of the many tribute bearers. "Since the English envoy has come far from the distant seas and for the first time visited a superior country," said the emperor Ch'ien-lung, "he should be treated with more consideration than the Burmese and Annamese who come here once every year." His Chinese escorts were instructed to teach him kowtow which, he was told, he must perform before the emperor. In Jehol where the emperor's summer palace was located, Lord Macartney was granted an audience (or audiences). Did he perform the kowtow? He said that he did not and that he had only bent one knee. On the other hand, Chinese sources, including those who were present during the audience, were equally sure that he did. Whether he did or did not, his request for diplomatic representation and others were rejected on the ground that they were inconsistent with Chinese custom. In 1816, the year after the battle of Waterloo, England sent another diplomatic mission to China. This mission, headed by Lord Amherst, was even less successful. His lordship was ordered to leave China immediately after he had made it clear that he would not perform the kowtow under any circumstances.

What was the kowtow? It consisted of kneeling and touching the forehead to the ground. It was a ritual performed by people of inferior status before their superiors, to show homage or deep respect. Ministers performed this ritual before kings, common people before government officials, and children before parents. The Chinese could not see any reason why the two English envoys would not perform it before their emperor as they did. The envoys were in Rome; therefore, they should do as the Romans did. When they refused to do so, the Chinese accused them of arrogance, bad manners, and bad faith. On the other hand, the two English gentlemen regarded this ritual as too humiliating. More than anything else, the controversy over the kowtow reflected the tremendous difficulties involved when two different cultures met head on for the first time. A Chinese had no objection to performing it before his parents or an emperor; many Westerners, on the other hand, preferred doing it before a beautiful woman.[1] What was humiliating to one side was glorified by the other. To a Westerner, trade was a right to be demanded; to a Chinese it was a privilege granted as a special favor. As a favor, it could be revoked. The Chinese looked down upon trade, whereas the Westerners attached great importance to it. Here was a cultural conflict which could not easily be resolved.

To compound the difficulties, the Chinese had no knowledge of the power and the civilization which England represented. The emperor K'ang-hsi often mentioned England and Burma and Annam in the same breath, and to him England was a remote, small, and uncivilized kingdom "impelled by humble desire to partake of our great civilization." The Chinese had no concept of international law as it was then known in Western Europe and would not have recognized it even if they had known it. The protocol and procedure that governed the normal conduct of trade and diplomatic relations were to them a new concept which they rejected. One century before, there had been the Jesuits in Peking who enlightened Chinese monarchs on Western countries, and their influence was partially responsible for the conclusion of a treaty with Russia in 1689. Now they were gone, and the Chinese had to grope in darkness.

As long as such ignorance persisted, the English traders in Canton had understandable grievances. At a time when mercantilism was the golden rule of Western Europe, the Chinese encouraged the import and discouraged the export trade. Ironically, this policy did not please foreign traders, because, having comparatively little to sell to China, their profits lay in buying as much as possible from China and reselling what they bought to Europe. There were also complaints against the tariff. Though the official rates as sanctioned by Peking were reasonable, local exactions were large. During each step of a business transaction, customs officials demanded payments for their services, and many such demands, in the eyes of the traders, were demands for bribes. As a result, the amount actually paid was several times larger than the statutory tariff. The monopoly of the Co-hongs was another source of irritation. The traders believed that if they were allowed to deal with whomever they pleased, their cost would have been smaller and their profits larger. Lastly, there was the problem of jurisdiction. The Chinese insisted that China had jurisdiction over all criminal cases in which a Chinese was involved. The foreign traders, considering Chinese law and court procedures "barbarous" and "uncivilized," were reluctant to agree to the Chinese demand, especially when they were the defendants.

In controversies of this nature, there are always two sides, perhaps equally persuasive. If the foreigners had to pay more duties than the

---

[1] Asked whether he would perform the kowtow before the Chinese emperor, John E. Ward, the American envoy to China in 1859, replied that he would only do so before God and women.

statutory tariff, the Chinese did not fare better if they were under similar circumstances. In other words, foreigners were not singled out for discrimination. There were times in Chinese history (such as the early Ming period) when government officials were honest and incorruptible. More often than not, bribery and corruption were a normal state of affairs. This argument, of course, did not excuse those Chinese officials who demanded bribes from foreign traders; it did, however, make their action understandable. As long as the "take" was reasonable, said one of the great Ch'ing emperors, it should be expected and should not cause undue alarm. Of course, there was the question whether the customs officials at Canton had been "reasonable." If the Co-hongs were monopolies (they were), so was the British East India Company. As to the jurisdictional problem, the Chinese had long maintained that whenever a Chinese was involved in a civil or criminal case in China, the Chinese government alone had jurisdiction and that a foreign government had jurisdiction only when both sides of a case were foreigners. In retrospect, the Chinese stand did not seem to be unreasonable in view of the fact that in accordance with the practice commonly recognized today, the territorial government alone has jurisdiction regardless of the nationalities of the parties involved unless the accused enjoys diplomatic immunity, which the foreign traders in Canton could not claim and did not have. Once a crime was committed, there was the difference in concept with regard to the ascertaining of responsibilities. The Chinese believed in joint responsibility; the Europeans, on the other hand, maintained that only the persons directly involved in a crime were subject to trial and punishment. From the Chinese point of view, a captain should be brought to account if one of his men had committed a crime and yet could not be found. To punish a captain because of a crime committed by one of his men was understandably "barbarous" to the Western world.

As each of the two sides insisted on the soundness of its own values and applied them accordingly, this problem of cultural conflict could only be solved if one side were strong enough to impose its will on the other. The Opium War (1839–1842), the first war between China and a European power, served exactly that purpose. When physical force was used, all alleged rights and wrongs became academic. It was the victor who dictated terms.

THE OPIUM WAR AND ITS AFTERMATH

Though mention of the opium-producing poppy can be found in ancient Chinese works, the use of opium as a habit-forming narcotic was of comparatively recent origin. Early in the seventeenth century the Spaniards introduced the smoking of tobacco in China, and shortly afterwards opium mixed with tobacco also appeared in China. Previously the Dutch had used this mixture in Java and in Taiwan which they then controlled, and from Taiwan it spread to nearby Fukien province. Once the mixture was in China, opium was separated from tobacco and was taken independently. Like every evil, opium possessed certain "charms" when it was first introduced to its victim: it reduced pain caused by headache, indigestion, and intestinal disorders, and midwives sometimes gave it to their charges during the time of childbirth. Even without any pain to reduce, a smoker nevertheless found it attractive. It cured depression, though only temporarily; it was even exhilarating while the effect lasted. However, once a person became an opium addict, he became a slave to his addiction. He was more concerned with the next puff than the next meal. If he had no money to buy it, he would sell whatever he had, including, sometimes, his own children. Opium, the black gold, was very expensive indeed. Its denial to an addict meant unbearable pain, and its continuous denial would reduce him to a state of hysteria which could only be cured with the first inhalation. Even though a wealthy person might be able to afford such a habit, addiction would eventually ruin his health. He could no longer live a normal life, not only because he was physically weak but also because each working day had to be interrupted by smoking. In most cases he became a useless person. Moreover, once the habit was acquired, rarely could one get rid of it. For the opium merchant it meant that once he had a customer, he would continue to have that customer.

The first shipment of opium in quantity to China was made by the Portuguese from Goa. In 1729 when the emperor Yung-cheng issued a decree to prohibit opium traffic, the annual import was still small, amounting to 200 chests (each chest weighed approximately 133 lbs.) on the average. The prohibition was not strictly enforced, and the import of opium continued to increase. In 1790 the import from India alone reached 4,054 chests. With the opening of the nineteenth century the import increased by leaps and bounds, and shortly before the Opium War, it amounted to more than 30,000 chests per year. By then England had become by far the largest shipper, though France and the United States also participated. Before the opium trade, Europe had purchased more from China than it sold, and there had been a continuous flow of bullion from Europe to China. With opium, Europe more than paid for all the silk, tea, and porcelain it purchased, and the flow of bullion was consequently reversed. Before 1823 the yearly outflow of silver from China amounted to one million taels; it increased to twenty million taels from 1831 to 1834 and reached thirty million taels shortly before the war. By then opium addiction had spread from the members of the gentry class to "artisans, merchants, women, and even Buddhist monks and Taoist priests." "If the opium traffic is not stopped," said Lin Tse-hsü, later the Imperial Commissioner at Canton, "the country will become poorer and poorer and its people weaker and weaker. Eventually not only will there be inadequate funds to support an army, there will be no useful soldiers at all."

Repeatedly the Chinese government had imposed bans on the opium traffic, but each attempt failed to achieve its purpose. The avarice of foreign traders and the corruption of Chinese officials combined to defeat whatever measures the government took. Moreover, the long coastline made smuggling extremely difficult to stop, and local interests, fattening on the opium traffic, connived at, if not actually encouraged it. In 1838 when the opium traffic had reached alarming proportions, the emperor Tao-kuang (1821–1851) sent one of his ablest servants, Lin Tse-hsü, to Canton, with the special charge to end it, "once and for all."

After Lin's arrival at Canton in the spring of 1839, he ordered that all foreign traders surrender the opium they possessed. They complied, and more than 20,000 chests of British-controlled opium were burned in public. However, the British refused to make a pledge that thereafter they would refrain from shipping more opium to China. Angered by their refusal, Lin threatened to ban all commercial traffic. In July, a Chinese was killed by a group of English sailors in Kowloon, and Lin demanded the surrender of the accused. As the British refused to surrender them, a fleet of Chinese war junks sailed towards the British naval force then staying at Hong Kong, with the ostensible purpose of seizing the accused seamen by force. The British fired, and the war began.

England could have gone to war before, but for reasons of its own it postponed the showdown until there was also the opium issue. To the Chinese, the issue was a moral one on which they believed that they could not make any compromise. Yet they did not want the war; nor were they prepared for it. It was unlikely that they had heard of Trafalgar or Waterloo; nor could their leaders foresee the grave consequences in having a war with a mighty power like England. In our modern concept of total war, the Opium War was no more than a skirmish. The British forces attacked and seized a few cities along the coast. When they threatened to attack Nanking, the Chinese sued for peace. There was no such concept then that a nation should fight to the last man and to the last inch of territory.

The Treaty of Nanking (1842), as the treaty which concluded the Opium War was called, contained thirteen articles. The major items were: (1) the opening of five ports (Canton, Amoy, Foochow, Ningpo, and Shanghai) for British trade, (2) the cession of the island of Hong Kong to Great Britain, (3) China's agreement to a uniform and moderate tariff on exports and imports which could not be changed save by mutual agreement, and (4) the payment by China of $21,000,000 as indemnity: $6,000,000 for the surrendered opium, $3,000,000 for the debts owed by Chinese to British merchants, and $12,000,000 for expenses occasioned by the war. A supplementary treaty, the Treaty of the Bogue, was signed one year later. With regard to this treaty, only two points need to be mentioned here. First, China agreed to grant Great Britain extraterritoriality in criminal cases, and second, Britain secured the most-favored-nation treatment. In accordance with this treatment, any additional privileges or immunities granted to any other power thereafter would automatically be enjoyed by British subjects. The most-favored-nation clause, though worded in different ways, was later included in every treaty concluded with a Western power, including Denmark and Mexico.

After Great Britain had obtained these concessions from China, other powers, through persuasion combined with the threat of physical force, demanded and received the same or even larger concessions. The American treaty (Treaty of Wang-hsia, July, 1844), for instance, extended the principle of extraterritoriality to include civil as well as criminal cases. France was given the right to build Roman Catholic missions at the treaty ports and the freedom to proselytize without interference from the Chinese government, though such concessions did not form a part of the official treaty (Franco-Chinese Treaty, October, 1844). Through the operation of the most-favored-nation clause, the new privileges were extended to all other countries which had, or were going to have, treaty relations with China. The concession given to France with regard to missionary activities, for instance, was granted to all countries which had Catholic or Protestant missionaries in China.

The Treaty of Nanking, hopefully hailed by many Westerners as the beginning of a new era in the relations between China and the Western world, created only a lull before another storm. The Chinese, who had behind them 4,000 years of ingrained ideas with regard to foreign relations, were slow to understand the new reality. Instead of boldly facing the future, they still dreamed about the golden past when the Son of Heaven chided barbarian chieftains for their unruly behavior and when there were no troublesome foreigners bent on making a profit at the expense of principle or morality. They were angered and frightened and were at a loss to know what to do. Their officials, caught between an antiforeign public and the demanding foreign powers, were a sorrowful lot; they evaded and stalled when the time arrived to implement the treaty provisions. In Canton, where the antiforeign feeling had been the strongest and was further intensified by the recent defeat, the mobs became violent and uncontrollable, and they refused to let foreigners enter their walled city. The foreigners were equally stubborn in their insistence, even though the treaty did not indicate explicitly that they had the right to enter the city. At this crucial moment when tension was building towards a climax, the viceroy of Kwangtung-Kwangsi, who was responsible for negotiating with the foreigners, was the inept, incredible Yeh Min-shen. He consulted a magician before he made any move, and the divine voice he heard always seemed to say: "Pay no attention to the trouble-some barbarians."[1] His superiors in Peking were equally unable to grasp the seriousness of the situation. "The object of the Manchu govern-ment," said a Western observer, "is to disgust Europeans, and break off all intercourse with them; it would gladly have nothing to do with them at any price." Yet, "China has now been brought too near to Europe for it to be permitted any longer to lead this isolated life in the midst of the world."

If the Chinese regarded the Treaty of Nanking as too harsh, the foreigners considered it too lenient. They wanted more ports opened for trade, especially in the interior, and they demanded diplomatic represen-tation at Peking. Since the Chinese government was reluctant even to honor existing obligations, it was clear to them that force had to be used if they wished to obtain additional concessions. The Opium War had revealed China's vulnerability, and there was reason to believe that an-other show of force would yield more rewarding results. "The time is fast approaching when we shall be obliged to strike another blow in China," said Palmerston, the Prime Minister of Great Britain. Now it was Eng-land's turn to play the role of the Son of Heaven, to punish, in the prime minister's own words, "these half-civilized governments such as those of China, Portugal, Spanish America," all of whom "require a dressing down every eight or ten years to keep them in order." Once minds were made up, the pretexts for starting another war were not slow in coming.

In the fall of 1856 a lorcha named *Arrow* was boarded by Chinese police and twelve of her Chinese crew of fourteen were arrested on the charge of piracy. The British consul at Canton protested on the ground that the ship had been registered in Hong Kong and was therefore legiti-mately British even though it was owned by a Chinese. The fact that the registry had expired before the arrest and consequently the ship was not legally entitled to British protection was apparently then unknown to both the Chinese and the British. The prisoners were eventually returned, but the British refused to accept the release as satisfactory because it was not accompanied by an apology. The British naval force at Canton at-tacked the city, and another war began.

Meanwhile, the French had decided to join the war. In February, 1856, a French Catholic missionary and some of his Chinese converts in Kwangsi were arrested and executed on the charge that they had insti-gated a rebellion. The missionaries' own admission that they had indoc-trinated their Chinese converts to look to "France as their support and liberation" against persecution seemed to have substantiated to some ex-tent the Chinese charge, though the exact circumstances of the so-called

[1] Yeh was later captured by the British during the ensuing hostilities and was taken to India as a prisoner. He wrote poems and calligraphy to be given to his captors as souvenirs before he died in 1859.

rebellion were not known. Moreover, no foreigners were allowed to step outside the treaty ports under the existing treaties, and the French missionary had been found deep in the interior. On the other hand, the Chinese, by arresting him and sentencing him to die, had obviously violated the extraterritorial right of France. Napoleon III had long dreamed of the spiritual conquest of China. When the news of the "judicial murder" arrived in Paris, he was eager to seize it as an opportunity to expand his spiritual empire.

The British and the French easily defeated the poorly trained, inadequately armed Chinese. When they threatened to attack Tientsin, the Manchu government sued for peace. The peace, called Treaties of Tientsin, granted new concessions and enlarged some old ones. Great Britain and France were to maintain resident ministers at Peking, and their nationals had the right of travelling in all parts of the interior of China. New ports were to be opened for trade, and foreign ships had the right of navigating the Yangtze River. Tariff rates would be adjusted downward from those that had been previously agreed, and China was to pay the two powers indemnities. There was also the article guaranteeing the protection of missionaries by Chinese authorities, since "the Christian religion, as professed by Protestants and Roman Catholics, inculcates the practice of virtue, and teaches man to do as he would be done by."

After the treaties had been signed, the Chinese refused to ratify them. This, of course, was the familiar Chinese delaying tactic, and the Western powers would have no part of it. Hostilities were renewed, and Tientsin and Peking were soon captured by the allies. In a vengeful mood, the British commander ordered the burning of the Yüan Ming Yüan, the Summer Palace ground which was the most beautiful place in the city and perhaps in all of China. The emperor Hsien-feng fled to Jehol, and China was again brought to its knees. Another treaty, the Peking Convention (1860) was signed. Kowloon was ceded to England, more ports were opened for trade, and more indemnities were paid. As other powers (including Russia and the United States) had the most-favored-nation clause in the treaties they had previously concluded with China, most of the privileges stipulated in the new treaties were also extended to them.

The treaties of 1858–1860, together with those of 1842–1844, provided the basis of the relationship between China and the Western powers until World War II. The Chinese called them "unequal treaties," because the benefits provided in these treaties went exclusively to the Western powers at the expense of China. They resented the special privileges foreigners enjoyed in China, privileges which they themselves did not have in their own country. The resentment against the special privileges was easily transformed into resentment against those who enjoyed them, and the Chinese, who had been tolerant towards peoples of different races and religions throughout their history, now became noticeably anti-foreign. For a century Chinese leaders blamed these unequal treaties for all real or imaginery ills that China suffered, and the call for abolishing them generated a patriotic fervor such as had never been seen in Chinese history. Though the Chinese case might often have been overstated, it is nevertheless true that we cannot understand the China of the last one hundred years unless we understand its grievances.

First, there was the right of extraterritoriality. Such a right denied the Chinese courts jurisdiction over foreign residents in China, and legally foreigners could do whatever they pleased without incurring the punishments provided by Chinese law. Only their consuls in the treaty ports had jurisdiction over them. In a case involving both Chinese and foreigners, the fairness of a consular trial was as much suspect by the Chinese as the fairness of a Chinese trial in a similar case had been suspect by foreigners before the treaty system. Moreover, when missionaries and other foreigners intervened on behalf of their Chinese protégés (converts and servants) who were involved in criminal or civil cases, local officials were expected to rule in their favor regardless of the merits of the case because these officials knew that their government was afraid that Western powers might seize any "mistrial" as an excuse to send troops to China to demand more concessions. If foreign powers intervened, they would be severely punished, as Lin Tse-hsü had painfully learned himself.[1] The fear of foreign intervention might or might not be justified, but such a fear did exist. As long as it existed, any court action involving a Chinese having foreign connections became a mockery of justice. Thus, with the passage of time, there developed in China a new privileged class, the foreigners and their protégés, above and beyond the reach of the law. Some of them learned to carry this exalted status with dignity, while others were eager to use it for their own advantage. All of them, of course, looked down upon the "natives" around them. This situation, as one would expect, caused great resentment on the part of the Chinese, and friction often occurred between Chinese and Chinese converts, especially in the interior regions. Since their government could not do anything to remedy the situation, eventually the people took this matter into their own hands. The result was the massacre of missionaries and Chinese converts, which will be discussed in the next chapter.

It was unfortunate that Christianity was reintroduced to China through the use of military force. It was elevated to a privileged position before it even had many followers. The way it was imposed on China and the privileged position it enjoyed made its failure almost a foregone conclusion. Ironically, its sponsors, insisting on a privileged position for their religion, did not give it a chance to compete fairly and equally with other religions in China. It could have succeeded, but it did not. To many

---

[1] Lin was stripped of his rank and title and was exiled to Ili after the Opium War.

Chinese the missionaries were an aggressive arm of Western imperialism, despite the many utilitarian things (such as schools and hospitals) they had brought to the Chinese people. To compound the difficulties, the early missionaries were not always well-trained. They were certainly not the best the West could have sent to China. Practically all of them were illiterate in the Chinese language, and some of them were barely literate in their own. Yet they were all determined to "lead the heathen Chinese out of the darkness." This attitude was of course not the best way of making friends and influencing people. While the Confucian scholars viewed their activities with a mixed emotion of bemusement and understanding, many lawless, unscrupulous elements swelled the Christian ranks because of the protection which the missionaries could provide in case they ran into difficulties with the law-enforcement officials. Thus, the Christian community, which had historically set an example in humility and virtue in many hostile lands, fell far short of being the ideal society in China which a good Christian would have wished. The Chinese attitude towards religion was similar to that of the ancient Romans. Christianity eventually conquered Rome, but it never made much headway in China. For this failure the unequal treaties were greatly responsible.

The low, conventional tariff (five percent *ad valorem*) as stipulated in the unequal treaties was declared by Chinese leaders to be an insurmountable barrier to China's industrial development. Tariff rates could not be raised save by mutual agreement, and it was virtually impossible to persuade foreign traders to agree to higher rates which increased the cost of their merchandise. No differentiation was made between luxuries and necessities, and the Chinese could not, for instance, impose higher duties on imported opium which had now become an open, legitimate item of trade. Deprived of tariff protection, native industries, still in an infant stage of development, could not compete with well-established foreign concerns. Only in certain industries, such as tea and silk, in which natural and geographical environment prohibited foreign competition, did the Chinese continue to prosper despite the unequal treaties. Moreover, as the Chinese government was not allowed to tax goods of foreign origins above the low, conventional tariff, it had to impose heavier taxation on the products of its own nationals in order to raise revenue for administrative expenses. Thus the unequal treaties forced the Chinese government to discriminate against its own nationals in favor of foreigners. It is difficult to say whether China could have developed a modern industry if the unequal treaties had never existed. As has been remarked in the Introduction, there were other factors in China unfavorable to industrial development. There is no denying the fact, however, that the regulated tariff was a great handicap to China's struggle to become a modern, industrialized society.

There were other provisions in the treaties which looked harmless at the beginning but which turned out to be detrimental from the Chinese point of view. The Treaty of Nanking stipulated the right of foreigners to reside in the treaty ports which, liberally interpreted, came to mean the right to reside in certain sections of the city over which the Chinese government had no jurisdiction. Originally intended for foreigners only, the "concessions," as foreign settlements in the treaty ports were called, eventually had more Chinese than foreigners who, with the passage of time, constituted only a small fraction of the total residents. The munici- pal government in each concession was controlled by the representatives of the foreign community and had sole jurisdiction over all its inhabitants, including the Chinese. Thus, within the boundaries of China there were numerous miniature "foreign countries" that were sovereign as far as China was concerned. They had their own tax systems, courts, and police. Deliberately or unintentionally, the foreigners in these concessions dis- criminated against the natives, and many Chinese have not forgotten the sign once hung on the entrance of one of Shanghai's parks: "Dogs and Chinese Not Allowed." What irritated local Chinese officials was the fact that a wanted criminal became immune from any penalty under Chinese law by simply stepping into a foreign concession unless the foreign gov- ernment in the concession chose to repatriate him. If a foreigner decided to take into his protection a Chinese accused of having committed high treason, even the Son of Heaven could not bring him to justice. Most foreigners used their power with discretion; there were others who did not. Shanghai, said one Western observer, was an adventurer's paradise.

It should be pointed out, however, that when the treaties were con- cluded, neither China nor the Western powers had foreseen their implica- tions. The Western powers were then interested in opening China for trade and, as if on second thought, also insisted on opening China for missionary activities. The extraterritorial rights, the regulated tariff, the foreign "concessions," and the freedom to navigate on China's internal rivers were not an end in themselves; they were aimed at enlarging profits and providing convenience for Western traders who, for business reasons, had to reside in China. If the treaty rights had been strictly interpreted, they would not have led to such abuses as later appeared. Their broad interpretations which caused such abuses clearly violated the intentions of the treaty makers. The Chinese, on the other hand, had no knowledge that these rights were a violation of their sovereignty when the treaties were concluded because few of them had any understanding of such a concept as national sovereignty, a concept which was Western in origin. As we have seen, China had long granted foreign residents (such as Persians and Arabs) a certain degree of extraterritoriality, and conces- sions of this sort did not seem to be incompatible with their dignity as a nation. Only when the treaty rights were abused was there a great deal of alarm. The agitation for the abolition of treaty rights provided the greatest driving force of Chinese nationalism. More than anything else, it united China as a modern nation.

THE TAIPING REBELLION

In the 1840's all evidence seemed to indicate that the Manchu dynasty had lost the mandate of Heaven. There were foreign invasions, domestic disturbances, natural disasters, famines, and a discredited, incompetent government which was unable to cope with them. The sequence was incomplete without a rebellion, and a rebellion there was. The Taiping Rebellion was the greatest social upheaval of nineteenth century China and the most serious challenge to the Manchu government before 1911. It was generated by indigenous forces, and it was suppressed by native resources. The professed Christianity of the rebels, however, was an indication of the Western influence.

From 1847 to 1849 natural disasters struck China repeatedly, and famines were reported in practically every province. The region most adversely affected was Kwangtung and Kwangsi where many peasants, driven by hunger, had appeared as organized bandits as early as 1847. Local officials were unable to maintain peace and order, and lawlessness spread over a large section of this region. The factors that had historically nourished a rebellion were present, and only a capable leader was required to organize it. In Hung Hsiu-ch'üan the dissatisfied peasants found their leader.

Hung Hsiu-ch'üan was born in 1812 near Canton to a small farmer. As the brightest member of the family, he was given the opportunity to study, while his two elder brothers continued to work on the family farm. He left school at the age of eighteen and, as was normally expected, went to take the lowest level of the civil service examination in Canton. He failed, and when he tried again in 1836, he did not fare any better. It was then that he was exposed to the teaching of Christianity for the first time, having read a pamphlet entitled *Good Advice to the World* (*Ch'üan-shih liang-yen*) handed to him by a street evangelist. He took the examination again the following year and failed for the third time. He then became seriously ill and was in a state of coma for forty days. When he woke up, he told an astonished audience that he had met God the Father and Jesus in his dream and that Jesus was God's elder son, whereas he, Hung, was His younger son. He was instructed by God the Father to kill the "demons," who later turned out to be the Manchus. It did not seem then that he had decided to lead a revolt, because as late as 1843 he took and failed the civil service examination for the fourth time. His bitterness could well be imagined, since he was an ambitious man. Of course, he had to bide his time until the opportune moment arrived. The moment did arrive when famine struck a wide area in his native province.

The base of his operation was a secret society called the Society of God Worshippers, efficiently organized under his command. It recruited its followers from poor peasants, and being looked down upon by Confucian scholars as another form of superstition, it was boycotted by the leaders of each community. Among the six "princes" whom Hung later appointed to assist him in establishing a Heavenly Kingdom of Great Peace, only three were educated, and the most powerful of the "princes," Yang Hsiu-ch'ing, had been a charcoal maker before he joined the rebellion. The society was very active in the southeastern section of Kwangsi, and as famine spread, it extended its influence towards other sections of the province. From time to time its members clashed with local militia men who were organized by the gentry leaders to combat the society as well as the widespread banditry. In the winter of 1850–1851, Hung raised the standard of revolt, calling for the overthrow of the Manchu dynasty.

The weakness of the Ch'ing regime had been shown in the Opium War. Now it could not even cope with the ill-trained, ill-equipped peasant rebels. The regular army collapsed before the rebels, and city after city fell into their hands. After each city was captured, the rebels singled out two groups for persecution: Ch'ing officials and Buddhist and Taoist priests. The persecution of the first group was to be expected; the persecution of the second group was unusual and was done on religious grounds, as the Buddhist and Taoist priests had allegedly worshipped "idols." A sizable number of these Buddhist and Taoist priests were killed, and their temples and monasteries were confiscated to provide homes for the homeless and the very poor. The discipline of the Taiping soldiers was generally good; a household only needed to paste the word "obedience" (*shun*) on its front door to assure that it would not be disturbed by the Taiping soldiers. In 1853 Nanking fell into the hands of the rebels. Hung proclaimed himself as *T'ien Wang*, or Prince of Heaven, and called his kingdom *T'ai-p'ing T'ien-kuo*, or Heavenly Kingdom of Great Peace. But there was to be no peace, not even an earthly one.

In retrospect, what made the Taiping regime unique was its attempted reforms. It decreed that all land belonged to the nation as a whole and that private property was forever abolished. Every household was to receive from the state a certain amount of land in proportion to its size. Since women were declared equals of men, they were entitled to an equal share. After a harvest, a household kept what it needed for its sustenance and handed over to the government the surplus. "Areas that suffer from famine shall receive help from areas that have had bumper harvests," said a Taiping decree, "so that everyone will enjoy the blessing of God, the Supreme Lord." "We shall till together and enjoy the fruits of

MAP 28

THE TAIPING REGIME
(1853–1864)

1853–1856

After 1857

Scale of Miles

0   150   300   450

YELLOW SEA

EAST CHINA SEA

SOUTH CHINA SEA

YELLOW RIVER

SI RIVER

Peking

Shanghai

Nanking

Anking

Hankow

Wuchang

Changsha

Kweilin

Chungking

A separate group led by Shih Ta-kai

our work in common. Food and clothing shall be shared; so shall money. No one shall have more than his neighbor has, and no one shall ever suffer from cold or hunger." Thus, four years after the *Communist Manifesto* (which nobody in China had then heard of) and one century before Mao Tse-tung's communes, a communistic society was established in China under the doctrine of Christian love.

The social reforms of the Taiping regime were equally drastic. Every twenty-five households were organized as a comradeship (*wu*), the basic administrative unit of the nation. Each comradeship was headed by a comrade leader (*wu-chang*), the military as well as the administrative chief. He was responsible for the training of the twenty-five soldiers (one from each household) under his command as well as the supervision of farming; he led his soldiers in police and war activities whenever the necessity arose. In carrying out his administrative duties he was assisted by a teacher-priest called *liang-ssu-ma* who was also the judge and treasurer of the comradeship. All children were required to go to the church school where they were taught the *Old* and *New Testaments*, together with the decrees of the Prince of Heaven (Hung Hsiu-ch'üan). *The Three-character Classic* was completely revised to emphasize religious indoctrination. The opening statements of the revised version read as follows:

> The Great Supreme Lord (*Huang Shang-ti*)
> Created Heaven and Earth (*tsao t'ien ti*).
> He Created Mountains and Seas (*tsao shan hai*);
> He Made the World Complete (*wan-wu pei*).

On Sunday the comrade leader led men and women to the comradeship church where they prayed and sang the glory of God. The aged, the orphans, the disabled, and all those who could not work were supported by the comradeship, and "none were to go hungry." All expenses occasioned by wedding, childbirth, and other festivities were drawn from the common treasury; during these festivities, "all heathen rituals should be dispensed with, and the participants had only to worship and pray to God the Father, the Supreme Lord."

The Taipings' communistic and collectivistic life may not appeal to us; some of their other reforms, however, were progressive and modern. They deplored the inferior role women had played in Chinese society and tried to elevate their position to the same level as that of men. Women were entitled to land distribution as has been said before, and were encouraged to attend school. In the Taiping government many talented women served as officials, and some of them even distinguished themselves on the battlefield. In the Taiping army women were a common sight. Civil service examinations were open to women as well as men, and candidates were asked to write an essay on such a topic as the refutation of Confucius' assertion that "Women and small people are the most difficult to deal with." Moreover, the Taiping law forbade concubinage, foot-binding, and prostitution. The transportation and smoking of opium were punishable by death.

Why did the Taipings fail? First, there was the lack of good leadership. Hung Hsiu-ch'üan was more a mystic than a statesman, and most of his top lieutenants were mediocre. His best friend and supporter, Feng Yün-shan, died in action early in the rebellion. After 1852 real leadership fell gradually into the hands of Yang Hsiu-ch'ing, while Hung withdrew more and more to a state of semiseclusion. As for Yang, the lack of a formal education was a great handicap; he had neither the foresight nor the statesmanship to steer the new regime through the first, most crucial years. He often went into a trance to speak in "the voice of God," forcing all, including Hung, to be obedient to him. He was a clever man, but not great. Once Nanking was captured, the Taiping leaders became complacent. After two attempts to conquer North China had failed in 1852–1853, they settled down in their new capital to enjoy the fruits of victory. This gave their enemy much needed time to prepare for a counter offensive. Even more damaging to their cause were the feuds that developed among the leaders themselves. Yang Hsiu-ch'ing, who often compelled Hung to kneel down before him to listen to "the voice of God," became arrogant and dictatorial, and Hung finally decided to get rid of him. When the massacre finally ended, Yang, his murderer, and the murderer of his murderer, together with hundreds of their lieutenants, were slaughtered in cold blood. Among Hung's top colleagues, only Shih Ta-k'ai, the only Taiping leader with a gentry background, was still alive. He left Nanking in disgust, went his separate way, and never returned. Being completely isolated, Hung could not trust anyone except his two half-brothers who, as has been noted before, had received no other training besides growing rice in the paddy fields. That the Taiping regime managed to last more than ten years in Nanking was largely due to the military genius of one man, Li Hsiu-ch'eng, who was not one of the original leaders of the rebellion. Eventually, however, even he was overpowered by the superior Manchu forces. The confession he made after his capture is one of the basic materials in studying the Taiping rebellion, especially its later stage.

Face to face with the Taiping regime and what it stood for were an ancient culture, the landed interests, some of the best brains of contemporary China, and finally, the Western interests in China. The odds against the Taipings were overwhelming. Their appeal to Chinese nationalism against "barbarian" Manchus fell on deaf ears because first, the Manchu regime had been Sinicized and had long been accepted by most, if not all Chinese; and second, whatever nationalist appeal the Taipings might have had was more than offset by the alien institutions and beliefs which they proposed for their new regime. Between the Sinicized Manchus and the "barbarized" Chinese, the Confucian scholars, supported by the majority of the Chinese population, did not hesitate to make a choice. The

Taipings were denounced as traitors to an ancient heritage, and the struggle against them was hailed as absolutely essential to the preservation of a great civilization. In the minds of these Confucian scholars, they were worse than the Western powers which had only recently defeated China, because the Western powers were only interested in making profits in China, whereas the Taipings deliberately undermined an established society and tried to destroy its ancient values. With the Taipings there could not be any compromise. Moreover, by proposing to nationalize all land, the Taipings infringed upon the vested interest of the most powerful class in China, the landed gentry. The same interests which had rallied to defeat Wang Mang eighteen centuries before now swarmed to the standard of the Manchus.

The man who symbolized and led the anti-Taiping forces to suppress the rebellion was Tseng Kuo-fan, one of the greatest Confucian statesmen of the nineteenth century. Tseng came from a gentry family in Hunan province and was well-schooled in Confucian learning during his boyhood. After passing the civil service examinations, he served successfully with the Ch'ing government and was eventually promoted to the vice-presidency of the Ministry of Rites. In 1852 he resigned his post to enter a period of mourning after the death of his mother, and it was then that he was ordered by the emperor Hsien-feng to organize a militia to defend his native province. He began his work earnestly in the following year, after the Taipings had swept across most areas south of the Yangtze River. The bannermen and the "green battalions" that had distinguished themselves on the battlefield early in the Ch'ing dynasty were now corrupt and useless, and the Ch'ing government had to depend upon provincial militias organized by local gentry to combat the rebels. While Tseng was busy in Hunan in organizing his army, a fellow gentry official named Li Hung-chang was doing the same in his native province, Anhwei. The Hsiang (Hunan) army led by Tseng and the Huai (Anhwei) army led by Li were the two major forces that eventually overthrew the rebel regime at Nanking.

In their war against the Taipings, Tseng and Li received help from an unexpected corner, the Western interests in China. Outwardly, it seems strange that the Western powers should assist the Manchu government against a Christian regime. At the beginning of the rebellion Christian missionaries showed considerable interest in the rebels who professed Christianity. A careful study of the Taiping beliefs soon disillusioned them because what Hung advocated could not be characterized in any way other than as outright heresy. The Taiping regime's prohibition of the opium traffic affected adversely the interests of Western traders who, together with their Chinese counterparts, had profited enormously by the spread of this vice. Moreover, the Western powers had only recently obtained many treaty concessions from the Ch'ing government, and there was no guarantee that the Taipings would honor these obligations if they replaced the Manchu regime. The feuds among the Taiping leaders and their inability to organize a real, respectable government dispelled whatever illusions some Westerners might once have had. When the showdown arrived, the Western interests sided with the Manchu government.

From 1860 to 1864 the bitterest fighting occurred in the Lower Yangtze. The Ch'ing forces were determined to take Nanking, and the Taipings, in order to defend their capital, were equally determined to occupy as large an area as possible. Shanghai, the most coveted prize in this region, was fought for by both sides. The Taiping commander Li Hsiuch'eng requested the Western powers to maintain neutrality, but his request was ignored. In Shanghai the Chinese as well as the Western commercial interests had grown enormously since the port had been opened for Western trade, and in view of the Taipings' communistic ideas, they understandably would do everything they could to prevent the Taipings from capturing the city. They sponsored and financed the organization of the so-called Ever Victorious Army, staffed by foreign officers and equipped with modern weapons. The army was first led by an American named John E. Ward, and after he was killed in action in 1862, the command was taken over by an Englishman, Charles G. Gordon. The Ever Victorious Army played an important role in the final campaign against the Taipings, as it captured many strategic cities for the Manchu regime in the Lower Yangtze.

In the summer of 1864, the Ch'ing forces, led by Tseng Kuo-ch'üan, a younger brother of Tseng Kuo-fan, made the final assault on Nanking. The city fell after a bloody battle which lasted fifteen days. Hung Hsiuch'üan, the Prince of Heaven, had committed suicide one month before, and his son and successor escaped from the city, only to be captured afterwards. "Not a single man of the 100,000 bandits in the city responded to the order of surrender," reported Tseng Kuo-fan to the imperial government, "and they burned themselves alive in groups as if they had no regret." Later he proceeded to Peking to report his victory in person. There he prostrated himself and kowtowed before the emperess dowager, Tz'u Hsi, who was then a co-regent for the boy emperor T'ung-chih.

۲ xiii

The Western Impact (2)

THE IMITATION OF THE WEST

Hu Lin-yi, Tseng Kuo-fan's top lieutenant and governor of Hupeh, went to a hill overlooking the city of Anking (Anhwei province) where the attacking Ch'ing army was fighting a bloody battle against the besieged Taipings. Pleased with the progress of the battle, he remarked to his retainers that it was not difficult to defeat the "bandits" despite their "stubbornness." Coming down to the bank of the Yangtze he saw two foreign ships sailing upstream like "two galloping horses with wind-like speed." He was silent and his face became pale. On his way to the barracks, he vomited blood and almost fell from his mount. He had not been well before and now his illness took a serious turn for the worse. Several months later he died while still commanding troops in the army.

Like Hu, many Chinese leaders felt that the real danger to China was not domestic rebels like the Taipings but the seemingly invincible West. "I wish I knew what the future holds for us," remarked Hu, whenever foreigners were mentioned in the course of conversation. Now that China's door was wide open, it seemed that there was no way to resist the ever-increasing Western demands. The issue, however, had to be faced. "If we continue to buy Western ships and arms," said Tseng Kuo-fan, "eventually we shall have enough weapons to resist England and France." This may sound naive today, but it marked the beginning of China's imitation of the West. By then it had become apparent to a few articulate leaders that to become strong enough to resist Western demands, China had to learn the advanced technology of the Western countries. Only by possessing a strong military force, they believed, could China negotiate peace with the West on equal terms and fight a more effective war when the necessity arose. However, the basis of such a military force would not be solid and stable so long as it had to be equipped with vessels and weapons purchased abroad. Thus, in the opinion of many Chinese leaders, China had to have factories of its own, to produce equipment for its own needs. In 1865 the first modern shipyard was established at Shanghai, and the very next year another one was founded at Mawei, near Foochow. In 1870 the Tientsin Machine Factory was renovated to manufacture modern weapons, and in 1872 the China Merchants' Steam Navigation Company was organized at Shanghai. In 1878 coal was mined by using Western technology for the first time at Kaiping, and in 1880 initial steps were taken to build a railroad with Chinese capital. Psychologically, the most important innovation was perhaps the establishment of the Tsungli Yamen (Foreign Office) in 1861 which replaced the traditional Bureau of Barbarian Affairs in handling diplomatic relations with Western countries. By such an action China relinquished its age-old claim that it was the center of power as well as the fount of civilization. In fact, China was making an agonizing reappraisal of itself and its own position in a fast-changing world.

One might call this reappraisal a mental revolution of the first magnitude because it was the first time in Chinese history that a sizable portion of the intelligentsia openly admitted that there was a great deal to be learned from the "barbarians." To learn from the "barbarians," they, of course, had to read "barbarian" books. In 1862 the first foreign language school was established at Peking (T'ung-wen kuan). Western instructors were employed to teach Manchu and Chinese students of "great native intelligence" as measured by a competitive examination. Four foreign languages were taught: English, French, Russian, and German. One year later another foreign language school was organized at Shanghai. The main purpose of these schools was to train interpreters and translators, especially the latter. Translation, a seemingly easy task, became extremely difficult when a Western language was to be translated into the Chinese language of the literary style. It required great skill in the handling of Chinese words and proficiency in Chinese literature as well as a thorough knowledge of the subject matter. Two of the greatest translators of the modern period, Yen Fu and Lin Shu, were not products of the language schools, and the latter did not even know any foreign language. Yen Fu translated more serious books such as *Man's Place in Nature* by Thomas H. Huxley, *An Enquiry into the Wealth of Nations* by Adam Smith, *Logic* by John Stuart Mill, and *Spirit of Laws* by Montesquieu. Lin Shu, on the other hand, translated books of a lighter vein, such as *Camille* by Alexandre Dumas.

The logical place to learn what was then known as "Western affairs" (*yang-wu*) was obviously the Western countries themselves. In 1870 the government decided to send thirty boys each year to be educated in the United States. In Hartford, Connecticut, it bought a house as a dormitory for the students, and a Chinese official was appointed as supervisor. Students were also sent to England and France, though the largest number of them went to the United States. The study-abroad program, beneficial as it might be, soon encountered sharp criticisms. It was not only financially expensive, said the critics, but it denied the students a more basic education, namely, the study of Chinese classics and the appreciation of Confucian vitues. These critics advocated the establishment of Westernized schools in China where students could "learn Western skills without abandoning Chinese virtues." As one might expect, the first Westernized schools were vocational, technical institutions. The Foochow Marine Academy was founded in 1866, and in 1880 a naval academy came into existence in Tientsin. It was not until 1898 that a university with emphasis on liberal arts was established in Peking. The university, later known as the Peking University, has been one of the most famous universities in China.

Significant as these programs were, they were far from adequate to meet the demands for modernization. They were all small in scope, and the goal of each program was not steadily pursued. The lack of adequate funds and trained personnel was one reason, and the frequent change of policy with regard to these programs was another. Moreover, the primary sponsors of these programs such as Tseng Kuo-fan and Li Hung-chang had only a limited objective. What they wished to learn from the West was science and technology, and nothing else. They believed in the superiority of China's political and social structure, the Confucian ideology behind it, and the moral values that governed the relationship among men. All reforms, they maintained, should be conducted within China's own historical framework. "Chinese values should govern the basic matters," said one of them, "whereas Western learning is applicable only in the technical sphere." If such a principle were followed, China would then incorporate the best from both the East and the West. In short,

China was to remain Confucian and authoritarian, while acquiring the technological and military capacity to defend itself.

Even this limited objective of Westernization encountered strong opposition from the majority of the Chinese intelligentsia. The opposition resulted partly from a genuine concern over the possible consequence of exposing Chinese to such "strange" ideas as freedom and democracy, but mostly from habits and beliefs ingrained in an ancient civilization. The opposition was so strong that Li Hung-chang, the undisputed leader of the progressive group after Tseng Kuo-fan's death in 1872, often complained that he was fighting a lonely battle. "The intelligentsia always criticize me for honoring strange ideas," said he in a letter to a friend, "and it is difficult to understand the minds of some Chinese."

If it was difficult for Li Hung-chang to understand the Chinese mind, it was doubly so for a Westerner. In 1874, for instance, the British built a railroad between Shanghai and Sungkiang. The Chinese opposed the construction of this railroad on the ground that it violated the natural harmony of the landscape and that this violation would bring bad luck to them for generations to come. There was a storm of protest and under public pressure the government had to buy the railroad from the British in 1876, wreck it, and carry the wreckage all the way to Taiwan where it was dumped into a lake as an ill omen. During the subsequent decades the preservation of the natural harmony of the landscape (called *feng-shui* by the Chinese) was a great handicap not only to railroad construction but also to mining, the erection of telegraph lines, and other Western projects. In 1880 a Chinese official arrived in the United States as a superintendent of Chinese students and ordered all his charges to come to Washington, D.C., to listen to his lecture on "morality and good behavior." Upon seeing him the students refused to perform the kowtow. He was so angry that he sent a memorial to the imperial government in which he suggested that all Chinese students in the United States be ordered to return to China on the ground that even if they could acquire Western skills they, corrupted by Western ideas, could never be the same Chinese. The imperial government, acting on the superintendent's proposal, ordered these students to return home in the following year.

Between a small group of progressives and the ultraconservatives who constituted the overwhelming majority of the Chinese literati the ultimate arbitrator was the empress dowager, Tz'u Hsi. There are so many legends about this woman that sometimes it is difficult to differentiate facts from mere hearsay. One thing, however, remains certain. She was a ruthless woman endowed with great ability, and she used every talent she had to fight for the one thing she loved most: power. Principle and morality meant nothing to her if the observance of them was incompatible with the fulfillment of her personal ambition. In her struggle for power her closest allies were the eunuchs who until then had not been an important factor in Ch'ing politics. Such an alliance should be expected because, as a woman, she was under great handicaps in negotiating political alliances with men outside the palace. Her eunuchs served as go-betweens as well as spies and informers. She was able to inspire fear or even respect, but never love. Despite her ruthlessness and lack of principle, her strong personality commanded the loyalty and obedience of many eminent men in the second half of the nineteenth century such as Tseng Kuo-fan and Li Hung-chang.

The life of Tz'u Hsi sounds more like fiction than biography, and here only the briefest outline can be presented. Selected as a concubine by the emperor Hsien-feng while in her teens, she worked her way into becoming his confidante through her charm, talent, and skillful maneuvering. Her position in the royal household was greatly enhanced after she bore the emperor a son who was then made the heir apparent. When the emperor died in 1862, she and the empress Tz'u An were made co-regents on behalf of the child emperor T'ung-chih, and three royal princes, in observance of the dead emperor's will, were to assist them in the management of state affairs. Tz'u Hsi soon liquidated the three princes on trumped-up charges and became regent in fact as well as in name. Though Tz'u An, as the former empress, out-ranked her in seniority, she was too pliable a person to offer resistance to Tz'u Hsi's ambition. Tz'u Hsi's ruthlessness eventually alienated even her own son who, as he grew up, resented being a mere puppet. The rivalry between mother and son reached a climax in 1872 when the time had arrived for the imperial marriage. The young man favored a girl approved by Tz'u An and rejected the one recommended by his own mother. Tz'u Hsi, as the story goes, prohibited her son from visiting his newly married wife, thus hoping to force him to visit the girl whom she favored, the girl who had by then been made an imperial concubine. The boy refused to have anything to do with this scheme and visited street girls instead. He contracted a venereal disease and died two years later (1874) at the age of nineteen.

To a Westerner one of the most interesting parts of Tz'u Hsi's political career was her successful exploitation of the Confucian virtue, filial piety, to advance her own ambition. As has been said in a previous chapter, an emperor might be the Son of Heaven before his subjects, but he remained his mother's son in the royal household. As such, he was required by custom and tradition to be obedient to her and cater to her wishes, even when, as sometimes happened, state policies were involved. While most empress dowagers in history did not interfere with state affairs and were satisfied with ritualistic deference from their imperial sons, the ambitious ones, such as Tz'u Hsi, could transform this maternal dignity into real power, and by controlling their sons they controlled the nation. If a son or adopted son were a minor, the empress dowager could rule the nation openly without using the emperor as a puppet, because in such case she customarily became the regent.

After the death of T'ung-chih, Tz'u Hsi placed on the throne her three-year-old nephew (the son of her sister) who, after accession, was

TZ'U HSI ON HER PEACOCK THRONE

known as Kuang-hsü. She considered the boy her own son, and such a claim enabled her to continue to rule as a regent. The fact that she violated the dynastic rule by installing as the new emperor another member of the same generation did not bother her so long as the new emperor was a minor whom she could control. In 1781 Tz'u An died and Tz'u Hsi became the sole regent. As he grew up, Kuang-hsü, like his predecessor T'ung-chih, resented the empress dowager's domination. When the time had arrived for him to select a queen, the empress dowager imposed on him a girl he disliked, while the girl of his own choice was made a mere concubine (later known as the Pearl Concubine). The two personalities continued to clash despite their outward correctness: the empress dowager was always "loving and protective" and the emperor was always "pious and obedient." The clash reached a new height during the so-called Hundred Days' Reform (1898) which will be discussed later in this chapter. (See pp. 424–427.) After the failure of the Reform, the emperor was kept a prisoner in his own palace; and isolated from outside contact, his only comfort was his Pearl Concubine. Even this comfort was taken away in 1900 when the empress dowager, in a burst of anger, ordered her to commit suicide. The clash between the two personalities finally ended in 1908 when both died only one day apart. Thus, for almost a half century (1862–1908), one of the most crucial periods in Chinese history, the real power in China was the empress dowager, Tz'u Hsi.

Had the empress dowager, with great power at her command, backed up the progressives and thrown China's resources behind the modernization programs, the China of the late nineteenth century would have been remarkably different from what it was. This, of course, she did not do. First, there was the honest ignorance of what Westernization meant and what it promised, and second, she had to look at the reforms from her stand as a Manchu princess. Would the reforms help her position in the government or the Manchus' position in China? The answer was obviously "no." Practically all progressive leaders were Chinese, and the most reactionary among the conservatives were Manchus. What would have happened to the dynasty and to her personally if, as a result of the modernization programs, the Chinese became so powerful as to tip the traditional balance between these two ethnic groups? Moreover, how was it possible to import Western technology without importing Western ideas such as representative government and democracy? On the other hand, she knew that without being modernized technologically, China could not resist the increasing demands from foreign powers. Caught in a dilemma, she gave some encouragement to the modernization programs, but not enough to make them succeed. She was only too happy when a sizable fund originally appropriated for building a new navy was transferred to another account for the purpose of building a palace ground (known as Yi-ho Yüan) for her personal enjoyment. She could have been

China's Meiji Emperor (See p. 418.) but for her own reasons she did not choose to become one. If she were forced to make a choice between the salvation of China and the preservation of her own power and the power of the Manchus, there was no question about her decision. "I prefer to give China to the foreigners rather than to surrender it to my own slaves [Chinese]," she once remarked. As far as her personal objectives were concerned, she succeeded remarkably well. She was in power and so were the Manchus, as long as she lived. Three years after her death, the Manchu dynasty went with her.

To balance what has been said above, it should be pointed out that by taking a more conservative stand Tz'u Hsi had on her side the over-whelming majority of the Chinese intelligentsia. If she had done other-wise, she would have faced an uphill struggle as all of the progressives did. Since the conservative stand was more compatible with her personal interests, she did no more than what could be expected.

Despite the half-hearted support on the part of the government, the ingrained opposition arising from Chinese customs and traditions, and the inertia of the majority of the Chinese people, the advantages of Western technology were too obvious not to be recognized by certain sections of the population. Some of the new industries were financed jointly by foreign and Chinese capital; others were solely Chinese enter-prises. Towards the end of the nineteenth century many railroads were built with the help of foreign capital, and several coal and iron-ore mines were operated by the use of Western technology. In the Wu-Han area the progressive governor-general Chang Chih-tung promoted Western-type industries with eagerness and energy, and financed them through local savings. In Shanghai small industries (such as textiles and flour mills) using machinery for production mushroomed overnight and attracted local capital which had been traditionally invested in landholdings. From 1864 to 1900 the total volume of China's foreign trade was more than trebled, though the excess of imports over exports also increased steadily. Economically, a new China was emerging, however slowly.

TERRITORIAL LOSSES

In the two decades after the Opium War, while England and France were battling China to enlarge their commercial interests, farther in the north another power was nibbling at Chinese territories. The emergence of Russia as an independent state after the overthrow of the Mongol overlordship was followed by a period of continuous expansion, and by the seventeenth century the Russian power had reached Siberia and clashed head-on with the rising power of the Manchu empire. Often there was friction between merchants and officials of both sides, and armed forces were sometimes called to resolve the differences. The situation was particularly serious in the Amur basin. As neither side could impose its will on the other in these remote areas, a compromise was reached in the Treaty of Nerchinsk in 1689. The Chinese granted Russian merchants the right to trade in the border areas in return for a generous boundary settlement. The boundary line ran along the Argun River, the Gorbitsa (a tributary of Shilka), and the watershed between the basins of the Lena and the Amur to the sea. This arrangement was supplemented by another treaty in 1727 (the Treaty of Kiakhta), which delimited the boundary line between the two countries west of the Gorbitsa, provided further details in the trade relations, and gave Russia a semirepresentation at Peking (a church, a priest, three curates, and five language students). This representation, unofficial as it was, provided Russia valuable information on China and enabled it to have direct access to imperial officials at Peking, a privilege which England sought in vain throughout the eighteenth century.

The northern frontier was comparatively quiet until 1847 when China's weakness as revealed in the Opium War was seized upon by Russia as a golden opportunity for expanding territorially at China's expense. In that year the tsar appointed Count Nicholas Muraviev as governor-general of eastern Siberia with special instructions to investigate the Amur region. The Count, one of the ablest empire-builders, pursued his task in earnest, and by 1854 he and his agents had explored and then occupied the entire region north of the Amur River which under the Treaty of Nerchinsk was Chinese territory. In 1858 when England and France were invading China from the sea and the Taiping rebels were ravaging South China on land, Muraviev presented to the local Chinese officials a set of territorial demands. These officials, knowing that they could not count on the central government to send reinforcements to counteract any military action the Russians might take, consented to the demands. The Treaty of Aigun, signed between Muraviev and Yi-shan, the governor of Heilungkiang, contained three major items: (1) the cession to Russia of all territories north of the Amur River, (2) joint control of the land lying between the Ussuri River and the sea (the present Maritime Province), and (3) the right of both countries to navigate the Amur, the Ussuri, and the Sungari rivers.

Before Russia had had time to digest these territorial gains, another opportunity for demanding more territories presented itself in 1860 after England and France had defeated the Chinese and captured their capital Peking. The Russian minister to China, General Ignatief, promised the Chinese that he would use his good influence to persuade the allies not to engage in continuous destruction of that ancient city if the Chinese could see their way to cede to Russia the territory between the Ussuri and the sea. Looking at the victorious allies on a rampage, Prince Kung, the

SEA OF
OKHOTSK

SIBERIA

SAKHALIN

Ceded to
Russia (1858)

AMUR RIVER

Ceded
to
Russia
(1860)

SHILKA RIVER

ARGUN RIVER

AMUR RIVER

USSURI RIVER

MANCHURIA

Lake
Khanka

Vladivostok

MAP 29
TERRITORIES CHINA CEDED
TO RUSSIA, 1858-1860

——— Present Boundaries

0   200   400

Scale of Miles

SEA OF
JAPAN

KOREA

highest Manchu official then in Peking after the emperor had fled, agreed
and subsequently signed the Treaty of Peking (1860). By the two treaties
(Aigun and Peking) Russia deprived China of 350,000 square miles of
territory, a territory larger than Texas (267,339 sq. mi.), without ever
firing a shot. At the southernmost tip of the newly acquired territory, the
city of Vladivostok was founded, and the city remains today as Russia's
largest naval base in East Asia.

Meanwhile in the south, England and France were engaged in conquering and annexing some of China's dependent states. These dependent states were sometimes called tributary states since their kings received investiture from China, adopted the Chinese calendar, and sent periodical tribute missions to the Chinese capital. China did not exercise actual control over these states and, as a rule, did not interfere in their domestic affairs. Generally speaking, the lord-vassal relationship was more a cultural than a political relationship. However, the dependent states did serve a political purpose in the sense that they formed a buffer zone between China proper and the less Sinicized and more hostile kingdoms and tribes beyond. The past showed that to protect China these dependent states had to be protected first, and that their loss to a foreign power would expose China itself to foreign invasions and might eventually even lead to the occupation of part or all of China. Throughout history China had striven to surround itself with a chain of friendly, dependent states, and the Ch'ing regime, like many Chinese dynasties before it, had a lord-vassal relationship with many of its border states such as Annam, Burma, Sikkim, and Korea.

Annam, which means "peace in the south" in Chinese, was known as Indo-China after the French conquest and comprises four independent countries today: North and South Vietnam, Laos, and Cambodia. France began to show interest in that country as early as 1843; however, it did not take military action until 1858. This military action and that which followed were taken on the ground that the Annamese government was hostile to Christians. In 1862 a treaty was concluded between the two countries which gave France the right to trade and proselytize in Annam and to navigate in the internal rivers. Besides, Annam ceded to France three provinces and paid indemnities to compensate French expenses occasioned during the military operation. To pave the way for annexation, France imposed another treaty on Annam in 1874 which recognized Annam as an independent country, thus cutting off its relationship with China. However, Annam continued to send tribute missions to China in 1876 and again in 1880. By 1884 the former Annam was quickly disappearing as a result of France's successful military operations, and French troops were pushing towards the Chinese border. China responded by sending troops to Annam, and amazingly, the Chinese, with native support, won victories against the French. Unable to make headway on land, France sent its fleet to ravage China's southeastern coast. Here the superiority of French naval power prevailed: it destroyed the Chinese naval base at Foochow and seized a naval port, Keelung, at Taiwan. Within the Ch'ing court, some officials favored continuing the war and others advocated a negotiated peace. The peace party, led by Li Hung-chang, eventually prevailed, after it had successfully convinced Tz'u Hsi that China was not prepared for a large-scale war and that continuing the conflict would subject the coastal cities to French bombardment or seizure. In 1885

China concluded a treaty with France in which China formally recognized Annam as a French protectorate.

Burma, an off-and-on Chinese tributary state since 1284, was conquered by Great Britain without provoking Chinese intervention. The conquest came about through three Burmese Wars (1824–1826, 1852–1853, and 1885), and, unlike the French conquest of Annam, this one did not involve missionaries. The Chinese formally recognized the conquest in 1886 when an Anglo-Chinese convention was signed. To save Chinese prestige, Great Britain promised to let the Burmese continue to send tribute missions to China once every ten years. However, only one such mission was sent, in 1895. Meanwhile, in 1890, Great Britain successfully "persuaded" the Chinese to recognize Sikkim as a British protectorate.

In retrospect, the country that proved to be more aggressive than either England or France was a neighboring Oriental country, Japan. During the initial stage of the Western impact, Japan reacted the same as China. However, it soon became convinced of the advantages of Westernization and began to apply Western technology to industry, commerce, and related fields. The modernization of Japan began with the Meiji Restoration (1867), and in one generation that country was transformed from a feudal, agricultural society to the most industrialized society in all Asia. The history of modern Japan is not our concern here; we can only relate those events that led to its conflicts with China. Japan's expansion began soon after its modernization began; in fact, a major purpose of the modernization programs was to provide Japan with the necessary economic and military capacity to play a more active role in East Asian affairs. Three years after Meiji became the emperor, a Japanese ambassador arrived in Peking asking for the same concessions that China had given to the Western powers. Li Hung-chang rejected the Japanese demand, saying that the unequal treaties had been forced upon China by the Western powers and that China had been duped into granting extraterritoriality to Westerners because it was unfamiliar with the European customs. "Now every time I see the dictatorial behavior of the Western consuls," he added, "I am grieved." However, a treaty of trade and commerce, minus the most-favored-nation clause, was signed between the two countries.

The first conflict between China and Japan involved Liu-ch'iu (Ryukyu) and Taiwan. Throughout the Ming-Ch'ing period Liu-ch'iu was China's vassal state and beginning in 1662 sent tribute missions to China once every two years. Japan, however, had claim on the islands too, as the king of Liu-ch'iu also sent tribute to the *Daimyo* of Satsuma from time to time. In 1871 some fifty-four Liu-ch'iu islanders, shipwrecked at Taiwan, were murdered by the aborigines. Japan proclaimed that Liu-ch'iu was its vassal state and asked China to punish the aborigines. Receiving no satisfaction from the Chinese, Japan sent a military expedition to Taiwan and occupied a strip of territory on the northern coast. When China responded by proposing to send a larger force to counteract the Japanese move, Japan requested England's good offices. The result was the treaty of 1874 which, by implication, recognized Japan's claim as protector of the Liu-ch'iu islands. Five years later, Japan deposed the Liu-ch'iu king and annexed the islands.

The conflict over Liu-ch'iu was the first of a long series of Japanese expansionist moves which were not to end until World War II. As Korea formed a natural bridge to mainland China, it was most logically Japan's next target. Since Han Wu-ti's conquest of Korea in the second century B.C., Korea had been sometimes a vassal state of China and sometimes independent. Military confrontations between China and Japan over Korea occurred in the seventh and again in the sixteenth century; in each case the greater manpower and economic resources China then possessed prevailed in the long run. Towards the end of the nineteenth century the power balance had shifted to Japan's favor, as that country had become militarily and technologically stronger. In 1876, as a result of a series of successful diplomatic maneuvers, a demonstration of force, and the outright occupation of some Korean islands, the Japanese secured a treaty with Korea which opened two Korean ports for Japanese trade and recognized that Korea as "an independent state, enjoys the same sovereign rights as does Japan." The detachment of Korea from its dependence on China, as the Japanese hoped, would enable them to have a free hand in that country. China, knowing its own military weakness, did not bother to protest. Instead, it persuaded Korea to open its ports to all Western countries, including England, France, the United States, and Russia, to counteract the increasing Japanese influence.

Meanwhile in Korea two political factions had developed, one progressive and the other conservative. The progressive group was led by returned students from Japan who wanted Korea to follow the Japanese example by initiating reforms. The conservative group, on the other hand, was headed by people close to the Korean king and leaned heavily on Chinese support. In 1884 the intrigues and strife between these two factions developed into open hostility, and both China and Japan, in the name of restoring peace and order, sent troops to Korea. The Chinese force, led by Yüan Shih-k'ai, dispersed the Japanese and placed the state power in the hands of the conservatives. In the following year a treaty was concluded between China and Japan in which each party pledged that in the case of future disturbances in Korea, it would notify the other party in advance before sending troops. By then it was clear that China was as determined to keep Korea as a dependent state as Japan was determined to detach it from China. If Korea were lost, the Ch'ing government reasoned, Manchuria, the home of China's royal house, would be exposed to Japan's attack. Between 1885 and 1894 China strengthened its control over Korea and made that country a protectorate, *de facto* as well as *de jure*. This was the first time that China had exercised such firm control since the beginning of the Ming dynasty.

In 1894 the Korean government had a rebellion to contend with. The rebellion was led by a semireligious group called the Eastern Learning Society which vowed to "expel and eliminate all Japanese invaders" and to "capture Seoul (Korean capital) to eliminate all aristocrats." The rebels occupied a large section of southern Korea and defeated the regular Korean army that was sent to suppress them. Korea requested China's help, and China responded by sending to Korea a military expedition, after notifying Japan of its intention. Japan moved quickly to counteract the Chinese move and succeeded in capturing Seoul. The Japanese deposed the Korean king and placed his natural father (known as Tai-wun-kun) on the throne. The new king concluded a treaty of alliance with Japan and requested his new ally to drive the Chinese troops out from Korea. Thus the war began.

After hostilities began, the Japanese won victories on both land and sea. From the Chinese point of view the most disastrous was the destruction of the Peiyang fleet, one of Li Hung-chang's most precious projects. After the Japanese troops had penetrated deep into South Manchuria and threatened Shanhaikuan, the Chinese sued for peace. Japan, enjoying the greatest victory it had ever won against China, refused to accept any man as China's minister plenipotentiary for negotiating peace except Li Hung-chang. Li, who had worked hard against great opposition to modernize China, was now compelled by circumstances to play a humiliating role: to go personally to Japan to ask the victors to moderate their demands. While in Japan he was shot by a Japanese citizen and was fortunate to escape serious injury. The incident, however, had no noticeable effect on the resultant treaty, one of the harshest China ever concluded with a foreign power. The Treaty of Shimonoseki (1895) called upon China (1) to recognize the independence of Korea, (2) to cede Taiwan, the Pescadores, and the Liaotung Peninsula to Japan, (3) to pay an indemnity of 200,000,000 taels, and (4) to open ports for trade and grant Japan the most-favored-nation treatment.

So harsh were the treaty terms that they sowed the seeds of hatred between the two countries for several decades to come. It was comparable to the Treaty of Paris of 1871 which helped to create a state of continuous hostility between Germany and France until the end of World War II. The Japanese were not merely interested in commercial expansion; their demand for large chunks of territories, the Chinese believed, revealed their ultimate ambition, the conquest of China. From 1895 on, Chinese nationalism was directed more at Japan than at any other foreign power, as Japan had shown herself to be the most aggressive of all foreign powers. From the Japanese point of view, however, the treaty was a masterpiece of diplomacy. The huge indemnity provided the much-needed capital for industrial expansion, and the most-favored-nation treatment enabled Japan to acquire the same tariff, extraterritoriality, and other concessions that Western powers enjoyed in China. Since Japan was geographically close to China, it was in a better position to exploit these concessions more effectively. Moreover, the treaty marked the beginning of the establishment of the Japanese empire. Korea, recognized as an independent state in 1895, became a Japanese protectorate in 1907, and was formally annexed by Japan in 1910. Taiwan was taken over by Japan outright and remained a Japanese possession until 1945.

In the case of the Liaotung Peninsula, however, the situation became more complicated. This peninsula, with its rich mineral resources, strategic location, and two excellent harbors (Dairen and Port Arthur), was as much coveted by Russia as it was by Japan. If it fell into the hands of a strong Japan, the Russian chance of securing it would become slim indeed. Shortly after the treaty was made public, Russia, supported by its ally France and also by Germany which had its own designs in this part of the world, demanded that Japan return the peninsula to China. Since Japan was in no position to fight a war against three major European powers, it reluctantly agreed to the Russian demand in return for a Chinese cash payment (30 million taels). The competition of the two countries for Manchuria eventually led to the Russo-Japanese War.

To Li Hung-chang the Treaty of Shimonoseki was as much a personal humiliation as a national disgrace. Moreover, he believed that Japan would not be content with what it had received and that sooner or later there would be another Sino-Japanese war. Knowing that China was unable to fight Japan alone, he was looking for a military alliance with a Western power. The memory of the recent wars with England and France was still fresh, and furthermore, it was unlikely that these two powers would fight a war against Japan to protect Manchuria for China. Russia, on the other hand, had a direct interest in seeing that Manchuria remain in Chinese hands because first, its occupation by Japan would threaten Russia's own security in Eastern Siberia, and second, Russia would like to reserve Manchuria as its own sphere for expansion. In 1896 Li Hung-chang went to St. Petersburg, outwardly to attend the coronation of Tsar Nicholas II but actually to negotiate a secret treaty of alliance with Russia. The treaty provided for mutual assistance against future Japanese aggression, for the use of Chinese ports by Russia in case of war, and for China's agreement to Russia's construction of a railroad (later known as the Chinese Eastern Railroad) across Manchuria to reach Vladivostok. Under no circumstances, said the treaty, should Russia use the construction of the railroad as an excuse to occupy Chinese territories.

Nevertheless, Russia was formally invited into Manchuria. The future of Manchuria was to be decided by the Russo-Japanese struggle, while the Chinese were forced to the sidelines.

CHINA'S STRUGGLE TO SURVIVE

The weakness of China as revealed during the Sino-Japanese War triggered a series of demands for Chinese territories on the part of Western powers. Germany, which was a newcomer among the imperialistic ranks and was anxious to secure a foothold in East Asia, made the first move. It notified the Chinese that it deserved a "reward" as a result of its intervention to force Japan to return to China the Liaotung Peninsula, and when the Chinese turned down its demand for the cession of the Kiaochow Bay (Shantung province), Germany decided to take military action. A gunboat was dispatched in July, 1897, but was destroyed by a typhoon while on its way to Kiaochow. Two months later two German Catholic missionaries were murdered by Chinese robbers in Shantung, and thereupon German troops landed in Kiaochow. Thus the Chinese government was forced to come to terms. The Kiaochow Bay was leased to Germany for ninety-nine years, and Germany was granted the right to build two railroads in Shantung and was also given the mining rights along the railroads. Moreover, "in all cases where foreign assistance, in persons, capital or material, may be needed for any purpose whatever within the Province of Shantung," the Chinese government bound itself to ask Germany for such assistance. In a term commonly used at the turn of the century, Shantung had become a German sphere of influence.

The German success was soon followed by Russian demands in the Liaotung Peninsula and French demands in southern China. Three weeks after Germany had acquired Kiaochow, China leased to Russia the southern tip of the Liaotung Peninsula (containing Dairen and Port Arthur) and gave Russia the right to build a railroad to connect Dairen with the main line of the Chinese Eastern Railroad in central Manchuria. Previously, France had acquired the right to exploit the mineral resources in Yunnan, Kwangsi, and Kwangtung as a "reward" for its intervention to force Japan to return the Liaotung Peninsula to China. Now, seeing that Germany and Russia had obtained new concessions from China, France demanded the same from the Chinese. In the spring of 1898 China agreed to give France (1) the right to build a railroad from Tonkin (Annam) to Kunming, (2) the lease of the Kwangchow Bay for ninety-nine years, and (3) the right to appoint Frenchmen as advisers to the newly proposed Chinese postal service. By virtue of this agreement, Yunnan, Kwangsi, and Kwangtung became the French sphere of influence.

England, whose interest in China had been so far more commercial

TRANS SIBERIAN RAILROAD

AMUR RIVER

Chita

RUSSIAN SPHERE OF INFLUENCE

CHINESE EASTERN RAILROAD

OUTER MONGOLIA

Harbin

Vladivostok

JAPANESE SPHERE OF INFLUENCE

Mukden

KOREA

Sea of Japan

YELLOW RIVER

Peking

Liaotung Pen.

Dairen
Port Arthur

Wei-hai-wei

Chefoo

JAPAN

Shimonoseki

GERMAN SPHERE OF INFLUENCE

Tsingtao
Kiaochow Bay

East China Sea

BRITISH SPHERE OF INFLUENCE

Shanghai

Pacific Ocean

YANGTZE RIVER

JAPANESE SPHERE OF INFLUENCE

PESCADORES

TAIWAN

FRENCH SPHERE OF INFLUENCE

Kowloon
Hong Kong

Kwangchow Bay

South China Sea

MAP 30

THE BATTLE OF CONCESSIONS, 1895-1905

◻ Capital ● Cities
╈╈╈╈ Railroads

0   150   300   450

Scale of Miles

than political, finally decided to join the other powers in the scramble for concessions. Three months after the French success England obtained from China the following concessions: (1) the promise by China that it would never alienate any territory in the Yangtze Valley, (2) British control of the Chinese Maritime Customs, (3) the lease of Weihaiwei to England as a naval station, and (4) the extension of the lease of Kowloon to ninety-nine years. Thus at the turn of the century, the economically most productive part of China had become divided into spheres of foreign influence. This was the procedure whereby Africa had been divided before, and the Chinese feared that the same fate would befall them. China, in the words of Sun Yat-sen, had become a subcolony with many masters. "Yet," said he, "none of the masters feels responsible for its welfare."

The defeat at the hands of Japan in the Sino-Japanese War and the territorial demands of the European powers stung China to a new realization that unless it was modernized quickly, it would not survive as a nation at all. Dismissing the cautious, gradual approach of Li Hung-chang as inadequate and ineffective, many Chinese believed that the nation must undergo speedy, drastic reforms before it was too late. The leader of the new sentiment was a Confucian scholar named K'ang Yu-wei. K'ang was born in 1858 to an aristocratic family in Kwangtung, a family which for generations had been prominent in scholastic and governmental circles. He was well educated in the traditional, Confucian scholarship and passed the provincial level of the civil service examination in 1894. On his way to Peking to participate in the metropolitan examination in the following year, he passed through Hong Kong and Shanghai where he was greatly impressed by the efficiency of the Western municipal administration. Previously he had petitioned the government for reforms, and now he was more than convinced that to survive, China had to imitate the West not only technologically but in a variety of other fields as well. In Peking he sent the emperor Kuang-hsü a petition on which he secured the signatures of hundreds of examination candidates. The petition, later known as the *Examination Candidates' Petition (Kung-che shang-shu)*, strongly urged immediate reforms. "The need is urgent, and the time is short," said the petitioners. Though there was no immediate response from the emperor, the petition caused a great stir among the gentry-scholars. A political star had arisen on the horizon, and a new crusade was on its way.

To achieve his purpose of reform, K'ang had to win the support of the members of the scholar-gentry class. The only way to win their support, as he well knew, was to convince them that the reforms were not only compatible with Chinese tradition but would have been supported by Confucius himself. This was the same technique that had been used by Wang Mang in the first century and Wang An-shih in the eleventh century. In this respect K'ang's erudition in Confucian learning served him well, and he found in the *Spring and Autumn Annals* support for his proposed reforms. To strengthen his ideological stand, he wrote two books, *A Study of Confucius as a Reformer* (*K'ung-tzu kai-chih k'ao*) and *A Study of Forged Classics of the Hsin Dynasty* (*Hsin-hsüeh wei-ching k'ao*). A new organization, called the Society of Learning and Study (Ch'iang-hsüeh hui) was organized on a nation-wide basis to propagate his ideas. K'ang's most gifted disciple, Liang Ch'i-ch'ao, became the editor of a newly founded newspaper, *Current Affairs* (*Shih-wu pao*), and spoke eloquently to win many supporters. The ideological groundwork having been carefully prepared, the next most important thing was to convince the emperor of the necessity of reforms because the emperor alone could initiate action. It should be noted that K'ang and his colleagues were not rebels, and that they wanted to effect their reforms through the existing monarchic system.

Fortunately Emperor Kuang-hsü, who had taken over the reins of government from Tz'u Hsi in 1889 when he reached his majority, was in a receptive mood. He felt deeply the humiliation China had suffered at the foreigners' hands and he wished to become, to quote court sources, another George Washington or Peter the Great. He had read K'ang's books and he liked them. In the spring of 1898 K'ang and some of his colleagues were appointed as imperial officials, and they lost no time going into action. From June 11 to September 16, 1898, a series of imperial decrees were handed down, which, if carried out, would mean, among other things: (1) the abolition of the eight-legged essays and the introduction of tests on current affairs in all civil service examinations; (2) the elimination of superfluous, unnecessary government organs such as the Bureau of Royal Butlers (Kuang-lu ssu, in charge of the emperor's food) and the Bureau of Royal Stables (T'ai-p'u ssu); (3) the establishment of Westernized schools; (4) the organization and training of armed forces according to Western methods and the increased use of modern weapons; (5) the establishment of modern banks, the opening of mines, and the construction of railroads; and (6) the establishment of an economic bureau coordinating all industrial and commercial activities across the nation. During the one hundred days (hence the name: Hundred Days' Reform) the reformers reigned supreme since they had the emperor on their side.

Mild as these reforms were, they were too radical for the conservatives. They rallied behind the empress dowager Tz'u Hsi and urged her to take over the government and force the emperor to abdicate. The capital was full of rumors, including the rumor that the conflict between the emperor and the empress dowager had reached a climax and that the emperor's life was in danger. Some of the reformers attempted to stage a coup d'état to seize the empress dowager. The coup, if successful, would save the emperor and therefore their reforms—so they believed. Yüan Shih-k'ai, whose troops were stationed at nearby Tientsin, was approached by a reformer to carry out the coup, but Yüan, for his own reasons, reported the plot to the empress dowager instead. Thus the attempted coup failed before it could even get started. In the dawn of September 21, five days after the last decree of reform had been issued, the emperor was found kneeling and kowtowing before the empress dowager. He was trembling and speechless. "Stupid son," scolded the empress dowager; "I have been feeding you and taking care of you for more than twenty years and yet you listen to the words of those churls to plot against me." Then she issued a decree that the emperor was ill and that it was necessary for her to attend state affairs. The emperor was ordered to live in confinement and the reform was finished. K'ang and Liang managed to escape to foreign countries. However, other reform leaders were captured; they were subsequently sentenced to death or long imprisonment.

Why did the reforms fail? A superficial answer can be found in the sharp contrast between the two leading personalities: the empress dowager was strong and ruthless and the emperor was weak and undecisive, though always well-intentioned. The real reason, however, went beyond the difference in personalities. The failure of the reform movement should be viewed in the broad context of the confrontation between the East and the West and between imported progressivism and traditional conservatism. It failed because in 1898 the progressive force was still in a minority. Fifty years after the Opium War the country was not yet ready to accept Western ideas and to abandon even a small fraction of its traditional values. The reforms were opposed not only by Tz'u Hsi and her conservative supporters but by the majority of the intelligentsia as well. Despite his justification of reforms on the basis of Confucian ideology, K'ang Yu-wei was denounced as a cultural traitor and deviationist and was regarded as a dangerous man. "Even if Confucius really wanted reform, he desired only to restore the ancient Sage Kings of the Three Dynasties," said one scholar; "he had no intention of replacing Chinese institutions with barbarian [Western] systems." "K'ang Yu-wei imitates Confucius in external appearance, but follows the barbarians [Westerners] in his inner mind," echoed another. One government official even suggested to the emperor that K'ang should be beheaded. Moreover, some of the reforms affected adversely the vested interests of many of the intellectuals. These intellectuals had spent years in studying the classics and perfecting the eight-legged essays, and they depended on their skill in the ancient training to open doors to officialdom, power, and prestige. The abolition of the eight-legged essays in the civil service examinations, as they rightly feared, would block their avenue to advancement. Thus, by introducing one educational reform, K'ang made millions of enemies.

After K'ang Yu-wei's reforms had failed, those Chinese who wished to see a modern China rise from its deadening past eventually concluded that the Manchu regime must go. They joined the standard of another man who by temperament and choice was a rebel and revolutionary. His name was Sun Wen, better known as Sun Yat-sen. As to the career of this remarkable man, we shall have a great deal to say later in this chapter.

THE BOXER REBELLION, THE OPEN DOOR, AND THE RUSSO-JAPANESE WAR

Tz'u Hsi, who in her advanced age was popularly referred to as the Old Buddha, remained outwardly placid and immobile after the storm over the reform movement had been blown away. Underneath the calm and almost kind appearance were anger, fear, and reinforced hatred. She wanted to depose the emperor, but she was not sure of the reaction of the foreign powers who, as generally understood, were in sympathy with the emperor and the progressive leaders. K'ang and Liang had escaped to foreign countries where they organized the Emperor Protection Society (Pao-huang hui) and openly criticized her and her reactionary policies. She wanted the foreigners to return the two "traitors" to China to be beheaded, but the foreigners refused to cooperate. Inside and outside the country there were numerous organizations working for her downfall and the downfall of her government. To her dismay even some of her own governors-general refused to consent to the deposition of the emperor. Who taught these Chinese to be "disloyal to their sovereign and impious towards their parents?" Of course, it was the foreigners. China would return to its virtuous path if all foreigners simply would leave China and take away with them all their gadgets such as railroads and telegraph poles. Yet she dared not say this to them because she was afraid of them, especially their fast ships and deadly weapons. If somehow these deadly weapons could be neutralized and could not do any harm to their intended victims! This would be a miracle, but miracles, as she was told, had happened before. Moreover, it was unthinkable that the great civilization of China would be trodden into pieces by these unscrupulous, contemptible barbarians. As she thought aloud, she increasingly surrounded herself with people of similar convictions. Around her were those who distrusted all books that were written in "illegible" horizontal lines and those who sincerely believed that sooner or later "Heaven will wipe out all barbarians who have recognized no ruler and no fathers for more than two thousand years." Their prayer seemed to have been answered when there appeared in North China the Society of the Righteous and Harmonious Fists (Yi-ho ch'üan). The society cried aloud: "Support the Manchus and eliminate the foreigners," and Tz'u Hsi and her reactionary advisers were greatly rejoiced. How could they eliminate the foreigners?

It was simple, said the Society's leaders. The foreigners had been able to defeat China because of their superiority in firearms, and "our members, when properly trained, are immune to bullets."

The Society of the Righteous and Harmonious Fists, better known in the English language as Boxers, was one of those numerous secret, semireligious organizations that have appeared time and again in Chinese history. Its religious beliefs were heavily dosed with superstition. It included among its dieties fictional as well as historical figures, including the monkey god invented by Wu Ch'eng-en in his romance, *Journey to the West* (Chapter X). Its followers were poverty-stricken peasants, the rural unemployed, disbanded soldiers, and all those who had nothing to lose except their lives. The nature and composition of this society would have implied that it was antilandlord and antigovernment, and for a considerable time it was. If it had been left alone to develop along its natural course, there would have been an open rebellion. However, by skillfully manipulating the Boxer leaders, local government officials were able to transform this antigovernment uprising into an antiforeign movement. As foreign pressure continued to increase towards the end of the nineteenth century, these officials had no difficulty in making the foreigners a scapegoat for China's miseries, especially the misery of the Boxers. The wrath of the Boxers, which at any other time would have been directed against the government, was now directed at the foreigners. Since the Boxers formed essentially a rural movement, they easily found their first target in the missionaries and their converts who lived in the rural areas.

That there had been friction between Chinese and missionaries has been said before; this friction was intensified as a result of Chinese misunderstanding of the nature of missionary activities. The Christians were accused of conducting immoral and illegal activities, such as "extracting eyes from infants to be compounded into direful drugs." Besides their extraterritorial status, their assumed superiority for having embraced the true faith and their alleged clannishness (in time of famine, for instance, the missionaries distributed rice only among their converts, derogatorily referred to by other Chinese as rice Christians) combined to make the situation worse. That most missionaries could not communicate in intelligible Chinese doubtless increased the confusion. During the nineteenth century there were isolated cases in which missionaries and converts were murdered, and in each case the foreign power from which these missionaries came quickly used the unfortunate occurrences as pretexts for demanding Chinese territories or other concessions. To the unsophisticated majority in China these missionaries were foreign agents and their Chinese converts were traitors to their own country and culture. Given the complexity of the situation, it was not surprising that the Boxers' first target was the missionaries and their Chinese converts.

The Boxer movement, like many other contentions between China and the Western powers, can best be understood in the context of an overall cultural confrontation during which friction and conflict were almost inevitable. Of all foreign groups in China, none was perhaps better motivated than the missionaries. One might argue about the desirability of sending missionaries to a country which had an advanced civilization of its own; there is no argument, however, about the sincerity of individual missionaries who believed that they were doing the most important thing that God willed. There was no question in their minds that the Chinese would eventually benefit from their work. They made great personal sacrifices by going to China, lived in uncomfortable, isolated places, and had to suffer and endure harassment, if not outright persecution, from the Chinese and their officials. If they did anything wrong, it was not intended. That their misfortunes had been often used by their home governments to advance their political and economic position in China was not their fault; as far as the missionaries were concerned, they preferred to see China converted to Christianity in a more peaceful way. "If the (Chinese) officials could be undeceived in regard to the real purposes of the missionaries, and if the missions in China could be conducted by really honest and sagacious men," said an American Minister to China in 1870, "I doubt if anything more than a passive resistance would be met with, which would soon be overcome by friendly intercourse and mutual forbearance." Unfortunately, not all missionaries were sagacious men; nor were Chinese officials always fair and wise. Thirty years after the above remark was made, a Chinese mob, called Boxers, fell mercilessly upon the missionaries and their Chinese converts. Their hatred was so bitter that they cared nothing for the consequences.

From the missionaries and their converts the Boxers broadened their targets to every Chinese who "smelt" foreign—people who advocated modernization and people who read books with horizontal lines. They burned churches, destroyed Westernized schools, dug out railroads, and cut telegraph lines. Had the local officials been wise, they would have suppressed this madness. They were not. The governor of Shantung, a bigoted Manchu named Yü-hsien, openly supported the Boxers' lawless activities. Only in South China did the governors take steps to suppress the Boxers despite the incitement from the empress dowager to do otherwise. One of the southern governors listened politely to a group of Boxer leaders who, appealing for his support, boasted about their magic powers, including their supposed immunity to Western bullets. The governor said that their claim had to be verified in front of impartial judges before he could give his support and ordered all of them to be shot in public, with, of course, Western bullets. Thanks to governors like him, the Boxer epidemic was confined to North China.

The question arises as to why such an intelligent person as the empress dowager believed this Boxer nonsense. It has often been said that her intense hatred of foreigners blinded her intellect and that in her advanced age she was no longer a rational person. This might be true, but still it does not explain adequately her obviously suicidal decision of declaring war on eight major powers all at once—any one of which could easily have defeated China. There is one lead to an otherwise puzzling situation. Shortly before the fatal decision was made, there had been a rumor that the foreigners had made new demands on China, one of which was that she should return the state power to the emperor. Knowing what she was, we can easily visualize how angry she would be. Without checking the validity of this rumor (which later turned out to be false), she plunged China into war because her position in China was always more important to her than China's position in the world.

Meanwhile in Peking the Boxers and their allies went on a rampage destroying everything foreign; among their victims was the German Minister to China, Von Ketteler. Their main target was the foreign legations which, against great odds, successfully defended themselves until reinforcements arrived. The rescue force consisted of 16,000 men sent by the allies: 8,000 Japanese, 4,500 Russians, 3,000 British, 2,500 Americans, and 800 French. Meanwhile, Russia was marching southward to seize Manchuria. The commander of the allied forces, Field Marshal Count Von Waldersee, was under the instruction from the Kaiser "to give no quarter and to take no prisoners," so that "no Chinese will ever again dare to look askance at a German." After the allied troops had arrived in Peking, there were large-scale massacre, rape, and looting, the like of which had not been seen since the days of the Mongols. The bulk of the German troops were held back to protect Kiaochow and the coast; otherwise the situation would conceivably have been worse. The empress dowager and the emperor fled to Sian, and China again lay helpless at the feet of the Western powers and Japan.

The existence of China could have ended then; it was saved by the disagreement among the powers as to how China should be divided among themselves. As they could not agree, they postponed their division of China by concluding a peace treaty with their vanquished foe. The main points of the treaty were: (1) the punishment of "war criminals"— some of them were later executed and others were exiled or demoted; (2) the destruction of all defenses ("now and forever") from Taku to Peking, (3) the right of foreign powers to station troops in legation sites; (4) the establishment by China of an effective 5 percent tariff; and (5) the payment of $333,000,000 in reparations of which Russia received the largest share. Against the background of a punitive vengeance the amount thus demanded was acknowledged to be far in excess of justifiable claims. A substantial portion of the American share, $25,000,000, was later voluntarily returned to China with the provision that the fund should be used to educate Chinese students in the United States. A similar arrangement was also made with England.

One of the products of the scramble for Chinese territories and the subsequent Boxer episode was the famed Open Door policy. It remained the basis of American foreign policy towards China until the Communists closed China's door in 1949. How did it come into being? It was a British idea at the beginning; only later was it revived by the United States. The British interests in China, as has been said before, were largely commercial. Such interests could be better served if China were to remain a free, open market. The scramble for spheres of influence in 1898 raised the unpleasant prospect that areas where another power had established a dominant position would be closed to British commerce and capital. Great Britain approached the United States for a joint pronouncement which would include the principle of equal commercial opportunity in all parts of China. When the Americans refused to cooperate, Great Britain went on to hunt for its own sphere of influence. After John Hay had become Secretary of State, he, unlike his predecessor John Sherman, was attracted to this Open Door idea. In September, 1899, he sent to Great Britain, Germany, and Russia his famous notes requesting that equal commercial opportunity for all powers be maintained within their spheres of influence. His notes did not attack the spheres of influence as such; nor did they explain how the incompatibility between two contrasting ideas, sphere of influence and equal opportunity of trade, could be resolved. The replies which Hay received from the three powers were noncommittal; even Great Britain conditioned its acceptance of the Open Door policy on the acceptance of it by other powers. However, the American Secretary of State announced in March, 1900 that the replies were "final and definitive."

The year 1900 was one of the least promising years to implement the Open Door. The Boxer uprising gave Russia the needed excuse to march into Manchuria, and it had intended to march further into North China until it was warned by Great Britain to keep out. Obviously, some of the powers, especially Russia and Germany, were bent on enlarging their spheres of influence and perhaps also gaining political control in them. If China were divided among them territorially, the Open Door idea would become meaningless, because naturally the power in control would introduce discriminatory measures against trade and capital from any other power within its territorial domain. In other words, the maintenance of China's territorial integrity was a prerequisite to the principle of equal commercial opportunity. In July, 1900, while Russian troops were pouring into Manchuria, Hay sent to the powers a circular note in which he stated that the United States aimed "to seek a solution which may bring about permanent safety and peace to China, preserve Chinese territorial and administrative entity, protect all rights guaranteed to friendly Powers by treaty and international law, and safeguard for the world the principle of equal and impartial trade with all parts of the Chinese empire." Except for Great Britain, none of the powers to which the note was addressed even bothered to answer.

The Open Door policy, like the Monroe Doctrine, was a unilateral declaration on the part of the United States. Its effectiveness relied on the willingness and capacity of the United States to enforce its observance. Since the United States did not attach such importance to the policy as to back it up with military force when the necessity arose, its effectiveness was rather limited. That the division of China was temporarily arrested in 1900 was due more to the rivalry among the powers than to the declaration of the American policy. However, to the Chinese who were in dire need of friends, this was a tremendous psychological lift. For the next fifty years China continued to seek help and support from the United States in its dealings with aggressors or potential aggressors, believing that the United States was the only major power that had no territorial ambition in China and could therefore be trusted.

The United States befriended China because, besides whatever sentimental reasons that can be cited, its interests in East Asia paralleled those of China. Though the American commercial interest was never large and accounted for only 2 percent of the total United States foreign trade at the turn of the century, there was always the hope that the volume could be considerably increased in view of the large Chinese population. Such a potential market could be best preserved for American goods if China remained independent and undivided. Politically, the American role in East Asia can best be understood in the context of the balance of power. From 1900 to 1949 China was the underdog in the power structure in East Asia, and during most of this period its potential or actual enemy was Japan. To be on the weaker side would have meant continuous support of China, and since this support was in line with America's commercial goal in China, the Open Door policy served both the political and economic interests of the United States. This, of course, only partially explains the American interest in China.

Among the different groups that influenced American policy towards China none was perhaps more important than the American missionaries. After 1900 the quality of all missionaries sent to China was greatly improved, and the approach to missionary work seems also to have changed. Now great emphasis was laid on educational and medical work, and the schools and hospitals thus established were among the best China ever had. These missionaries, like the early Jesuits, were scholars and teachers as well as evangelists. With tact and understanding they won respect and admiration from the Chinese among whom they lived. As the Chinese admired the missionaries, they also admired the country from which the missionaries came. For fifty years no foreign country was more popular in China than the United States. The missionaries, on their part, were equally enthusiastic about the Chinese and their culture, and their optimistic reports to their home churches unquestionably affected the attitude of Americans at home. Through the home churches the influence of the missionaries was eventually felt in the State Department and in Congress.

After the Boxer Protocol had been signed, the Russians stalled and delayed their evacuation from Manchuria. They were, in fact, exercising pressure on the Chinese government to legalize their occupation through the signing of a convention. The United States responded to the Russian threat with a reaffirmation of the Open Door, while England and Japan responded with a military alliance. England feared Russian penetration into North China, and Japan was uneasy about Russia's intention with regard to Korea. From England's point of view, the Anglo-Japanese Alliance (January, 1902) was merely a part of its global policy of containment against Russian expansion, "in Tibet, in Persia, in Turkey" as well as in Manchuria. To the Japanese, however, the Russian expansion had to be stopped if Korea were to be safeguarded and preserved as a stepping stone for the fulfillment of their own ambitions in Manchuria. The Anglo-Japanese Alliance pledged one party to neutrality if the other party was at war and to come to the other party's assistance if it had been attacked by more than one power.

In the summer of 1903 Japan proposed to Russia an arrangement whereby Russia would recognize Japan's special interests in Korea in return for Japan's acceptance of Russian rights in Manchuria "based on recognized treaties." If Russia agreed to this arrangement, it would mean, among other things, that its troops would have to withdraw from Manchuria. This the Russians would not do. The Japanese at home cried for war, and war came in the spring of the next year. Since the war had to be fought in Chinese territory, the Chinese government notified both belligerents that they should confine their fighting to the areas east of the Liao River so to minimize damage to Chinese life and property. This pleading, however, was ignored. During the hostilities Japan won victories on both land and sea. However, being a small country with limited resources, it could not continue the war indefinitely. Meanwhile, a revolution broke out within Russia; so both parties were ready for a negotiated peace. Through the good offices of the American President, Theodore Roosevelt, the Treaty of Portsmouth (September, 1905) was concluded. The major items of the treaty were: (1) the transfer to Japan by Russia of the Liaotung leased territory (including the two ports Dairen and Port Arthur), the southern section of the Chinese Eastern Railroad, and all the mining rights along the said section of the railroad; (2) Russia's acknowledgement of Japan's "paramount political, military, and economic interests in Korea"; and (3) the cession to Japan by Russia of the southern half of the island of Sakhalin.

By virtue of this treaty Japan not only safeguarded its interest in Korea (which it annexed later) but also acquired South Manchuria as its own preserve for economic activities. Meanwhile, Russia withdrew to North Manchuria which it regarded as its sphere of influence. Both parties, however, consented to withdraw their troops from Chinese territory and promised "not to obstruct any general measures common to all countries, which China may take for the development of the commerce and industry of Manchuria."

THE DOWNFALL OF THE MANCHU REGIME

After she returned from Sian where she had fled during the allied occupation of Peking, Tz'u Hsi was more than convinced of the Western superiority and was in a receptive mood for Westernized reforms. The measures that had been suppressed after the failure of the Hundred Days' Reform were reintroduced, and outwardly at least the empress dowager went along with enthusiasm. An imperial decree called for the organization of a national school system with a new curriculum which included not only the ancient classics but also "Western learning" such as European history, literature, and science. Students who possessed the financial means were encouraged to go abroad to study. Most of these students went to Japan because of its geographical proximity, while others went to Europe and the United States. In 1907 the American government made available the Boxer indemnity funds, and the number of Chinese students in the United States had increased to eight hundred on the eve of the revolution. Meanwhile in China the enrollment in Westernized schools continued to increase, reportedly reaching 1.6 millions by 1910. It was clear then that the old type of Confucian training would never come back again as the government had decided in 1905 to abolish the civil service examination once and for all.

Other reforms included the reorganization of the army and the navy and a newly found determination to stamp out the opium traffic. Though the Opium War was fought over the opium traffic, there was no mention of opium in the Treaty of Nanking. In 1858 the opium trade was legalized and importation of the drug continued to increase. As it increased, the Chinese began to grow opium poppy themselves. When the nation was again in a mood to carry out reforms, opium reappeared as a political issue. In 1906 the government adopted a policy of taxing domestic opium out of existence, and two years later Great Britain agreed to decrease annually its opium exports to China. In 1911 further agreement was reached with other powers besides Great Britain: all of them promised to cooperate with the Chinese government to stop the smuggling of the drug into China and to close opium shops and dens in the areas under their control. One year later the agreement came to naught, as the Manchu dynasty was overthrown and China entered the warlord period. Opium was to plague China for another forty years.

More interesting, if not more significant, was the attempted constitutional reform. To many Chinese it was the most basic of all reforms. The agitation for a written constitution began during the Russo-Japanese War, and many reformers optimistically predicted that "the outcome of this war depends on which nation has gained a constitutional government." When a small Japan with a constitution defeated a giant Russia without a constitution, it seemed to them that the merits of a constitution had been truly vindicated. Both the Chinese intellectuals and the Manchus wanted a constitutional government, though for different reasons. To the Chinese intellectuals it meant the opening of new opportunity to go into politics and secure government positions after the abolition of the civil service examinations. "In free political competition," said Liang Ch'i-ch'ao, "there will be no question as to whether the Manchus or the Chinese will have the predominant position under a constitutional government, since the political ability of the Chinese is far greater than that of the Manchus." The Manchus, for their part, wanted a constitution to legalize their control of the central government. There were also the Changs and Lis who honestly believed that a constitution was the first step to the modernization of China and would eventually make China as strong as Japan.[1] With all parties clamoring for a constitution, the empress dowager threw up her arms in despair and remarked majestically: "You say a constitutional monarchy can really make the nation strong; I will immediately send high officials to make a careful study of all constitutional monarchies."

It was unthinkable that Tz'u Hsi, who would not even share power with her nephew the emperor, would agree to share it with an elected parliament. Before the study group began to study "all constitutional monarchies," everybody knew what it would recommend: the Japanese model. In fact, under the draft constitution of 1908 the emperor enjoyed greater power even than the mikado. He was sacred and inviolable and he alone had the power to sanction or proclaim a law. The parliament whose deputies were chosen from a limited franchise could be opened or closed, prolonged or disbanded, at his choice. He was the commander-in-chief of the army and the navy, and he alone had the right of declaring war and concluding peace. The rights of speech, press, residence, and assembly could be exercised freely "within the boundary of law." Since the law could be changed by the government at any time, its boundary

[1] Chang and Li are two of the commonest surnames among the Chinese. They are like Brown and Smith among the English.

was extremely flexible, and the guarantee of civil rights existed mostly on paper.

Limited as these reforms were, if they had been introduced at the time when Tz'u Hsi became a co-regent in 1862 rather than at the year of her death (1908), the situation would have been vastly different. Now it was a matter of "too little and too late." The majority of the Chinese intellectuals who had until recently supported the Manchu regime became either apathetic or outright hostile. K'ang Yu-wei's Emperor Protection Society slowly but steadily lost its popularity; even his disciple Liang Ch'i-ch'ao had joined the revolutionary chorus: "The Manchus must go." Though the revolution drew its primary support from the intellectuals (especially those who lived abroad), it was supported by a large section of the people. China's numerous secret societies, which had a long tradition of rebelling against recognized authorities, could easily be transformed into a revolutionary potential. The overseas Chinese who had been discriminated against or even persecuted were anxious to see a modern, strong China that could extend to them a protective hand. Numerous young army officers saw the revolution as a new avenue for their own advancement, and many local gentry, if not openly sympathetic to the revolutionary cause, nevertheless wished to use it as a leverage to advance local autonomy. Finally there were the adventurers who joined the revolution for the sake of excitement, or for want of a better career to follow. Whatever motives each group of people might have, all agreed that China must be modernized and strong and that to build a modern China they must overthrow the Manchu regime.

The divergent elements of the revolution had to be organized before they could become a single striking force. They needed a leader, and they found him in Sun Yat-sen. Sun was born to a peasant family in a village near Canton in 1866, where for generations his family had had to work hard to wring a meagre subsistence from a small farm. He began his schooling at seven and at fourteen left his home to visit his elder brother in Hawaii, who by then had become a prosperous cattleman on a small island. He attended a missionary school in Honolulu and returned home in 1883. In 1886 he decided to enter the medical profession; he was enrolled at a medical school in Canton and one year later was transferred to the Alice Memorial Hospital at Hong Kong. It was then that he made valuable contacts with the anti-Manchu underground and won recognition as a potential leader. "I was using the school as headquarters for propaganda and using medicine as a medium for entering the world," said he many years later. Why did he forsake the profitable medical profession to enter the dangerous career of a revolutionary? Because the number of lives a doctor could save was rather limited, he replied, whereas a great statesman could save the lives of an entire nation.

To win supporters for his cause, Sun was at a disadvantage in competing with the reformer K'ang Yu-wei. K'ang came from an aristocratic family, had passed the civil service examinations, and was a brilliant Confucian scholar. Sun, on the other hand, came from a poor family, and his education was mostly Western. While K'ang appealed to the intellectual elite, Sun had to build his revolutionary base among the less respectable, many of whom were the members of the secret societies. "At first I despised Sun Yat-sen because I suspected that he was illiterate," said Wu Chih-hui who later became one of Sun's colleagues and friends. In 1894 when Sun organized his first revolutionary society (Hsing-Chung hui, or Society to Rejuvenate China) in Hawaii, his only followers were his brother and a dozen others. The headquarters of his organization was moved to Hong Kong the next year and there was some increase in membership. In that year he sent his close followers to Canton to stage a coup d'état. The plot, however, was discovered before it could be carried out, and the plotters were arrested and put to death. This was the first of a series of attempted coups that ended in failure. The Manchu government, which had been helpless in fighting against the foreigners, was nevertheless still capable of handling a small band of ill-organized and ill-equipped revolutionaries.

After the failure of his first attempted coup, Sun went to the United States and then to England. In London he was kidnapped by the Chinese legation personnel who planned to ship him back to China as a "bandit." During his captivity he managed to slip two notes out to his former teacher James Cantlie asking for help, and he was released after Cantlie notified Scotland Yard and the press. He stayed in London for the next two years where, according to a Scotland Yard report, "he went to the British Museum every day and spent most of his time there." It was then, he said later, that his basic ideas regarding the Three Principles of the People (Nationalism, Democracy, and People's Livelihood) first took shape. When the allies occupied Peking in 1900, he hastened back to organize another coup; but again he failed. From 1900 to 1905 he travelled between Japan, Southeast Asia, the United States, and Europe, concentrating his efforts on winning supporters and raising funds among the Chinese living abroad. By then many revolutionary societies had mushroomed both inside and outside China; some of them devoted themselves to the spread of revolutionary ideas through the clandestine publication of newspapers and magazines, and others took direct action by inciting open revolt and the assassination of "public enemies." In Japan there were several such "patriotic societies" among the 10,000 Chinese students. In the summer of 1905 Sun succeeded in persuading them to merge with his own and announced the formulation of the Alliance for Chinese Revolution (Chung-kuo ko-ming t'ung-meng hui), better known by its abbreviation, the Alliance, or T'ung-meng hui.

The organization of the Alliance was an important landmark in Sun's revolutionary career. Until then his organization had been small and attracted only a scattered following. Into the new organization came not only the young and idealistic students but also the veteran revolutionaries such as Huang Hsing who until then had headed his own revolutionary group. On November 17, 1905 the party organ, *The People* (*Min pao*), first appeared in Tokyo. Its first editorial, written by Sun himself, emphasized the importance of the Three Principles of the People and the necessity of completing national, democratic, and social revolutions simultaneously:

> While it is clear that there should be no delay in beginning our national and democratic revolution in view of the present circumstances, such as thousands of years of autocratic rule, the oppression by an alien people [Manchus], and the intensified encroachment of China by foreign powers, it should also be kept in mind that the causes of social revolution which have accumulated themselves for a long time in Europe and the United States and which have not become serious in China should also be given adequate attention. As the disease is not serious, it is easy to cure. . . . People say that to strive for a strong China, we should imitate Europe and the United States. Strong as the Westerner powers are, their people remain poor. Labor strikes occur often, and the anarchists and the socialists have become increasingly active. In the near future a social revolution is bound to occur. . . . The seeds of evils in the Euro-American society were sown several decades ago, and such evils cannot be easily disposed of even after they have been discovered. If we can foresee these evils before they occur and prevent their occurrence by practicing the Principle of People's Livelihood, we can catch two birds with one stone: to complete political and social revolution at the same time. The day will arrive when we look over our shoulder and find Europe and America lagging far behind. . . .[1]

The above passage should be read against the background of 1905 when the labor movement in the West was still in its infant stage and when organized labor had yet to win a strong voice in legislation and in the formulation of governmental policy. Sun could not foresee what form the social revolution would take; he did see, however, that such a revolution would occur, given the existing social and economic injustices. By then his revolution had taken on a new dimension; it was social and economic as well as political. The overthrow of the Manchu regime, whenever it occurred, was to be merely the beginning rather than the end of his revolution. It was clear to him even then that the establishment of economic and social justice was much more difficult to achieve than the overthrow of a discredited, corrupt regime. The Principle of People's Livelihood,

---

[1] Translated by the author from a photographed copy of the original that appears in *The Pictorial Biography of Dr. Sun Yat-sen* (*Kuo-fu hua-chuan*) (Taipei, 1954) by Lo Chia-lun, p. 43.

said he many years later, was the basis of the other two principles: Nationalism and Democracy.

Meanwhile, there was the Manchu dynasty to overthrow. From the establishment of the Alliance to the abdication of the last Manchu emperor in 1912, Sun was responsible for eight attempted coups and uprisings within China: six in Kwangtung, one in Kwangsi, and one in Yunnan. If an important city or a sizable area could successfully be brought under the control of the revolutionaries, Sun reasoned, a call for national uprisings would receive favorable response from various groups within China that wished to overthrow the existing regime but did not dare to take the first step. If the entire nation were in revolt, the Manchu regime would have to collapse. Sun's last coup was made in the spring of 1911 when Huang Hsing led his rebels to attack the governor-general's office at Canton. The promised military supplies did not arrive in time, and eighty-six revolutionaries died without seeing the establishment of the republic.

Ironically, what triggered the downfall of the Manchu regime was none of Sun's coups but an incident which was completely bourgeois in origin. In 1910 the Manchu government had concluded an agreement with an international banking agency (composed of banking interests of England, France, Germany, and the United States) to build a railroad linking Hankow and Canton. With the capital assured, it announced in May, 1911, the nationalization of railroads and revoked the construction rights which had been previously granted to private capital. Local interests in the provinces regarded the government's move not merely as an infringement on private enterprise but also as a deliberate attempt to break provincial autonomy which by then had become too precious to lose.

The increasing autonomy of provinces began in the 1860's when men of great influence and prestige such as Tseng Kuo-fan and Li Hung-chang were appointed as governors-general. Once begun, the process of decentralization accelerated. Towards the end of the nineteenth century even Tz'u Hsi made it a habit to consult the most important governors-general before she made an important move, though, being a strong ruler, she did not have to listen to their advice. The large measure of provincial autonomy was shown during the Sino-Japanese War when the North, under Li Hung-chang, was fighting a war against Japan and the South did not send one soldier to help. It was again shown during the Boxer Rebellion when the southern governors-general remained factually, if not legally, neutral, while the allies were marching towards Peking. In 1911, the empress dowager was gone, and there was not a single man in Peking, including the child emperor Hsüan-t'ung, who commanded the unswerving loyalty of the provincial authorities. Even without the revolution, the disintegration of the empire was already in sight.

More than anything else, the nationalization of railroads aligned the provincial interests against those of the central government and evoked a storm of protest such as none of Sun's coups had been able to do. Provincial leaders and local gentry, businessmen and bankers, intellectuals and students—all of them suddenly found that they had one aim in common: to preserve the railroads for their respective provinces. Organized by professional revolutionaries, radical students paraded in the streets, calling for the end of the Manchu regime. The situation was particularly serious in Szechuan where a general strike was called in all the railroads and related industries. In Chengtu many people were killed by police when they went to the governor's office to protest against the imprisonment of students. The news of Szechuan's defiance spread to other provinces, and the nation was in a mood for rebellion.

After the failure of Sun's last coup, his revolutionaries moved northward and concentrated their efforts in the Wu-Han area. They infiltrated the newly organized battalions of the Manchu regime where the young officers gave a sympathetic ear to the professional agitators. Their so-called secret meetings were nevertheless semiopen affairs, and it was reported that even the commander of the local garrison had sat in their meetings. However, the revolutionary leaders remained scrupulously in the background, and to avoid a repetition of past mistakes, they were carefully planning each step of a scheduled uprising. On October 9 the Manchu government discovered and seized the rebels' ammunition dump, and worse still, it got hold of a list of army officers who had secretly joined the revolutionary party. To forestall their arrest, the revolutionaries in Wuchang decided to take immediate action. On the night of October 10 they seized the government's ammunition dump and then attacked the governor-general's office. Instead of fighting the rebels, both the governor-general and the commander of the local garrison chose to flee, and the revolutionaries scored a victory far beyond their own expectations. After their successful coup, the most pressing need was to find a man of prestige to serve as their commander. Fortunately, in a routine search of the enemy's camps, they found a frightened colonel named Li Yüan-hung hiding underneath his bed. They dragged him out, put him under arrest, and then demanded that he become their commander. "I was surrounded by guns at the time, and I might have been killed instantly if I had not complied with their request," wrote Li a few days later to one of his friends.

The successful uprising at Wuchang prompted similar actions in other cities and provinces. In some cases the revolutionaries took control through the use of force, while in other cases the governors and governors-general declared their independence from the Manchu government and switched their loyalty to the revolution. By the end of the year practically all provinces south of the Yangtze had been freed from Manchu control.

Sun Yat-sen, who had been in London, England, when the revolution fire began to spread, now came back to China to assume leadership. On January 1, 1912, he was sworn in as the first president of the Provincial Government of the Chinese Republic at Nanking, and the amiable Li Yüan-hung was named vice president. The new government pledged, among other things, to emancipate domestic slaves and to clean up, once and for all, the opium poison.

The Nanking government proved to be short-lived. In the north there was a strong, conservative force with which the revolutionaries had to reckon. This force was not led by the Manchu government but by the ambitious Yüan Shih-k'ai. The compromises which the revolutionaries had to make with this man paved the way for a new era of turbulence, popularly known as the period of warlords. The Manchu regime formally ended in 1912; China's woes, however, were far from being ended.

ꙮ xiv

The Republic (1)

THE WARLORDS

The abdication of the last Manchu emperor, Hsüan-t'ung, on February 12, 1912, marked the formal end of the Manchu regime. Yet there was not a single force strong enough to replace it. In the south the revolutionaries were divided among themselves. Many governors who switched to the side of the revolution after the Wuchang uprising were more motivated by the preservation of their personal domains than the creation of a unified republic. Sun Yat-sen, the titular head of the revolution, had little or no influence over them. He was admired and respected, but he was not listened to. Equal confusion existed in North China where governors and military commanders fought among themselves and worked at cross purposes. The struggle for supremacy in China was a struggle among the political realists: the governors and military commanders who had the

442

physical power to back up their demands. Meanwhile, China was plunged into chaos and war unlike that which occurred at the end of any previous dynasty. If the past indicated anything, the country was looking for a strong man to emerge who could fight his way to supremacy and eventually unify all of China.

For a while the candidate most likely to succeed was Yüan Shih-k'ai whose name has been mentioned before in connection with the Sino-Japanese War. After that war he was given the important task of training a new army in the area near Tientsin, and it was then that he built a strong following among the young officers under his command. His role in the Hundred Days' Reform pleased Tz'u Hsi who later rewarded him with the governorship of Shantung. As the governor of Shantung, he suppressed the Boxers without in the meantime antagonizing the empress dowager, and by his successful maneuvers in a most difficult situation he won acclaim from both the Chinese and the foreigners as a clear-thinking, far-sighted statesman. In 1900, on the day before his death, Li Hung-chang recommended Yüan as his successor to govern Chihli (later known as Hopeh). "As I am looking around for men of ability all over the nation, I find no one better than Yüan," said Li in a memorial to the throne. As governor-general of Chihli and concurrently Superintendent of Trade in the Northern Ports (*Pei-yang ta-ch'en*), Yüan became one of the most powerful men in the nation. Once in a powerful position, he placed his followers in responsible and strategic positions in the imperial army as well as in the provinces. His army, called the Peiyang Army, was the most powerful fighting force in North China, and the Manchu government relied on it for the defense of the capital. Yüan's personal following constituted what was later known as the Peiyang clique, which produced many warlords in the years to come.

The Manchus in Peking were not unaware of the threat that Yüan's power posed for their own security. When Hsüan-t'ung was placed on the throne after the death of Kuang-hsü in 1908, the child emperor's father, Tsai-feng, dismissed Yüan from all the offices he held and ordered him home to "recuperate from the leg ailment which affected his gait." Rumor had it that he would have put Yüan to death had he not been afraid of violent reactions on the part of the officers of the Peiyang Army. In 1911 when most provinces had switched their loyalty to the revolution, the only thing that stood in the way of the revolutionaries' march towards Peking was the Peiyang Army, whose officers made it very clear that they would not fight "to the best of their ability" if Yüan were not made their commander-in-chief. The tables were now turned, and Yüan notified Tsai-feng that he would not resume his command until his conditions were satisfactorily met. He demanded the opening of parliament in the following year, the organization of a responsible cabinet, the legalization of political parties, and "full authority over, and the power to organize, all the armed forces." The Manchu government, under the dictate of circumstances, complied with all these demands. Shortly afterwards Yüan was made premier of the Manchu government. Thus, by one master stroke, Yüan became the ultimate arbitrator between the Manchu government in the north and the revolutionaries in the south.

The assumption of power by Yüan Shih-k'ai in the north was followed by negotiation with the revolutionaries in the south. Yüan's insistence on the legalization of political parties and other friendly gestures pleased the revolutionaries who promised him the presidency once the Manchu government was overthrown. On the day that he became president of the provisional government at Nanking, Sun Yat-sen telegraphed Yüan that he had accepted the office on a temporary basis, and that Yüan was to occupy it whenever he was ready. Why did the revolutionaries go so far as to make such extensive concessions? For one thing, Yüan was in command of the most powerful military force then in existence, and an open break with him would mean not only the continuance of the Manchu regime but also a prolonged civil war which the revolutionaries could not be sure of winning. The revolutionaries hoped that Yüan, as the president of the republic, could be made responsible to an elected parliament which they themselves would doubtless control. Obviously they underestimated their opponent's ambition, and because of their misjudgment, the new republic was destined for a turbulent beginning.

Under Yüan's pressure, the last Manchu emperor abdicated, and as previously agreed, Yüan was elected president of the new republic. Since he refused to come to Nanking to accept the presidency, the capital of the new republic was moved to Peking. No sooner did he take office than difficulties developed between the legislative branch of the government (the parliament) and the executive branch headed by the president. The provisional constitution which had been adopted in Nanking prior to the abdication of the Manchu emperor provided for a strong parliament which the new president would not tolerate. As the revolutionaries controlled the parliament, he proceeded to break their strength by all the means at his command. Early in 1913, Sung Chiao-jen, a key member of Sun Yat-sen's party, the Kuomintang, and a deputy in the parliament, was assassinated in Shanghai, and since Sung had been one of the most severe critics of Yüan's dictatorial behavior, all fingers pointed at the new president. Meanwhile, through persuasion, coercion, and outright bribery, Yüan strove to build a personal following among the parliamentary deputies. The outcome was the Progressive Party (Chinputang), composed of opportunist politicians as well as those who believed that Yüan alone possessed the power and the ability to unify China, and that they could honestly support him. Facing the opposition of the revolutionaries, in June of 1913, Yüan ordered the dismissal of three Kuomintang governors. The revolutionaries staged an armed revolt, only to be suppressed by

Yüan's powerful army. After the revolt, all Kuomintang members were disqualified as parliamentary deputies by the president's orders, and the provisional constitution was revised to give dictatorial power to the president.

Thus, less than two years after the establishment of the republic, Yüan achieved what he had set out to achieve: a personal dictatorship. The foreign powers strengthened his regime by advancing him a loan amounting to 25 million pounds, despite vigorous protests from Sun Yat-sen, who believed that Yüan would use the loan to strengthen his personal control. Had Yüan been satisfied with being a dictator, he would have been remembered differently in history, but instead, he chose to become emperor. By doing this he not only antagonized the Kuomintang but all those to whom monarchy had come to mean the most reactionary rule. Early in 1915 an organization called the Peace Planning Society was launched by Yüan's followers to prepare the way for transforming the republic into a monarchy with Yüan as the first emperor. In August an American professor, Frank J. Goodnow, who then served as Yüan's constitutional adviser, prepared a memorandum in which he pointed out the desirability "of establishing a constitutional monarchy if there was general demand for it." In view of the patronage the president possessed and the ceaseless activities of the Peace Planning Society, the "general demand" was not slow in coming. In each province Yüan's followers were busy creating "public opinion" and choosing the "right" people as provincial delegates to decide the basic structure of the government: constitutional monarchy or republicanism. When they finally cast their ballots, the count was 1,993 for monarchy and none for republicanism. Armed with this mandate, Yüan declared that a constitutional monarchy should be established in June, 1916.

What followed could not have been foreseen by the president, as he had been too much blinded by his own ambition. Led by Yunnan, several provinces successively declared independence, and Yüan, to save his presidency, belatedly relinquished his royal pretensions. By then it was already too late; the rebels insisted that he should resign from the presidency as well. Beset with worry and grief, he died on June 6, 1916.

Upon the death of Yüan Shih-k'ai, the man around whom China could have been unified was gone. The office of the presidency changed hands several times until Tuan Ch'i-jui, a member of the Peiyang clique and one of Yüan's early followers, managed to restore a semblance of order in the capital as the premier. The so-called national government controlled no more territory than Peking and its surrounding areas, though internationally it was recognized as representing China. The rest of China was divided among the so-called warlords, conquering and annexing the territory of one another with impunity. The disintegration of China which began as early as the 1860's was now complete. As the central authority all but disappeared, there was nothing left except political anarchy. This situation was neither unique nor strange in Chinese history; it had always been that way during the change of dynasties. Those familiar with the course of history only blamed themselves for being born in a wrong time, a wrong age. While the Westernized intellectuals were discussing the comparative merits of republicanism and constitutional monarchy, the peasants were waiting patiently for the next Son of Heaven (or his modern equivalent, the Leader) to emerge who could lead China back to peace and prosperity. Meanwhile, as the civil war raged on, they had to endure the hardships inherent in a transitional period. The lesson of history was not lost, either, in the minds of China's ambitious leaders. They knew that to achieve supreme power one had to fight his way with a superior military force. With such a force Yüan Shih-k'ai almost succeeded in unifying China, and without it Sun Yat-sen had had to relinquish his presidency almost as soon as he had acquired it. Thus, despite the Western impact, the political game was played according to the ageless rule: might was right. Those who wished to succeed had to build a strong military following around themselves, just as the founders of the old dynasties used to do.

Before they succeeded in winning some respectability for their governments, the local strong men were called warlords. A warlord was a man who fought for personal gains, territorial or otherwise, rather than principles. His position might be that of a governor-general, a governor, or simply a military commander with enough following to make his weight felt. He was sovereign within the territory he controlled; he recruited his own bureaucratic and military personnel, levied taxes, and administered justice. With no lofty principles to claim the loyalty of the people he ruled, his major and perhaps only asset was his army. His army was composed of mercenaries recruited from the rural unemployed who would fight for anyone as long as they were regularly paid. Generous warlords promised bonuses if their soldiers helped them win a victory. As each battle involved no higher principle than the victory or defeat of two equally selfish warlords, most of the soldiers went through the motions of fighting and were not interested in heroism which would make them unnecessary casualties. As they were the best assets a warlord had, he was concerned for their safety, especially on the battlefield. The best victory was won by an impressive show of force to scare the enemy away rather than that won in a bloody battle which brought benefit to neither side except a third warlord. Often the outcome of a prospective battle was mutually agreed upon before it was actually fought after each side had objectively compared its strength with that of its enemy; the weaker side simply fled. Bloody battles did, however, occur from time to time when both sides had grossly underestimated the strength of each other. One battle fought in North China resulted in reported casualties of 20,000 for the two sides, only to benefit a third warlord in the south. Generally speaking, battles like this were the exceptions rather than the rule, and all warlords agreed that war, as an instrument of policy, should be indulged in only as the last resort.

As the wars between the warlords involved no lofty principles, they were among the most polite ever recorded in history. A warlord did not hate his enemy; he only wished to acquire his opponent's territories. He held no grudge against the people living on the other side of the battle-line; he merely wanted to rule them so that they would pay taxes to him instead of his opponent. As far as the people were concerned, it did not make much difference which side won, because one warlord was as good or bad as the other. One warlord might promise lighter taxes than another; this consideration, however, was not important enough to cause one to commit himself fully to his side. In each battle the people were neutral, ready to welcome whoever happened to be the winner. Respecting the neutrality of the people, the warlords tried to disturb them as little as possible during each battle, for they all knew that killing taxpayers defeated the very purpose of warlordism. It was not unusual for two gentlemanly warlords to arrange a fight in a sparsely populated area to prevent unnecessary damage to life and property, while in the nearest city the people waited patiently for the outcome of the battle. When the news finally arrived, the city fathers opened the city gates; the victor, whoever he happened to be, rode in at the head of his army, to receive the city's tribute which was his due. Thus, despite what might be said about the evil of warlords, their war was much more civilized than other wars in which religious and other important issues were involved and when the principle of one side was the direct opposite of the principle of the other.

From 1916 to 1927 there were dozens, if not hundreds, of warlords. Small warlords attached themselves to big warlords as necessity arose but declared their independence as soon as they were strong enough to do so. Some of the big warlords had under their control two or three provinces, while in other cases two or three warlords might share one province. Under the nominal control of each of these warlords there were numerous small warlords feuding constantly among themselves. As wars were fought almost constantly, the territory within each warlord's control was in a continuous state of flux. As for the backgrounds of these warlords, they varied a great deal. Some were outright bandits, and others succeeded in maintaining a remarkable degree of respectability. At least one of them was a scholar of sorts who had passed the lowest level of the civil service examination during the Manchu regime.

Early in the 1920's power struggles revolved around three main personalities: Tuan Ch'i-jui in the capital and the surrounding areas, Wu P'ei-fu in the middle Yangtze, and Chang Tso-lin in Manchuria. Tuan Ch'i-jui, as premier of the republic, attempted to use force to unify China and bring all China under his control. He was challenged by Wu P'ei-fu, then a divisional commander in Hunan. Wu, with the help of his allies in the north including Chang Tso-lin, defeated Tuan in a battle fought near Peking (July, 1920). After Tuan was out of the way, Wu and Chang fought each other over the control of North China. In the spring of 1922 Chang marched southward and captured Peking, only to be driven back by Wu. Chang retreated to Manchuria where he continued to rule, and Wu became for the time being the overlord of North China. In South China the numerous warlords fought one another until Sun Ch'uan-fang succeeded in bringing under his control the Lower Yangtze and its surrounding areas in 1925. Outside the regions mentioned above there were numerous other warlords who remained beyond the control of the central government long after Chiang Kai-shek and his Nationalists had declared the establishment of a national government in 1927.

FOREIGN PRESSURE

The young republic, weak and divided, was an easy prey to foreign aggressors. After its advance in Manchuria had been stopped by the Russo-Japanese War, Russia shifted its expansion efforts to Outer Mongolia where resistance, if any, was not expected to be effective. In 1912, Outer Mongolia, supported by Russia, drove out the Chinese minister in residence and declared its independence. China protested to Russia in vain, and in an agreement concluded in the following year the Chinese consented to grant Outer Mongolia an autonomous status, in return for Russia's recognition of Outer Mongolia as a part of China. The political agreement was followed by a commerical treaty in 1914 whereby China agreed to give Russia the right to trade, to exploit the mineral, forest, and fishing resources, and to purchase land for farming and pastoral purposes in Outer Mongolia. Besides, all Russian goods exported from or imported into the Mongolian territory were to be duty-free. By virtue of this treaty Outer Mongolia became in fact a Russian sphere of influence, though nominally it was still a part of China.

In 1917 a revolution broke out in Russia; with the Russians engaged in civil war, China reasserted its control of Outer Mongolia in 1919. A Chinese general named Hsü Shu-tseng was named the Minister of Mongolian Affairs, with special instructions to "pacify and solace" the Mongolian people. Hsü, however, turned out to be a bad choice, and his ruthless, reckless behavior soon antagonized the powerful Mongol princes who, in cooperation with a group of White Russian mercenaries, drove Chinese officials out from the Mongolian capital. The establishment of a Mongolian empire was proclaimed, and the Living Buddha of Urga was declared emperor. In the summer of 1921 the Bolsheviks entered Outer

Mongolia, defeated the White Russians, and transformed the country into a Russian protectorate.

Previously, in the summer of 1919, the Soviet Union announced its willingness to give up all special rights and privileges which Tsarist Russia had acquired in China and to establish new relations with China based upon the principle of complete equality. Whatever motives prompted this announcement, it was greeted with great enthusiasm; many Chinese openly opined that the road to China's salvation was to follow the Soviet example, since the Soviet Union, they believed, was the only country that had no imperialistic ambitions in China. Two years after the Soviet announcement, the Chinese Communist Party was organized in Shanghai. In 1924 China concluded a treaty and supplementary agreements with the Bolshevik regime in which the latter agreed (1) to recognize Outer Mongolia as a part of China and to withdraw Russian troops; (2) to give up all special rights and privileges in China such as extraterritorial rights and concessions; and (3) to renounce the balance of the Boxer Indemnity which had not yet been paid. With regard to the Chinese Eastern Railroad, the treaty specified that it was a joint enterprise, "purely commercial," and that it might be redeemed by China in the future with "Chinese capital." Lenin might not have said that the road to world communism was through Peking; the fact that the Soviet Union was the first Western power to renounce the unequal treaties did, however, create a favorable impression. As such an impression spread, so did communism.

The early years of the republic saw not only Russian penetration into Outer Mongolia but also British penetration into Tibet. Previously, as Tibet was a center of contention between Russia and England, both powers had agreed to Chinese suzerain rights in that territory, thus making it a buffer zone between the two rival powers. In two conventions signed by Great Britain—the convention of 1906 with China and the convention of 1907 with Russia—Britain pledged itself not to annex Tibetan territory and not to enter negotiation with Tibet except through China, the suzerain power. In 1910 the ruler of Tibet, Dalai Lama XIII, revolted, and the Manchu government responded by sending troops to Lhasa. The Dalai Lama escaped to India where he stayed until the following year when revolution broke out within China. As the Chinese could no longer give adequate attention to Tibet, the Dalai Lama returned to Lhasa and, with British support, drove out the Chinese garrison. In 1912 the new Chinese republic ordered the re-entry of Chinese troops into Tibet, only to cancel its plans when Great Britain protested. In 1914 a conference between British, Chinese, and Tibetan delegates was held in the Indian city of Simla where a draft agreement was reached; the agreement was to become effective when it was ratified by the delegates' respective governments. The Chinese government refused to ratify it on the ground that the agreement, if carried out, would mean the loss of a considerable piece of Chinese territory. Meanwhile, World War I broke out in Europe and England was too busy at home to put pressure on the Chinese; so the matter was dropped for the time being. It reappeared after World War II when India and Communist China debated the legality of the Simla agreement. The disagreement eventually led to a border war, as we shall see in another chapter.

The Russian maneuvers in Outer Mongolia and the British penetration in Tibet were conducted under the pretence of supporting local autonomous movements against an inefficient, corrupt central authority; and as such, justifications could be advanced, however flimsy they were. Japan's intervention in China, on the other hand, was brazenly brutal and lacked any of the arguments one might advance to defend the Russian or British actions. For one thing, Japan's territorial ambition was directed against the heavily populated China proper rather than the outer territories sparsely inhabited by Mongolian and Tibetan minorities. Japan's ambition with regard to China was common knowledge to all parties concerned, but until World War I Japan had not been able to translate its ambition into reality, partly because of China's distrust of Japanese motives and designs after the Sino-Japanese War and partly because of the lack of adequate capital on the part of Japan to pursue an effective dollar diplomacy such as Western powers then pursued in China. Meanwhile Japan, to use the words of one of its statesmen, was waiting patiently for the arrival of a "psychological moment" when it could fulfill its ambitions.

Such a moment arrived with the outbreak of World War I. All major powers in Europe were engaged in a life-and-death struggle, and Japan finally was free to do whatever it pleased in East Asia. After the war broke out, it attacked Germany's Kiaochow leasehold at Shantung, "as a voluntary expression of friendship," said the Japanese foreign minister, "toward Great Britain under the Anglo-Japanese Alliance." The German garrison surrendered and Japanese troops not only took over the leasehold but also Chinese territories along the Kiaochow-Tsinan Railroad. Despite Chinese protests, it seemed that Japan intended to occupy Shantung indefinitely. Knowing Japan's ambition, China appealed to the United States for diplomatic support, the only country then in a position to give such support. The United States, however, did not wish to get involved because, to use the words of Acting Secretary of State Lansing, while the United States was prepared to promote China's welfare by peaceful methods, "it would be quixotic in the extreme to allow the question of China's territorial integrity to entangle the United States in international difficulties." China was now isolated, and Japan was in a position to press on towards its goal.

Early in 1915 Japan presented to China the world-shaking Twenty-One Demands, acceptance of which would have reduced China to a Japanese protectorate. The demands were divided into five groups, and the harshest was the fifth or last group. The implementation of Group I would mean the transformation of Shantung from a German into a Japanese sphere of influence. Group 2 would give Japan extensive industrial, commercial, and residential rights in South Manchuria and eastern Inner Mongolia, in addition to the extension of the lease of Port Arthur and Dairen from twenty-five to ninety-nine years. Group 3 concerned the Han-yeh-ping Company, the largest iron mining and smelting concern in Hupeh. The Japanese demand called for the transformation of the company into a Sino-Japanese joint enterprise, with actual control in the hands of the Japanese. Group 4 contained one article which called upon China "not to cede or lease to any other Power any harbor or bay or any island along the coast of China." By "any other Power" was meant, of course, any other power except Japan. Group 5 was the most drastic and was aimed at bringing all of China, rather than just a section of it, under Japanese control. Its major items were: (1) the employment of Japanese as political, financial, and military advisers in the Chinese central government; (2) the right of Japanese to own land for the construction of hospitals, temples, and schools; (3) the joint control of Chinese police force; (4) the purchase of Japanese arms by China and the establishment of ammunition factories jointly controlled by China and Japan; (5) the granting of railroad construction rights to Japan in the central lakes region; (6) China was to consult Japan if it wished to borrow foreign capital to finance railroad construction, mining, and other economic activities such as harbor improvement in Fukien province; and (7) China was to grant Japan the right of "preaching religion" in China. The last article was perhaps the most ironical; obviously the Japanese had in mind the Western missionaries who allegedly served the imperialist interests of their respective countries.

While the delegates of both countries were still negotiating on the demands, Japanese fleets sailed towards Chinese harbors and the Japanese army suddenly increased its strength in Shantung and South Manchuria. As great pressure was exercised, the Chinese president Yüan Shih-k'ai agreed to all the demands as listed in the first four groups and the one demand in relation to Fukien in the fifth group. China rejected, however, all the other demands in the fifth group, as their acceptance would have meant the end of China as a sovereign state. The Japanese could have pressed the matter further, but facing a violent reaction from Chinese in all walks of life, they decided to drop the most obnoxious demands for the time being. If the Sino-Japanese War of 1894–1895 marked the beginning of the Sino-Japanese hatred, the Twenty-One Demands solidified it. To the Chinese Japan's ultimate goal was the conquest of China, and to the Japanese China was a "power vacuum" which was a temptation not easily resisted.

In the summer of 1917 China joined the Allies and declared war on

Germany, partly because of the diplomatic pressure exercised by the Allies and partly because it wished to be represented in the peace conference after the war. It hoped, particularly, to regain the German leasehold in Shantung. It did not know then that early in the year England and France had agreed to support Japan's demand with regard to the said leasehold. During the Paris Peace Conference China demanded the return of the leasehold, but the Allies, bound by their secret agreements with Japan, sided with their stronger ally in the East in insisting that it be transferred to Japan. President Wilson of the United States, though sympathetic to the Chinese cause, could not do anything to help, as the Japanese delegation threatened to leave the conference if its demand were not met. The angry Chinese delegation left Paris without signing the Versailles Peace Treaty.

The Shantung question reappeared in the Washington Conference in 1921–1922. This conference was called for two purposes: naval disarmament and the consideration of the "Far Eastern question" that threatened international peace. The rapid expansion of the Japanese navy had caused considerable apprehension in Washington as it posed a threat to the security of such American possessions as the Philippines. As the relations between the United States and Japan continued to worsen after World War I, the American government was anxious to seek a multilateral agreement to maintain the *status quo* in the Western Pacific so that Japan would not change the existing power structure and thus disrupt a delicate balance to its own advantage. To complicate the matter, Japan had a military alliance with England, so that in case of a shooting war between the two governments across the Pacific the United States might conceivably be at war with England too, and possibly even Canada which was then a British Dominion. As one recalls, the Anglo-Japanese Alliance of 1902 was formed having in mind Russia and possibly Germany as potential enemies. Now that Germany had been defeated and Russia after the Bolshevik revolution was no longer a threat to British interests in East Asia, England was anxious to leave the alliance without in the meantime making Japan "lose face." Like the United States, it was also seeking a multilateral agreement to replace the Alliance. In November, 1921, at the invitation of President Harding of the United States the delegates of nine countries (England, France, the United States, Italy, Japan, China, the Netherlands, Belgium, and Portugal) gathered in Washington, D.C. for the scheduled conference.

Three important treaties emerged from their consultations. The Four Power Pacific Treaty (between the United States, Great Britain, Japan, and France), which replaced the Anglo-Japanese Alliance, called upon the contracting parties to respect one another's rights in the regions of the Pacific in respect to their "insular possessions and insular dominions" and to settle any controversy "arising out of any Pacific question" by peaceful means. The Five Power Naval Treaty called for a ten-year holiday in capital ship construction and the limitation of the tonnage of capital ships and aircraft carriers in a ratio of 5:5:3:1.75:1.75 for England, the United States, Japan, France, and Italy, respectively. Moreover, the *status quo* in the Western Pacific with regard to each other's territorial possessions and "fortifications and naval bases" was to be maintained. As far as China was concerned, the most important document was the Nine Power Open Door Treaty signed by all powers represented in the conference. The treaty called upon all signatories, other than China, "to respect the sovereignty, the independence, and the territorial integrity of China" and "to use their influence for the purpose of effectually establishing and maintaining the principle of equal opportunity for the commerce and industry of all nations throughout the territory of China." On paper the treaty was a great victory for China and the United States, as it incorporated the two basic principles of the Open Door. For the first time the Open Door became an international committment as well as a statement of American policy. However, the treaty did not provide sanctions, economic or military, in case its terms were violated by one or more of the contracting parties. As it was worded in the most general and abstract terms, the treaty was subject to different interpretations. Naturally each signatory would interpret it to advance its own interests in China.

Unsatisfactory as the treaty might be, the Chinese delegation did not go home empty-handed. The concessions they won from the powers were noteworthy in view of the fact that China had no bargaining power whatsoever in the conference and that it relied solely on the good will of the powers concerned and the "righteousness" of its case. Shantung was to be returned to China, though Japan would retain control of the Kiaochow-Tsinan Railroad. France agreed to return to China the Kwangchow Bay, Japan the Kiaochow Bay, and England the Bay of Weihaiwei. Japan, however, refused to discuss the return of Port Arthur and Dairen, and England was equally determined to keep Kowloon. As to the main objectives of China such as the restoration of tariff autonomy, the abolition of extraterritoriality, and the withdrawal of foreign troops and police from foreign concessions in China, the Chinese delegation was woefully unsuccessful. The powers, however, agreed to discuss these matters at a future date. In the case of extraterritoriality, a commission composed of the treaty powers was to be organized to study Chinese law and the judicial system before each treaty power would consider "gradual" steps to be adopted for the eventual abolition of the extraterritorial system. As to the foreign spheres of influence in China, they were a subject so touchy that none of the major powers wished to discuss it.

However unsatisfactory from the Chinese point of view, the various treaties and agreements concluded during the Washington Conference enabled the existing power structure to be maintained and initiated a ten-year period of international peace and stability in the Pacific region. In the 1920's a moderate group was in power in Japan which preferred economic and commercial expansion to outright military aggression. To be sure, there were occasional armed clashes between China and Japan, none of which, fortunately, developed into full-scale war. It was not until 1931 when militarism re-emerged in Japan that armed aggression was again undertaken to extend Japanese control over mainland China.

CHINA REAWAKENED

During the past one hundred years each major military or diplomatic defeat was followed by a reappraisal of Chinese values and an increasing interest in Western culture. The Opium and *Arrow* Wars were followed by Li Hung-chang's advocacy of a Westernized armed force; the Sino-Japanese War and the creation of foreign spheres of influence precipitated the Hundred Days' Reform; and the Manchu government's incompetence in handling the Boxer Rebellion gave rise to intensified activities among the revolutionaries who eventually overthrew the Manchu regime. In each case the process of Westernization was not pursued on a sustained basis, and the conservative force representing the indigenous culture prevailed in the end. After the passing of each crisis China returned to its long slumber, unchanged and seemingly unchangeable. It should be added, however, that while the conservatives continued to win each round, their strength also steadily declined; and with each round the progressive forces began to gain ground, however slowly. For instance, the concept of a Chinese republic sounded fantastic in the 1890's, but it became a reality in 1912, imperfect though it was.

In the long run the winds of progress blew ever stronger. Each new generation was more receptive to new ideas than the preceding one, and Confucianism, the ideological stronghold of the conservative forces, became less sacred and more vulnerable with the passage of time. Confucian ideology, as has been said before, was the product of a sedentary, agricultural society, and the changed conditions resulting from the Western impact necessitated a more liberal interpretation of the ancient doctrine. Moreover, with the abolition of the civil service examination system in 1906 the mastering of Confucian classics, which had been traditionally the key to officialdom, power, and influence, was no longer emphasized as it had been. As the sanctity of Confucianism was subject to question, the traditional Chinese society built on Confucian virtues was slowly undermined. The process was speeded up by an annual inflow of the so-called returned students who had received part or most of their education abroad. Though not all returned students advocated "complete Westernization," they favored the change of the traditional Chinese society in one way or another. As they became leaders of the new China, their beliefs inevitably affected the thinking of the Chinese people as a whole.

As foreign pressure continued to mount in the early years of the republic, it was not surprising that the reawakening of China should initially take the form of strong nationalism. Though Chinese nationalism in its modern sense could be traced back to the years immediately following the Opium War, it had been confined to a small group of sensitive intellectuals who felt that the Chinese nation as well as its culture had been threatened by "barbarian" invasions. Most Chinese knew nothing about it and perhaps did not even care. However, the basis of nationalism continued to broaden with successive defeats at the hands of the Western powers and Japan, and as the loss of territories and the significance of the unequal treaties became better known, more Chinese became nationalistic. In 1915 when the supposedly secret Twenty-One Demands were intentionally leaked to the press and became public knowledge, there was such a violent reaction among the Chinese that even the Japanese were surprised. A modern press, introduced to China in the latter part of the nineteenth century, played an important role in the spread of nationalistic ideas. The Confucian gentry who had been concerned mostly with local affairs were aroused by the possible consequence of a China completely dominated by Japan. Wherever newspapers were found, the seeds of nationalism were sown.

In 1919, when news arrived in China that the Chinese delegation had failed to secure the return of Shantung in the Paris Peace Conference, thousands of students demonstrated in the streets of Peking; they beat one Chinese diplomat and burned the house of another, both of whom were accused of having sold China out when they negotiated with Japan on the Twenty-One Demands. Similar demonstrations occurred in all parts of China, and the students demanded "the preservation of Chinese sovereignty and the abolition of the unequal treaties." In large cities like Shanghai and Hankow, workers supported the students' demands by calling strikes, and merchants responded by closing their shops. Chinese were warned not to purchase goods of Japanese origin, and when the Japanese government protested, the students changed their slogan from "Boycott Japanese goods" to "Purchase Chinese goods only." This patriotic movement was later known as the May Fourth Movement because the first student demonstration occurred in Peking on May 4, 1919.

The May Fourth Movement was of course more than an antiforeign movement. It reflected the dissatisfaction of the new generation of intellectuals with China's domestic as well as international status. The Manchu regime had been overthrown, but China's difficulties were far from over. The country was divided among numerous warlords, fighting ceaselessly to advance their personal gains. The foreign powers, especially Japan, took advantage of this sad state of affairs and exploited it to their own advantage. This domestic disunity, as many Chinese readily conceded, was the cause, rather than the result, of foreign encroachments. Therefore, China should first "put its own house in order" before its voice could command any respect in international conferences. The yearning for a unified China was shared by people of all walks of life who had everything to lose in the long war conducted by the warlords. The merchants, for instance, resented the repeated taxation whenever their merchandise passed through a warlord's domain with the resultant increase in cost. Farmers were sometimes forced to pay land taxes twenty or thirty years in advance, only to see another warlord come to power who demanded the same preferential treatment. This legalized robbery was accompanied by an illegal variety conducted by the soldiers in the countryside. These soldiers, unpaid or underpaid, lived on the peasants like parasites. They stole their food, besides tampering with the chastity of their daughters. How long would this miserable state of affairs continue? Who could deliver the people from their sufferings? When Chiang Kai-shek finally arrived with a strong force of well-disciplined soldiers, the nation sighed with relief. Perhaps he could achieve what others had failed to do: the unification of China under a strong, centralized government.

While the intellectuals could do nothing to change the political situation, they attempted to create a new atmosphere in which a modern China could emerge. These intellectuals were not the Confucian scholars of the old type; they were the products of Western schools abroad or Westernized schools in China. Each year many students who had been educated in Europe, America, and Japan returned home, and many of them found employment in the newly established universities and colleges. They preached in their classrooms what they had learned abroad, and their students who subsequently became secondary and primary school teachers transmitted their ideas to an even larger audience. None of their ideas were original, and more often than not they mimicked their more illustrious professors in Europe or America. But for the Chinese who had lived for more than two thousand years in a staid Confucian atmosphere, these new ideas were more than welcome. From France came vitalism; from England, utilitarianism; and from the United States, pragmatism—plus a number of other "isms" too numerous to mention. It is difficult to assess the net impact of these ideas on China's intellectual life; superficially understood, as philosophies, they perhaps served no better purpose than arousing curiosity and stimulating inquisitiveness. Their advocates needed battering-rams to tear down the ancient stronghold of Confucianism which they blamed for China's "backwardness," and to use ideology to combat ideology, they wielded whatever weapon they had recently learned to use, be it pragmatism or utilitarianism. A nihilistic attitude characterized many of the new intellectuals who were determined to destroy the old values but were at a loss to find new ones to replace them. Some of them called for "complete Westernization," and others cried aloud for "science and democracy." Few of them, however, wished to be bothered with details and went beyond the stage of shouting slogans.

The intellectual aspect of the May Fourth Movement has often been referred to as the Chinese renaissance. The most concrete outcome of this intellectual revival was the colloquial (*pai-hua*) movement. As has been said in a previous chapter, all writing in China, to be presentable and respectable, had to be composed in a literary or classical style. To be able to write in a literary fashion required a tremendous amount of preparation in traditional literature on the part of the learner. The question often arose as to whether the colloquial language, the language as it was actually spoken, could be used as a means of literary expression. The traditionalists said "No," and for more than two thousand years no writer, except occasionally novelists, ever attempted to use it for serious writing. As democracy, in whatever form, was the goal of the new intellectuals, it naturally occurred to them that an informed public, upon which a workable democratic government ultimately depended, could not come about unless the written language was made easier to learn. The old question was again raised, and this time a small group of intellectuals answered "Yes."

What ensued was perhaps one of the most important though bloodless revolutions in Chinese history. The leader of this colloquial movement was the American-educated Hu Shih who demonstrated through his own writings that the spoken language could be literary and that in a piece of literature it was the content rather than the form that really counted. *The Marsh Heroes* and *The Dream of the Red Chamber,* which most people had read and yet pretended to look down upon, acquired new halos as great masterpieces of literature, even though they were written in colloquial Chinese. Following Hu's example, other writers began to experiment with colloquial Chinese, and it was proved beyond doubt that works written in the new medium could also be literary. All of a sudden the colloquial style acquired a respectability that it had never enjoyed before; it soon replaced the classical style as the standard form in newspapers, magazines, and all other means of communication aimed at large audiences. School textbooks were rewritten in the easily understood style, and students wrote letters home in the spoken language, much to the chagrin of their more conservative parents. Their parents perhaps became angry when they found in the letters punctuation marks which, according to the ancient custom, should never be used unless they were meant as a deliberate insult to the literary ability of the prospective reader. As the popularity of the colloquial style increased, writers also introduced the punctuation marks like those used in English.

The continuous inflow of Western ideas not only caused the intellec-

tuals to reappraise their ancient beliefs; it slowly undermined the traditional Chinese society which we described in Chapter XI. Old and new
values met head-on, and nowhere was the conflict so evident as it was
within the family. The conflict was most acute in families whose children
had received education abroad or in Westernized schools in China. Filial
loyalty, a cardinal Confucian virtue and the strongest tie which held the
Chinese family together, suddenly became a form of "parental oppression," and many parents could not understand how all of a sudden they
had become "intolerable tyrants" in the eyes of their children. Boys revolted when their parents proposed to arrange their marriages; some of
them ran away from home when wedding dates had already been set.
They had read many books which emphasized love and romance as the
correct basis of marriage, and they could not see why they should marry
women whom they had never met. Their parents, on the other hand, were
equally adamant in proclaiming the soundness of their own values and
condemned in unequivocal terms this "love-and-romance nonsense" which
to them was not only indecent but outright immoral. "No decent girl
would let a man talk to her while she remains a maiden," said the parents;
"if she does, we certainly do not wish to have her as our daughter-in-law."
The battle between the older and the younger generations went on, sometimes with heartbreaking results. The parents might decide to disown
children who had been openly rebellious, and their children, unable to
change the "old-fashioned" ideas of their parents, might prefer to cut off
the family relations anyway.

Thus during the transitional period when old values were slowly
losing their grip and when new ideas had not been fully accepted, difficulties were bound to occur. Arranged marriages were denounced as "out-
dated" and "unscientific"; yet the dating system had not been approved
by even the "most broad-minded" people. Under the circumstances, how
could a young person ever find a husband or wife? In many instances a
happy compromise was worked out: the parents would consult their son
before they decided on his future bride and might even arrange meetings
when the prospective life partners could see each other at a safe distance.
Once the engagement was announced, it was a golden contract almost
sacred. If it were violated, the family whose daughter had been "scorned"
would suffer a disgrace which neither the society nor itself could ever
forget.

A much publicized incident which occurred in the 1920's may help to
illustrate the intensified conflict between the old and the new. A group of
bandits raided a train and carried away many passengers to hold for
ransom. Among the people seized was the daughter of a distinguished
gentry family. After the girl had been released following the payment of a
handsome ransom, the question arose as to whether her fiancé should
honor the engagement by marrying her, since, presumably, she had been

compromised by the bandit chieftain. The debate went on in many news-papers and magazines, with progressives and conservatives lining up on the opposite sides of the argument. The progressives, led by returned students from Europe and America, urged the young man to honor the engagement on the ground that his fiancée was not responsible for the unfortunate happening and that the bond of marriage was love, not chas-tity. The conservatives, on the other hand, maintained that chastity was one of the great virtues of maidenhood and that even though the unfortu-nate circumstance was not of her own making, she should be willing to make a personal sacrifice by refusing to marry the young man in order to maintain the good custom of China. In fact, this kind of argument could have occurred only in China!

It should be added that such a cultural conflict as this was confined to families which had been more or less influenced by the Western cul-ture. For the overwhelming majority of the Chinese people, especially those on the peasant level, the old values still reigned supreme. Generally speaking, cultural conflict was more evident in the cities than in the rural areas, more wide-spread along the coast than in the interior regions, and more pronounced among the educated than the uneducated. In large sections of China two criteria were often used to measure the degree of Western influence: whether the parents had stopped binding their daugh-ters' feet and whether the women, married or unmarried, had cut their hair short to resemble the hairdo popular in the West. Prior to the West-ern impact, a maiden braided her hair into a long pigtail hanging on her back, and a married woman coiled it into a bun on the back of her neck. It took great courage for the first woman in a community to cut her hair short, and once it was done, other women, finding the new hairdo more easily managed, began to follow suit. The short hairdo became a symbol of "Westernization" (yang-hua) or "emancipation," but more often than not the so-called emancipation was more apparent than real. Most girls were still taught to obey their fathers at home and their husbands after they were married.

The lessening of family ties was made inevitable by the increase of geographical mobility resulting from the introduction of modern means of transportation (first railroads and then automobiles) and the establish-ment of new industries. This situation was particularly noticeable in large cities and their immediate environs. The new industries needed workers, and this need was met by the influx of the unemployed or semi-employed from the rural areas. Once people lived in the cities, they acquired many urban characteristics such as independence and individualism as far as their families were concerned. This did not mean that their families had completely lost control; it did mean that as individuals they were more self-reliant in regulating their personal lives. In the 1920's the Nationalist and Communist agents were active in organizing them into unions and

often urged them to go on strikes for political as well as economic purposes. If they could challenge the authority of their employers, why could
they not challenge that of their parents? This newly acquired independence was not only discernible among the workers but also among other
groups who had to live and make a living in the cities.

The establishment of new industries also changed the old concepts
regarding industrialists and merchants—a group of people who had
been traditionally looked down upon. As Western influence spread, the
old concepts began to change until Western values eventually became the
norm. Profit was no longer an unsavory word as long as the profit was
legitimately realized. Nor was wealth something to be modestly hidden or
to be ashamed of; it was to be proudly displayed. The traditional image
of an ideal young man, poor but studying diligently for the civil service
examinations, gave way to a new brand of young men who, shrewd and
aggressive, knew how to turn a fast profit. This trend was particularly
noticeable in large cities, a trend which made China look more and more
like an industrial society in Europe or America. It should be remembered,
however, that by and large the old values still existed in most parts of
China and that there was a vast difference between a few Westernized
cities and the large rural areas.

Though large industries such as railroads and maritime shipping
were mostly controlled by foreigners, there was enough room left for
native entrepreneurs. Rural savings, which had been traditionally invested
in land, were channeled into industrial development, and new factories
mushroomed in many large or medium-sized cities. The new industries
were for the most part light industries catering to the needs of consumers
and were not impressive by European or American standards. For one
thing, capital outlay could not be large because the Chinese, true to their
ancient tradition, preferred to raise capital on a family rather than a
corporate basis. Most of these new industrialists were former landlords
who found investment in modern industry more profitable than landholdings. As more landlords invested their money in industrial and commercial enterprises, the traditional distinction between the gentry-scholars
and merchants was no longer so clear as it once had been. Needless to
say, the stigma traditionally attached to the merchant class had all but
disappeared.

SUN YAT-SEN AND HIS PHILOSOPHY

While the various warlords were fighting among themselves and annexing each other's territories, Sun Yat-sen, the founder of the Chinese republic, was a disappointed man. He was respected as an honorable man
but, not having a military following of his own, his words carried little

weight with the realistic warlords. His old revolutionary comrades were scattered all over the country—some gave him polite attention and others joined the warlords. In 1917, together with a few of his followers, he set up an independent government in Canton; but he left this government after only one year because the southern warlords had skillfully taken it over. In 1920 he returned to Canton; and the following year with the help of a warlord named Ch'en Hsiung-ming, he proclaimed the establishment of a new national government with himself as the president. Thus two governments existed simultaneously in China, one in Peking and another in Canton, each claiming that it represented all of China. It was then that Sun asked the Western powers, especially the United States, for financial and diplomatic support, and the Western powers, recognizing the Peking government, turned down his request. Undaunted, he organized an expedition to "crush the northern warlords." His army, poorly organized and poorly led, was defeated, and one of his key supporters, Ch'en Hsiung-ming, deserted him. He was forced to resign from his presidency and left for Shanghai in May, 1922.

It was during Sun's stay in Shanghai that a very important event occurred, entailing enormous consequences for decades to come. In June, 1922, Sun met the Soviet emissary Adolph Joffe, and they issued a joint statement after their conferences. In this statement the Soviet Union pledged its assistance to Sun for the realization of China's political unity and independence and, to allay Sun's fear of Communist domination over China, it declared that Communism and the Soviet system were unsuited to China's present needs. Late in that year the Soviet agent Michael Borodin arrived in Canton where he helped to reorganize the Kuomintang (National People's Party) after the Bolshevik model. Members of the Chinese Communist Party joined the Kuomintang as "individuals" and pledged to support Sun as their revolutionary leader. Meanwhile, their own party was not dissolved and existed side by side with the Kuomintang. In the reorganized Kuomintang emphasis was laid on party loyalty and discipline, indoctrination and propaganda among the masses, and the creation of a revolutionary army under the command of the party. The new programs were formally approved by the party's first national congress convened in January, 1924. To train officers for the revolutionary army, the Whampoa Military Academy was established. Chiang Kai-shek, who had been sent by Sun to study the organization and training of the Red Army in the Soviet Union in the summer of 1923, then returned home as the president of the new school.

Early in 1924 Sun Yat-sen gave a series of lectures to his followers in Canton. These lectures, later compiled into one volume, were known as *San Min Chu-yi*, or *Three Principles of the People*. This volume, together with Sun's other works such as *Plans for National Reconstruction* (*Chien-kuo fang-lüeh*), the *Fundamentals of National Reconstruction* (*Chien-kuo ta-kang*), the *Political Philosophy of Sun Yat-sen* (*Sun Wen hsüeh-shuo*), and the *First Step to Democracy* (*Min-ch'üan ch'u-pu*), provided the ideological basis for the Nationalist revolution. To the members of the Kuomintang or Nationalists, Sun's philosophy was the ultimate in truth and wisdom. In areas within the Nationalist control it was a standard course taught in every school, from grade to college level and is still taught in Taiwan today.

Sun believed that his political philosophy was a combination of the very best from "the East and the West." While borrowing extensively from the prevailing Western ideologies, he hoped to preserve for his new China what he regarded as the best in China's ancient heritage. He was not an originator of any philosophical system in a metaphysical sense; the merits of his works lay more in their practical wisdom. He strove to solve the problems China then faced and hoped eventually to build a new society in which economic prosperity and social justice would exist simultaneously with political independence. He was a great patriot, and all his works should be read in that context. The basic ideas in the *Three Principles of the People* had been conceived as early as the turn of the century and matured with the passage of time. It was not until 1924, however, that they were put down in a more systematic form. Sun became seriously ill and then died before he had time to complete his lectures on his third and last principle, the *Principle of People's Livelihood*. The lectures, hastily composed, present many imperfections in organization and style. Had he lived a few years longer, he would doubtless have corrected them. The lectures have been published as they were originally delivered, because no one in the Nationalist government has had the audacity to suggest correction and improvement. To the Nationalists it is the bible.

In the *Principle of Nationalism*, Sun appealed to the national pride of the Chinese, with their ancient culture and great heritage. This great nation was in danger, said he, unless all Chinese transformed their traditional loyalties to families and clans into a new loyalty as embodied by the nation. The problem of the Chinese was not that they had too little individual freedom as had been the case with many European countries before the modern period, but that they had too much. They were like sands on the beach, said Sun, which, being too individualistic, produced no strength. They should be cemented together to from a solid rock, and in that case they would be able to resist foreign aggression and abolish the unequal treaties. The abolition of the unequal treaties should be China's first concern because, as long as these treaties existed, China could never be the master in its own house. China's status in the international family, Sun maintained, was worse than that of India, because India, being a colony of Great Britain, served only one master, whereas China, having unequal treaties with so many powers, was a subcolony of many masters all of whom exploited China without rendering anything in return. It was suicidal to practice internationalism while one's own country was in danger of being submerged, and only when China became a free, independent country in the truest sense could it become a member of the international community as an equal partner. Before that day arrived, nationalism, instead of internationalism, had to be its goal. To achieve national independence, "China should ally itself with all countries that treat us as equals." The countries that treated China as an equal presumably included the Soviet Union which was then helping Sun to unify China.

The achievement of international equality for China should be accompanied by a similar achievement among the various peoples within China, according to Sun. The traditional chauvinistic attitude of the Han (Chinese) people towards the minority groups should be condemned and dispensed with, and all peoples in China, regardless of their ethnic backgrounds, should enjoy the same social, economic, and legal rights. They should choose their own representatives to sit in the National Assembly when a constitutional government was established, and all policies with regard to the minorities should be aimed solely at the betterment of their welfare. Eventually, Sun continued, a new nation would be created in which all people in China would identify themselves as Chinese, regardless of their original ethnic backgrounds. This could be done, said Sun, and he cited the United States as an example. "The United States was composed of a variety of peoples originated from Europe; yet, today these are only one people, the American people, one of the most glorious peoples in the entire world."

In advancing his *Principle of Democracy,* Sun pointed out that men, contrary to the general belief, were not born equal. Men were endowed differently by nature, and within any group of people, some were wise and others were stupid, while most of them were somewhere between the two extremes. Equality, therefore, was created rather than inherited, and equality should mean equality in opportunity rather than achievement, because no two persons could achieve the same. In the political sense, everyone should have the same political rights (which were "created" for him) such as the right to vote, but the actual operation of the government should be in the hands of the able and the wise. The people were like bus riders and the government officials were like bus drivers, said Sun. The people should hire the best bus driver they could find; but once they hired him, they should not keep on telling him how to drive. How could one know that he was a good driver? He should take a road test, of course. Therefore, before any man was allowed to run for political office, he should pass a written examination in political science and related fields, impartially administered like the old civil service examinations. A man's popularity with the voters was a poor measurement of his ability; an uneducated or inadequately educated man should not be entrusted with public office, however popular he was. The right to vote, on the other hand, should be enjoyed by all above the legal age, without property, sex, education, and other limitations.

To make the government responsible to the people and yet to conduct an efficient administration without their constant meddling, the powers of the government and the rights of the people should be separated and well balanced, according to Sun. The government should have five powers (*ch'üan*): executive, legislative, judiciary, examination, and censorship. The examination branch of the government was not only responsible for administering examinations to government employees but would keep an objective record of their services for promotion or demotion purposes. The censorship (sometimes translated as control) branch of the government was a revival of the censorate of the imperial days; it was empowered to criticize or impeach all government officials who had failed in their assigned duties or who for personal reasons were unfit for public office. To balance the five powers which the government possessed, the people should have four rights (*neng*): the right to elect and recall public officials, the right to initiate legislation when their representatives had failed to introduce it, and the right of referendum with regard to all important legislation. The government, said Sun, should be like the board of directors of a corporation, and the people like the stockholders. The directors were experts and their way of conducting business should not be interfered with unnecessarily. On the other hand, they were hired employees and should be held responsible for the welfare of the stockholders.

Having lived under autocratic government for thousands of years, the Chinese, said Sun, were not yet prepared to exercise the political rights described above. The democratic or constitutional government could not be achieved overnight, he warned. Instead, there should be three stages in the revolutionary process, and the main tasks during each of the stages should be successfully completed before the arrival of the next stage. The first of these would be the military period during which the revolutionaries would use military force to unify the country and subject it to military rule. Once the country had been unified, the second stage, that of political tutelage, would arrive. During this period, the actual control of the government would be vested in the revolutionary party, the Kuomintang, whose main task was to educate the people in the use of the four rights. Self-government should begin with the lowest administrative unit, the subprefecture, and then be extended to the provincial level. Only after each province had functioned under a provincial constitution would come the third and last period, the establishment of a national, constitutional government. Then the historical rule of the Kuomintang would be completed and it should hand over the control of the government, happily and willingly, to the representatives of the people. What could the people do if the Kuomintang, long entrenched in power, refused to surrender its power or even order elections? This question was not answered.

Sun's economic theory, as described in the *Principle of People's Livelihood,* can best be described as a moderate socialism. Seeing the increasing conflicts between capital and labor during his lifetime, he rejected capitalism as an economic system. On the other hand, he was equally unwilling to accept socialism of the Marxist version. For one thing, he believed that the motivation of social progress was not class struggle as expounded by Karl Marx; it was cooperation, he said. The problem China faced was not how to distribute wealth of which it had little but how to create it. To create it, people must be given an incentive. While large industries that "affect the welfare of the people as a whole" should be government owned and controlled, there should be enough room left for private enterprise and individual initiative. Transportation and communication systems, for instance, should be made government monopolies because competition in this field was costly and uneconomical. On the other hand, there was no reason that industries that "are not monopolistic in nature and do not affect the life of the people as a whole" should not be left in private hands where free competition would be most beneficial. In the development of China's industrial potential, foreign capital was to be welcomed as long as foreign investment did not affect China adversely as a sovereign nation. Communism was at best a distant goal; for the time being the most important task was to create wealth, by private as well as public resources. "In China there is no such difference as that between the rich and the poor," Sun declared; "there is only the difference between the extremely poor and the moderately poor." "We shall strive to eliminate poverty before we can talk about the distribution of wealth."

Sun's land policy can be summarized in the often repeated statement: "Land belongs to the tillers." This purpose, however, should be achieved by peaceful, gradual means rather than radical methods such as nationalization of all land and its redistribution among peasants. In a speech made in 1921 Sun suggested some initial steps for the eventual realization of this important goal. Under his plan a landlord was allowed to assess the cash value of his land estates and report his assessment to the government. If the government believed that the assessment was above the true worth of his landholdings, it would tax him in accordance with his own assessment. If, on the other hand, the assessment was below that measured in terms of market price, the government would purchase the reported land by paying a price according to the landlord's own assessment. Presumably, land thus obtained would be resold to tillers on easy terms. Any appreciation of land values resulting from circumstances other than the landlord's own improvement should be credited to the society as a whole and be expropriated by the government. Sun believed that his plan would not only prevent land concentration in the hands of a few but would also lead to the acquiring of land ownership by tillers. Moreover, as land was no longer a profitable field for investment, the nation's savings could be channeled to industrial development which was badly in need of capital investment.

To millions of Chinese, Sun's works summarized the wishes and aspirations of a new China. To them Sun was not merely a politician or even a statesman; he was a Messiah. Personally, he was honest and selfless; even his enemies had never doubted the sincerity of his motives. In December, 1924, he was invited by the northern warlords (Tuan Ch'i-jui, Chang Tso-lin, and "Christian General" Feng Yü-hsiang) to Peking to negotiate a peaceful unification of all China. Already seriously ill, he was moved to Peking on his sickbed. As it happened, this became his final attempt to unify his beloved country; his health deteriorated further after his arrival in the capital. He died on March 12, 1925. After the establishment of the Nationalist regime his body was moved to Nanking where it was housed in a magnificently built mausoleum.

CHIANG KAI-SHEK

After Sun's death a power struggle developed among his followers. Chiang Kai-shek, a long time disciple, eventually emerged triumphant. Chiang was born in 1887 in Ch'ik'ou, a village on the coast of Chekiang province. The family had been farmers for generations and were well-to-do according to local standards. His father died when Chiang was only nine and it was his mother, said he many years later, who gave him love and protection so essential to the healthy growth of a fatherless child. She was somewhat disappointed when Chiang, after his graduation from high school, decided to pursue a military instead of a scholarly career. However, she gave her consent after the young man had definitely made up his mind. He applied and was accepted by the Paoting Military Academy (Hopeh province), then the leading school for training army officers in accordance with Western standards. After his graduation he was sent by the Manchu government to Japan for additional training where he was greatly impressed with the discipline and hardship which accompanied the training of a Japanese soldier. In 1910 he enlisted in a Japanese artillery battalion as a trainee with the rank of private, second class, but was soon promoted to a higher rank. His battalion commander, when interviewed many years later, said that he knew that Chiang would accomplish a great deal; yet, he could not even dream that the young soldier would become a "great, historical figure." In Japan Chiang joined the Alliance [1] and was introduced to Sun Yat-sen shortly afterwards. "He is

---

[1] The Alliance was a revolutionary organization headed by Sun Yat-sen. For more details, see pp. 437–438.

an unusual man," commented Sun. He was said to be serious, sincere, and full of enthusiasm about the revolution. In 1911 he returned to China to participate actively in the overthrow of the Manchu regime. He led a group of revolutionaries to attack the Manchu governor's office at Hangchow and returned that city to the newly established republic at Nanking. However, when Yüan Shih-k'ai banned the Kuomintang, Chiang, like other revolutionaries, went underground.

We know little about Chiang's activities during the early years of the republic. When he reappeared on the political scene early in 1922, he joined Sun Yat-sen's government at Canton. Two years later he was appointed president of the Whampoa Military Academy, the first major break in his political career. When Sun died in 1925, Chiang had built a strong following among his student-officers. They formed what was later known as the Whampoa clique, one of the bases of Chiang's political strength. They, in turn, trained other officers who all pledged loyalty to Chiang as their leader. Later when the Whampoa Military Academy was renamed the Central Military Academy and was moved to Nanking, Chiang remained its president. Several hundred cadets graduated each year and they, when they joined the army as second lieutenants, not only carried their loyalty to Chiang with them but also indoctrinated their soldiers with their own beliefs. In a country where political victory was ultimately decided on the battlefield, it is not difficult to see what a political asset this strong following was. With such an asset, Chiang was able to achieve what Sun had failed to bring about: the defeat of most of the warlords and a symbolic unification of all China. Early in the 1930's he was officially proclaimed the Leader (*ling-hsiu*), demanding and receiving absolute loyalty from all government officials, civilian or military, in the Nationalist government. He was the ultimate power, regardless of the official positions he happened to hold at any given moment. One might find ample grounds to criticize a personal power so vast; it should be remembered, however, that throughout Chinese history political power had always been built around men instead of institutions or ideologies.

In the summer of 1926 Chiang Kai-shek was appointed by the revolutionary regime in Canton commander-in-chief of all armed forces, with special instructions to eliminate the warlords and unify China. The military campaign, known as the Northern Expedition, was accompanied by speedy and overwhelming success. The Wu-Han metropolis was captured in October and Nanking was occupied in March, 1927. Why did the warlords collapse so quickly? For one thing, their soldiers had neither the training nor the fighting spirit possessed by the revolutionaries who had been indoctrinated to fight for a cause: a unified, strong China as outlined in Sun Yat-sen's *Three Principles of the People*. Moreover, because the Northern Expedition became as much antiforeign as it was antiwarlord, the belief that the warlords were supported by foreign interests damaged their position in the eyes of their countrymen. Chang Tso-lin and Wu P'ei-fu, for instance, were regarded as Japanese and British puppets, respectively.

The antiforeign sentiment was intensified immediately before and during the Northern Expedition as a result of a number of incidents. Early in 1925 a group of Chinese workers called a strike for higher wages against a Japanese textile mill in Shanghai, and the management dismissed the leader of the strikers, shot to death another worker, and wounded many others. Supporting the workers' stand, the angered students demonstrated in Shanghai's International Settlement and made speeches condemning "the imperialists and their brutalities." During one of the demonstrations (May 30th) the students were fired upon by British police and many of them were killed and injured. A general strike of protest was called: workers left factories, merchants closed their shops, and students vacated classrooms. The antiforeign movement soon spread to other large cities, and England resorted to the use of force to suppress it. In Hankow, British troops machine-gunned demonstrators on June 10, while in Canton several hundred were killed and injured on June 23 when British men-of-war opened fire from the nearby harbor. The entire nation was aroused, and the partriots urged all Chinese to boycott English and Japanese products. Chiang Kai-shek's Northern Expedition, which had been launched primarily for the defeat of the warlords, now became increasingly nationalistic. To millions of Chinese the success of the Northern Expedition would not only mean the unification of China but also the abolition of the unequal treaties.

After the revolutionaries reached the Yangtze Valley, the Kuomintang split into two rival factions. The revolutionary regime, which had been moved to Wu-Han after the capture of that metropolis, was then controlled by the Kuomintang leftists and their Communist allies. It had forcibly taken over the British concession at Hankow and was violently anti-foreign. Chiang Kai-shek, then fighting in the Lower Yangtze, was greatly concerned over the possible consequence of the official policy which to him had unnecessarily invited so many foreign enemies. Moreover, the Communists and the Kuomintang leftists were converting the Northern Expedition from an antiwarlord campaign into a social and economic revolution. They had successfully organized peasants and workers, expropriating land from landlords and calling strikes for political purposes. Within areas under the Kuomintang control, production stood at a standstill and no property owners were safe against mob violence. It was then that Chiang Kai-shek decided to change the course of the revolution and took a step so drastic that it affected Chinese history for decades to come.

In March, 1927, Chiang sent his troops to seize Shanghai and ordered the liquidation of all Communists who had been active in organizing strikes and demonstrations to prepare in advance the taking over of that city by the revolutionaries. With the help of Shanghai's conservative businessmen and secret societies he scored a quick victory. Not only was Shanghai captured, but countless Communists and leftists were captured and shot. Chou En-lai who was then a primary organizer of the Communist activities in Shanghai barely escaped. This marked the beginning of the intense hatred between Chiang and the Communists which has been intensified with the passage of time. As Chiang's coup was not authorized by the Central Committee of the Kuomintang, the Wu-Han govern-

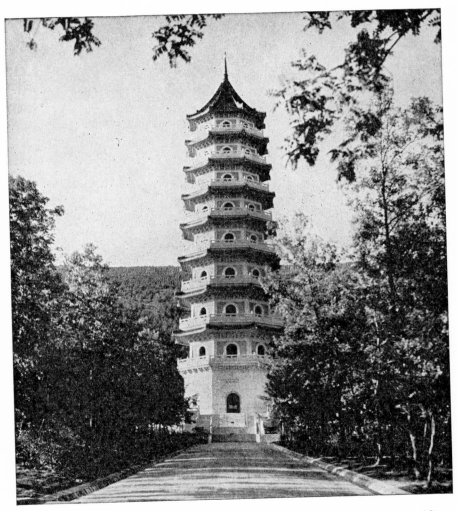

MEMORIAL PAGODA This pagoda is located outside of Nanking where soldiers killed during the Northern Expedition are buried.

ment dismissed him from his post as the commander-in-chief. Chiang retaliated by setting up a separate government at Nanking. As the intra-party struggle continued, the war against the warlords was temporarily suspended. Under strong party pressure, Chiang finally resigned from his post and went into exile in Japan.

Meanwhile, even the leftist Kuomintang members began to suspect Communist motives and came closer to Chiang's point of view: that the Communists were Moscow agents and that their ultimate purpose was to eliminate the Kuomintang and subject China to Soviet rule. A supposedly secret telegram from Joseph Stalin to the Chinese Communists became known to Wang Ching-wei, a leader of the Kuomintang, in which the Soviet leader outlined the steps to be taken by his Chinese comrades for the control of the Kuomintang and the liquidation of the "recalcitrant" elements who refused to cooperate with the Communists. Wang and his colleagues were alarmed and proceeded to do the same thing for which they had criticized Chiang before, which was the purging of Communists from the Kuomintang ranks. The Communists, being a minority, offered only ineffectual resistance. The Communist purge paved the way for a reconciliation between the left and right factions of the Kuomintang. In August, 1927, the separate Nanking government was abolished, and the Wu-Han government moved to Nanking. Chiang returned to China early in 1928. The Northern Expedition was resumed, and despite Japanese obstruction Peking was eventually captured. Chang Tso-lin, the last of the strong warlords, was murdered (presumably by the Japanese) while retreating to Manchuria. His son and successor Chang Hsüeh-liang (the "Young Marshal") declared his allegiance to the revolutionary regime in December, 1928. In name at least, China was unified.

As the radical elements had been either purged or had voluntarily left the party, the new government at Nanking (officially, the National Government of China) was conservative in tone. In the fall of 1927 Chiang was converted to Christianity as a Methodist and late in that year he was married to Soong Meiling, a beautiful, talented young woman who came from a businessman's family and had been educated in the United States. These two happy occurrences well foretold the national and international policies the Nationalist government was going to follow. The *Three Principles of the People* was still the ideological basis of the new regime, but it was not to be interpreted literally. The equalization of land ownership, for instance, had come to mean the reduction of rent charged by landlords, and the pro-Soviet policy originated by Sun Yat-sen was abandoned. Sun's widow, Soong Ch'ing-ling, accused Chiang of having betrayed her husband's trust and left China for Moscow. The new regime was supported wholeheartedly by the landowners and the bourgeoisie, as it was more consistent with their concept of a revolutionary regime. In foreign policy, China was to be more Western orientated, and the goal of abolishing the unequal treaties, while not abandoned, should be achieved through peaceful means and by negotiation. By and large, the conservative policy of Chiang and his colleagues was supported by the nation as a whole, and the Communists, through their constant agitation for violence, had antagonized not only property owners but all those who wanted nothing better than peace after so many years of civil war. Upon the new leader, Chiang Kai-shek, China placed much of its hope, as he was young, energetic, and self-assured.

THE NATIONALIST REGIME

After Peking had been captured by the Nationalists and when China was again nominally unified, the Nationalist government in Nanking formally declared that the military period had come to an end and that the second period of the revolution, that of political tutelage, had begun. During the period of political tutelage, the state power was vested in the Kuomintang which formulated policies and appointed government personnel. No other political party was allowed to function because the Kuomintang alone, according to Sun Yat-sen, had the right and obligation to prepare the country for the eventual realization of a democratic, constitutional government. The highest organization of the party was the National Party Congress, composed of delegates from all provinces and overseas Chinese communities. When the congress was not in session, party power was vested in a Central Executive Committee and a Supervisory Committee; the members of both committees were elected by the congress. The standing committee of the Central Executive Committee was in fact the most powerful organ of the party. As the government was responsible to the party, the man in control of the party was also the strongest man in the government. He might not occupy the position of president of the republic, but whatever position he held, he made the final decisions with regard to government as well as party policies. During most of the period under discussion, 1927–1949, Chiang commanded the majority vote in the standing committee as well as the Central Executive Committee.

Even during the prime of the Nationalist regime, the unification was more apparent than real. Recognized by all foreign powers as China's legal government, it had no more than one-third of the nation under its direct jurisdiction in the 1930's—the central lakes region, the Lower Yangtze, part of North China, and later, Fukien and Kwangtung provinces. The other two-thirds were controlled by local strong men who were given such titles as governor as long as they were not in open rebellion. Time and again they revolted, and the central government had to use force to suppress them. Once they were defeated, they were either al-

MAP 31
CHINA, 1931

□ Capital
● Provincial Capital

Scale of Miles

0   150   300   450

Sea of Japan

East China Sea

Yellow Sea

South China Sea

Bay of Bengal

HEILUNGKIANG

● Tsitsihar

SUNGARI RIVER

KIRIN

● Kirin

● Mukden

LIAONING

YALU RIVER

OUTER MONGOLIA

● Urga

CHAHAR

JEHOL

● Chengteh

● Kalgan

HOPEH

Tsingyuan (Paoting) ●

● Tsinan

SHANTUNG

Chinkiang □
Nanking ●

KIANGSU

Hangchow ●
CHEKIANG

Foochow ●
FUKIEN

SUIYUAN

● Kweihsui

SHANSI

Taiyuan ●

HONAN

Kaifeng ●

ANHWEI

Anking ●

Nanchang ●
KIANGSI

NINGSIA

● Ningsia

Lanchow ●

KANSU

SHENSI

Sian ●

HUPEH

Wuchang ●

HUNAN

Changsha ●

Canton ●
KWANGTUNG

● Tihwa (Urumchi)

SINKIANG

TARIM RIVER

CHINGHAI

Sining ●

SZECHUAN

Chengtu ●

Tatsienlu ●

KWEICHOW

Kweiyang ●

Kunming ●
YUNNAN

Nanning ●
KWANGSI

TIBET

SIKANG

● Lhasa

TSANGPO RIVER

BRAHMAPUTRA RIVER

MEKONG RIVER

SALWEEN R.

lowed to retain their territories or were brought back to Nanking to occupy some high but powerless positions. In some cases they were "advised" to go abroad for a prolonged vacation. Why did Chiang not pursue the goal of unification to its logical conclusion by conquering all warlords? To him these warlords were merely selfish, unprincipled men who could be easily pushed aside once he successfully defeated the real enemy, the Communists. Having an ideology, a program, and strong and able leadership, the Communists were the greatest challenge to everything he stood for, and he did not mind making alliances with the warlords to help bring about the defeat of the Communists. With communism there could not be any real compromise. From time to time he was called upon to deal with other problems such as warlords' rebellions and Japanese aggression, but he never let those problems distract him from his main political goal: the destruction of communism in China. As far as he was concerned, the die was cast as early as 1927.

Despite recurrent warfare against warlords, continuous conflict with the Communists, and Japanese aggression after 1931, the Nationalist regime was not without significant achievements during its short stay in Nanking (1927–1937). For the first time since the overthrow of the Manchu regime, there was a fairly honest government which most Chinese could support with good conscience. Though much has been said about Nationalist corruption, it was perhaps no worse than what could be found in many other countries. It was not until the end of World War II when a runaway inflation had eaten up the income of most wage earners that corruption became a major disease. Chiang was personally incorruptible, though we cannot say the same thing about all of his followers. He practiced and glorified a Spartan type of life, and he invited others to do the same. Despite criticism of his foreign and domestic policies, his popularity continued to grow. His popularity was never so high as when he decided to make a stand against Japan in 1937.

Before the war with Japan began, the Nationalist government made conscientious efforts to improve the nation's economy. Thanks to the fact that China was largely agricultural, the world-wide depression of the 1930's did not affect China as it did more industrialized countries. However, the devaluation of currencies in foreign countries affected adversely the Chinese monetary system. Silver, which had been the standard medium of exchange for many centuries, began to flow abroad, following the raising of silver price in the United States. In 1935 the government decreed the nationalization of silver and imposed severe penalties for using it in business transactions. All silver was to be handed over to the government in exchange for the "legal tender" (fa pi) issued by government-controlled banks. All bullion thus collected was the bank reserve backing the soundness of the paper currency. The currency reform was more successful than had been expected; for one thing, it enabled the government to finance the war against Japan which began in 1937. However, towards the end of World War II the continuous printing of unredeemable paper money resulted in an inflation unprecedented in modern history which eventually destroyed the financial structure.

Other economic achievements of the 1930's included the construction of railroads and highways. The Che-Kan (from Hangchow to Nanchang) Railroad and the Yüeh-Han (from Canton to Hankow) Railroad were both completed in 1936. The construction of highways was also emphasized, reaching 68,000 miles by 1937. A Sino-American enterprise, the China Aviation Company, was founded in 1930 with regular flights between major cities in China. Meanwhile, efforts were made to convert the middle and lower Yangtze—areas under the direct control of the Nationalist government—into a highly industrialized region. Heavy and light industries were equally emphasized, and the government took initial steps towards the exploitation of China's mineral resources. Unfortunately, most of the industrial programs were still in the blueprint stage when war began in 1937.

On the rural level, a land law passed in 1930 was intended to reduce some of the worst evils in tenancy. Rents were not to exceed 37.5 percent of the main crop, and tenants could not be evicted unless they had failed to pay rent consecutively for two years or had not worked the land for a year without good reason. Unfortunately, the law was not strictly enforced, and ingenious landlords had schemes for obtaining the same rent without violating the letter of the law. For one thing, tenancy was difficult to obtain and tenants did not have the bargaining power possessed by landlords. As credit was rare and not easily available, usurious interest was a rule rather than an exception. When the government made available low-interest loans in rural areas, more often than not such loans wound up in the hands of landlords whose credit rating was certainly higher than that of the peasants. Moreover, flood and drought were a recurrent problem. In 1931 an unprecedented flood along the Yangtze caused the death of more than 100,000 and affected an area of more than 70,000 square miles. Following the disaster, the government built a long dyke along the middle and the lower valley of the river, extending more than 2,600 miles. This extraordinary work reduced damages in the subsequent floods, though it could not eliminate them. Despite the government's efforts, the majority of the peasants were no better off than they had been before. The government's inability to solve the rural problems gave the Communists a great opportunity to exploit them. As to this, we shall have more to say in the next chapter.

To prepare the nation for the eventual realization of a constitutional government, the Nationalist government launched an extensive educational program. However, due to the lack of adequate funds and trained personnel, the result was anything but impressive. All children were supposed to have at least six years of schooling, but this goal proved to be impossible to reach. In the rural areas children began to work in the fields at a tender age, and even if the tuition were free, their parents simply could not afford to take them away from the field to send them to school. Whenever schools were established in rural areas, only the comparatively well-to-do could take advantage of the opportunity. Unable to promote education on a mass scale, the government concentrated its attention on institutions of higher learning. Many universities, colleges, and teacher-training schools were established. They were of uneven quality, of course; but the best among them could be compared favorably with the leading institutions in other countries. For one thing, high school graduates had to pass rigid entrance examinations before they were admitted; in many cases, only one in twenty candidates could be accepted. Academic learning was universally emphasized; sports and other forms of recreation had been looked down upon and still were. However, as institutions of learning were few and expensive, only a few could ever enter their doors. The waste of the nation's talent was simply enormous.

In the field of foreign relations the Nationalist government directed its major attention to the abolition of the unequal treaties. German, Austrian, and Hungarian rights in China were liquidated in World War I, and Russia renounced its special privileges following the Bolshevik revolution. Now China under the Nationalist regime wished other Western powers and Japan to do the same. During the two year period (1928–1929) a series of treaties were concluded with these powers which conceded to China the principle of tariff autonomy. Thus after eighty-seven years (1842–1929) the system of regulated tariff finally came to an end. The government was only partially successful, however, in securing the return of the concessions. Some were regained, but others, including the International Settlement at Shanghai, remained in the hands of foreigners. As to extraterritoriality, the Western powers and Japan refused to give ground. They criticized China's judicial system and would agree to the gradual abolition of the extraterritorial system only after China had revised its legal codes, modernized its prisons, and conducted a variety of other reforms. As negotiations were stalemated, the Nationalist government announced that extraterritoriality would come to an end on January 1, 1932. When the powers refused to budge, the Chinese government capitulated in December, 1931. By the beginning of World War II China was one of the few "sovereign" countries where foreigners still enjoyed extraterritorial rights. Both Turkey and Siam had successfully eliminated them.

ᐇ XV

The Republic (2)

THE COMMUNISTS

The forerunner of the Chinese Communist Party was the Marxist Study Association organized by a group of intellectuals in Shanghai in the spring of 1920. Until this time the leader of this group, Ch'en Tu-hsiu, had been an ardent advocate of American republicanism; but then, impressed with the Soviet Union's anti-imperialist stand and its willingness to relinquish its special rights in China, he saw communism as the cure-all of China's foreign and domestic ills. In the summer of that year he and his colleagues organized the Communist Youth Corps as a prelude to the organization of a Communist Party. The party formally came into being in July, 1921. The total number of registered Communists was no more than fifty, and when the First Party Congress was called into session that year there were only thirteen delegates from "all parts of China" to attend the

476

meeting. The party had little strength then, and it needed a popular hero to bolster its prestige. G. Maring, the Comintern agent who had been sent to China to help organize the Chinese Communist Party, contacted Sun Yat-sen for a possible alliance, and Sun, believing that the New Economic Policy as then pursued in Russia under Lenin was similar to his own idea of economic development, agreed to the alliance. The alliance with the Soviet Union was formally announced after Sun's meeting with another Soviet agent Joffe. When the Kuomintang held its First Party Congress in January, 1924, all Communists pledged their loyalty to Sun as their leader, and some of them were elected as alternate members of the Central Executive Committee of the Kuomintang—including an obscure young man named Mao Tse-tung.

During the Northern Expedition (1926–1927) the Communists were very active in propaganda work and in the organization of peasants and workers. They took a strong antifeudal and anti-imperialist stand by which they meant the elimination of landlordism as an economic institution and the liquidation of the special privileges and rights which the treaty powers then enjoyed in China. To achieve their purpose, they did not hesitate to use the most dubious methods. When Nanking was captured in the spring of 1927, the Communist-inspired mobs, waving anti-imperialist flags, invaded British and American consulates and churches, killed foreigners indiscriminately, and did much damage to property. The British and American ships in the nearby Yangtze opened fire and bombarded the city, and for a while it seemed that a severe punishment of the Boxer type was in order. It was against this background that Chiang Kai-shek struck back against the Communists, and his success in Shanghai was followed by a mass purge. The Nationalists and the Communists went their separate ways, and ever since then the Communists have accused him of betraying the revolution.

The victory of Stalin over Trotsky in Russia in 1927 was followed by a similar change of leadership among the Communists in China. Ch'en Tu-hsiu and his colleagues were replaced by the Stalinists, headed by a Moscow-trained Chinese named Li Li-san. Goaded by Stalin, the Communists staged a series of uprisings in southern and central China in the latter part of 1927. All of them failed, including the "autumn harvest" uprising in Hunan led by Mao Tse-tung. After the failure, the Communists were a dispirited and disorganized force; each group was more concerned with its survival than with the proletarian revolution. One group, led by a Communist militarist named Chu Teh, arrived at Ching-kangshan, a mountainous area in southern Kiangsi. Soon it was joined by Mao Tse-tung and his group. The Chu-Mao coalition became the nucleus around which a strong Communist force was eventually built up. Meanwhile, other Communist groups were scattered in many isolated areas in South China, each fighting for its own existence. To coordinate the efforts of the various groups and to plan a unified strategy, a party congress was called in Shanghai in May, 1930. The congress passed a resolution reaffirming the "correctness of the leadership of the proletariat" and condemning those comrades (such as Mao Tse-tung) who elevated the peasants above the workers as the basis of the revolution. The party leadership remained in the hands of the doctrinaires who believed that to succeed the Communists had to capture large cities where the proletarians lived, while the peasants, traditionally conservative and politically inert, could only be considered auxiliaries to the revolution. In June, 1930, the Communists felt strong enough to carry out the resolution. They attacked Changsha and the Wu-Han cities with the purpose of building an urban, revolutionary base. They succeeded in capturing Changsha, only to be driven out by the reinforced Nationalists a few days later. Though the action had been planned and urged by the Comintern, the Kremlin dropped Li Li-san after his failure, and party leadership passed into the hands of a group of students who had recently returned from Moscow.

Meanwhile Mao and Chu, who had been the reluctant partners in Li's *putschism*, went their separate ways and practiced their own brand of communism. The failure of Li and his Moscow-dictated strategy had convinced them of the correctness of their own theory: that in an industrially backward, agricultural China where industrial workers were few, the basis of the revolution could not be any other group except the peasants who constituted the majority of the population. Of the two, Mao was the leader who formulated policies and planned strategy. More versed in Chinese history than in Communist ideology, he was in closer touch with reality than those doctrinaire Communists trained by Moscow.

Mao Tse-tung was born in 1893 to a peasant family in Hunan. His father, a shrewd farmer who also speculated in the rice market, brought prosperity to the family much to the envy of the neighborhood. He was a strict disciplinarian, however, and ruled the family with an iron hand. Many years later his son still remembered vividly how he had hated the "dictator." Being intelligent and promising, young Mao was sent to school where, we are told, he hated his teacher with equal intensity because the teacher forced him to study Confucian classics which he disliked. Defiant of authorities and established conventions, he imagined himself as a Chinese Robin Hood, striking against the rich and helping the poor. Had there been no Karl Marx and Lenin, he would have been a rebel in the traditional sense, perhaps like those in *The Marsh Heroes*, a book which he enjoyed reading and greatly admired.

To say that Mao was a born rebel is of course not enough. Like any other Chinese who knew how to read, he was greatly disturbed by China's international status. The thought that China might be conquered by Japan or divided among foreign powers aroused in him a strong sense of nationalism. "It was the duty of all people to help save China." he declared. How could China be saved? His early solution was a simple one: China had to possess Western inventions—railroads, telegraphs, steamships, and "machines of all kinds." After he grew older, he realized that this would not be enough. The real solution, he declared, lay in the conversion of China to a Communist society because "the emancipation of China depends upon the successful liberation of all colonial and semicolonial countries from capitalist, imperialist rule." By reaching such a conclusion he made China's struggle for freedom and independence a part of the world Communist movement. Thus three facets appeared in Mao's personality: the rebel, the nationalist, and finally, the Communist.

After finishing his education in the village school, Mao went to Changsha, capital of Hunan, where he was enrolled as a student in a normal school. A prospective teaching career, however, was not to his liking, and he left the school one year later so that he could devote his entire time to "patriotic work." He read avidly the newspapers and pamphlets put out by the various revolutionary groups. Among the revolutionaries, he admired Sun Yat-sen and hoped to join his organization. In 1918 he went to Peking where he found a job as an assistant librarian with the Peking University. This position gave him an opportunity to read books of different ideologies and also to audit the lectures of many prominent professors, including Hu Shih. The head of the library and his immediate superior was Li Ta-chao, an avowed Marxist, and under Li's guidance, he became Marxist orientated. In 1921 when the Communist Party was organized, he was one of its charter members. During the first Kuomintang-Communist cooperation (1924–1927) Mao strongly urged his own party to rely upon the peasants as "the most dynamic, most revolutionary force" because "they have been despised and trodden down by the gentry for centuries." "The leadership by the poor peasants is very essential," he continued; "without them there will be no revolution." His proposal was rejected by the party leaders who regarded his idea as unorthodox and heretical.

After the failure of Li Li-san's *putsch* in 1930, Mao's prestige within the party increased. Many Communists, while still giving lip service to the dictatorship of the proletariat, began to accept Mao's strategy as the most feasible. In 1931 the establishment of a Soviet Republic was proclaimed in southern Kiangsi with Mao as its chairman. Within the area under their control, the Communists liquidated the landlords, expropriated their land, and distributed it among the peasants. This gave the peasants a stake in defending the republic. Quickly the Communists applied their organizational ability and mobilized all men and women on a permanent, military basis. Even small children were mobilized to spy on their "enemy," the Nationalists. A program of intensified indoctrination was conducted, and the peasants were taught to hate "the imperialists, the landlords, and their lackey, Chiang Kai-shek." By the early 1930's the Communists had extended their control over a great part of Kiangsi and large areas of Fukien and Hunan provinces.

Meanwhile the Nationalists, under the leadership of Chiang Kai-shek, had not been idle. From December, 1930, to June, 1932, they launched four military campaigns against the Red republic; all of them, however, ended in failure. The failure was partly due to the strength of the thoroughly indoctrinated peasant Communist army and partly due to other circumstances beyond the Nationalists' control. For instance, the third campaign was called off after Japan had invaded Manchuria in September, 1931, and the fourth campaign came to nought when the Nationalists had to move troops to North China to face another Japanese invasion early in 1933. Ironically, the Japanese militarists had been the Communists' inadvertent allies throughout the civil war. They put pressure on China whenever the Nationalist government was busy fighting its domestic enemy; by doing so they reduced the pressure that the Nationalists had been exercising on the Communists. In 1933 the Nationalist government obtained a truce from Japan by signing away part of North China, and in the following year it launched the fifth and the best planned campaign against the Soviet Republic in Kiangsi. The military offensive was accompanied by an economic blockade so thorough that soon the Communists began to feel the pinch. For one thing, the lack of an adequate supply of salt had become so serious that the peasant soldiers were simply too weak physically to continue the fight. Rather than risk total annihilation the Communists left Kiangsi and began the so-called Long March. Breaking through the encirclement with 80,000 men, they walked 6,000 miles until they reached Yenan in northern Shensi in the fall of 1935. When they arrived at their destination, only 20,000 men remained. Meanwhile the Nationalist troops were pressing northward for the final campaign of liquidating the Communist remnants.

It seemed that the Communists, as an organized group, would have ended then, but they were saved by a totally unexpected event, the Sian Incident. When Japan invaded Manchuria in 1931, the Manchurian army, under the leadership of the "Young Marshal" Chang Hsüeh-liang, was ordered by the Nationalist government to withdraw southward to China proper. After the Communists had arrived in northern Shensi, this army was deployed face to face with the Communists in the north. The Communist agents immediately began to work among the officers and soldiers of the Manchurian army, and their line of argument, from the point of view of people who had recently lost their homes in Manchuria, was very convincing indeed. The civil war should cease at once, said the Communists; and all Chinese, regardless of geographical and ideological differences, should form a united front against the Japanese invaders. The deployment of the Manchurian army along the front, the Communists continued, was Chiang's standard way of using one enemy to eliminate another, since the Manchurian army was not trained and commanded by Chiang's personal followers. The Communist strategy worked well; even the "Young Marshal," after a meeting with Chou En-lai, became convinced of the Communists' sincerity. Not only did the two opposing armies cease to fight; they fraternized. Angered by this development, Chiang flew to Sian, the "bandit-extermination headquarters," on December 12, 1936, for a personal inspection. He was seized by the Manchurian army under the "Young Marshal's" order, and his bodyguards were either killed or captured. The mutineers demanded the termination of the civil war and the formation of a united front against Japan. Chiang, however, refused to negotiate with them and ordered them to release him immediately and to accept the consequences of their mutiny. On December 25 not only was he released; he brought his captor, the "Young Marshal," as his prisoner back to Nanking.

What had happened between December 12 and 25? The official explanation was that the "Young Marshal," after conferring with Chiang, was greatly moved by the latter's uprightness and selfless devotion to the state and agreed to release him. On the other hand, there was no question that the Communists had played a decisive role in the final outcome. Why did the Communists want their bitter enemy to be released? Paradoxical as it might seem, the answer is not difficult to find. By insisting on Chiang's release, the Communists acted according to their own best interests. Soon after the news arrived in Nanking that Chiang had been kidnapped, the Nationalist air force began to drop bombs on Sian, and Chiang's best army, then stationed in the Lower Yangtze, began to move northward. If Chiang were killed, there would have been a bloodbath which the Communists would not wish to face as their force, even with the help of the Manchurian army, was much inferior. By insisting on Chiang's release, they hoped to strike a bargain with him which would prolong their own existence. Moreover, despite their personal feelings, it was clear to them that there was no man except Chiang Kai-shek behind whom the nation could rally for a prolonged effort against the Japanese aggression. In the spring of 1937 Chou En-lai held a series of discussions with Chiang and his representatives, as a result of which the second period of cooperation between the Kuomintang and the Communists began. Before the agreement was even completed, Japan struck again. The war with Japan was not to be ended until August, 1945.

JAPANESE INVASIONS

For two decades after the establishment of the Nationalist regime in Nanking, there were three major forces in China's political arena: Japanese militarists, Chinese Nationalists, and Chinese Communists. The triangular conflict between the three groups overshadowed all other events during this period. If Japan were to conquer China, nothing would be more to her advantage than for that country to remain continually weakened and divided. A unified China, better utilizing its vast manpower and natural resources, would be an insurmountable obstacle to the fulfillment of Japan's ambition. In April, 1928, when the Nationalists were marching northward to capture Peking, Japan sent its troops to Shantung and interposed them between the northern militarists and the Nanking forces, ostensibly for the purpose of protecting Japanese residents in that province. A clash ensued which ended with the withdrawal of the Nationalist forces from Tsinan and its occupation by the Japanese. It was not until March, 1929, after a long period of painful negotiation, that Japan agreed to withdraw from Shantung. Meanwhile the almost perennial conflict between the two countries also took a turn for the worse in Manchuria. The "Young Marshal" who succeeded his father as the overlord of Manchuria proved to be more nationalistic than his father had ever been. After he had pledged his allegiance to the Nanking regime in December, 1928, a large number of Kuomintang agents came to Manchuria with his blessing, and these agents, preaching an anti-imperialist gospel, found an attentive audience among the local Chinese who resented the privileged position enjoyed by the Japanese. Japan's privileged position in Manchuria was secured through a series of treaties and agreements between these two countries dating from 1905 to 1915. China, weak as it was, never resigned itself to the *status quo,* as it believed that the existence of Japan's privileges in Manchuria was a violation of its sovereign rights. On the other hand, Japan was anxious to enlarge the existing concessions whenever the opportunity presented itself. After Russia had agreed to relinquish its special privileges in Manchuria (with the exception of the Chinese Eastern Railroad) following the Bolshevik revolution, the primary target of Chinese nationalism in Manchuria was Japan. Neither side would retreat from its established position, and this eventually led to an armed conflict, with Japan, the stronger power, playing a more aggressive role.

One of the many difficulties between the two countries concerned the South Manchuria Railroad (from Changchun to Dairen), the primary agent of Japan's economic interests in Manchuria. It was more than a railroad; it was a vast industrial complex organized to exploit the economic resources of South Manchuria. To safeguard the monopolistic interest of the railroad, Japan obtained from China a promise in 1905 that the Chinese government would not "construct any main line in the neighborhood of and parallel to that railway, or any branch line which might be prejudicial to the interests" of the South Manchuria Railroad. When the "Young Marshal" came to power, he proceeded to carry out an economic development of his own, including the building of railroads in South Manchuria with Chinese capital. This infuriated the Japanese who viewed the Chinese program as a challenge to their dominant position.

The Chinese contended that since Manchuria was their territory, they had every right to develop it the way they thought fit.

Another difficulty between China and Japan had to do with Korean residents in Manchuria. On the Manchurian side of the Yalu River a large number of Korean farmers had settled. As the number of Koreans increased, the Chinese took various measures to restrict Korean immigration, as they feared that the continuous acquisition of land by Koreans would eventually lead to the alienation of that part of the country to Japan, of which Korea was then a part. This fear was intensified when Japan made it clear that under no circumstances would it recognize the naturalization of Koreans as Chinese. Invoking its extraterritorial rights, it declared that it alone had jurisdiction over Koreans in China. Whenever clashes occurred between Chinese and Korean farmers, China and Japan each proceeded to use force to protect its own group. It was one of these clashes that became the immediate cause of what has been known as the Manchurian Incident.

At Wanpaoshan, a small village near Changchun, a dispute occurred in 1931 over the right of some Korean farmers to construct an irrigation ditch across the lands of some Chinese farmers. Both Chinese and Japanese police appeared on the scene, and their appearance resulted in bitter feelings between the Chinese and Korean farmers. The sensational accounts of this seemingly minor incident in the Japanese and Korean press led to anti-Chinese riots in Seoul and Tokyo; the aroused mobs killed and injured several hundred Chinese. The Chinese responded with a vigorous boycott of Japanese goods. While the feelings of both sides ran high, a Japanese military officer named Nakamura was killed by Chinese soldiers in northwestern Manchuria. It was then that the Japanese militarists decided to make a drastic move: to occupy all of Manchuria. Japan could not have chosen a more propitious moment. The world had just entered the worst depression in modern history, and it was unlikely that the major powers would interfere with the implementation of Japan's "grand scheme."

On the night of September 18, 1931, Japanese forces seized Mukden. This was followed by an almost unopposed occupation of all large cities in Manchuria. Towards the end of that year the victorious Japanese army pushed its operation towards the Great Wall and occupied the province of Jehol. The Nationalist government, then busy fighting a domestic war against the Communists, decided not to oppose the Japanese invaders. Such a policy aroused public anger, and students demonstrated in the streets and demanded Chiang Kai-shek's resignation. Chiang resigned in December, 1931, only to regain power shortly afterwards.

Why did the Nationalist government let China's richest territory go without offering military resistance? First, the China of 1931 was certainly in no position to fight against a strong, industrialized Japan. The Chinese hoped that if Japan met with no opposition, it would be satisfied with Manchuria. If China decided to resist, went the argument, large parts of China, especially the coastal areas, would be under Japanese attack or even occupation. Moreover, as far as Chiang was concerned, the Communists (whom he termed a "disease of the heart") were a much worse and more deadly enemy than Japan (which he termed a "disease of the skin"), and he would yield to Japanese demands in order to gain time to eliminate the Communists. However the Japanese militarists, for obvious reasons, would not give him time. Flushed with their easy victory in Manchuria, they attacked Shanghai early in 1932. A warlord's army (the Nineteenth Route Army), which was then stationed at Shanghai and over which Chiang had no direct control, decided to take up the battle against the Japanese. Fighting against great odds, it held the invaders at bay for more than two months. Overnight the soldiers of the Nineteenth Route Army, composed mostly of Cantonese, became national heroes. As the Japanese invasion of Shanghai threatened the commercial interest of foreign powers in that city, they exercised pressure on both sides to negotiate for a truce. They succeeded and the Battle of Shanghai was over. Subsequently, the Nineteenth Route Army withdrew to Fukien where its commanders proclaimed the establishment of an independent republic. Striking with flashing speed, Chiang liquidated their republic before it could get off the ground.

Unable to resist Japanese aggression single handed, China appealed to the League of Nations and the United States for help. The Western powers were sympathetic but decided to do nothing aside from giving verbal and moral support. They were opposed to sanctions of any kind "other than the sanctions of adverse public opinion and official nonrecognition of conquests or settlements achieved by other than peaceful means." The nonrecognition of conquests was later known as the Stimson Doctrine, as it was first enunciated by the American Secretary of State Henry L. Stimson. Later the League incorporated the doctrine in a resolution proposed by Great Britain. It appointed a commission of inquiry to study the dispute between China and Japan with regard to Manchuria. In its report (known as the *Lytton Report*, named after the chairman of the commission, the Earl of Lytton), the commission criticized Japan's military action as unwarranted and proposed ten conditions as indispensable to any satisfactory solution. The last condition was perhaps the most interesting and significant. It said in effect that as long as China was without a strong central government and remained politically unstable, the difficulties with Japan would continue. To put it more bluntly, Japanese aggression would continue as long as China was weak and divided and did not possess the physical strength to resist such aggression. The commission urged "temporary international cooperation in the internal reconstruction of China, as suggested by the late Dr. Sun Yat-sen."

Meanwhile, Japan was consolidating and expanding its military gains. It created a puppet regime called Manchukuo early in 1932, consisting of Manchuria and the Jehol province. The last Manchu emperor Hsüan-t'ung, who had then acquired the unbelievable name of Henry P'u-yi, was "kidnapped" by Japanese agents from Tientsin to serve as the figurehead of the new regime.[1] One year after the establishment of Manchukuo, Japan renewed its military operations. By the spring of 1933 it drove out all Nationalist forces in eastern Hopeh where it succeeded in establishing another puppet regime. In May, 1933, the Nationalists signed the so-called Tangku truce whereby they agreed to withdraw from the Peking-Tientsin area where, under the Boxer Protocol, Japan was entitled to, and did, station troops. By then it was clear that Japan intended to bring all of North China under its control. In 1935 it proceeded to create a North China autonomous region, embracing five provinces: Chahar, Suiyuan, Shansi, Hopeh, and Shantung. It was on the verge of succeeding when China decided not to retreat any more. In Lukouchiao (Marco Polo Bridge), south of Peking, fighting broke out between Chinese and Japanese troops on the night of July 7, 1937. In August, Japan attacked Shanghai, and a full-scale war began.

Why did China finally decide to fight? The answer has to be found in the domestic situation. When Japan invaded and then occupied Manchuria, Chinese patriotism was aroused, and as Japan continued to advance in North China, the nationalistic fervor steadily built to a climax. That China could not militarily cope with Japan was brushed aside as unpatriotic thinking, and in a wishful mood, swords were glorified as more effective weapons than tanks. Students went repeatedly to the streets, calling for resistance against Japan, and they caused such an uproar that at one time they even forced Chiang Kai-shek to resign. The boycott of Japanese goods was vigorously pursued; sad to say, it had no noticeable effect on either the policy or the military strength of the Japanese government. Newspapers and magazines that were not controlled by the Nationalist government continued to agitate for a war of resistance regardless of consequences. "If China as a nation has to be terminated, let it be terminated by a war rather than continuous retreat." The fires of patriotism were fanned by the Communists who called for the cessation of the civil war and the formation of a united front against the Japanese. As Japan

[1] P'u-yi was captured by the Russians towards the end of World War II and was subsequently repatriated to Communist China. "What is he doing now?" asked a Western correspondent in 1962. "He is having a happy life in the People's Republic," replied a high-ranking Communist Chinese official. "What does he do for recreation?" "He loves gardening."

continued to advance in North China, their appeal became more convincing to a large section of the Chinese.

While the nation was clamoring for a war of resistance, Chiang Kai-shek was immobile. Yet, in view of the position he held, he was the only man who could lead the nation in war. There was no question that he resented Japanese aggression as other Chinese did, but he hated the Communists more. He had to liquidate the Communists first before he could think seriously about an all-out war against Japan. "Until all hopes are exhausted, we shall not forsake peace," he announced; "until the last moment arrives we shall not talk casually about sacrifices." Meanwhile, some of the leaders who had talked too loudly about sacrifices were sent to jail. How long could he withstand public pressure? This question was answered for the nation by the Sian Incident. When a rapprochement was reached between the Kuomintang and the Communists, the Nationalist government agreed to go to war if Japan pushed further for territorial gains. Ten days after the Lukouchiao Incident, Chiang announced that the "last moment" had arrived. "Once we go to war to save the nation," he continued, "there is no alternative to victory." "We will fight to the bitter end, whatever the sacrifices. If we compromise with our enemy in the course of the war, we compromise our very existence. What Japan has done to us cannot be tolerated by any nation with self-respect." Throughout the war, time and again Japan proposed peace negotiations. True to his words, Chiang turned them down without the slightest hesitation.

THE UNDECLARED WAR

The undeclared war that began in the summer of 1937 was referred to by Japan as the "China Incident"; but to the Chinese it was a life-and-death struggle. It was, to use an ancient Chinese metaphor, like an egg trying to make a stand against a rolling rock; and the Japanese rock, rolling on and on, captured the two major cities in North China, Tientsin (Map 5) and Peking, shortly after the hostilities began. When Japan attacked Shanghai in August, Chiang Kai-shek threw his best troops into the battle. Overnight there was such national unity as had never been seen before in modern history. Even the warlords sent their representatives to Nanking, offering their services in the hour of common peril. They were requested to dispatch troops to the front and they responded without hesitation. Their response was selfless indeed, in view of the fact that once a warlord lost his army he ended his career as a warlord. Most of the warlords' soldiers left their home provinces for the first time, determined to exchange their lives for those of the invaders. Some gave a good account of themselves; most of them, however, served no better purpose than to consume Japanese bullets, as they were equipped with nothing better then knives, swords, and a variety of odd weapons. These soldiers and their commanders who had never done anything more bellicose than bullying peasants and fighting the most polite of battles panicked when they saw Japanese tanks rolling towards them. Ironically, as they were destroyed *en masse*, the warlordism which had plagued China since the beginning of the republic thereby faded out of the Chinese scene. What the central government had not been able to achieve was accomplished by the warlords' own selfless patriotism.

In Shanghai where the Nationalist government's crack troops were committed, the Chinese performance surprised even the foreigners who watched the battle from the French and the International Settlements whose neutrality the belligerents respected. The day after hostilities began in that city carrier-based Japanese aeroplanes were sent out to destroy the nascent Chinese air force, and some of the aeroplanes, painted with Chinese emblems, destroyed many Chinese aircraft that failed to take off in time.[1] During the initial stage of the war, the Chinese air force did well in the air as long as planes and pilots lasted. Eventually the overwhelming numerical superiority of the Japanese prevailed, and Japan obtained complete control of the air. On the ground it was the same story. Chinese forces fought well for almost three months in Shanghai until they were flanked by the invaders who had landed near Hangchow. They retreated hastily to Nanking which was quickly surrounded by the Japanese. The fall of that city was followed by what has been called the rape of Nanking. For a whole week's period, the victorious Japanese plagued the city with plunder, rape, and mass murder. Thousands of civilians were slaughtered in cold blood, in addition to countless numbers of surrendered soldiers.[2]

After the capture of Nanking Japan waited for China to sue for

[1] In the afternoon of August 14, 1937, the author was playing with other boys in the family backyard when he saw two single-engined planes fly over the house roof. The planes flew so low that the Chinese emblems on the planes were clearly visible. The boys jumped and waved. A few minutes later bombs were dropped on the nearby airport, and the city was in a panic. The magistrate ordered the evacuation of all residents to the countryside, as he was afraid that the Japanese planes would come back to bombard the city. The Japanese planes, however, did not come back that evening. They waited until the Japanese had captured Shanghai. Then they destroyed the city (Kwangteh, Anhwei Province) with incendiary bombs.

[2] How far man can degenerate during the time of war may well be illustrated by the following incident. After the capture of Nanking two Japanese soldiers entered a murder contest, each claiming that he could kill more in a given day than the other. In the morning they went for a killing spree and met again in the evening to compare statistics, each claiming several hundred murdered men, women, and children to his credit. As their "heroic deeds" were also described in detail in the Japanese press, the Chinese government, after the end of the war, insisted on the return of the two "heroes" to be tried as war criminals. The two Japanese said that they had done this only to impress their girl friends at home. On their way to the execution ground they shouted repeatedly: "Long live the friendship between China and Japan!"

peace, but Chiang Kai-shek refused to oblige. The China of 1937 was completely different from that of the nineteenth century when the capture of a few key cities by a foreign power would usually bring about China's surrender. More than three decades of nationalistic indoctrination had thoroughly changed the mental outlook of every Chinese, and no political leader within the Nationalist government dared to speak openly for a negotiated peace, whatever his private opinion. Instead, he spoke bravely of the scorching of every inch of earth before the advancing invaders and of China's ultimate victory, however remote it might be. Facing a stubborn Chiang, Japan announced early in 1938 that it would no longer deal with him. In the fall of that year Japan renewed its offensive. Canton fell on October 21, and Hankow, the provisional capital after the fall of Nanking, was captured by the invaders on October 25. Still refusing to surrender, Chiang moved his capital to Chungking. The frustrated Japanese, who had wished to put a quick end to the "China Incident" so that they could concentrate their efforts on their prospective, more formidable enemies such as the Soviet Union and the United States, decided to create their own Chinese leaders to deal with. They created two puppet regimes, one for North China with its capital at Peking and one for the Yangtze region with its capital at Nanking. Yet they were unable to persuade any prominent Chinese, not even the old warlord Wu P'ei-fu, to head the two puppet governments. Their fortunes in this respect took a turn for the better in December, 1938, when Wang Ching-wei, a high-ranking Nationalist official, deserted his own government at Chungking to collaborate with the enemy. Wang, a long time disciple of Sun Yat-sen, made the important move on the ground that continuous resistance against Japan was hopeless and suicidal and that by cooperating with Japan he might be able to mitigate the harsh Japanese rule in the occupied areas. He did not know then that World War II would break out in Europe in a few months. Nor had he any idea that he would be treated as merely another puppet once he was installed as "President of China." Within the occupied territories the Japanese organized development companies to explore and exploit China's natural resources. The Chinese refused to cooperate in this endeavor and used such negative methods as work stoppage and sabotage to defeat practically every Japanese move. Thus, despite great efforts, the utilization of Chinese resources to meet Japan's military and financial needs was largely unsuccessful.

By the end of 1939, two years after the outbreak of hostilities, Japan had conquered the northeastern one-third of the country, the most populous and productive region in China. By then Japan had overextended itself and its forces were spread too thin. The battle line remained substantially the same until towards the end of the war when Japan made the final attempt to force China to surrender by penetrating deep into Kwangsi and Kweichow. After the outbreak of World War II in Septem-

MAP 32
CHINA: 1939-1940
Areas under Japanese Occupation

0   300   600
Scale of Miles

Peiping

YALU RIVER

OCCUPIED

Yenan

YELLOW RIVER

Yellow
Sea

FREE   CHINA

CHINA   Nanking

Hankow   YANGTZE RIVER   Shanghai

Chungking

East
China
Sea

SI RIVER

Amoy

Swatow

Canton

ber, 1939, Japan had other enemies to think about, and the "China Incident" became more and more a liability. As for China, it was nearly
exhausted. It could not launch a massive offensive on its own, though by
its very existence it was able to tie down a large number of Japanese
troops on Chinese soil. A stalemate was thus reached, without the prospect of a decisive victory for either side. Meanwhile Japan, with complete

control of the air, continued to send planes to bomb Chungking, a terror technique designed to force Chiang out of the war. Chungking, China's wartime capital, is a mountainous city on the upper Yangtze. During the war the Chinese dug into the mountains and constructed numerous connecting tunnels as air shelters. When the sun rose, the air raid alarm sounded and everyone entered the tunnels, only to emerge after the sunset when the Japanese planes had gone. One summer day, while enemy aeroplanes were still overhead, people were pushing one another towards the tunnel gates which were locked and guarded by soldiers. The soldiers, under the orders of their commander, refused to open the gates until the air was clear of enemy planes. When they finally opened the gates, they saw nothing except dead or half-dead bodies in the tunnels. Anywhere between 5,000 and 10,000 persons were reported to have suffocated to death on this occasion.

As the best troops of the Szechuan warlords had been sent to the front at the beginning of the war and were destroyed by the Japanese, the Nationalist government was able to move to that province without encountering much opposition. Szechuan, in fact, was the economic as well as the political center of unoccupied China. Before the fall of such industrial cities as Shanghai and Hankow, the Chinese had managed to move some of their industrial plants to the interior where they were reassembled for renewed production. They were carried by river boats and by animal and human strength, since there was not a single operative railroad within the unoccupied areas. These plants enabled the Chinese to continue the manufacturing of small arms and daily necessities such as soap and matches. The greatest difficulty was of course the supply of trucks and gasoline because the Chinese did not produce the former and had only a limited supply of the latter. Transportation was a serious problem, and every old motor vehicle was patched up again and again to keep it moving. Many trucks were converted into alcohol and charcoal powered vehicles; they did not move as fast as they should, but they moved.

As the Nationalist government moved to the interior, so did China's better universities. The Peking University was merged with two sister universities of North China and, renamed the Southwestern University, found its new home at Kunming. The National Central University was moved from Nanking to Chungking, and the National Chekiang University, after a long and eventful journey, finally settled down at Tsungyi in Kweichow, hundreds of miles away from its original home in Hangchow. Two students from these three universities, then operating under the most difficult circumstances, eventually became China's first Nobel Prize winners. Thanks to the richness of the Szechuan soil, there was no starvation on a mass scale, as had often been the case in North China. However, there was a great shortage of industrial products.

For interior China, the war was not without its compensating factors. The arrival of new industries from the coastal areas gave this region a new orientation in economic life; it was hoped that a more balanced economy could be achieved even after the coastal Chinese returned home at the end of the war. Culturally, the interior region had been less advanced than the coastal areas. The arrival of eastern universities such as those mentioned above slowly raised the educational standard of the area, and parents did not have to send their children afar to receive the best kind of education then available. As the institutions of higher learning improved, they eventually benefited secondary and primary schools, since better teachers became available. Socially, the impact was even greater. The war had increased geographical mobility and brought together people of different regions. Provincialism which had always been strong in China was now greatly reduced, and people were more inclined to think of themselves as Chinese rather than as Cantonese or Szechuanese. Though friction did occasionally occur between the interior and coastal Chinese, it never reached serious proportions. In fact there was a harmony far beyond any previous expectations. Warlordism was by and large eliminated, and the Nationalist regime was perhaps the most enlightened the interior Chinese had seen for a long time. For example, opium addiction which had been common before the war was now vigorously suppressed. New hospitals, public or private, were established to attend to the needs of the addicts, though the supply of drugs and medicine was a serious problem. Opium traders, once they were caught, could expect long imprisonment or capital punishment.

Before December, 1941, the Chinese hope for an ultimate victory was not more than an unshakable faith; it bore no relation to a realistic appraisal of the existing domestic and international situation. China had been pushed towards the poor, interior regions; economically and militarily, it had a difficult time maintaining itself, let alone launch an offensive to recover the lost territories. To be sure, China received some outside help, first from the Soviet Union and then from the United States. The American help consisted of lend-lease aid, technical advisers, and the famed Flying Tigers, an American volunteer air force formed by Claire Chennault to challenge the Japanese domination of the air. This help prevented a bad situation from deteriorating faster; it deteriorated nevertheless. When the United States entered the war against Japan after Pearl Harbor and officially became China's ally, the international situation, if not the domestic one, completely changed. For one thing, China then no longer fought alone. Though there was no immediate relief, there was a real hope for the future for the first time since the war began. Despite the initial setbacks which the United States and Great Britain suffered in the Western Pacific, there was no question in the Chinese mind that the allies would win because, for one thing, the alternative was simply unthinkable.

Whatever doubt they might have had before about ultimate victory, they did not have it any more.

After Pearl Harbor American aid, in the form of military and financial assistance, became much more substantial. Believing that Chinese soldiers, properly trained and equipped, could make a great contribution to the defeat of Japan, President Franklin D. Roosevelt ordered the delivery of military equipment to China and a training program for Chinese soldiers. A financial grant of $500,000,000 was a great help in stabilizing the Chinese currency at a time when a runaway inflation, rather than any Japanese offensive, had become the major concern. The man sent by the President to implement American policy was General Joseph Stilwell who arrived in China early in 1942. His major objective was to hold Burma so as to keep open the Burma Road over which, it was hoped, American supplies would be transported to Chungking. Burma fell to Japan despite his efforts, and American supplies then had to be flown over "the Hump" (the Himalayas) from India. The amount of military equipment thus supplied could not be large, and to make the situation worse, the overall strategy as decided in Washington and London was "Europe first, the Pacific Ocean area second, and the China-Burma-India theatre last in terms of priorities."

The Sino-American cooperation was not without its difficulties. Soon after Stilwell's arrival, disagreement developed between him and Chiang Kai-shek. This disagreement involved not only a conflict in personalities but also a basic difference in policy. Stilwell, a soldier who placed victory against Japan above anything else, insisted on the arming of all anti-Japanese elements in China, including the Communists. Chiang, more a statesman than a soldier, saw easily the serious consequence to his Nationalist government if the Chinese Communists were armed with American weapons. Though the Kuomintang and the Communists were officially allies, tensions between them had been slowly building up by 1942. Eventually Chiang insisted on Stilwell's dismissal, and in October, 1944, Roosevelt agreed and appointed a more diplomatic general, Albert Wedemeyer, as his successor. Chiang and the new American general got along beautifully. The Ledo Road (later renamed as Stilwell Road) was then constructed, linking Assam (India) and the upper Burma Road in Yunnan. A large quantity of American equipment came in; as a result China was able to create new armed divisions with modern weapons. Before they could be committed to the battlefield against the Japanese, the atomic bombs were dropped, and the war was over. Later, these divisions were used against the Chinese Communists when the civil war broke out again.

Chinese victories were much more impressive on the diplomatic front than they were on the battlefield. In January, 1943, the United States and Great Britain concluded treaties with China providing for the immediate relinquishment of extraterritorial rights and the settlement of related matters. This meant that the Chinese courts, for the first time in one hundred years, had jurisdiction over British and American citizens in China; it also meant that the powers concerned could no longer maintain troops on Chinese soil without Chinese consent and that the remaining concessions would be returned to China. The last remnants of the unequal treaties were thus eliminated. Later in the same year, urged by President Roosevelt, Congress passed a law which permitted a small number of Chinese—105, to be exact—to migrate to the United States as immigrants each year. For the first time since 1882 (Chinese Exclusion Law) a Chinese could be naturalized as an American citizen. China's greatest diplomatic victory, however, was scored at Cairo, where Roosevelt, Winston Churchill, and Chiang Kai-shek met in November, 1943, to discuss policy matters concerning Japan. The policy statement, known as the Cairo Declaration, pledged the allies to continue the war until Japan accepted "unconditional surrender." Manchuria, Taiwan, and the Pescadores would be returned to China, and Korea would become free and independent "in due course." When the news of the agreement reached Chungking, never had there been a foreigner so popular as Franklin D. Roosevelt. And as far as Chiang Kai-shek was concerned, his popularity and prestige reached a new height.

The enthusiasm, however, proved to be somewhat premature. In February, 1945, Roosevelt, Churchill, and Stalin met at Yalta to discuss the final phase of the war with regard to Germany and Japan. In exchange for the Soviet Union's promise to enter the war against Japan "two or three months after Germany had surrendered," the two Western statesmen promised Stalin the following concessions: (1) Outer Mongolia over which China claimed jurisdiction would become independent; (2) Dairen would be internationalized and Port Arthur would be leased to the U.S.S.R. as a naval base; and (3) the Chinese Eastern Railroad and the South Manchuria Railroad would be jointly operated by China and the Soviet Union and "the preeminent interests of the Soviet Union shall be safeguarded." In other words, Manchuria was to become a Soviet sphere of influence, though "China shall retain full sovereignty" in that area. The special privileges which Lenin had condemned and renounced in 1919 were returned to his successor Stalin with extra bonus. Since the Yalta Agreement was reached without Chinese knowledge, "the President [Roosevelt] will take measures in order to obtain this concurrence [from Chiang Kai-shek] on advice from Marshal Stalin." Chiang was not informed of the contents of this agreement until months later; when the Chinese people learned of them after the war, there was strong resentment. However, as long as China depended upon the United States for military and diplomatic support, there was nothing it could do with regard to the agreement made by the Big Three. In July, 1945, Chiang sent his brother-in-law T. V. Soong to Moscow to negotiate a treaty with the Soviet Union. The treaty called for China's recognition of the independence of Outer Mongolia "if a plebiscite indicates that result" and the implementation of other Yalta terms. In return the Russians promised assistance and support for the Nationalist government as headed by Chiang Kai-shek.

Following the dropping of the first atomic bomb on Hiroshima on August 6, the Soviet army marched into Manchuria. The Japanese army offered little resistance, and the invaders soon took over Manchuria. After Japan surrendered on August 12, the Russians were in a good position to help their comrades, the Chinese Communists.

COMMUNIST ASCENDENCY

After the war broke out in July, 1937, the Communist army was renamed the Eighth Route Army and fought side by side with the Nationalists against the Japanese invaders. Since they had no heavy equipment, their contribution to the war efforts was confined largely to guerrilla activities. The aggressiveness of a common enemy had temporarily forced the two old rivals (Nationalists and Communists) to cooperate; but, as the war reached a stalemate towards the end of 1939, the old enmity returned and tensions began to develop. From hindsight it seems that their cooperation had never been intended to be more than a temporary arrangement; distrust and hatred of long standing could not be wiped out simply by a joint declaration of good will. Early in 1941 the tensions which had been slowly building up flashed into the first open conflict as Nationalist troops attacked and partly wiped out the Communist New Fourth Army, a guerrilla force then operating in the Lower Yangtze. This turned out to be only the beginning of a long struggle to come. When the United States entered the war after Pearl Harbor, both sides acted as if the war against Japan had already been won, and they began to think in terms of a postwar struggle between themselves. From the Nationalist point of view the areas controlled by the Communists should be contained and if possible reduced. The Communists, on the other hand, were anxious to bring as many areas under their domination as possible, so that they would be in a better position to challenge the Nationalist authority when Japan was out of the picture. Both sides were more concerned with their struggle against each other than their common war against Japan, and they deployed their forces accordingly. When General Stilwell suggested the arming of the Communists with American weapons, the reaction of Chiang Kai-shek was predictable.

Knowing what lay ahead, Mao Tse-tung planned his strategy accordingly. He was reported to have ordered his comrades to devote 70 percent of their energy to Communist expansion and 20 percent to "coping with" the Kuomintang, leaving 10 percent to be used against Japan. He might not have used exactly the same words, but the policy he followed during the war coincided well with what he had allegedly said. The Japanese invaders could at best control large cities, strategic points, and main lines of communication and transportation after they had driven out the Nationalists. For one thing, they simply did not have enough forces to cover every town and village. The puppet Chinese force they created was anything but reliable; the presence of the Japanese and their Chinese collaborators in the countryside was bitterly resented by the villagers. This situation offered the Communists a unique opportunity. They infiltrated the Japanese lines in small groups and went to the villages to organize. They called for a united effort against Japan and brought under their banner people from all walks of life, including former Kuomintang officials. Since they had abandoned their extreme methods such as land confiscation, even conservative landlords chose to cooperate with them. Their basic support came of course from the peasants who constituted the overwhelming majority of the people in the rural areas. To win their support, the Communists lowered rent and interest rates and encouraged the organization of cooperatives and the establishment of schools. They even allowed peasants to choose their own administrative officials on the village level, while reserving for themselves the power of control. Their efforts did not go unrewarded; to the villagers, including many landlords, the Communists were patriotic Chinese who desired nothing for themselves except the nation's survival. As they continued their efforts, large areas within the occupied territory were brought under their control. The Japanese held the big cities, but the Communists dominated the countryside. However, when the Communists attempted to extend their organizational work to areas nominally within the Nationalist control, the Nationalists struck back, as they had done in the case of the New Fourth Army early in 1941.

The physical struggle between the two parties on the wide expanse of China was accompanied by an ideological battle of sorts. Mao Tse-tung and Chiang Kai-shek spoke out from their respective capitals, Yenan and Chungking, about the kind of society they wished to create for the Chinese people. Mao, in a major speech made early in 1940, outlined the New Democracy which he said was an integration of the truths of Marxism and China's nationalist characteristics. There was no place for doctrinaire Marxists in China, he declared. In economic matters he pledged his support to Sun Yat-sen's principle of people's livelihood. Big banks and big industrial and commercial enterprises should be owned by the government. However, the government should not take over other capitalist production that "cannot dominate the livelihood of the people." It would "adopt certain necessary measures to confiscate the land of landlords and distribute it to those peasants having no land or only a little land, abolish the feudal relations in the rural areas, and turn the land into the private property of the peasants." In other words, there would be no compromise with the landlords.

Who, then, should wield political power in the New Democracy? Mao divided the existing governments in the world into three groups: (1) "republics under bourgeoisie dictatorship" such as most of the Western countries, (2) "republics under the dictatorship of the proletariat" such as the Soviet Union, and (3) "republics under the joint dictatorship of several revolutionary classes." China, said he, belonged to the third category, where the power of the government should be vested in the proletariat, the peasantry, the intelligentsia, and other sections of the petty bourgeoisie. Lest anyone forget that he was a Communist, he added that the "several revolutionary classes" should be led by the proletariat, even though from the vantage point on top of his Yenan cave there was not a single proletarian in sight. The kind of government described in the third category, he continued, was not only correct for China; it was "the transitional form of state to be adopted by revolutionaries in colonial and semicolonial countries." "So long as there are revolutions in colonies or semicolonies, the state and political form will of necessity be basically the same in nature, *i.e.*, a new democratic state under the joint dictatorship of several anti-imperialist classes." The New Democracy, however, was the party's present or minimum program. The ultimate objective was the creation of a socialist or Communist state. Mao did not say when it would be the most propitious time to implement socialism or communism. For the time being, he was most interested in making his program moderate enough to attract the support of the largest possible number of people.

In 1943 Chiang Kai-shek published two books in succession, *China's Destiny* and *Chinese Economic Ideology*. Like Mao, he blamed imperialism and the unequal treaties for China's past ills and pledged the implementation of Sun Yat-sen's three principles of the people. Whereas Mao regarded such implementation as appropriate only during what he called the transitional period, Chiang considered it the final fulfillment of China's political and economic goals. The theoretical basis of the new society was not such alien ideologies as Marxism or *laissez-faire*; it was such ancient virtues as loyalty and filial piety. Marxism with its theory of class struggle had no place in China which had always been a society of cooperation and mutual help, and to preach class struggle was to artificially create class hatred which had never existed. On the other hand, Chiang had no use for such Western virtues as individualism, because in his opinion, they were motivated by man's selfishness and could not be properly called virtues. Private enterprises were allowed, but they should be carefully controlled so as to protect the people from the evil of economic exploitation. Politically, the new society should practice democratic centralism. Power was to be created by a democratic process, but once created, it should command the obedience and respect of the people as a whole. Only when the government was "able," said Chiang, could it successfully carry out Sun Yat-sen's three principles of the people.

Ideologies notwithstanding, the outcome of the struggle between the Nationalists and the Communists was to be decided in a contest of physical strength. At the end of World War II, the Communists controlled large areas inside the former Japanese-occupied territory and within marching distance of some of the large eastern cities, whereas the main strength of the Nationalist army was far away in the interior. The Allied Command ordered Japanese troops not to surrender to any Chinese groups except those authorized by Chiang Kai-shek. When the Communists attempted to seize some of the major cities, the Japanese repulsed them. Thanks to American help, the American equipped Nationalist Chinese divisions were airlifted to these cities, disarmed the Japanese, and took over control. The Communists protested, but there was not much they could do.

In Manchuria, however, the situation was somewhat different. The Russians, who had been scheduled to withdraw from Manchuria "three months after the defeat of Japan," decided to stay longer. They used this valuable time to strip Manchuria of industrial equipment to be shipped to Russia as "war booty" and also to provide a protective wing for the activities of their Chinese comrades. They turned over the surrendered Japanese arms to the Chinese Communists who thereby for the first time were equipped with modern weapons, including tanks and heavy artillery pieces. By doing this the Russians violated the Sino-Soviet treaty of 1945 as well as the Yalta Agreement which specified that they should not assist any Chinese group other than the Nationalist government. With such assistance the Chinese Communists were eventually able to drive the Nationalists from Manchuria.

China's internal development during and immediately after World War II was a great disappointment to the United States which had been hoping for the emergence of a "friendly, unified China as a stabilizing influence in the Far East." Largely through Roosevelt's insistence and efforts China was elevated to be one of the "Big Five" and later became a permanent member of the Security Council of the United Nations. As the prospect of civil war loomed larger, the United States government instructed its Ambassador to China, Patrick T. Hurley, to play an active role in bringing the Nationalists and the Communists together. As a result of his efforts Mao Tse-tung arrived at Chungking on August 28, 1945, to confer with Chiang Kai-shek for a peaceful settlement of their differences. Mao's six-week stay in Chungking did not bring about any constructive results, as the two sides were far apart in their views about the methods to

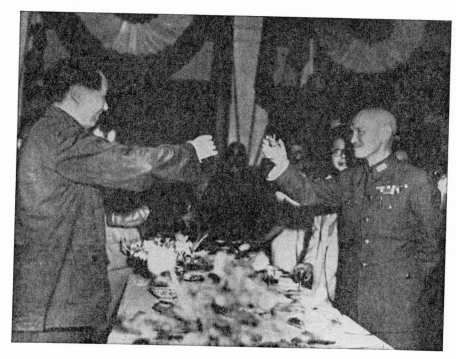

MAO TSE-TUNG (LEFT) AND CHIANG KAI-SHEK DRINKING A TOAST   This picture was taken in the fall of 1945 after Mao Tse-tung had arrived in Chungking to talk with Chiang Kai-shek on the terms to organize a coalition government. During his stay in the Nationalist wartime capital Mao's personal safety was said to have been guaranteed by the American government. The negotiations between the two Chinese leaders came to nought. Four years later, the Communists overran mainland China and drove Chiang Kai-shek to his island stronghold, Taiwan.

be used in unifying China. For one thing, the Nationalists insisted on the complete integration of the Communist army with the Nationalist force, a condition which the Communists would not accept. Later, when they agreed to the existence of a separate Communist army, there was no agreement as to how large such an army should be. The Nationalists would not agree to more than twenty divisions, and the Communists would not be satisfied with less than forty-three. As a result, they were hopelessly deadlocked. The nature of their disagreement would mean that even if a coalition government had been formed, it would not have been a national government in the true sense of that term, because no government could function "nationally" as long as there was a separate military force operating within its territory over which it had no control.

In December, 1945, the United States proposed the convocation of a national conference to end the civil war, while pledging continuous assistance to the Nationalist government as the only legal government of China. Early in 1946 President Harry S. Truman sent General of the Army George C. Marshall as his special ambassador to China with special instruction to effect a compromise between the Nationalists and the Communists which, it was hoped, would eventually lead to the establishment of a democratic coalition government. Marshall's efforts came to nought and he returned to the United States early in the following year. Before his departure, he blamed the recalcitrance of both parties for the failure and regarded the assumption of leadership by the liberals as the only hope for the future. The liberals, consisting mostly of intellectuals who had received their education in Europe and America, had their own organization, called the Democratic League. They had good intentions and constructive ideas, but they lacked one thing most essential in Chinese politics: an independent army. Nevertheless, they played an important part in the political consultative conference which came into session early in 1946. The conference, called to "broaden the democratic basis of the Nationalist government," eventually broke down as the Nationalists and the Communists could not agree to the composition of the state council, the policy-making organ in the proposed coalition government. When the political consultative conference was finally dissolved, the members of the Democratic League were forced to choose sides. As one might expect, the leftists switched their loyalty to the Communists, and the rightists to the Nationalists. With the departure of Marshall and the dissolution of the political consultative conference the civil war was renewed in earnest.

What followed is a familiar story. At the beginning of the renewed civil war, Mao Tse-tung warned his followers that there was a long struggle ahead. He predicted that it would take five years before they could match the Nationalists in military strength and that they would triumph at the end of ten years. In all likelihood, his quick victories on the battlefield amazed even himself. Manchuria fell to the Communists in the fall of 1948, and this was followed by the conquest of North China. Sometimes entire divisions switched to the Communist side and carried with them their American weapons. One of the best Kuomintang armies of some 300,000 strong which had been pampered for more than ten years just for this occasion evaporated with hardly a fight. As the Communists marched southward and threatened Nanking, the Nationalists decided to make a strong stand at Hsuchow (northern Kiangsu) where one of the most decisive battles was fought. There was heroism on both sides, but the Nationalist troops went to defeat when the flanking Communists cut off their logistical support. After this battle Chiang resigned from the presidency and his successor Li Tsung-jen proceeded to negotiate peace with the Communists. The Communists demanded virtually unconditional sur-

A GATE STRUCTURE LEADING TO THE INNER CITY OF PEKING   The Chinese characters in the background read: "Eliminate anarchy to reconstruct the country; exterminate bandits (Communists) to save the people." The city was then under the Nationalists' control. In the foreground is the ornate *p'ai-lou*, or arch.

render and the punishment of "war criminals" headed by Chiang Kai-shek. As there was no common basis for a negotiated peace, the Communist offensive was resumed in April, 1949. The capture of Nanking was followed by the surrender of Shanghai one month later. By the end of that year all of China proper was brought under Communist control. Meanwhile, Mao Tse-tung and his colleagues proclaimed the establishment of a People's Republic on October 1, 1949.

THE DEFEAT OF THE NATIONALISTS

The causes of the Nationalists' defeat were many-fold, and we can easily overemphasize one at the expense of others which were perhaps equally valid. Just as in many other wars, the weaknesses of the vanquished combined with the strength of the victor to bring about the final outcome. Moreover, there were factors working to the advantage or disadvantage of one side or the other that were beyond the control of either. The Japanese invasions, for instance, helped the Communist cause immensely, even though they were never meant that way by the Japanese. In the final analysis, however, the blame has to be placed upon the Nationalists themselves. At the end of World War II they were far superior to the Communists militarily. It is clear that the subsequent change of political fortunes was due to factors other than the military, and that these factors were advantageous to the Communists.

Politically, prior to 1948 when a constitution went into effect, the Nationalist regime operated under the theory of political tutelage. The power of governing was vested in the Kuomintang, and all important government officials were appointed by and responsible to the party. In view of the Chinese circumstances (the lack of a democratic tradition, for instance) a great deal could be said for this theory, and it could have worked had the Kuomintang remained the dynamic, revolutionary party conceived by Sun Yat-sen. No political party is better than its members, and the members, being human, are subject to human frailties. Once power was secured, the Kuomintang leaders were more interested in the power itself and what it could bring to them than in the social and economic programs which they had pledged themselves to carry out. Had there been popular elections threatening to oust them or an opposition party to serve as a watchdog, this abuse could have been reduced if not prevented, but the theory of political tutelage under which the Nationalist government operated ruled out either of these two possibilities. Party leaders became the power elite, and not subject to popular control, gradually they lost touch with the masses and became isolated from them. As the party leaders were essentially the same people from 1927 to 1949, so, by and large, were the government officials who formulated and carried out policies. A change of cabinet meant no more than a reshuffling of a few "infallible" men, and public offices were granted as a reward for loyalty to party leadership rather than party programs. Among the best qualifications that many of these high-ranking officials possessed was that they were once members of the Alliance and had heard an excellent speech made by Sun Yat-sen. To be sure, not all of them were bad men. Yet by occupying these high positions without either the inclination or the ability to accomplish something worthwhile, they frustrated the ambitions of younger aspirants to leadership, and in that sense they were harmful to their own party.

A political organization such as this inevitably encouraged the maintenance of the *status quo* and discouraged social and economic reforms. A man in power would naturally abstain from doing anything that might jeopardize his own position. To assure his security in power, he measured the worth of his subordinates not in accordance with their ability or performance but upon the evidence of their loyalty to him. It was not an ordinary kind of loyalty: it was the sort of blind, absolute obedience such as that once given to the ancient emperors. By insisting on such a condition for employment or promotion, the Kuomintang leaders isolated themselves from the country's most talented people who naturally had independent opinions of their own. Moreover, a man of strong moral fibre would not humiliate himself by being so slavish. As personal loyalty was generally emphasized, there was a proliferation of political cliques within the Kuomintang; each clique was built around one or two party leaders who evaluated and rewarded men in accordance with their loyalty towards them. Above these cliques was Chiang Kai-shek who was "the greatest, the wisest, and the most virtuous." Personal loyalty was of course not a bad thing in itself as long as the followers had other qualifications as well. Only when it became the only virtue overshadowing all others was it an abuse. A man could be corrupt and incompetent, but he could still hold his office as long as his loyalty to his superior was not in doubt.

Thus overemphasized, the expression of loyalty often degenerated into a shameless contest of adulation and flattery. Many clever but unscrupulous men literally flattered their way to some of the highest positions in the land. In this respect we cannot give a better example than by citing the career of a man named Chang Chih-chung. An ex-policeman who used to direct traffic at Hankow, Chang had no great talent or ability as far as we know. Yet in a short time he rose to become a general of the army, a governor, and a member of the Central Executive Committee of the Kuomintang. During the Japanese war he was given a military command to defend Changsha. He set fire to the city and fled as fast as he could even though there was not a ghost of the enemy nearby. Despite vigorous protests from the Hunanese who had seen their beloved capital reduced to ashes, he was not brought to trial; instead, he rose to even higher and more responsible positions. Why was he not punished? Because, said his apologists, his loyalty to the Leader was invaluable. In 1949 when he was sent by the Nationalist government to negotiate a truce with the Communists, he quickly switched sides and proclaimed that Mao Tse-tung, after all, was the true savior of China. Chang, unfortunately, was not an isolated case; there were thousands of his type within the Nationalist government.

In rural areas the Kuomintang members were inevitably the "recognized leaders of each community," namely, the gentry. The party did not attempt to attract membership from among the peasants and it did not have peasant members. To the peasants the local Kuomintang headquarters was just another government they had to support, if they noticed its existence at all. The new gentry in the countryside was different from the scholar-gentry of the old type whose members, because of their Confucian training, had a strong sense of obligation towards the less fortunate peasants. Since Confucian virtues had become "old-fashioned," the members of the new gentry enjoyed power and used that power for their own advantage without feeling an "old-fashioned" obligation. They could then exploit the hapless peasants with a clear conscience since they may also have gone to Western schools and heard of such ideas as *laissez-faire*. Whatever laws the central government might have enacted to improve the lot of peasants (such as the land law of 1930), those laws could not be carried out without the cooperation of the gentry class. Since their implementation worked to the disadvantage of this class, it is not difficult to understand the hostile attitude of this class towards these laws. The gentry obstructed, stalled, and used every means available to see to it that these laws were not strictly enforced. Usually the gentry members succeeded.

The accumulated evil of a bureaucratic rule became all too evident at the end of the Japanese war. Thousands of Kuomintang officials took the first aeroplanes to the formerly occupied areas to perform the function of *chieh-shou* (literally, take and receive) which in numerous cases was a legalized robbery of the people in the occupied areas. The situation was most serious in Taiwan where it eventually provoked an open revolt. These carpetbaggers who had been regarded as liberators from Japanese oppression behaved like conquerors and damaged the reputation of the Nationalist regime beyond repair.

In the countryside the landlords who had been driven out by the Japanese came home to reclaim their land which was now tilled by those left behind. By accusing those who had been left behind as collaborators, these landlords not only regained their lost land but often enlarged it too, as they could easily force the "collaborators" to sell out at a nominal price. The once tranquil countryside became a battleground of land grabbing, setting relatives against relatives and friends against friends. Whoever won, the peasants could not see any difference. Much land had been laid waste during the war, and without proper care land productivity had been greatly reduced. Yet the landlords, old or new, demanded the payment of the same amount of rent. In many cases they demanded the payment of all rents that were due but were not collected during the war years. By spring when the sowing season began, most of the peasants had exhausted their food supply, and to borrow from the landlords they had to pay an annual interest of something like 200 percent. In a more or less typical case a peasant who borrowed one bushel of rice in May would have to pay the lender two bushels in September when harvests were collected. Once he paid his debt, he was on a starvation diet. Whether there had been Communists or not, the situation had become too serious to continue.

What was happening in the countryside was either unknown or brushed aside as insignificant by the Nationalist hierarchy. At this crucial moment the formulation of policy was in the hands of a group of professional soldiers who looked at everything in military terms and resolved to solve every problem by military methods. It never occurred to them that communism was more a socio-economic than a military problem and that to eliminate communism one had to eliminate the social and economic ills upon which communism thrived. Those who were not military-minded enough were accused of being soft on communism and were dealt with accordingly. The militarists did not succeed in eliminating communism, but they did succeed in silencing those who believed that there were better, more effective ways of combatting communism.

The social and economic ills were reflected most poignantly in the runaway inflation. The war against Japan had been financed largely through inflation, especially during the latter stage of the war when the most productive areas in China had been lost to the Japanese. The ratio of exchange between Chinese and American dollars was 3 to 1 before the war began in 1937. In August, 1945, when the war ended, the official rate was 20 to 1, though the black market price, which reflected more correctly the true worth of the Chinese dollar, was many times larger. Early in 1946 the official rate was raised to 2,020 to 1 and was again raised to 73,000 to 1 at the end of that year. By the summer of 1948 to print a paper bill cost more than the face value it bore, and the government lost money every time a piece of paper money came off the printing press. Early in 1949 shortly before the government made a last attempt to reform the currency, one American dollar was worth 1.2 million Chinese dollars. According to independent newspapers, the maintenance of an official exchange rate which bore no relation to reality enabled a few high government officials and their relatives to enrich themselves. They purchased American dollars according to the official rate and then resold them in the black market where the exchange rate was many times larger. By repeating the same process they made themselves fabulously wealthy. It was widely rumoured that a sizable portion of the American financial aid designed to stabilize the Chinese currency reappeared in America and other foreign countries under private accounts and was invested in such profitable businesses as oil wells in Texas.

The runaway inflation prevented capital from being invested in industrial enterprises which produced goods and created jobs. As it continued, a businessman found it more profitable to hoard than to produce. When every businessman thought along the same line and acted accordingly, hoarding itself became a cause of inflation, as prices were forced to go up when businessmen refused to part with their merchandise. By 1949, shortly before the Communists took over, a decent meal cost a million dollars, and a pair of shoes several millions. In the countryside, people resorted to barter trade, since they no longer trusted the government's "ghost money." In the Lower Yangtze, for instance, every salable product, from chairs to chickens, was priced in terms of rice. Thanks to the thoroughness of the government's currency reform in the 1930's, rarely could one find a Mexican dollar which had been in circulation before the currency reform.[1] Rice, bulky and perishable, was not the best kind of medium of exchange, but the peasants had to do what they could under the existing circumstances. After four thousand years of civilization, they went back to the prehistoric ways.

Despite what has been said above, the Nationalist regime was perhaps no better or worse than most Chinese regimes in history. What made its shortcomings so striking was that in the twentieth century the requirements for a good government were a great deal higher and more substantial. The numerous problems a modern government had to face were also more complicated. The broadening of education made people more politically conscious and consequently less fatalistic. For every problem they demanded a solution, and solutions were difficult to find. The Western impact brought with it the force of nationalism which, in its modern form, had never been in existence before. After a century of humiliation at the hands of the Western powers and Japan, people demanded the abolition of the unequal treaties, the recovery of lost territories, and the restoration of China as an independent, sovereign state. In view of China's political and military weaknesses these were difficult goals to reach. The Western impact also brought the concept of democracy, and authoritarian rule was no longer taken for granted. People became more articulate in demanding that government existed for the governed only and that their voice be heard in the council of government. Right or wrong, many believed that the Nationalist government was too slow in achieving either the nationalistic or the democratic goal.

While the question as to whether the Nationalists or the Communists were more nationalistic or democratic was a subject of great controversy, what tipped the balance in favor of the Communists was their success in convincing the peasants that they could do better for them in the field of social justice and economic welfare. In the countryside the most serious had been and still was the land problem. All attempts to resolve it had failed, the last of these attempts having been made by the Taipings.[2] The Communists resolved it by liquidating landlords and dividing the expropriated land among the peasants. This was not a true solution because the Chinese problem was essentially a problem of shortage rather than of distribution. For the time being, however, their program appealed to the peasants who fought their wars and fought so well that they conquered mainland China for the Communists. Why did the same peasants not fight for the Nationalists? Here we return to one of the basic weaknesses of the Nationalist government: its inability to think in social and economic

---

[1] The Mexican dollars may have been brought to China by the English (who had taken them from the Spanish) in the seventeenth and eighteenth centuries.

[2] See Chapter XII, pp. 400–406.

terms in its anti-Communist crusade. It regarded communism as a military issue which, unfortunately, it was not. If it were, it would have been eliminated a long time ago.

THE NATIONALIST REGIME ON TAIWAN

In the spring of 1949 when it became increasingly clear that mainland China could no longer be defended against the seemingly invincible Communists, Chiang Kai-shek began to move part of the Nationalist troops to Taiwan. Previously he had ordered the transfer of China's gold reserve to the island, and now with the men and the money it was hoped that Taiwan could make a successful last stand against the Communists and perhaps serve as a base of operation for the eventual reconquest of the mainland as well. The hope for the future, however, contrasted sharply with the grimness of the present. The Communists were pushing relentlessly towards the Southwest, and the remaining Nationalist troops were either defeated or chose to surrender without a fight. Li Tsung-jen, then the Acting President, wanted Chiang to send back his troops to hold the Southwest, and Chiang wisely refused, as it was unlikely that any Nationalist forces could stop the Communist advances on the mainland. Taiwan, on the other hand, could be better defended. The Communists had no amphibious forces, and the Nationalists, by virtue of possessing a few naval ships, could give a good account of themselves. The Taiwan Strait, one hundred miles wide, thus saved the Nationalist regime from total extinction.

Gloomy as the domestic situation was, the international situation was even worse. In the summer of 1949 the United States issued the famous *White Paper* in which it placed the blame for the Nationalists' downfall on their own "corruption and incompetence" and adopted the policy of "waiting for the dust to settle." In January, 1950, President Truman said that the United States did not have "any intention of utilizing its armed forces to interfere in the present situation" and would "not provide military aid or advice to the Chinese forces on Formosa." The Nationalist fortunes had never looked worse. There was confusion, uncertainty, and despair. In view of what the Communists had done to the so-called counter-revolutionaries on the mainland, the Nationalists had no illusion about what lay ahead for them if the Communists captured the island. At least two high-ranking Nationalist officials—two of the most decent ones—had committed suicide, and others were prepared for the worst to come. On March 1, 1950, Chiang resumed the presidency after Acting President Li Tsung-jen, who was then staying in the United States to "seek American aid," failed to return. Whatever shortcomings Chiang might have, he was not a quitter. His assumption of leadership inspired confidence and hope among the otherwise dispirited Nationalists. They were all in one ship which had to be kept afloat at all costs. Across the Taiwan Strait on the mainland the Communists amassed a large invasion force. Farther north in Peking the commander-in-chief of the People's Liberation Army, Chu Teh, announced that the urgent task of the nation was to "liberate" Taiwan from the "Chiang Kai-shek clique."

From hindsight it seems that what saved Taiwan from Communist conquest was neither Taipei nor Washington but a miscalculation on the part of Moscow. In June, 1950, North Korea invaded South Korea, and the United States, which had been anything but enthusiastic about the Nationalist regime on Taiwan, was then forced to reverse its policy. It declared that "in these circumstances [North Korean invasion] the occupation of Formosa by Communist forces would be a direct threat to the security of the Pacific area" and ordered the Seventh Fleet to prevent any attack on Taiwan. The intervention by the Chinese Communists in the Korean War and their subsequent animosity towards the United States drew Washington and Taipei closer each day, culminating in the conclusion of a mutual defense treaty in December, 1954. The American government embarked on a program of military and economic assistance which for a thirteen-year period (1950–1963) amounted to more than three billion U.S. dollars. The long-range policy of the United States regarding Taiwan is anything but clear, but in the foreseeable future it is fully committed to the defense of that island and the Pescadores against Communist attack.

The Nationalist regime on Taiwan is noticeably different from what it was on the mainland. Its defeat at the hands of the Communists was not without its blessings. The opportunists who had used their party label to get rich quick or to exercise power for whatever it could bring to themselves were cleaned out under the impact of disaster. Some retired to enjoy their ill-gotten wealth and others were either liquidated by the Communists or became turncoats and joined them. Those on Taiwan knew that they had to make their government either a respectable going concern or to suffer final defeat. Moreover, there were too many people in the world who were anxious to compromise with the Communists at the expense of the Nationalists. To be sure, the regime is not a great democracy in the true sense of that term; it is still a one-party government which tolerates no opposition. Nominally, the highest organ of the government is the National Assembly, consisting of those delegates who had been elected on the mainland and then fled to Taiwan at the end of the civil war. Though they have not seen their constituents since then, they supposedly represent their interests. Somehow the legal fiction has to be maintained because the government claims that it represents all of China, while the Communists on the mainland are merely "bandits." The real power of governing is in the hands of those whom Chiang personally trusts, such as Ch'en Ch'eng who, as the vice president, has all but openly been designated as his successor. They are not bad men by any standards, and they are thoroughly dedicated to their anti-Communist cause.

In recent years the Taiwanese have been given an increasingly important role in governing the island. After fifty years of Japanese rule they welcomed the opportunity of joining their mother country at the end of World War II, only to be shocked by the ruthless behavior of the mainland carpetbaggers headed by the ex-warlord Ch'en Yi who was appointed their first governor. They staged an open revolt early in 1947; the revolt, however, was quickly suppressed by the Nationalist troops. Since then the mainlanders have gone a long way towards placating the injured feelings of the islanders, and there have not been any major incidents. We do not know what the Taiwanese would decide in a plebiscite held to determine their political future. It is reasonable to assume that they would prefer the Nationalist rather than a Communist type of government. Though disagreements between the mainlanders and the Taiwanese do exist, in the long run the problems do not seem so formidable as they did a few years ago, because, despite statements to the contrary, the Taiwanese are racially and culturally Chinese. Today the local governments are by and large in the hands of the Taiwanese, though the government at Taipei, the "national" government, is controlled by the mainlanders. As marriages between the two groups multiply and as their children go to the same schools and are taught the same subjects, it is reasonable to suppose that the superficial differences between these two groups will eventually disappear.

Political stability on Taiwan is accompanied by an economic progress which is equally impressive. To begin with Taiwan is naturally wealthy, as has been pointed out in a previous chapter. During the Japanese occupation, the island was developed industrially as well as agriculturally. Thanks to Chinese diligence and the generous provision of American aid, both agricultural and industrial outputs have far outdistanced peak performances during the Japanese occupation. It is a good example, showing that given an honest and cooperative government, American aid can achieve a great deal. During the last few years the gross national product has been growing at the rate of 7.7 percent a year, and industrial production increased by 11 percent from 1962 to 1963. Per capita income has been rising steadily during the past decade, and the people enjoy a material well-being such as they had never experienced before. This material prosperity is shared by all sections of the population, including the small, independent farmers. As early as 1949 the Nationalist government embarked upon a program of land reform which began with the reduction of rent to 37.5 percent of the main crops. The eventual goal was the full realization of Sun Yat-sen's teaching that "all land belongs to the tillers." Today all but a small fraction of arable land is owned by the tillers, and a large portion of that small fraction is owned by the government. By and large the land reform has been a great success. Had the Nationalist government done the same thing on the mainland, the history of the past forty years might have been remarkably different.

Economically, there are two factors overshadowing the otherwise rosy prospect. One is the continuous increase of population which will eventually cancel any economic progress that can be made. The island (13,866 square miles), less than half the size of South Carolina, supports a population of presently more than eleven million. Sooner or later it will not be able to produce enough food to feed the ever-increasing population. Secondly, the economic progress has been possible largely through American aid. What will the situation be if American aid is suddenly stopped? Will the island's economy be able to stand on its own feet? Moreover, a large portion of the national income is swallowed up by the maintenance of an armed force of some 600,000 men. The maintenance of such a huge force is justified by the necessity of constant readiness for the reconquest of the mainland. Here again the Nationalist government allows political considerations to override the soundness of economic reasoning. In the event of a mainland invasion, the decision is more likely to be made in Washington or Peking than on the island. For the time being, the costly display of an impressive armed force serves no other purpose than to keep a distant hope alive.

℞ xvi

The People's Republic

THE POWER STRUCTURE

On the morning of October 1, 1949, hundreds of thousands of people gathered at the Tien-an-men Square in Peking. Thousands of red flags fluttered against the autumn wind, and a two-hundred-piece band played one martial song after another. The crowd was joyful and anxious. Finally it heard the band play the familiar tune:

> The East is Red;
> The Sun is Rising.
> On the Horizon of China
> Appears the Great Hero Mao Tse-tung.

High on the Tien-an-men Tower a tall, plump man in grey uniform slowly ascended the marble stair towards the central platform decorated

510

STUDENTS PARADE ON THE TIEN-AN-MEN SQUARE Mao Tse-tung's picture appears on the upper left. The Chinese slogans on the wall read: "Long Live the People's Republic of China" and "Long Live the Grand Unity of All People in the World."

with huge red lanterns. Flanked by other dignitaries, he at last reached the central position of the platform and, with a faint smile, turned and waved to the crowd below. Thunderous applause followed which drowned out even the loud band. By then the band had come to the last line of the music:

He is the Great Savior of the People.

Immediately after the last music note subsided, a clear, masculine voice roared from the loudspeaker: "Ladies and Gentlemen, our national anthem." The band struck up again:

Arise, you brave men
Who do not wish to become slaves;
Let us use our blood and flesh
To build a new Great Wall of national defense.

The colorful but solemn ceremony marked officially the beginning of the People's Republic of China, sometimes called Communist China in the Western world. The central figure of the show was Mao Tse-tung who only one year before had predicted that it would take four years for his Communist legions to win the civil war. Now standing on the top of the Tien-an-men Tower where many ancient emperors may have stood before, he must have viewed with great satisfaction his own career, from an insignificant librarian making eight Chinese dollars (U.S. $2.70) a month to the dictator of all China, commanding the absolute obedience of 600 million people. How many people in the world had achieved so much in such a short time? Every place where he had been—the farm where he had once tended his father's pigs, the normal school at which he had once been a student, and the little room where he had once worked as an assistant librarian—was subsequently declared a national shrine. Since the last days of the emperors many people had fought for the position he now held; yet only he had succeeded. Why? For one thing, he knew how to make the finest promises. "We will work bravely and industriously to create our own civilization and happiness and will at the same time promote world peace and freedom. Our nation will never again be an insulted nation. We have stood up." To hundreds of thousands of people who stood on Tien-an-men Square on that memorial day, the sweetest word was perhaps "peace." The war had lasted too long; the sufferings had been too heavy to bear. Was it chance that chose Tien-an-men Square as the place to announce the establishment of the People's Republic because Tien-an-men, literally, meant the Gate of Heavenly Peace? Could Chairman Mao lead the Chinese people successfully through that gate?

Since the disintegration of the Manchu empire no Chinese regime had a more propitious beginning. For the first time since 1911 the country was unified and the power of the central government was effectively exercised over all parts of China. The Kuomintang enemy had been decisively defeated, and people of all walks of life, regardless of their personal feelings, had no choice but to accept the new regime. Would the new regime be one of the greatest in Chinese history like Han, T'ang, and Ming, or would it last only a short time like Ch'in? Whatever future historians might record, Mao had no doubt about his own position in history. Without a blush, he thought that he was the greatest conqueror China had ever produced. Witness his poem:

> Snow (To the Melody Shen Yüan Ch'un)
> This is the scene in that northern land;
> A hundred leagues are sealed with ice,
> A thousand leagues of whirling snow.
> On either side of the Great Wall
> One vastness is all you see.
> From end to end of the great river
> The rushing torrent is frozen and lost.

The mountains dance like silver snakes,
The highlands roll like waxen elephants,
As if they sought to vie with heaven in their height;
    And on a sunny day
You will see a red dress thrown over the white,
    Enchantingly lovely!
Such great beauty like this in all our landscape
Has caused unnumbered heroes to bow in homage.
But alas, these heroes—Ch'in Shih Huang and Han Wu Ti
Were rather lacking in culture;
Rather lacking in literary talent
Were the emperors T'ang T'ai Tsung and Sung T'ai Tsu;
    And Genghis Khan,
Beloved Son of Heaven for a day,
Only knew how to bend his bow at the golden eagle.
    Now they are all past and gone:
To find men truly great and noble-hearted
We must look here in the present.[1]

Minus the modern, Marxist trimmings, the position of Mao Tse-tung was the same as that of the strongest emperors in China's past. Theoretically, his government was the New Democracy, a "joint dictatorship of all the revolutionary classes" headed by the proletariat, and this dictatorship was to be exercised through a process called democratic centralism. As defined by Mao, the revolutionary classes were the proletariat, the peasants, the national capitalists, and finally, the petty bourgeoisie which meant the intellectuals and their allies who, while of a gentry or bourgeois background, had chosen to cooperate with the Communists. Opposite the revolutionary classes were the "reactionaries" such as the landlords, the capitalists who had cooperated with foreign interests in China (as opposed to the national capitalists), and the Kuomintang officials under Chiang Kai-shek's leadership. The New Democracy, said Mao, was a "democracy for the people and dictatorship for the reactionaries." "We certainly have no benevolent policies towards the reactionaries," he declared.

While the emperors of imperial China spoke of the mandate of Heaven to justify their rule, Mao and his colleagues repeated endlessly the mandate of the people which really amounted to the same thing because in both cases the mandate was secured on the battlefield. The theory of democratic centralism was, to use a popular Chinese metaphor, merely a new bottle for the same old wine: a true dictatorship disguised

---

[1] This poem was written by Mao Tse-tung in August 1945. The great heroes mentioned in this poem can be found elsewhere in this book. T'ang T'ai Tsung and Sung T'ai Tsu were the imperial or "temple" titles for Li Shih-min and Chao K'uang-yin respectively. Source of this poem: Mao Tse-tung, *Nineteen Poems*, Peking: Foreign Language Press, 1958, p. 22.

under an attractive, modern phraseology. Theoretically, state power was created through popular elections, but once such power was created, it commanded absolute authority over the entire Chinese people. Since the Communist Party controlled every level of popular election, nobody could be elected without its approval. The man who controlled the party also controlled the government. As long as he remained head of the party, his power was absolute, whatever position he happened to hold within the government. In 1959 Mao Tse-tung stepped down as the Chairman (President) of the People's Republic and was replaced by his lieutenant Liu Shao-ch'i. Nevertheless, his power remained the same because he did not relinquish his post as head of the Communist Party. To be sure, minority parties such as the reconstructed Democratic League were still allowed to function. Each of them, however, had to write into its constitution the statement that it accepted the Communist Party's leadership; and such provision of course ruled out the possibility of its functioning as a genuine opposition party. In fact, the minority parties were never meant to be anything except a democratic window dressing for the one-party dictatorship.

Prior to the formal establishment of the People's Republic, a People's Political Consultative Conference was called on September 21, 1949, and was attended by 662 delegates of Communist and pro-Communist parties. The Conference passed three fundamental laws as the basis of the new government before a general election could be called. They were the *Organic Law of the People's Republic, Organic Law of the People's Consultative Conference,* and the *Common Program.* The Political Consultative Conference was declared the supreme organ of the state pending the convocation of the National People's Congress. The *Common Program* incorporated Mao's concept of a democratic dictatorship in which political and civil rights were to be enjoyed by the "people" but to be denied to the "reactionaries." Besides, it described in broad outlines the organs of state power, the military system, economic policy, cultural and educational policy, policy towards minorities, and foreign policy. By September, 1954, the Communists had established firm control over the entire country, and the government decided to call a general election to choose delegates to the First National People's Congress. One of the major purposes of this congress was to ratify a constitution proposed by a draft committee headed by Mao Tse-tung. The constitution was subsequently adopted to replace the three fundamental laws mentioned above. The Constitution of 1954 is still in force today.

The Constitution consists of a preamble and 106 articles in four chapters. Article 1 states that the People's Republic of China is a people's democratic state led by the working class and based upon the alliance of workers and peasants. The highest organ of the state is the National People's Congress whose deputies are elected for a four-year term by provinces, municipalities directly under the central government, autonomous regions, the armed forces, and Chinese residents abroad. It is empowered to amend the Constitution, to enact laws, and to elect the high officials of the government such as the chairman and the vice-chairman of the People's Republic, the premier of the state council, president of the Supreme People's Court, and others. Moreover, it examines and approves the state budget; decides on questions of war and peace; and exercises such other functions and powers as it considers necessary. The congress meets once a year for a few weeks, and when it is not in session its powers and functions are transferred to a Standing Committeee whose members are elected and subject to recall by the congress. Under the Standing Committee are various subcommittees that propose budget, draft legislation, and perform a variety of other functions.

The head of the state is the chairman of the People's Republic who is elected by and responsible to the congress. He receives foreign diplomatic representatives and appoints and recalls Chinese representatives to foreign countries. He supervises the operation of the State Council and nominates its premier. He commands the armed forces and is the chairman of the National Defense Council. In performing his state functions he is assisted by one or sometimes two vice-chairmen who exercise whatever power the chairman chooses to entrust to them. Under the chairman of the republic is the State Council, headed by a premier, whose function is to carry out policies formulated by the National People's Congress or its Standing Committee. If the congress can be compared with a Western parliament, the State Council is its cabinet, the executive branch of the government. Under the jurisdiction of the premier are more than thirty ministries, commissions, bureaus, and agencies. The ministers are chosen by the congress upon the recommendation of the premier. They are supervised and controlled by the premier in the same manner and to the same extent as the premier is supervised and controlled by the chairman of the republic. Though key ministries (defense, foreign affairs, etc.) are held by Communists as a rule, from time to time leaders of minority parties are given less important portfolios such as ministries of culture and public health.

Chapter 3 of the Constitution lists the "fundamental rights and duties of citizens." All citizens are required to abide by the Constitution and the law, pay taxes, and serve in the armed force "to defend the homeland." Also, they must "uphold discipline at work, keep public order, and respect social ethics." The rights of citizens include freedom of speech, freedom of the press, freedom of assembly, freedom of association, freedom of procession and demonstration, and freedom of religious beliefs. "No citizens may be arrested except by decision of a people's court or with the sanction of a people's procuratorate." All citizens who have reached the age of eighteen have the right to vote and stand for election regardless of nationality, sex, occupation, etc. They also have the right to work and to education.

Outwardly, the Constitution does not seem to have differed greatly from parliamentary constitutions of Western countries. However, it makes clear that political and civil rights are to be enjoyed by the "people," not "traitors and counter-revolutionaries." In practice the Communist Party alone determines the difference between these two groups; it can deprive any one of his constitutional rights by simply classifying him as a "traitor" or "counter-revolutionary." In other words, those who are opposed to the Communist Party are not "people" in the legal sense and therefore cannot enjoy constitutional rights. The overriding and extra-legal power possessed by the Communist Party makes a farce of the civil liberties guaranteed by the Constitution. To understand the power structure of the People's Republic is, in fact, to understand the nature and organization of the Chinese Communist Party.

From a total membership of about fifty in 1921 when it was first organized, the Chinese Communist Party has grown to become the largest communist party in the world. As of 1963, it had approximately 17,000,000 members. Constitutionally, the highest organ of the party is the National Party Congress composed of delegates chosen by party members. The congress elects the Central Committee which in turn elects the Political Bureau. The Standing Committee of the Political Bureau, composed of six or seven members, constitutes the power center of the Chinese Communist Party. Its members are Mao's close associates who have followed his leadership since the days of the Long March. Mao's power is derived from the fact that he is the chairman of both the Political Bureau and its Standing Committee and that he commands the absolute loyalty of other members of the two organizations. Under Mao, in the order of political importance, are Liu Shao-ch'i, Chou En-lai, and Chu Teh. At present (1964) Liu is the chairman of the People's Republic, Chou En-lai is the premier of the State Council, and Chu Teh is the Commander-in-chief of the People's Liberation Army. Generally speaking, party leadership corresponds with government leadership, and party leaders are also government leaders. Since Mao resigned from his post as chairman of the People's Republic in 1959, he has not been the highest government official. However, his control of the party enables him to continue to control the government.

Though power is centralized and comes from above, the effectiveness of the Chinese Communist Party as a revolutionary organization depends ultimately upon individual members to carry out the party instructions and directives and to influence non-party members to do likewise. By carefully screening each candidate for membership, the party recruits to its ranks thoroughly indoctrinated individuals. They are not party members in the ordinary sense; they are fanatics devoted to the implementation of

Communist ideology as interpreted by party leaders. "The test of a Communist Party member's loyalty to the Party and to the task of revolution and communism is his ability, regardless of the situation, to subordinate his individual interests unconditionally and absolutely to those of the Party," wrote Liu Shao-ch'i. "He should see that his own individual interests are completely identical with Party interest, to the extent that they are fused. When conflicts arise between the interests of the Party and the individual, he can without the slightest hesitation or feeling of compulsion submit to Party interests and sacrifice individual interests." Upon the blind, unswerving loyalty of the party members the power of the Chinese Communist Party ultimately depends. From time to time purges are conducted among the rank and file to eliminate the so-called weak and undesirable elements. Those who remain are constantly reminded of their sworn loyalty to party leaders and party programs. Throughout Chinese history there has never been an organization so authoritarian and effective as the Chinese Communist Party.

Whenever there are three or more party members, they are organized as a cell. Many cells form a party branch covering a mine, factory, or an army unit. Above the branches are party organizations that operate in a city, county, or commune. Further above are headquarters with jurisdiction over entire provinces, special municipalities, and autonomous regions. The party branch, however, is the basic operational unit. Its members are responsible for propaganda and organizational work among the non-party individuals among whom they work and live. Together with the non-party activists, they carry out instructions given by higher party organizations, whether they be the raising of production quotas or the selling of war bonds. They organize mass meetings against what the party considers as "traitors and counter-revolutionaries," and conduct indoctrination classes for non-party individuals. Through constant "criticism and self-criticism" meetings they strive to maintain themselves as "pure, incorruptible" Communists, immune to and free from bourgeois influences. In 1956 about 69 percent of the party members were of peasant background, 14 percent were industrial workers, and the rest were from other groups. Since the overwhelming majority of party members are of peasant and worker background, their educational level is low. In carrying out party instructions, they are more noted for their enthusiasm than for their good judgment. In many cases their single-mindedness defeats the very purpose which the party has attempted to achieve. During the national drive for higher steel production in 1958 village Communists encouraged peasants to contribute their pots and pans to local furnaces to be smelted into crude steel. The steel production increased and looked good on paper (though most of it was useless), but the peasants, after their "patriotic" gesture, had nothing to cook with.

To isolate party members as well as the rest of the Chinese people from undesirable, bourgeois ideas, the party, through governmental agencies, monopolizes all means of communication such as newspapers, magazines, radio, and movies. No ideas except those approved by the party can be presented, and those who do not follow the party line are liars by definition. In trains, buses, and public lounges can be found the ubiquitous loudspeakers which keep on urging people to be polite, unselfish, and work harder for the socialist and Communist reconstruction of China. There is no value except the Communist value and no truth except the Communist truth. A person has either to accept it or face universal condemnation. Listening to their own endless propaganda and having no other values with which they can compare their own, the party members become prisoners within the confines of their own creations. To them communism is a matter of faith subject to no reason or objective evaluation. They believe in their own propaganda and they persuade or coerce others to do the same. Those who do not agree with them are "the enemies of the people," who should be either liquidated outright or "reformed" through labor.

INDUSTRIAL DEVELOPMENT

Thought control and life regimentation are justified by the Communists and their allies on the ground that they are necessary for the development of a prosperous, classless society. Before the work of socialist reconstruction is completed, they say, the inconveniences to individuals are unavoidable. Socialist reconstruction means not only the elimination of the "feudal" relationships of the past and the establishment of a socialist society based upon the alliance between workers and peasants; it also means the transformation of China from an economically backward society based upon agriculture to an economically advanced society dominated by modern industries. The ultimate purpose is to build an economy so productive that the Socialist maxim "To each according to his needs and from each according to his ability" will finally be realized. Meanwhile, if Communist China can solve many of its economic problems, its gravitational pull would be so great that other Asian countries, facing the same problems, would have to fall in line. If communism can work such magic, it would become irresistible.

While the Communists could dream about the future when they took over power in 1949, the immediate tasks were stupendous. Wars had been an almost normal state of affairs since the fall of the Manchu regime in 1912, and whatever economic accomplishments had been made before 1937 were more than cancelled during the Sino-Japanese War and the civil war that followed. The Communists themselves did an effective job in wrecking railroads and destroying mines that were then under Nationalist control. In Manchuria, which had been built up as an industrial showcase during the Japanese occupation, industrial equipment and sometimes entire plants were dismantled by the Russians and were then shipped to Russia as "war booty." Much of what was left suffered heavy damage during the civil war that followed. In 1949 the output of producer goods dropped by 70 percent from its previous peak, and the decline in the production of consumer goods was 30 percent. The shortage of technical and managerial personnel, the inadequate supply of raw materials, the diffusion of labor forces, and the disruption of rail and water transportation all combined to make reconstruction work extremely difficult. The Nationalists did not help the situation by staging a naval blockade shortly after they were driven out from the mainland. Shanghai, once a booming city of industry and commerce, was virtually dead.

Slowly and gradually the Communists succeeded in overcoming their initial difficulties. They took possession of the enterprises that formerly belonged to the Nationalist government or officials. They took over foreign assets either by outright confiscation as in the case of American firms upon the outbreak of the Korean War or by a more devious method in which foreign owners, having encountered numerous Communist-inspired labor disputes, were forced to sell their assets to the Communist government at a nominal price. As for those capitalists who could not be classified as either reactionaries or counter-revolutionaries, the government decided not to liquidate them for the time being because, for one thing, it needed their experience and managerial skill to keep production going during a time when there was serious shortage of manufactured products. This lenient attitude towards the so-called national capitalists contrasted sharply with the harsh policy the new regime then pursued with regard to the landlords who were liquidated *en masse*.

In due course this attitude was to be changed. After the government had entered the Korean War, it launched the so-called Three-Anti and Five-Anti campaigns and many businessmen were liquidated on a variety of trumped-up charges. Their properties were confiscated and the confiscated assets were extremely helpful in financing the costly Korean War. Those businessmen who were spared during these campaigns were persuaded to take the government as their partner to form joint state-private enterprises. Private ownership diminished steadily, and by 1956 the government reported that 98.7 percent of the value of industrial output was produced by state-controlled enterprises. In each of the enterprises which the government took over, more often than not the managers were asked to stay on their jobs until the Communists trained enough managerial personnel to replace them. Generally speaking, the Communists exercised more restraint in the cities and caused less bloodshed in carrying out their socialist transformation than they did in the countryside.

Through strenuous efforts, the government was able to restore industrial production to the pre-1949 peak by the end of 1952. The production of crude and rolled steel, for instance, rose from 250,000 metric tons in 1949 to more than a million tons (pre-1949 peak: 1.4 million metric tons). Confident and ambitious, the government launched its First Five Year Plan in 1953. The plan called for speedy development of heavy industry and creation of new industrial centers in the Northwest and the Southwest, away from the coastal areas. Of the 42.74 billion *yuan* (*ca.* 17 billion U.S. dollars) earmarked for capital expenditure, more than 77 percent was to be spent on heavy industry, while the remaining was divided between agriculture, forestry, water conservation, and cultural, educational, and health activities. The new regime believed that heavy industry was the basis of all industries and had to be developed first, even though such development caused great hardship among the people who despite their toil saw no immediate improvement in their standard of living. By 1957 when the First Five Year Plan was completed, it reported fulfillment and over-fulfillment of all production quotas. The output of capital goods was increased by more than 204 percent with an average growth rate of 24.9 percent per year, and the production of consumer goods was increased by 85.1 percent with an average growth rate of 13.2 percent per year. The production of steel was increased from 1.8 million metric tons in 1953 to 5.4 million metric tons in 1957, a total increase of 296.6 percent. In consumer goods the production of sugar was increased from 298,000 metric tons in 1953 to 864,000 metric tons in 1957, a total increase of 247 percent. The increases in production for cotton yarn and cotton piecegoods were less impressive, amounting to 28.5 and 53.1 percent respectively. The inability of this key section of industrial output to keep pace with the rest of the economy, together with the failure in agriculture, spelled trouble for the entire economy in the years to come.

Having scored a tremendous success in the production of capital goods, a more cautious planner would have called for the concentration of energy in other sections of the economy to achieve a more balanced growth. This was of course not the case with the Chinese Communists. Carried away by their recent successes, they pushed relentlessly towards even higher goals along the same lines. When the Second Five Year Plan began in 1958, the prospect for continuous economic growth had never looked better. Yet by the end of the year the whole economy began to fall into pieces. Discarding all precautions, the government called for "The Great Leap Forward": the increase of production by 100 percent in key industries. The Chinese were urged to work even harder, "concentrating twenty years' progress in a single day" and surpassing Great Britain in fifteen years. Thousands of small blast furnaces appeared on the countryside, producing tons of iron and steel which looked good in the statistics but were mostly useless, even to make farm implements. The government claimed an increase of 131 percent in pig iron production to 13.7 million metric tons, and an increase of 107 percent in crude steel to 11.1 million metric tons, all in a single year. The increases in the production of other industrial items were less spectacular but were nevertheless substantial. As more and more production figures were released by governmental sources, experts outside of China became increasingly skeptical. In most cases they turned out to be correct in their skepticism. For one thing, local Communists, to impress their superiors in Peking, sent fantastic reports about their achievements on the economic fronts, achievements which could not be substantiated by on-the-spot inspections. The Peking government had quickly to revise its claims downward, much to its own embarrassment.

The year 1958 marked the peak of Communist China's industrial growth. Since then it has been beset with one economic difficulty after another. Factories lay idle because of the shortage of raw materials, and thousands of workers had to be sent to the countryside to increase agricultural production. Transportation broke down; demand could not find supply and vice versa. The most crucial area was in the key section of consumer goods: food and cloth were rationed and re-rationed as there was not enough to go around. Many people were actually hungry and some of them did not have enough clothing to cover their bodies. All of a sudden, the bright, rosy picture became dismal and bleak.

What had happened? First, there were serious errors in both planning and implementation with regard to the various industrial projects. The plans were too ambitious, exceeding the capacity of both natural and human resources then at the government's disposal. Coordination was poor among the various governmental agencies responsible for industrial development; each pursued its own goals with little or no regard for supplementary and complementary work done by other agencies. The major resource the government had was manpower; yet manpower would be used in vain if it were not wisely and correctly applied. Serious errors in design and construction resulted in many flood control and irrigation projects that were faulty or useless after millions of man-hours had been spent in building them. In such cases, the applied manpower became a negative rather than a positive asset, because additional manpower was needed to undo what had been completed. Though the government paid practically nothing to the millions of peasants recruited for the construction of its various projects, these peasants had to be fed if they were expected to work twelve or thirteen hours a day. When they were hungry and totally exhausted, no indoctrination or coercion would make them work harder.

Second, the failure to expand agricultural production to keep pace with industrial development resulted in the inadequate supply of industrial raw materials as well as food. Textile plants became idle when cotton production fell below expectation. The government's limited amount of foreign exchange had been earmarked for the purchase of heavy equipment and was not available for the purchase of industrial raw materials; when cotton crops failed, textile plants had to be closed or worked on a part time basis. The situation was not helped when the government took millions of peasants away from their farms to work in factories and on public projects. As agriculture continued to deteriorate, a point was eventually reached when the supply of food became dangerously low and people simply did not have enough to eat. Under these circumstances it was senseless to talk about industrial development.

Third, there were serious floods and droughts that occurred repeatedly and successively after 1959. The government had either to abandon its ambitious industrial projects or face mass starvation and possibly mass revolt. Naturally it took the former course. Millions of peasants were shipped back to the farms to increase agricultural production and, temporarily at least, industrial production was relegated to a position of secondary importance.

Finally, the increasing economic difficulties came at a time when the ideological conflict between the Soviet Union and Communist China continued to widen. Not only did the Soviet Union fail to lend a helping hand, it withdrew the assistance which it had formerly pledged. As China's export trade dwindled, its foreign exchange reserve continued to shrink, and it could not obtain heavy equipment from the Soviet Union even if there had not been an ideological conflict. Many industrial plants could not be completed when the Soviet Union decided not to send additional equipment. Subsequently Soviet technicians left China *en masse*, and the Chinese had a difficult time operating the equipment that had already arrived.

Underlying the various causes of the recent economic disaster is the basic question involving the very nature of a planned economy. While a planned economy admittedly possesses many advantages, it is also true that no planners, however capable, can anticipate the operation of numerous economic forces, many of which are clearly beyond human control. This difficulty is compounded by the inflexibility of Communist dogmas and the eagerness to accomplish what simply cannot be accomplished in a short time. Under the capitalist system when each corporation plans separately with regard to its expansion and production, its failure to anticipate market demand will not affect the economy as a whole, and its failure will be compensated by the success of other corporations, because it is inconceivable that all corporations should make the same mistakes at the same time. Moreover, since the scope of its planning is small and since its planning affects only a small section of the economy, its misjudgments can have only a limited impact on the entire economy as compared with a planning involving the economy of the entire country and affecting hundreds of millions of people. In the latter case, a minor error on the planning board will be magnified a million times on the implementation level and might result in irreparable damage to the economy as a whole. To complicate the matter, the Communist planners, under the dictate of political considerations, were often inclined to disregard economic realities.

Despite what has been said above, there is no denying the fact that the Communist regime has made substantial economic progress. Through its tight control of an almost unlimited supply of labor forces which it compels to work for long, inhuman hours, it has been able to achieve what ordinarily cannot be achieved. New railroads have been built, including the Ch'eng-Yü Railroad, the Peking-Ulan Bator Line, and the Hsining-Lanchow Railroad. From Lanchow the Lung-Hai Railroad has been extended westward to the eastern section of Sinkiang province. Thousands of miles of highways have also been completed, extending even to such remote areas as Tibet. For the first time in Chinese history all provincial capitals are linked to the capital by mechanized transportation. Many irrigation and flood control projects have been either completed or are still under construction. The most ambitious is the Yellow River project which has been mentioned earlier in this book. Despite the recent setback, all forms of industrial production have exceeded the pre-1949 peaks. Given two or three good harvests, the Communists will doubtlessly push towards even higher goals. There is a dedication to industrialization among the Communist leaders such as has never been seen in recent history. If they choose to benefit from their past mistakes, they will no doubt make their future plans along more realistic lines. Recent reports from Communist China indicate that the economic situation of that country has changed for the better.

AGRICULTURE

Agriculture has been the most important section of the Chinese economy, and the problems it poses are also the most difficult to solve. These problems become more serious as the population continues to grow while the amount of arable land remains substantially the same. The Communists rose to power on their promise to solve the land problem; the success or failure of their regime has ultimately to be judged by their ability or inability to fulfill that promise.

The role of traditional agriculture was a simple one: to provide enough food to meet the basic needs and to produce enough cotton, hemp, and silk for clothing. This goal, however, is no longer sufficient for the new regime. Besides producing necessities for domestic consumption, it has to produce a large surplus to be shipped abroad in exchange for industrial equipment and fuels necessary for China's industrialization programs. The demand on agriculture is greater than it has ever been. If historically China has not been able to produce enough to meet domestic needs, how can the new regime hope that it can produce huge surpluses to meet the new demand? The Communists say that it can. They assert that if "feudal" relationships in the countryside are abolished, if land ownership is socialistic rather than private, and if modern science and technology are applied to farming, then the historical problem will be solved. With fanatic zeal, they began, a long time ago, to apply their brand of Marxism-Leninism to the Chinese land problem.

Knowing that they would encounter great resistance if they attempted to carry out their socialist reconstruction in one giant step, the Chinese Communists decided to advance towards their eventual goal by stages. The first stage was the reduction of rent paid to landlords and interest charged by rural money-lenders. This was the policy they followed during the Sino-Japanese War in areas within their control, and its moderation won them great admiration as agrarian reformers, especially in the Western world. Before the summer of 1950 the same policy was also followed in Central and South China.

The second stage was that of land redistribution which came into being after the Communists had brought an area under their effective control. It was not enforced in the Yangtze region until the fall of 1950, though it had been carried out in Manchuria and North China before this time. It was accompanied by hatred and bloodshed whenever it was carried out, and it was during this period that the Communists committed their most wanton brutalities. Communist cadres went to work in each village in a campaign to stir up hatred among the villagers. They divided the rural population into five classes: landlord, rich peasant, middle peasant, poor peasant, and farm laborer, and the instruction from Peking was to make alliance with poor peasants and farm laborers, neutralize rich and middle peasants, and strike against landlords. Engineered by Communist cadres, mass "struggle" meetings were called, and each landlord was brought before his fellow villagers to confess his sins, real or imaginary. If he had no sins to confess, he had better invent some if he were wise, because the more he pleaded innocence, the more ugly the mob would become. He could be shot on the spot if he were lucky or be tortured to a slow death if he were not. In some cases his life was spared and he was declared a social outcast, begging for food for the rest of his life. How many landlords were killed during the period of land reform? A conservative estimate would place it somewhere between two and three millions, though the number could have been considerably larger. After land redistribution, each peasant received anywhere between 0.15 to 0.45 of an acre of land, depending upon the localities. By the spring of 1953 land reform had been completed for more than 80 percent of the Chinese villages.

The small amount of land each peasant received after the land had been redistributed reflected the tragic nature of the problem: too little land and too many people. The Communists knew that land redistribution could not be the final solution because, as land was further fragmented, its productivity became smaller still. Their land policy defeated the very purpose they had attempted to achieve, which was more efficient cultivation and higher production. While economically this policy could not be described as sound, politically it gave the middle and poor peasants a stake in the new regime because the return of landlordism would have meant bloody retaliation.

What would be the government's next step? If it took away the redistributed land from the peasants, it might lose the political support it had recently won. It had to proceed slowly towards its goal of collectivization. Beginning in the spring of 1953 it called for the organization of mutual-aid teams in the rural areas and laid down in detail the methods for promoting them. The organization of mutual-aid teams may be called the third stage of the government's socialist reconstruction program. Within each mutual-aid team peasants shared manpower, draft animals, and agricultural tools, mostly on a seasonal or temporary basis. This form of cooperation was readily accepted because it benefited all parties involved. From 1954 to 1956 the mutual-aid teams were gradually transformed into agricultural producers' cooperatives, the fourth stage of socialist reconstruction. All members in a cooperative pooled their land, draft animals, farm implements, and labor and were remunerated in accordance with their contributions. Labor, however, carried more weight than land in the division of harvested crops. By the summer of 1956 more than 90 percent of the peasant households had been organized into cooperatives.

The government encountered considerable resistance from peasants in its efforts to organize them into cooperatives. To bring reluctant peasants into line, it exercised a variety of pressures. One of the most effective weapons it used was the granting or withholding of credit by government-controlled banks. Those peasants who refused to join the cooperatives (and later, collective farms) were denied the much needed credit and therefore could not compete with the cooperatives which the government favored. Loans were also used to influence the direction of agricultural production. If the government decided that certain farms should produce industrial raw materials (such as cotton) instead of food crops, it threatened to withhold credit unless the farms concerned abided by its decision. Monopolizing the credit market, it succeeded in every case.

While the agricultural producers' cooperatives were still being organized in South and Central China, the government ordered the amalgamation of cooperatives into collective farms in such areas as Manchuria and North China where the cooperative movement had been completed earlier. The collective farms may be said to be the fifth stage of the government's socialist reconstruction program. At the beginning the state-owned collective farms, mechanized or semimechanized, were more or less demonstration pieces and were designed as examples for cooperatives to follow at some future time. As the organization of cooperatives was rewarded with success, the government did not wait long before it pushed towards the organization of collective farms. The displaced rural manpower would, it hoped, be quickly absorbed by the newly developed industries in the cities. As things turned out, neither were industries so highly developed as to be able to absorb labor from the countryside nor were there enough machines and technical knowledge to operate the newly created collective farms. The exodus of peasants to the cities seeking employment increased the city problems such as housing, while in the countryside the inexperienced cadres were groping in darkness in their attempts to solve the production problems.

While pressures from cities and rural areas were mounting, the government resorted to more organization to solve the existing problems. The year 1958 was declared the year of The Great Leap Forward, and agriculture had to leap together with industry, said the government. Cooperatives and collective farms were ordered to be amalgamated into communes, the final stage in socialist reconstruction for the rural population. The communes were said to be communism *par excellence,* outdistancing the collective farms of the Soviet Union. Peasants were ordered to hand over all that they possessed to the communes with the temporary exception of houses, courtyards, and trees. Overnight private ownership had completely disappeared and all peasants became the rural proletariat, working for the communes and paid in wages. Each commune had an average of five thousand households and a labor force of ten thousand. In the spring of 1959, the government announced that 99 percent of China's rural population had joined the communes.

Despite its social implications which will be discussed later, the commune possessed certain advantages as well as disadvantages. The enlargement of farms enhanced the prospect of using larger and better machines; it gave rise to labor specialization among participating peasants. It made irrigation, flood control, and field drainage much easier; it facilitated the use of fertilizers and the application of insecticides. Moreover, each commune was encouraged to build its own industries—small plants that produced goods to meet local demand and provided employment for peasants who were not needed on the farm. The rural unemployed did not have to travel to faraway cities to seek employment; the arrival of unskilled labor from rural areas had in the past complicated city problems. The establishment of commune plants would reduce the pressure on state-owned enterprises which could then concentrate on the production of goods that required advanced knowledge and technology. Culturally as well as economically each commune was to be as self-sufficient as possible. It was to have its own schools, job-training centers, and entertainment facilities. Every peasant was to be trained as a farmer in the field, a worker in the factory, and a soldier in the army. He worked as if he were fighting a battle, and he was to be rewarded or punished in proportion to his contribution. Strict discipline was imposed on each commune member, and at no time was he to disobey the decisions of the commune council which, of course, was controlled by the Communists.

One would search in vain for the commune concept in the teachings of Marx and Lenin, but it has been put into practice time and again in the course of Chinese history. It was basically a Legalist concept, dating from the time of Shang Yang of the fourth century B.C. (Chapters I and II). Later Confucians such as Wang Mang of the first century A.D. (Chapter III) and Wang An-shih of the eleventh century (Chapter VI) incorporated it to various degrees in their policies. As late as the nineteenth century the leaders of the Taipings attempted to do likewise (Chapter XII). Stripped of its modern embellishments such as the establishment of factories and the use of tractors, the so-called pure communism was really Legalism in disguise. While none of the previous statesmen had carried rural organization to such an extent as that practiced by the present Communist regime, their basic ideas, such as the mobilization of manpower to the fullest extent to maximize production, the combination of production, military training, and education as one single, continuous operation, the regimentation of life and the elimination of individuality for the alleged common good, and the interdependence and mutual responsibility among all members of each organizational unit, were the same as those of Mao's communes. While it is difficult to predict how long the commune system will last, it is interesting to note that none of the systems similar to it survived for long in China's historical past.

If for the time being we disregard the political and social implications of Communist China's agricultural policy, its success or failure has to be measured by two major standards: total production and the corresponding share each peasant receives. The first standard reflects the increase or decrease of agricultural wealth which in turn affects capital accumulation, and the second standard indicates the increase or decrease of each peasant's standard of living. Agricultural production rose steadily from 1949 to 1958. In the latter year total grain production reached 250 million metric tons (soy bean production not included) as compared with a production of 113 million metric tons in 1949 and 164 metric tons in 1952 (soy beans included in both cases). Meanwhile, cotton production rose from 445,000 tons in 1949 to 1.3 million tons in 1952 and reached an unprecedented height of 2.1 million tons in 1958. While it is true that production would have increased in any event after the restoration of peace and order, it is also true that the intensive use of fertilizers, insect control, and better irrigation and flood control all played a substantial role in the increased production. On the other hand, the abolition of "feudal" relationships to which the government gave the largest credit for such success may have had little or nothing to do with it.

While agricultural production continued to rise from 1949 to 1958, the standard of living of the peasants did not rise proportionately because a large portion of farm produce was taken away by the government in the form of taxes and contributions. The government justified such heavy taxation on the ground that it needed farm surpluses to finance its industrialization programs. It was estimated that about 52 percent of an average peasant's gross income was taken away as taxes and contributions between 1950 and 1952. Subsequently, this percentage was reduced, though it remained substantial. Moreover, as the population continued to increase, a large portion of the increased production was consumed by the accrued population, leaving only a small amount to be added to per capita income. All things considered, it is difficult to say to what extent the standard of living of an average peasant has been increased. One thing, however, remains significant. No longer is there any difference between rich and poor peasants; all of them have a similar, if not the same, standard of living. The leveling of income has its disadvantages as well as advantages. Before the Communist revolution, a famine inevitably struck the poorest peasants first and only slowly worked its way towards the rest of the population. The leveling of income, together with the increase of total production, might have reduced the frequency of famine. However, when it does occur, it affects the entire population rather than just a section of it. Ironically, the reduction of its frequency might thus increase its intensity.

The year 1958 marked the highest peak on all production fronts, agricultural as well as industrial. After that year deterioration set in; it reached disastrous proportions by 1961. While millions of people in China were facing starvation, the Soviet Union and other Communist countries watched with folded arms, and the Chinese Communists had to shop in such Western countries as Canada, Australia, and France for grain needed to feed the hungry millions at home. While the Communist regime blamed natural disasters—flood, drought, and destructive insects—for its economic debacle, experts outside of China believed that Communist mismanagement was at least equally responsible. The sudden, sharp drop in agricultural production affected adversely the development of industry that depended upon the supply of farm products as raw materials. Exports of farm products were sharply reduced, and Communist China could no longer pay for the industrial equipment it had planned to purchase. New factories could not be built, and those upon which construction had begun could not be completed. As agriculture deteriorated, so did industry.

SOCIAL AND CULTURAL CHANGES

The Chinese Communists, like Communists everywhere, believed that a society's social and cultural pattern was determined by its economic relationships and that as economic relationships changed, social and cultural life would also have to change. They called the pre-Communist era "feudalistic" during which landlords and bureaucratic capitalists formed the oppressing class bent on the exploitation of workers and peasants. Now that the Communists had successfully overthrown the "oppressive" Nationalist regime, it was time to build a new society based upon the alliance of the two revolutionary classes formerly exploited. However, the new regime that came to power in 1949 did not propose the immediate liquidation of all other classes, but declared instead that all except the reactionaries would have their proper functions to perform in the new society. This conciliatory policy won for it many friends who, after years of foreign and domestic wars, were ready to accept any government that could restore peace. But disillusionment followed swiftly. The moderate policy was reversed soon after the new regime had successfully consolidated its power. The so-called national capitalists were "persuaded" to surrender their assets and become silent partners in the joint state-private enterprises. In the countryside the rich and middle peasants lost their land ownership and were reduced to the same level as that of the poor peasants. The leftist intellectuals who had vigorously supported the new regime eventually lost favor; most of them were put under close surveillance. Thus within three years after the establishment of the People's Republic, all "revolutionary classes" except workers and peasants had virtually disappeared.

The elimination of private ownership and the control by government of all means of production meant that virtually all Chinese, to earn a livelihood, had to become government employees. Since the Communist Party controlled the government, literally no man could live without its open or implied consent. All classes had disappeared; organized forces not in sympathy with communism had been destroyed; all men were equal in the sense that they all had to be obedient to the Communist Party. Even the differences between workers and peasants were all but obliterated because the party, by invoking the authority of the government, could assign any section of the people to perform whatever task, rural or industrial, it pleased. No man was important as compared with the overwhelming importance of the Communist Party. Thus, upon the ruins of the old society was built a new social structure in which the Communist Party constituted the ruling class and the people were the ruled.

With the destruction of the traditional Chinese society went also the collapse of the Confucian family system. The Confucian family system had been slowly undermined since the 1920's, and the Communists gave it the *coup de grace* in recent years. In 1950 the new regime promulgated a marriage law aimed at the reorganization of family relations. Outwardly, the law was reasonable and modernistic. It banned bigamy, concubinage, child betrothal, and arranged marriages of any nature. It emphasized the importance of individual consent in the negotiation of a marriage contract. If a marriage did not work, either the wife or the husband could initiate divorce proceedings. Generally speaking, the law itself was not radically different from the general practice in a Western society and was similar to the marriage law incorporated in the Nationalist government's civil code of 1931. The difference had to do with enforcement. While other societies relied on individual initiative to start suits in civil cases such as divorce, Communist cadres agitated for such suits on behalf of allegedly injured individuals on the ground that the individuals involved had been too much "poisoned" by feudal ideas to demand their own rights. They investigated family and sexual relationships, held "confession" meetings so that grievances could be aired in public, and called upon the masses to "struggle" against reactionary husbands and mothers-in-law. Again it was the extra-legal power of the Communist Party that made a mockery of the law. The credulous wives and daughters-in-law who did stand up against their "oppressors" found themselves shunned by the entire society; and shamed and disgraced, many of them had only one honorable way to get out of the impasse: suicide. According to the government's own estimate, between seventy and eighty thousand people were killed or committed suicide over marriage difficulties in a single year, 1952. Meanwhile, the divorce rate soared. In most cases, it was women who, egged on by Communist cadres, took the initiative.

What did the government expect to gain by loosening family relationships? First, measured by modern standards, the Confucian family system was anything but perfect. It harbored a great deal of injustice, especially to the female members such as wives and daughters-in-law. Admittedly, some form of redress was long overdue. Second, by breaking down the close relationship among family members the government wished to strengthen their loyalty towards the state which, according to the government, was superior to any other form of loyalty, including the loyalty towards one's husband and parents. To achieve this purpose, it used the most dubious methods such as the holding of "confession" and "struggle" meetings in which wives were encouraged to denounce their husbands and children were asked to denounce their parents. One family member was urged to inform upon another, and such information was used as evidence for prosecution in "struggle" meetings or people's courts. The local cadres became the confession receivers, and knowing the innermost secrets of every individual within their jurisdiction, they held a weapon which no Chinese official had ever possessed. Lastly, the breaking-up of the Confucian family released millions of women from family control and enabled the government to put them to work in the field, factories, and public projects. In 1958, for instance, 73 million women were reported to have worked on water conservation projects alone.

The utilization of human resources reached the highest stage after the establishment of the commune system in 1958. In each commune, mess halls were set up to feed all peasant-workers, and nurseries and kindergartens were established to take care of babies and children. Released from household chores, women were put to work in the field or in factories. Older women who were too weak to do strenuous work joined the sewing squads, sewing and mending for all people in the commune. Those men and women who were too old to do any type of work were sent to the "happy home of the aged." Husbands and wives were encouraged to live in separate dormitories and see each other only on weekends so that their private affairs would not interfere with the sacred task of working for the common good. Husbands should call their wives "lovers" (and *vice versa*) instead of wives because the word "wife" was "feudalistic" and implied a person of inferior status. Wages earned by women were paid to them directly; the Communists hoped that after acquiring a degree of economic independence, these women would acquire social independence as well.

As the Legalists had learned more than two thousand years ago, thought control was absolutely necessary if a government expected its citizens to act and behave in the manner dictated or approved. In the imposition of thought control, the People's Republic naturally encountered the strongest resistance from the intellectuals, whose very profession implied that they should be able to think freely and independently. Before it had enough time to educate the children of peasant and worker background to replace them, the government needed the knowledge and skill of the old-type intellectuals who, almost without exception, came from gentry or bourgeois families. Some concessions were made to them out of necessity during the early years of the new regime; many of them even served the government as high officials. The government hoped that by intensive indoctrination these intellectuals would purge themselves of their bourgeois beliefs and remodel their thinking along the Marxist-Leninist line. In 1957, for reasons never adequately explained, Mao Tse-tung invited the old-type intellectuals to express their opinions about the new regime. For a short period when freedom of speech was allowed, these intellectuals launched a scathing attack upon the government's foreign and domestic policies; even top leaders like Mao were subject to strong criticism. By then the government concluded that they had abused their freedom of speech and ordered an immediate crackdown. After this episode it was announced that from then on freedom of speech could be granted only to the "people," namely, those who would unconditionally support the Communist line.

In the exercise of thought control the government was generally more lenient towards natural scientists who were not interfered with in their teaching or research as long as they did not express opinions openly hostile to the Communist regime. It was a different matter, however, with social scientists, humanists, men of letters, and artists. The historians were expected to write and teach history in accordance with the dialectic truth of Marxism; the novelists and the artists were supposed to create socialist realism. All intellectuals were urged to live with workers and peasants to taste in person the "sweetness of labor" and to draw inspiration from them. Literary and artistic works were to depict the oppression of the reactionaries, the struggle of the masses, and the glory of labor. *The Dream of the Red Chamber* was not merely a tragic love affair; it was an exposition of the degenerated "feudalistic morals" which the hero and the heroine had "gloriously" combatted. All forms of entertainment, such as dramas and movies, should correctly reflect the point of view of the masses; that is, they should serve as media of propaganda. Every man should have the freedom of religious belief as long as his religious beliefs were "patriotic" and did not contradict the basic truth of Marxism and Leninism.

The paucity of literary and artistic creations did not mean that there were no achievements whatsoever in the field of education and culture. On the contrary, a great deal of credit should be given to the new regime for its concentrated efforts in pushing education on all levels. In 1960 it was reported that nine out of ten children of school age were attending schools and that more than twelve million students were attending middle (high) schools. The quality of instruction seemed to be low due to the insufficient training of teachers, the lack of adequate facilities, and the large amount of time required to be spent on indoctrination and manual labor. As a matter of principle as well as that of necessity, students had to devote much of their time to raising crops, vegetables, and livestock for their own support. Spare-time schools for adults were established in the countryside as well as in the cities and scored one of the most impressive gains in the educational scene. The government claimed that from 1949 to 1958 more than 120 million illiterates had been taught to read. The simplification of Chinese characters might have had something to do with this impressive result.

As the government emphasized the importance of industrialization, it naturally gave great attention to technical and higher education. The total number of schools of higher learning rose from 227 in 1950 to more than 1,000 by 1958. Total enrollment was estimated between 600,000 and 700,000 in the latter year. Though the quality of these schools was uneven, the best among them could be compared favorably with the best in many Western countries. As one would expect, the government favored colleges of science and engineering. While Peking University remained a college of general studies, its sister institution, Tsinghua, was reorganized as a vast polytechnic university. It coordinated its research with governmental projects, whether the project was the construction of a dam or the designing of a new jet engine. In 1958 the famed Chinese University of Sciences and Technology was established in Peking which admitted students of exceptional academic ability and high political reliability. The faculty was drawn from the research members of the Academy of Sciences, the leading center of research in Communist China. In 1957 the Academy had 68 research institutes with a total personnel of more than 17,000. It purchased books and subscribed to magazines from all scientifically advanced countries, including the Soviet Union and the United States. It had many of China's renowned scientists as its research fellows.

In the field of cultural activities efforts were made by the Communist regime to popularize folk music, art, and dancing. The three major art forms for intellectuals—calligraphy, traditional painting, and the composition of classical poetry—required advanced education and a long period of training and were therefore unsuitable for the proletarians. Folk art and music, on the other hand, were plebeian in origin and were more in line with the spirit of the new society. The government not only patronized the Peking opera, a form of folk music originated in Hupeh, but also the lesser known music forms such as the Canton opera and the Shaohsing (a subprefecture in Chekiang) opera. *Yang-ko*, a fertility dance in North China, was popularized by the Communists during the civil war and shortly afterwards. Puppet shows and shadow plays, two of the most popular entertainments among the peasants, were now used to tell the stories of the masses, instead of kings and princesses. Paper cuts, woodcuts, and bamboo articles which had been traditionally looked down upon were revived as major art forms under the new regime. Moreover, each ethnic or regional group in China was urged to develop further art forms peculiar to itself. Interestingly enough, the Western ballroom dance was not only permitted but actually encouraged. For one thing, it provided an opportunity for young comrades of opposite sexes to meet one another.

FOREIGN RELATIONS

The China after 1949 was a different China from that of the pre-Communist era. No longer was it a geographical expression, a pawn in international politics; it was unified, strong, and confident. Not only did it assert vigorously what it regarded as its national rights; it dedicated itself to another goal, the spread of communism abroad. As it pursued a more aggressive foreign policy, it ran into resistance from foreign countries.

We shall divide our discussion of Communist China's foreign relations into three groupings: (1) with the Soviet Union and other Communist countries; (2) with the neutral, nonaligned countries; and (3) with the Western countries headed by the United States.

In view of the fact that the Communist success in China was achieved without substantial help from the Soviet Union, it had been hoped in Western circles that once the regime was established, it would pursue a foreign policy independent of Moscow. Such a hope was dashed in the summer of 1949 when Mao Tse-tung announced to the whole world that China would "lean to one side," the side of the socialist camp as headed by the Soviet Union. On October 2, 1949, the day after the new regime was formally inaugurated, the Soviet Union extended its recognition; the leadership of the Soviet Union in this respect was soon followed by other Communist countries. In December Mao travelled to Moscow to confer with Stalin—his first trip outside China—and brought home in February a treaty of friendship and alliance designed to last thirty years. The military alliance was ostensibly directed against Japan but was actually against the United States and American power on the Western Pacific. The conclusion of this treaty was followed by the negotiation of trade and loan agreements in which the Soviet Union pledged financial and technical support for China's reconstruction programs.

The test of this new alliance came in the summer of 1950 when North Korea, egged on by Moscow, invaded South Korea. The United States, with some help from other members of the United Nations, came to the aid of the South Koreans. By October, 1950, the United Nations forces had not only recovered all the territories the South Koreans had lost, but were pushing northward to the Yalu River, the boundary between China and Korea. For a while, it seemed that Korea would be unified under United Nations sponsorship. Much to the surprise of the outside world the Chinese Communist regime, then barely one year old, intervened and fought the United Nations forces to a stalemate. The final settlement restored Korea to its prewar status, divided as it had been before. Despite staggering losses it had suffered, Communist China emerged from the Korean War with accrued prestige because it had successfully prevented the United Nations from unifying Korea under a pro-Western regime. The significance of Communist China's military "success" was not lost to the Kremlin; as long as the Soviet Union had China as its ally in East Asia, its eastern flank would be safe against the attack of the so-called imperialist warmongers.

The years 1950–1958 marked the heyday of Sino-Soviet cooperation. A series of agreements were reached between the two Communist countries and were generally in favor of China. The Soviet Union agreed to provide China with industrial equipment and technical advice, and such help was uninterrupted by Stalin's death in 1953. Though China had to pay for everything it received, the Soviet Union agreed to take whatever products China could deliver, even though it might not need these products itself. There are evidences that it took these products at a bargain price and then dumped them in the international market for a handsome profit. Since China could not trade in the international market itself because of the Western powers' embargo following the Korean War, it did not have much choice. However, the equipment and technical assistance it received from the Soviet Union were of great help to its industrialization programs and were at least partially responsible for the economic progress it made during the period from 1950 to 1958.

Economically stronger and more self-assured, Communist China began to ask the Soviet Union to relinquish the economic privileges which the latter had acquired before 1949. We may recall that the Yalta Agreement of February, 1945, gave Russia vital concessions in Manchuria such as the joint control of the Chinese Eastern (Changchun) Railroad and the lease to Russia of the naval base of Port Arthur. These concessions were finalized in a treaty between Nationalist China and the Soviet Union later in the same year. After the establishment of the Chinese Communist regime, further concessions were made to the Russians in the form of four Sino-Soviet joint stock companies organized to exploit China's natural resources. In the fall of 1952 the Soviet Union agreed to transfer to China, with full title and without compensation, all Russian rights in the joint management of the Chinese Eastern Railroad and all property belonging to it. Three years later, China took full control of the four joint stock companies. This was followed by the transfer of Port Arthur to Communist China in May, 1955. Thus for the first time since 1842 (Treaty of Nanking) the last vestige of the much denounced unequal treaties was wiped out. Ironically, the Soviet Union was the first country to renounce the unequal treaties but was also the last country to relinquish its special privileges as stipulated in the unequal treaties.

Within the Communist bloc the influence of China continued to grow vis-à-vis the Soviet Union and other Communist countries. In 1956 when the Soviet Union faced mass revolt in Eastern Europe after its de-Stalinization campaign, the Chinese premier Chou En-lai travelled to Poland and Hungary as a peacemaker. Chou's successful mission marked the apex of China's prestige and influence within the Communist bloc. After this point, the relationship between the two Communist giants soon began to deteriorate; the deterioration became all the more evident after Nikita Khrushchev had successfully purged his opponents (the anti-party group) and consolidated his own power in the Soviet Union. Ideologically, the disputes involved such questions as the feasibility of peaceful coexistence with the capitalist countries and the best method—war or peaceful competition—to communize the world. The Moscow Declaration of November, 1957, signed by the Soviet Union and Communist China as well as other Communist countries, was a compromise of the two conflict-ing points of view, to the satisfaction of neither of the two parties. The schism continued and the conflict became more serious with the passage of time. Khrushchev's degradation of Stalin had antagonized many Chi-nese diehards who believed that the old dictator was the greatest savior of mankind since Lenin, while Khrushchev's open criticism of Mao's com-munes touched the most sensitive point. In 1960, Chinese students were called home from Russia, and Russian technicians were recalled from China. This was followed by the closing of Russian consulates in many Chinese cities. Meanwhile, Chinese trade with Russia slumped from about two billion U.S. dollars in 1959 to less than one billion in 1961. For the time being, both parties camouflaged their attacks on each other by ostensibly criticizing some other Communist countries—China denounc-ing Yugoslavia's revisionism and Russia denouncing Albania's Stalinism. But an alert outside world was not in the least deceived.

The quarrel between the two Communist giants came into the open during the Cuban Crisis of October 1962. Communist China character-ized Khrushchev's withdrawal of offensive weapons from Cuba under U.S. pressure as "100 percent appeasement, a Munich pure and simple," and called the United States a paper tiger to be relentlessly struggled against. Khrushchev, on the other hand, reminded Mao Tse-tung that the American paper tiger had nuclear teeth and compared Communist China to a frog which, by constantly croaking for "struggle," would eventually have to burst. At the East German Communist Party Congress held in Berlin in January, 1963, Communist delegates from various countries, led by the German Communist leader, Walter Ulbricht, launched a scathing attack on Communist China's disagreement with Khrushchev on peaceful coexistence. When the Chinese delegate went to the rostrum to defend the Chinese position, he was met with boos and catcalls and could not even finish his speech.

By July, 1963, when the Soviet Union and Communist China finally agreed to talk over their ideological differences in Moscow, the conflict between these two countries had become so intense that the talk consisted merely of the statements of each other's rigid position. After the failure of the Moscow talk, the Soviet Union went ahead to sign a nuclear test-ban treaty with the United States and Great Britain. Communist China ac-cused the Soviet Union of having betrayed the Communist cause by "making an alliance" with the United States and called upon the Russian people to overthrow the Khrushchev leadership. Meanwhile it promised the world that "the present attempt of a small number of countries to control the destiny of the people of the world by means of monopolizing nuclear weapons will certainly be smashed in the not too distant future."

Though Communist China had only a few allies (Albania, North Korea, and North Vietnam) in the ideological dispute, it was convinced that the "minority" would eventually become the "majority," and counted heavily on the eventual support of the Communist parties in Asian, African, and Latin American countries that were dissatisfied with the *status quo* and were plotting for the overthrow of the existing regimes. Meanwhile party members in the non-Communist countries were widely split: some followed the hard line of Peking and others, at least outwardly, echoed Khrushchev's peaceful coexistence. Whatever course it would eventually take, world Communism had ceased to be a monolithic structure.

While Communist China had no difficulty in formulating its policy towards "capitalist and imperialist" countries ("eternal enemies") and "People's Republics" ("eternal friends") by following a simple, Marxist formula, it was hesitant and uncertain with regard to nonaligned, neutral countries. To be sure, Mao Tse-tung had called for the formulation of a united front among all "revolutionary classes" in colonial and semicolonial countries to overthrow the colonial regimes; but he and his colleagues were far from sure what their policy would be if, after independence had been achieved, the new regimes were non-Communist or even anti-Communist. The problem was further complicated when these newly independent countries such as those in Southeast Asia had sizable Chinese minorities whose interests Communist China declared that it would protect. Generally speaking, it abstained from any overt act that might antagonize these newly independent countries and sometimes even provided them with material aid whenever it was able to do so. On the other hand, it doubtless hoped that a strong Communist movement would develop in these countries and would eventually establish more friendly Communist-type governments. Meanwhile, it maintained a correct, though not particularly cordial, relationship. As its ideological conflict with the Soviet Union deepened after 1961, these neutral, nonaligned countries were the only group with which Communist China was not in open quarrel. The bankruptcy of its foreign policy was virtually complete.

Though Communist China had generally maintained a friendly relationship with the neutral, nonaligned countries, there was one major exception: India. Since the establishment of the People's Republic, there had never been a country outside the Soviet bloc more friendly towards Communist China than India who, among other things, continued to sponsor its membership in the United Nations. Yet in October, 1962, open warfare erupted between these two countries. The conflict involved two pieces of territory, one in eastern Ladakh (Kashmir) and the other in the eastern end of the Himalayas between Bhutan and Burma. The basic cause of this conflict can be traced back to the first decade of this century when Great Britain, then ruling India, played "the great game" (as Lord Curzon called it) by penetrating deep into Tibet (Chapter XIV). The then weak, divided China could do nothing about the British penetration. During the

SOVIET
UNION

AFGHANISTAN

WEST
PAKISTAN

Sinkiang

C H I N A

Tibet

Kashmir

NEPAL

HIMALAYA MOUNTAINS

SIKKIM

BHUTAN

BRAHMAPUTRA RIVER

EASTERN
PAKISTAN

I N D I A

B U R M A

Bay of
Bengal

MAP 33

THE SINO-INDIAN
BORDER DISPUTE, 1962

- - - - - McMahon Line
· · · · · National Boundaries
· · · · · Internal Boundaries
Disputed Territories

Scale of Miles

0   100   200   300

Simla meeting of 1914, Britain's representative, Sir Arthur McMahon, determined the eastern portion of the border by drawing a line on a map along the Himalayan peaks from Bhutan to Burma. This line was later known as the McMahon line. The Chinese government refused to ratify the Simla Agreement and repudiated the McMahon line on the ground that the traditional demarcation line, based on ethnic factors, was the one located further in the south. Subsequent Chinese governments, both Nationalist and Communist, have taken a similar stand. After India became independent, it inherited the British claim with regard to these territories. Communist China accused India of being expansion-minded; India said the same thing about Communist China. When nationalist fervor was aroused, reason was thrown overboard. Since by that time Communist China had been diplomatically isolated from the Soviet bloc as well as the Western world, there was not a single country in the world that openly supported its case. Ironically, the only exception was Nationalist China, its bitterest enemy which, as we have said before, had never recognized the Simla Agreement and the McMahon line. By 1963, Communist China had concluded boundary agreements with all of its Himalaya neighbors except India.

Whatever justifications one might find to support Communist China's case in its border dispute with India, its foreign policy towards the so-called capitalist, imperialist countries was characterized by an almost unbelievable rigidity. Under the dictate of its Marxist dogma that these countries were the enemies of the "oppressed peoples" to be relentlessly "struggled" against, theoretically Communist China had no foreign policy towards them as such; it had only tactics for their ultimate defeat. Its attitude was inflexible and did not allow any room for compromise and maneuverability. It believed that capitalism would eventually collapse because of the inherent contradictions within the capitalist system itself and that communism would rise to replace it. While Karl Marx had advocated the theory of the inevitable triumph of communism against a nineteenth century background, the Chinese Communists still believed it literally, completely ignoring the history of the past one hundred years.

Among the "capitalist, imperialist" countries, the People's Republic singled out the United States as its number-one enemy. It went even further by saying that the United States had always been China's enemy. This accusation cannot be substantiated historically; specifically, the United States has never annexed one inch of Chinese territory. Why did the new regime regard the United States as its greatest enemy? First, prior to the Communist conquest of the mainland the United States had steadily supported the cause of the Nationalist regime, its civil war enemy. Second, the new regime obviously believed that during the postwar period the United States alone had the power that could block the fulfillment of China's own ambition in East Asia after the power of Japan had collapsed and that of Great Britain and France was diminishing because they had lost or were in the process of losing their colonial empires. Finally, there was an ideological conflict. Every other condition being equal, a Communist regime was more likely to be hostile to a capitalist country than to a fellow Communist regime.

Despite these differences, a more realistic Chinese regime would have attempted to reach an understanding with the United States because, the power situation being what it was, a foreign policy openly hostile towards the United States was bound to be fraught with danger and frustration. Whatever chance there might have been for a Sino-American rapprochement, it was lost as a result of the Korean War. After the Korean War the center of contention was shifted to Taiwan which Communist China vowed to "liberate" and which the United States was equally determined to defend. The off-and-on Communist bombardment of the two Nationalist-held islands of Matsu and Quemoy was merely a side issue of this major difference between these two countries. The United States did not recognize Communist China, and as far as anyone can tell, still does not intend to do so. Nevertheless it decided to hold ambassador-level talks with Communist China in Warsaw. The talk went on intermittently for several years with no noticeable, constructive result. The major block, as it was understood by people outside the conference room, was still the Taiwan issue.

The complaints of Communist China included also the Western defenses known as the Southeast Asia Treaty Organization (SEATO) and the leadership taken by the United States in barring Communist China from joining the United Nations. Since its establishment in 1954 SEATO has been by and large a paper alliance and will perhaps remain so as long as the Southeast Asian members of the alliance such as Pakistan, Thailand, and the Philippines do not feel any immediate threat from Communist China in the form of armed aggression. As to Communist China's entry into the United Nations, the question has been debated in the General Assembly ever since the establishment of the Communist regime in 1949. Communist China declared that it would not become a member of the United Nations even if it were invited, as long as Nationalist China remained a member. On the other hand, the United States, recognizing the Nationalist regime as the government representing China, would oppose its admission under any circumstances, let alone agree to the Communist conditions. As both Nationalist and Communist China insisted on being considered the only government of China and were opposed to the concept of two Chinas, the discussion of the Communist regime's admission to the United Nations became academic. In other words, the admission would not have materialized even if the United States had not opposed it. While debate went on in the United Nations concerning the advisability of admitting the new regime, Communist China, confident of its own importance, did not even seem anxious to join the international body. "The United Nations needs us more than we need the United Nations," Chou En-lai declared. Arrogant as this remark was, many people outside China agreed that it did contain an element of truth.

THE PAST AND THE FUTURE

There are three elements in the Chinese Communist movement: socio-economic, nationalist, and Communist. The Chinese Communists rose to power by exploiting fully and successfully the socio-economic and nationalist forces that had been in existence long before the organization of the Chinese Communist Party. As far as the outside world is concerned, the most important question is: in what ways will the People's Republic pursue its nationalist or Communist goals and how does the pursuance of these goals affect the rest of the world? Its socio-economic policies do not affect the outside world directly except in the sense that if such policies prove remarkably successful in solving China's social and economic problems the Chinese brand of communism would have great appeal to countries that have problems similar to those in China.

For the past two thousand years the basic economic problem of China has been too little arable land and too many people, as we have said repeatedly in this book. While all Chinese might be said to have been poor, poverty became more unbearable when the limited amount of land was concentrated in the hands of a comparative few. Those few who owned land were the gentry class which provided the country with scholars and government officials; those who owned little or only a small amount of land were the peasants and they constituted the overwhelming majority of the Chinese people. Though social mobility was great, at any given time the dividing line between gentry-scholars and peasants was nevertheless distinct. Since most government officials came from gentry families, the socio-economic relationship between gentry-scholars and peasants corresponded fairly well with the political relationship between rulers and the ruled. Though a typical landlord might not own more than ten acres of land, the fact that most of his fellow villagers owned little or nothing was a constant source of frustration and discontent. Chinese statesmen, from Wang Mang to Hung Hsiu-ch'üan, resolved to solve the land problem by drastic measures, but none of them succeeded because the problem was not one of distribution but one of shortage. The problem became more acute as population continued to grow throughout the last three centuries. While in power on the mainland, the Nationalist regime attempted to carry out a mild form of land reform, and the result, as we have noted before, was almost nil. Rural discontent continued and was intensified during and shortly after the Sino-Japanese War. It was ruthlessly and successfully exploited by Mao Tse-tung and his comrades.

The Communists came to power by riding on rural discontent, and authoritarian as the government is, its continuance in power ultimately depends upon the peasants' continuous support, or more correctly, the absence of withdrawing such support. If the history of the past 3,500 years indicates anything, the peasants revolt only as a last resort. Used to suffering, they prefer to suffer more instead of launching a bloody rebellion. In practical terms, it means that they revolt only when they are hungry. Freedom and democracy, the noble ideas that inspire many men to rise in anger against tyranny, do not impress a Chinese peasant who, used to authoritarian government, is more concerned with a practical need: food. As far as he is concerned, a good government is a government that leaves him enough to eat after he has paid his taxes.

To provide enough food for so many people out of a limited amount of land, the People's Republic introduced a series of rural reforms, including the commune which was in fact a desperate attempt to solve economic problems at the expense of social and human values. Despite the recent setback it is expected that continuous efforts will be made to increase food production. Improvements in irrigation and flood control, the use of better and more fertilizers, and rigid insect control will be emphasized. Meanwhile, much hope is placed upon continuous industrialization to absorb surplus population from rural areas and to produce industrial goods to be shipped abroad in exchange for much needed food. If industrialization cannot reduce the pressure of population or alleviate the shortage of food, birth control will be the next logical step, a step which every Chinese regime, including that of the Communists, has been extremely reluctant to take. Should all these measures fail and when millions of people are starving at home, the temptation of the rich rice-producing areas in Southeast Asia will become irresistible. However, any overt act on the part of Communist China will not only antagonize the entire world but will perhaps bring immediate retaliation from the Western powers against mainland China. Any economic gain China might be able to receive by an armed aggression will not compensate for the losses it will suffer. While an armed aggression cannot be completely ruled out, it is unlikely that it will take place in the foreseeable future. Communist China will perhaps prefer trade to obtain what it needs from the food-producing countries in Southeast Asia.

Chinese nationalism in its modern sense can be dated from the Opium War. For more than one century it has been one of the most dynamic forces in shaping the national life. The Chinese are a proud people, conscious of their cultural heritage and identifying themselves with a glorious past. The humiliations which they have suffered during the past century contrast sharply with the position which they once occupied as a center of power and of a great civilization. At one time China was divided into spheres of influence among the Western powers and Japan, and it even seemed that the end of the Chinese as a nation might be in sight. The loose talk about "yellow peril" in the Western world struck terror in the heart of every literate Chinese, and to the most sensitive of them it could have been a rationalization of the West's ultimate goal of wiping out the yellow race. The slow disappearance of many colored peoples on earth and Hitler's policy of genocide towards the Jews portended ill for those who were perhaps too willing to believe the worst. Whatever the justification, this fear of being submerged, if not exterminated, was one of the most formidable, psychological blocks to an effective birth control program. This fear did not come from rational reasoning; rather, it was a product of the history of the past one hundred years. Reading modern history, the Chinese developed a persecution complex. Chinese leaders in modern times, from K'ang Yu-wei to Mao Tse-tung, shared the same sentiment, and regardless of their ideology and background they all wanted to build a strong China, strong enough to demand its rightful place in the world. Without taking into consideration Chinese nationalism, it is difficult to explain why many intellectuals, all of bourgeois and gentry background, swarmed to the standard of Mao Tse-tung. Mao, a crafty politician, exploited their nationalist sentiments as effectively as he had exploited the economic discontent of the peasants. When he declared that China had stood up, he was echoing the wishes of millions of Chinese, including the "reactionaries" whom he had vowed to liquidate.

To the outside world, the most important question is: into what kind of action will Chinese nationalism be translated, now that it is directed by the Communists? Will it be aimed at the fulfillment of China's legitimate aspirations or will it develop into a mass force of aggression? If it is the former, the outside world can learn to live with it. If it is the latter, it is no longer genuine nationalism; it becomes imperialism, the same "crime" which Communist China has accused the Western powers and Japan of having committed against China during the past one hundred years. In other words, if Communist China confines its ambition to legitimate, nationalist aspirations, there is no reason why the Western world cannot meet it halfway and make enough accommodations for the fulfillment of such aspirations. If, on the other hand, the Chinese Communists intend to use China as a base of operation for the communization of the world, any compromise with them is clearly ruled out. In such a case, they become a danger and threat to international peace, and the people who ultimately have to suffer most would be the Chinese people themselves.

What could be the legitimate, nationalist aspirations which a responsible Chinese regime would pursue? It would desire friendly relations with its neighboring states which, in any event, would not serve as bases for hostile nations to launch attacks upon China itself. It would desire freedom of trade with all nations in the world to obtain what it needs and to sell what it can sell. It would desire to be represented in international councils such as the United Nations. Would the demand for the return of "lost" territories such as Hong Kong and Macao in the south and the Amur region in the north be also considered as legitimate? Whatever the answer to this question might be, it is easy to see that a Chinese government, pursuing purely nationalist interests, will perhaps have more difficulty with the Soviet Union than with any other country in the world because China shares the longest boundary with the Soviet Union, and the Amur region constitutes one of the largest "unrecovered" territories. We may recall that Communist China waged a short but hot war with India in 1962 because of boundary disputes. As far as the Western world is concerned, it has no quarrel with a Chinese government that follows a policy of legitimate nationalism. Colonialism is dead or at least is dying, and the Chinese know it. However, even legitimate aspirations cannot be fulfilled if, in the meantime, the Chinese government intends to export communism abroad. With expansionist communism the Western world cannot and will not compromise. In practical terms, it means that Communist China has to make a rapprochement with the United States if it wishes to attain what it might regard as its nationalist goals; such rapprochement is impossible as long as China remains militantly communistic. Any government that bases its foreign policy upon the assumption that the United States is a paper tiger is unrealistic to the greatest extreme and can do so only at its own peril. This is clear to everyone except the Communist leaders who happen to live in the Forbidden City.

A Chinese government, serving the interests of the Chinese people, will have much to gain by cooperating with the Western world. It needs help to solve its many economic problems; the past shows that such help is more obtainable from the West than from the Communist countries. The comparatively high standard of living in Taiwan as compared with the bleak life of mainland China is a case in point. All that an average Chinese needs and wants is a tolerable livelihood, education for his children, and the dignity and respect due to any decent individual. What has he to gain by communizing such remote areas as Latin America? Why should he make great sacrifices which bring good neither to himself nor to the rest of the world? The dogmatic Communists, by pursuing their own grand illusion, create an irreconcilable contradiction between themselves and the Chinese people whom they rule. The more they pursue such an illusion, the faster such contradiction grows; and the intensification of such contradiction might prove to be the cause of their eventual downfall. With the Chinese people the outside world has much in common; for one thing, they face a common danger.

Suggested Readings

Students who can read Chinese are strongly urged to read primary sources in Chinese. The books usually recommended for beginners are *Historical Records* (*Shih chi*) by Ssu-ma Ch'ien, *History of the Han* (*Han shu*) by Pan Ku, and *History As A Mirror* (*Tzu-chih t'ung-chien*) by Ssu-ma Kuang. The following list consists entirely of books in English, most of which are secondary works.

General:

Chi Ch'ao-ting, *Key Economic Areas in Chinese History*. London: G. Allen & Unwin, Ltd., 1936.

De Bary, Wm. Theodore and others, *Sources of Chinese Tradition*. New York: Columbia University Press, 1960.

Feng Yu-lan, *A History of Chinese Philosophy*, 2 vols. (trans. by D. Bodde). Princeton: Princeton University Press, 1952–1953.

Giles, H. A., *A History of Chinese Literature*. New York: Groves Press, 1958.

Goodrich, L. Carrington, *A Short History of the Chinese People*. New York: Harper and Brothers, 1959.

Grousset, Rene, *The Rise and Splendour of the Chinese Empire*. Berkeley: University of California Press, 1953.

Latourette, Kenneth S., *The Chinese: Their History and Culture*. New York: Macmillan, 1946.

Needham, Joseph, *Science and Civilization in China*. Vol. 1, Introductory Orientations; vol. 2, History of Scientific Thought; and vol. 3, Mathematics and the Sciences of the Heavens and the Earth. Cambridge, England: Cambridge University Press, 1954–1958.

Reischauer, Edwin O. and John K. Fairbank, *East Asia: The Great Tradition*. Boston: Houghton Mifflin Company, 1960.

Willetts, William, *Chinese Art*, 2 vols. London: Penguin Books Ltd., 1955.

Introduction

Cressey, George B., *China's Geographical Foundations; A Survey of the Land and Its People*. New York: McGraw-Hill, 1933.

Cressey, George B., *Land of the 500 Million*. New York: McGraw-Hill, 1955.

Chapter I

Creel, Herrlee G., *The Birth of China*. New York: Frederick Ungar, 1954.

Li Chi, *The Beginnings of Chinese Civilization*. Seattle: University of Washington Press, 1957.

Chapter II

The Analects of Confucius. Translated by Arthur Waley. London: G. Allen and Unwin, 1938.

The Book of Songs. Translated by Arthur Waley. London: G. Allen and Unwin, 1937.

The Chinese Classics, 5 vols. Translated by James Legge. Hong Kong: Hong Kong University Press, 1960.

The Complete Works of Han Fei-tzu, 2 vols. Translated by Liao Wen-Kuei. London: A. Probsthain, 1939 and 1959.

Creel, Herrlee G., *Confucius, the Man and the Myth*. New York: John Day Co., 1949.

Hsü, Leonard Shih-lien, *The Political Philosophy of Confucianism*. New York: E. P. Dutton Co., 1932.

Lin Yutang (ed.), *The Wisdom of China and India*. New York: Modern Library, 1955.

Mei Yi-pao, *The Ethical and Political Works of Motse*. London: A. Probsthain, 1928.

Shryock, John K., *The Origin and Development of the State Cult of Confucius*. New York: Appleton, 1932.

Waley, Arthur, *Three Ways of Thought in Ancient China*. London: G. Allen and Unwin, 1939.

Waley, Arthur (ed.), *The Way and Its Power; A Study of the Tao Te Ching and Its Place in Chinese Thought*. Translated by Arthur Waley. London: G. Allen and Unwin, 1934.

Chapter III

Bodde, Derk, *China's First Unifier*. Leiden: E. J. Brill, Ltd., 1938.

Bodde, Derk, *Statesman, Patriot, and General in Ancient China*. New Haven: American Oriental Society, 1940.

Dubs, Homer H., *History of the Former Han Dynasty*, 3 vols. Baltimore: Waverly Press, 1938, 1944, 1955.

Forke, Alfred, *Lun-heng*. London: Luzac & Co., 1907–1911.

Swann, Nancy Lee, *Food and Money in Ancient China*. Princeton: Princeton University Press, 1950.

Swann, Nancy Lee, *Pan Chao: Foremost Woman Scholar of China, First Century A.D.* New York: D. Appleton-Century Co., 1932.

Watson, Burton, *Records of the Grand Historian of China*. New York: Columbia University Press, 1961.

Watson, Burton, *Ssu-ma Ch'ien: Grand Historian of China*. New York: Columbia University Press, 1958.

Chapter IV

Acker, W. R. B., *T'ao the Hermit, Sixty Poems by T'ao Ch'ien (365–427)*. London & New York: Thomas & Hudson, 1952.

Buritt, E. A. (ed.), *The Teachings of the Compassionate Buddha*. New York: Mentor, 1955.

Parker, E. H., *A Thousand Years of the Tartars*. New York: Alfred A. Knopf, Inc., 1924.

Zürcher, E., *The Buddhist Conquest of China: The Spread and Adaptation of Buddhism in Early Medieval China*, 2 vols. Leiden: E. J. Brill, 1959.

Chapter V

Bingham, Woodbridge, *The Founding of the T'ang Dynasty*. Baltimore: Waverly Press, Inc., 1941.

Biography of An Lu-shan. Translated by Howard S. Levy. Berkeley: University of California Press, 1961.

Edwards, Evangeline Dora, *Chinese Prose Literature of the T'ang Period*, 2 vols. London: A. Probsthain, 1937–1938.

Fitzgerald, Charles Patrick, *The Empress Wu*. Melbourne: F. W. Cheshire, 1956.

Fitzgerald, Charles Patrick, *Son of Heaven, a Biography of Li Shih-min*. Cambridge, England: University Press, 1933.

Hung, William, *Tu Fu, China's Greatest Poet*. Cambridge: Harvard University Press, 1952.

Ladies of the T'ang. Translated by Elizabeth Te-chen Wang. Taipei: Heritage Press, 1961.

Pulleyblank, E. G., *The Background of the Rebellion of An Lu-shan*. Oxford: Oxford University Press, 1955.

Reischauer, Edwin O., *Ennin's Travels in T'ang China and Ennin's Diary*. New York: The Ronald Press, 1955.

Siren, Osvald, *Chinese Sculpture from the Fifth to the Fourteenth Century*. New York: Charles Scribner's Sons, 1925.

Wiley, Arthur, *The Life and Time of Po Chü-i*. New York: The Macmillan Company, 1949.

Chapters VI and VII

Bruce, Joseph Perry, *Chu Hsi and His Masters*. London: A. Probsthain, 1923.

Carter, Thomas Francis and Goodrich, L. Carrington, *Invention of Printing Press in China and Its Spread Westward*. New York: The Ronald Press, 1955.

Huang Siu-chi, *Lu Hsiang-shan, a Twelfth Century Idealist Philosopher*. New Haven: American Oriental Society, 1944.

Kracke, Jr., Edward A., *Civil Service in Early Sung China*. Cambridge, Mass.: Harvard University Press, 1953.

Lin Yutang, *The Gay Genius: the Life and Times of Su Tungpo*. New York: John Day Co., 1947.

Liu, James T. C., *Reform in Sung China: Wang An-shih (1021–1086) and his New Policies*. Cambridge, Mass.: Harvard University Press, 1963.

Meskill, John (ed.), *Wang An-shih—Practical Reformer?* Boston: D. C. Heath and Company, 1963.

Williamson, Henry R., *Wang An-shih: A Chinese Statesman*. London: A. Probsthain, 1935.

Wittfogel, Karl A. and Feng Chia-sheng, *History of Chinese Society, Liao (907–1125)*. New York: Macmillan, 1949.

Chapter VIII

Hsiung, S. I., *The Romance of the Western Chamber (Hsi Hsiang Chi)*. London: Methuen & Co., Ltd., 1935.

Martin, Henry Desmond, *The Rise of Chinghis Khan and his Conquest of North China*. Baltimore: The Johns Hopkins Press, 1950.

Polo, Marco, *The Travels of Marco Polo*. London: Penguin Books, Ltd., 1958.

Schurmann, Herbert Franz, *Economic Structure of the Yüan Dynasty*. Cambridge: Harvard University Press, 1956.

Zucker, Adolph E., *The Chinese Theater*. Boston: Little, Brown and Co., 1925.

Chapter IX

Hobson, Robert Lockhart, *The Wares of the Ming Dynasty*. London: Benn Brothers, Ltd., 1923.

Hucker, Charles O., *The Traditional Chinese State in Ming Times (1368–1644)*. Tucson: University of Arizona Press, 1961.

Instructions for Practical Living and Other Neo-Confucian Writings by Wang Yang-ming. Translated by Chan Wing-tsit. New York: Columbia University Press, 1963.

Wang Yi-t'ung, *Official Relations Between China and Japan (1368–1549)*. Cambridge: Harvard University Press, 1953.

Chapter X

Brewitt-Taylor, Charles Henry, *San Kuo or Romance of the Three Kingdoms*, 2 vols. Shanghai: Kelly & Walsh, Ltd., 1925.

Buck, Pearl S., *All Men Are Brothers (Shui Hu Chuan)*. New York: John Day Co., 1933.

Egerton, Clement, *The Golden Lotus*, 4 vols. London: G. Routledge & Sons, Ltd., 1939.

Giles, Herbert Allen, *Strange Stories from a Chinese Studio*. New York: Boni, 1925.

Goodrich, L. Carrington, *The Literary Inquisition of Ch'ien-lung*. Baltimore: Waverly Press, Inc., 1935.

Ho Ping-ti, *Studies on the Population of China, 1368–1953*. Cambridge: Harvard University Press, 1959.

Hsiao Kung-chun, *Rural China: Imperial Control in the Nineteenth Century*. Seattle: University of Washington Press, 1960.

Hummel, Arthur W. (ed.), *Eminent Chinese of the Ch'ing Period*, 2 vols. Washington: U.S. Government Printing Office, 1943–1944.

Michael, Franz, *The Origin of Manchu Rule in China*. Baltimore: Johns Hopkins Press, 1942.

Waley, Arthur, *The Monkey, by Wu Ch'eng-en*. New York: John Day Co., 1943.

Wang, C. C., *Dream of the Red Chamber, by Tsao Hsueh-chin*. New York: Twayne Publishers, 1958.

Chapter XI

Buck, John L., *Chinese Farm Economy*. Chicago: University of Chicago Press, 1930.

Buck, Pearl S., *The Good Earth*. New York: John Day Co., 1931.

Chang Chung-li, *The Chinese Gentry: Studies on their Role in Nineteenth-century Chinese Society*. Seattle: University of Washington Press, 1957.

Fei Hsiao-tung, *China's Gentry*. Chicago: University of Chicago Press, 1953.

Fei Hsiao-tung, *Peasant Life in China*. London: Routledge, 1939.

Hsu, Francis L. K., *Americans and Chinese: Two Ways of Life*. New York: Henry Schuman, 1953.

Hsu, Francis L. K., *Under the Ancestors' Shadow*. New York: Columbia University Press, 1948.

Lin Yutang, *My Country and My People*. New York: John Day Co., 1936.

Menzel, Johanna M. (ed.), *The Chinese Civil Service—Career Open to Talent?* Boston: D. C. Heath and Co., 1963.

Williams, S. Wells, *The Middle Kingdom*, 2 vols. New York: Charles Scribner's Sons, 1901.

Chapters XII and XIII

Allen, G. C. and A. G. Donnithorne, *Western Enterprise in Far Eastern Economic Development: China and Japan*. New York: Macmillan, 1954.

Boardman, Eugene P., *Christian Influence Upon the Ideology of the Taiping Rebellion, 1851–1864*. Madison: University of Wisconsin Press, 1952.

Buck, Pearl S., *Imperial Woman*. New York: Pocket Books, Inc., 1958.

Cameron, M. E., *The Reform Movement in China*. Palo Alto, Calif.: Stanford University Press, 1931.

Fairbank, John K., *Trade and Diplomacy on the China Coast, The Opening of the Treaty Ports, 1842–1854*, 2 vols. Cambridge: Harvard University Press, 1953.

Gallagher, Louis Joseph, *China in the Sixteenth Century: the Journals of Matthew Ricci, 1583–1610*. New York: Random House, 1953.

Hail, William James, *Tseng Kuo-fan and the Taiping Rebellion*. New Haven: Yale University Press, 1927.

Hsü, Immanuel C. Y., *China's Entrance into the Family of Nations: The Diplomatic Phase, 1858–1880*. Cambridge: Harvard University Press, 1960.

Hudson, Geoffrey F., *Europe and China; A Survey of Their Relations from the Earliest Times to 1800*. London: E. Arnold & Co., 1931.

Latourette, Kenneth S., *A History of Christian Missions in China*. New York: Macmillan, 1929.

Li Chien-nung, *The Political History of China, 1840–1928*. Princeton, N.J.: D. Van Nostrand Co., Inc., 1956.

Morse, Hosea B., *International Relations of the Chinese Empire*. London: Longmans, 1918.

Moule, Arthur Christopher, *Christians in China; Before the Year 1550*. New York: Macmillan, 1930.

Olschki, Leonardo, *Marco Polo's Precursors*. Baltimore: Johns Hopkins Press, 1943.

Purcell, Victor, *The Boxer Uprising*. New York: Cambridge University Press, 1963.

Teng Ssu-yü, *Chang Hsi and the Treaty of Nanking, 1842*. Chicago: University of Chicago Press, 1944.

Teng Ssu-yü and Fairbank, John K., *China's Response to the West*. Cambridge: Harvard University Press, 1954.

Wright, Mary C., *The Last Stand of Chinese Conservatism: The T'ung-chih Restoration, 1862–1874*. Stanford: Stanford University Press, 1957.

Chapters XIV and XV

Buell, Raymond L., *The Washington Conference*. New York: Appleton, 1922.

Chiang Kai-shek, *China's Destiny*. New York: Macmillan, 1947.

Chiang Kai-shek, *Soviet Union in China: A Summing-up at Seventy*. New York: Farrar, Straus, 1958.

Chiang Monlin, *Tides from the West*. New Haven: Yale University Press, 1947.

Chou Tse-tsung, *The May Fourth Movement: Intellectual Revolution in Modern China*. Cambridge: Harvard University Press, 1960.

Hu Shih, *The Chinese Renaissance*. Chicago: University of Chicago Press, 1934.

Linebarger, Paul, *The Political Doctrines of Sun Yat-sen*. Baltimore: Johns Hopkins University Press, 1937.

Liu Chih-pu, *A Military History of Modern China, 1924–1949*. Princeton: Princeton University Press, 1956.

Malraux, Andre, *Man's Fate*. New York: Modern Library, 1934.

Riggs, Frederick W., *Formosa Under Chinese Nationalist Rule*. New York: Macmillan, 1952.

Sharman, Lyon, *Sun Yat-sen; His Life and Its Meaning*. New York: John Day Co., 1934.

Snow, Edgar, *Red Star over China*. New York: Random House, 1938.

Sun Yat-sen, *The Three Principles of the People*. Translated by F. W. Price. New York: Chinese News Service, Inc., 1943.

United States Relations with China. Washington, D.C.: The Department of State, 1949.

Chapter XVI

Center for International Affairs and the East Asian Research Center, Harvard University, *Communist China, 1955–1959*. Cambridge: Harvard University Press, 1962.

Hughes, T. J. and D. E. T. Luard, *The Economic Development of Communist China, 1949–1958*. London: Oxford University Press, 1959.

Li Tieh-tseng, *Tibet: Today and Yesterday*. New York: Bookman Associates, 1959.

Mao Tse-tung, *China's New Democracy*. New York: International Publishers, 1955.

Mao Tse-tung, *Selected Works, 5 vols*. New York: International Publishers, 1954–1960.

Payne, Robert, *Portrait of a Revolutionary: Mao Tse-tung*. New York: Abelard-Schuman, 1961.

Rostow, W. W., *The Prospects for Communist China*. New York: John Wiley, 1954.

Schwartz, B. I., *Chinese Communism and the Rise of Mao*. Cambridge: Harvard University Press, 1951.

Snow, Edgar, *The Other Side of the River: Red China Today*. New York: Random House, 1962.

Tang, Peter S. H., *Communist China Today: Domestic and Foreign Policies*. New York: Praeger, 1957.

Yang, C. K., *The Chinese Family in the Communist Revolution*. Cambridge, Mass.: The Technology Press, 1959.

Yang, C. K., *A Chinese Village in Early Communist Transition*. Cambridge, Mass.: The Technology Press, 1959.

Wu Yuan-li, *An Economic Survey of Communist China*. New York: Bookman Associates, 1956.

Zagoria, Donald S., *The Sino-Soviet Conflict, 1956–1961*. Princeton: Princeton University Press, 1962.

Romanization
of Chinese Names

There is no unanimity among scholars as to how Chinese names should be romanized. The easiest way out of this difficulty is to follow the Wade-Giles system throughout regardless of other considerations. In that case, Confucius becomes *Kung ch'iu* or *Kung Fu-tzu;* Chiang Kai-shek becomes *Chiang Chieh-shih* or *Chiang Chung-cheng*. This, certainly, will not do. In general, the following rules are followed in this book:

1. All historical names of persons and places, with the exception of those which have long been standardized (such as Confucius and Mencius), are romanized according to the Wade-Giles system: *Chao K'uang-yin, Li Shih-min, Ch'üanchou,* etc.

2. The names of people in modern China are the same names they themselves prefer to be called or the names which have long been used in con-

temporary literature: *Sun Yat-sen, Chiang Kai-shek,* etc. With the exception of these two cases, personal names are romanized according to the Wade-Giles system.

3. Postal names are used for all major Chinese cities: *Peking, Nanking,* etc. For cities little known in Western literature or cities whose postal names cannot be easily located, the Wade-Giles system is used: *Ch'ench'iao,* for instance.

4. Whenever historical cities bear the same names and are on the same sites as their modern counterparts, postal names are used: *Kaifeng, Yangchow,* etc.

5. Whenever a name is romanized identically as another name according to the Wade-Giles system even though they are indicated by two entirely different Chinese characters or two different sets of Chinese characters, they are romanized differently in order to avoid confusion. A Chinese kingdom during the Spring and Autumn period bears the same Chinese character as a Chinese regime flourishing between the third and the fifth century, and both are romanized as *Tsin,* even though they could have been romanized as *Chin* according to the Wade-Giles system. On the other hand, the Nuchen regime established in the twelfth century is romanized as *Chin* because it bears a different Chinese character which means *gold.*

6. A personal name which consists of two Chinese characters is linked with a hyphen: *Hung-chang, Tse-tung,* etc. A hyphen is used even when the name is not really a name but a title: *Wen-ti* (Emperor Wen), *Wu-ti* (Emperor Wu), etc. As a general rule, only a person's real name (*ming*) is given, rarely his courtesy name (*tzu* or *hao*). This is done in order to reduce the number of names that have to appear in this book.

7. Geographical names, whether they are the names of cities, mountains, or seas, have no hyphens even though they contain two or more Chinese characters: *Pohai, Ch'angan,* etc. Hyphens appear only when the names are Sinicized foreign names: *Hsiung-nu, Wu-sun,* etc. An exception is made in cases when there have been standardized English equivalents long in usage: *Genghiz Khan* instead of *Ch'eng-chi-ssu Han,* for instance.

In summary, the Wade-Giles system is followed unless there are compelling reasons for not doing so. However, the system provides only approximate pronunciation for Chinese words; the pronunciation of most Chinese words simply does not have its equivalent in English. A useful purpose will be served if students observe the following simple guide:

a as in f*a*r
i as the first *e* in *e*vade
o as in *o*ver
ai as the *i* in time
ao as the *ow* in n*ow*
ch' as in *ch*urch
p' as in *p*ay
ts' as in boa*ts*
ch as the *j* in *j*est

e as in *e*rror

u as in r*u*le
ou as the *o* in *o*bey
ü as *ü* in German
k' as in *k*ite
t' as in *t*ie
tz' as in quar*tz*
k as the *g* in *g*o

p as the *b* in *b*oy

ts and *tz* as *dz*

j has no English equivalent but
   is pronounced more like *r*
   than like *j*.

ss is pronounced as *s*

t as the *d* in *d*ay

hs as *sh* in *sh*arp

Chronological Chart

Dynasties	Government and Politics
Hsia (c.2205–c.1766 B.C.)	Yü, founder of the Hsia dynasty The Great Flood (legend?) Chieh, last Hsia ruler
Shang (c.1766–c.1122 B.C.)	T'ang, founder of the Shang dynasty Frequent shift of capital until it was settled at Yin (modern Honan province) in 1401 B.C.
Chou (c.1122–249 B.C.) West Chou (c.1122–771 B.C.) East Chou (770–249 B.C.) Spring and Autumn period (722–481 B.C.) Warring States period (403–221 B.C.)	King Wen, King Wu, and Duke Chou Feudalism established, c. 1122 B.C. Feudal states: Lu, Ch'i, Tsin, etc. Interstate warfare after 771 B.C.; interstate conferences; decline of feudalism Duke Huan of Ch'i and Duke Wen of Tsin Rise of Ch'u Warring States: Ch'in, Ch'i, Ch'u, Chao, Han, Wei, and Yen
Ch'in (221–207 B.C.)	Shih Huang-ti; Li Ssu China unified, 221 B.C. Legalism adopted as the state philosophy: the burning of books Central control and bureaucratic administration over all parts of China
Han (202 B.C.–220 A.D.) Former Han (202 B.C.–9 A.D.) Hsin dynasty (9–23 A.D.) Later Han (25–220 A.D.)	Liu Pang (Han Kao-tsu) Han Wu-ti Defeat of Hsiung-nu and conquest of Korea Usurpation of the Han throne by Wang Mang Liu Hsiu Usurpation of power by eunuchs Massacre of eunuchs, 189 A.D. Ts'ao Ts'ao

Socio-economic Developments	Culture
Domestication of animals Cultivation of wheat and millet Sericulture	Black pottery Animism
Trade; cowrie shells being used as medium of exchange	White incised pottery Bronze vessels and weapons Carved ivory and jade Written language (*chia-ku wen*) Ancestor worship Oracle bones
The "well-field" system (*ching-t'ien chih*) The rise of the merchant class and the growth of cities after the eighth century B.C. Sinicization of South China Iron Age Introduction of metallic coins Shang Yang's social and economic reforms Roaming scholars	*Book of Odes* Confucius Mo Ti *Book of Taoist Virtue* Chuang Chou Mencius Ch'ü Yüan and Sung Yü Han Fei *Chou-pi Mathematics*
Standardization of weights and measures *The Ch'in Code* Irrigation projects and public works	*Small Script* declared as standard for all writing
Persecution of merchants Wang Mang's reforms Resurgence of the landed class under the Later Han regime Personal loyalty	Tung Chung-shu Confucianism declared as the state philosophy Ssu-ma Ch'ien Ssu-ma Hsiang-yü Alchemy Compass Pan Ku; Pan Chao Invention of paper Introduction of Buddhism Wang Ch'ung *The Peacock Flies Southeast*

Dynasties	Government and Politics
Three Kingdoms	Ts'ao P'i; Liu Pei; Sun Ch'üan
Wei (220–265) Shu (221–265) Wu (222–280)	
Tsin (265–420) West Tsin (265–317) East Tsin (317–420)	Tsin Wu-ti Barbarian invasions Sack of Loyang, 311 and 316 Tsin Yüan-ti
Southern and Northern Dynasties South: Liu Sung, 420–479; Ch'i, 479–502; Liang, 502–557; Ch'en, 557–589 North: Later (North) Wei, 386–535; East Wei, 534–550; West Wei, 535–556; North Ch'i, 550–577; North Chou, 557–581	China divided Liu Yü Wei Hsiao-wen-ti Liang Wu-ti
Sui (590–618)	Sui Wen-ti Sui Yang-ti Civil service examination introduced
T'ang (618–906)	Li Shih-min (T'ang T'ai-tsung) T'ang Kao-tsung: conquest of Central Asia and Korea Empress Wu The Three Secretariat system; six ministries Fu-ping chih T'ang Hsüan-tsung An Lu-shan's revolt Hui-heh; T'u-fan
Five Dynasties (907–960) Later Liang, 907–923 Later T'ang, 923–936 Later Tsin, 936–947 Later Han, 947–950 Later Chou, 951–960	Warlordism Loss of the Sixteen Yen-Yün Districts Chou Shih-tsu

Socio-economic Developments	Culture
The nine rank system	Decline of Confucianism Taoism; Buddhism
Mass migration to the Yangtze region, fourth century Clans Moral decline of the gentry class	Pilgrimage to India: Fa-hsien Calligraphy: Wang Hsi-chih T'ao Ch'ien Seven Sages of the Bamboo Grove
Invaders Sinicized Hsiao-wen-ti's land reform Elite families	"Parallel form" Golden age of Buddhism
Ever-ready granaries Grand Canal	Block-printing
Land distribution Liang-shui fa Arab and Persian traders	Hsüan-tsang Ch'an Buddhism Zoroastrianism; Manicheanism; Nestorianism, Islam Cultural expansion Essayists: Han Yü; Liu Tsung-ch'üan Poets: Li Po; Tu Fu; Po Chü-yi Painters: Li Ssu-hsün; Wu Tao-tzu; Wang Wei Dance and music
Foot-binding	Printing of Confucian classics Li Yü

Dynasties	Government and Politics
Sung (960–1279) North Sung, 960–1126 South Sung, 1127–1279 Liao, 907–1125 West Hsia, 990–1227 Chin, 1115–1234	Chao K'uang-yin (Sung T'ai-tsu) "Disarmament beside the wine cups" Agreement of River Shan The Tangut war Sung Shen-tsung Fang La rebellion Fall of Kaifeng, 1126 Sung Kao-tsung Yo Fei Rise of the Mongols
Yüan (1260–1368)	Genghiz Khan Kublai Khan Corruption of Mongol princes
Ming (1368–1644)	Chu Yüan-chang (Ming T'ai-tsu) Yung-lo (Ming Ch'eng-tsu) Seven Voyages to the "Western" Ocean The tribute system Japanese pirates Eunuchs Chang Hsien-chung; Li Tzu-ch'eng
Ch'ing (1644–1912)	K'ang-hsi Ch'ien-lung Opium War Taiping Rebellion Sino-Japanese War Boxer Rebellion K'ang Yu-wei: Hundred Days' Reform Tz'u-Hsi
Republic (1912–)	Yüan Shih-k'ai Warlordism Sun Yat-sen Chiang Kai-shek Nationalist Government at Nanking Manchurian Incident, 1931 Sino-Japanese War Communist ascendency Nationalist Government in Taiwan

Socio-economic Developments	Culture
Wang An-shih's reforms Decline of women's status Paper currency	Four Colleges Movable type Philosophers: Chou Tun-yi; Chu Hsi; Lu Chiu-yüan *Tz'u* poets: Liu Yung; Li Ch'ing-chao; Hsin Ch'i-chi Essayist: Su Shih Historians: Ou-yang Hsiu; Ssu-ma Kuang Painting: Mi Fei Vernacular tales
Caste system	Road construction; Grand Canal Music drama: *The Romance of the West Chamber* *The Marsh Heroes* *The Romance of the Three Kingdoms*
Plantations Commercial expansion Gentry Deterioration of peasantry	*Yung-lo Encyclopedia* Wang Shou-jen T'ang Yin and Tung Ch'i-ch'ang School system "Eight-legged" essays Ku Yen-wu Jesuits *Flowering Plum in a Golden Vase*
Population increase Opium addiction Taiping's social and economic reforms Introduction of modern industries	The Han Learning *Four Treasuries* Introduction of Western culture Christianity *The Dream of the Red Chamber* *An Unofficial History of the Literati*
The May Fourth Movement Three Principles of the People Emancipation of women Traditional society undermined	The *pai-hua* (colloquial) movement Modern schools Science and democracy Hu Shih

Dynasties	*Government and Politics*
People's Republic (1949–)	The Chinese Communist Party Mao Tse-tung: New Democracy and democratic centralism The Russo-Chinese alliance, 1950 Korean War The Constitution of 1954 Split in the international Communist movement

Socio-economic Developments	*Culture*
Land reform	Marxism; Leninism; Maoism
Cooperatives	Mass education
Collective farms	Thought reform ("brainwashing")
Communes	Science and technology
Planned economy: industrialization	Folk art and dance
Destruction of the Confucian family system	
Regimented life	

Index

Index

ILLUSTRATION ACKNOWLEDGMENTS

American President Lines: 500

Brown Brothers: 412

Chicago Natural History Museum: 72, 236

The Cleveland Museum of Art: 61 (Edward L. Whittemore Fund); 114 (Gift of Mr. and Mrs. Harold T. Clark, In Memory of Flora L. Terry); 157 (Gift of Mr. and Mrs. Ralph King); 177 (John L. Severance Fund); 240 (Gift of Hanna Fund); 305 (John L. Severance Fund)

Charles Phelps Cushing: 20; 21, middle, bottom left and right (all by Sawders)

Eastfoto: 511

Ewing Galloway: 21, top; 22, 24, 160, 254, 277, 469

The Metropolitan Museum of Art: 239 (Rogers Fund, 1923)

The New York Public Library: 179, 282 (Manuscript Division); 322 (Spencer Collection)

Peabody Museum of Salem, Courtesy of: 388

The Smithsonian Institution, Courtesy of: 45 (Freer Gallery of Art, Washington, D.C.)

Victoria and Albert Museum (Crown Copyright): 339, 340

United Press International Photo: 498